the Unofficial Guide® to

Skiing and Snowboarding in the West

1st Edition

the Unofficial Guide® to Skiing and Snowboarding in the West

1st Edition

Lito Tejada-Flores   Kurt Repanshek
Claire Walter   Peter Shelton
Seth Masia   Bob Sehlinger

WILEY

Wiley Publishing, Inc.

Please note that prices fluctuate in the course of time, and travel information changes under the impact of many factors that influence the travel industry. We therefore suggest that you write or call ahead for confirmation when making your travel plans. Every effort has been made to ensure the accuracy of information throughout this book, and the contents of this publication are believed correct at the time of printing. Nevertheless, the publishers cannot accept responsibility for errors or omissions or for changes in details given in this guide or for the consequences of any reliance on the information provided by the same. Assessments of attractions and so forth are based upon the author's own experience, and therefore, descriptions given in this guide necessarily contain an element of subjective opinion, which may not reflect the publisher's opinion or dictate a reader's own experience on another occasion. Readers are invited to write the publisher with ideas, comments, and suggestions for future editions.

Published by:
John Wiley & Sons, Inc.
111 River Street
Hoboken, NJ 07030

Produced by Menasha Ridge Press
Cover design by Michael J. Freeland
Interior design by Michele Laseau
Cover photo by Josef Frankhauser/Getty Images

For information on our other products and services or to obtain technical support, please contact our Customer Care Department within the U.S. at (800) 762-2974, outside the U.S. at (317) 572-3993 or fax (317) 572-4002.

John Wiley & Sons, Inc. also publishes its books in a variety of electronic formats. Some content that appears in print may not be available in electronic formats.

ISBN 0-7645-3927-2

ISSN 1544-063X

Manufactured in the United States of America

5   4   3   2   1

Contents

About the Authors

Lito Tejada-Flores was born at 13,000 feet in the Bolivian Andes and spent much of his life in high places. Lito is known for both his ski travel and ski technical writing. Lito's three *Breakthrough on Skis* videos—*Expert Skiing Simplified, Bumps and Powder Simplified,* and *The New Skis*—have opened the doors to expert skiing for thousands of American skiers. Lito's website, www.BreakthroughOnSkis.com, is an alternative on-line skiers' journal featuring monthly articles on ski travel, ski technique, and impressionistic and personal ski writing of all sorts.

Claire Walter is an award-winning ski and travel writer based in Boulder, Colorado. She is a contributor to national magazines and has authored or co-authored more than a dozen books, including *Rocky Mountain Skiing,* which garnered the 1994 Harold Hirsch Award in the ski book category, and *Snowshoeing Colorado,* one of three finalists in the non-fiction category for the 1999 Colorado Book Awards. Her most recent book, *Culinary Colorado,* is a food-oriented guide to the number-one ski state.

Seth Masia began skiing in Chamonix in 1968 and joined the staff of *Ski Magazine* in 1974. He was technical editor of the magazine for 20 years, while also writing for *Outside* and other national publications. Seth has worked as ski product manager for K2 Corp. and as general manager of skinet.com. He has written half a dozen books on the sport. Seth is a fully certified ski instructor and currently teaches at Beaver Creek. He divides his time between Boulder, Beaver Creek, and Lake Tahoe.

Kurt Repanshek is an outdoors and travel writer based in Park City, Utah. During the 2002 Salt Lake Games he worked for the organizing committee as a supervisor for the Olympic News Service. Kurt was the Northern Rockies correspondent for *Snow Country* magazine Before its demise.

Peter Shelton is a long-time ski instructor and a well-regarded ski industry freelance writer. He is a contributing editor for *Ski Magazine.*

Bob Sehlinger is the creator of the *Unofficial Guide* series and author of more than two dozen travel guides.

Introduction

About This Guide

Why "Unofficial"?

The material in this guide originated with the authors and researchers and has not been reviewed, edited, or in any way approved by the ski resorts and the ski areas profiled. In this "unofficial" guide we have elected to represent and serve the *skier*. If a resort is plagued with congested slopes, awful food, or intolerable lift queues, we can say so. We are also free to highlight everything we love best about a ski resort, even if it doesn't fit the official image. In this way, we hope we can make your ski experience more fun, efficient, and economical.

Westward Ho

Look at a 3-D relief map of North America, and if you love mountains, your gaze will automatically swing to the west. The western side of the continent is full of mountains, more mountains, bigger mountains, long chains of mountains. There are the Rockies, not one range but a confabulation of many ranges and subranges. Taken together, in their intricate braided complexity, they define the backbone of the continent and here, in the United States, span six states. West of the Rockies, there are still more mountains—Sawtooth, Wasatch, Tetons, Sierra Nevada, Cascade, Carson—interior ranges, coastal ranges, snowy ranges blanketed with crystallized moisture from the Pacific. Snow is why we care about these mountains. We're skiers. We're in love with snowy mountains, and the West is our mecca.

Let's be fair. American skiing began in Norwegian farming and mining towns in the Midwest—places like Ishpeming, Michigan, and Red Wing, Minnesota. But western ski snobs like to point out that what passes for a mountain in the East is more like a big rounded hill (ancient mountain ranges do wear down through the ages into rounded hills). And you don't have to be a chauvinist to admit that there are not just more mountains

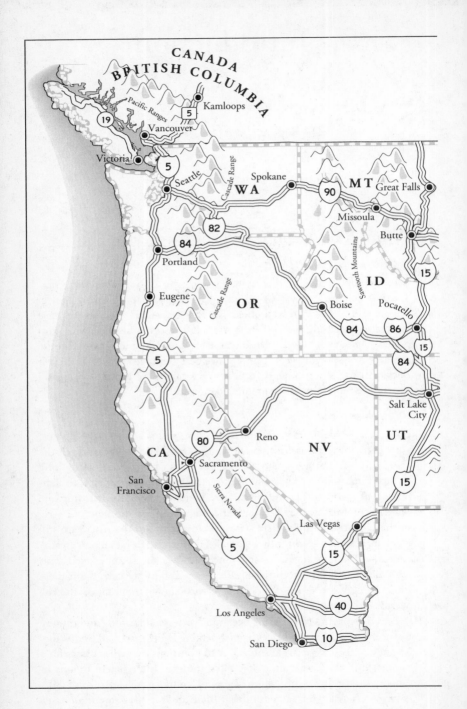

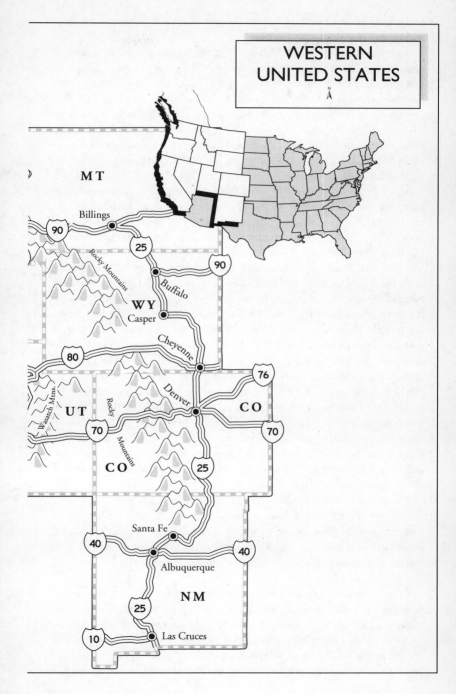

WESTERN
UNITED STATES

MT

Billings

90

25

90

Rocky Mountains

Buffalo

WY

Casper

Cheyenne

80

76

Denver

CO

UT

Wasatch Mtns.

70

70

Rocky

CO

Mountains

25

Santa Fe

40

40

Albuquerque

NM

25

10

Las Cruces

and more snow out west, but more ski areas and ski resorts, more skiing, and more great skiing.

And that's what this book is about: it's a guide—an altogether new kind of guide—to the very best skiing in the West. Where it is, how to get there, but more important how to get the most out of every mountain, every run, every turn. This book is, first and foremost, about *skiing*. I mean *skiing,* not ski-resort lodging, not dining, not ski-town shopping, but *skiing.* The real thing, the poetry in motion underneath the predictable prose of airline tickets and hotel reservations and dollars spent. The magic of movement down surreal snow-covered peaks. Skiing. The real thing.

After a life of skiing, my bookshelves are full of skiers' guidebooks—dozens of them promising the lowdown on American ski slopes, even more for the Alps. But when I look closer, I find that the heart of the matter, the skiing itself, generally gets short shrift. In all these ski guidebooks you'll find statistics aplenty: vertical feet; elevations; numbers of lifts and trails; percentages of terrain devoted to beginners, intermediates, experts. You'll find phone numbers and addresses; recommendations for hotels, condos, and lodges, either chic and pricey or low-budget bargains; you'll even find restaurant reviews—but precious little about the skiing. And I can tell you why—a little secret, just between us: most ski travel writers can't ski very well. There, the cat's out of the bag. I know travel writers whose bylines and stories have appeared in leading American ski magazines for decades, but who still haven't learned to make a parallel turn on skis; writers who spend weeks on assignment at the best ski resorts in the Rockies or in Europe but somehow manage to spend only a few hours on their skis. And that's why most skiing guidebooks scarcely talk about what the skiing is really like at the different areas and resorts they cover; seldom paint a clear picture of why the skiing on one mountain can be so different from that on another mountain; never offer the sort of insider's tips that can unlock the secrets of a ski mountain for any level of skier.

The authors of this guidebook are a different breed. Three of us, Seth, Peter, and myself (Lito), have spent years as successful, dedicated ski instructors—working, skiing, teaching at some of the biggest important ski resorts in the West—and we bring that perspective to the book. An instructor's perspective and an insider's perspective. Let me expand on this double idea for a moment.

When an experienced ski instructor starts teaching on a new mountain, the first task is to figure out all the basic types of information that we are going to share with you in this book: *Which are the best runs to warm up on in the morning? Which are the best ways down in the evenings? Where are the traffic bottlenecks and how to avoid them? How to find the best ski lunch without wasting time or standing in line. Above all, what slopes offer just the right blend of challenge and comfort for each student—that is to say, for each level of skier.* It's a real art to figure all this out in a day or two, in order to give your students the absolute best experience possible from the very first day of the season. But that's exactly what good ski instructors do, what we've all done for years, and exactly what we've tried to do in this book.

And what about the role of the skiing insider? Who are we talking about? Someone who lives the ski life daily, someone who has explored a mountain year after year, from the first autumn snowfalls to the last corn-snow day of spring. Someone who has spent years ferreting out a mountain's secrets and who's willing to share them. Someone who sets the alarm clock for 5 a.m. to go up with the patrol on a powder morning and who still knows where to find the last untracked stash two days after a storm. Someone who can find the warmest, sunniest run on the coldest day of winter, the best-shaped moguls, the most interesting groomed runs. Someone who knows the best boot fitter, or the best ski tuner in town, and wants to tell you about them. The sort of skier you'd like to meet when you first visit a new ski area.

Peter, Seth, and I have lived this life—we've called more than one ski resort *home.* And we are ready to take you on an insider's tour of *our* favorite ski mountains. Sure, it's a tall order to give you the inside scoop on the fifty major western ski areas and resorts visited in this guide. We have lived for years at some, taught skiing at others, and visited still others so often they feel like second homes. No, we can't claim total, intimate, in-depth "insider's" knowledge of every one of these amazing ski areas, although—to answer an obvious question—yes, we really have skied every area we've written about. So our solution is to offer a multiple look at things, to give our own impressions and very personal views of skiing in our respective regions of the West. But we've also gone out of our way to consult local insiders in virtually all these ski resorts and ask them for the sort of information that we could only know about our own "home" mountains.

Veteran ski journalist Claire Walter has worked on this and the previous edition. Claire has been writing about skiing for more than 20 years and, unlike many ski writers, has spent most of that time on the slopes instead of in the spa. For this edition, our team welcomed Kurt Repanshek, an expert skier and highly respected writer.

Bob Sehlinger, the creator of the *Unofficial Guide* series and the sixth author of this guide, is known for his detailed, consumer-oriented travel journalism. While the rest of us flexed our legs over the bumps, cruised the bowls, and tracked up the fresh powder, Bob was unraveling the mysteries of finding the perfect condo, shopping for ski vacation packages, and getting discounts on lift tickets. Equally important, Bob brought to this collaboration the singular perspective of an avid intermediate skier. His sensitivity to the aspirations and fears of beginner, novice, and intermediate skiers is central to our focus throughout the guide.

This combination of an instructor's perspective and practical consumer tips, we know, really works. This *Unofficial Guide* to the best skiing across the West grew out of several earlier volumes, which focused on Colorado and Utah—books that quickly became the most trusted and most useful skiers' guides to those states. This more comprehensive guide has expanded the concept, the geographic range, and the number of ski areas and resorts covered. It will take you a skier's lifetime to explore and enjoy every ski mountain covered here. It won't be a wasted lifetime.

—Lito Tejada-Flores

Skiing the West: An Overview

OK, we confess. It was somewhat arbitrary to divide this guidebook to Western skiing, as we have, into three sections. It could have been two: the Rockies and the coastal mountains. Or we could have taken a state-by-state approach. But there's a certain logic, and a lot of practicality, in the way we divided our coverage of the western ski scene.

To begin with, Rocky Mountain skiing differs from West Coast skiing, because Rocky Mountain snow is so different from the denser, moister snow that falls near the Pacific. Snow is lighter and drier throughout the entire Rocky Mountain region than anywhere else in the country. And while Colorado and its Rocky Mountain neighbors can't really dispute Utah's claim to the lightest, driest snow of all, to visitors it all seems feather-light.

Why is this snow so light, so dry, so fine? It's because the Rockies enjoy (and occasionally suffer from) an altogether different climate—a so-called "continental" rather than a "maritime" climate. All other ski regions in the United States are close to the coasts or the Great Lakes. And water means wet: wet sand at the beach, wet snow at Tahoe, at Sugarbush in Vermont, at White Pass in Washington. But when storms travel a thousand miles or so, over intervening ranges and rain-shadowed desert basins, losing moisture all the way, what they finally drop on mountain ranges in the center of the continent is light, dry fluff. The name's the same (only Eskimos, we're told, have over thirty separate words for different types of snow) and so is the color, white on white on white, but there the similarity ends. Rocky Mountain snow is drier, lighter, fluffier than can possibly be described or imagined if you haven't already skied it.

And why is light snow important? Light, dry "continental" snow versus wetter, heavier "maritime" snow? Simple: people tend to ski better—much better—on light, dry snow. That's a promise. You'll ski better in the Rockies than you do at home (unless the Rockies are your home). This is the real reason skiers from all over tend to get hooked on Rocky Mountain skiing and return, year after year after year. This promise—that you'll actually ski better—is not clearly articulated on the cover of any of the hundreds of thousands of ski/tourist brochures that tout the virtues of the Rocky Mountain ski experience. But an enormous segment of the tourist economy of Colorado and Utah depends on this particular promise being legitimate. It is.

In the Rocky Mountain ski region Colorado and Utah often get the lion's share of attention. Not, we hasten to add, because their ski resorts are that much better than those in nearby states, but simply because there are more major resorts in those two states than in the rest of the Rockies put together. That's why we've divided our Rocky Mountain ski coverage into two sections. Colorado and New Mexico form a natural pairing. In terms of climate, skiing in the southern Rockies is a sort of luxury experience, in part because of the abundant sunshine and the seldom bitter winter temperatures. By contrast, winter in Utah and the northern Rockies states of Wyoming, Montana, and Idaho is perhaps a harsher, more hard-core experience. This is not to say that ski areas in these states aren't blessed with sunny days too; they are, but maybe fewer of them. And these states are also blessed with the same phenomenal, light Rocky Mountain snow. And since Utah's mountains intercept eastward-moving storms long before they hit Colorado, their powder dumps are often larger and deeper. In the last analysis, storms, not sunshine, define a skier's experience, a skier's memories. But when contrasting skiing in the northern and southern Rockies, the best one can come up with is a difference of degree, not of kind. Sharper differences emerge when one looks at California and West Coast skiing.

West Coast snow has its own pluses, its own charms, its fanatical aficionados too. But it's different. The maritime climate of the coastal states makes this snow wetter (relatively speaking) and denser; but the snow makes up in depth and in abundance what it lacks in lightness. Ski resorts out west don't generally have to invest millions in snowmaking systems to guarantee early openings before Christmas. And surprise: West Coast snow actually lets you ski more terrain, since it fills in rocky shapes (even cliffs) with something more than light fluffy powder. As the season progresses, more and more unlikely spots become skiable. At areas like Squaw Valley, Mammoth Mountain, and Whistler-Blackcomb, this deep, dense snow allows bold skiers to leave their tracks on slopes that would be suicidal in the Rockies. And the not-so-bold, or the rest of us, can enjoy a far longer ski season in California's High Sierra or in the Pacific Northwest than anywhere else in the country. Late-spring skiing is the norm, not the exception, in this region.

There is another subtle and rather intriguing difference between skiing in the far West and skiing in the Rockies. In general, you'll find more ski *resorts* in the Rocky Mountain states and more ski *areas* along the West Coast. This is not a facetious or merely semantic distinction. By ski *resort* we mean a skiing destination where the village beneath the ski mountain is part and parcel of the skier's experience. A ski *area,* by contrast, need be nothing more than a mountain, a lift system, and a parking lot. Generally a ski resort invites you for at least a week-long ski vacation or longer, while a ski area tempts you only for the day or maybe a weekend. Now that's a very broad generalization, as is the claim that there are more resorts in the Rockies. Generalizations invite exceptions, and there are many.

You'll notice immediately that we've been very inclusive, describing both major ski resorts and smaller ski areas. But not all of them. Our goal was simple: write an insider's guide to the *very best skiing in the West.* We've looked for the best skiing across our vast region, and described it in detail. And we have left out ski areas, ski resorts, ski mountains, ski places that were not exciting enough to really capture and captivate distant skiers. (It's always reasonable to visit and enjoy your local ski area, no matter how small or limited—as thousands of dedicated midwestern skiers prove every weekend of the winter on ski hills only a couple of hundred feet high.)

Typically, Rocky Mountain ski resorts draw skiers from both coasts, from all over the country, and from abroad, while for the most part, West Coast skiing attracts residents of California, Oregon, and Washington. High Sierra ski resorts, for example, have been hard put to convince East Coast skiers to fly over the Rockies to visit Lake Tahoe. However, they attract Europeans and Japanese by the thousands. Nevertheless, we'd encourage skiers from any corner of the country to explore this whole region—including California and the Pacific Northwest—where they'll find great resorts and legendary skiing. Where will you find your favorite skiing? Where will you live your most memorable days on skis? That's impossible to say, but we can promise you this: in another 20 ski seasons you are not going to run out of exciting ski destinations or snowy surprises here in the West.

Although we've focused our eyes, our hearts, and our word processors primarily on the skiing itself—describing how skiers of every level, beginner, novice, intermediate, advanced or expert, can enjoy a peak experience on each mountain—we haven't really neglected the resort life below the slopes. Our favorite lodges, restaurants, and local hangouts are spotlighted, even though we didn't think it necessary, or appropriate, to turn this skiing guidebook into an encyclopedia of travel details.

How to Use This Guidebook

This book is designed for browsing, for reference, for fun. But above all, it's designed to encourage you to visit new and different ski destinations across the West. And to get the most out of each mountain once you get there. If you were the kind of skier who was content to visit the same local ski area forever, you probably would never have picked up this book. But now that you've been touched by a winter wanderlust, where to start? And how to choose?

To help you navigate your way through the in-depth chapters covering each ski destination (the heart of the book), we've put together mini-descriptions of each ski mountain that summarize what differentiates the skiing and vacation experience there. You'll find an innovative rating comparison of ski area statistics in the section on planning your trip. And of course, you'll probably want to browse through the different chapters in your own particular order of interest. You can read summaries of ski resorts that friends have told you about or ski destinations that have been written up in the national ski press, to see whether we agreed or disagreed with *Skiing, Snow Country, Ski,* or *Powder* magazines. Eventually you may read every chapter in this book (but please, not straight through, not from beginning to end).

Yet when the time comes to make plans for next season's ski vacation, don't trust statistics, don't take out a pencil and make a list of pluses and minuses. Instead, listen to that little voice inside you that whispers: "Wouldn't it be neat to go out to Utah and see if the snow's as good as they say," or, "Why don't we visit one of those little unknown places this time," or, "I've never skied in California, wonder what it's like," or, "Let's go somewhere really hard and see if we're up to it." In short, choose your ski vacation destination for the same inexplicable, unjustifiable sort of reasons that made you a skier in the first place. For romance. For adventure. For the hell of it. The West, as they say, is a big place. You'll find all the snow, all the adventure, all the romance you can handle out here. And more.

Tech Tips

Because three of us are ski instructors, we would feel remiss if we didn't encourage you a little to improve your technique. To this end we have sandwiched some instructional tips between our profiles of the resorts. We call these tips "Tech Tips."

There's no way to become an accomplished skier without paying your dues. Frustration, falls, occasional failure, lots of days—and miles—on skis are part of the recipe. But there are also shortcuts, learning strategies that will make your practice time pass quicker and will get you faster where you want to go. Here are our suggestions for more efficient progress on skis.

Terrain will be your best teacher. It's humbling for a ski instructor to admit this, but it's true. You should learn to distinguish between three types of ski terrain: practice/learning slopes, pleasure/performance slopes, and challenging slopes. Basically "learning terrain" is ski terrain that's a little *too* easy for you: slopes so easy there is absolutely no doubt in your mind that you can make every mistake in the book and still recover. This is essential if you are going to concentrate 100% on new, hence psychologically risky, moves. It's even true in bumps. You will master medium-size bumps by practicing in trivial minibumps, and will learn to ski giant man-eating moguls by practicing the moves in comfy medium-size ones. Always pick practice/learning terrain that's too easy; it frees your mind.

At the other end of the scale you'll find "adventure" or "challenge" terrain: slopes that are honestly too hard, where you're scrambling just to survive. It's okay to ski over your head from time to time, which can be a confidence builder of a sort. But don't let friends, or your own ego, push you over your head too often. It will permanently retard your progress as a skier by reinforcing awkward survival moves to the point of ingrained habits. Your best bet for rapid progress is to spend about two-thirds to three-quarters of your skiing day on performance slopes (slopes in your comfort range) and the rest of the time concentrating on practicing key moves on easier, learning terrain. But don't practice anything all day long, or even for hours on end; you'll burn out. Better to ski three runs for the hell of it, and then slow down and focus your attention on skiing form for just one good run. A good instructor will automatically strive for this sort of balance between concentrated, focused practice and relaxed pleasure skiing where you can slowly "ski in" the new habits.

While constant attempts to practice new skills, hour after hour, are usually counterproductive, it is still a good idea to devote a week of time to achieving some sort of major goal or breakthrough in your skiing. Whether a simple week of group lessons, or a more focused program, the effect of such commitment is cumulative and dramatic. On the other hand, one- or two-hour lessons are a waste of time for most skiers. And half-day lessons or three-hour "clinics" are about as successful as any other quick-fix remedies and not effective at all in terms of changing your basic skiing habits. Change takes time. And the advantage of longer lessons (all day at a minimum or week-long if possible) is that your instructor will have sufficient time to guide and adjust the alternation of focused practice periods with spontaneous skiing mileage in such a way as to achieve the greatest results and the longest-lasting ones.

Finally, focus on one thing at a time: one movement, one skill, one skiing pattern. No one can do more. Don't let your concentration get fragmented by half a dozen well-intentioned tips. A good instructor may express the same point in a variety of ways, but he or she will continue to guide you toward one goal at a time.

Good skiing!

Letters, Comments, and Questions from Readers

Many of those who use the *Unofficial Guides* write to us asking questions, making comments, or sharing their own strategies for planning and enjoying a trip. We appreciate all such input, both positive and critical, and encourage our readers to continue writing. Readers' comments and observations are frequently incorporated into revised editions of the *Unofficial Guides* and have contributed immeasurably to their improvement. Please write to:

Lito, Peter, Seth, Claire, Kurt, and Bob
The Unofficial Guide to Skiing and Snowboarding in the West
P.O. Box 43673
Birmingham, AL 35243

When you write, be sure to put a return address on your letter as well as on the envelope; sometimes envelopes and letters get separated. It's also a good idea to include your phone number. And remember, our work often requires that we be out of the office for long periods of time, so forgive us if our response is a little slow.

How to E-mail the Authors

You can e-mail the authors at UnofficialGuides@Menasharidge.com. Although *Unofficial Guide* e-mail is *not* forwarded to us when we're traveling, we will respond as soon as possible when we return.

Map Legend

First-Aid Station	⊕		Highway	══════
Dining	✕		Cross-Country Skiing	··········
Rest Room	♥♥		Green Trail	··········
Back Country Gates	❶		Blue Trail	▦▦▦▦▦
Shopping	$		Black Trail	──────
Half-pipe	▥		Ski Boundary	─ ─ ─ ─
Handicap Access	♿		Ski Lift	──────
Terrain Park	⬭		Express Ski Lift	═════
Cat Area	⬳		Proposed Lift	── ──
Danger No Skiing Area	⬮		Proposed Express Lift	──▬──
Cliff Area	⬮			

Part One

Planning Your Ski Trip

Bob Sehlinger

Things to Consider before You Go

This guide has a double function: first, to help you select the right ski destination for your specific skill level, preferences, and enthusiasm; and second, to help you get the very most out of your visit to any skiing resort in the West. However, before you leave home, in the early stages of planning your perfect ski trip, there are a number of issues that also must be considered.

When to Go

The resorts are busiest, the slopes most crowded, and the lodging at capacity during the Christmas/New Year's week and over the Presidents' Day holiday weekend in February. When there is early snow, the Thanksgiving holiday period is also very busy. If you are crowd-averse, these are times to avoid.

All of February and the first three weeks of March are high season for most ski resorts, though the specific dates vary from area to area. While February is still quite busy, crowds during this month almost never approach the levels seen during the holiday periods in December and January.

December *before* Christmas week and January *after* New Year's, as well as late March and early April, are considered low or value season. Lodging is less expensive and the slopes are usually less crowded during this time.

The best time of year for sparse crowds, good snow conditions, *and* good deals on lodging and airfare is in January after New Year's. Mountain conditions in November, December, late March, and April can be iffy.

Having written about Walt Disney World for 20 years, I know that the day of lowest attendance, year after year, is Superbowl Sunday. The good news is that Superbowl Sunday and the following week are also very slow times for ski resorts. I skied Breckenridge, Keystone, and Copper on Superbowl Sunday and during the following week and never waited more than three to five minutes tops to board the lifts. Crowds began to pick up the Friday after the Superbowl. This was the only day during our ski vacation when crowds were a factor. Even then, the lines topped out at about eight minutes for the most heavily trafficked lifts.

Where to Go

A major objective of this guide is to help you find the perfect mountain for your skill level and taste in skiing. Prior to embarking on that quest, however, we thought we would share some insider knowledge that will make you a more savvy shopper.

Special Events

In addition to snowfall, holidays, and high and low seasons, you need to consider special events. The Sundance Film Festival, for example, held during the second half of January in Park City, Utah, puts quite a strain on lodging and restaurants and also adds significant numbers of skiers to nearby slopes. Spring break brings increased business to ski mountains, as do ski races, music festivals, and conventions.

Local Skier Impact

If skiing conditions are good and a resort is located within two hours of a large city, you can expect to be joined on the mountain by an army of locals. This is particularly true on weekends. If you truly hate crowds, you might consider going to a more isolated resort, such as Telluride, Steamboat, Crested Butte, Jackson Hole, Big Sky, or Sun Valley. While isolation does not guarantee that you'll have the mountain to yourself, you will avoid the throngs of day skiers pouring out of the large cities.

If you choose a resort region accessible to locals, head for the least difficult mountains on weekends. Beaver Creek, for example, will be less crowded than Vail on weekends. Likewise, Buttermilk will be less populated than Aspen Mountain or Snowmass. In the Salt Lake City area, avoid Alta, Snowbird, and Park City on weekends. Instead try Brighton, Snowbasin, and the Canyons. You get the idea.

Games Ski Mountains Play

Ski mountains are like politicians: they want to be all things to all people. Every mountain, for example, represents itself as providing a complete skiing experience. This means, of course, that there *must* be beginner terrain, intermediate terrain, and advanced/expert terrain. Even if the whole mountain consists of three runs drooping off a 200-foot moraine, you can bet that one of the trails will be rated green, one blue, and one black.

The grand result of this denial and wishful thinking is a ski-trail rating system that has its origins in Fantasyland and lacks any hint of objective rating criteria. If you can handle the black diamonds at Ober Gatlinburg in Tennessee, does that mean you are ready to ski advanced terrain at Telluride? Hardly. In fact, you would be much better off preparing for Telluride by skiing the green runs at Snowbird!

The more benign manifestation of marketing-driven ratings is seen in the easier mountains that tend to overrate their trails. Skiing black-marked trails that are really blue, and blue-marked trails that should be rated green, makes the skier feel more skilled than he actually is. This builds confidence, reinforces the ego, and enhances enjoyment of the day. Regardless of the objective validity of the trail ratings, this skier is skiing within his skill level and probably will not get into anything seriously over his head unless, of course, he decides to go to another mountain.

While those who ski overgraded mountains might form an exaggerated opinion of their ability, skiers skiing undergraded mountains have the potential for getting into real trouble. Mountains that do not offer much, if any, easy terrain owe it to the skier to acknowledge this fact. Aspen Mountain, for example, states forthrightly that there is no easy terrain. Read my lips, "no green runs." Most mountains, unfortunately, are less forthcoming. In our mountain profiles, therefore, we have taken pains to identify mountains where trail difficulty is over- or undergraded. Take this into consideration when choosing a resort.

Another deceptive, though less dangerous, marketing trick is the exaggeration of skiable acreage. Skiable acreage is the statistic used by resorts to describe size. Supposedly, the more skiable acreage, the larger the resort. Skiable acreage at many resorts, however, has little to do with the number or length of maintained trails. Instead, it is the total number of acres within the resort boundaries where skiing is allowed. Some resorts count all of their acreage, including those acres occupied by roads, parking lots, buildings, unskiable cliffs, and streams. Others count parts of the ski area not serviced by lifts. In the final analysis, because every resort uses a different calculation, it is impossible to compare resorts on the basis of skiable acreage.

Ski mountains are also notorious for exaggerating their vertical—the difference in altitude from the top of the resort to the base. The most common prevarication here is to measure from the top of the highest peak, even though the lifts don't go up that high. Additionally, on many mountains, you cannot ski all the way from the top (whatever that may be) to the bottom. Instead, you must interrupt your descent with a lift ride to reposition yourself for the continuation of the run to the bottom.

Then there is the "longest trail" ruse. While resort promotional literature could boast a trail 3.5 miles long, the run in reality often may be either a catwalk or three or four different trails somehow tenuously connected.

Lift capacity—the number of skiers the lift system can move up the mountain in an hour—is another misleading descriptor. For most resorts, the number is derived by adding the hourly capacity of all lifts. This bears little resemblance to actual conditions on the mountain, because it assumes an optimal distribution of skiers to all of the lifts. In reality, some lifts are inundated with skiers, while other lifts dispatch chair after empty chair up the mountain. Quite a few resorts have lifts that are not even opened unless the mountain is really swamped with business. In any event, lift capacity and mountain design are vastly different animals. A resort can have an impressive lift capacity on paper but function inefficiently as a result of poorly designed or badly placed lifts.

A Word about Grooming

Many American skiers love smooth, manicured, machine-groomed slopes. Some skiers even choose a ski mountain on the basis of the resort's reputation for grooming. As long as the sun shines, life is good for the well groomed. When it snows, however, it usually takes the cat operators a day or two to get the new snow smoothed and packed down. If you are a skier who by preference or skill limitations demands groomed runs, here are a few things you should know.

Although some mountains groom more than others, every mountain has a basic grooming plan, and most are similar in several respects. Grooming usually begins as soon as the mountain shuts down for the night. Advanced/expert runs scheduled for grooming are tackled first, followed by intermediate runs. Lower intermediate and beginner runs are groomed last, often in the early morning just before the mountain reopens.

If new snowfall stops by midnight, many blue and almost all green trails will be groomed before morning. When the snow continues past midnight into the wee hours, new snow will fall on many runs where grooming has been completed. While some resorts take a second crack at popular green runs just before opening, there's generally not much that can be done until the next evening's crews go out. If you are looking for the best-groomed mountain around after a new snow, odds are it will be the mountain that caters more to beginners and intermediates.

Special Considerations

When determining where to go, there are some situations that require special consideration. If you are not in as good physical condition as you would like to be, you might give some thought to looking at mountains less than 10,000 feet high. There are more of them than you might expect. Also look at resorts where there is good skiing of the type you prefer (cruising, bumps, whatever) lower on the mountain. Conversely, if you are skiing in November, late March, or April, higher mountains provide the greatest assurance of good skiing conditions.

If you are a party animal and like to stay out late, or if you just enjoy sleeping in mornings, you might be happier skiing in Utah, Montana, or Idaho. Because these states are situated in the westernmost part of the mountain time zone, it stays light later in the day, and some of the resorts remain open an hour or so longer than many Colorado resorts.

If you want to ski in the West, but have a limited number of days available, you can increase your time on the mountain by skiing on your travel days. If you are flying, travel-day skiing is most easily accomplished at one of the nine resorts within 45 minutes of Salt Lake City. An early flight from most cities will get you to Salt Lake City before noon, even with a connecting flight. If you have your own equipment, you can be on the slopes by 1 p.m. Most Utah resorts keep lifts running until 4 or 4:30 p.m. On your return, you can ski until 2 p.m. or so and still make it to the airport in plenty of time to catch a flight home.

If you are flying from the Pacific Coast states, you can enjoy travel-day skiing also by flying into Reno, Nevada, and hitting the slopes at one of the Lake Tahoe resorts, or flying into Vancouver, British Columbia, and skiing Whistler or Blackcomb. Travel-day skiing in Colorado is difficult, even if you take a commuter flight to the resort area. If you fly into Denver International Airport and rent a car, you are really at a disadvantage. You must drive from one-and-a-half to four hours to reach the resorts. If you are really avid, however, and if you can get an early direct flight to Denver, it is possible to arrive, rent a car, and drive to Loveland, Keystone, or Breckenridge in time for a half day of skiing. When the mountain closes, you can continue on to your final resort destination.

Comparing Ski Mountains

The essence of this guide can be found in the comprehensive profiles of the ski mountains. There we take you on a detailed tour of each mountain, pointing out all the characteristics that make this mountain special. By reading the ski-mountain profiles, you will discover the particular features, style, and atmosphere of the resorts, and you will be able to confidently select a resort that fits your skiing and vacation preferences. At the same time, we understand that you may want to narrow your range of choices before you dig into the profiles. Thus we have attempted to rate the ski mountains in a number of areas that are of interest to skiers of all skill levels. The ratings are presented specifically to facilitate a quick comparison of the ski mountains. It should be stressed that many important aspects of a ski vacation, such as restaurants, nightlife, and the character of the overall resort community, are not included in the ratings.

Because the *Unofficial Guides* are known for their strong consumer orientation, we are accustomed to being direct, evaluative, and critical. Thus it is our preference to compare, rate, and rank according to measurable and verifiable objective standards. When we initiated the process of comparing ski mountains, however, we encountered strongly held personal differences within our research/author team. One point of view is that a ski mountain, by virtue of changes in season, temperature, visibility, weather, slope grooming, and the number of skiers on the mountain, provides a totally different experience every day. This immense variability of conditions, it follows, precludes drawing conclusions from ratings that compare different mountains. Moreover, mountains with very similar statistics and physical characteristics can have a very different feel.

The counterargument is that every ski area starts with a mountain, a unique physical presence that is designed and arranged in a definite way. Trails can be measured in terms of top-to-bottom elevation differential and length of run. Mountain design and lift placement likewise can be analyzed and rated for adequacy, convenience, and efficiency. According to this argument, there is, for any ski area, a baseline measurement that represents that mountain's design and physical characteristics.

After much discussion, we agreed to rate all of the major western ski mountains (as well as a sampling of the smaller mountains) and allow the reader to determine whether or not the rating comparisons are useful. Variables such as inclement weather, poor visibility, changing surface conditions, unusually light or heavy skier traffic, seasonal thawing or freezing, and/or inadequate snowbase are not considered. Instead, the mountain is evaluated on a mythical average day when the snowbase permits operation of the entire mountain, when visibility is perfect, when normal slope-grooming schedules are followed, and when skier traffic is average. Rating each mountain's characteristics, serviceability, and design sometimes calls for a physical measurement, sometimes for a personal opinion, and sometimes for both.

Mountain Size

Maintained Trails The relative size of the resort in terms of developed and maintained (but not necessarily frequently groomed) trails—trails depicted as green, blue, and black on the resort trail map.

Size ratings run along a continuum and are scored as follows:

Very Large	Large	Medium	Small	Very Small
▲▲▲▲▲	▲▲▲▲	▲▲▲	▲▲	▲

Off-Trail Skiable Terrain This is a rating primarily of interest to advanced and expert skiers. Using the same rating scale as above, the area is rated in terms of the size of its off-trail skiable terrain. This rating wholly *excludes* all developed trails, but includes bowls.

Skiable Vertical Top-to-bottom skiable vertical served by lifts. This excludes any vertical where the skier must climb to a higher elevation from the lift exit.

3,100 feet & higher	2,600–3,099	2,100–2,599	1,600–2,099	1,599 feet & less
▲▲▲▲▲	▲▲▲▲	▲▲▲	▲▲	▲

Average Length of Run Excludes catwalks and nearly flat run-outs at the end of runs. On average, the designated runs/trails are:

Very Long	Long	Average	Short	Very Short
▲▲▲▲▲	▲▲▲▲	▲▲▲	▲▲	▲

Mountain Size

	Maintained Trails	Off-Trail Skiable Terrain	Skiable Vertical	Average Length of Run
Alpine Meadows	▲▲▲▲	▲▲▲	▲▲	▲▲▲
Alta	▲▲▲	▲▲▲▲▲▲	▲▲▲	▲▲▲
Arapahoe Basin	▲▲	▲▲▲▲	▲▲▲	▲▲▲
Aspen Highlands	▲▲▲	▲▲▲	▲▲▲▲▲	▲▲▲
Aspen Mountain	▲▲▲	▲▲	▲▲▲▲▲	▲▲▲
Bear Valley	▲▲▲	▲▲▲▲	▲▲	▲▲▲
Beaver Creek	▲▲▲▲	▲▲	▲▲▲▲▲	▲▲▲▲
Big Mountain	▲▲▲▲	▲▲▲▲	▲▲▲	▲▲▲▲
Big Sky	▲▲▲▲	▲▲▲▲▲	▲▲▲▲▲	▲▲▲▲
Blackcomb	▲▲▲▲▲	▲▲▲▲▲	▲▲▲▲▲	▲▲▲▲▲
Breckenridge	▲▲▲▲	▲▲▲	▲▲▲▲	▲▲▲
Brian Head	▲▲▲	▲	▲	▲▲▲
Bridger Bowl	▲▲	▲▲▲▲	▲▲	▲▲▲
Brighton	▲▲▲	▲▲▲	▲▲	▲▲▲
Buttermilk	▲▲▲	▲	▲▲	▲▲▲
The Canyons	▲▲▲	▲▲▲	▲▲▲▲	▲▲▲
Copper Mountain	▲▲▲▲	▲▲▲▲	▲▲▲▲	▲▲▲
Crested Butte	▲▲▲	▲▲▲▲	▲▲▲▲	▲▲▲
Crystal Mountain	▲▲▲▲	▲▲▲▲▲	▲▲▲▲▲	▲▲▲
Deer Valley	▲▲▲▲	▲▲▲	▲▲▲	▲▲▲
Durango	▲▲▲	▲	▲▲	▲▲▲
Fernie Alpine	▲▲▲	▲▲▲▲	▲▲▲	▲▲▲
Grand Targhee	▲▲▲	▲▲▲▲	▲▲▲	▲▲▲▲
Heavenly	▲▲▲▲	▲▲▲▲	▲▲▲▲	▲▲▲▲
Jackson Hole	▲▲▲▲	▲▲▲▲▲	▲▲▲▲▲	▲▲▲▲▲
June Mountain	▲▲▲	▲▲	▲▲▲	▲▲▲
Keystone	▲▲▲▲	▲	▲▲▲	▲▲▲▲
Kicking Horse	▲▲▲	▲▲▲▲▲	▲▲▲▲▲	▲▲▲▲▲

Mountain Size *(continued)*			
Maintained Trails	**Off-Trail Skiable Terrain**	**Skiable Vertical**	**Average Length of Run**
Kirkwood ▲▲▲	▲▲▲▲	▲▲	▲▲▲
Loveland ▲▲	▲▲▲	▲▲▲	▲▲▲
Mammoth ▲▲▲▲▲	▲▲▲▲	▲▲▲▲▲	▲▲▲
Mission Ridge ▲▲▲	▲▲▲▲	▲▲▲	▲▲
Mount Bachelor ▲▲▲▲▲	▲▲▲▲	▲▲▲▲▲	▲▲▲▲
Mount Baker ▲▲▲	▲▲▲	▲▲	▲▲
Northstar ▲▲▲	▲▲	▲▲▲	▲▲▲▲
Panorama ▲▲▲▲	▲▲▲▲	▲▲▲▲▲	▲▲▲▲
Park City ▲▲▲▲	▲▲▲▲	▲▲▲▲▲	▲▲▲
Powder Mountain ▲▲▲	▲▲▲	▲▲	▲▲▲
Santa Fe ▲▲▲	▲▲	▲▲▲	▲▲▲
Schweitzer Mountain ▲▲▲	▲▲▲▲	▲▲▲	▲▲▲▲
Sierra-at-Tahoe ▲▲▲	▲▲	▲▲▲	▲▲▲
Snowbasin ▲▲▲	▲▲▲	▲▲▲	▲▲▲
Snowbird ▲▲▲	▲▲▲▲▲	▲▲▲▲▲	▲▲▲▲
Snowmass ▲▲▲▲▲	▲▲▲	▲▲▲▲▲	▲▲▲▲
Solitude ▲▲▲	▲▲▲▲	▲▲	▲▲▲
Squaw Valley ▲▲▲▲▲	▲▲▲▲▲	▲▲▲▲	▲▲▲
Steamboat ▲▲▲▲▲	▲▲▲	▲▲▲▲▲	▲▲▲▲
Stevens Pass ▲▲▲	▲▲▲▲	▲▲	▲▲▲
Sugar Bowl ▲▲▲	▲▲	▲	▲▲▲
Sundance ▲▲	▲	▲▲▲	▲▲▲
Sun Peaks ▲▲▲▲	▲▲▲	▲▲▲	▲▲▲
Sun Valley ▲▲▲▲	▲▲▲	▲▲▲▲▲	▲▲▲▲
Taos ▲▲▲▲	▲▲▲	▲▲▲▲	▲▲▲▲
Telluride ▲▲▲	▲▲▲	▲▲▲▲▲	▲▲▲▲
Vail ▲▲▲▲▲	▲▲▲▲▲	▲▲▲▲▲	▲▲▲▲
Whistler ▲▲▲▲▲	▲▲▲▲▲	▲▲▲▲▲	▲▲▲▲▲
Winter Park ▲▲▲	▲▲▲	▲▲▲▲	▲▲▲▲

Skiable Terrain Available for Specific Skill Levels

This rating is designed to allow you to make comparisons between ski mountains of different sizes concerning the availability of a particular type of terrain.

The rating has nothing to do with a resort's percentage breakdown of terrain (i.e., 25% beginner, 50% intermediate, 25% expert). A small resort may have 90% intermediate terrain, but still not have enough runs to keep an intermediate skier happy for half a day. A high rating (5) for intermediate terrain availability would indicate that an intermediate skier would have a large and varied selection of suitable terrain, so much, in fact, that it would take two days or more to explore it all. Conversely, a resort where the intermediate terrain could be exhausted in a morning would receive a low score.

Extensive Availability		Moderate Availability		Limited Availability
▲▲▲▲▲	▲▲▲▲	▲▲▲	▲▲	▲

Available Skiable Terrain

	Beginner	Novice	Inter-mediate	Advanced	Expert
Alpine Meadows	▲▲▲	▲▲▲	▲▲▲▲	▲▲▲▲	▲▲▲▲
Alta	▲▲	▲▲▲	▲▲▲	▲▲▲	▲▲▲▲▲
Arapahoe Basin	▲	▲▲	▲▲▲	▲▲▲	▲▲▲▲
Aspen Highlands	▲▲	▲	▲▲▲▲	▲▲▲	▲▲▲
Aspen Mountain	none	none	▲▲▲▲	▲▲▲▲▲	▲▲▲▲
Bear Valley	▲▲▲	▲▲▲	▲▲▲	▲▲▲▲	▲▲▲▲
Beaver Creek	▲▲	▲▲▲	▲▲▲▲	▲▲▲	▲▲▲▲
Big Mountain	▲▲▲	▲▲▲▲	▲▲▲▲	▲▲▲▲	▲▲
Big Sky	▲▲▲▲	▲▲▲▲	▲▲▲▲	▲▲▲▲	▲▲▲▲▲
Blackcomb	▲▲▲▲	▲▲▲	▲▲▲▲▲	▲▲▲▲▲	▲▲▲▲▲
Breckenridge	▲▲▲▲	▲▲▲▲	▲▲▲▲▲	▲▲▲▲	▲▲▲
Brian Head	▲▲▲	▲▲▲	▲▲▲▲	▲▲▲	▲
Bridger Bowl	▲▲▲	▲▲▲▲	▲▲▲	▲▲▲	▲▲▲▲
Brighton	▲▲	▲▲▲	▲▲▲▲	▲▲▲	▲▲
Buttermilk	▲▲	▲▲▲▲	▲▲▲▲▲	▲	none
The Canyons	▲▲▲	▲▲▲	▲▲▲	▲▲▲	▲▲▲
Copper Mountain	▲▲▲	▲▲▲▲	▲▲▲▲▲	▲▲▲	▲▲
Crested Butte	▲▲▲	▲▲	▲▲▲▲	▲▲▲▲▲	▲▲▲▲▲
Crystal Mountain	▲▲▲▲	▲▲▲	▲▲▲▲	▲▲▲▲▲	▲▲▲▲▲
Deer Valley	▲▲	▲▲	▲▲▲	▲▲▲▲▲	▲▲▲
Durango	▲▲	▲▲	▲▲▲▲	▲▲	▲
Fernie Alpine	▲▲	▲▲▲	▲▲▲	▲▲▲▲	▲▲▲▲
Grand Targhee	▲▲	▲▲	▲▲▲▲	▲▲▲▲	▲▲
Heavenly	▲▲▲	▲▲▲	▲▲▲▲▲	▲▲▲▲▲	▲▲▲▲
Jackson Hole	▲▲	▲▲▲	▲▲▲▲	▲▲▲▲	▲▲▲▲▲
June Mountain	▲▲▲▲▲	▲▲▲▲▲	▲▲▲▲▲	▲▲▲▲	▲▲
Keystone	▲▲	▲▲▲	▲▲▲▲▲	▲▲▲	▲
Kicking Horse	▲▲	▲▲▲	▲▲▲▲	▲▲▲▲	▲▲▲▲▲
Kirkwood	▲▲▲	▲▲▲▲	▲▲▲▲▲	▲▲▲▲	▲▲▲▲
Loveland	▲▲	▲▲▲	▲▲▲	▲▲▲	▲▲
Mammoth	▲▲▲	▲▲▲▲	▲▲▲▲▲	▲▲▲▲▲	▲▲▲▲▲
Mission Ridge	▲▲	▲▲▲	▲▲▲▲	▲▲▲	▲▲▲
Mount Bachelor	▲▲▲▲	▲▲▲▲	▲▲▲▲▲	▲▲▲▲	▲▲▲▲
Mount Baker	▲	▲▲	▲▲▲	▲▲▲	▲▲▲▲
Northstar	▲▲▲▲	▲▲▲▲▲	▲▲▲▲▲	▲▲▲▲	▲▲▲

Available Skiable Terrain (continued)

	Beginner	Novice	Inter-mediate	Advanced	Expert
Panorama	▲▲	▲▲▲	▲▲▲▲	▲▲▲▲	▲▲▲▲
Park City	▲▲▲	▲▲▲	▲▲▲▲	▲▲▲▲	▲▲▲
Powder Mountain	▲▲	▲▲▲▲	▲▲▲▲	▲▲	▲▲▲
Santa Fe	▲▲▲	▲▲▲	▲▲▲	▲▲	▲▲
Schweitzer Mtn.	▲▲▲	▲▲▲	▲▲▲▲	▲▲▲▲	▲▲
Sierra-at-Tahoe	▲▲▲▲	▲▲▲▲	▲▲▲▲▲	▲▲▲▲	▲▲▲▲
Snowbasin	▲▲▲	▲▲	▲▲▲▲	▲▲▲	▲▲▲
Snowbird	▲▲	▲▲	▲▲▲	▲▲▲▲	▲▲▲▲▲
Snowmass	▲▲	▲▲▲	▲▲▲▲▲	▲▲▲▲	▲▲▲
Solitude	▲▲▲▲	▲▲	▲▲▲	▲▲▲	▲▲▲
Squaw Valley	▲▲▲	▲▲▲	▲▲▲▲	▲▲▲▲▲	▲▲▲▲▲
Steamboat	▲▲▲	▲▲	▲▲▲▲▲	▲▲▲▲	▲▲▲
Stevens Pass	▲▲▲	▲▲▲▲	▲▲▲▲	▲▲▲▲	▲▲▲▲
Sugar Bowl	▲▲▲▲	▲▲▲▲	▲▲▲▲▲	▲▲▲▲	▲▲▲
Sundance	▲▲	▲▲▲	▲▲	▲	▲▲
Sun Peaks	▲▲▲	▲▲▲	▲▲▲▲▲	▲▲▲▲	▲▲▲
Sun Valley	▲▲▲▲	▲▲▲	▲▲▲▲	▲▲▲▲▲	▲▲▲
Taos	▲▲	▲▲	▲▲▲	▲▲▲▲▲	▲▲▲▲▲
Telluride	▲▲▲	▲▲▲	▲▲▲	▲▲▲▲▲	▲▲▲▲▲
Vail	▲	▲▲	▲▲▲▲▲	▲▲▲▲	▲▲▲▲
Whistler	▲▲▲▲	▲▲▲	▲▲▲▲▲	▲▲▲▲	▲▲▲▲
Winter Park	▲▲▲	▲▲	▲▲▲▲	▲▲▲▲	▲▲▲▲▲

Mountain Characteristics and Design

The following categories rate how well the mountain is designed, taking into consideration design elements that are particularly vexing to beginner and intermediate skiers. All categories are rated on 0–5 scale, with 5 stars considered best and 0 considered worst.

Ease of Orientation   How easy is it to find your way around the mountain? This considers quality of resort maps and signage. An easy mountain to navigate will score 5 stars.

Forgivingness   Can a beginner or intermediate really get into a bind by taking a wrong turn, or is there usually an escape route? A very forgiving mountain will score 5 stars.

True Fall Lines   This is the natural line of travel down the slope. A mountain with all or almost all true fall lines will score 5 stars. We realize that some more experienced skiers may prefer irregular fall lines, but as mentioned, the scoring is in accordance with the preferences of less skilled skiers.

Run Width   A mountain with a high percentage of wide runs will score 5 stars. For most beginners and intermediates, wider is better.

Line of Sight   This relates to the skier's ability in clear weather to see what is coming up during the run. Areas with a lot of blind drops and sharp turns score low in this category.

Intersections   This relates to the crossing of trails and the potential for collision. The fewer intersections the better, and the higher the score.

Confluence   This relates to some or many trails feeding into a single, congested trail or runout. A ski area where most of the mountain feeds into a primary trail to the resort center will score low.

Cat Tracks or Difficult Traverses   An area where skiers (beginner and intermediate, especially) must use cat tracks and/or difficult traverses to get down the mountain will score low.

Visual Intimidation   This psychological dimension relates to how intimidating the run appears from the top. A ski area with a number of visually frightening runs will score low.

Interesting All the Way Down   This rating characterizes whether, on average, runs maintain interest and challenge to the skier from beginning to end. Mountains where many runs traverse long flat sections and/or feed into long, uninteresting run-outs will score low.

Mountain Characteristics and Design Table I

	Ease of Orientation	Forgivingness	True Fall Lines	Run Width	Line of Sight
Alpine Meadows	▲▲▲	▲▲▲▲▲	▲▲▲	▲▲▲	▲▲▲
Alta	▲▲▲▲	▲▲▲	▲▲▲▲▲	▲▲▲▲	▲▲▲▲
Arapahoe Basin	▲▲▲▲	▲▲▲	▲▲▲▲	▲▲▲▲▲	▲▲▲▲▲
Aspen Highlands	▲▲	▲▲	▲▲	▲▲▲	▲▲▲
Aspen Mountain	▲▲▲▲	▲▲▲▲	▲▲▲▲	▲▲▲	▲▲▲▲
Bear Valley	▲▲▲▲	▲▲▲	▲▲▲▲	▲▲▲▲	▲▲▲▲
Beaver Creek	▲▲▲▲	▲▲▲	▲▲▲▲▲	▲▲▲▲	▲▲▲▲
Big Mountain	▲▲	▲▲▲▲	▲▲▲▲	▲▲▲▲▲	▲▲▲▲
Big Sky	▲▲▲	▲▲▲▲	▲▲▲▲	▲▲▲▲	▲▲▲
Blackcomb	▲▲▲	▲▲	▲▲	▲▲▲▲	▲▲▲
Breckenridge	▲▲	▲▲▲▲	▲▲▲	▲▲▲▲	▲▲▲▲
Brian Head	▲▲	▲▲▲▲	▲▲▲	▲▲▲	▲▲▲
Bridger Bowl	▲▲▲▲	▲▲▲▲	▲▲▲▲	▲▲▲▲	▲▲▲▲
Brighton	▲▲▲▲	▲▲▲	▲▲▲▲	▲▲▲	▲▲▲
Buttermilk	▲▲▲▲▲	▲▲▲▲▲	▲▲▲	▲▲▲▲	▲▲▲▲▲
The Canyons	▲▲▲	▲▲▲▲	▲▲▲	▲▲▲▲	▲▲▲

Mountain Characteristics and Design Table I *(continued)*

	Ease of Orientation	Forgiv- ingness	True Fall Lines	Run Width	Line of Sight
Copper Mountain	▲▲▲	▲▲▲▲	▲▲▲▲	▲▲▲▲	▲▲▲▲
Crested Butte	▲▲▲	▲▲	▲▲▲▲	▲▲▲	▲▲▲
Crystal Mountain	▲▲▲▲	▲▲▲	▲▲▲▲	▲▲▲▲	▲▲▲▲
Deer Valley	▲▲▲	▲▲▲▲	▲▲▲▲▲	▲▲▲▲	▲▲▲▲
Durango	▲▲	▲▲▲	▲▲▲▲	▲▲	▲▲
Fernie Alpine	▲▲▲	▲▲▲	▲▲▲	▲▲▲	▲▲▲
Grand Targhee	▲▲▲▲▲	▲▲▲▲	▲▲▲▲▲	▲▲▲▲▲	▲▲▲▲▲
Heavenly	▲▲	▲▲▲▲	▲▲	▲▲▲	▲▲▲
Jackson Hole	▲▲	▲▲▲	▲▲▲▲▲	▲▲▲▲	▲▲▲
June Mountain	▲▲▲▲	▲▲▲▲▲	▲▲▲	▲▲▲▲	▲▲▲▲
Keystone	▲▲▲▲	▲▲▲▲	▲▲▲▲▲	▲▲▲	▲▲▲▲
Kicking Horse	▲▲▲	▲▲▲	▲▲▲	▲▲▲▲	▲▲▲▲
Kirkwood	▲▲▲▲	▲▲▲	▲▲▲▲	▲▲▲	▲▲▲▲
Loveland	▲▲▲	▲▲▲	▲▲▲	▲▲▲▲	▲▲▲▲
Mammoth	▲▲	▲▲▲▲	▲▲▲	▲▲▲▲	▲▲▲
Mission Ridge	▲▲▲▲	▲▲▲▲	▲▲▲	▲▲▲	▲▲▲
Mount Bachelor	▲▲▲▲▲	▲▲▲▲	▲▲▲	▲▲▲	▲▲▲▲
Mount Baker	▲▲▲	▲▲▲	▲▲▲	▲▲	▲▲▲
Northstar	▲▲▲▲	▲▲▲▲▲	▲▲▲	▲▲▲	▲▲▲▲▲
Panorama	▲▲▲	▲▲▲	▲▲▲	▲▲▲▲	▲▲▲▲
Park City	▲▲▲	▲▲▲▲	▲▲	▲▲▲▲	▲▲▲▲
Powder Mountain	▲▲	▲▲▲	▲▲▲▲	▲▲▲	▲▲▲▲
Santa Fe	▲▲▲▲	▲▲▲▲	▲▲▲	▲▲▲	▲▲▲
Schweitzer Mtn.	▲▲▲▲▲	▲▲▲▲	▲▲▲▲▲	▲▲▲▲▲	▲▲▲▲▲
Sierra-at-Tahoe	▲▲▲	▲▲▲▲	▲▲▲▲	▲▲▲	▲▲▲▲
Snowbasin	▲▲▲▲▲	▲▲▲	▲▲▲▲	▲▲▲▲	▲▲▲▲
Snowbird	▲▲▲▲	▲	▲▲▲▲	▲▲▲▲	▲▲▲▲
Snowmass	▲▲▲	▲▲▲▲	▲▲▲▲	▲▲▲▲▲	▲▲▲▲▲
Solitude	▲▲▲▲	▲▲	▲▲▲▲	▲▲▲▲	▲▲▲
Squaw Valley	▲▲▲	▲▲	▲▲▲▲	▲▲▲	▲▲▲
Steamboat	▲▲▲	▲▲▲	▲▲▲▲	▲▲▲▲	▲▲▲▲
Stevens Pass	▲▲▲▲	▲▲▲▲	▲▲▲▲	▲▲▲▲	▲▲▲▲
Sugar Bowl	▲▲▲▲	▲▲▲▲	▲▲▲	▲▲	▲▲▲
Sundance	▲▲▲	▲▲▲	▲▲▲	▲▲	▲▲▲
Sun Peaks	▲▲▲	▲▲▲	▲▲▲	▲▲▲	▲▲▲▲
Sun Valley	▲▲▲	▲▲▲▲	▲▲▲▲▲	▲▲▲▲	▲▲▲▲▲
Taos	▲▲▲	▲▲	▲▲▲▲	▲▲▲	▲▲▲
Telluride	▲▲▲	▲▲	▲▲▲▲	▲▲▲	▲▲▲
Vail	▲▲▲▲	▲▲▲▲▲	▲▲▲▲	▲▲▲▲▲	▲▲▲▲
Whistler	▲▲▲	▲▲	▲▲	▲▲▲	▲▲▲
Winter Park	▲▲	▲▲▲	▲▲▲▲▲	▲▲▲	▲▲▲

Mountain Characteristics and Design Table II

	Intersections	Confluence	Cat Tracks/ Traverses	Visual Intimidation	Interesting All the Way Down
Alpine Meadows	▲▲▲	▲▲▲	▲▲▲▲	▲▲▲▲	▲▲▲
Alta	▲▲▲	▲▲▲▲	▲▲▲	▲▲▲	▲▲▲▲
Arapahoe Basin	▲▲▲	▲▲▲	▲▲▲▲	▲▲▲	▲▲▲▲
Aspen Mountain	▲▲▲	▲	▲▲▲▲	▲▲▲	▲▲▲▲
Bear Valley	▲▲▲	▲▲▲	▲▲▲▲	▲▲▲	▲▲▲▲
Beaver Creek	▲▲▲	▲▲▲	▲▲▲▲	▲▲▲▲▲	▲▲▲▲
Big Mountain	▲▲▲	▲▲▲	▲▲▲▲	▲▲▲▲	▲▲▲▲
Big Sky	▲▲▲▲▲	▲▲▲▲▲	▲▲▲▲	▲▲	▲▲▲
Blackcomb	▲▲▲	▲▲▲▲	▲▲▲	▲▲	▲▲▲▲▲
Breckenridge	▲▲	▲▲▲	▲	▲▲▲▲	▲
Brian Head	▲▲▲▲▲	▲▲▲▲	▲▲▲▲▲	▲▲▲▲▲	▲▲▲
Bridger Bowl	▲▲▲▲	▲▲▲	▲▲▲▲	▲▲▲▲	▲▲
Brighton	▲▲▲▲	▲▲▲	▲▲▲▲	▲▲▲▲	▲▲▲▲
Buttermilk	▲▲▲▲▲	▲▲▲▲▲	▲▲▲▲	▲▲▲▲▲	▲▲▲
The Canyons	▲▲▲	▲▲	▲▲	▲▲▲	▲▲▲
Copper Mountain	▲▲	▲▲▲▲	▲▲▲	▲▲▲▲▲	▲▲▲
Crested Butte	▲▲▲▲	▲▲▲	▲▲▲	▲▲	▲▲▲▲
Crystal Mountain	▲▲▲▲	▲▲▲▲	▲▲▲▲	▲▲▲▲	▲▲▲▲
Deer Valley	▲▲▲▲	▲▲▲▲	▲▲▲▲▲	▲▲▲▲▲	▲▲▲▲
Durango	▲▲▲	▲▲▲▲	▲▲	▲▲▲▲▲	▲▲
Fernie Alpine	▲▲▲	▲▲	▲▲▲	▲▲▲	▲▲▲
Grand Targhee	▲▲▲▲	▲▲▲▲	▲▲▲▲	▲▲▲▲▲	▲▲▲▲
Heavenly	▲▲	▲▲	▲	▲▲▲▲	▲▲▲
Highlands	▲▲▲▲	▲▲▲	▲▲	▲▲▲	▲▲
Jackson Hole	▲▲▲▲▲	▲▲▲▲	▲▲	▲	▲▲▲▲▲
June Mountain	▲▲▲▲	▲▲▲▲	▲▲▲▲	▲▲▲▲▲	▲▲
Keystone	▲▲▲	▲▲▲	▲▲▲▲	▲▲▲▲	▲▲▲▲
Kicking Horse	▲▲▲	▲▲▲	▲▲▲	▲▲▲	▲▲▲▲
Kirkwood	▲▲▲▲	▲▲▲▲	▲▲▲▲	▲▲▲	▲▲▲▲
Loveland	▲▲▲	▲▲▲	▲▲▲▲	▲▲▲▲	▲▲
Mammoth	▲▲▲	▲▲	▲▲▲▲	▲▲▲▲	▲▲▲▲
Mission Ridge	▲▲▲	▲▲▲	▲▲▲▲	▲▲▲▲▲	▲▲▲▲
Mount Bachelor	▲▲▲▲▲	▲▲▲▲▲	▲▲▲▲	▲▲▲▲	▲▲▲▲
Mount Baker	▲▲	▲▲	▲▲▲	▲▲▲	▲▲▲▲
Northstar	▲▲▲▲	▲▲▲	▲▲▲▲	▲▲▲▲	▲▲
Panorama	▲▲▲	▲▲▲	▲▲▲	▲▲▲	▲▲▲▲
Park City	▲▲	▲▲	▲▲▲	▲▲▲▲	▲▲▲
Powder Mountain	▲▲▲▲	▲▲▲	▲▲	▲▲▲▲▲	▲▲▲▲
Santa Fe	▲▲▲	▲▲▲	▲▲	▲▲▲	▲▲▲
Schweitzer Mtn.	▲▲▲▲	▲▲▲	▲▲▲▲	▲▲▲▲	▲▲▲▲
Sierra-at-Tahoe	▲▲▲▲	▲▲▲▲	▲▲▲▲	▲▲▲▲	▲▲▲▲

Mountain Characteristics and Design Table II (continued)

	Inter-sections	Confluence	Cat Tracks/ Traverses	Visual Intimi-dation	Interesting All the Way Down
Snowbasin	▲▲▲▲	▲▲▲	▲▲▲	▲▲▲	▲▲▲▲▲
Snowbird	▲▲▲	▲▲▲▲	▲▲	▲	▲▲▲▲▲
Snowmass	▲▲▲▲	▲▲▲	▲▲▲▲	▲▲▲▲	▲▲▲
Solitude	▲▲▲	▲▲▲▲	▲▲▲	▲▲	▲▲▲▲
Squaw Valley	▲▲▲▲	▲▲	▲▲▲	▲▲▲▲	▲▲▲▲
Steamboat	▲▲▲	▲▲▲	▲▲▲▲	▲▲▲▲	▲▲▲▲
Stevens Pass	▲▲▲▲	▲▲▲	▲▲▲▲	▲▲▲▲	▲▲▲▲
Sugar Bowl	▲▲▲▲	▲▲▲	▲▲▲▲	▲▲▲▲	▲▲▲
Sundance	▲▲▲▲	▲▲▲	▲▲▲▲	▲▲▲	▲▲▲
Sun Peaks	▲▲	▲▲	▲▲▲	▲▲▲▲	▲▲▲▲
Sun Valley	▲▲▲▲	▲▲	▲▲▲	▲▲▲▲	▲▲▲
Taos	▲▲	▲▲▲	▲▲▲	▲	▲▲▲▲
Telluride	▲▲▲	▲▲	▲▲	▲▲	▲▲▲▲
Vail	▲▲	▲▲▲	▲▲	▲▲▲▲▲	▲▲▲
Whistler	▲▲▲▲▲	▲▲▲▲	▲▲	▲▲	▲▲▲▲
Winter Park	▲▲▲▲	▲▲▲	▲▲▲	▲▲▲	▲▲▲

Crowd Conditions and Skier Traffic Control

These items rate how well the mountain handles skier traffic on an average high-season weekday. If a mountain scores low, assume that the congestion will be significantly worse on weekends and holidays.

Lift Design, Adequacy, Placement   This relates to the number of lifts, the types of lifts, and the extent to which the lift system distributes skiers effectively around the mountain. The more efficient the system, the higher the score.

Lift Line Crowding   Can the lift system accommodate the average number of skiers on the mountain with little or no wait? This item is scored in terms of the more popular lifts and parts of the mountain, as opposed to averaging all of the lifts. A resort where skiers wait less than five minutes to board a lift that services a popular part of the mountain will rate high.

Beginner/Novice Area Congestion   Is there enough beginner/novice terrain on the mountain relative to the average number of beginner/novice skiers? The less congestion, the higher the score.

Intermediate Run Congestion   Is there enough intermediate terrain on the mountain relative to the average number of intermediate skiers? The less congestion, the higher the score.

Crowd Conditions and Skier Traffic Control

	Lift Design, Adequacy, Placement	Lift Line Crowding	Beginner/ Novice Area Congestion	Intermediate Run Congestion
Alpine Meadows	▲▲▲▲	▲▲▲	▲▲▲▲	▲▲▲
Alta	▲▲▲▲	▲▲▲	▲▲▲▲	▲▲▲▲
Arapahoe Basin	▲▲▲	▲▲▲	▲▲▲▲	▲▲▲
Aspen Mountain	▲▲▲▲	▲▲▲▲▲	n/a	▲▲▲
Bear Valley	▲▲	▲▲▲	▲▲▲	▲▲▲
Beaver Creek	▲▲▲▲	▲▲▲▲	▲▲▲▲	▲▲▲▲
Big Mountain	▲▲▲	▲▲▲▲	▲▲▲▲	▲▲▲▲▲
Big Sky	▲▲▲▲▲	▲▲▲▲	▲▲▲▲▲	▲▲▲▲
Blackcomb	▲▲▲▲	▲▲▲	▲▲▲▲▲	▲▲▲
Breckenridge	▲▲	▲▲	▲▲▲▲	▲▲
Brian Head	▲▲▲	▲▲▲	▲▲▲▲	▲▲▲▲
Bridger Bowl	▲▲▲	▲▲▲	▲▲▲▲	▲▲▲▲
Brighton	▲▲▲▲	▲▲▲▲	▲▲▲	▲▲▲
Buttermilk	▲▲▲▲	▲▲▲▲▲	▲▲▲▲▲	▲▲▲▲
The Canyons	▲▲▲▲	▲▲▲▲	▲▲▲▲	▲▲▲▲
Copper Mountain	▲▲▲	▲▲	▲▲▲▲	▲▲▲▲
Crested Butte	▲▲▲	▲▲▲▲	▲▲▲	▲▲▲▲
Crystal Mountain	▲▲▲	▲▲▲▲	▲▲▲▲	▲▲▲
Deer Valley	▲▲▲▲	▲▲▲▲	▲▲▲	▲▲▲
Durango	▲▲	▲▲▲▲	▲▲▲▲	▲▲▲
Fernie Alpine	▲▲▲	▲▲▲▲	▲▲▲	▲▲▲
Grand Targhee	▲▲▲▲▲	▲▲▲▲	▲▲▲	▲▲▲▲▲
Heavenly	▲▲▲	▲▲	▲▲	▲▲▲▲
Highlands	▲▲▲▲	▲▲▲▲▲	▲▲▲	▲▲▲
Jackson Hole	▲▲▲▲	▲▲▲▲	▲▲▲▲	▲▲▲▲
June Mountain	▲▲▲	▲▲▲▲	▲▲▲▲▲	▲▲▲▲
Keystone	▲▲▲▲	▲▲▲	▲▲	▲▲
Kicking Horse	▲▲▲	▲▲▲▲▲	▲▲▲	▲▲▲▲▲
Kirkwood	▲▲▲	▲▲▲	▲▲▲▲	▲▲▲
Loveland	▲▲▲	▲▲▲	▲▲▲	▲▲▲
Mammoth	▲▲▲▲▲	▲▲	▲▲▲	▲▲
Mission Ridge	▲	▲▲▲	▲▲▲	▲▲▲
Mount Bachelor	▲▲▲▲▲	▲▲▲	▲▲	▲▲
Mount Baker	▲▲	▲▲▲	▲▲▲	▲▲▲
Northstar	▲▲▲	▲▲▲	▲▲▲▲▲	▲▲▲
Panorama	▲▲▲	▲▲▲▲▲	▲▲▲▲	▲▲▲▲
Park City	▲▲▲▲▲	▲▲▲	▲▲▲	▲▲
Powder Mountain	▲▲	▲▲▲▲	▲▲▲	▲▲▲▲▲
Santa Fe	▲▲▲▲	▲▲▲	▲▲▲▲	▲▲▲▲
Schweitzer Mtn.	▲▲▲▲	▲▲▲	▲▲▲▲	▲▲▲▲
Sierra-at-Tahoe	▲▲▲▲	▲▲▲▲	▲▲▲▲	▲▲▲
Snowbasin	▲▲▲▲	▲▲▲▲	▲▲▲▲	▲▲▲▲

Crowd Conditions and Skier Traffic Control (continued)

	Lift Design, Adequacy, Placement	Lift Line Crowding	Beginner/ Novice Area Congestion	Intermediate Run Congestion
Snowbird	▲▲▲▲▲	▲▲	▲▲▲	▲▲▲
Snowmass	▲▲▲▲	▲▲▲▲	▲▲▲	▲▲▲
Solitude	▲▲▲▲	▲▲▲▲	▲▲▲▲	▲▲▲▲
Squaw Valley	▲▲▲▲	▲▲▲	▲▲▲	▲▲
Steamboat	▲▲▲	▲▲▲	▲▲▲	▲▲▲▲
Stevens Pass	▲▲▲	▲▲▲	▲▲▲▲	▲▲▲
Sugar Bowl	▲▲▲	▲▲▲	▲▲▲	▲▲▲
Sundance	▲▲▲	▲▲▲▲	▲▲▲	▲▲▲▲
Sun Peaks	▲▲▲	▲▲▲▲	▲▲▲▲	▲▲▲▲
Sun Valley	▲▲▲▲▲	▲▲▲	▲▲▲▲	▲▲▲
Taos	▲▲▲	▲▲▲	▲▲▲	▲▲▲
Telluride	▲▲▲	▲▲▲▲	▲▲	▲▲▲
Vail	▲▲▲▲	▲▲▲▲▲	▲▲▲	▲▲▲▲
Whistler	▲▲▲▲	▲▲▲	▲▲▲▲▲	▲▲▲
Winter Park	▲▲▲	▲▲▲	▲▲▲	▲▲▲

Beginning Skier Considerations

These ratings take into account two items of interest to beginner and novice skiers.

Nonbeginner Traffic in Beginner/Novice Areas   Relates to the amount of nonbeginner traffic passing through beginner trails or practice areas. Ski areas where a lot of nonbeginner traffic is present on beginner trails will score low. "Beginner trails" in this context refers to the first-timer area(s) and to those green trails that first-timers would logically graduate to after a few days.

Beginner Terrain Transition   Relates to the availability of trails of incrementally increasing difficulty, thus allowing first-timers and novices to transition gradually to more challenging terrain. A ski area with good transitional terrain will score high.

Beginning Skier Considerations

	Nonbeginner Traffic in Beginner/ Novice Areas	Beginner Terrain Transition
Alpine Meadows	▲▲▲▲	▲▲▲▲
Alta	▲▲▲▲▲	▲▲▲
Arapahoe Basin	▲▲▲	▲▲
Aspen Mountain	n/a	none

Beginning Skier Considerations *(continued)*

	Nonbeginner Traffic in Beginner/ Novice Areas	Beginner Terrain Transition
Bear Valley	▲▲▲	▲▲▲▲
Beaver Creek	▲▲▲	▲▲▲▲▲
Big Mountain	▲▲▲▲	▲▲▲▲
Big Sky	▲▲▲▲	▲▲▲
Blackcomb	▲▲▲	▲▲▲▲▲
Breckenridge	▲▲▲▲	▲▲▲▲
Brian Head	▲▲▲	▲▲▲▲
Bridger Bowl	▲▲▲	▲▲▲▲
Brighton	▲▲	▲▲▲▲
Buttermilk	▲▲▲▲▲	▲▲▲▲▲
The Canyons	▲▲▲▲	▲▲▲
Copper Mountain	▲▲▲▲▲	▲▲▲▲
Crested Butte	▲▲▲▲	▲▲▲
Crystal Mountain	▲▲▲▲	▲▲▲▲
Deer Valley	▲▲▲▲▲	▲▲
Durango	▲▲▲▲	▲▲▲
Fernie Alpine	▲▲	▲▲▲▲
Grand Targhee	▲▲▲▲	▲▲▲
Heavenly	▲▲	▲▲▲
Highlands	▲▲	▲▲
Jackson Hole	▲▲▲	▲
June Mountain	▲▲▲▲	▲▲▲▲
Keystone	▲▲▲▲▲	▲▲▲
Kicking Horse	▲▲▲	▲▲▲▲
Kirkwood	▲▲▲▲	▲▲▲▲
Loveland	▲▲▲	▲▲▲▲
Mammoth	▲▲▲▲	▲▲▲▲
Mission Ridge	▲▲▲▲	▲▲▲
Mount Bachelor	▲▲	▲▲▲▲▲
Mount Baker	▲▲	▲▲
Northstar	▲▲	▲▲▲▲
Panorama	▲▲▲	▲▲▲▲
Park City	▲▲▲	▲▲▲
Powder Mountain	▲▲▲	▲▲▲▲
Santa Fe	▲▲	▲▲▲
Schweitzer Mountain	▲▲▲▲	▲▲▲▲▲
Sierra-at-Tahoe	▲▲▲	▲▲▲▲
Snowbasin	▲▲▲▲	▲▲▲▲
Snowbird	▲▲▲▲	▲▲
Snowmass	▲▲▲	▲▲▲▲▲
Solitude	▲▲▲	▲▲▲▲
Squaw Valley	▲▲▲	▲▲

Beginning Skier Considerations (continued)		
	Nonbeginner Traffic in Beginner/ Novice Areas	Beginner Terrain Transition
Steamboat	▲▲	▲▲
Stevens Pass	▲▲▲▲	▲▲▲▲
Sugar Bowl	▲▲▲	▲▲▲▲
Sundance	▲▲▲	▲▲▲
Sun Peaks	▲▲▲	▲▲▲▲▲
Sun Valley	▲▲▲▲▲	▲▲
Taos	▲▲▲▲	▲▲
Telluride	▲▲▲▲	▲▲▲
Vail	▲▲▲▲▲	▲▲▲
Whistler	▲▲▲	▲▲▲▲▲
Winter Park	▲▲▲	▲▲▲

Groomed Cruising Terrain and Bumps

These categories rate the availability and plentifulness of groomed cruising as well as entry-level moguls. All three categories assume normal grooming operations. The higher the number of stars, the more this type of skiing is available.

Groomed, Friendly-Angle Cruising   Relates to the availability and abundance of mellow, "friendly angle," groomed cruising runs.

Groomed Steeps   Relates to the availability and plentifulness of steep groomed runs.

Entry-Level Bumps   Relates to the availability of entry-level bumps. An ideal situation offers smaller bumps adjacent to a groomed run, thus allowing the learning skier to enter and exit the bumps easily (without committing to an entire bump run).

Groomed Cruising Terrain and Bumps		
	Groomed, Friendly-Angle Cruising	Groomed Steeps	Entry-Level Bumps
Alpine Meadows	▲▲▲▲	▲▲	▲▲▲
Alta	▲▲▲	▲▲	▲▲▲▲▲
Arapahoe Basin	▲▲▲	▲▲▲	▲▲
Aspen Mountain	▲▲▲	▲▲▲▲	▲
Bear Valley	▲▲▲	▲▲	▲▲▲
Beaver Creek	▲▲▲▲	▲▲	▲▲▲
Big Mountain	▲▲▲▲	▲▲▲▲	▲▲▲▲

Groomed Cruising Terrain and Bumps (*continued*)

	Groomed, Friendly-Angle Cruising	Groomed Steeps	Entry-Level Bumps
Big Sky	▲▲▲▲▲	▲▲▲	▲▲▲▲▲
Blackcomb	▲▲▲	▲▲▲▲▲	▲▲
Breckenridge	▲▲▲▲	▲▲▲	▲▲▲
Brian Head	▲▲▲	▲▲▲	▲▲▲▲
Bridger Bowl	▲▲▲▲	▲▲	▲▲
Brighton	▲▲▲▲	▲▲▲	▲▲▲
Buttermilk	▲▲▲▲▲	▲	▲▲
The Canyons	▲▲▲▲	▲▲▲	▲▲▲
Copper Mountain	▲▲▲▲▲	▲▲▲	▲▲▲▲
Crested Butte	▲▲▲	▲▲	▲▲
Crystal Mountain	▲▲▲	▲▲▲▲	▲▲▲▲
Deer Valley	▲▲▲▲	▲▲▲▲▲	▲▲
Durango	▲▲▲	▲▲	▲▲▲
Fernie Alpine	▲▲▲	▲▲▲	▲▲▲
Grand Targhee	▲▲▲	▲▲▲▲	▲▲▲▲
Heavenly	▲▲▲▲▲	▲▲▲	▲▲
Highlands	▲▲▲	▲	▲▲▲
Jackson Hole	▲▲	▲▲▲▲	▲▲
June Mountain	▲▲▲▲▲	▲▲	▲▲▲
Keystone	▲▲▲▲	▲▲▲	▲▲▲▲▲
Kicking Horse	▲▲▲▲	▲▲▲	▲▲▲▲
Kirkwood	▲▲▲	▲▲▲▲	▲▲▲▲
Loveland	▲▲▲	▲	▲▲▲
Mammoth	▲▲▲▲▲	▲▲▲▲	▲▲
Mission Ridge	▲▲▲▲	▲▲	▲▲▲
Mount Bachelor	▲▲▲▲▲	▲▲▲▲▲	▲
Mount Baker	▲▲	▲▲▲	▲▲▲
Northstar	▲▲▲▲▲	▲▲▲	▲▲▲▲▲
Panorama	▲▲▲▲	▲▲▲	▲▲▲▲
Park City	▲▲▲▲	▲▲▲	▲▲▲▲
Powder Mountain	▲▲▲▲	▲▲	▲▲
Santa Fe	▲▲▲▲	▲▲	▲▲
Schweitzer Mountain	▲▲▲	▲▲▲▲	▲▲▲▲
Sierra-at-Tahoe	▲▲▲▲	▲▲▲	▲▲▲
Snowbasin	▲▲▲▲	▲▲▲	▲▲▲
Snowbird	▲▲▲	▲▲▲	▲▲▲▲
Snowmass	▲▲▲▲▲	▲▲▲	▲▲▲▲▲
Solitude	▲▲▲	▲▲▲▲	▲▲▲▲
Squaw Valley	▲▲▲▲	▲▲▲	▲▲▲
Steamboat	▲▲▲▲	▲▲	▲▲▲
Stevens Pass	▲▲▲	▲▲	▲▲▲
Sugar Bowl	▲▲▲▲	▲▲	▲▲▲

Groomed Cruising Terrain and Bumps *(continued)*		
	Groomed, Friendly-Angle Cruising	Groomed Steeps	Entry-Level Bumps
Sundance	▲▲▲	▲▲▲	▲▲▲
Sun Peaks	▲▲▲▲	▲▲▲▲	▲▲▲▲
Sun Valley	▲▲▲▲	▲▲▲▲▲	▲▲
Taos	▲▲	▲▲	▲▲
Telluride	▲▲	▲▲▲▲	▲▲
Vail	▲▲▲▲	▲▲▲	▲▲▲
Whistler	▲▲▲▲	▲▲▲▲▲	▲▲
Winter Park	▲▲▲	▲▲	▲▲

Weather

While just about any kind of weather can be encountered on any mountain, the fact is that certain conditions are experienced more frequently on some mountains than on others.

Ice   Relates to the probability and extent of ice forming on ski runs during the heart of the season—late December through the third week in March. The more pronounced the tendency to ice, the lower the score.

Wind   Relates to the probability of high winds. Areas with frequent high winds score low.

Cold   If the mountain, for whatever reason, is unusually cold, the score will be low.

Weather		
	Ice	Wind	Cold
Alpine Meadows	▲▲▲	▲▲▲	▲▲▲▲
Alta	▲▲▲▲▲	▲▲▲▲	▲▲▲▲
Arapahoe Basin	▲▲▲▲	▲▲	▲▲
Aspen Mountain	▲▲▲	▲▲▲	▲▲▲
Bear Valley	▲▲▲▲	▲▲▲	▲▲▲▲
Beaver Creek	▲▲▲	▲▲▲	▲▲▲
Big Mountain	▲▲▲▲	▲▲▲	▲
Big Sky	▲▲▲▲	▲▲	▲
Blackcomb	▲▲	▲▲	▲▲
Breckenridge	▲▲	▲	▲▲
Brian Head	▲▲▲	▲▲▲▲	▲▲▲▲
Bridger Bowl	▲▲▲▲	▲▲▲	▲▲
Brighton	▲▲▲▲	▲▲▲	▲▲▲
Buttermilk	▲▲▲	▲▲▲▲	▲▲▲

Weather *(continued)*

	Ice	Wind	Cold
The Canyons	▲▲▲	▲▲▲▲	▲▲▲
Copper Mountain	▲▲▲	▲▲	▲▲▲
Crested Butte	▲▲	▲▲▲	▲▲▲
Crystal Mountain	▲▲▲	▲▲▲	▲▲▲▲
Deer Valley	▲▲	▲▲▲	▲▲▲
Durango	▲▲▲▲▲	▲▲▲▲▲	▲▲▲
Fernie Alpine	▲▲▲▲	▲▲▲	▲▲▲
Grand Targhee	▲▲▲▲	▲▲	▲▲
Heavenly	▲▲▲	▲▲	▲▲▲▲
Highlands	▲▲▲	▲▲▲	▲▲▲
Jackson Hole	▲▲▲	▲▲	▲▲
June Mountain	▲▲▲	▲▲▲▲	▲▲▲▲▲
Keystone	▲▲▲	▲▲▲	▲▲
Kicking Horse	▲▲▲▲	▲▲▲	▲▲▲
Kirkwood	▲▲▲▲	▲▲▲	▲▲▲▲
Loveland	▲▲▲▲	▲▲▲	▲▲▲
Mammoth	▲▲▲▲	▲▲	▲▲▲▲
Mission Ridge	▲▲▲	▲▲▲	▲▲▲▲
Mount Bachelor	▲▲▲	▲	▲▲▲
Mount Baker	▲▲▲▲	▲▲▲	▲▲▲▲
Northstar	▲▲▲	▲▲▲▲	▲▲▲▲
Panorama	▲▲▲▲	▲▲▲	▲▲▲
Park City	▲▲▲	▲▲▲▲	▲▲▲
Powder Mountain	▲▲▲▲▲	▲▲▲▲	▲▲▲
Santa Fe	▲▲▲▲	▲▲▲	▲▲▲▲
Schweitzer Mountain	▲▲▲	▲▲	▲▲
Sierra-at-Tahoe	▲▲▲	▲▲▲	▲▲▲
Snowbasin	▲▲▲▲	▲▲	▲▲▲
Snowbird	▲▲▲▲	▲▲▲	▲▲▲
Snowmass	▲▲▲	▲▲▲	▲▲
Solitude	▲▲▲	▲▲▲	▲▲▲
Squaw Valley	▲▲	▲▲	▲▲▲▲
Steamboat	▲▲	▲▲▲	▲▲
Stevens Pass	▲▲	▲▲▲	▲▲▲▲
Sugar Bowl	▲▲▲▲	▲▲▲	▲▲▲▲
Sundance	▲▲▲	▲▲▲	▲▲▲▲
Sun Peaks	▲▲▲	▲▲▲	▲▲▲
Sun Valley	▲▲	▲▲▲▲	▲▲
Taos	▲▲▲▲	▲▲▲▲	▲▲▲▲▲
Telluride	▲▲▲	▲▲▲	▲▲▲▲▲
Vail	▲▲	▲▲▲▲	▲▲▲
Whistler	▲▲	▲▲	▲▲
Winter Park	▲▲▲	▲▲▲	▲▲▲

Getting There

Flights are cheaper and more readily available if you can come and go on a weekday. Tuesday is generally the slowest day of the week for airlines, followed by Thursday and Wednesday. Book the earliest flight possible even if it means setting off before the sun rises. According to the department of transportation, flights that leave before 9 a.m. are 33% more likely to arrive on time than flights departing after 9 a.m. Also, taking an early morning flight makes for an easier day. Even if you do not intend to ski on your arrival day, the early start will ensure that you have plenty of time to drive to your final destination, check in, rent equipment, and get settled in.

If you want to use frequent-flyer miles, start calling in July for major air destinations like Salt Lake City, Reno, San Francisco, Vancouver, and Denver. For smaller mountain destinations like Aspen, Gunnison, Steamboat, Bozeman, and the like, don't call until the seasonal air service is downloaded into the system in September. If you can't find a seat on a weekend, try for a Tuesday, Thursday, or Wednesday.

Most airlines review their bookings for January and February in December. If business is soft you can expect a big cut-rate fare sale to ensue around December 7 for travel in January and February. We recommend hedging your bet by buying tickets at the best rate you can obtain in mid-September. If a sale occurs in December, some airlines will credit the difference between the price you paid and the sale price, while others will allow you to switch to the lower fare after deducting a change fee. Each airline is a little bit different, so ask, "What are my options if I buy now and you run a fare sale later?"

Because flying is always problematic during the winter months, try to keep your itinerary as simple as possible. Let's say you live in Louisville and want to fly to Bozeman, Montana (for Big Sky). The airline will try to sell you an itinerary where you fly from Louisville to Cincinnatti, connecting to Salt Lake, with a second connection from Salt Lake to Bozeman. In the winter this is one connection too many. You're better off eliminating one connection by driving from Louisville to Cincinnati and initiating your flight itinerary there. If you live in a city served by two or more airports, you can bet that one of the airports is better designed and equipped to handle winter weather than others. In the New York area, for example, Newark and Kennedy airports are better winter alternatives than LaGuardia.

Before you head to the airport, check the weather channel for winter storm advisories affecting your hub city. If the weather is iffy, see if your carrier will reroute you through another hub. Returning to Atlanta from Whistler out of Vancouver, we discovered that our hub airport, Chicago O'Hare, was experiencing major weather delays. On request, our airline gladly rerouted us through Phoenix. If a reroute is not possible, we advise booking a hotel room at the hub city in case you get stuck. If you don't need it you can always cancel the reservation. Incidentally, in the event of weather delays or weather-related flight cancellations, the airlines will not arrange or pay for a hotel.

If you can afford it, commuter flights from a major airport to the resorts make life a lot easier, providing the weather is good. When the weather is bad, the smaller airports in the mountains are sometimes forced to suspend operations. If you are en route to the mountains, you may be seriously delayed or, alternatively, be forced to drive from the nearest major airport. On your return trip, weather delays and flight cancellations at the smaller airports also may cause you to miss your connecting flights.

Five major airports serve most of the ski mountains described in this guide. From these five you can continue on to your resort destination either by rental car, resort shuttle service, or in some cases, by commuter flight. The big five are Denver International Airport (Colorado), Salt Lake International Airport (Utah), Vancouver International Airport (British Columbia), Reno-Tahoe International Airport (Nevada), and Albuquerque International Airport (New Mexico).

The Reno and Albuquerque airports are small and efficient. Baggage handling is expeditious, it's easy to rent a car, and the airports are convenient to town. Vancouver International is undergoing a major renovation that will occasion delays, hassles, and additional expense for the foreseeable future. The really big players in the ski market, however, are Denver International and Salt Lake International airports.

The Denver International Airport (DIA) opened in the spring of 1995. Technologically state-of-the-art, the new airport is designed to minimize the kind of traffic and weather delays that plagued Stapleton Airport (the old Denver airport). DIA for pilots is a dream come true. DIA for passengers, however, is a mixed bag. For starters, the airport is in the middle of nowhere, 30 miles from Denver on the desolate prairie. For skiers, the location of DIA adds about 30 minutes to the commute to the mountains.

Much of the cost burden of the $5 billion airport is passed along to user airlines, which (surprise!) pass it along to their customers. The cost of doing business at DIA was so great that Continental Airlines abandoned Denver as a hub and cut departures by 80%. Continental's bailout left United with more than 68% of the market and not much in the way of competition. Bottom line for skiers: inconvenient location, less service, and higher ticket prices.

All of the rental-car agencies except U.S. Rent-a-Car, Affinity, and All America have processing counters on the fifth level (baggage claim) of the terminal. We recommend that you complete your paperwork while you are waiting for your skis and luggage. Be prepared to pay more for your rental car than you were quoted by your travel agent. You will be hit with a $3-a-day surcharge for the privilege of using this wonderful airport in addition to 11% taxes.

Paperwork, luggage, and skis in hand, head out the level-5 doors to catch a van or bus to the rental-agency lots where you will pick up your car. To save time at the car lot, designate one of your party to sprint to the counter as soon as the bus arrives, while the remainder of the group handles the luggage and skis. If you have completed your rental agreement at the airport and want to pick up your car while the rest of your group waits for the luggage and skis, proceed through the level-5 door to the courtesy shuttles and from there to the car lots. After picking up your rental car, return to the airport via Pena Boulevard. Follow the Passenger Pickup sign to the fourth level, where you can meet your group and load at the curb.

Though the situation has improved at DIA, you should still anticipate burning one-and-a-half to two hours from the time you get off the plane to the time you drive away in your rental car.

On the return trip, be sure to fill your rental car with gas before you leave Denver, or at the new gas station just inside the DIA grounds, near the toll booth on Pena Boulevard. Assume a 45-minute commute (longer during rush hours) from Denver to the airport, 15 minutes to turn in your car and catch the courtesy bus, 5–10 minutes to get to the terminal, 30 minutes to check in, and 25 minutes to reach your departure gate. All told, about two hours and some change. Rental-car courtesy vehicles, incidentally, will drop you off on the fifth level. To reach the ticket counters and baggage check, you must haul your luggage and skis up the escalator to the sixth level.

Compared to DIA, western skiing's other major hub, the Salt Lake International Airport, is a breeze. The airport is almost never shut down due to inclement weather, luggage and skis are delivered expeditiously, and best of all, the facility is only 10 minutes from downtown Salt Lake City and 45–60 minutes from ten different ski resorts.

The only thing we don't like about Salt Lake International is the location of the car-rental counters. To reach the rental car facility you must haul your baggage and skis up one story (via escalator or crowded, slow elevator), cross over a road on an enclosed pedestrian bridge, and then descend again to ground level. If you pile all of your stuff on one of those handy luggage carts you'll be stuck with the pokey elevator. If you try to lug your things up the escalator, you may have to make more than one trip. Either way, it's a hassle. The only way to avoid the pedestrian bridge is to exit the terminal, bear left, and proceed to a crosswalk across from the rental-car counters. This is the easiest option for anyone lugging a lot of gear (provided you can find the crosswalk).

A nice thing about all aiports serving ski areas is the ready availability of information. DIA and Salt Lake International particularly have well-equipped ski information centers offering trail maps, snow base and weather conditions, shuttle information, as well as hotel and restaurant info. The larger airports even have ski equipment rental shops on site. Think twice about renting gear from these shops, however, unless they have sister shops where you'll be skiing. You don't want to drive all the way back to the airport if a binding or boot buckle breaks on your rented equipment.

A Word about Checked Luggage

Twice in the past three years, our ski gear has missed an air connection and was missing in action for a day or two. Now we pack ski boots, goggles, long underwear, ski socks, parka, and gloves in a carry-on bag along with such necessities as prescription medication. Everything else needed to ski can be rented, so there's no worry about missing the first day of skiing because of lost luggage.

Rental Cars

If a rental car is part of your ski vacation plans, remember that you might have to drive through mountainous terrain in less than optimal driving conditions. At the very least, rent a vehicle with front-wheel drive. If conditions warrant, upgrade to a four-wheel-drive vehicle. If you rent your car in a desert or Pacific Coast city that doesn't see much snow, make sure that the car has tires suitable for driving in snow. Also check the windshield wiper cleaning fluid and look to see if a windshield scraper is provided.

Take into consideration that you will require luggage space on arrival and departure days. Be certain you rent a car large enough to comfortably accommodate your entire party as well as your luggage and skiing equipment. For convenience and maximum space utilization, rent ski racks (most hold five pairs of skis), and have members of your group pack their belongings in soft luggage.

If you rent a van or an SUV with a factory-installed roof rack, and if you bring along some good rope, you can lash down both skis and luggage up top, thus making more room for passengers inside. When we tie down luggage on top, we always place it in big plastic garbage bags first. If we run into snow, slush, or rain our stuff stays dry and clean. Do not try to lash luggage onto ski raks.

Try to avoid itineraries that involve long drives into the mountains after dark. If you are contemplating such a drive and the weather is bad, seriously consider getting a hotel for the night and starting fresh in the morning.

Lift Tickets

Except in unusual situations, you should not have to pay full price for lift tickets. For starters, ski mountains compete for local skiers by discounting tickets in major urban areas within driving distance of the resort. In Denver, King Soopers (a supermarket chain) sells discounted tickets to several mountains. Discounts average $5–$9 per day depending on the resort. If you are driving to the mountains from Denver International Airport, the most convenient King Sooper is on Youngfield Street, 300 yards from the West 32nd Avenue exit off I-70. Call (303) 238-6486 for information. In Salt Lake City, try Harmon's and Smith's (supermarkets) for discounted lift tickets. Smith's (phone (801) 328-1683) sells Snowbird and sometimes Deer Valley tickets; and Harmon's (phone (801) 967-9213) sells only Brighton tickets.

Lodging

Ski resort lodging is unique in the tourism and hospitality industry. Because skiing is social, it has great appeal to parties, families, and groups of various sizes. This translates into a tremendous demand for lodging that not only furnishes sleeping accommodations, but also provides space where members of the group can come together to dine and socialize. In ski resort communities, the accommodation of choice is increasingly the condominium or rental home. While hotels continue to serve solo travelers and couples, most of the lodging growth in western ski venues is in condos and homes.

The resort towns at the base of most ski mountains are more than a service infrastructure for tourists. In the main, these towns are well-established communities with strong identities and sizable year-round populations. The beauty of the mountains in conjunction with civic pride, a largely affluent population, and cultural resources seldom found outside of major cities make ski-resort towns very desirable places to live any time of year.

Ski-resort communities usually have more in common with real-estate developments than with tourist destinations. The ski mountain is a recreational centerpiece used to attract buyers in the market for a primary or vacation residence and serves the same function as golf courses in real-estate developments elsewhere in the country. In most ski resorts, condos and homes have eclipsed hotels as the most prevalent form of lodging. For example, in Aspen, Colorado, arguably the capital of American skiing, there is only one chain hotel.

From a consumer point of view, the explosion of condominiums and rental homes has resulted in a very decentralized lodging inventory. Whereas a central reservations service or convention authority in Chicago or Miami might be expected to know what is available and which hotels have vacancies, it doesn't work like that in ski venues. There is usually a central reservations service in a ski resort community, but owing to the diverse private ownership of most of the accommodations, it is practically impossible for that service to keep track of what is available.

Because demand for accommodations in the mountains is very predictable, rates are established and remain fairly stable. Hotel and condo owners in popular ski destinations know that, barring a bad snow year, they can pretty much charge full rack rate. There is, in fact, little discounting of ski resort accommodations. Half-price clubs and room consolidators are conspicuously absent in the ski vacation industry. There is less emphasis on negotiating price than on matching specific skiers with accommodations that meet their physical and budgetary requirements. When deals are made, they are usually promoted through high-volume tour operators who sell ski vacation packages.

The Sellers

There are a lot of different players selling lodging to skiers—so many, in fact, that sometimes the market is very confusing. The trick is to differentiate the "order takers" from the really knowledgeable agents who can provide valuable information and dig up the best deals.

Ski Vacation Tour Operators   Also called packagers, these are companies that sell complete ski vacations, including airfare, lodging, lift tickets, rental car or airport transfers, and, if needed, ski equipment. Most packagers offer both condo and hotel accommodations. Large tour operators offer ski packages to most major western resorts. Later in this section we will tell you how to evaluate ski vacation packages and how to elicit the best deals from tour operators.

Central Reservations Services   Most large resorts have one, and they are usually operated by the resort management company, the local chamber of commerce, or the tourist bureau. Central reservations services book both hotels and condos and attempt to function as a lodging clearinghouse. Though many central reservations services are very good, very few are able to keep track of all the lodging inventory available in their area. If you can specifically define your budget and lodging requirements, a well-organized central reservations service can be very helpful in locating accommodations. Seldom, however, will central reservations services be aware of available discounts or other special deals. Usually the central reservations service represents the resort management as well as various local realtors and property management enterprises that have private condos and homes to rent. Central reservations operates in a passive, responsive mode, and you must be able to ask the right questions in order to obtain useful information. Most central reservations agents are order takers. Furthermore, central reservations agents do not usually have the authority to negotiate rates or make special arrangements. Central reservations services will deal directly with you or work with your travel agent.

Receptive Operators   These are local, independent lodging agents who intimately know the local hotel and condo scene. Receptives often come from, or are involved in, the local real-estate market and have physically inspected the properties they suggest. Best of all, most are aware of condos and homes not listed with the local central reservations service. A good receptive operator will work hard to find the perfect place that fits both your budget and your lodging requirements. Though receptives work directly with consumers the majority of the time, most are willing to assist travel agents. When this occurs, the receptive and the travel agent usually split the available commission. To locate a receptive, call the tourist bureau (or its equivalent) in the resort town of your choice and ask for the names of some good receptive operators. Sometimes the tourist bureau will even assist in sorting out which receptive can help you best. Occasionally you may reach someone unfamiliar with the term "receptive operator." When this occurs, explain that you are looking for a local independent reservations service.

Local Realtors and Management Agencies   These are companies that maintain, manage, and rent privately-owned condos and homes for absentee owners. While most realtor and management agency rentals are arranged by the central reservations service or by receptive operators, the realtors and property managers will rent to you or your travel agent if you contact them directly. Sometimes they have nice properties that have recently become available and have not been listed or publicized. Unlike central reservations services and receptive operators, most realtors and management agencies do not work on sales commissions. Instead, they are paid a monthly fee by the owners of the properties they represent. Properties they rent, however, are usually commissionable to your travel agent. The local tourist bureau or association of realtors will put you in touch with management agencies and realtors that rent the type of condo or home you are looking for. As you might guess, the rental condo or home inventory of a particular realtor or management agency will be much more limited than that offered by a good receptive or even central reservations. On the other side of the coin, you might unearth some special property that is never available in the general market.

Individual Property Owners   Some property owners, for a variety of reasons, elect to manage the rental of their own condo or home. Their properties are advertised in the classified ad sections of major skiing specialty magazines, and sometimes in the travel sections of newspapers. While you can occasionally save some money dealing directly with property owners, you may not be able to resolve maintenance or other problems that arise once you have arrived. Properties booked through central reservations, receptives, realtors, or management agencies usually have people on call 24 hours a day to attend to problems in rental units. Likewise, individual owners can be more elusive when it comes to issuing confirmations, arranging for the transfer of keys, and getting back your damage deposit.

A Word about Ski-In/Ski-Out Accommodations

Believe us, there is nothing more wonderful and liberating than being able to walk out your door and commence skiing. Unfortunately, only a fraction of the accommodations billed as ski-in/ski-out provide this convenience. Usually, either coming or going, you will have to shoulder your skis and take a hike. What ski-in/ski-out really means is that you will not have to use your car or catch a shuttle. It does not necessarily mean that you can access the slopes or the lifts right outside your door.

If you are thinking about ski-in/ski-out lodging in a large hotel, consider that you might have a long walk to the elevator from your room and another long walk to the slope or lift access. Also, most hotels require that guests check their skis as opposed to taking them to their rooms. If the ski-check room is run efficiently, it's a labor-saving service; if improperly manned, however, it can be a bottleneck.

Ski-in/ski-out condos and homes are frequently connected to the slopes by cat tracks, sidewalks, or roads. Although it's possible to access the slopes and lifts, access is neither direct nor easy. In the final analysis, if you are willing to bear the additional expense of a ski-in/ski-out hotel, condo, or home, make sure you qualify what ski-in/ski-out actually means before you book.

Condos and Rental Homes versus Hotels

Now that you know who the sellers are, let's examine the differences among rental homes, condos, and hotels. Hotels, of course, provide public areas like lobbies, lounges, restaurants, swimming pools, and exercise rooms, as well as daily maid and other services. Hotels in most resorts are not any more likely to be closer to the slopes than condos or rental homes.

Rental homes are freestanding, while condominiums are usually part of a large development and almost always share a common wall with adjoining units on either side. Many condos offer the same features as rental homes. While rental homes do not usually offer swimming pools, condominium complexes frequently do. Very, very few condominium complexes, however, include restaurants or lounges or the type of services usually associated with a hotel. There is no daily maid service in most condominiums, though a mid-week tidying up and change of linens on a weekly rental is not uncommon.

If you are considering a multimountain resort area such as Vail/Beaver Creek, Aspen/Snowmass, the Lake Tahoe area, or Park City, Utah, there will often be some part of the overall area where lodging is less expensive. Snowmass, for example, is usually less expensive than Aspen, which is nine miles down the road. At Park City, you can get a better deal on rooms and condos at the Canyons than at Park City Ski Resort or at Deer Valley (the other two nearby ski mountains). Some of the best deals on accommodations in the West are at stand-alone mountains like Big Sky in Montana, or at smaller ski venues such as Powder Mountain or Snowbasin in Utah, or Monarch in Colorado.

Condos and Rental Homes

If there are three or more adults in your party, you will usually be better off in terms of both accommodations and cost to go for a condo or home as opposed to a hotel. In addition to being roomier, the condo (or home) will have a living area where you can be together with the others in your group, and a kitchen and dining area. Eating in your condo instead of in restaurants can save hundreds of dollars.

In addition, although there are some extraordinary hotels at ski resorts, many motels and hotels in the mountains offer not-so-beautiful views of highways, parking lots, and the backs of other buildings. While there are exceptions, we nevertheless recommend a condo or a rental home as the best way to enjoy the mountains. Many private homes and condos can be had for less than the price of a hotel room and include such amenities as decks, fireplaces, and even hot tubs. Most important, in our estimation, is that the condos and rental homes provide exactly the kind of quiet, solitude, and remote beauty that most folks come to the mountains to experience.

The way to go about renting a condo or home is to make a list of features that are important to you. How many beds, bedrooms, and baths do you require? Do you need a full kitchen? When you get your list together, call (or have your travel agent call) a receptive operator and order your home or condo like you would order a pizza. We phoned a receptive in Aspen/Snowmass, Colorado, and said, "We want a two-bedroom, two-bath condo for two adult couples. We prefer to be high on the mountain, with a good view, in a remote quiet area. We don't care about a hot tub, but we do want a fireplace and a nice big deck."

Whether you get what you want depends on how far in advance you make your reservation, when during the ski season you want to visit, what you are willing to spend, and how close you want to be to the lifts, the resort center, or the main shopping and restaurant district. Regarding proximity to the lifts, you can usually get a much nicer condo or home for the money if you are willing to lodge a little farther from the lifts. All large and most medium-size ski resorts have efficient free shuttle service to the slopes. If you have a car, feel free to use it. Even at large resorts like Vail and Snowmass, parking is no problem except on very busy weekends.

When you have figured out what features you want, where you want to be, and when you want to go, then you can start shopping. Initiate your search by calling the local chamber of commerce or tourist information office at your chosen destination. Information specialists will provide you with the names and phone numbers of local-area receptive operators, realtors, and management companies that rent the kind of accommodations you are looking for.

The better homes and condos are reserved well in advance. Some renters sign up for next year during this year's stay. The earlier you plan, therefore, the better your chances of getting what you want. If you are picky, or are looking for something special, start your shopping early. If there is a ski area you visit every year, take a day off skiing and go look at some possible rental properties for next year's trip.

When you talk with a receptive or rental agent about a particular home or condo, ask how old the property is. If it's older than five or six years, ask if it has been recently renovated. If the property sounds appealing, request that you be mailed photos of both the exterior and interior. Color is better than black and white, but either will do. Some agents have only one set of color photos. If this is the case, suggest that the agent send photocopies in black and white or color. Write off any agent that will not supply some sort of photograph or copy. Never reserve a property strictly on the basis of a rendering, sketch, or line drawing. Insist on a photograph. As an aside, be aware that many homes and condos, while beautiful outside, offer interiors that range from truly tasteless to absolutely bewildering. Mining Town Bordello, Decorator Tepee, and Longhorn Anatomy are but three of the major decorating styles alive and well in western mountain rental properties.

Particularly during the busier times of year, some agencies require a five- or seven-day minimum rental. We were able to work around the minimum, however, by finding properties with two-, three-, and four-day gaps between renters. We found a three-bedroom condo, for example, that was reserved from January 11 through January 17, and from January 21 to January 27. The agency was more than happy to rent us the condo for the short intervening period (January 18, 19, and 20). Reservation gaps, as well as cancellations, are common but unpredictable. You have to call around and ask the right questions to uncover the deals. For weekly rentals, check-in and check-out are usually on Saturday, though sometimes other arrangements are possible.

Once you have found a suitable property, you will usually have to prepay with a credit card or check. Some agencies will mail you a rental contract to sign and return, while others will process the whole deal over the phone. Cancellation policies vary, so be sure to inquire. Some agencies charge a set price for the rental property, while others charge on a per-head basis for the number of persons accommodated. If you are asked for a damage deposit, make sure it's refundable and that you understand your obligations. For most rentals, check-out is essentially the same as at a hotel. Some rental agencies, however, request that you strip the beds, take out the garbage, and clean up the kitchen. A few demand that you sweep and vacuum. The easiest way to preclude being unpleasantly surprised is to nail this kind of stuff down before you book.

Once the reservation is made, most agents will provide written confirmation. If written confirmation is not routinely provided, ask for it. Along with your confirmation, the agent will also provide directions to the rental office. Most rental offices operate seven days a week during ski season. Here, you will register, pick up your keys, and be given directions to your rental unit. Once in your home or condo, check to make sure that everything is in order. If there is a problem, most agencies offer 24-hour maintenance service.

If you plan to cook a lot of your meals, as opposed to going to restaurants, be aware that grocery markets in resort communities are often expensive and sometimes may not offer the variety to which you're accustomed at home.

Hotels and Lodges

Hotels in ski resorts run the gamut from large chain hotels to small, cozy, privately owned inns. We recommend hotels for couples or solo travelers, for folks who intend to eat their meals in restaurants, and for skiers who require such amenities as swimming pools, lounges, nightclubs, and daily maid service.

During ski season, except for lodging sold by packagers, there are few discounts offered. For each property, by and large, there is an established rate for each month of the ski season. That is the rate that is quoted and that is the rate you will pay. Chain hotels, to a degree, constitute an exception. Because they are part of a chain, they usually must offer the same discounts as their sister hotels across the country. These include corporate discounts, preferred rates, and other specials. Most hotels in ski venues are listed in the *Hotel & Travel Index,* an industry reference work that your travel agent has.

If you are considering a hotel, you can check its quality as reported by a reliable independent rating system such as those offered by the *AAA Directories* or *Mobil Guides.* Checking two or three sources is better than depending on one. If the hotel is not listed, it may be because it is a privately owned hotel with a loyal repeat clientele.

Before you book, ask how old the hotel is and when the guest rooms were last refurbished. Locate the hotel on a local street map to verify its proximity to the lifts, restaurants, and shops. If you will not have a car, make sure that there is bus or shuttle service that satisfies your needs.

To protect yourself, always guarantee your first night with a major credit card (even if you do not plan to arrive late), send a deposit if required, and insist on a written confirmation of your reservation. When you arrive and check in, have your written confirmation handy.

Getting a Good Deal on a Hotel

The benchmark for making cost comparisons is always the hotel's standard rate, or rack rate. This is what you would pay if, space available, you just walked in off the street and rented a room. In a way, the rack rate is analogous to an airline's standard coach fare. It represents a straight, nondiscounted room rate. In the mountains, you assume the rack rate is the most you should have to pay.

To learn the standard room rate, call room reservations at the hotel(s) of your choice. Do not be surprised if there are several standard rates, one for each type of room in the hotel. Have the reservationist explain the differences in the types of rooms available in each price bracket. Also ask the hotel which of the described class of rooms you would get if you came on a ski vacation package sold by a tour operator or travel agent. This information will allow you to make meaningful comparisons among various packages and rates.

Tour Operator/Packager Deals

Recognizing that an empty hotel room is a liability, various travel entrepreneurs have stepped into the breach, volunteering to sell rooms for the hotels. These entrepreneurs, who call themselves tour operators and travel packagers, reserve or "block" at a discounted rate a certain number of rooms that they in turn resell at a profit. As this arrangement extends the sales outreach of the hotels, the hotels are only too happy to cooperate with this group of independent sales agents. Although a variety of programs have been developed to sell the rooms, most are marketed as part of ski vacation packages.

This development has been beneficial to both the skier and the hotel. Predicated on volume, some of the room discount is generally passed along to consumers as an incentive to book. By purchasing your room through a tour operator or packager, you may be able to obtain a room at the hotel of your choice for considerably less than if you went through the hotel's reservations department. The hotel commits rooms to the wholesaler or tour operator at a specific deep discount, usually 18–30% or more off the standard quoted rate, but makes no effort to control the price the wholesaler offers to his customers.

Packagers and tour operators holding space at a hotel for a specific block of time must surrender that space back to the hotel if the rooms are not sold by a certain date, usually 30 days in advance. Since the wholesaler's or tour operator's performance and credibility are determined by the number of rooms filled in a given hotel, they are always reluctant to give rooms back. The situation is similar to when a particular department at a university approaches the end of the year without having spent all of its allocated budget. The department head reasons that if the remaining funds are not spent (and the surplus is returned to the university), the university might reduce the department budget for the forthcoming year. Tour operators and packagers depend on the hotels for their inventory. The more rooms the hotels allocate, the more inventory they have to sell. If a packager or tour operator keeps returning rooms unsold, it is logical to predict that the hotel will respond by making fewer rooms available in the future. Therefore, the packager would rather sell rooms at a bargain price than give them back to the hotel unsold.

Incidentally, the relationship also works in the other direction. If the hotel is sitting on a goodly number of unsold rooms, it will contact the tour operator and ask for his or her help in selling them. When this happens, it is usually under "fire sale" conditions, and the skier can sometimes score a truly remarkable deal.

You and your travel agent do not have to buy an entire package from a tour operator to get a good rate on a hotel room (some packages offered by airline travel companies are an exception). Also, be aware that some of the really hot deals become available at the last minute, one to four weeks before the dates in question. If you have your heart set on getting a bargain, make your reservations through a tour operator about two weeks or so before your departure date. Could you get stuck without a room? It's possible, but not likely, particularly if your party consists of just two people. If your party is larger than two and there is no room at the inn, you always have the option of going the condo route.

Casino Hotels

If you plan to ski one or more of the Lake Tahoe, California/Nevada mountains, consider rooming at a casino hotel on the Nevada side of the lake. You may be a little farther from the slopes and the ambience will resemble Las Vegas more than Aspen, but the price of your hotel room will be a bargain. Likewise, food and après-ski entertainment will be plentiful and affordable.

For even greater savings, try the ski deals offered by Reno casinos. Last year Circus Circus and the Biltmore, among others, featured room rates as low as $45 a night. Some casinos threw in buffets, welcome cocktails, and transportation to Squaw Valley (about 50 minutes west). A brochure about Reno casino deals for skiers can be obtained by calling (800) 367-7366.

Hotel-Sponsored Deals

In addition to selling rooms through tour operators, most hotels periodically offer deals or packages of their own. Sometimes the deals are specialized or the packages are offered only at certain times of the year, for instance in November and December. Promotion of hotel specials tends to be limited to the resort area's primary markets. If you live in other parts of the country, you can take advantage of the packages, but you probably will not see them advertised in your local newspaper.

An important point regarding hotel specials is that the hotel reservationists do not usually inform you of existing specials or offer them to you. In other words, you have to ask. Finally, if you are doing your own legwork and are considering a hotel that is part of a national chain, always call the hotel instead of using the chain's national 800 number. Quite frequently, the national reservations service is unaware of local specials.

AAA and AARP

Members of the American Automobile Association and the American Association of Retired Persons are eligible for discounts at many ski area hotels. Call your local AAA office or check the AARP monthly magazine for additional information.

Special Weekend Rates in Big Cities

Hotels in Denver, Santa Fe, and Salt Lake City—all within easy driving distance of the slopes—are good prospects for weekend lodging deals. Most downtown hotels that cater to business, government, and convention travelers offer special weekend discount rates that range from 15 to 40% below normal weekday rates. You can find out about weekend specials by calling the hotel or by consulting your travel agent.

Getting Corporate Rates

Many hotels offer discounted corporate rates (5–20% off rack). Usually you do not need to work for a large company or have a special relationship with the hotel to obtain these rates. Simply call the hotel of your choice and ask for their corporate rates. Many hotels will guarantee you the discounted rate on the phone when you make your reservation. Others may make the rate conditional on your providing some sort of *bona fides,* for instance a fax on your company's letterhead requesting the rate or a company credit card or business card upon check-in. Generally, the screening is not rigorous.

Preferred Rates

If you cannot book the hotel of your choice through a half-price program, you and your travel agent may have to search for a lesser discount, often called a preferred rate. A preferred rate could be a discount made available to travel agents to stimulate their booking activity or a discount initiated to attract a certain class of traveler. Most preferred rates are promoted through travel industry publications and are often accessible only through an agent.

We recommend sounding out your travel agent about possible deals. Be aware, however, that the rates shown on travel agents' computerized reservations systems are not always the lowest rates obtainable. Zero in on a couple of hotels that fill your needs in terms of location and quality of accommodations, and then have your travel agent call for the latest rates and specials. Hotel reps are almost always more responsive to travel agents, because travel agents represent a source of additional business. As discussed earlier, there are certain specials that hotel reps will disclose only to travel agents. Travel agents also come in handy when the hotel you want is supposedly booked. A personal appeal from your agent to the hotel's director of sales and marketing will get you a room more than half of the time.

Ski Vacation Packages

Hundreds of ski packages are offered to the public each year. Some are created by members of the National Ski Tour Operators Association, a consortium of packagers that combines the buying power of its members to negotiate bulk discounts on lodging (both condos and hotels), airfare, rental cars, and lift tickets. Other packages are offered by airline touring companies, independent travel agents and wholesalers, the resorts themselves, and local or regional ski clubs. Big ski clubs are usually nonprofit social organizations that negotiate lodging and lift-ticket packages directly with ski resorts and secure group air discounts with the carriers. By our observation, the big ski clubs strike some of the best deals going, because they normally are able to bypass all the middlemen. It is probably worth your while to join a good ski club just to take advantage of their ski packages.

While most ski packages include airfare, lodging, and lift tickets, it is possible to buy the "land only" part of the package. When you purchase land only, you must make your own air transportation arrangements. This is a good strategy if you can take advantage of an airfare price war or if your city enjoys below average rates for air travel. Be aware that November, December, and January, except for the holiday periods, are usually low-volume months for the airlines. It is quite likely to see discounted airfares and other promotions during this period.

On the other side of the coin, package airfare prices are locked in. If you get an urge to go skiing but are too late to buy a 7-, 14-, or 21-day advance purchase ticket from the airlines, a tour operator can almost always find you an affordable fare. Likewise, when the airlines are sold out, tour operators frequently have seats available. You may not be able to fly on your favorite airline, and you may not be eligible for frequent-flyer mileage, but you will be able to go skiing.

Ski package prices vary seasonally, with the Christmas/New Year holiday period and Presidents' Day weekend being the most expensive. Next most expensive is early February through the third week of March. Least expensive are November (excluding Thanksgiving), the first three weeks of December, January, and late March through the end of the ski season.

If you can book at the last minute, you might be able to get a highly discounted package even in high season. Here's how it works: If a lodging property has a group cancellation, or advance bookings are slow for certain dates, management will get on the phone with high-volume ski packagers and cut a special deal to sell the rooms. The packager in turn will promote the deal to customers who call in. It's a win/win situation all around. The hotel fills the rooms, the packager sells packages, and the skier gets an amazing deal. On March 3, as an example, we called Any Mountain Tours, a large packager that handles 24 different resorts, and asked for their best Colorado deal for March 10 through 17. We indicated that we wanted hotel accommodations for two nonsmoking adults traveling from Chicago. In response, Any Mountain Tours suggested the Pines at Beaver Creek Resort (just west of Vail), a plush ski-in/ski-out lodge. The price quoted was $1,581 per person, or $3,162 altogether for the couple. When we called Vail/Beaver Creek Resort Management (the central reservations service that handles bookings for Vail Associates lodging properties), we were quoted $2,877 for the same room and dates!

Almost all package ads feature a headline stating "Vail for Three Days from $498" or "Five Days at Crested Butte from $705" (or some such). The prices quoted are per person, and the key word in the ads is "from." The rock-bottom package price connotes the least desirable hotel accommodations. If you want better or more conveniently located digs, you'll have to pay more, often much more.

Most packages offer a selection of four or more hotels and several condos at each featured resort. Though some properties are very good, others run the quality gamut.

Packages should be a win/win proposition for both the buyer and the seller. The buyer only has to make one phone call and deal with a single salesperson to set up the whole vacation: transportation, rental car, lift tickets, lodging, and even equipment rentals. The seller, likewise, has to deal with the buyer only once, which eliminates the need for separate sales, confirmations, and billing. In addition to streamlining selling, processing, and administration, many packagers also buy airfares in bulk on contract like a broker playing the commodities market. Buying a large number of airfares in advance allows the packager to buy them at a significant savings from posted fares. The same practice is applied to lodging, lift tickets, and rental cars. Because selling ski vacation packages is an efficient way of doing business, and because the packager can often buy in bulk individual package components (airfare, lodging, etc.) at discount, savings in operating expenses realized by the seller are sometimes passed on to the buyer so that, in addition to convenience, the package is also an exceptional value. In any event, that is the way it is supposed to work.

All too often, in practice, the seller realizes all of the economies and passes nothing in the way of savings on to the buyer. In some instances, packages are loaded additionally with extras that cost the packager next to nothing but run the retail price of the package sky-high. As you might expect, the savings to be passed along to customers are still somewhere in Fantasyland.

When considering a package, choose one that includes features you are sure to use. Whether you use all the features or not, you will most certainly pay for them. Second, if cost is of greater concern than convenience, make a few phone calls and see what the package would cost if you booked its individual components (airfare, rental car, lodging, etc.) on your own. If the package price is less than the à la carte cost, the package is a good deal. If the costs are about the same, the package is probably worth it for the convenience.

Listed below are airlines and tour operators that offer ski vacation packages:

Any Mountain Tours   (800) 296-6686 or www.anymtn.com, is a large tour operator that sells nothing but ski packages. A good source of discounts and last-minute deals, Any Mountain sells packages and land-only to 24 U.S. and Canadian resorts.

Central Holidays   (800) 935-5000 or www.centralh.com, sells ski packages through travel agents to Italy, Austria, France, and Switzerland, as well as to the U.S. and Canadian Rockies. In addition to competitive prices, Central Holidays features a deal where a sixth person receives free accommodations with five paid packages.

Daman-Nelson Travel   is a full-service travel retailer specializing in packages to Sun Valley, Jackson Hole, Banff, Whistler, and most major Colorado and Utah ski areas. For a free newsletter, call (800) 343-2626 or check out www.skirun.com on the Internet. Clients include both individual skiers and travel agents.

Delta Airlines   (800) 872-7786 or www.deltavacations.com. Delta Dream Vacations offers ski packages to the western United States and to the Alps. Delta's package prices for American resorts are reasonable but do not represent a great bargain. From the eastern United States, Delta has some of the best routes to Salt Lake City, Utah, as well as to Montana.

Mountain Vacations, Inc.   www.mountianvacations.com, sells through travel agents and offers competitive packages to 21 western U.S. and

Canadian ski resorts. Mountain Vacation packages feature many upscale properties.

Northwest Airlines (800) 800-1504 or www.nwa.com, features packages to some of the more remote western resorts, including Big Sky in Montana. Package prices are very competitive for resorts in Northwest's service area.

Rocky Mountain Tours (800) 525-SKIS or www.skithewest.com is a New Jersey packager that sells ski vacations to the U.S. and Canadian Rockies. Clients include both individual skiers and travel agents.

Southwest Airlines (800) 423-5683 or www.swavacations.com, runs affordable packages to Taos, the Salt Lake City–area resorts, and the Lake Tahoe–area resorts.

Aspen Ski Tours (800) 525-2052 or www.skitours.com, focuses on the American and Canadian West. Its packages have been fairly competitive, especially its ski vacations to Whistler/Blackcomb in British Columbia.

Helping Your Travel Agent Help You

Most travel agents do not ski and consequently have only a limited knowledge of the major ski areas. This lack of information translates into travelers not getting reservations at the more interesting hotels, paying more than is necessary, or being placed in out-of-the-way or otherwise undesirable lodging.

When you call your travel agent, ask if he or she has been to the ski area you wish to visit. First-hand experience means a lot. If the answer is no, be prepared to give your travel agent a lot of direction. Do not accept any recommendations at face value. Check out the location and rates of any suggested hotel or condo and make certain that the hotel or condo is suited to your needs.

Because travel agents are often unfamiliar with ski venue alternatives, your agent may try to plug you into an airline travel company ski vacation or some other preset package. This essentially allows the travel agent to set up your whole trip with a single phone call and still collect an 8–10% commission. The problem with this scenario is that most agents will place 90% of their ski business with only one or two tour operators. In other words, it is the path of least resistance for them and not much choice for you.

To help your travel agent get you the best possible deal, do the following:

1. Determine which ski areas you are interested in. Decide whether you prefer a hotel, condo, or rental home.

2. Check out the skiing travel ads in the Sunday travel section of your local newspaper and compare them to ads running in the newspapers of your preferred destination's key markets. A key market for the Lake Tahoe–area resorts, by way of example, is San Francisco. Dallas, Houston, Los Angeles, Chicago, and New York are key

markets for most Colorado resorts. Mammoth and June Mountain resorts heavily target Los Angeles. Because the competition among resorts and tour operators in key market cities is great, you will often find deals that beat the socks off anything offered in other parts of the country. Scan the ads in the papers of these primary market cities and see if you can find hotel discounts or packages that sound good.

3. Call the packagers, hotels, or resorts whose ads you have collected. Ask any questions you might have, but do not book your trip with them directly.

4. Tell your travel agent about what you found and ask if he or she can get you something better. The packages in the paper will serve as a benchmark against which to compare alternatives proposed by your travel agent.

5. Choose from among the options uncovered by you and your travel agent. No matter which option you select, have your travel agent book it. Even if you go with one of the packages in the newspaper, it will probably be commissionable (at no additional cost to you) and will provide the agent some return on the time invested on your behalf. Also, as a travel professional, your agent should be able to verify the quality and integrity of the package.

Part Two

Colorado and New Mexico

Claire Walter

Lito Tejada-Flores, who developed the Colorado and New Mexico chapters for the first edition of *The Unofficial Guide to Skiing in the West* back in 1995, and I both live in Colorado, in distant parts of the state. In many years of living here, neither of us has run out of reasons to love Colorado skiing. Originally this section was written by Lito, who also shepherded it through two revisions. His observations, opinions, and words formed the platform which I have now twice updated and revised.

Of course, the magic of Colorado skiing starts with the light, dry, Rocky Mountain snow. And we'll admit that Colorado holds no monopoly on it. Partisans of Utah claim their snow is deeper, drier; aficionados of New Mexican *nieve* swear it's the lightest of all; locals in the northern Rockies claim that their dry snow falls more frequently and piles up higher; and Pacific Coast skiers will trade our ultralight powder for their mammoth accumulations of wetter, denser snow any day. And so it goes. But if Colorado snow is not absolutely unique here in the Rockies, it is still a small miracle—the stuff of which skiers' dreams are made. Not only does Colorado snow fall from the sky as fluff, as true powder, but lowering temperatures after a storm will often dry it out even further. Colorado's high elevation keeps the snow light and dry, as much as (or more than) winter cold does. If it hasn't been packed down, the snow sometimes gets lighter and drier a day after it's fallen. In skiers' terms, this translates into less resistance, less friction, less work to turn and slide. It's as though one's skis are always better waxed on Colorado slopes. Untracked powder snow is for play not penance, an invitation with no strings attached; and when it's groomed and packed down into pistes, this stuff becomes a sort of velvet where skis can perform to 110% of their design potential.

But that's just the beginning. As important as its snow, but surely more unique, are Colorado's ski towns. The resort flavor is unlike anything elsewhere. It's fair to say that what distinguishes Colorado from other ski regions in our country is not the number of great ski areas, but the number of great ski resorts. This is not mere hair-splitting. A ski area is a mountain equipped for skiing, period. A ski resort ideally offers far more than just skiing, for life at the bottom of the mountain must be as intriguing and as intoxicating as turns on the hill. A real ski resort has to offer more than strip development, motel-style or minimalist condo accommodations, and endless parking lots. Most Colorado ski areas are real "resorts" in this sense. The very best are actually true villages, towns, communities where the whole rhythm and fabric of life, the atmosphere in the streets, the focus and passion of locals as well as visitors, are inextricably tied to mountains, snow, and skiing. Great ski villages, which are easy to find in the Alps, are all too rare in the States, and most of those are in Colorado.

But we're taking you on a tour of the *best skiing* in Colorado, not just the best resorts, so we'll also be visiting a couple of areas that don't qualify as proper resorts but do offer dynamite skiing. Still we've been very choosy. Of Colorado's 26 ski areas, we'll visit only 16, plus two great destinations in New Mexico. It was easy to slip New Mexico skiing into a section devoted to Colorado. The resorts of both states, after all, lie in the southern Rockies, which means slightly warmer winter temperatures, more sunshine, and blue skies.

It's also easy for us to promise you a tour of Colorado's "best skiing," but some readers may already be wondering where they'll find *the* best skiing, *the* best ski mountain, *the* best ski town. Lito has lived in one Colorado ski town, Telluride, and I live in Boulder, with Vail two hours from my front door and seven places closer than that. But neither of us would point to any one resort as "the best." Every good ski resort is somebody's favorite. The special quality of light, snow, friends you're skiing with, your own state of mind and body—all this makes one day, one place, one memory the best. With any luck you'll have numerous "best days" on Colorado slopes. So we leave ultimate judgments to each reader.

Yet there is still a pecking order. If Colorado can be called the capital of American skiing, then it must be said that the twin capitals of Colorado skiing are Vail and Aspen. Our insider's tour of the southern Rockies begins with these two ski towns that set the standards by which all others are judged. These resorts (or, more accurately, the corporations running them) are two leaders in a wave of change that is altering the nature and quality of Colorado skiing. Lito calls it a white revolution.

With so many skiers now in Colorado, both locals and out-of-state vacationers, the competition between resorts to attract them is so fierce that the average level of service and amenities—what you get for your skiing dollar—seems higher here than anywhere else in the country. Just as important, however, you're getting something *new* for that dollar.

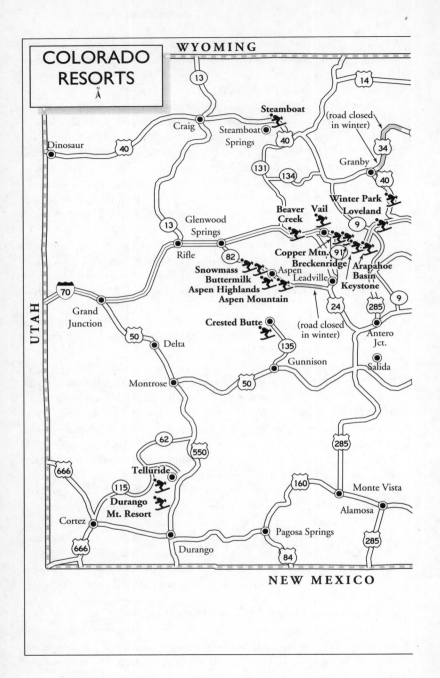

COLORADO RESORTS

N

WYOMING

13

14

Dinosaur

40

Craig

Steamboat

Steamboat
Springs

40

131

134

(road closed
in winter)

34

Granby

40

Glenwood
Springs

13

Rifle

82

Snowmass
Buttermilk
Aspen Highlands
Aspen Mountain

Beaver
Creek

Vail

Winter Park
Loveland

9

Copper Mtn.
Breckenridge

91

Arapahoe
Basin
Keystone

Aspen

Leadville

9

70

Grand
Junction

50

Delta

Crested Butte

135

24

(road closed
in winter)

285

Antero
Jct.

Montrose

Gunnison

50

Salida

50

285

62

550

666

115

Telluride

Durango
Mt. Resort

160

Monte Vista

Cortez

666

Durango

Pagosa Springs

84

Alamosa

285

NEW MEXICO

UTAH

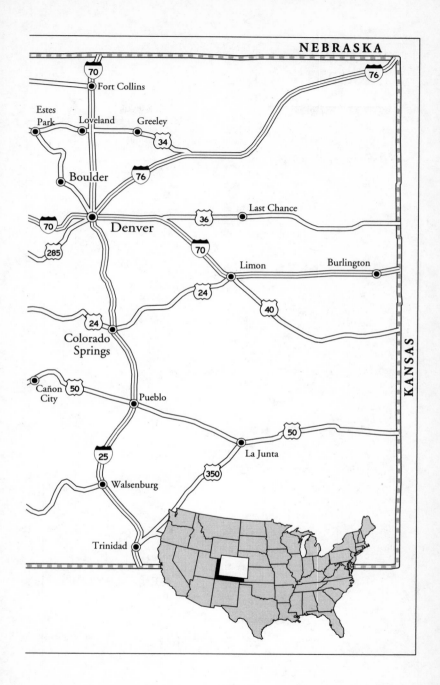

NEBRASKA

KANSAS

70
Fort Collins

Estes
Park
Loveland
Greeley
34
76
Boulder
70
Denver
36
Last Chance
285
70
Limon
Burlington
24
40
24
Colorado
Springs
Cañon
City
50
Pueblo
50
La Junta
25
350
Walsenburg
Trinidad

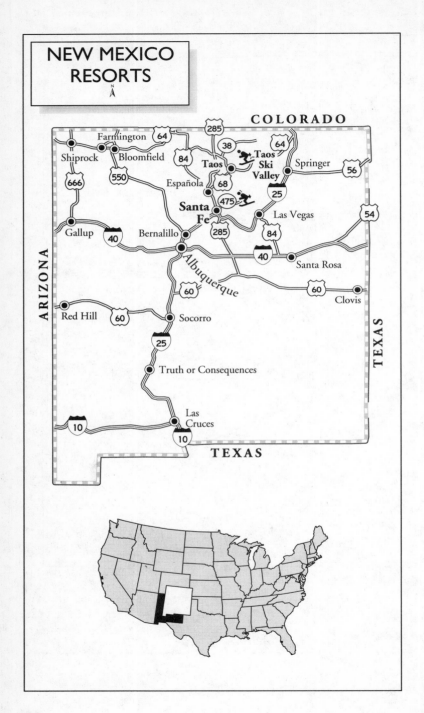

NEW MEXICO RESORTS

N

COLORADO

Farmington — 64 — 285 — 38 — 64

Shiprock — Bloomfield — 84 — Taos — Taos Ski Valley — Springer — 56

666 — 550 — Española — 68 — 25

Santa Fe — 475 — Las Vegas — 54

Gallup — 40 — Bernalillo — 285 — 84

ARIZONA

40 — Santa Rosa

Albuquerque

60 — 60 — Clovis

Red Hill — 60 — Socorro

25

Truth or Consequences

TEXAS

Las Cruces

10

10

TEXAS

For generations, lift lines have been the bane of downhill skiers' existence. The vast majority of the lifts installed in Colorado since the late 1980s boast higher capacity and dramatically faster uphill speeds that not only have eliminated long liftwaits, but have dramatically cut the uphill ride time. The cunning machines responsible for this white revolution are high-speed, detachable, four- and six-person chairlifts, which are also known as express lifts or superchairs. It's a brave new world, and skiers who never managed to get enough runs in one day now find themselves quitting at 2:30 p.m. because they've skied so much and so fast that their legs are tired. A nice feeling. And a new feeling in American skiing. Of course, high-speed lifts are not a Colorado monopoly—they're found everywhere today—but Colorado has more of them.

For years, lift-ticket prices rose steadily, largely due to these new high-speed lifts. At the dawn of the twenty-first century, however, local skiers have been the beneficiaries of fierce competition between resorts, which have embarked on the most amazing lift-ticket wars. Astonishing as it may seem, especially for season pass–purchasing locals, the cost of quality skiing has actually come down.

The radical revamping of lift infrastructure is only the most obvious change in the Colorado ski scene. Many areas have greatly extended their snowmaking—already nearly universal as a form of pre-Christmas, early-season insurance. Some have recently opened large, steep, formerly out-of-bounds zones to adventurous skiers willing to hike for their adrenaline runs. Many areas have completely remodeled their base facilities and created entire new villages. On-mountain, sit-down restaurants have proliferated as alternatives to the usual dreadful cafeteria fare. All told, Colorado ski corporations have undertaken a cycle of investment in the future of a magnitude never before seen. Fifteen years ago, snowboarding was a controversial rarity. Now skiers and riders share the slopes at all Colorado ski resorts and all but one in New Mexico. Snowboarding's initial appeal was to youngsters who, on the slopes as in everyday life, delight in anything that sets them apart from their parents' generation. But those first-wave young riders have now grown up, and even their parents have taken up the sport. Snowboarding has actually brought more families to the slopes together and has given more kids a reason to accompany their parents willingly rather than grudgingly on annual Colorado ski jaunts. Mountain snowboarding is challenging and graceful, while Colorado's abundant half-pipes, quarter-pipes, and terrain parks still bring on that adrenaline rush, not just for single-plank snowboarders but for new-school skiers.

Colorado ski resorts have been consolidating on the business end. Vail owns not only Beaver Creek but also Keystone and Breckenridge. Intrawest, the sophisticated company that owns or manages some of the biggest and most sophisticated ski resorts in North America (like Whistler/Blackcomb, Mont Tremblant, and Stratton Mountain), has been redeveloping Copper Mountain and at the end of the 2002–2003 ski season also took over Winter Park. The struggling Utah-based American Skiing Company still owns Steamboat, and the Aspen Skiing Company owns and operates all four ski areas there (Aspen Mountain, Aspen Highland, Buttermilk, and Snowmass.) Even little SolVista (formerly Silver Creek) operates Berthoud Pass, the state's oldest ski area and a high-elevation powder mecca that has now developed into a snowcat-served ski adventure skiing and riding area. Despite certain amount of predictable grumbling about Colorado ski resorts becoming homogenized corporate amusement parks, such consolidation of ski-resort ownership has resulted in continued and even accelerated upgrading of skier services.

The white revolution, first in Colorado and today across the country, remains the final and perfect justification for this guidebook. High-speed lifts, season-extending snowmaking, and sophisticated grooming have changed the way we think about our ski mountains, the best way to ski them, the best way to plan a day for maximum enjoyment. That's what this book is all about.

Enough introductions. We have 18 major ski mountains to visit and a lot of glorious white miles to cover together. Needless to say, doing the "research" for this guide—skiing and re-skiing all these Colorado and New Mexico areas—has been fantastic. A ski writer's fantasy. One that's waiting for you too, on Colorado ski slopes.

The Vail Valley

Vail   The original American mega-resort, Vail is an enormous ski area with the most advanced lift system and the greatest number of high-speed detachables in Colorado; groomed trails plus ungroomed Back Bowls (but a little shy on true beginner terrain); a great kids' program; and evening activities to beat the band. The town of Vail is a large, diverse, Alpine-style pedestrian village whose twin centers and abundant outlying lodging are seamlessly linked with swift, free buses.

Beaver Creek   Vail's smaller sister resort offers better novice terrain, really splendid, not-too-steep, introductory bump skiing and, of course, fewer skiers on a mountain that, although still of respectable size, is a good deal smaller than Vail. The village is handsome, upscale, and exclusive; more modest accommodations can be found down the hill, close to Avon.

Vail

In a sense, it is impossible to write about Vail or Aspen—in fact, the broader picture of Rocky Mountain skiing—without comparing these high-priced, high-profile resorts. They, and their satellites, are the skiing capitals not only of Colorado but of American skiing. That being said, there are differences between them: Aspen is older and richer in history and community, but its slopes—quite diverse and never crowded—are spread out across four separate ski mountains that are not linked with one another. Vail, a newer and brasher resort, has it all, all together, all in one area. Closer to Denver, Vail also attracts day skiers. It is never as packed as its Summit County neighbors, because it is one pass farther west. The mountain is big enough to absorb crowds without feeling crowded. Vail is the most complete all-around ski mountain and seamlessly polished vacation-resort machine you can imagine. It's probably the easiest place where a skier, any skier, can have a perfect day, any day.

The Vail Advantage

It's no accident that Vail is the first ski resort discussed in the Colorado section of this guidebook. Vail comes in first by most terms with which the ski world measures success: number of visitors, size of ski school, sheer boggling sum of money that vacationing skiers leave in this jewel of a ski-resort town, and above all, the size of its skiable terrain. Vail's mountain is enormous. A comparison gives you an idea of just how big Vail really is. In 1989, when Vail doubled its total skiable acreage by opening five new Back Bowls, collectively named The Far East, it could boast that it had more skiable acreage than its Summit County neighbors—Keystone, Arapahoe, Breckenridge, and Copper Mountain—put together. Of course, since then, those resorts have added new terrain of their own, but they still don't come close. In 1999–2000, Vail took another initiative with the first phase of a two-year expansion to *Blue Sky Basin* with another pair of bowls.

The town and mountain work in ways that other ski areas only dream about. To serve its vast ski terrain, Vail boasts more high-speed lifts than any other mountain in the West. Also, Vail Village, the first true pedestrian ski town in North America, became a role model for resort planners everywhere.

Virtually every one of the 18 ski areas in this guidebook can boast one or two special facets of the skiing experience in which it absolutely excels: the grandest views, the best beginner area, the finest glades. Vail, too. It is distinguished by multiple back bowls that are easily the best open-slope skiing and powder preserve in the whole state after a snowfall. But—and this is an important "but"—no other American resort offers as complete a spectrum of ski options for every level of skiing on one mountain. A family group spanning three generations and twice that many skiing or snowboarding styles and ability levels can ski Vail Mountain, meet for lunch, separate, and meet again in the evening. (Perhaps making lunch optional, because this mountain is so huge that the logistics of having everyone at the same midday meeting place can be daunting.) Individuals, like the proverbial blind men describing an elephant, will be skiing their own version of Vail Mountain. This kind of all-around ski mountain, where no one need be bored, frustrated, or over-challenged, is a rarity.

Vail's first trails and runs were cut by early-day ski fanatics, veterans of the Tenth Mountain Division, armed only with chainsaws and visions of the wide-open skiing they had enjoyed in the Alps after World War II. Unencumbered by yet-to-be-invented university degrees in ski-area design, computer-generated mountain models, and environmental impact statements, they just went and cut themselves exceptionally wide runs. Wide runs have a subconscious, but critical, effect on a skier's frame of mind: with no potential obstacles looming on either side, all skiers ski better. Because Vail's runs are wider than the norm, they feel more "natural" than what most skiers are used to. A liberating experience. Enough generalizations. Let's look at this beauty of a ski mountain in detail.

The Multiple Worlds of Vail Mountain

Looking up from Vail Village, the original town center and still the resort town's heart and soul, one can easily underestimate Vail Mountain. Organize your mental map into nine zones. On the front side, from west to east: (1) Lionshead, (2) "the middle mountain," for lack of an official name (3) the Mid-Vail area above, (4) the northeast section, and (5) Golden Peak, the easternmost section of the base. Tucked in behind Lionshead, on the west end, is (6) Game Creek Bowl, set in a side valley that's neither on the front nor the back side of the mountain. On the back side are (7) the two classic Back Bowls, and (8) the five newer bowls collectively called China Bowl after the biggest and most significant of the quintet. Finally, facing China Bowl, is (9) Blue Sky Basin.

Sure it's big, or, more accurately, wide, very wide, but all you can see from below is a forest cut here and there by white ribbon runs, rising gently, then sloping back out of sight. Most of the mountain, in fact, is out of sight. From the village, you catch a couple of tantalizing glimpses of steep ridge runs high up. From Lionshead, the second resort center to the west, the upper mountain is totally invisible. But it's up there, waiting.

A long ridge running roughly east to west defines Vail, a wide mountain rather than a tall or narrow one. The ski area measures over seven miles across. It's also a two-faced ski mountain, not merely in the sense that the ski terrain faces both north and south, but that it exhibits a totally different character on each side. Dropping down toward the twin resort centers of Vail Village and Lionshead, the front or north face is classic of Colorado ski country: a dark-green mountainside of dense forest that only ingenuity and chain saws could have transformed into a big ski area. The front side offers mostly trail skiing, with only a few wide-open clearings and small bowls high up.

Forest fires in the late nineteenth century stripped the back-side slopes of timber, and the intense solar radiation and evaporation have kept the trees from reestablishing themselves on these high, south-facing slopes. Hence the Back Bowls, Vail's not-so-secret advantage. Not just one back bowl, but a whole series one after the other, mile after mile.

From Vail's opening in 1962 until 1988, only two bowls, Sun Down and Sun Up, were part of the lift-served ski area, yet they literally made Vail's reputation as a ski mecca. Huge as they are, they have been dwarfed in size, if not in reputation, by the five additional bowls—China, Tea Cup, Siberia, and Inner and Outer Mongolia bowls—that were opened up in 1988–1989. The newer bowls are somewhat easier angled, hence

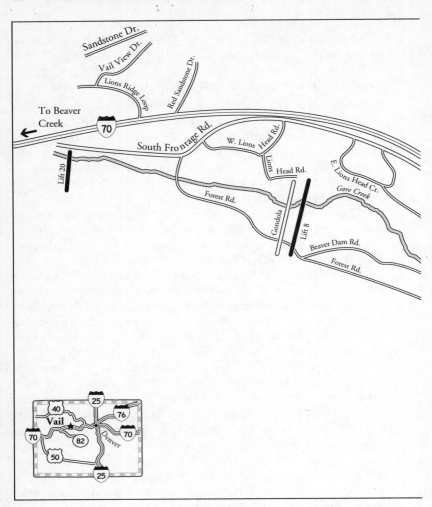

more accessible to average skiers, than the original two. These bowls are definitely not experts-only terrain, but they're just as imposing— empty, white, and breathtaking as the two classic bowls.

The Back Bowls face south, enabling people to ski in the strong Colorado sunshine. However, that same sun, beating down on the ungroomed snow does create an unpalatable melt-and-freeze cycle that often produces crusted morning snow, followed by gummy afternoon conditions—especially in the later part of the ski season. After years of planning and permitting, the lift service in *Blue Sky Basin* debuted in 1999–2000 and was significantly expanded the following winter. This

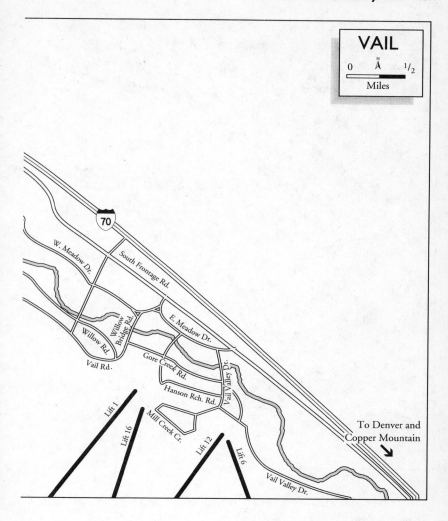

expansion area sits across Two Elk Creek from China Bowl, and its north-facing slopes—some open, some elegantly gladed—further rounded Vail's already-rounded skiing mix.

Vail Mountain is so large that skiers often spend whole days skiing only one part of it without running out of new runs to try. After a week, they might have explored only portion of the mountain's vastness, especially if they used part of their multiday ticket to ski Beaver Creek, Breckenridge, Keystone, or A-Basin. To those who know Vail Mountain well, it is like a collection of separate but contiguous ski areas, each with its own feeling, character, and style of skiing.

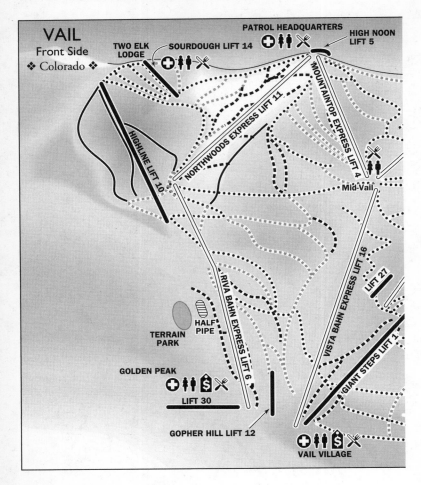

Let's start with a thumbnail sketch of each area, then we'll visit them in more detail for different levels of skiers.

The Lionshead runs, located at the extreme western side of Vail Mountain, comprise a labyrinth of long, sinuous, cleanly separated paths through elegant forests of lodgepole and spruce. The Lionshead side, well served by one eight-passenger gondola and three detachable quad chairs, may not offer a lot of steep or difficult skiing, but it does offer an abundance of good, relaxed cruising. Also, there is often a pleasing feeling of solitude, because the runs are visually cut off from one another. Many of them, especially the westernmost off the Pride Express, rarely seem to have too many people in sight at one time. Eagle's Nest, the large complex at the top of the gondola (and at the top of a series of high-speed chairs) has also been turned into Adventure Ridge. It's a sort of nighttime

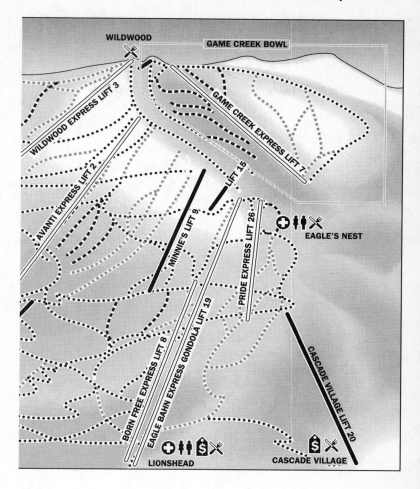

amusement park with an ice-skating rink, a snowboard terrain park, a tubing area, and a novice skier area, all under the lights. It's just a fast ride in the heated gondola from the valley floor.

With abundant uphill capacity and fast-moving lift lines (when there are any queues at all), Lionshead invites skiers to spend more time cruising lovely sinuous trails like *Pride, Bwana,* and upper *Simba*. These trails are never crowded, even on big weekends, and offer the sort of high-speed cruising that would be imprudent on the more peopled slopes above Mid-Vail.

The middle mountain, which is not an official name on a trail map but our designation of convenience, is a nebulous zone that is somewhat underskied and underappreciated. The runs drop below *Eagle's Nest Ridge* east of the Lionshead trails, and in fact some look and feel quite similar to

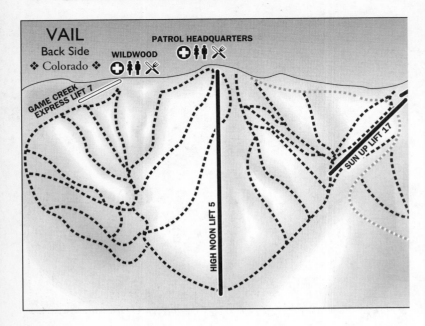

Lionshead runs. The Avanti Express serves these runs, which range from *Avanti* to *Columbine* plus their lower extensions, and drop all the way down into Vail Village. Because this section doesn't have a real name, a unique geographical identity, or mystique, it is skied less than it deserves. Sure, it is used for World Cup and World Championship ski races, but people usually tend to ski it only as a way home at the end of the day. These runs are very long and interesting. The Avanti Express is also the easiest way to cross the front face from Vail Village to Lionshead or vice versa.

If the middle mountain has a nebulous image, Mid-Vail is just the opposite. The network of runs is known by the same name as the giant mid-mountain hub at the top of the Vista Bahn Express lift. Mid-Vail terrain is not quite a bowl in the pure sense, but rather two open Alpine valleys served by two fast quads. The section is chock-full of a great variety of relatively short but interesting runs. If any zone on Vail Mountain seems crowded, this is the one. The Vista Bahn Express (Lift 16) delivers an endless stream of skiers, many of whom, through some sort of gregarious herd instinct, tend to stay right there. Don't fall into this trap. Mid-Vail skiing is like a visit to a lovely but small ski area within a giant ski area; if you spend all day there, you will be enjoying only a fraction of what the entire resort has to offer. Additionally, the two lifts carrying skiers and snowboarders above Mid-Vail tend to be among the mountain's most crowded.

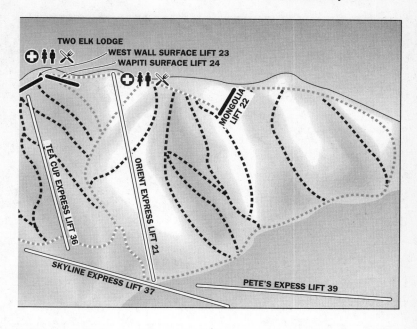

The Mountaintop Express (Lift 4) carries skiers to the top of Vail Mountain. Calling this a summit would give too much dignity to what is little more than the highest bump on a system of ridgelines, but it's still the top, which locals call "PHQ" (for Patrol Headquarters). Unprepossessing at it looks, it is the key crossroad on the mountain, where the High Noon triple (Lift 5) comes out of the original Back Bowls and the Northwoods Express (Lift 11) arrives from the northeast side.

The northeast side of Vail's front face lies just around the corner, east of the Mid-Vail basin. Subtly referred to on the trail map as the Northeast Bowl, although its deep forests prevent it from looking or feeling bowl-like in the context of Vail, this is an area of heavy timber, deep forests, steep runs, and hard skiing. In fact, the most challenging skiing in Vail—if not the most beautiful—and the greatest concentration of black-diamond runs on the front side are all in the Northeast Bowl. There are rolling, swooping, "easy" black trails, steep and moguled ridgelines, and even a kind of bump skiers' ghetto off the Highline chair (Lift 10), with its demanding double blacks, such as *Highline* and *Blue Ox*. The Northeast is where serious Vail skiers head, at least once a day, for a real workout. Nearby is *Northwoods* with both gladed steeps and broad cruisers, served by a high-speed quad called the Northwoods Express (Lift 11). On a high gentle face of the Northeast Bowl sits an unprepossessing gateway to Vail's sprawling China Bowl, a long, long way from

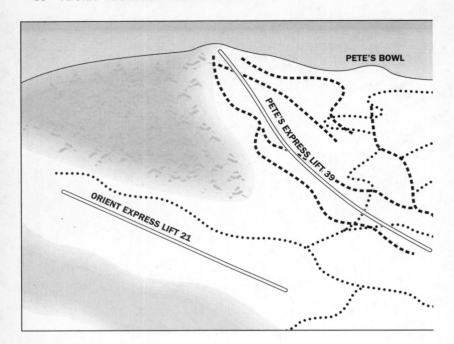

where we began in Lionshead. The trails off the Sourdough triple (Lift 14) comprise a novice skier's paradise of gentle, friendly, low-angle but high-mountain runs where inexperienced skiers can cut loose and soon transcend their novice limits. It is also the obvious gateway into the new bowls. This transition area can be reached by taking the Riva Bahn Express and the Northwoods Express (Lifts 6 and 11) or the Vista Bahn Express and the Mountaintop Express (Lifts 4 and 16), then to cut across to Lift 14 on the usually crowded *Timberline Catwalk*. The top of Lift 14 is only a stone's throw from Two Elk Lodge, a giant log-and-glass structure with the best views on Vail Mountain. Two Elk made headlines in October 1998, when it was torched by eco-terrorists protesting Vail's then-proposed expansion into what is now *Blue Sky Basin*. The summit restaurant was swiftly rebuilt, bigger than the original.

At the eastern base of the mountain's front side is Golden Peak, a separate subpeak named for the glowing autumn colors displayed by its dense aspen stands. Golden Peak boasts a beautifully arranged children's skiing area, a sensational terrain park, and a few comfortable intermediate runs, and has also always been known as a ski-racing and race-training enclave. The Riva Bahn Express (Lift 6) starts from a beautiful and totally rebuilt base complex and climbs up Golden Peak, dropping some skiers at an intermediate unloading point. The lift then continues above Golden Peak to the bottom of the Northwoods Express (Chair 11).

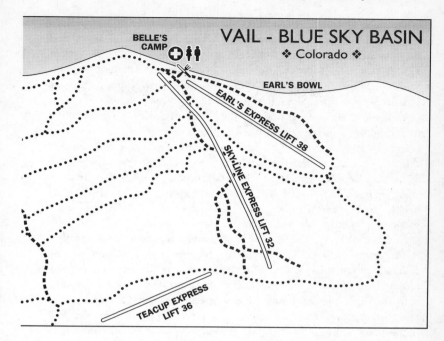

And then there are the bowls. Vail simply wouldn't be Vail without these huge white spots on the map. In skiers' minds, these are empty, delicious, open white-on-white arenas. Game Creek Bowl, introduced earlier, lies over the ridge west of Mid-Vail via the Wildwood Express (Lift 3). The runs on its north-facing flank, served by the Game Creek Express (Lift 7), have become one of the most complete intermediate ski zones on the mountain, evidenced by the lines that form at the bottom of the chair.

The two classic, original Back Bowls, the five newer bowls collectively referred to as China Bowl, and the two *Blue Sky Basin* bowls are the frosting on Vail's cake. We'll visit them in more detail in the following sections. But in your bird's-eye overview, remember that the two classic Back Bowls—Sun Down and Sun Up—lie just behind PHQ. There are three routes into these bowls. The traditional main entrance is from the top of the mountain. Other options are to enter Sun Down from Wildwood, at the top of the Wildwood or Northwoods Express chairs (Lifts 3 and 11), or enter Sun Up from Sourdough chair (Lift 14). To return, take the High Noon chair (Lift 5) back to PHQ or the Sun Up chair (Lift 17) to the west end of the China Bowl area.

The marketing name for the five bowls added in 1988 was the Far East. Now they are called China Bowl—even though there are five of them. Whatever the name, together they boast a skiing acreage equal to the rest of Vail Mountain! The bowls are most easily entered from Lift 14 but can also be reached from PHQ via *Sleepytime Catwalk.* From west to east, you'll encounter Tea Cup Bowl, China Bowl, Siberia Bowl, and Inner and Outer Mongolia bowls. To return to the top, ride the Orient Express (Lift 21). A short platterpull to 11,455 feet, the highest point on the Vail Mountain ride, accesses Outer Mongolia. Two additional surface lifts simply pull skiers along flats toward the Two Elk Lodge.

Vail's most recent expansion was the bold move to *Blue Sky Basin,* the tempting north-facing terrain on the other side of Two Elk Creek that skiers had long eyed from the Far East. Four high-speed chairs brought this exquisite parcel into the Vail skiing fold. The Skyline Express (Lift 37), Pete's Express (Lift 38), and Earl's Express (Lift 39) directly serve *Blue Sky Basin's* terrain, while the Tea Cup Express (Lift 36) hauls riders back up to Two Elk. Contemporary standards of trail cutting, with routes roughed out among the tress, were put into play here.

And that's Vail, a totally diverse mega-mountain, a world of subworlds; the biggest of the big ones. The common denominator is its user-friendly character. Most runs lie square in the fall line, most steeps offer a way around for skiers who suddenly realize they don't belong there, and most runs are steady and continuous. Vail is perhaps more of a cruiser's mountain than an adventurer's mountain. But Vail cruising is sensational, and there are still enough challenges on this monster to keep hyperactive hotshots happy for a long time. Let's get more specific.

Vail for Beginners

Vail has two separate beginner areas on different sides of the mountain. On the Vail Village side, first-time and beginner classes meet at Golden Peak, and students are soon riding Lift 12, which serves an area that's nicely roped off from traffic but is still, for beginners, a bit steep. Lionshead beginners can ride to the top on the gondola, make their first moves off Lift 15, and soon progress to handle the wonderful, gentle slopes off Minnie's chair (Lift 9). A nearly effortless experience. Lionshead instructors have put together the absolutely easiest way down their side of the mountain, combining bits and pieces of various runs into what they call the "teaching trail." If you're looking for an extremely gentle way down the mountain from Eagle's Nest, do as they do. At the bottom of Lift 15, turn right onto *Owl's Roost.* Follow this catwalk straight past several steeper bluish runs until it turns a sharp corner and zigs back left across the same runs to the middle green section of *Ledges,* a series of gentle pitches around small tree islands that leads you to another road, *Cub's Way* to the top of the little-used Giant Steps lift (Lift 1). From there, *Gitalong Road* takes you to the bottom of the mountain. It's a mighty roundabout journey, but it works, even for virtual first-timers. Also, because it's long, it begins to provide new skiers with the mileage they need to gain confidence and skill. Much of the upper part of this teaching trail and the top sections of other trails have been designated as slow-skiing zones, so that learners won't be distracted or scared by stronger skiers whooshing by—in theory at least.

Special Ski-School Programs, Special Tips

Vail boasts the largest ski school in the country and certainly one of the best. Vail's children's ski school is incredible, perhaps the best anywhere. Within it are a number of special programs. The *Small World Play School* is a nursery at Golden Peak for youngsters from two months to two-and-a-half years old (or nonskiers to age six). From there, kids graduate into Mini-Mice (beginner three-year-olds), Mogul Mice (four years to kindergarten) and then to Super Stars (advanced beginners and better, ages three and older). The "regular" kids' ski school teaches children from six years old and up, and teenagers are grouped together in their own classes. Of course, snowboarding is the peer of skiing in this progressive children's ski school, which has been the most creative branch of Vail's giant ski school. There's even a kids' trail map that points the way to mysterious mine shafts, Indian villages and burial grounds, a mountain lion's den, and more for young skiers and snowboarders to explore. The children's program has been as much a contribution to the future of skiing as all of Vail's quad chairs, and it has been widely and successfully copied at other ski resorts.

What about adults? Lito, a Vail veteran, confesses to being less sanguine about the quality of grown-up instruction, for a curious reason. Vail has the largest and most affluent private lesson clientele of any North American ski mountain. Since instructors make a far better living teaching private than group lessons, all the hot instructor talent at Vail winds up booked for the season with private lessons. (Some moneyed folk hire an instructor to ski with them for days on end just so that they can cut the lift lines.) That's all well and good if you can afford the tab, which is upwards of $110 per hour and well over $400 for an all-day private lesson. But an unfortunate side effect is that instructors teaching group lessons on Vail Mountain are apt to be less experienced, less motivated, and less skilled, and the chances of getting a great group lesson are correspondingly low.

Recognizing the importance of remedying this situation, Vail offers multiday beginner packages and also the Three-Day Breakthrough program designed to help intermediates move on to the next level. Ski School Desks are located at Golden Peak, Vail Village, and Lionshead and on-mountain at Mid-Vail and Eagle's Nest, so there's no reason not to sign up if you have the sudden urge to improve.

Vail for Less-Experienced Skiers

Inexperienced skiers, both novices and emerging intermediates who lack either mileage or confidence or both, can have a great time on this mountain. In all honesty, though, Vail's choices for this level of skier are somewhat limited compared to what's available for better skiers. Inexperienced skiers, in search of green runs, can wind up spending a lot of time on Vail's long and fairly boring catwalks—and if they're on a snowboard, the day can be completely agonizing. They will probably enjoy themselves more, and certainly make more progress, if they spend a few days at Beaver Creek, the closest of Vail's sister resorts, where they'll find more ideal terrain.

The very best novice and low-intermediate skiing at Vail is served by Lifts 3, 7, and 14—although you'll have to also use some other lifts (and ski down some other runs) to take full advantage of these hyper-friendly zones.

One of the most congenial greens is *Lost Boy,* the ridge run around the rim of Game Creek Bowl. It's long and arcs around the far end of the ridge, presenting wonderful high-Alpine views and a big-mountain experience. Cruise *Lost Boy* to your heart's content—but remember, it's the only run in Game Creek that's really suitable for fairly inexperienced skiers. When leaving Lift 7, bear left down *Eagle's Nest Ridge,* from which you can either return to Mid-Vail via *The Meadows, Jake's Jaunt,* or *Over Easy,* or continue on down *Eagle's Nest Ridge* to the Lionshead side of the mountain. From Mid-Vail, egress from the mountain begins with *Lion's Way,* a gentle packed road at the end of which is a series of broad, open slopes. *Gitalong Road* leads back to Vail Village. You can ski sections of *Bear Tree* when you cross them if they look groomed and inviting. The best option if you're heading to Lionshead is to continue traversing across the mountain past *Bear Tree* to *Born Free,* the main drag down into Lionshead. If you are a hesitant skier, avoid the one steep spot near the bottom by following *Village Catwalk* in a long zigzag that takes you around the last steep pitch.

As noted earlier, all the runs off Lift 14 on the eastern end of the front side are optimal for inexperienced and learning skiers. The only flaw here is the trip home, which necessitates following *Flapjack* all the way to the bottom of Lift 11. It is easy if it's been groomed recently but daunting if it hasn't, so check the grooming report. From the bottom of Lift 11, slide down *Skid Road* to the back-side loading station of Lift 6, and from the top of the lift, ski *Ruder's Run,* an easy blue straight back to the bottom of Golden Peak, or you can angle over to Vail Village.

If you are pretty good at coping with average, mid-level blue runs, even though you don't "bomb" them the way good skiers do, you have many more choices. Above Mid-Vail, take Chair 4 and start with *Swingsville, Christmas,* and *Ramshorn. Avanti* and *Pickeroon* are two of the beautiful cruising runs on the middle mountain. Each has one steep, black face, which you can go around on convenient escape paths. Farther west, try *Columbine* and *Ledges.* Finally, the westernmost run on the whole mountain, *Simba,* is easy, wide, and inviting for most of the way down until you reach *Post Road.* Follow *Post Road* right to *Born Free,* and you'll be home free.

Another option, of course, is to get out of the novice mode as quickly as possible by enrolling in the Vail–Beaver Creek Ski & Snowboard School, the biggest in the country. Investing a few hours with an instructor can pay big dividends at Vail.

Vail for Good Skiers

The term "good skiers" refers to those who feel at home on skis, who have probably been skiing for quite a few seasons, who spend most of their time on blue slopes (and look pretty spiffy on moderate terrain), who can definitely get down a black-diamond slope, or two, or three, but don't hang out all day on these steep, moguled runs. Such skiers can cope with fresh snow and powder, but don't exactly dance through it. They ski the whole mountain, but don't yet "own" it. They don't make heads turn with admiration as they flash by, but flash by nonetheless and enjoy skiing at a pretty good clip when the slopes are comfortable. For such skiers, Vail is paradise, Valhalla, the ultimate joy.

If you start your day at Vail Village (as opposed to the Lionshead side), you'll hop the Vista Bahn Express (Lift 16) and warm up with a couple of runs on the wide cruising slopes above Mid-Vail. The relatively obscure and narrow entrance from the popular *Swingsville* hides a gem called *Cappuccino,* which is more varied in pitch than the runs flanking it. Wonderful stands of widely spaced trees invite you into a kind of natural, giant slalom game. *Ramshorn,* the widest run, is marked green but virtually indistinguishable from the blue runs around it. (Someone apparently felt the need to show green runs on the map from the top of the mountain down to Mid-Vail, which must be why *Ramshorn* and *Swingsville* are colored green, in defiance of common sense.) For the many other skiers who bomb down it, *Ramshorn's* extra width is a real incentive to make fast, big turns. You too can indulge in a few extra miles per hour here without disturbing (or even coming close to) other skiers—but remember that it can be intimidating for novices to share even a wide trail with fast skiers.

After a Mid-Vail warm-up, take a couple of morning cruises down *Northwoods* and *Northstar* on the northeast side. This terrain captures the morning sun; additional charms are its length and its continuously changing mountain shapes—rolls, dips, short flats, and inviting drops. *Northstar,* half hidden in the forest to the left of *Northwoods,* looking downhill, is the same sort of run, only more so. Its steeps are somewhat steeper and the rolls and drop-aways are more inviting. Although marked black on the trail map, *Northstar* isn't really very hard, but, unlike

Northwoods, there is no way around the steeper pitches. Return to the top via Northwoods Express (Lift 11).

Swingsville also leads to the fabled run called *Riva Ridge,* an "easy" black. Once an intimidating mogul-studded steep with a scary neckdown in mid-slope, it has long been tamed with grooming and widening its narrow spot. Still, *Riva Ridge* is a name that carries a great reputation with it. To follow it with *Northwoods* runs, bear right onto *Trans Montane Catwalk* at the bottom of *Riva Ridge's* actual ridge, which leads back to Lift 11. If you miss the cutoff, you'll find yourself down at the base.

If you begin your day at Lionshead, you'll follow a different path. Instead of heading for Mid-Vail and *Northwoods,* take your warm-up runs on the Pride Express (Lift 26). Let your skis run over the big rollercoaster humps and hollows of *Bwana* and *Safari,* where there are no obstacles, no sudden surprises. (As a bonus, on a powder day when the world seems to be cutting up the bowls' new snow, you can snare first tracks off Pride for a couple of hours, and there's hardly ever a lift line.) Then drop over the back side of *Eagle's Nest Ridge* into Game Creek Bowl, another paradise for good skiers, where the black runs feel almost "bluish" and the blue runs are continuous enough to feel "blue-black," dramatic if not difficult. *Deuces Wild, Faro, Ouzo,* and *Dealer's Choice* on skier's right, are marked black, but they are short and very wide. Neighboring these sparsely treed runs are friendly, nonthreatening powder lines after a storm—a good place to develop your deep-snow skills. The Game Creek Express (Lift 7) keeps you circulating at a brisk clip—especially if you enter the right side of the maze, which seems to have a shorter wait than the left side.

What about the Back Bowls? Sure, why not? But please, not every run back there. Sun Up and Sun Down, the original Back Bowls, are far more challenging than the newer (but no longer new) China Bowl sector. The bowls are so vast that you can actually find almost every kind of skiing there, but the eastern (skier's left) sides of both China and Siberia bowls are fairly low-angle slopes, ideal for your first Vail bowl adventure. Drop off the catwalk into *Poppyfields East* and *West,* the two main groomed routes into China Bowl and the only top-to-bottom blue runs in all seven Back Bowls. Even strong skiers find themselves skiing them often, because the south-facing bowls often undergo real melt-freeze cycles which can make the ungroomed sections impossible at worst and unpleasant at best under various conditions. *Shangri-La,* on the east side of China Bowl, is an area of sparse trees with multiple gladelike paths, none of which is truly hard. You can ski run after run here and never dive through the same grove twice. These trees are an important exception in the middle of the wide-open treeless terrain, for they allow, and even encourage, bowl skiing on stormy days by providing extra visibility and shelter from wind.

Next door, in Siberia Bowl, the easiest, most stress-free runs are *Gorky Park* right down the center and *Bolshoi Ballroom* on the eastern (skier's left) flank. Conditions are likely to be best in springtime, corn-snow conditions. The easternmost bowls, Inner and Outer Mongolia (known to locals as "Innie" and "Outie"), are big and friendly, and are also too far beyond the main traffic pattern to attract a lot of skiers. To reach them, traverse past China, Tea Cup, and Siberia Bowl and then ride the Mongolia surface lift (Lift 22). The farther east you go in Mongolia Bowl, the gentler the terrain. The return to the Far East Express is via a gentle road along Two Elk Creek, another factor that keeps the Mongolias from crowding.

Blue Sky Basin, a pair of north-facing cirques across from China and Tea Cup Bowls, offers even more for good skiers. Of the two bowls, Pete's Bowl on the east offers the most beguiling terrain for upper intermediates. Designed with routes laced through glades and clearings rather than the wide trails that characterize Vail Mountain's front side, Pete's finest blue-square offerings are long, sinuous routes: *Cloud 9, Big Rock Park,* and *The Star.* Ski them ten times, and you can find ten very different lines down—all within an intermediate's ability. *Earl's Bowl* is more open, while the best intro runs are *In The Wuides* (named for Vail's Resorts longtime employee Paul Testwuide), an often-groomed wide-open run, and *Champagne Glade* and *Montane Glade,* both incredible on powder days.

If you start out on the Lionshead (western) end, you may stay there for hours. Hardly any black shows on the Lionshead side of the trail map. The finest runs are *Simba* with its branches and variants, *Safari, Pride,* and *Cheetah,* all very long and steady. The continuous fall-line pitch of the terrain gives these runs a special feeling that shorter runs of the same difficulty lack. This is Vail cruising at its finest. Cruising is a sport, or addiction, best practiced on newly groomed runs, "virgin corduroy" as some call it, referring to the patterns made in the snow by the grooming vehicles' big rollers. In addition to grooming reports at the top of most lifts, Vail posts a highly visible grooming symbol at the top of any run that's been groomed in the last 24 hours. A nice touch. High-speed, high-capacity chairlifts and one gondola mean few lines. If you're in reasonably good shape, try to ski nonstop, top to bottom, or at least in longer sections than normal. Pure exhilaration.

Vail for Experts

A certain lingering snobbishness in Colorado ski circles insists that Vail is a great cruising mountain for average skiers and that real experts will sooner or later get bored there. Nonsense! Vail's trail map does not look like a forbidding grill of black bars, but with its enormous size, Vail still has more serious expert runs than most other Colorado mountains. Expert terrain comes in two flavors: steep, fierce bump skiing and ungroomed, all-terrain, all-snow skiing primarily on the back side. Bump skiing isn't everyone's cup of tea, but moguled runs are a daily challenge that few expert skiers can resist. At Vail, you'll encounter the challenge of the steep and lumpy in two main areas: off the Highline Chair (Lift 10) and on a stellar run called *Prima*.

The runs of Lift 10 comprise bump city. The three main ones, *Blue Ox, Highline,* and *Roger's,* deserve their double black-diamond designation. *Blue Ox* is the easiest of the lot and the first one to try if you're hesitant. *Highline,* right under the lift, is steepest and most continuous, and provides the best long, pure bump run in Vail. That's where the hot young bumpers with their 20-year-old knees pound the fall line. This is straightforward, clean bump skiing on big moguls down an obvious fall line, with plenty of width and options for changing lines. In short, it's a beauty. By contrast, *Roger's* (pronounced Roh-zhay's after early Vail Ski School director Roger Staub) is very narrow and generally messy.

Follow *Swingsville Ridge* from the top of Lift 3, drop off the ridge toward the village, and eventually you'll reach a fork. On the left are the smoothed-out steeps of *Riva,* and on the right is *Prima,* Vail's classic bump run. For years the ski school awarded Prima Pins to students who managed to ski it with a bit of grace and composure. Brown's Face is the first major steep on *Prima.* The skier's left side lies back at a slightly gentler angle and therefore attracts the majority of skiers, but some experts, like Lito, find the skiing much better on skier's far right. The *Pronto* cutoff below Browns' Face is a bailout from *Prima* and a legitimate shortcut back to Lift 11.

Bump specialists on their way from the top to the Highline chair ski what they call "PPL," a killer combination of *Prima, Pronto,* and *Logchute.* But Lito doesn't recommend *Pronto* for mere mortals. The bumps (or more accurately the troughs and gullies) on this short steep face are gnarly and gouged beyond belief. Although marked only black, not double black, *Pronto,* in Lito's opinion, is the meanest, most technically difficult skiing at Vail—and that's saying a lot. Most skiers, even most experts, would do better to follow *Trans Montane Catwalk* back around to Lift 11. *Prima Cornice,* an extremely steep exit near the top of *Prima,* is surely the scariest run at Vail. In low snow years it often remains closed, because its cliff bands aren't sufficiently covered. Don't even consider *Prima Cornice* unless a steep pitch like *South Rim Run* seems easy to you.

For true experts who don't want to ski moguls all the time, much of Vail's magic is found in the two classic Back Bowls. A day there in fresh powder is the finest experience the resort has to offer. Other Colorado resorts also have terrific bumps and even a smattering of bowls, but there are simply no other Back Bowls. If you're good, they're always good. There is nonetheless a sort of hierarchy of adventures—lines to ski first, lines for later.

Despite their names, Sun Up Bowl has no monopoly on early morning light, and Sun Down does not get great sunsets. The names simply are a poetic alternative to East Bowl and West Bowl. Neither bowl has any traditional runs at all, only generalized lines that have been given their own names. All are marked black on the trail map, but some are much blacker than others. The *Slot* into Sun Up Bowl is sometimes machine groomed, so before you venture in, check the grooming report.

Sun Down and Sun Up bowls are separated by High Noon Ridge, a massive central ridge. The first gate east of Lift 5 leads to the flat top of the central ridge for a few hundred yards. The slopes down and left are the first ones to hit on a powder morning. They're steep, direct, and easy to reach, and they get tracked up quickly. There is no best place to drop off. Simply turn and dive off where there are few or no tracks. First is *Milt's Face,* which pretty much represents the whole side or flank of this ridge, and then *Cow's Face,* the name given to the nose at the end of the ridge. Skiing here is so wide and free that where one named zone stops and the next one starts is quite vague, and even the trail maps are not always helpful. There's room for at least a hundred sets of non-overlapping tracks.

Another gate just west of the Lift 5 top station seems to usher you into a narrow tree slot rather than a proper bowl, but the trees quickly thin out into a few hundred yards of beautiful glades before disappearing altogether at the top of *Forever.* Less steep but just as broad and even longer is *Forever* on the left side of Sun Down Bowl, immediately west of the Lift 5 lift line and close to High Noon Ridge. Farther right is *Wow.* Both runs are best reached through a gate.

Because most skiers seem to circulate in the Back Bowls' central area, closest to Lift 5, many lovely lines on the extreme sides of Sun Up and Sun Down don't get tracked out as fast and often yield great powder late in the day or even a day or two after a snowstorm.

From the ridge between the Sun Up and Tea Cup Bowls, you can access *Yonder Gully, Yonder,* and *Over Yonder,* which offer wonderful, obscure skiing on the far west-facing flank of Sun Up Bowl. This area has a feeling all its own with patchy, widely spaced trees that offer the most skiable lines on a stormy day.

On the extreme western side of Sun Down Bowl, via a traverse from the top of Lift 7, are two other remote zones, known as *Seldom* and *Never,* that also provide the away-from-it-all feeling. Be mindful of a few rock bands and minicliffs, but nothing extreme. Other lines on this side, like *Morningside Ridge* and *Ricky's Ridge,* provide pretty good skiing but lack the wild character of the classic bowls.

Two of the finest lines in the Back Bowls are *Après Vous* and *Chicken Yard,* both in Sun Up Bowl. To find *Après Vous,* head for Cow's Face and hug the right-side control fence. *Après Vous*'s triangular face often has a gentle cornice wave at its crest and typically receives deeper wind-drifted snow than the rest of the bowl. Its beauty is not so much the skiing, which is splendid, but the sensation of being out of sight of everything and everyone else. Eventually, the route narrows into a gully that cuts through sparse aspen forests down to the *Sun Up Catwalk*. Even wilder and more isolated is *Chicken Yard,* which you reach by once again hugging the right side of the *Après Vous* control fence and ducking through a marked gate in the ropes. The top of this run gives the peculiar sensation of being suspended high above the valley floor—a sensation only conveyed by convex, fall-away terrain. Despite this suspended-in-the-sky feeling, *Chicken Yard* isn't really very steep. The hardest moment comes in the exit gully, which is barred by small cliffs. When there isn't enough snow to negotiate the cliffs, the patrol closes the *Chicken Yard* gate.

The lines on either side of the Back Bowls ultimately lead down to roads that lead back to the High Noon chair (Lift 5). The action is all over when you reach these catwalks, so be sure to look around and enjoy the view. *Sun Up Catwalk,* in particular, brings you around a corner to a sudden splendid view of the peaks of the Holy Cross Wilderness framed between two snowy ridges, one of Vail's most dramatic Alpine views.

Another great bit of expert-only terrain that many skiers never find is the *Ouzo Glade* (or the *Ouzo Trees*) in Game Creek Bowl. Use the *Eagle's Nest Ridge* entrance to *Ouzo* and then traverse right for a hundred yards or so on a grooming road before peeling down into the forest. There are many lines here, with continual surprise openings in the trees. In winter the snow is fantastic, but on spring afternoons it turns heavy because of its direct western exposure.

The western sides (skier's right) of China and Siberia Bowls are fairly steep and should be considered legitimate black-expert terrain. They also receive a good deal more windblown snow than the two original Back Bowls, so that when the patrol records 6 or 7 inches of new snow at PHQ, lines like *Jade Glade, Bamboo Chute,* and *Genghis Kahn* can capture 18 to 24 inches. *Rasputin's Revenge,* the steep face directly beneath Siberia Bowl's western ridge, is a great Back Bowl powder shot and also ranks as the single steepest pitch in the back, definitely experts' turf.

Blue Sky Basin offers its share of black-diamond terrain too. Follow the ridgeline separating Pete's and Earl's Bowls, enjoy the sensational views, and then enter an increasingly steeper and more heavily timbered section to *The Divide* or *Encore* down the sheerest section. Another option is to drop off the cornice along the upper section of the east flank of the Pete's Bowl, where you'll find a quartet of gladed steeps: *Lover's Leap, Iron Mask, Little Ollie,* and *Heavy Metal.* Traverse out toward the center of Pete's Bowl, and you can ski *Steep & Deep* or *Scree Field.* Earl's Bowl has fewer trees and an overall gentler pitch; if you hanker after steeps, head for *Champagne Glade,* the first run into the bowl from the Belle's Camp summit area.

Vail is a more intriguing playground for expert skiers than many believe. This is true not only because of its hard runs and Back Bowls, but because of the sheer amount of nonstop skiing available. There is enough terrain here—both obvious and hidden—to keep your sense of discovery and surprise alive for many seasons. The only reason for one Vail ski day to resemble another is lack of imagination.

All of Vail's bowls, by the way, are separately controlled areas entered through marked gates in roped-off control fences. Generally, they are closed earlier than the front side of the mountain to give skiers a chance to get back up to the summit and down to the village by a reasonable hour—and to give the patrol a chance to sweep this entire massive mountain.

Snowboarding

Vail caters to snowboarders and freeriders, as it does to everyone else, with superb facilities. The Highlight of the Golden Peak Terrain Park is the Vail Superpipe, whose 15-foot walls and 17-foot tranny, groomed nightly, are known for their consistency as well as challenge. Vail was one of the first resorts to use the Superpipe Dragon, a state-of-the-art machine that literally revolutionized freestyle snowboarding by providing consistent, sculpted superpipes. Throughout the park is a huge variety of jibs, rails, and boxes of all shapes and sizes. In fact, the Jib Park is like a park within the park, enclosed in a glade of trees, where riders can spend a day on all different kinds of rails and jib boxes. It has become a true hangout for terrain-park riders. The park offers a quarter-pipe plus a variety of jumps, including tabletops, spines, and hips, some with rail options. In addition to the Superpipe Dragon, which grooms the big pipe nightly, Vail uses the Park Bully to groom terrain-park features to perfection. The Burton Super Center, located at the top of the park, is a heated yurt that offers Burton snowboards and tuning benches equipped with snowboard tools. Excellent rider-friendly routes are scattered around the mountain too, discreetly signed so that they are difficult to miss. *Hairbag Alley* off *Flapjack* and *Chaos Canyon,* a former recreational bobsled run on a natural snow track, off *Lion's Way,* draw riders like magnets draw iron filings.

Strategies and Tactics at Vail

While bottlenecks and crowding are, generally speaking, not problems during a day's skiing on Vail Mountain, the same can't be said of the evening traffic jams as skiers and snowboarders return to the valley by the most obvious trails. At Lionshead, most people ski home via *Born Free.* An alternative is *The Glade,* a most delightful, semi-hidden spot. This series of openings in a beautiful aspen forest is usually half-deserted when *Born Free* is choked with bodies. If you're a strong skier, several short black pitches into Lionshead avoid the evening congestion. It's also more pleasant to ski home on the western side of the gondola line, following lower *Simba* instead of *Born Free.*

You can return to Vail Village sans crowds via the same route. Head for the Lionshead side, ski *The Glade,* and when you emerge on the last shoulder of *Born Free,* follow the *Village Catwalk* back across to the village.

And one final skiing tip: In stormy weather forget the Back Bowls without trees. Visibility is often so marginal that it just isn't worth it. In fact, the lower mountain is much better than the upper ridges. Lionshead really comes into its own in storms. For one thing, you can ride the gondola and stay warm and dry. For another, the timber on this side of the mountain is denser, so the runs not only feel more sheltered, but your visibility will be at a maximum. The basic strategy for a stormy day, anywhere, is to ski right next to the trees and avoid the featureless center sections of wider slopes.

Lunchtime

Despite the sincere, well-deserved praise heaped on Vail Mountain, the best lunches are actually in Vail Village or in Lionshead. Although food service on the mountain is certainly adequate, the food is not up to the standards of the skiing—and it is expensive. And Vail's mountain restaurants, whether cafeteria style or sit-down, simply lack charm. **Two Elk** on the ridge above China Bowl is a beautiful building on a grand scale, but it is still just another ski-area cafeteria. **Eagle's Nest** has been vastly upgraded and offers several levels of dining—both actual levels in the building and levels of food and formality. Mid-Vail offers the **Cook Shack,** a popular table-service restaurant, a huge cafeteria, and a great sunny deck. **Belle's Camp,** the day lodge atop *Blue Sky Basin,* was originally designed as a bring-your-own lunch spot. Tables indoors and out, mountaintop grills where you can cook your own lunch, and limited beverage sales were going to make this a low-key lunch experience. But a degree of customer demand (most Vail skiers aren't in the habit of brown-bagging their lunches) and the corporation's apparent unease at letting a potential profit center go untapped signaled a change. Basic food service is now offered. Several smaller snack stops—including **Buffalo** where Lifts 3, 4, and 11 unload; **Wildwood** at the top of Lifts 3 and 7; and **Northwoods** near the bottom of Lift 11—are scattered around Vail's wide-ranging slopes.

However, unless you are staying just on the Back Bowls and *Blue Sky Basin* and don't want to spend ski time getting to lunch and back, you can eat in many fine eateries off the mountain. This way you can enjoy a better lunch at lower prices and be back up on the mountain in time to wear your legs to a frazzle long before the lifts close. Several Vail Village and Lionshead restaurants serve luncheon specials at a fraction of their dinner costs.

If you're in the mood for a true romantic lunch up on the mountain and the weather looks good, another option is to pick up a classic French *pique-nique* (in a small backpack) from **Les Délices de France** in Lionshead and enjoy it on one of the several picnic decks marked on the trail map.

Around Town, Vail Ambience

In little more than 40 years, Vail has grown from less than modest beginnings (a single homestead in a green and grassy valley) to an Alpine urban center with three (count them!) exits from I-70. It's really a mountain city more than a town or a village, and despite (or perhaps because of) its size and bustle, it's still a remarkable place to spend a ski vacation.

Vail has two main resort centers, Vail Village and Lionshead. Both are true pedestrian zones, where life and living people—not cars and exhaust—fill the streets, and this is an enormous part of its ongoing success. Vail has banished America's worst urban plague, the automobile, to the outskirts of town and to the outer reaches of vacationing visitors' consciousness. If you bring your car to Vail (which certainly isn't necessary), you're probably going to park it and forget it for the rest of the week—and love living without it. Vail's free bus system, Colorado's second largest after metro Denver's, is extraordinary.

It takes only one ride to get oriented. The town loop is continuous and obvious, and even young kids ride the bus on their own. Between the Village and Lionshead, there is a key bus stop for the **Dobson Ice Arena** (public skating at various hours as well as fierce local-hockey action). The ride from one side of Vail to the other is only about five minutes—at least in the evening, when people aren't dealing with ski gear or climbing on and off the bus in boots. Other routes lead to outlying developments. Both Vail Village and Lionshead are so crammed full of shops, boutiques, galleries, eateries, and lodges that you'll need a week to explore the place—and you'll need a lot of money to take advantage of it all too.

The price of success, this much success, is price. And Vail is as pricey as they come, with *nouveau riche* overtones that are so up-front they don't really offend. The flow of people and commerce in Vail Village sweeps you along **Bridge Street,** which runs from a three-story underground parking structure, over the landmark **Covered Bridge,** and on up to the Vista Bahn Express. Within half a block of this axis of Vail Village social life you'll find the two most chic sports/fashion stores, **Gorsuch** and **Pepi's,** a few too many designer fur shops and jewelers, and all the ritz and glitz of a big-time resort. But Vail Village isn't a one-block shopping stop. There are backstreets, arcades, tucked-away courtyards, and shops.

The après-ski scene is intense too. You'll soon discover the basic Vail Village pub crawl, known as the **Bridge Street Shuffle. Los Amigos** is the slope-side center of the nachos-and-Margarita set, and its deck is wall-to-wall tanned bodies on spring afternoons. The **Christiania** at the foot of the slopes is definitely "old Vail," and its old-fashioned bar/lounge is surely the least trendy après-ski rendezvous in town. The deck at the **Gasthof Gramshammer** is packed on warm afternoons, but the cozy indoor bar is crowded every evening, no matter what the weather. The **Hong Kong Café,** just off Bridge Street, has its adherents as well. In truth, the finest après-ski show is the view of the Gore Range high over town turning rose and purple in the evening alpenglow—but not too many people bother to look.

Lionshead, a more free-form resort center, has open plazas and stairways, as well as more condos and condotels than Vail Village. In addition to such long-running watering holes as **Bart-n-Yeti's,** the top floor of the old gondola building was converted into the **Kaltenbach Brewery,** a 100% authentic German brewery and beer hall, a perfect replica of the Musicians' Hall in the Neuschwanstein castle in Bavaria. Its Kaltenberg Pils is one of the best beers available in Colorado, and Kaltenberg Weiss beer is the ultimate après-ski drink on a warm spring afternoon.

Vail has no night skiing as such, but it pioneered family-friendly evening diversions by opening and perfecting **Adventure Ridge,** beside Eagle's Nest at the top of the Eagle Bahn gondola. Ice skating, snowmobiling, laser tag, tubing, ski biking, or rollicking down the mountain on a Thrill Sled are among the almost-nightly amusements. The gondola is free to foot passengers after 2:00 p.m. daily.

Dining and Lodging in Vail

In Vail, as in Aspen, the problem is not of finding a really good meal but rather one of an embarrassment of riches—and perhaps requiring riches to enjoy the best restaurants. Vail now stretches beyond the Vail Village–Lionshead orbit, from East Vail to Cascade Village on the far west. Lodging abounds there, as well as at West Vail (which is really Vail-across-the-Interstate), but most of the best dining options remain in the two main resort centers.

Sweet Basil is a tastefully decorated, low-key sort of "California nouveau" restaurant that simply serves the most consistently interesting fare in town (which is quite a compliment, considering the competition!). The **Sonnenalp** harbors several restaurants, from the Western-style **Bully Ranch** to the **Ludwig's,** a classic Alpine eatery. Another spot for traditional European mountain fare is **Pepi's** in the Gasthof Gramshammer, which has been around almost as long as Vail itself, dishing up schnitzel and such. Of the several fairly classic French and Frenchified restaurants, **The Left Bank** and **La Tour** are the best known. **The Chop House** at the Cascade Resort & Spa serves up huge portions of steaks, chops, and nonmeaty fare. If the prices and pretensions of some Vail restaurants start to get to you, consider an evening in nearby Minturn. This still somewhat scruffy, true-grit sort of town lies ten minutes from Vail, tucked away in a side canyon under the rocky crag that gave Lionshead its name. Minturn owes both its existence and half its population to the railroad yards. The **Minturn Country Club** is a funky, cook-your-own-steak emporium, and the **Saloon** is a giant, barn-like Mexican restaurant. Both are longtime local favorites and both provide a lively counterpart to the more formal Vail dining. Once the kind of place that vacationers delighted in discovering, these Minturn watering holes have been doing the "lively counterpart" bit for so long, that have now become something of an act too.

Vail accommodations come in such abundance that it's difficult to focus on just a few. Naturally, Vail has a central reservation service (see the Vail Data section), which can book anything from very posh, full-service hotels to luxury apartments and private homes to quite basic condos. Issues to consider include price, style, and location, which in such a sprawling resort are not trivial. If you want to be within a short walk of the lifts, your choices are relatively limited; if you want a good view, you won't want to look directly at I-70; and if you want a quiet neighborhood or reasonable rates, you'll have to take a bus to the lifts.

For atmosphere, architecture, and charm, the Sonnenalp's **Bavaria Haus** is hard to beat. The Bavaria Haus, which seems more old world than old Vail, is a magical building remodeled from a once-boring block of 1960s apartments into an authentic Bavarian, wood-and-plaster masterpiece. It is the nucleus of a sprawling resort that now includes the **Austria Haus Club, the Bavaria Haus,** and the **Swiss Hotel and Spa.** Owned and operated by the Johannes Fässler, scion of the family that have operated an eponymous resort in the Bavarian Alps for four generations, the **Sonnenalp** is one of the top resorts in the Rockies. The **Christiania** and **the Lodge at Vail** are well located, old Vail favorites. The Lodge, in fact, sits just steps from the Vista Bahn and is an immaculately run Vail Village property. The **Cascade Resort & Spa** is the center of a satellite village connected to Lionshead by a quad chairlift outside the door and by a skiway back at the end of the day. This full-service luxury hotel has the biggest and arguably the best spa in the valley.

Lodging a bit out of town, say in West Vail on the north side of I-70 or slightly west in the direction of Eagle–Vail, costs somewhat less than staying right in Vail Village or Lionshead. Despite its outrageously deluxe reputation—and its outrageously deluxe reality—most of Vail lodging is comparably priced with similar lodging in other major Rocky Mountain ski resorts. Many of the outlying lodging complexes offer their own shuttle-van transport to and from the center so you can still enjoy the pedestrian quality of a Vail vacation.

Vail Data

Mountain Statistics

Vertical feet	3,450 feet
Base elevation	8,120 feet
Summit elevation	11,570 feet
Longest run	3 miles
Average annual snowfall	346 inches
Snowmaking	380 acres
Number of lifts	33: 14 high-speed quads; 1 eight-passenger gondola; 1 fixed-grip quad; 3 triple chairlifts; 5 doubles; 9 surface lifts
Skiable terrain	5,289 acres
Opening date	Mid-November
Closing date	Mid-April
Snowboarding	Yes

Vail shares a common lift ticket with Beaver Creek, Keystone, Breckenridge, and Arapahoe Basin.

Transportation

By car 100 miles (2 hours in good road and weather conditions) west of Denver and a little longer from the Denver International Airport (DIA) via I-70.

By bus or limo Colorado Mountain Express from DIA. Call (800) 525-6363.

By plane As an alternative to DIA, many direct flights land at the Vail/Eagle County Airport, just 35 miles west of Vail. United Express has year-round service from DIA, and recently five major airlines have offered seasonal nonstops from many major U.S. cities.

Key Phone Numbers

Ski-area information	(970) 476-5601
Activities desk	(970) 476-9090
Snow report	(970) 476-4888
Reservations	(800) 427-8308 or (970) 845-5745
Website	www.vail.com

Lito's TECH TIP

A Powder Primer

Powder skiing is a great liberation from gravity, effort, and worldly cares. But you have to defeat the powder paradox first. The paradox is this: once you know how to ski in deep snow, it seems much easier than skiing on the packed snow; but learning to ski powder is always harder than learning to turn on packed slopes. Here's a simplified approach to get you as quickly as possible past the frustrations of learning to ski powder.

Balance first. Or, as I used to tell my students, stability before mobility. You'll need a new sort of balance in deep snow—standing two-footed, weight roughly equal on

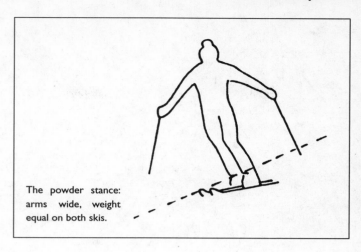

The powder stance: arms wide, weight equal on both skis.

both skis. If you stand on one ski, which is the normal mode for hardpack, that weighted ski will dive down while the other one floats up, and whoops! To develop two-footed powder balance, be sure you do a bit of straight running and traversing before you start turning downhill in deep snow. Bounce and flex up and down on both skis as you descend in a straight line, and adapt your stance for better balance by spreading your arms wider than normal.

Slow-motion speed control. Everything takes longer to accomplish in deep snow: skis don't just whip around, they come about slowly and gently. You'll feel as if you are skiing in slow motion. This is normal and is due to the extra resistance from your skis being buried inside the snow rather than just sliding over the top of it. Get used to finishing turns gently and pulling smoothly out of the fall line much slower than normal. A jerky attempt to pivot your skis sideways in powder will inevitably

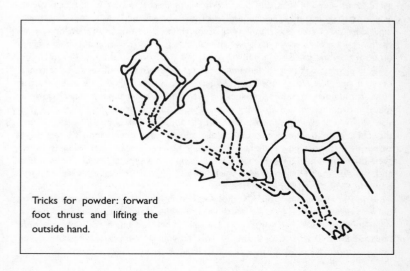

Tricks for powder: forward foot thrust and lifting the outside hand.

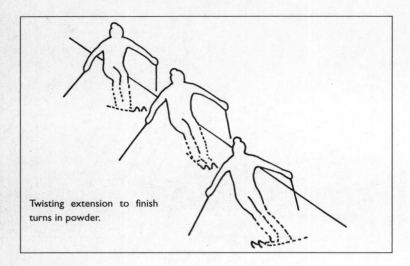

Twisting extension to finish turns in powder.

produce a fall. From a steep traverse, sink down and then slowly, smoothly twist your skis uphill while extending your legs and pushing and grinding your heels sideways. Twisting extension is the key to a strong finish for a powder turn.

Launching your turns down the hill. Here we have another powder paradox: For experienced powder skiers, short-linked turns are easiest, but newcomers will find that individual medium- to long-radius turns result in more success. Launch these turns by using a couple of "powder tricks," either separately or together. The first trick is to vigorously lift your outside hand as you start your turn. This will help to unweight the fronts of your skis and bank you neatly in the direction of the turn—a real secret weapon in extremely deep snow and a big help when you're learning. The other trick is more subtle. If it works for you, great; if not, don't give it a second thought. I'm talking about pushing both feet forward as you start your turn. This is a hard-to-observe move, but believe me, good powder skiers do it a lot and often subconsciously. By thrusting both feet forward in the direction of the new turn down the hill, you will be guaranteeing equal weight on both skis, and once again, helping to lighten the fronts of the skis.

And please, don't be too demanding or too judgmental about your performance on your first few excursions into powder snow. Falling is inevitable and, with the right attitude, almost fun. At first, surviving turns in the deep and just staying on your feet is more important than doing them right. After you've proven to yourself that you can make it down a slope covered with a foot and a half of fluff, it's easier to find the confidence to work out the details and ski the same slope better, more smoothly, and more gracefully. Like everything else on skis, powder skiing is a progression. Remember the sequence: First develop a new type of balance on two feet and two skis, then work on a slow-motion finish to your turns, and, finally, master a powerful "lifting" start to launch them.

And I have one more tip. A secret weapon: fat skis. In recent years, the introduction of extra-wide and slightly shorter powder skis has thrown the door to deep-snow performance wide open. These skis have so much flotation that they never seem to get stuck or "railed" in the powder snow. Skiers who have never really had the time to go out and practice in deep snow will find these wide skis simplify the whole problem of developing deep-snow balance. You very nearly can't make a mistake on them, and if you do make a mistake, you almost can't fall. Known affectionately as "fat boys" or "powder pigs," these extra-wide skis have become ubiquitous in just a few seasons. Rent a pair the next time you find yourself looking at a foot or more of new snow. You will be amazed and delighted.

And that's the powder story. Soon you'll be connecting medium-radius turns through knee-deep powder that used to psych you out. At first, you shouldn't try to link turns too closely—that will be your final step. Initially, you'll want to use the space between turns to catch your breath, smile in amazement that you made it, and get yourself together for that next turn. After your first few successes, you'll know why skiers rave about powder. It really is the ultimate. It is very close to flying.

Beaver Creek

When Beaver Creek was first launched in 1980, it carried the image of being Vail's little sister. The resort was created and is still owned and managed by Vail Associates (now Vail Resorts, Inc.), one of the most sophisticated ski companies in North America. It was to be expected that they would do a good job, and they did. Initially, however, the mountain didn't seem interesting enough to hold a good skier's full attention, no matter how well designed the lifts, how efficient the snowmaking system, or how attractive the luxurious new village at its base. Vail's little sister has grown up into quite a beauty. Maybe all new ski resorts (though admittedly, nowadays there are virtually no totally new ones) have to go through the same awkward years before everything clicks into place and the sophisticated skier can finally say, "Wow, that's quite a mountain!"

In skiing terms, what made all the difference was the opening up of Grouse Mountain. This separate and well-defined ridge rising at the head of a side valley located between the original ski mountain and Larkspur Bowl provides lots of the playful, yet not stressful, advanced terrain that Beaver Creek previously lacked. That's made it a complete, well-balanced ski mountain. In addition, Beaver Creek incorporated into its lift-and-trail system a formerly independent golf-and-ski development called Arrowhead. This was done via a linked valley called Bachelor Gulch, which debuted with homesites in the seven figures and mountain mansions built to reflect that price tag. Resort marketers refer to each of these residential centers as a village, so that the resort is able to boast of "the only village-to-village skiing" in America. In fact, Vail Resorts, Inc. is so proprietary of the concept that they've trademarked it, and it is properly called Village-to-Village Skiing.

The original base village at Beaver Creek has grown up too. The finished architecture is rather distinctive and monumental, with a handsome mix of stucco, stone, and slate. It is less of an Alpine look-alike and has more of its own personality than nearby Vail. And best of all, this

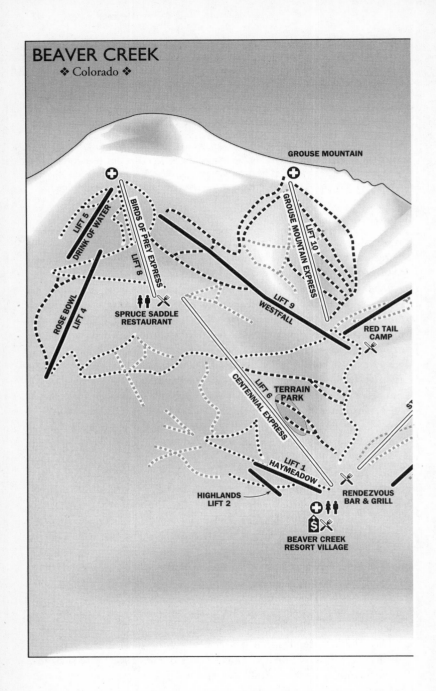

BEAVER CREEK
❖ Colorado ❖

GROUSE MOUNTAIN

LIFT 5

DRINK OF WATER

BIRDS OF PREY EXPRESS

LIFT 8

GROUSE MOUNTAIN EXPRESS

LIFT 10

ROSE BOWL

LIFT 4

SPRUCE SADDLE RESTAURANT

LIFT 9
WESTFALL

RED TAIL CAMP

LIFT 6
CENTENNIAL EXPRESS

TERRAIN PARK

LIFT 1
HAYMEADOW

HIGHLANDS LIFT 2

RENDEZVOUS BAR & GRILL

BEAVER CREEK RESORT VILLAGE

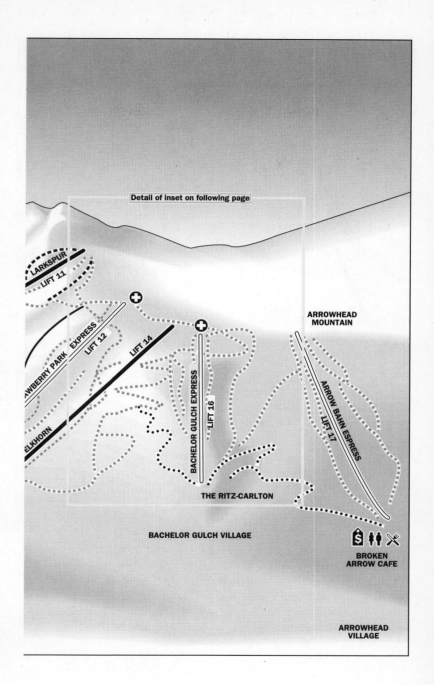

Detail of inset on following page

LARKSPUR

LIFT 11

ARROWHEAD
MOUNTAIN

AWBERRY PARK EXPRESS

LIFT 12

LIFT 14

BACHELOR GULCH EXPRESS

LIFT 16

ARROW BAHN ESPRESS

LIFT 17

ELKHORN

THE RITZ-CARLTON

BACHELOR GULCH VILLAGE

BROKEN
ARROW CAFE

ARROWHEAD
VILLAGE

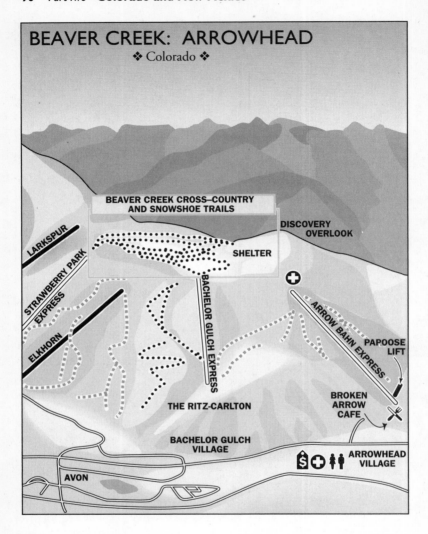

BEAVER CREEK: ARROWHEAD
❖ Colorado ❖

BEAVER CREEK CROSS–COUNTRY
AND SNOWSHOE TRAILS

DISCOVERY
OVERLOOK

SHELTER

LARKSPUR

STRAWBERRY PARK
EXPRESS

ELKHORN

BACHELOR GULCH EXPRESS

ARROW BAHN EXPRESS

PAPOOSE
LIFT

THE RITZ-CARLTON

BROKEN
ARROW
CAFE

BACHELOR GULCH
VILLAGE

AVON

ARROWHEAD
VILLAGE

base village really works well as a pedestrian space. A handsome network of plazas, passageways, easy-angle stairs, and even escalators make strolling around Beaver Creek's stores, galleries, and lodges a real pleasure. An outstanding performing-arts center is topped by a meticulously maintained skating rink, which is popular by day and well into the evening and is a true focal point of the resort. Beaver Creek Village, and the satellite villages too, say "Money" with a capital M.

The skiing public hasn't been immune to Beaver Creek's charms. The lingering reservations about what a splendid place Beaver Creek is, have become concerns about the rather exclusive and pricey nature of the resort itself, not the ski terrain. Beaver Creek Village and Bachelor Gulch Village are tucked up at the heads of narrow canyons. So perhaps this sense of chic exclusivity literally comes with the terrain. Even so, forbidding entrance gates to Beaver Creek Village and Bachelor Gulch Village are not most people's idea of a warm welcome. Day skiers are presently relegated to parking lots along U.S. Highway 6, from which shuttle buses lead to the resort.

Even though Beaver Creek is now a successful destination resort in its own right, its proximity to Vail makes it easy for many skiers to split their Vail Valley experience by skiing at both Vail and Beaver Creek during a week-long holiday.

The Lay of the Land, Valley, and Mountain

You don't just drive up to Beaver Creek and go skiing. The resort center is located at the upper end of a steep side valley that enters the larger Eagle River Valley by the new town of Avon, a few miles west of Vail. Avon and Beaver Creek are as different as night and day. Avon provides lots of relatively affordable housing, economical dining, and budget shopping (enormous, totally nonresorty Wal-Mart and Home Depot outlets have sprung up there), while Beaver Creek's base village provides a compact assortment of resort amenities, elegant mountain architecture, ultraluxury accommodations, and boutique shopping and dining experiences.

Unless you're staying at Beaver Creek or riding the bus from Vail, you'll have to park in one of the large lots at the mouth of the canyon and take a shuttle bus up to the area. The shuttles leave every few minutes, and the ride is quite short. It is also possible to start skiing from Arrowhead or Bachelor Gulch. Both are accessible by vehicle but have extremely limited parking; currently, most people (except those staying at either of those centers) begin at Beaver Creek Village. A plan to build a gondola into the resort from Avon is in the works and will short-circuit this traditional route. When that happens, Beaver Creek will feel like a more egalitarian place to ski. Whichever way you reach the heart of Beaver Creek's ski terrain, just above the original village, lifts and runs veer off in two directions. With the McCoy Park day lodge and the plaza area behind you, the main mountain rises straight ahead, directly above the center of the village. A spacious beginner pasture lies at the bottom, and the Centennial Express (Lift 6) charges right up the center of a massive rounded peak where ribbon runs alternate with dark evergreen forests.

The main mountain is a large central ridge, essentially two lifts high. The Centennial Express climbs most of the way up to the large mid-mountain restaurant at Spruce Saddle, and from there the Birds of Prey

Express (Lift 8) continues to the top. The upper mountain is as gentle as can be. The Drink of Water chair (Lift 5) rises from the east and serves a fantastic network of easy and forgiving novice trails. Lower on the east side of this big ridge, the Rose Bowl chair (Lift 4) serves a slanting side drainage called Rose Bowl. On the opposite, or western, side of the main ridge, the Westfall chair (Lift 9) serves Beaver Creek's most serious and celebrated terrain, the three Birds of Prey runs: *Golden Eagle, Peregrine,* and *Goshawk.*

If you are looking up the main mountain sector, the Strawberry Park Express (Lift 12) is behind you. It climbs through open aspen trees up what looks like a different mountain altogether, which it is. What you can't yet see at all from the base is Grouse Mountain, way in the back, rising between these two. The Bachelor Gulch/Arrowhead area is also well out of sight behind, to the west. Beginning with the Strawberry Park Express, you need to ride a series of lifts and ski a series of runs to get to the end. The Arrowhead/Bachelor Gulch sections of Beaver Creek's terrain are served by three lifts, including the Arrow Bahn (Lift 17) from the Arrowhead base and the Bachelor Gulch Express (Lift 16) from Bachelor Gulch Village. The skiing in this westernmost part of Beaver Creek is mostly blue runs through mixed aspen forests, with quite a few of the trails cut simply as real-estate amenities. No matter—more space to ski and new runs to cruise are always welcome, and a ski jaunt from Beaver Creek over to Arrowhead for lunch and back is a worthy excursion.

Back at Beaver Creek Village, a small canyon separates the main mass of Beaver Creek from the Strawberry Park–served "side mountain." This canyon dead-ends in a sort of mid-mountain cul-de-sac, from which the Westfall chair (Lift 9) climbs toward the Birds of Prey, and the Larkspur chair (Lift 11) rises into Larkspur Bowl. At the dead-end back of this small valley, the Grouse Mountain Express (Lift 10) climbs straight up Grouse Mountain. The Elkhorn Chair (Lift 14) begins near the golf course below Beaver Creek Village, crosses the main access road, and serves as a "real-estate chair" for luxurious ski-in, ski-out homes on the hillside.

Beaver Creek for Beginners and Less-Experienced Skiers

Beaver Creek is a novice skier's dream. It offers much more suitable and intriguing skiing terrain, and more of it, than does Vail. That famous first-day mountain experience—where skiers leave the cradle, forego the comfort of the beginner slope, and head up the mountain like everyone else—is a snap at Beaver Creek. Novices can experience the very top on runs like *Red Buffalo, Booth Gardens,* and *Powell*—all gentle, barely inclined rivers of snow, designated as slow-skiing zones. At the end of the ski day, novices can follow *Cinch* or *Dally* back to the bottom, all without a traumatic moment. *Cinch* especially is a big road that doesn't have a cramped, narrow "catwalk" feel.

This is not to say that the whole mountain is flat. There is simply a lot of gentle skiing at the very top, connected to the base by easy well-designed and well-groomed descent routes. They are well marked with clear signs at the tops of all relevant lifts and also at many trail intersections. The aforementioned Village-to-Village Skiing experience uses long green traverses, so that fairly new skiers—if they have the stamina—can experience one of Beaver Creek's truly unique offerings. Although it's the easy upper-mountain terrain that makes Beaver Creek such a standout for novice and learning skiers, first-timers and small children are also well served at the base. The Haymeadow beginners' area, with its slow East Haymeadow chair (Lift 1), assures a successful first day on skis.

Each of the other villages offers something pleasant for novices too. At Arrowhead Village, *Piece o' Cake* and *Smooth Moos* are long and lovely novice trails, and at Bachelor Gulch Village, it's *Sawbuck* that wins the praise of new skiers.

Beaver Creek for Good Skiers

Beaver Creek offers good skiers a very straightforward gradation of terrain, steady pitches, excellent grooming, no nasty surprises, no blue runs suddenly turning black and ugly, and, for the most part, uncrowded and reasonably wide slopes. Lower-mountain runs below *Cinch*, like *Assay, Fool's Gold,* and *Latigo,* are all a little harder because they're narrow. Others, like *Centennial,* Beaver Creek's longest run, and especially *Red Tail,* are absolutely perfect, wide-open sheets of snow, where intermediate skiers can stretch their wings and fly. *Red Tail* (which, despite the name, is not one of the infamous double-diamond Birds-of-Prey runs) leads from the Centennial Express/Spruce Saddle complex at mid-mountain to Red Tail Camp, a wonderfully intimate luncheon hut, and to the bases of three chairlifts—Westfall (Lift 9), Grouse Mountain (Lifts 10), and Larkspur (Lift 11).

On Grouse Mountain itself, all the runs but two are black. *Camprobber Road,* a switchback trail, crosses most of the other runs, enabling skiers to bail from the steeps, and *Raven Ridge* is only marginally gentler than the others. Grouse Mountain is one of the best places in Colorado to begin to master moguls. The slopes are so wide and inviting (for bump runs, that is) that they may be a perfect transition for good skiers who want to tackle something more serious. Good skiers should start on *Raven Ridge,* and if all goes well, try *Ptarmigan* or *Ruffled Grouse.*

Directly across the valley from *Red Tail,* the Larkspur chair (Lift 11) climbs *Larkspur Bowl,* another "perfect" upper-intermediate run—very wide, very free. This true bowl leads into wide aspen-lined avenues at the bottom and ranks as the sort of run on which everyone skis just a little bit better than normal. On a powder morning, the main face of this paradise is not aggressively steep, so that good skiers just getting their powder legs under them feel comfortable.

The runs served by the Strawberry Park Express (Lift 12), lower down on Beaver Creek's west-side mountain, are beautifully, even poetically laid out, but they suffer from less than idyllic conditions. The combination of lower elevation and direct sun exposure works against the snow conditions, meaning that runs like *Pitchfork* and *Stacker* have a tendency to turn icy, especially near the bottom.

Arrowhead Village and Bachelor Gulch have one high-speed quad apiece, a profusion of high-ticket slopeside homes, and fine networks of green-circle boulevards and blue-square cruisers. *Saddlehorn, Grubstake,* and *Gunders* are lovely intermediate runs served by the Bachelor Gulch Express (Lift 16), while *Back to the Bahn, Golden Bear,* and *Cresta* are the favorite cruisers off the Arrow Bahn Express (Lift 17). Just because Village-to-Village Skiing is a pleasure that novices can enjoy doesn't preclude intermediates from experiencing the same touring pleasure too.

Beaver Creek for Experts

Some of Beaver Creek's more challenging terrain is sprinkled here and there around the sprawling ski area. Several steep black pitches—*Loco, S. Star,* and *Lupine*—drop into the right bank of Larkspur Bowl. Similarly, a few short steep slots—*Cataract, Spider,* and *Web*—drop into Rose Bowl. And a trio of short black stretches—*Bootleg, Moonshine,* and *Buckboard*—are alternatives to *Centennial* on the lower main mountain. But really, there are two main areas that will delight expert skiers at Beaver Creek: Grouse Mountain and the Birds of Prey.

Grouse Mountain deserves praise as a zone of easy-to-learn-on bump runs, but it is also attractive to dyed-in-the-wool expert skiers. What an expert skier can do with these bumps is ski them faster than usual. It's a place for dash and style, for getting a little air between bumps, and for something between cruising and bumping. Delicious. On the left side of the lift, looking down, the runs are a bit steeper, demand more concentration, and are appropriately labeled with double diamonds. But the best adventure is *Royal Elk Glades,* a steep flank just beyond all the cut runs that is really more dense forest than open glades. Although a boundary rope will keep you from straying too far, this skiing demands cunning route-finding, quick feet, and powerful turns. It's never groomed, of course, seldom packed out, and always interesting.

Until Grouse Mountain was opened, expert skiing at Beaver Creek was synonymous with the Birds of Prey, and the Birds of Prey remain synonymous with steep, demanding moguls. They're hemmed in by trees, a factor that can inhibit even expert skiers, and they also tend to get a bit wind-scoured, which can create some sudden, rocky surprises early in the season. A lot of skiers find the three Birds of Prey runs daunting. *Goshawk,* the shortest, is a good run on which to test yourself. *Golden Eagle* was lengthened, widened, and somewhat recontoured into an international-class downhill course, site of the men's downhill at the 1999 World Alpine Championships, and is still a commendable challenge when the bumps build. The run starts from the very top of the mountain, and it's still a real thrill. *Peregrine* is the show-off run directly under the lift.

Snowboarding

Beaver Creek has two terrain parks, one with a superlative half-pipe. The Moonshine Terrain Park, off Lower Centennial, boasts a 400-foot-long, 18-foot-wide superpipe, while Zoom Room is an easier park set for beginning and intermediate riders.

Après-Ski and Extra-Ski in Beaver Creek

Beaver Creek lodging is of such a high level that no accommodation is less than luxurious, a sense that also permeates the after-ski scene. (A drink at the **Rendezvous Bar & Grill** in the spacious base lodge at the bottom of the Centennial lift is as casual as anything gets.) Restaurants are equally high-end. With the exception of **Mirabelle,** a fine French restaurant in a classic ranch house near the resort entry, Beaver Creek Village restaurants are in the core of the village or in one of the many elegant inns nearby. **Toscanini** at rinkside, the **Grouse Mountain Grill** in the Pines Lodge, **Bivans** for what passes for family dining and the ultra-elegant **Vue,** both in the Hyatt Regency Beaver Creek, **TraMonti** in The Charter, **Splendido** in The Chateau, and the **Saddle Ridge Restaurant** in the exclusive townhome development of the same name are acclaimed for their cuisine, atmosphere, and service.

A Beaver Creek–style experience is a trip to **Beano's Cabin.** The word "cabin" is a misnomer. Beano's, a large, handsome building (call it "designer rustic" for its stone and logs, but a cabin it ain't), and **Allie's Cabin** above the Haymeadow slope are both members-only, on-mountain luncheon clubs by day and an open-to-all dinner restaurants in the evenings. If you can combine dinner at Beano's, good weather, and a full-moon night, then you've really got something. Allie's can also be reached by sleigh or on snowshoes. In the same vein—only more so—would be an overnight stay at **Trapper's Cabin.** This beautiful lodge (a cabin grown up and gone to heaven) in McCoy Park above the Beaver Creek connection to Bachelor Gulch, is surely Colorado's most exclusive B&B. An overnight stay includes dinner and breakfast. Trapper's Cabin is designed and priced to make you feel like a featured guest on *Lifestyles of* *the Rich and Famous.* If you happen to be rich or famous or just want to splurge, this is the place.

High on the mountain, above Beaver Creek Village, is the resort's outstanding Nordic and snowshoe trail system. It is set at McCoy Park at the top of the Strawberry Park Express, where the great views live. It's a real delight just to be there, and even more so to ski or snowshoe there. Trails are trackset for classical skiing and groomed flat for skating and snowshoeing. Picnic tables are positioned so that you can take advantage of the best views, and a trailside heated yurt provides shelter on blustery days. If and when the gondola from Avon is added, this may compromise the tranquillity along part of the Nordic system, but the area is extensive enough to always be a quiet place to ski or snowshoe.

The outdoor skating rink in the heart of Beaver Creek Village is a picture-perfect ice surface, and underground beneath it is the magnificent Vilar Center for the Arts. This tasteful and luxurious theater offers family shows, comedies, Broadway musicals, and more. Sometimes, big-name entertainers are booked. For more information, call (970) 845-TIXS (8497).

Beaver Creek Data

Mountain Statistics

Vertical feet	4,040 feet
Base elevation	7,400 feet
Summit elevation	11,440 feet
Longest run	2.75 miles (Centennial)
Average annual snowfall	331 inches
Snowmaking	605 acres
Number of lifts	13: 6 high-speed quads; 3 triple chairs; 4 doubles
Lift capacity	24,739 skiers per hour
Skiable terrain	1,625 acres
Opening date	Mid-November
Closing date	Mid-April
Snowboarding	Yes

All Beaver Creek lift tickets are also good at Vail, Breckenridge, Keystone, and Arapahoe Basin.

Transportation

By car From Denver, west on I-70 to Exit 167 (Avon exit) 210 miles (2.5 hours in good road and weather conditions), then south 1 mile through four roundabouts to the Beaver Creek gate.

By bus or limo Colorado Mountain Express from Denver International Airport. Call (800) 525-6363.

By plane See Vail Transportation information, page 84.

Beaver Creek Data (continued)

Key Phone Numbers

Ski-area information	(800) 404-3535 and (970) 845-9090
Snow report	(800) 404-3535 and (970) 476-4888
Reservations	(800) 427-8308
Website	www.beavercreek.com

Lito's TECH TIP

Polishing Parallel

This is the age of parallel skiing, but it might be more accurate to call it the age of "sloppy parallel skiing." Nowadays it's easier than ever to make turns with your skis parallel. In fact, two out of three skiers on the slopes don't do anything special to turn their skis, they just twist 'em around in the direction they want to go. By twisting both skis more or less together, they pull off more or less parallel turns.

Most intermediate skiers know what I'm talking about. They turn their skis together, but the result is a kind of sloppy, ill-defined, wide-track skid rather than a graceful carving arc, where the two skis slice around in a narrow, elegant track. Parallel turns of a sort, but not the sort that instructors and experts make. Let's do something about it. The secrets of a polished parallel turn are fewer than you think, and relatively easy to master.

The first critical step is learning to ride the arc of the turn. This one is easy, if I can convince you to stand exclusively, 100%, on your outside ski. That's right. Average skiers who make rough-and-ready, hit-or-miss parallel skids, skis wide apart, always stand almost equally on both skis. What's the difference? Modern skis are softer in flex than earlier skis; this allows them to bend under the skier's weight (so-called reverse camber), and this bent ski is what "carves" a pure round arc in the snow. But in order to make your skis bend, you really have to load them up

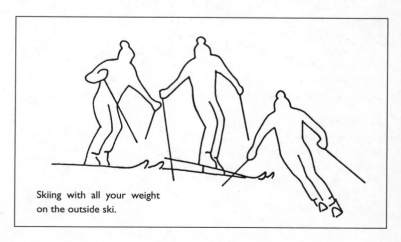

Skiing with all your weight on the outside ski.

with maximum weight. Suppose you weigh 150 pounds and stand equally on both skis; then each ski only supports 75 pounds. But if you stand completely over one foot, it's like dropping an additional 75-pound sandbag onto that ski. You've doubled the weight on that ski, and it will bend and carve for you. It's that simple. Modern skis are designed to turn best with the full weight of your body pressing down on only one ski, the outside ski of the turn. (By the way, the reverse bend, or reverse camber, in the ski is hard to observe—you can see it best in still photos— but it's always there in a good turn.)

So your first step in mastering modern parallel is to develop the balance needed to put all your weight on one foot. Practice one-footed skiing on gentle flats and catwalks. Lift the light foot up off the snow just to check whether or not you're cheating. Play with the idea, make it a habit. Your turns will improve immediately, and, believe it or not, your legs will be less tired at the end of the day. In actual skiing you don't want to lift that light inside ski up off the snow—that's too much work. Just let the light inside ski float along on the snow next to the loaded outside ski that's doing all the work. Skiing this way is like walking in slow motion: first one foot . . . then the other . . . one complete turn on one foot . . . then another on the opposite foot. . .

You'll discover an interesting bonus. Not only are your turns rounder, more carved, and more efficient, but your skis will stay closer together. Say good-bye to that old wide track. It's very easy to change the position of the light inside ski in relation to the weighted outside ski. If you stand on both skis equally, trying to move one closer to the other is as impossible as lifting yourself off the ground by your bootstraps.

Nothing else can change your skiing as much as learning to stand exclusively over that outside ski. I call this the best-kept secret in modern skiing, because it's so hard to observe that great skiers are really standing exclusively on one foot— first on one foot, then on the other. But they are, and you can too. Naturally, that's not all there is to polishing your parallel turns, but it is the most important step.

Greater Aspen

Aspen The town of Aspen is the most sophisticated ski town in the Rockies, with more good restaurants, galleries, and elegant boutiques than any other Colorado resort. Bracketed by mountains and set hard against the winter closure of the state highway leading over Independence Pass, Aspen maintains an ethereal end-of-the-road quality. For skiers, the Aspen area works more like a large European ski region than like a single resort. Its four separate mountains offer a range of skiing choices and diverse terrain. A splendid bus system links the town and its four ski areas. Aspen is expensive and exclusive. The rich and famous (or infamous) people who could afford to ski (or establish second or third homes) anywhere select Aspen more than anyplace else in the country, but don't be intimidated by the resort's rep. The mountains and the lodgings welcome the rest of us too.

Aspen Mountain Located directly south of downtown, Aspen Mountain is only one of four Aspen-area ski mountains, just the tip of the iceberg—but a very impressive tip. No green beginner slopes at all here. Instead, inviting steeps, rather modest cruising, and a high-speed gondola to maximize slope time.

Buttermilk This is a perfect learning and practice hill just outside Aspen's city limits, with a dynamite ski school and mostly lazy, laid-back terrain. A few steeps but virtually no bumps. Buttermilk is an underappreciated, uncrowded, and truly splendid ski area.

Highlands Also on the outskirts of town and Buttermilk's closest neighbor but its polar opposite, Highlands is a gnarly performance arena for skilled and athletic skiers. Good bumps, steeps, trees, and hike-to bowls, but an awkward mountain layout for cruisers. High-speed lifts have made Highlands an attractive alternative for strong skiers.

Snowmass   Greater Aspen's best all-around, all-skier mountain. Immense, with a modern lift system serving long, wide-open runs that make this resort the cruising capital of the Aspen ski region. And there are just enough ungroomed steeps to keep experts from getting bored. Snowmass Village is more about lodging than resort life; it's still just a suburb of Aspen.

Aspen

Aspen is the quintessential Colorado ski town in exactly the same way that Vail is the quintessential Colorado ski mountain. Aspen is the place every other ski town gets compared with. The one that's got it all: history and tradition, money and chic, Victorian architecture and postmodern boutiques, culture and clout, narrow streets and tall views, remarkable sophistication and unquenchable enthusiasm. And . . . oh, yes, good skiing too.

The old mining town has lived through it all—discovery, abuse, prostitution, development, more development, good and bad snow years, good and bad economic times. It has sold or pawned everything it ever held dear, and somehow continues to enchant.

Aspen is hipper, trendier, and more expensive than ever, but it's also just as exciting, just as real a place as it ever was. Paradoxically, the secret of Aspen's enduring fascination as a resort is that, despite everything, it's still more of a community than a resort. Real people—unusual and creative people—have put down deep roots here, have made this town different and, in a nonsuperficial way, more sophisticated than any other ski town or mountain town in America.

Aspen Mountain has always been interesting, and you can ski yourself silly there any day. The Aspen Skiing Company has gone the extra mile to provide extra services: in addition to the common cadre of mountain hosts ready with smiles, trail maps, and directions, all four mountains have on-slope Guest Service Centers, which dispense all of the above plus sunscreen, refreshments, message boards, courtesy phones, and direct links to resort concierges who can arrange anything from ski lessons and day care to evening baby-sitting, dinner reservations, and spa bookings. You can also pick up free postcards, which the ski company will mail, free, to your friends. The ski bus between Aspen, where many people sleep, and Snowmass, where many people ski, is free, and so are the cookies and beverages served to those waiting in the bus line.

Aspen's Own Mountain: An Introduction

Aspen Mountain, which some locals persist in calling Ajax after an old mining claim, has come a long way since its discovery and launching as a ski area shortly after World War II. There's an inescapable snob appeal, a built-in cachet, to a ski area that doesn't have a single green run! Aspen

Mountain deserves its reputation. The skiing is not formidably difficult, but it is serious—exciting, continuous, but not always challenging for the most accomplished skiers and snowboarders. Good skiers will find Aspen Mountain as good as they are. There are more strong skiers on this mountain than on any other in Colorado. The average skier on Aspen Mountain skis better than the average skier elsewhere in the state. Now snowboarders are part of the mix too. On April 1, 2000, Aspen Mountain lifted its prohibition against snowboarding, the last ski area in the state to do so.

Aspen Mountain is a long, narrow ski area extending back from the valley floor along the flanks and tops of a couple of long ridges that run down perpendicular into the Roaring Fork Valley. Gaze up from anywhere in town and the ski mountain looks damn serious but not very big. Don't be fooled. It goes back and back and back. What you see from town is only the tip, or actually the foot, of the iceberg.

Two parallel topographic shapes define the ski area. On the west side—the right side looking up from town—is a ridge and the mountain's World Cup downhill course peeling down the front face. This steep swath drops off a long ridge that for most of its length is called *Ruthie's Run.* It starts near the summit and continues clear back to the valley, marking the western edge of the ski area. The parallel valley below and east of *Ruthie's* represents the middle of the ski area and finishes in a classic Aspen run, *Spar Gulch*—the path most skiers take off the mountain. In the evening, however, *Spar* can be too crowded for comfort. In fact, it was where Michael Kennedy skied into a tree and died. A last run down *Ruthie's* or *Copper Bow*—or even a download on the gondola, if *Spar* is scraped-off—is a better bet (and certainly would have been for the Kennedy clan.)

The east side of *Spar Gulch* (that is, opposite from *Ruthie's* on the left, looking up) is formed by the flank of Bell Mountain, a second long, ridgelike shape. Bell Mountain has its own mystique and absolutely no easy-angle runs. Of the several runs on the far eastern side all seem to belong to the Bell Mountain half of the ski area. These runs finish in a second rounded gully called *Copper Bowl,* which is analogous to *Spar Gulch* although shorter and narrower. It brings skiers back around the bulk of Bell Mountain to join the down-mountain traffic flow from *Spar* at a merge appropriately called *Grand Junction,* which in turn feeds onto the *Little Nell* slope and the bottom of the gondola. In short, if you're skiing continuous runs down the mountain, you'll either be skiing somewhere on the *Ruthie's* side or somewhere on the Bell Mountain side or in the valley between them. With this general picture in mind, you can find your way around Aspen Mountain like an old hand.

Long continuous runs are definitely one of Aspen Mountain's most significant characteristics and a key to the strategy of skiing the mountain. But it wasn't always so. Since the high-speed, six-passenger Silver

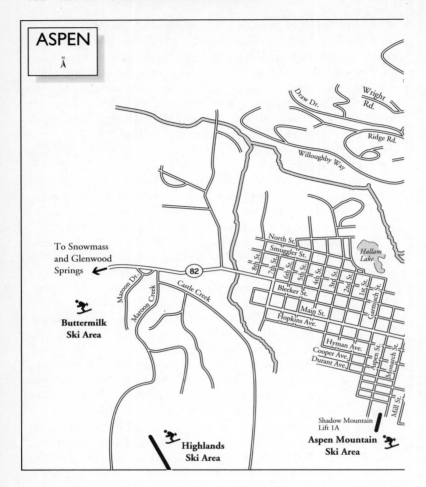

Queen gondola was inaugurated in 1987, climbing the entire 3,267 vertical feet in 14 minutes, it altered the way people skied the mountain. At most areas, a lift that was installed over a decade-and-a-half ago would seem to have been there forever, but on a mountain with so many veterans with long memories, it still seems like a new lift. Lito reminiscences about having spent many memorable days on Ajax, skiing himself "right into the ground only on top-to-bottom runs, and never riding any lift except the gondola."

A natural tendency that makes sense at most ski areas is to ride lifts to the top in the morning and then stay on the upper slopes all day. Most Aspen skiers seem to do this too, perhaps as a habit of the old, slow chairs that the gondola replaced. This pattern ensures that the gondola rarely

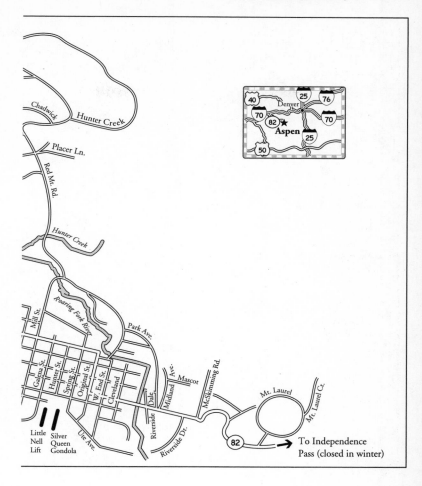

gets really crowded. It moves so fast that even what looks like a monster line in the morning gets you on board in a few minutes. And finally, even though the very bottom slopes aren't very interesting in themselves, strong skiers can shoot across them in a hurry and actually save time by simply skiing down to the bottom every run. This strategy would have been unthinkable in the past, when riding a daisy chain of slow chairlifts was required to get to the top.

Along with the gondola, chairlifts on the upper middle mountain were upgraded. Lift 3, a high-speed detachable quad, serves the not-very-steep or difficult central basin above *Spar Gulch,* where many of Aspen Mountain's blue-square trails are located. Skiers who previously wouldn't have dared ski on Aspen Mountain can now ski there. Ride Silver Queen

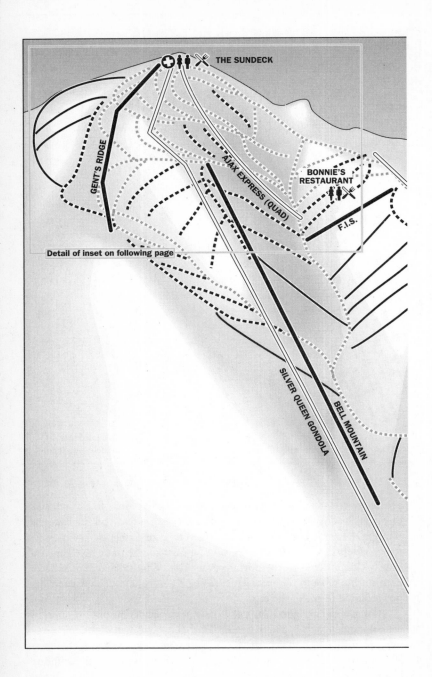

THE SUNDECK

GENT'S RIDGE

AJAX EXPRESS (QUAD)

BONNIE'S RESTAURANT

F.I.S.

Detail of inset on following page

SILVER QUEEN GONDOLA

BELL MOUNTAIN

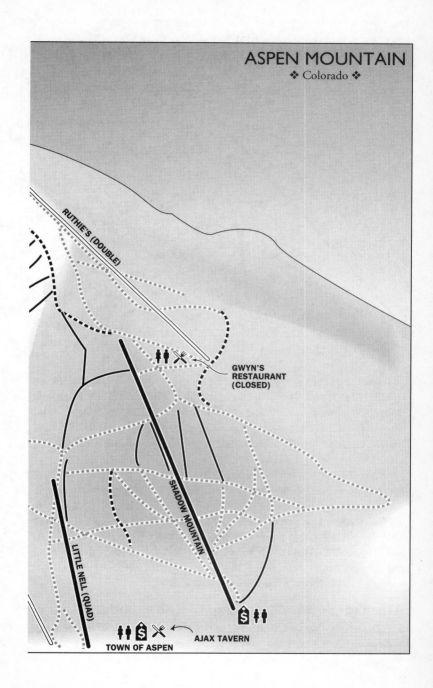

ASPEN MOUNTAIN
❖ Colorado ❖

RUTHIE'S (DOUBLE)

GWYN'S
RESTAURANT
(CLOSED)

SHADOW MOUNTAIN

LITTLE NELL (QUAD)

AJAX TAVERN

TOWN OF ASPEN

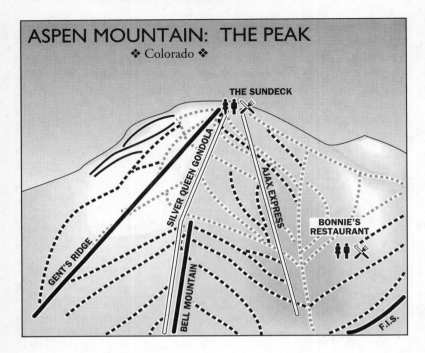

ASPEN MOUNTAIN: THE PEAK
❖ Colorado ❖

THE SUNDECK

GENT'S RIDGE

SILVER QUEEN GONDOLA

BELL MOUNTAIN

AJAX EXPRESS

BONNIE'S RESTAURANT

F.I.S.

to the top and then just yo-yo around on the easier blue runs like *Pussy-foot, Silver Bell,* and *1&2 Leaf* served by Lift 3, and even take the gondola down in the afternoon if you don't feel comfortable on *Spar Gulch.* A lot of weaker skiers—weaker by this mountain's standards, anyway—have figured this out, which has inevitably led to some serious crowding on these Lift 3 runs.

Aspen Mountain has the big reputation in these parts, and it is where the local heroes ski. Some skiers try to buy into this mystique before they're ready for it. Lito's long-held opinion is that unless you're truly comfortable on Aspen Mountain (which means, at a minimum, short turns on steeper blue slopes), you should spend most of your Aspen vacation at Snowmass and Buttermilk. No, you certainly won't be bored, and yes, you will make phenomenal progress as a skier. Progress is just about impossible if you start hanging out on Aspen Mountain before you're ready.

Aspen Mountain: Close-up of Classic Experiences

A good-quality Aspen Mountain experience divides neatly into steep giant-slalom-style cruising and even steeper bump skiing. If you hate moguls, you just won't get all this mountain can offer, but you don't need to spend all day abusing your knees either.

When Aspen hosts World Cup downhill or Super-G races, they are held on the *Ruthie's* side, but anyone can enjoy the sequence of slopes that together constitute one of the most exciting downhill courses in North America. The route begins at the lower end of *Ruthie's* and strings together a number of separately named runs—*Aztec, Spring Pitch, Straw-pile*—into a steep, exciting, and remarkably continuous run. The best nonmogul skiing is on the big ridge around *Ruthie's,* with such variations and detours as *Roch Run, International,* and *Buckhorn* that delight the cruising skier. Take the Ruthie's lift, a unique high-speed double chair. The Aspen Skiing Company intentionally did not put in a quad, because they wanted to eliminate the previously long ride but still preserve some of the tête-à-tête, conversational intimacy of riding a double chair, a classic component of the ski experience that has become an unintended casualty of the white revolution.

Aspen Mountain has a reputation as a mogul mountain, and a quick glance at the trail map shows why. Even without greens, there are still three marked levels of difficulty: blues, blacks, and double-black diamonds at the top of the scale. Anything marked double-black is not merely steep and moguled but with moguls of the extra-demanding sort rather than garden variety. Let's start with some friendlier bump lines.

The *Face of Bell* is a beaut. Ski down *1&2 Leaf* and cut left just under the top of Bell Mountain, traversing out on its flank to the first of a series of open moguled faces separated by long lines of evergreens. Below, as the slope steepens, is a sea of bumps that, until the advent of snowboards and short skis, were usually large and round and well spaced. Start anywhere and ski most of the way down, but before you actually reach *Spar Gulch,* bear right in a long horizontal traverse across to the next open face. Locals refer to this as "going back up." Since *Spar Gulch,* which is effectively the "floor" beneath the *Face of Bell,* keeps dropping away, each traverse brings you back up to the top of another bump slope. You can repeat the process again and again for one of the most satisfying bump runs around.

Bell Mountain's other less-than-fierce bump lines on its far, or eastern, side include *Christmas Tree* and a generalized area called *Back of Bell.* The trees on this side were denser, but the skiing company thinned out the best tree lines to make them more skiable. Very quickly you'll find that this mountain pushes you onto steeper, more challenging, double-black runs with tighter, less rhythmic bumps and the sharper troughs between them. For experts in search of a workout, the *Ridge of Bell,* a long steep nose facing straight down toward Aspen, offers some of the most challenging skiing on this side of the mountain. Aspen Mountain's exciting double-black gullies on the front face above town are steep and rather narrow, but there's not always enough snow on these lower slopes to cover all the rocks. *Corkscrew* and *Corkscrew Gully* are the best of these lower bump slots, best skied in really big snow years.

Aspen Mountain's toughest bump runs are found in two separate zones, the *Mine Dumps* and *Walsh's Gulch*. The former is a series of thrilling, half-open gashes through the steep aspen forest on the west bank of *Spar Gulch*. *The Dumps* were originally created when miners pushed the slag and rubble from their "holes" down the mountainside. On the trail maps, you'll see them marked as *Bear Paw* through *Last Dollar*. Unless you can successfully launch a turn, anytime, on any bump, no matter how weird, don't tempt fate over here. Try to ski the *Mine Dumps* early in the morning, since they catch the first sun beautifully.

Walsh's Gulch used to rank among the most infamous, out-of-bounds skiing at Aspen (along with nearby *Difficult Gulch,* which is still out of bounds). These renegade powder paths lead down steep, cliff-cut slopes into the Roaring Fork Valley, several miles upvalley from Aspen. Over the years they have claimed a respectable number of avalanche victims. The ski company now avalanche-controls the place and has opened the best of it—the upper slopes of *Walsh's* and a couple of parallel lines next door on *Hyrup's* and *Kristi,* short but fierce runs that are steep enough to make even brilliant skiers pay attention. A must if you want to say you've skied the most serious slopes on Aspen Mountain.

If you take the Gents Ridge chair (Lift 7) back to the top when you come out of *Walsh's,* you might feel as if you are on the world's slowest quad. It diminishes a thrilling run with a boring aftermath. Better to head on down the eastern border of the ski area and enjoy the most obscure skiing on Aspen Mountain, *Gentleman's Ridge* and the gladed trees below it. These runs are so far off the beaten path they don't see much traffic, but they don't get groomed much either, which means more bumps. They also catch the afternoon sun so there's no hurry to get there early. You can complete the circuit by continuing to the gondola to return to the summit.

Given the number of bump runs, Aspen Mountain is not the greatest powder skiing venue, even after a serious dump. Except on the *Ruthie's* side, you're more likely to ski powder-covered moguls than real powder-blanketed slopes. The very best powder days at Aspen always seem to be during heavy storms, when Aspen's many fair-weather skiers tend to stay home. In addition to almost no one on the mountain, you can ride the gondola back up after each run, warm and dry.

Snowboarding

Aspen Mountain was the last ski area in Colorado to permit snowboarders. It did so with an end-of-season test in April 2000 and followed with full access by riders during the 2000–2001 season. The mountain's secret steeps, gulleys, and glades are super snowboarding terrain, though single-plankers, as well as skiers using today's short, shaped skis, have changed the geometry of the mountain's fabled moguls. Aspen Mountain's terrain park is a seasonal wonder. Called the Spring Jam terrain park, it is built on *Little Nell* every April in celebration of the month when snowboarding was first permitted on Aspen Mountain.

Lunchtime

Lunch, on mountain and off, is better around Aspen than in most ski resorts. The Aspen Skiing Company has begun taking over restaurants that were formerly leased to individual owner operators, but wisely, the company has kept the individual style and flavor of each restaurant, rather than subjecting them all to corporate homogenization. This is true at all four of the mountains, and food-loving skiers benefit enormously.

Aspen Mountain's prime on-mountain lunch spot is **The Sundeck** at the summit. It offers awesome views off the back side of the mountain into the heart of the Elk Range with 14,000-foot summits lined up like a special effect for a Spielberg film. An elegant 22,000-square-foot summit lodge was built for the 1999–2000 season, and with it came food that is the peer of the scenery. Chefs under the supervision of the five-star **Little Nell Hotel** preside at the double wok station, the grill, the rotisserie, and the sandwich station, which can customize combinations as basic or as Bumstead as you might wish. There is now a private lunch club under the **Sundeck** roof, too, and if you're lucky, you might score an invitation from a new friend from the gondola. **Bonnie's,** located at Tourtelotte Park above *Spar Gulch,* is the most traditional Aspen Mountain lunch stop, serving German-inspired food and a real see-and-be-seen lunch scene. The restaurant along *Ruthie's Run* that was first known as **Ruthie's** and later **Gwyn's** is shuttered, for the foreseeable future in any case. In-town lunch options are plentiful and easy to enjoy without sacrificing any ski time, as the gondola makes it easy to eat at the bottom and get back up the mountain quickly. Two top choices are right at the base of the *Little Nell* slope. Rating high, in terms of convenience, cuisine, and also price, is **Montagna** in the Little Nell Hotel. When it comes to creativity, cachet and, yes, price again, the **Ajax Tavern** shines. Operated by the same folks who run Napa Valley's Tra Vigne and Mustards Grill, this is a top lunch spot and also boasts an excellent après-ski scene.

Aspen Ambience, Aspen Style

Because, as mentioned earlier, Silver Queen gondola gives you so much vertical so quickly that you can really hurt yourself, lots of skiers, even strong skiers, hang it up before the lifts close, because their legs are saying, "Please! Enough!" In Aspen it's okay to quit early. There's more than enough to do off the slopes.

For years and years, Aspen après-ski began as regular as ritual at **Little Nell's**—the funky, old-fashioned, rundown, crowded, and wonderful slope-side bar at the bottom of the slope of the same name. But Little Nell's is dead—long live Little Nell's! The bar was sacrificed some years back on the altar of a massive base-redevelopment project, and the Little Nell name now adorns a very chic and pricey hotel beside the gondola terminal (and its bar does boast good jazz). The **Ajax Tavern** also attracts a good afternoon crowd. But where do the ski patrollers and instructors, debutantes, and *demimonde* stop for a drink after skiing? In Aspen today, number-one locals' après-ski bar is probably **Little Annie's,** a few blocks from the base of the mountain. It's a draught beer kind of place, so don't bother to order a Kir royale.

Hotel Jerome's **J-Bar,** even though it's blocks from the lifts, has a loyal following. I've been seduced by the tiny wine bar at the **Cooking School of Aspen**—a sommelier pours, with as little or as much information about that wine as a group might choose. Not exactly classic après-ski either, but Lito's favorite after a long day of skiing is a cappuccino at the upstairs café in the **Explore Bookstore** across from the Hotel Jerome. An Aspen treasure, this wonderful Victorian house/bookstore/café is one of the last things you'd ever expect to find at a ski resort. But then, Aspen is different.

It's a complex, intriguing, and hard-to-pin-down ski town that is arty, design-conscious, too sophisticated for its Levi's britches, and still just right. If Vail represents *nouveau riche* ski society, then Aspen could be characterized as old money with an overlay of *Entertainment Tonight* celebrity chic. Aspen's real secret isn't money at all, but the large underground of writers, artists, and other creative refugees from the so-called real world who have gravitated to the Roaring Fork Valley over the last 30 or 40 years and have given this town an unexpected and disarming sophistication. Even the newly arrived visitor, who obviously doesn't have a circle of fascinating Aspen friends and fringe types, can feel this sophistication. Galleries show serious art by nationally known artists, not just cowboy art and fun prints; Aspen fashions are real fashions, not just fun furs. *Aspen Magazine* is arguably the most polished and ambitious resort magazine in the country, showcasing writing and cultural reporting you'd expect to find in New York, L.A., or Santa Fe. The Aspen public, local and transient, is tuned into the arts in a way that no other ski town can imagine, much less equal.

Consumer opportunities run rampant in Aspen. Some visitors seem to come to town just for the shopping. Art galleries, high-toned boutiques, jewelers, furriers, expensive shoe stores, sporting goods stores, and home furnishings emporiums abound—and so do the well-heeled shoppers who frequent them. But you don't have to spend a fortune to dress like a millionaire in Aspen. The town's thrift and consignment shops—notably **Gracy's, Susie's,** and **For You Shoppe**—often carry last season's designer ski- and streetwear at bargain prices.

No other ski town has anything like the Aspen Museum of Art either. This old, brick powerhouse a few blocks from downtown, transformed into a postmodern palazzo, is a must if you're into contemporary art. There is no permanent collection, but rotating exhibitions of some of the most cutting-edge modern works.

As for eating out, there are too many good choices for serious reviewing in this short chapter. Suffice it to say that you can find almost anything and spend any size fortune in Aspen's restaurants. **Range** is a new creation by owner/chef Charles Dale, who has twice been a James Beard Foundation nominee for the best American chef in the Southwest. Its focus is on food and wines of what Dale calls "the Gold Rush states." **Olives Aspen,** in the St. Regis Hotel, is the Colorado outpost of superstar chef Todd English. It serves huge portions of upscale American cuisine.

The **Ajax Tavern** at the foot of the slopes, mentioned for lunch or après-ski, is also an excellent dinner choice. These guys challenged Aspen's long-established restaurateurs with astonishing San Francisco Italian food and style at relatively attractive prices that are distinctly un-Aspen: understated *trattoria* decor, white tablecloths, and wild mushrooms—heaven. Former Ajax Tavern chef Greg Topper has his own small, informal spot behind the Hotel Jerome. Called **Topper's,** it serves casual, chef-prepared food at some of the best prices in town. **Cache Cache** is another restaurant where you won't spend a fortune (though it is more expensive than Topper's). It's intimate, unpretentious, and delicious. Aspen also boasts three superb sushi houses—**Kenichi, Matsuhisa,** and **Takah Sushi**—with fresh seafood flown in from far-off coasts and sushi-masters to prepare it. **Asie** is a sleek, trendy, quite reasonably priced, and fairly new Asian fusion restaurant on Main Street.

It's really not hard to find things, places, and addresses in Aspen. Its downtown core, a classic Western grid, is compact and intimate. Two one-block pedestrian malls define the center of the grid. If you ask for directions, the reply will probably be in terms of a number of blocks north or south, or up or down from the malls. Aspen doesn't function perfectly as a true pedestrian village, and some people insist on thinking of it as a place to drive. Parking downtown is a nightmare of meters and 90-minute-only signs, although the multilevel parking garage on Main Street has alleviated the problem. It's a better bet to take the bus to and from town. The **Rubey Park Transit Center** two blocks from the gondola is the hub for frequent buses to Aspen's other mountains and to Snowmass Village. With the exception of a daytime shuttle between the parking garage and the gondola, in-town transportation remains somewhat awkward. However, once you've made your way downtown, you can walk everywhere.

So, naturally, the recommended hotels are within walking distance of everything. For those who have budget constraints, the **Hotel Jerome,**

Hotel Lenado, the **Little Nell Hotel,** and the **St. Regis Aspen** are all rather expensive—actually very expensive—but they're also very wonderful. The Jerome remains Aspen's pearl. This classic historic structure from the glory days of Aspen's silver mining was renovated in time for its centennial in 1989. If you can't afford to stay at the Jerome, as most of us can't, at least raise a glass in the **J-Bar**—it's the hotel's dark, warm *fin-de-siècle* bar.

Two blocks west, the **Carriage House Inn** is behind the Sardy House, a Victorian landmark mansion that is once again a private residence. The **Hotel Lenado,** diagonally across from Paepcke Park, is a modern pocket hotel designed by Aspen architectural wizard Harry Teague. It is an intimate, low-key, postmodern masterpiece in pale wood.

Other posh addresses, like the Little Nell Hotel and the St. Regis Aspen, are definitely in the running for most expensive and most luxurious, but even in Aspen money isn't everything. Known for high-end lodging, Aspen nevertheless offers a surprising number of moderately priced accommodations in simpler, older properties. These include the **Mountain Chalet,** the **Boomerang Lodge,** the **Limelight,** and the **Ullr Lodge.**

Whatever your budget or style, at the end of a week-long stay you'll have the impression that you're just beginning to get the hang of this remarkable ski town. You'll be back.

Aspen Mountain Data

Mountain Statistics

Vertical feet	3,267 feet
Base elevation	7,945 feet
Summit elevation	11,212 feet
Longest run	3 miles
Average annual snowfall	300 inches
Snowmaking	210 acres
Number of lifts	8: 1 six-passenger gondola; 1 high-speed quad; 1 high-speed double; 2 fixed-grip quads; 3 fixed-grip doubles
Uphill capacity	10,755 skiers per hour
Skiable terrain	673 acres
Opening date	Mid-November
Closing date	Mid- to late April
Snowboarding	Yes

Aspen Mountain shares a lift ticket with Buttermilk, Aspen Highlands, and Snowmass.

Transportation

By car 4.5-hour drive from Denver, via I-70 west to Glenwood Springs (Exit 116), then south on Highway 82 to Aspen.

By van Colorado Mountain Express from Denver International Airport and Eagle County Airport (call (800)525-6363 or (970) 926-9730).

Aspen Mountain Data (continued)

Transportation (continued)

By bus The Roaring Fork Transit Agency (RFTA) operates free local buses and inexpensive schedules from downtown Aspen's Rubey Park Transit Center 40 miles down the Roaring Fork Valley to Glenwood Springs, with connections from Amtrak or interstate buses.

By plane Denver International Airport (220 miles) is Colorado's major gateway airport, with nonstop service from many North American cities. Aspen/Pitkin Airport (aka Sardy Field), just 3 miles from Aspen and 6 miles from Snowmass, has flights (some year-round, some seasonal) from Denver, Los Angeles, and San Francisco on United/United Express, from Minneapolis and Memphis on Northwest Jet Airlink, and from Phoenix on America West Express. Airline service changes annually, so this is not carved in stone. Eagle County Airport (70 miles), an increasingly popular alternative, is currently served by six carriers.

The unique Aspen Ski Plane enables front-range skiers to visit Aspen or Snowmass for the day. Priced at $99 round-trip during its first two seasons, this United Express service uses 88-passenger jet aircraft, departing Denver International Airport in the morning and returning from Aspen in the evening. It operates weekdays (except over the Christmas–New Year period) between mid-December and early April. Flight time is just 25 minutes. Overnight packages are available with this special offer. Travel must be booked 48 hours in advance through Stay Aspen Snowmass (call (877) 230-5077) or via email at skiplane@stayaspensnowmass.com

Key Phone Numbers

Ski-area information	(970) 925-1220 or (800) 525-6200
Snow report	(970) 925-1221 or (888) 277-3676
Reservations	(800) 262-7736
Website	www.aspensnowmass.com

Lito's TECH TIP

Short Turns—The Key to Black Slopes

What is it that keeps some skiers off steep slopes while others can't get enough steep black skiing? Short turns—not just short, but smoothly, crisply linked short turns right down the fall line, tick-tock, side-to-side, as inevitable and rhythmic as a pendulum. Short swing, as it's often called, is the key that unlocks steep, narrow, and challenging terrain. (Medium and long turns build up too much speed too fast.) And as usual, there's a trick to it. I call this trick, or technique, dynamic anticipation. This is how it works.

Suppose, before turning your skis down the hill, your whole upper body—hips, shoulders, head, and arms—was already turned and aimed downhill. Then your skis would turn faster and easier, pivoting rapidly around to line up beneath your body, which was already in the fall line. Less mass to turn means less effort needed, which in turn means faster, snappier results—the very essence of short-linked turns. In skiing, this pretwisting of the upper body in the direction of the coming turn has always been called anticipation. But we can do better.

Our goal is not to turn the body first and then let the skis catch up, but instead to let our bodies move straight down the slope while legs and skis pivot back and forth beneath us. That's where the action is, down below the stable quiet mass of the upper body. And it's this back-and-forth, wind-up and release, preturn-and-return sort of action that I call dynamic anticipation. Everyone has seen and admired this type of skiing, but how do you learn it?

It isn't so very easy. Dynamic anticipation is the watershed skill that divides average good skiers from extremely good skiers. But here's a simple game plan.

First, be sure you're skiing in a loose upright stance with a very relaxed lower back. This is the region that acts as a pivot point, or hinge, letting your legs and skis turn beneath you without the body itself turning. If you're bent forward with a hollow, tight lower back, nothing will work.

Next, try a few hockey stops. Slide straight down the hill and twist your legs and skis sideways to a stop beneath you. They turn, you don't. After you get the hang of it, smooth out your hockey stops into round uphill curves that work the same way: skis turning up the hill but body floating along motionless above them, still facing down the fall line. We call these uphill curves with anticipation (that uninvolved, motionless upper body) preturns.

Then use your preturns to launch new turns down the hill. Just add a pole plant while shifting your weight to the top ski and, wham, the skis will (or should) turn back downhill almost on their own. That's the reaction from the action of the preturn. And, of course, you'll want to capture this feeling and prolong it in a continuous series of turns—the end of each turn becoming the preturn—or wind-up for the next turn.

What I've just given you is only the bare outline of a game plan to develop dynamic anticipation (for the details, see Chapter 4 of my book Breakthrough on Skis from Random House or my videotape of the same title) but it should give you a sense of what's involved in developing short turns. The more natural your anticipation becomes—that is, the more your upper body relaxes and floats instead of actively turning from side to side with your skis—the easier it will be for you to link short turns.

One last tip. The trigger, the signal that launches one turn right after another down the fall line, is always a pole plant. By reaching straight down the hill with your pole, rather than letting it swing around and across the hill with your skis, you will help to keep your body lined up in that going-down-the-mountain direction. Short turns in a nutshell: you keep going down the mountain while your skis twist back and forth beneath you.

The Ski Mountains Next Door

Buttermilk and Highlands are in what was once the suburbs or outskirts of Aspen, but with the rapid development of the land between town and these mountains, as well as at these mountains themselves, they now seem closer to Aspen. More importantly, they are different enough from Aspen Mountain to balance and complete the town's ski offerings. Both of these areas have changed dramatically in recent years; both are better than ever.

Buttermilk, founded and named by Friedl Pfeifer, one of Aspen's pioneers, is composed of two sectors, Buttermilk and Tiehack. What's in a name? Tiehack refers to the forest stands where loggers cut trees for railroad ties. In early-day Aspen, the Sterner family had a homestead and dairy farm right about where the ski-area base lies today. As the story goes, when the Sterner daughters took fresh milk up the mountain to the loggers hacking ties from the forest, the jolting of their buckboard on the rough track turned the milk into buttermilk. Buttermilk, in any case, has become synonymous with Aspen's prime beginner area, but it is more. It is an ideal learning and teaching mountain for virtually every level of skier and snowboarder. There's no question that Buttermilk is certainly the most underrated ski experience in Aspen. Sure, skiing here is fairly easy for the most part: no heroes, no hotdoggers, *ni trompettes, ni tambours,* no guts, no glory associated with skiing on this mountain with its beautifully cut runs and laid-back ambience. The terrain is mostly medium- and low-angle, seldom steep, with lots of variation and lots of character. The Summit Express accesses abundant top-to-bottom runs, many of uncommon width that pleases the eye and soothes the skiing ego. *Savio,* a huge expanse near the top, feels quite bowl-like, and for those who really like that kind of terrain, a short chairlift permits lap after lap.

Highlands, long the maverick of the Aspen ski scene, for years was run by an independent ski company that clung stubbornly to archaic lifts and an eccentric, rather old-fashioned ski school method. Highlands was always proud of its low-priced lift ticket and of being the first of the Aspen ski areas to actually welcome freestylers, bump skiers, and snowboarders, but that's now ancient history. Over the last few years, everything changed so much that it's a feat of memory to recall what it used to be like. Now also operated by the Aspen Skiing Company, Highlands has become a brand-new mountain. Like Aspen Mountain, Highlands is really more of a ridge formation rising toward Highland Peak between the Castle Creek and Maroon Creek valleys. It's not a "natural" ski mountain, since all the fall lines lead down one side or the other of the ridge, but it creates a distinctive layout that makes you think. Inevitably with such topography, there's a certain amount of traversing to get "back to center," which makes the ski terrain feel smaller than it really is. Since the Aspen Skiing Company took this little country cousin in 1994–1995, it has totally upgraded the lift system and developed a sparkling base village at the bottom. Now three high-speed quads whisk you to the top in a fraction of the time it used to take via a succession of slow doubles. Runs have been widened, some that weren't previously groomed are now, and skier services are vastly upgraded. In one day you can ski more than twice the vertical you could with the old lifts. Highlands' real glory is its steeps, which include narrow shots through the trees and high, wild bowls, chutes, and wide glades off Loge Peak chair on top.

And that's not all. An actual base village at the bottom of Highlands replaces acres of muddy parking lots and a quaint but dated day lodge.

Like all such projects, we won't see the final result of this expensive new development for years, but the nucleus is there, with a fine plaza, après-ski bar, and luxurious lodgings.

Now let's zoom in on "suburban" Aspen skiing.

Buttermilk: Aspen's Biggest Little Ski Area

Buttermilk is an easy mountain to understand. It's a three-pronged area with three major, branchlike skiing zones slanting down from its summit ridge. The front side, or Main Buttermilk, is a tongue of interlaced blue and green runs that drop northward in two steps toward the main base. The main lift at Main Buttermilk is the Summit Express quad that whisks you 1,834 vertical feet from base to top in nine-and-a-half minutes. A short double chair called Savio serves the upper third of the mountain for skiers who don't want to circulate back to the base on every run. This upper area is a fanlike bowl of beautiful wide blue runs: *Savio, Friedl's, No Problem,* and the top of *Buckskin.*

One has to get around an awkward gap in the mountain's downhill flow either on the *Homestead Road Catwalk* or *Lover's Lane,* a wide, flat, roadlike gully. Below this gap, the runs to the bottom are more roundabout than the upper slopes, but still quite aesthetic. Skiers display a tendency to stay on *Midway Avenue,* the main drag to the bottom, but excursions to the left and right, such as the long snaking grooves of *Jacob's Ladder* and *Bear,* are worthy alternatives.

The second branch of the area is Tiehack, which slants eastward from the top in the direction of town—east. *Main Tiehack* offers blue-square cruises, while *Tiehack* is considerably steeper and full of blue and black runs (although the blacks feel more blue-black and are not too demanding). The two most continuous runs are *Tiehack Parkway* and *Sterner* on the very edge of the crest overlooking Maroon Creek. *Tiehack Parkway* feeds into *Racer's Edge* and *Javelin,* while black *Sterner* turns into blue *Sterner Gulch.* With one long, slow double chairlift back to the top and a short one to nowhere right at the bottom, the Tiehack side rarely gets crowded—except on powder days when knowledgeable locals come to ski the trees. You'll find them in *Timber Doodle Glade* and *Ptarmigan Glade,* where the powder lingers longer than on all but the most secret spots on Aspen Mountain.

Finally, slanting down diagonally on the other side of Main Buttermilk is West Buttermilk, the third branch of the mountain. It is another gentle area of blue and green runs. Although at a lower angle than the runs of Main Tiehack, these runs are no less beautiful, with long sweeping views. This pod offers five easy green runs, plus a couple of blues and a couple of blacks. Remember that a Buttermilk black is a lot gentler than an Aspen Mountain black. Again, there's an obvious main-drag way down. *West-*

ward Ho is an inviting green highway until the last broad blue face. But there's more to explore. Check out *Red's Rover,* a gentle white arc through the woods, and two short, surprise black pitches, *Little Teaser* and *Lower Larkspur,* which actually have some moguls. Tiny and intimate, with the flavor of a lunch chalet or *stube* lost high in the Alps, **Café West** at the bottom of Buttermilk West is known for its luncheon crêpes and a killer artichoke soup. The Buttermilk West lift takes you slightly higher on the rounded summit than the Summit Express. From there, you can begin one of the loveliest runs at the area, a ridge run via *Tom's Thumb, Tiehack Parkway,* and *Racer's Edge* all the way down to the bottom of Tiehack. This edge of the ski area is particularly impressive because it overlooks Maroon Creek, the deep Alpine valley separating Tiehack from Highlands. Tiehack has also become an active ski-racing site in recent years. There are new electronic timing facilities for the National Standard Race (NASTAR) and self-timer courses, and lots of junior and amateur races are run on the eastern flank of the mountain. A natural giant-slalom flavor to Tiehack terrain makes you want to ski it in big fast turns as well, even if you haven't worn a racing bib for years or ever.

No matter where you ski, you're sure to get hungry. The **Cliffhouse** at the top of the Summit Express has introduced the Mongolian barbecue concept to Aspen—chunks of seasoned chicken, beef, pork, or shrimp dramatically flash-cooked on a hot metal plate called a *tea.* The view from the terrace over Maroon Creek, with Pyramid Peak looming up like the Matterhorn at the end of the canyon, is one of the grandest at Aspen. Enjoy the Cliffhouse terrace on sunny spring afternoons. For the best ski-area cafeteria meal, ski all the way to the bottom of Main Buttermilk and eat lunch at **Bumps.** This remarkable example of lowly ski-area cafeteria elevated to another level is run by the folks who operate the Ajax Tavern at the base of Aspen Mountain, and it shows. Fresh-baked *focaccia* sandwiches, made-to-order Greek or baby-green salads, and four-cheese white pizza would pass muster with even fussy foodies.

Both Tiehack and West Buttermilk have their own bases with small parking lots. As a beginner, novice, or low-intermediate area, Buttermilk works exactly as you would expect it to. The green runs are an honest green. You can't get in trouble, and you can't get lost. If you're a beginner or novice vacationing in Aspen and interested in taking lessons but don't want to go all the way out to Snowmass every day (where you'll also find superb learning terrain) then Buttermilk is the place! In fact, the Buttermilk ski school is one of the very best in Colorado. There's only one reason an instructor would choose to stay at a smaller mountain like this year after year rather than moving over to the ritz and glitz of any of Aspen's three larger ski mountains, and that is that he or she really loves to teach. That's precisely the story of the Buttermilk ski school: gifted, motivated ski teachers and ideal terrain to work on.

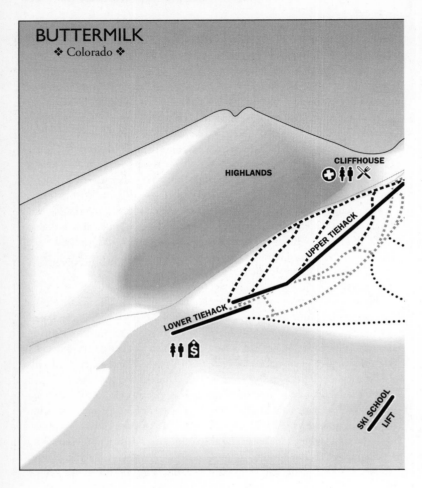

Solidifying Buttermilk's position atop the pantheon of learning hills is the focus on a relatively new learn-to-ski, learn-to-ride program called Beginner's Magic. (The program is also used at Snowmass, but Buttermilk is where it really shines.) This one- or three-day program takes never-evers (the ski industry's nickname for someone who has "never ever skied" or snowboarded) and turns them into confident navigators of green-circle slopes after one day and of blue-square terrain after three days. Picture yourself as a first-timer, and imagine how practical Beginner's Magic is.

Rental equipment is new and high-quality, and your pro will walk through the process with you to help you get comfortable with your gear from the get-go. He or she will work with you on some centering and

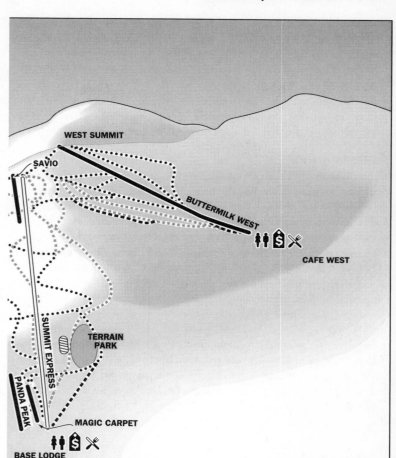

balancing techniques, address the mental, physical, and even mechanical aspects of your new sport. As a beginner, you'll spend a short time making your first turns on a ski deck, a moving artificial sliding surface, and then move quickly to real snow. Pros work with small groups, seamlessly introducing the skill and art of turning down a snow-covered slope on two boards or one. So confident is the ski school, now grandly named the Ski & Snowboard Schools of Aspen, that a money-back guarantee is part of Beginner's Magic. They don't give very many refunds!

Finally, another Buttermilk exists as a sort of parallel universe to the one we know. This is Buttermilk for kids. In addition to its regular adult ski and snowboard programs, Buttermilk is also home to the Powder

Pandas, a day-care/skiing program for miniskiers three to six years old, and Pandas on Boards, a day-care/snowboarding program for slightly older kids, age five to seven. For older children, a special kids' trail map (for both Buttermilk and Snowmass) points out mountain highlights like *Toad's Road,* the *Wall of Death,* and the *Black Hole.* Aside from the log palisades of Fort Frog, adult skiers seem quite unaware of this other mountain—perhaps because most Buttermilk kids' runs are secret mini-trails snaking through dense trees beside the regular runs.

Snowboarding

Buttermilk might be small potatoes in the realm of Aspen skiing, but it's big-time, world-class, top-of-the-heap in the realm of snowboarding and freeriding. When the area built a generous terrain park on *Spruce,* a previously little-used intermediate run, Buttermilk catapulted itself into the conscious of the free spirits of the snows. And that was just the beginning.

Aspen now hosts the Winter X Games, and Buttermilk is action central. The two-mile long "Crazy T'rain" park, one of the longest continuous parks in the world, first opened during the 2001–2002 season and was improved and expanded for 2002–2003. New terrain has been cleared through Uncle Chuck's Glades, giving the Crazy T'rain its own dedicated run. The park, home of the 2002 and 2003 ESPN Winter X Games, features over 30 rails and 25 jumps, including tabletops, hips, and spines (on the advanced side) and easier tables, hits, and spines (for intermediate riders). A permanent X-Games slope-style course within the park ratchets this up to the pantheon of the best parks in the land. Additionally, riders have a 350-foot-long superpipe with 15-foot-high walls, a 17-foot transition, and a 15-degree pitch slope.

Buttermilk Data

Mountain Statistics

Vertical feet	2,030 feet
Base elevation	7,870 feet
Summit elevation	9,900 feet
Longest run	3 miles
Average annual snowfall	200 inches
Snowmkaing	108 acres
Number of lifts	7: I high-speed quad; 5 double chairs; I handle-tow
Uphill capacity	7,500 skiers per hour
Skiable terrain	420 acres
Opening date	Mid-December
Closing date	Early April
Snowboarding	Yes

All four Aspen ski areas share a common lift ticket.

Buttermilk Data (continued)	

Key Phone Numbers (continued)

Ski-area information	(800) 525-6200 or (970) 925-1220
Snow report	(970) 925-1221 or (888) 277-3676
Reservations	(800) 262-7736 or (970) 925-9000
Website	www.aspensnowmass.com

Highlands: Former Maverick Now Mainstream

Except perhaps in terms of spectacular views, nature hasn't exactly favored Highlands, a difficult mountain to ski well or to serve well. Like Aspen Mountain, Highlands is a long, narrow area extending back from the base on a north-south axis. But where Aspen Mountain has several ridges and valleys for a pleasing variety of terrain, Highlands is really only one long ridge—a crest from which the terrain drops off steeply on both sides. This means there's a serious lack of natural fall-line skiing. Straight descents to one side or the other of the central ridgeline often exact a toll in tiresome come-back traverses. And even though it boasts one of the greatest vertical drops in Colorado (some 3,635 vertical feet), Highlands doesn't really have as much truly skiable terrain as this statistic might suggest. Of topographic necessity, most runs are concentrated on the crest of Highlands' long ridge, but by sticking close to this crest and utilizing the new fast lifts, skiers can enjoy longer-than-average continuous runs of up to three-and-a-half miles.

Highlands wins kudos for marking its runs accurately and honestly. Some ski areas without much hard skiing often jack up the ratings to make their trail maps look a little more serious, while others, shy on good intermediate terrain, consistently underrate the difficulty of their runs to make average skiers think they have more terrain to play on than they really do. Not so with Highlands. Here the double-diamond runs on Steeplechase and Olympic Bowl are legitimate experts-only terrain. The blacks are honestly hard. The blues are real cruisers, and so on. How does this mountain work? Highlands offers a few welcoming novice runs, notably *Smuggler,* a wide slope right at the base. Off to the left side as you are looking toward the mountain is a large open area whose west side is called Thunderbowl. The east side is known as Powder Bowl, which is strange, because the sun hammers the snow on this exposure, especially in spring, so, despite the name, powder doesn't stay powder for long. Feeding into these two base-area bowls is *Golden Horn,* a long, steady fall-line cruising run of uncommon width.

But this section, served by the Thunderbowl chair, is a kind of diversion. The main route up the mountain starts with the Exhibition chair, a high-speed detachable quad rising through steep forests to a plateau

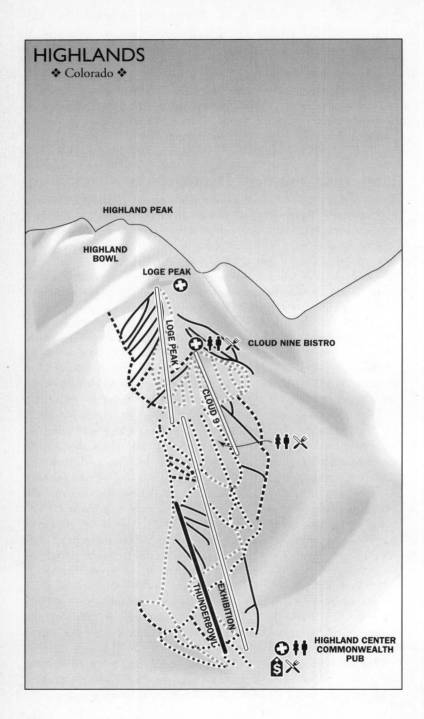

HIGHLANDS
❖ Colorado ❖

HIGHLAND PEAK

HIGHLAND
BOWL

LOGE PEAK

LOGE PEAK

CLOUD NINE BISTRO

CLOUD 9

THUNDERBOWL

EXHIBITION

HIGHLAND CENTER
COMMONWEALTH
PUB

two-thirds of the way up the mountain, where the famous Merry-Go-Round Restaurant is located. Below the Merry-Go-Round are easier-angled runs, which serve as Highlands' upper-novice to intermediate area—a braid of friendly, mostly green runs with a few blues. Inexperienced skiers who wish to spend most of their day up there have to extend themselves on some blue-square terrain from the top of the Cloud Nine Express to reach the more benign green-circle runs. Otherwise, they have to ski back to the base via *Park Avenue,* the easiest trail down the lower third of the mountain. This means that a novice skiing laps on these will get variety at the beginning of each run but none at the end. In contrast, there is quite a bit of truly steep and challenging skiing dropping off on either side of the uppermost end of Highlands' long ridge. Everything above Merry-Go-Round is blue, black, or blacker. To ascend beyond the Merry-Go-Round, you have two options: either ski down to the left and take the Cloud Nine high-speed quad partway up, or hop on the Loge Peak high-speed quad for a spectacular ride above the crest of the final ridge with breathtaking drops and views to either side. Once on top of Loge Peak, strong skiers have three very stimulating choices. On the eastern or Maroon Creek side (skier's right) is a zone of compelling steep faces known collectively as Steeplechase. From top to bottom the routes are called *Hyde Park, Mushroom, Lucky Find, Kessler's Bowl, Snyder's Ridge, Sodbuster, Garish,* and *St. Moritz. Kessler's Bowl* is barely wide enough to deserve the name "bowl." The others all turn into fiery, exciting bump pitches as soon as each new snowfall gets packed out. Their top-of-the-mountain location guarantees the sort of cold, dry, firm snow that makes steep skiing a pleasure, and being east-facing, they are all bathed in lovely morning light. When conditions are good, experts may want to spend all morning here.

The west side of the summit ridge (skier's left) harbors a pitch that gets the adrenaline pumping a lot harder than Steeplechase. Olympic Bowl isn't a bowl at all, no matter what the trail map says, but rather several tricky entrances through the trees that open into one very steep and exposed bump face, *Deception,* and a collection of semi-treed, semi-open lines like *Aces & Eights, Aerobie, Why,* and *Why Not.* The views here, across steep and wild out-of-bounds country toward Pyramid Peak, are as dramatic as any you can find in Aspen. And *Deception* is steep enough that a fall would be terribly unpleasant. The various glades just to the right are a little more forgiving and a lot more varied, and they have the advantage of a shorter come-back traverse to the base of the Cloud Nine lift or all the way across to the Merry-Go-Round and the base of the upper quad via the *Midway* trail. In general, you're better off cutting right at the base of all of these Olympic Bowl runs rather than continuing down the flank of the mountain.

The third and arguably the best choice for really strong, confident skiers is to shoulder their boards and make their way through the control gate and hike up to Highlands' newest in-bounds terrain. Highlands Bowl is an immense, treeless bowl, dropping a thousand vertical feet from the summit of Highland Peak. It had haunted and enticed skiers' imaginations for years, but with 45-degree slopes, conventional wisdom long held that this giant bowl, the scene of a major avalanche tragedy that killed a group of patrollers, was simply too dangerous to ever become part of the ski area. The Aspen Skiing Company snow-safety experts spent years studying avalanche hazards in Highlands Bowl and found that it could be controlled. You can now enter the bowl through several gates. The first is relatively close to the 11,675-foot Loge Peak summit, and the highest is some 700 breath-sapping feet above. The higher you climb, the longer and steeper the runs. Therefore *Ozone* and *Be One,* just under Highland Peak's 12,392-foot summit, are the most demanding, while *Flip's Leap* and *Whip's Veneration* are the shortest of this pantheon of double-black diamond chutes and faces. A portion of this exquisite, high-Alpine terrain opened to skiers and snowboarders in the 2000–2001 season and overnight turned Highlands into one of the most exciting and extreme ski destinations in the state. Two winters later, the whole bowl was brought inbounds, solidifying its reputation.

Before we leave Highlands, a couple of final tips: Even without being a high expert, you can ride the Loge Peak lift, enjoy the sensational views, and make it down in one piece. Sturdy intermediates not given to vertigo can also ride this highest Highlands lift and follow *Broadway* to *Hayden, Meadows,* or *Kandahar* back to mid-mountain. The Cloud Nine isn't solely for experts either, accessing several great blue-square cruisers. If you are a strong skier, be sure to check out *Bob's Glade* on your way down the mountain. Seldom packed out, never bumped out, this wonderful slope of widely spaced trees gets very little traffic and, after a good storm, offers some of Highlands' most intriguing powder skiing. Although marked double diamond, *Bob's Glade* is nowhere near as steep as Steeplechase or Olympic Bowl, and there's plenty of room to maneuver between the trees. To reach this gem, bear left off *Golden Horn.* Or just stay on *Golden Horn,* whose width and pitch will inspire you to shift into overdrive.

Actually, the whole area has become a real gem with the addition of the four high-speed lifts that replaced nine antiques and their frustrating "forever" lift rides. These expensive lift replacements actually cut the hourly capacity from over 9,100 riders to 5,400, but the new chairs move so quickly that lines move faster—and, of course, ride time has been shaved dramatically. Highlands offers lots of serious, intense skiing, complimented by a new upscale base development.

Snowboarding

Even without a big terrain park or gonzo half-pipe, Highlands is a snow-boarder's dream. With its abundant chutes, big bowls, tight trees, and secret stashes, the mountain is rife for exploration on a super-maneuverable board. The trail map is considerately drawn with hatchmarks to indicate flat catwalks that skiers can pole and skate through but snowboarders either avoid or walk.

Highlands Data

Mountain Statistics

Vertical feet	3,635 feet
Base elevation	8,040 feet
Summit elevation	11,675 feet (lift served); 12,382 feet (hike-up)
Longest run	3.5 miles
Average annual snowfall	300 inches
Snowmaking	110 acres
Number of lifts	4: 3 high-speed quads; 1 triple chair
Uphill capacity	5,400 skiers per hour
Skiable terrain	790 acres
Opening date	Mid-December
Closing date	Early April
Snowboarding	Yes

Key Phone Numbers

Ski-area information	(800) 525-6200 or (970) 925-1220
Snow report	(970) 925-1221 or (888) 277-3676
Reservations	(800) 262-7736 or (970) 925-9000
Website	www.aspensnowmass.com

Bob's TECH TIP

Collision Avoidance

Mountain maps always seem to incorporate some version of the Skier Responsibility Code. Among other things, the code admonishes you to "ski under control so you can stop or avoid other skiers or objects" and to "avoid skiers who are ahead of you—they have the right of way."

Some of the worst injuries on the slopes result from skiers colliding; collisions that are not only avoidable, but also predictable. Most ski wrecks involve one or more of the following:

Icy slopes. Two of the most attractive characteristics of western skiing are good snow and (compared to the East) very little ice. Both of these translate into an added measure of control for all skiers. In the West, icy conditions are generally localized and easy to avoid.

Poor visibility. Poor visibility can affect any mountain. When the mountain is weathered in, stay on trails that are familiar and preferably tree lined. Cut back on your speed and anticipate unexpected stops. Ski tight, controlled turns, avoiding wide cross-slope traverses. If you stop for a breather, stop on the far side of the trail.

Crowded slope conditions. A mountain or trail with fewer skiers provides fewer opportunities for a collision. You cannot, after all, run into people who are not there. If you are a beginner or intermediate skier who sometimes struggles with control, try to ski on weekdays on mountains with less traffic. If you are skiing on a popular mountain, ask the ski patrol or ski school which runs have fewer crowds.

Marginal to gross lack of control. The Skier Responsibility Code aside, all skiers lose control from time to time. While occasional loss of control is part of the learning process, there are things you can do to avoid collision. First, rein yourself in quickly and deliberately when you feel your control slipping. Stop if necessary and collect yourself. There is no excuse for flailing and careening down the mountain. If you find yourself on a trail that is more challenging than you expected, and your control is marginal or worse, stop and wait to proceed until there is a gap in the traffic.

Skiing too fast relative to other skiers. In the main, your skiing speed should be roughly compatible with that of the other skiers on the slope. If you are blowing past other skiers or if they are zipping by you left and right, you need to find another trail. This goes double when visibility is bad.

Erratic, unpredictable movements and stops. Remember that skiing is a rhythmic pattern of linked turns. The path of a good skier down a mountain is as predictable as a road map. Beginners and even intermediates, however, ski more erratically, sometimes stopping suddenly or breaking out of their turn pattern. If you are still learning, remember that your unanticipated movements can wreak havoc on skiers behind you. Check out the traffic uphill every time you turn, and try to keep your skiing as predictable as possible. If you are more advanced, expect that less-experienced skiers in your path will do truly weird things. Spot struggling skiers while you are considerably upslope and give them a wide berth.

Stopping where not visible from above. Stopping below dips and rises is a no-brainer. Do it and you will probably get creamed.

Stopping in a place that obstructs the trail. Obstructing or partially obstructing a trail is asking for trouble as well as being inconsiderate. Find some-place else to stop.

Failing to yield the right of way. Skiers downhill of you have the right of way. Period. They may be staggering beginners or timid intermediates traversing back and forth across the trail like a turkey in a shooting gallery. Either way, it's your responsibility to watch out for them. When you merge, entering a trail or starting downhill, skiers who are already on the trail—both above and below you—have the right of way.

Skiing while intoxicated. Dumb and dangerous. Don't do it.

Snowmass

If Snowmass were somewhere else, all by itself, it would still be one of the big three in Colorado, right up there with Vail and Steamboat. But interestingly enough, Snowmass isn't, never has been, and perhaps never will be a stand-alone type of ski resort. Still, Snowmass worked hard to develop an independent resort identity ever since its first lifts opened, trying to persuade skiers to love it for itself and not as part of greater Aspen—except when it markets itself based on its proximity to Aspen.

Snowmass Village is located in a lovely rolling side valley above the Roaring Fork, only a 20-minute drive from Aspen. There's a variety of condominium lodging that makes for a fine place to stay, not just to ski—especially with a family—but . . . The "but" in this case is that beds alone don't make a resort, much less a ski town. Snowmass Mall, the central plaza that is the shopping area and heart of this resort, is little more than a block long and two stories tall. One modest mall and a big convention center simply don't add up to an exciting ski town. As soon as they've kicked off their ski boots, savvy Snowmass skiers head for Aspen. And a very efficient RFTA bus system makes it easy to commute between Snowmass and Aspen. Judged as a ski mountain, Snowmass garners rave reviews from Lito, from me, and from virtually everyone who has every skied there. It is an all-around ski area for every family member and every skill level, with separate zones that feel like separate ski mountains. As at all the other Aspen Skiing Company mountains, the level of skier service at Snowmass is very slick, polished, and gracious.

The Shape and Feel of the Mountain

Snowmass is a very wide, spread-out mountain, and the only challenge with so much room is that, without a clear mental picture of the whole area, you can wind up wasting a lot of time just getting from one part of the sprawling ski area to another. If you start your skiing day on one side of the mountain and discover that you really want to be on the other side, it may take you a couple of hours to get there. This is a fact of life on any really big ski mountain—and Snowmass is that: really big. There are some good strategies for different levels of skiers in search of different experiences on this friendly giant.

Although the development of the Two Creeks base area was much heralded when it debuted a few years back, and although a new Base Village is in the works from Intrawest, traditional Snowmass Village remains the main port of entry for most skiers—and will remain so until Base Village begins to come on line. The slopeside development, revolutionary when it was designed and built in the mid- to late 1960s, snuggles against some of the lower (but by far not the lowest) terrain. The staggered tiers of lodging units rising uphill past the village provide a most convenient ski-in/ski-out situation. The terrain divides more or less naturally into five sections. Looking straight uphill from Snowmass Village, you'll see the lifts and runs of Sam's Knob, not a very poetic name but an apt one for what is essentially just a big bump on a long high ridge. The restaurant on top of Sam's Knob has the best on-mountain views, because you eat looking directly out over the bare white summits of the Snowmass/Maroon Bells Wilderness. This high-traffic area is full of skiers heading toward the back of Snowmass. The

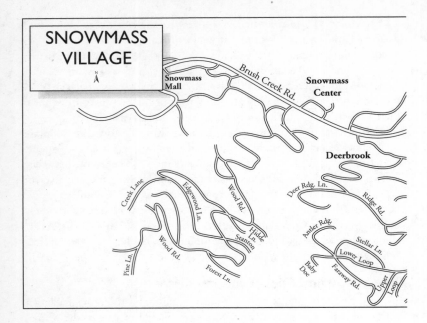

upper slopes of Sam's Knob are wide blue freeways. The very bottom
turns into *Fanny Hill,* a gentle beginners' slope that laps up against
Snowmass Village. Dropping down to the right, or north, from the top
of Sam's Knob is the Campground area, a very important part of the
Snowmass skiing spectrum. Its long elegant runs are marked black on
the map, although they would be dark blue almost anywhere else. *Slot,
Campground,* and *Wildcat* are the finest sustained upper-intermediate
skiing on the whole mountain—pure fall lines, continuous pitches,
runs that go on and on and on.

On the southeastern side of Sam's Knob is the Big Burn area, the most
celebrated ski terrain at Snowmass—and one of the single best-known
runs in the Rockies. The Burn is a large half-mountainside, denuded of
trees by an ancient fire. While it is only a modest section of modern
Snowmass, it is still an effective symbol of the flavor and feel of this
mountain with room to move. The *Big Burn* itself is segmented into a
number of lines named on the trail map as regular ski runs: *Wineskin,
Dallas Freeway, Timberline,* and others, but these names seem artificial.
The beauty of this terrain, which is more vast than not steep, is that you
can ski anywhere and everywhere without once encountering the sort of
obstacles, either natural or man-made, that so often delimit the edges of
a run or trail. Equally remarkable is the terrain just east of the Burn itself,
Coyote Hollow and *Sheer Bliss* served by the Sheer Bliss lift. They are not
the result of a long-ago forest fire but instead represent the finest job of

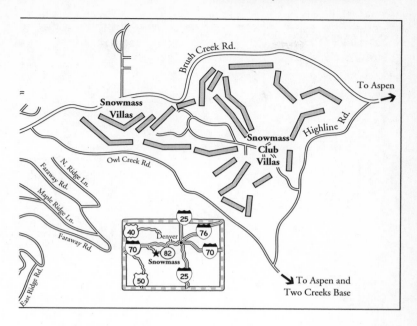

man-made glading. Given enough money, manpower, and Forest Service permission, it's relatively easy to create wide-open treeless slopes. It's a lot harder to create slopes that have a forested feel to them yet ski as if they were wide-open treeless slopes. That's exactly what you'll find on both sides of the well-named Sheer Bliss lift. It's also a good deal harder to groom such gladed terrain, but Snowmass does it after the first fresh blanket of powder has been tracked up.

Next door, to the east of and above the Burn, the Cirque scoops out a big chunk in the mountain. A platterpull lift from the Sheer Bliss lift unload takes skiers to the very top of Snowmass, at 12,510 feet. Ride this modest lift to access the Cirque. Sturdy intermediates can negotiate *Rocky Mountain High,* but it takes more skill to ski the *Cirque Headwall, East Wall,* or some of the other double-black lines. High winds or insufficient snow can keep this uppermost extension of the Big Burn zone closed for weeks, but when it's open, it offers wonderful skiing and endless views.

Farther to the east, beyond the Cirque, is the High Alpine pod, which indeed feels a long, long way from the village. High Alpine's lower section is served by the Alpine Springs and Naked Lady chairlifts and offers a lot of fairly ordinary ho-hum sort of blue runs with lots of mileage but not much charm or character, and a terrific upper section served by the High Alpine lift, which contains some moderately steep and very pleasant bump skiing and one long, roundabout blue adventure named *Green Cabin* that winds its way into and down the side of the Cirque. The High Alpine chairlift is

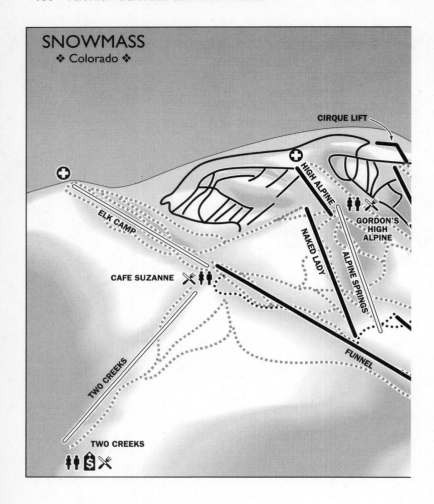

SNOWMASS
❖ Colorado ❖

CIRQUE LIFT

HIGH ALPINE

GORDON'S HIGH ALPINE

ELK CAMP

NAKED LADY

ALPINE SPRINGS

CAFE SUZANNE

FUNNEL

TWO CREEKS

TWO CREEKS

also the gateway to the most exciting terrain at Snowmass, the *Hanging Valley*. Although you ride High Alpine to get there, *Hanging Valley* is a separate world that we'll look at in more detail a little later.

Beyond High Alpine are Elk Camp, a low-angle novice paradise that is the last stop on our west-to-east trip across the ski area, and Two Creeks below. Elk Camp is strictly a one-shot deal: one lift, one type of skier, one restaurant, basically one type of trail—comfortable, easy-to-moderate runs that are marked blue but would not have produced a single lifted eyebrow if they had been graded green. The connection from Elk Camp down to the Village is a long, diagonal boulevard called the *Funnel*, a fun route for coasting home in the afternoon. The quickest way to reach Elk Camp is by the Two Creeks high-speed quad from the newish base area of the same

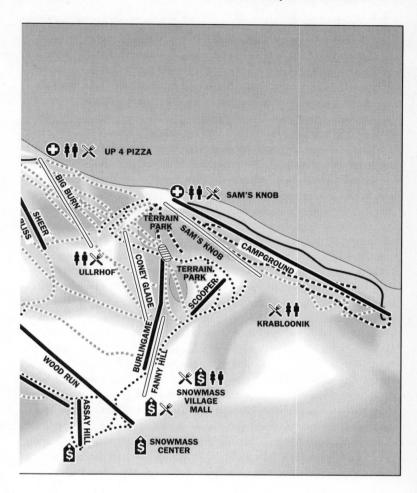

name. If you leave a vehicle at the Two Creeks parking lot, your return run will be on a winding blue-green road that is more of a ski-in/ski-out amenity for the expensive homes lining the trails than a true ski experience.

Snowmass for Families

Snowmass is a great family area for the slopeside lodging that makes family vacationing logistically easy. Further, the array of kids' programs is the greatest in the four Aspen-area mountains. Snowmass's stratification accommodates guests' offspring from the cradle to college. Snow Cubs at Snowmass is the nursery for wee ones as young as eight weeks and as old as three-and-a-half years. Big Burn Bears (to age four), Grizzlies (ages five and six), Bears on Boards (ages five to seven), group ski and snowboard lessons (ages seven to twelve) and even Teens First Turns and Teens "Too Cool for School" Groups (ages 13 to 19) cover the age gamut of any skiing family. There are also kids' and teens' Extreme Camps. Snowmass's tubing hill, called Tube Town, is a kid-pleasing facility off the Assay Hill chair on the lower section of the mountain. Evening childcare, called Nighthawks, enables mom and dad to have an evening to themselves.

Snowmass for Learning Skiers

If you're just starting out, know that Beginner's Magic, a hallmark of the Buttermilk operation, is also practiced at Snowmass. Same dedicated instructors, same format, same philosophy, same results. Snowmass doesn't have better learning terrain than Buttermilk, just a lot more of it. Newcomers are initiated into the friendly mysteries of snow sliding on *Fanny Hill,* doubtless in a ski-school context, which is always the best way to go—and especially so with Beginner's Magic. Fanny Hill's advantage is that it's right off the Snowmass Village mall, which makes it convenient for new skiers. Fanny Hill's disadvantage is that it's right off the Snowmass Village mall, which makes it crowded with skiers and riders of all skill levels coming and going. This can be disconcerting to beginners without a lot of confidence or control. But once they have acquired even a modest repertoire of basic moves, even fairly skiers can move around far more easily than the trail map seems to indicate.

A close look doesn't reveal many green runs. The three most obvious are the *Funnel* (via *Funnel Bypass*), *Assay Hill* served by a lower-mountain chairlift of the same name, and a long, meandering route composed of *Max Park* to *Lunchline* to *Dawdler* from the top of Sam's Knob. However, many Snowmass blue runs are so benign and well groomed that skiers who normally look for the easiest way down can easily handle them. But which blue runs are they? In a way, the trail marking system breaks down here, because some blue runs are easy green-plus routes, while others are more demanding and serious black-minus.

The entire Elk Camp area is ideal for anyone who can make some sort of skidded turn. Elk Camp and *Funnel* are reached via two high-speed quads. Also on the eastern side of the mountain, *Adams Avenue* (from the bottom of Elk Cabin) and *Green Cabin* (from High Alpine down) barely nudge into the blue category. Novice skiers can also escape from the green-only world by making a big loop from the top of Sam's Knob via *Trestle* and lower *Green Cabin* back. By contrast, the blue runs on the front face of Sam's Knob are all rather serious for novices. Inexperienced skiers can even do the *Big Burn* for thrills as long as they remember that there's no rule that says they have to ski straight down. The Burn is wide enough to allow for very long side-to-side traverses, while being mindful of faster, more accomplished skiers who take straighter lines.

Snowmass for "Cruisers"

In skiers' lingo, "cruising" has a special, even privileged, meaning. A cruising skier is at one with the terrain, not struggling, not solving problems, not even responding to challenges, but simply savoring the rush of snow, air, and speed. A cruiser prefers the natural lines and flows that the mountain offers. The cruiser instinctively dials in big turns and long, smoothly blended curves, heads for open spaces, and prefers a steady nonstop pace down the mountain. Does it sound like fun? It would be easy to argue that cruising is the most fun you can have on skis; and Snowmass is a good place to find out if that's true. In fact, like Vail, Snowmass is a cruising mountain *par excellence.*

The cruiser can find true happiness on terrain accessed by the Big Burn and Sheer Bliss lifts. It's easy to spot the most popular lines and to consciously ski away from them, so that a touch of extra speed won't disturb other skiers—elementary cruising courtesy. A creative skier can cruise these sections all day without ever repeating exactly the same line. *Slot* and *Wildcat* off the Campground chair are slightly steeper runner-ups to the Burn as cruisers' heaven. The "front" terrain on Sam's Knob would seem ideally pitched for cruising too, but it is typically a high-traffic area, and fast skiing and crowds don't mix. Also, Sam's Knob introduces a short uphill stretch into the otherwise continuous slope between the Big Burn and Campground. But by schussing the last section of *Sneaky's,* keeping your speed up, and cutting south around the knob itself, you can put together a truly enormous and memorable cruising run, and continue to the bottom of the Campground lift in one fell, thigh-burning swoop.

The blue runs of the Alpine Springs area are less interesting, less open, and less exciting for serious cruising than the western side of the mountain, but often they're also less crowded and are suitable for a tentative intermediate who wants to notch it up and get the feel of cruising. These runs are cut through a dense forest and offer both better visibility and more sheltered conditions on stormy days.

Snowmass for Adventure

Don't get the idea that Snowmass has a reputation as a cruising mountain simply. It doesn't lack steeper, harder slopes. The mountain offers pitches that will wake you up, make you concentrate, and leave you feeling proud of yourself after a successful run. Proportionally, there isn't as much hard skiing at Snowmass as on Aspen Mountain or at Highlands, but because of the vast total acreage, there is still a considerable amount of challenge. Remember that on such a balanced mountain, so well regarded as a place to learn and an intermediate's haven, only a minority of skiers look for that kind of excitement, and there's enough to keep that minority happy.

The biggest thrills at Snowmass are in the high Alpine terrain of the Cirque and Hanging Valley. Ski from the top of the Sheer Bliss lift and ski down along the edge of the Cirque, the large central amphitheater that looks as if it was excavated out of the Snowmass ridge with a giant ice-cream scoop. The single easiest route is a spectacular advanced blue run called *Rocky Mountain High*, but the rest of the Cirque wears double diamonds. The gnarly western bank of this hole (skier's left) is a long series of cliffs, but there are a few ways through. These gaps in the wall are intensely exciting. Signs and ropes lead to *KT Gully* and *Rock Island*, which also deserve their double-black-diamond designations. Once you have performed your obligatory short swing dance down these steep gullies, the skiing mellows out as you slide down to *Green Cabin*. Even more stimulating is *AMF*, a steep Alpine gully dropping into the very top of the Cirque. *AMF*, a local tag that has found its way onto the trail map, may (or may not) stand for *adiós, my friend*. If you have the legs for laps on *AMF*, ski all the way down to the Cony Glade quad and take it and the Burn quad back up. Next door to *AMF* is *Gowdy's*, an even steeper gully sometimes nicknamed *80/20*, allegedly because 80% of the skiers who look over the edge chicken out.

Even finer, even longer, and much more remote are the "runs" from the top of the High Alpine lift into Hanging Valley. These "runs" are named zones on a big Alpine mountainside. Opening Hanging Valley to the public was an enlightened move. For many years the Snowmass ski patrol kept it to themselves as a kind of insiders' powder preserve, but now they control, patrol, and sweep this difficult and remote powder preserve, sort of an "inbounds" outback situation. Hanging Valley gives Snowmass a dimension it would otherwise totally lack. Nice.

Hanging Valley is so remote and dramatic that the double-black rating is certainly fair. The *Hanging Valley Glades* branch to the right off the *Edge*, an easier black bump slope accessed from the High Alpine lift. The *Hanging Valley Wall* is a longer, more intriguing route than the *Hanging Valley Glades*. The extra ten minutes you'll spend walking east from the top of the High Alpine lift to the *East Wall* are well worth it. The first pitch is a steep but short face dropping from a high, bare ridge down onto a timbered bench in the middle of nowhere. There seem to be a lot of choices, and the first impression is that you'll get more vertical and more powder by trending right down to the second, longer step. In fact, left is better. Drop down along the left edge of the final high wall until you spot your perfect line. These lower pitches are known locally as *Wall 1, Wall 2, Strawberry Patch, Cassidy's*, and *Union 1 & 2*. Hanging Valley is real adventure terrain, so don't expect trail signs, warning signs, or other ski-area information. Still, even in the wilds of Hanging Valley, the ski area has been worked. It's easy to reach the best lines on the *Wall*, because the forest along its edge has been discreetly thinned. Even when you fly out across the rolling flats where the *Wall* joins *Sandy Park,* you owe your last dozen turns to the efficient, subtle glading. Hanging Valley's vertiginous runs might forever be beyond you, but you can admire them from Elk Camp's gentle cruisers. Hanging Valley's beautiful steep Alpine slopes overhang Elk Camp like a perpetual dare. They seem to tell Snowmass skiers: No matter how good you become, there'll always be a challenge waiting for you. Numerous control ropes and gates in both Hanging Valley and the Cirque at first don't seem to make sense, because sometimes runs enter from both sides of the ropes. They are not closure ropes but rather control ropes to separate different areas that the patrol checks and sweeps at different times, so it's important to respect them. They weren't put there just to irritate or confuse you.

On powder days, strong Snowmass intermediate and advanced skiers tend to head for the *Big Burn,* but experts in the know often strike out for the *Wall* first thing on a powder morning. The quickest way from the village is via the Wood Run, Alpine Springs, and High Alpine lifts in succession. If you use the high-speed quads up the front side, the *Wall* might be tracked up by the time you get there. Double status boards at the bottom of the Sheer Bliss and High Alpine lifts will tell you what's open.

Snowboarding

Another Aspen area mountain. More great riding. In 2002–2003, Snowmass doubled the length of the Trenchtown terrain park and is now top-to-bottom off the Coney Glade chairlift. Park builders also added more rails and jumps while they were at it. Also, fine new interactive kids' ski/snowboard trails were added—solidifying the resort's reputation both as a place to ride and as a place for youngsters to find adventure.

Snowmass Data

Mountain Statistics

Vertical feet	4,406 feet
Base elevation	8,104 feet
Summit elevation	12,510 feet
Longest run	5 miles
Average annual snowfall	300 inches
Snowmaking	160 acres
Number of lifts	20: 7 high-speed quads; 2 triples; 6 doubles; 3 platter pulls; 2 moving carpets
Uphill capacity	27,978 skiers per hour
Skiable terrain	3,010 acres
Opening date	Mid-November
Closing date	Mid-April
Snowboarding	Yes

Snowmass Data *(continued)*

Transportation

By car 4.5-hour drive from Denver, via I-70 west to Glenwood Springs (exit 116), then south on Highway 82. Turn right on Brush Creek Rd. to Snowmass. (Do not turn off Highway 82 at the earlier Old Snowmass sign.)

By van Colorado Mountain Express (call (800) 525-6363 or (970) 926-9730) from Denver International Airport and Eagle County Airport.

By plane See Transportation section for Aspen, page 112.

Key Phone Numbers

Ski-area information	(970) 925-1220 or (800) 525-6200
Snow report	(970) 925-1221 or (888) 277-3676
Reservations	(800) 598-2996 pr (970) 923-2000
Websites	www.aspensnowmass.com and
	www.snowmassvillage.com

Lito's TECH TIP

Cruising—Big Turns for Big Mountains

The cruiser's secret weapon is an effortless, energy-saving, long-radius turn—more elegant and more efficient than the way most intermediate skiers hack their way down the slope. To ski this way, you'll need two skills: a smoother beginning to your turn and a means of controlling your speed that doesn't depend on skidding or digging your edges into the snow.

A smoother start to the turn Having polished up the arc or trajectory of your turn by learning to ride that outside ski exclusively, your next step is to start into the turn with less oomph and less effort. If you just twist, swing, or throw your skis around sideways, you're not only wearing yourself out, but you make it harder for the ski to follow its own bent curve in the snow. You'll skid down the mountain in short bursts of motion rather than cruising it in big effortless arcs. The ideal cruising turn starts slowly, progressively, with the skis peeling gradually off into an arc and not jammed quickly around the corner. How does it work?

The pure, smooth start to your parallel turn depends on an early weight shift. Most skiers try to turn their skis and feet before they shift weight to the outside ski. I'm going to ask you to try a very curious thing: Stand on your new outside foot before you twist it into the turn. At first, you won't be able to do this on a steep or impressive slope. Play with this idea on wide-open, gentle green runs just to see what it's like. Shift your weight first, then turn. Surprise—the start of the turn will take more time. And because you're already standing on the top, soon-to-be-outside ski of the turn, you won't be able to twist it as much. The turn itself will slow down, and you'll find yourself carving a cleaner, longer arc. As the habit develops, you will notice that even when you get in trouble, even on steep slopes, even in bumps, as long as you shift your weight onto the new ski before turning, both skis will always pivot smoothly together into the new turn. (That's right, it really is the top ski I want you to step on before turning downhill.)

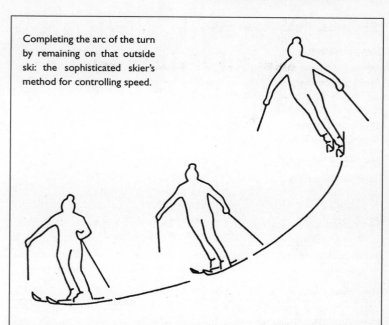

Completing the arc of the turn by remaining on that outside ski: the sophisticated skier's method for controlling speed.

Speed control Speed control in a long radius turn is easy—if you simply keep on turning. And that's easy. As long as you keep all your weight on your outside ski, the bent shape of the ski will keep it turning. As soon as you equalize your weight on both skis, the turning action disappears. But how about speed control? Long-radius turns give you more time in the fall line to pick up speed, so slowing down at the end of each turn is important. The theory is simple: If your ski keeps turning, it will eventually turn uphill and bring you to a stop. Even if you don't turn that far, the slope is still decreasing underfoot, so it is the shape of the hill and not the resistance from your edges digging into the snow that slows you down. Control your speed by "completing the turn" and turning longer rather than harder. This is, in fact, the way expert skiers control their speed—by guiding their skis farther around the arc rather than by scraping, skidding, and edging. And you can too. Smooth, long, round turns—pure pleasure.

West and North
of Denver

The commonality among these three ski areas—two that qualify as destination resorts and one that is a ski area in its simplest, purest, and most traditional sense—is they are not clustered. Each is a stand-alone destination, and each, in its own way, exemplifies the quality of Colorado skiing.

Steamboat Steamboat is a perfectly balanced mountain, but with elegant tree skiing taking the place of open bowls at the upper end of the spectrum. It's an easy mountain to move around on, with great fall lines, great valley views, and efficient lifts. An informal skiers' village has evolved at the base of the ski mountain, but the real Steamboat Springs, an authentic ranching town with deep roots, is just a few miles away, close enough to enjoy as an integral part of a ski vacation.

Winter Park Strong on skiing and still weak on resort and vacation atmosphere (though that is changing fast), Winter Park was first developed more than 60 years ago but remains a young, athletic, gutsy sort of mountain that doesn't pamper its guests with too many luxuries. Mary Jane, heaven for serious bump skiers, seems almost like a separate ski area, but it's just another side of this big, varied ski complex. Enduringly popular with Denver locals.

Loveland Loveland straddles Interstate 70 but is far more impressive than it looks from the highway. Charming, and charmingly old-fashioned, this day ski area offers the closest big-mountain skiing to Denver—just skiing, no resort, no condos, no glitz. Interesting terrain right under the Continental Divide and the highest quad chairlift in Colorado.

Steamboat

Steamboat ranks right up there with Vail and Aspen in quality, size, and importance as a Colorado ski resort—one of the big three for sure. But it is no clone. While Vail adopted the style of a European Alpine village and

Aspen clung to its silver-mining roots, Steamboat has worked awfully hard to craft an old-time Western ranching image composed of cowboy hats and chaps, horses belly deep in snow, and soulful old barns, a kind of daguerreotype frozen on the pages of ski magazines and in skiers' minds. But the image is misleading and has little to do with Steamboat skiing, which is thoroughly modern and simply outrageous. Steamboat is a far better ski resort than any of its ad campaigns would lead you to believe.

The Western metaphor is nevertheless a natural one because the town of Steamboat Springs, three miles from the ski area, really was a regional ranching center and a market town for cattle raisers up and down the wide Yampa Valley, but a Wild West theme park it ain't. Steamboat Springs is a traditional Western strip town with a long main street. There are few historical touches, no cutesy false fronts, and, thank God, no staged shoot-outs for tourists on the main drag. Steamboat Springs, at its core, has largely remained an everyday working Western town with a vacation-destination overlay.

The Steamboat ski area was founded by locals in the early 1960s and passed through various corporate hands, ranging from a U.S. conglomerate called LTV Corporation to a Japanese ski operator. At this writing, it was still owned by the American Skiing Company, which also operates The Canyons in Utah and several New England ski areas. (Lately, the company endured severe financial problems, however, and was at one point a heartbeat away from being taken over by the folks who operate Okemo, Vermont.) Over this time, Steamboat matured as a ski resort, a ski village was built at the base of Mount Werner, and lifts were added and steadily upgraded, creating a place that is far more contemporary than historic Western. Development at the resort center rambles with several levels, two central plazas, and condos, hotels, second homes, and retail and restaurant space wrapping around the base of the massif rising from U.S. 40 well up both sides of the ski mountain's lower slopes. With such facilities at the resort, going downtown for a good meal or a little après-ski action is not the only option, but no ski trip to Steamboat is complete without exploring the town of Steamboat Springs.

The Look and Feel of the Mountain

Steamboat does not provide merely good skiing, but great skiing. Steamboat's ski terrain is sometimes still loosely referred to as Mt. Werner, the topographical honorific for the beef massif with a rounded summit and several sub-peaks. From the flat, rolling ranch country of the Yampa Valley below, you can see much of it—a series of massive steps covered with a frosted net of white-ribbon runs. But it's almost impossible to guess the scale, to know how much you're seeing at once, or to judge how far away the upper runs really are.

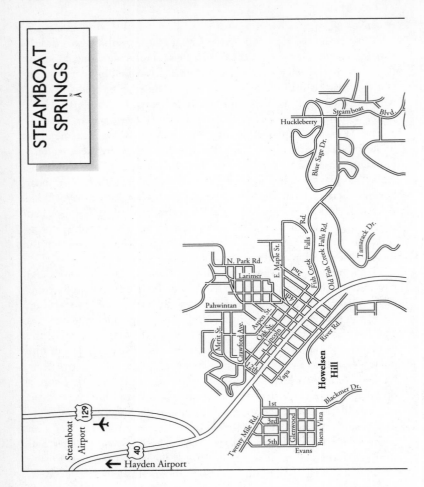

Every ski mountain has its own feel, its own flavor, its own atmos-phere—the result of a hard-to-analyze combination of snow conditions, terrain, scenery, trail design, and even the attitudes of skier service person-nel. Two mountains with the same statistics (vertical, uphill capacity, etc.) can feel different. Not only are Steamboat's stats impressive, but it has a wonderful feel to match. Special qualities include the steady nature of most runs, which go on and on in long, uninterrupted pitches, not in fits and starts, not in flats and drops, not in sudden constrictions and sudden widenings; expansive, plunging views and a suspended-in-the-sky feeling that makes skiers feel like privileged characters; and, finally, the aspen trees. Steamboat is not as high as resorts farther south, so its magnificent aspen stands grow right to the top of Sunshine Peak (10,385 feet). These aspen groves are incredible to ski through, but they're also fabulous to look

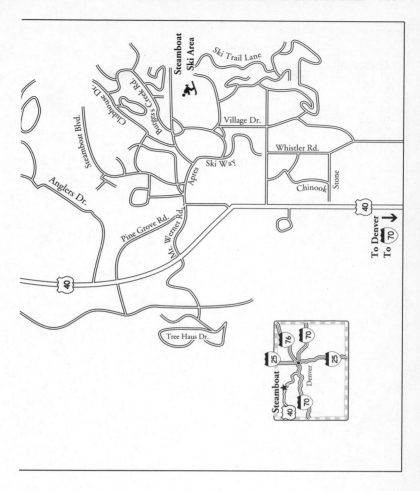

at. Aspens are everywhere and are like no trees you've ever seen. Taller, whiter, and straighter than aspens on other Colorado ski mountains, their lacy, fringy tops seem to glow against the deep winter sky.

Somebody should be praised for deciding to paint the lift towers a deep, rich midnight blue; they seem to come right out of the dark north-Colorado sky. Dramatic color and its corollary, dramatic light, are part of the everyday Steamboat ski experience, because this mountain faces west. Most ski areas are laid out facing primarily north to assure cold, dry snow conditions, but many slopes are therefore gray and somber, especially in the short days of early winter when the light is low. On this primarily west-facing peak, the afternoon light is intense and golden, and even the morning shadows seem deep and dramatic. Yet Steamboat is high enough and far enough north that its snow conditions don't seem to suffer from

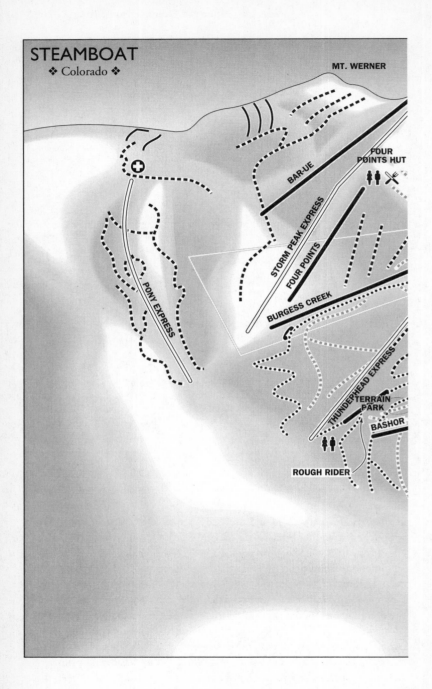

STEAMBOAT
❖ Colorado ❖

MT. WERNER

FOUR POINTS HUT

BAR-UE

STORM PEAK EXPRESS

FOUR POINTS

BURGESS CREEK

PONY EXPRESS

THUNDERHEAD EXPRESS

TERRAIN PARK

BASHOR

ROUGH RIDER

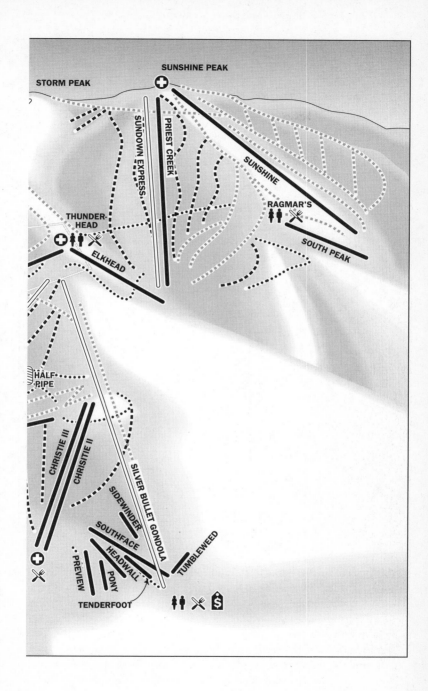

STORM PEAK

SUNSHINE PEAK

SUNDOWN EXPRESS

PRIEST CREEK

SUNSHINE

RAGMAR'S

THUNDER-HEAD

ELKHEAD

SOUTH PEAK

HALF PIPE

CHRISTIE III

CHRISITIE II

SILVER BULLET GONDOLA

SIDEWINDER

SOUTHFACE

HEADWALL

PREVIEW

PONY

TUMBLEWEED

TENDERFOOT

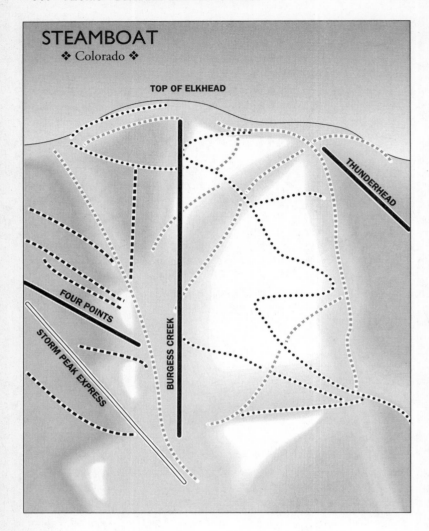

this western orientation. (In fact, Steamboat invented the phrase "champagne powder" to describe its snow.) The view from the mountain presents a wide westerly panorama of broad white valleys and rolling, receding, snow-crusted foothills stretching on and on because there are no high peaks to the west and no bare south-facing slopes in sight. This stunning, wintry view seems to be built into just about every run.

Steamboat skiing comes across as having three parts: the lower mountain and the two separate sides of the upper mountain. The most recent lift expansions have added a couple of new zones to this picture, but it remains basically accurate. The lower mountain is a kind of frontal peak called Thunderhead. A number of chairlifts are scattered over the slopes, but the main route up Thunderhead is via Steamboat's eight-person Silver Bullet (the ride is rapid—only nine minutes, covering the significant 2,200-foot vertical). When you exit the Thunderhead gondola terminal, you realize that you are still separated from the upper slopes by a kind of long, rounded saddle. Instead of going right on up, you must ski down into one of the basins on either side of Thunderhead and only then continue up to the crest of either of the two upper peaks. Decisions, decisions: right or left? Down to the left is the Burgess Creek side, with Storm Peak chairlifts rising to the northernmost region of Steamboat's twin upper summits. Down to the right is the Priest Creek side and the Sunshine Peak lifts. So far, so good: one large lower mountain, sitting out in front of two broad upper peaks. Each of these "mountains" functions as a separate ski domain with its own character, its own views, its own type of skiing, and each feels about as big as many respectably sized ski areas in their entirety.

It's possible to ski across from the Storm Peak side to the Sunshine Peak side, and vice versa once you're up there, but the natural tendency is to ski on one side or the other, and then take a comeback chairlift to Thunderhead Saddle. There, it's decision time again: visit the opposite side of the upper mountain, ski on the lower slopes, or maybe lunch in one of the various restaurants in the massive Thunderhead gondola building.

The slopes below Thunderhead offer an enormous amount of good skiing, and if there weren't something about human nature that makes us all want to head for the summits, this lower mountain could hold your attention all day. On your first days at Steamboat, you'll probably just ski down from Thunderhead in the afternoon, but it's worth some serious exploration if you spend a week at Steamboat. Note the phrase "week at Steamboat," because this is definitely a vacation resort, not a weekend ski destination, even though many front-range skiers do, in fact, escape there for the weekend a couple of times a winter. Although the drive from Denver is not really that much longer than to Summit County resorts like Breckenridge, Copper, and Keystone, or to Vail, it is still perceived as both much longer and tougher. As a result, weekend skiers don't flock here in great numbers as they do in Summit County—and there are virtually no day-trippers at all. This is a big plus for Steamboat.

Another plus is a very intelligent lift layout. Steamboat was one of the last big Colorado resorts to install high-speed, detachable quad chairlifts, preferring instead to double up its conventional chairs, with newer fixed-grip triples running parallel to the earlier doubles. It worked very well for a while. But Steamboat, too, finally joined the white revolution of high-speed lifts, initially with two express quads right where they would do the most good—up the center of the two upper mountains. Two more high-speed detachables followed soon after. In many key locations, there is redundancy to the lift layout, with the conventional fixed-grip lifts (doubles, triples, and a fixed quad) placed in strategic spots to give skiers the option of several ways back up. In this fashion, Steamboat has eliminated most of the natural bottlenecks where everybody skis down into a cul-de-sac from which there's only one direction and one chairlift out. For instance, on the Storm Peak side, instead of taking the slower Bar-UE, Four Points, or Burgess Creek chairlifts, you have the option of riding the Storm Peak Express every time. Even when the maze is full, the line moves fast and chair travels fast, so you'll get in more skiing with less ride time.

From the top of Storm Peak, you can ski down toward town and the Yampa Valley or ski the back side into Morningside Park or northside slopes known collectively as Pioneer Ridge. This network of intermediate and advanced terrain is served by a triple chairlift, which brings you back up to Storm Peak. This area has several sinewy trails, such as *Rooster, Frying Pan,* and *Wake-Up Call,* but is best known for shots through the well-spaced conifers. From the top, you can also drop into steep chutes etched between the trees of beefy Mount Werner itself.

The Pony Express quad serves Pioneer Ridge, the northernmost sector of Steamboat skiing and another relatively recent expansion area. You can choose one of several single-black-diamond trails and more enticing glades, and best of all, because this terrain is on the far perimeter of the Storm Peak side, you'll seldom encounter a lift line. This part of the ski area has more mid-level terrain as well as tight trails and incredible aspen glades flanking the Sundown Express and parallel Priest Creek chairs. Beyond are the wide and handsome cruising runs off the Sunshine chair. These three lifts unload very near each other on the Sunshine summit. On a knob near the ski area's southern perimeter (the Sunshine Peak side) is Rendezvous Saddle, with a day lodge, cafeteria, and restaurant service, so that skiers can stay on this part of the mountain all day, dancing through the trees or sailing down the cruisers.

Steamboat for Less-Experienced Skiers

Steamboat has a super learning area at the base that is served by a couple of chairlifts and a tiny, Mitey-Mite surface lift, where the ski school starts first-timers. Beginners soon graduate to the practice runs on the lower mountain, served by the Christie lifts. Even new skiers can ride the Silver Bullet gondola and take one of two long green trails, *BC Ski Way* and the more interesting *Why Not,* which wind completely around the lower mountain. Other than those, Steamboat does not have a lot of green on its trail map; in fact, there are almost no green runs at all on the upper mountains. Still, recent graduates from the beginner slopes at the base can explore wonderful runs on top that are only nominally blue and are very, very friendly to less-experienced skiers. The runs on the far side of the Sunshine lift, especially *Tomahawk, Quickdraw* and the short connecting runs between them, are so low-key and friendly that locals call this zone of long, gentle, and extremely wide trails "Wally World." To exit Wally World, novices should take *Duster,* a cross-mountain catwalk, from near Rendezvous Saddle. This route cuts behind Thunderhead peak, eventually turning into a greenish run called *Park Lane* connecting with several easy ways down the lower mountain.

Steamboat for Good Skiers

When cruising fever takes hold, Steamboat skiing really starts to get exciting. *Buddy's Run* provides lots of room and lots of variations. No pressure to turn here, there, or any particular spot. No reason not to accept a bit more speed. This classic cruiser, along with runs like *High Noon* on the Sunshine Peak side and *Heavenly Daze* on the front face of the lower mountain, spells bliss for strong skiers who just don't want to bother with short turns, putting on the brakes, or, above all, bumps.

Many of Steamboat's black runs are just plain inviting for good skiers but don't require expert skiing skills at all. Runs like *The Ridge* and *Crowtrack* on Storm Peak and *Valley View* below Thunderhead require short turns and fall-line skiing but rarely seem to throw any awkwardly shaped bumps in your way. If it's friendly bumps you're searching for, you'll often find them on *Twilight, One o' Clock,* and *Two o' Clock,* which are slightly steeper lines dropping down and right from the *High Noon* ridge run on the Sunshine Peak side.

A good strategy is to explore one section of the mountain in depth on any given day, working lunch into your plans. For example, spend a morning on Sunshine Peak's blues and the easy blacks past Rendezvous Saddle and back to the Sundown Express quad, and then treat yourself to a real Norwegian lunch at Ragnar's at Rendezvous Saddle. Or spend a morning cruising both sides of the Storm Peak Express lift. *Rainbow* and *Buddy's Run* and all their variations funnel into the bottom of the Burgess Creek drainage. The Four Points Hut, a tiny, low-key eatery with an immense view of the Yampa Valley, is a good lunch spot. Afterwards, pump yourself up again by exploring the blue runs and black tree glades (shading into expert country) on both sides of the Pony Express quad, that distinct zone mentioned above with its own distinct flavor.

Or, as a final option, after spending a morning on the lower mountain skiing the pleasant runs on both sides of the Arrowhead chair, leave the crowded mountain eateries and enjoy quiet lunch off the slopes in one of the Ski Time Square or Gondola Square restaurants. After lunch, the Silver Bullet will get you back up the mountain in no time.

Steamboat for Experts

A great ski mountain should improve as skiers do. Steamboat qualifies. You'll go nuts here if you're an expert or near-expert skier. You don't have to be a hotshot with rubber knees and thunder thighs, but simply a very strong skier who's at home on moderately steep bumps, comfortable in powder, and capable of turning not just where you want to but where you need to. A lot of skiers fit this description.

While there is a fair number of steep and moguled black runs on both the upper and lower mountain, Steamboat's most exciting skiing is found among its aspen trees. The slender, white aspen trunks are almost perfectly spaced, with enough room between them to weave through forests without feeling pinched, pressured, or wondering if you're going to make it. This classic, open aspen lines abound in the Priest Creek area on the Sunshine Peak side. The angle steepens a bit, and skiing is more exciting to the north of the Sundown Express and Priest Creek lifts (to the left of the lifts as you ride up). You'll see two main lines, *Shadows* and *Closet,* on the trail map, that are generally, rather than clearly, defined runs. Really good skiers still have the deep trees largely to themselves, sharing the lift with their less skilled compatriots who, nevertheless, like the cachet of skiing Priest Creek. Steamboat's combination of trees and powder is one of the mountain's real signatures. The reason for this can be credited to weather patterns and Steamboat's western orientation The typical westerly winds that accompany big storms, transform the abundant aspen forests into fairy groves and festoon the delicate bare branches with white hoarfrost lace. Incredible skiing and incredible beauty! Steamboat tends to catch northern storms out of Wyoming that often miss central and southern Colorado resorts. In fact, a lot of skiers think that, after Vail's Back Bowls, Steamboat offers the best powder skiing in the state. A lot of skiers further contend that Steamboat has even better snow, because it simply doesn't get the traffic that Vail does. In any case, the tree–powder combination creates an experience that's greater than the sum of its parts.

For unusual tree skiing, and perhaps some stashes of late powder long after Priest Creek is tracked out, explore the forest zones in between the zigzags of *Why Not,* an easy green comeback trail on the lower mountain—some of the best hidden tree skiing at Steamboat.

Elsewhere, Pioneer Ridge, the chutes off the back of Morningside Park, and the far-north glades off the Pony Express—all mentioned previously—offer various levels of challenge to strong skiers. They don't have the distinctive flavor of the Priest Creek aspens, but they are satisfying in their own right and provide some change of scenery.

Snowboarding

Terrain parks and pipes just don't get much biggest than Steamboat's 11.8-acre SoBe Terrain Park, which is located in Bashor Bowl and served by its own lift. The terrain park boasts 11 professionally designed rails, ranging from beginner rails to "mailbox sliders." Mavericks, the awesome superpipe, has quickly established itself as one of the go-to places in the freeride world. Measuring up to 650 feet long, with 15-foot-walls, and a 17-foot transition, it provides a really big ride. In fact, it is reportedly North America's longest half-pipe. Steamboat cut a pipe skeleton and installed new snowmaking, so that Mavericks opens sooner each winter than most pipes in Colorado, attracting freeriders from afar to ride the longest pipe on the continent. Pipe tyros use nearby Mini-Mav, a 200-foot-long beginner half-pipe with five-foot walls.

Mountain Dining

Most days, it makes more sense to eat lunch on the mountain than to ski down to the base. There are three mountain restaurant locations but considerably more than three restaurants to choose from.

Thunderhead, the massive mid-mountain crossroads at the top of the Silver Bullet gondola, includes four separate restaurant/cafeteria facilities, thus offering Mexican, Italian, midland American, country and western, pizza, barbecue, etc. Hazie's, the fancier of Thunderhead's two sit-down restaurants (named for Steamboat ski champion Buddy Werner's mom, the late Hazie Werner), offers a menu full of gourmet touches. It is an even better place to spend an evening. Ride the Silver Bullet gondola in the early evening, when the lower edge of the winter sky is still a band of pale orange. Enjoy a knockout dinner, an excellent wine list, and with luck, a table by a window with a panoramic view that invites you to reach out and touch the lights of Steamboat Springs sparkling below. Reserve at least one Steamboat evening for this treat.

At Rendezvous Saddle below the Sunshine chair, you'll find a regular mountain cafeteria, barbecue on the deck, as well as Ragnar's, the mountain's most popular sit-down lunch restaurant. The wild Norwegian names on the menu are equaled by the good Norwegian cooking (not an oxymoron). Try the *fyldt pandekager* (shrimp crêpes) or the *stekt rødspaette trondheim* (sautéed sole with asparagus and leeks). Ragner's also provides atmospheric dinner some nights a week. Access is via gondola and snowcat-towed sleigh. The experience is intimate and the food is wonderful.

The tiny but cool Four Points Hut at the top of Four Points lift, halfway up Storm Peak, is a miniature mountain restaurant. It has fewer choices than the multistory Thunderhead lodge, but it is Steamboat USA's equivalent of the fabulous little lunch huts set smack in the middle of long ski runs in the Alps.

Steamboat Extras

At Steamboat you can ski with a champion—for free. Stetson-topped, Bogner-clad Billy Kidd, Olympic silver medalist and enduring American skiing icon, calls Steamboat home. Whenever he's in town, he takes a run with any visitor who shows up, dispensing tips and charm along the way.

Check with skier services for time and meeting place. The Billy Kidd Performance Center, while far from free, is a racing workshop sure to improve recreational racers' technique in the gates and while free skiing too.

Not all of Steamboat's winter adventures are found up on the mountain. Buffalo Pass, just north of town, is a known powder skiing center. Steamboat Powdercats—Blue Sky West is arguably the best-known snowcat-skiing operation in Colorado. Established over two decades ago, it has more terrain to choose from than any other snowcat operation. The terrain, high on Buffalo Pass north of Steamboat Springs, offers sensational tree skiing that is the peer of the glades at the ski area (or perhaps even surpasses them). Another plus is that this snowcat operator sincerely tries to divide groups by ability, so that everyone moves at roughly the same pace. Strong intermediate skiers and riders are grouped with their ability peers, and all groups stop for lunch at a lovely mountain hut. With Steamboat Powdercats–Blue Sky West, you'll sometimes be making tracks in virgin snow a week to ten days after the last storm has blown through. This expansive, wide-open terrain, plus fresh snow, equals poetry in motion.

The Bridgestone Winter Driving School is a unique experience—and one that can save your butt when you're out on a winter road. On safe courses of watered ice, you'll learn all the tricks of keeping yourself and your car on the road in the most treacherous conditions. Courses are offered daily, and the school's office is at Ski Time Square.

For families vacationing with youngsters under driving age, Steamboat is *the* place. Some 20 years ago, this resort pioneered Kids Ski Free—free lift tickets, free lodging, and even free rentals for kids to age 12 with parents on a multiday stay at the many participating properties. There's also a reduced teen ticket, and the nursery and kids' ski school comprise some of the biggest and most respected children's programs in the Rockies.

Finally, if you have any extra time at all—a big *if* at Steamboat—you may want to consider a hot-air balloon ride. These are offered at several Colorado resorts, but the wide Yampa River Valley below the ski mountain is ideal for ballooning. Several companies offer a variety of silent excursions in their multicolored *montgolfiers.*

Down in the Valley, Below the Mountain

Steamboat is definitely a mountain to fall in love with, but there is not so much visual charm about the base—either the newish ski village at the base of Mount Werner or old-town Steamboat a few miles away—to make you lose your head. The functional base development offers good facilities, hotels, lodges, and condo-style units; a good selection of eateries, sport stores, conventional and even offbeat shops; and good service with a good attitude. In short, it has all the amenities you'd expect at a first-class Rocky Mountain ski resort, but not a lot of character.

The main centers at the base of the ski mountain, Gondola Square and Ski Time Square, are integrated multilevel plazas and arcades. No matter where you stay, you'll probably partake of some après-ski merriment here. Among the end-of-day hotspots is the Bear River Bar & Grill, with a mammoth 5,000-square-foot outdoor deck. You can easily stroll from one cluster of activity to another in minutes, and it will probably be several nights before you've explored it thoroughly.

Lodging at the base is mainly in stylish, modern condo/apartment blocks that are all within easy walking distance of the slopes. There are two full-service hotels, the Sheraton Steamboat, which has recently undergone much-needed renovation and refurbishment, and the newer and larger Steamboat Grand Resort Hotel, a timeshare (oops, fractional ownership) property with attractive units, full hotel services, and The Cabin, one of the Yampa Valley's top fine-dining choices. The base development has sprawled from this quasi-village core, up both sides of the ski terrain and down toward the highway. Relatively few properties are now ski-in, ski-out or within walking distance of the lifts, but the free bus service is good—so park your vehicle and leave it.

Downtown Steamboat Springs retains much of is laid-back ambience. Just look at Howelsen Hill, the ultimate locals' sports facility, where Steamboat youngsters train for slalom or mogul skiing, ski jumping, or cross-country skiing—or sometimes play hockey, skate, or just hang with their friends at the rink or base lodge for the evening. Winter Carnival, a late-January or early-February highlight that started in 1913 and is still going strong, features such attractions as the local high school's marching band on skis, a snowcat ballet, ski-joring, sleighs on parade, and all manner of merriment—right down Main Street. Still, the town has morphed from being only a working-class ranch town to a full-blown ski resort as well. Now in addition to such classic Western-wear purveyors as F.M. Light's, that has been selling to real cowpokes and visiting dudes for decades, downtown offers the usual resort compliment of fine restaurants, lively nightspots, shops, boutiques, home-furnishing emporiums, and art galleries.

One advantage of having an honestly Western ranch town nearby is that you can organize a week's lodging at almost any price range imaginable, from slope-side deluxe to a modest downtown motel. Even though real-estate values have skyrocketed, second (and third) homes creep up hillsides and side valleys, and restaurants and shops now are beginning to match those elsewhere in the Rockies. Yet no one can call Steamboat pretentious, nor is it self-consciously pricey. It's just a neat place to ski and stay at.

Steamboat Data

Mountain Statistics

Vertical feet	3,633 feet (top of Morningside lift);
	3,668 feet (hike to)
Base elevation	6,900 feet
Summit elevation	10,533 feet (top of Morningside lift);
	10,568 feet (hike to)
Longest run	3+ miles
Average annual snowfall	337 inches
Snowmaking	438 acres
Number of lifts	20: 1 eight-passenger gondola; 4 high-speed quads;
	1 fixed-grip quad; 6 triples; 6 doubles; 2 surface lifts
Uphill capacity	36,195 skiers per hour
Skiable terrain	2,939 acres
Opening date	Late November
Closing date	Mid-April
Snowboarding	Yes

Transportation

By car About 160 miles northwest of Denver. Take I-70 west through the Eisenhower Tunnel to the Silverthorne exit (exit 205), then north on Colorado Highway 9 to Kremmling and west on U.S. 40 over Rabbit Ears Pass to Steamboat Springs.

By plane Yampa Valley Regional Airport, about half-an-hour from Steamboat Springs, has nonstop ski-season flights from a number of major cities via American, Continental, Northwest, and United, and connecting flights from Denver on United/United Express.

By limo or bus Alpine Taxi operates airport transportation; (800) 343-7433.

Key Phone Numbers

Ski-area information	(970) 879-6111
Snow report	(970) 879-7300
Reservations	(800) 922-2722 or (970) 879-0740
Website	www.steamboat-ski.com

Lito's TECH TIP

Trees without Fear

Becoming an expert is a reasonable, practical goal that I really believe most skiers can achieve with enough patience and practice. (In fact, my book *Breakthrough on Skis* and my videos of the same title are based on this premise, and they both outline a straightforward path to expert skiing.) So just what does Steamboat reserve for expert skiers? Powder. Aspens. And often both together. The combination is dynamite.

When skiing the trees, the ability to make good short turns is a must. In periods between storms, you'll even encounter moguls, not mean moguls but still moguls, among these trees. But I repeat: Steamboat tree skiing is not just for heroes; these are actually the easiest forests to ski in Colorado. For a strong skier, the experience involves far more pleasure than challenge. For much of this last section I've been raving about the beauty of Steamboat's trees, aspen glades that are universally considered to offer the finest tree skiing in Colorado. But I know that not everyone feels at home among these tall, slender, white trunks. When compared with the middle of a large, well-groomed run, tree skiing—even friendly, Steamboat-style tree skiing—can seem cramped, restrictive, and, with so many arboreal obstacles, downright intimidating. Here are a few tips to help you make peace with these noble trees.

True, you need good short turns to ski among trees. You also need an antici-pated style, a quiet upper body aimed more or less down the hill while legs and skis turn from side to side beneath you, and, above all, a rapid decisive pole plant. Your pole plant is the trigger that launches a good short turn, and if you hesitate with your pole, you'll probably hesitate to turn your skis too, and, whoops! Here comes that tree trunk.

To ski well among trees, whether tight trees or widely spaced Steamboat trees, you have to plan ahead and you have to get rid of that "what if" anxiety. What if I don't make the next turn? What if I hit a tree? You won't. Because if you're about to hit a tree you can just sit down in the snow. Not very elegant to be sure, but very safe. You certainly won't be skiing at high speeds among trees, so you can always "save yourself" from disaster by just bailing out and sitting down. Once you realize this, and maybe do it once or twice, you just won't worry about hitting trees anymore. As I've said, Steamboat has some of the friendliest, most widely spaced aspen groves in the West. Tree skiing is almost too easy.

Like a chess player, you'll want to plot your strategy several moves or turns in advance. Look up, look ahead, and keep adjusting your line to take you toward the widest gaps between tree trunks. If you look at your ski tips, you're lost.

Any time you're skiing through or near trees, you should also make a point of taking the straps of your ski poles off your wrists. If you snag a pole on a twig or branch, this will keep you from spraining your wrist, or worse.

Finally, at an area where tree skiing is as popular as it is at Steamboat, you'll often find moguls between the trees. What then? No big deal; simply use these moguls—incipient or fully formed—to ski with less effort than you might other-wise. By always initiating your turns on the high spot or crest of the bump, which serves as a free pivot point for your skis, you can turn with far less speed than you usually use. While you're getting used to navigating through trees, less speed is definitely a blessing. It gives you that much more time to look ahead and plan your route through these giant, inviting, but inflexible slalom poles.

Winter Park

In Colorado skiing, Winter Park is an exception to the norm in more ways than one. It's a very big ski mountain (two mountains, really—or more, depending on the way you parse the peaks), but it is neither a major nor a particularly well-known ski-vacation destination. For decades, Winter Park has been a publicly owned ski area, whose lifts and runs were owned by the city of Denver and operated by a not-for-profit corporation). The ski area's tradition included a wonderful management philosophy, focused exclu-sively on delivering the best ski experience for the best price, rather than

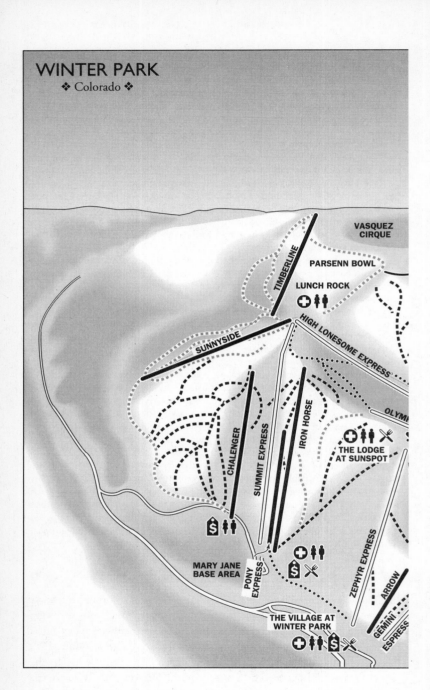

WINTER PARK
❖ Colorado ❖

VASQUEZ CIRQUE

PARSENN BOWL

TIMBERLINE

LUNCH ROCK

HIGH LONESOME EXPRESS

SUNNYSIDE

OLYMP

CHALENGER

SUMMIT EXPRESS

IRON HORSE

THE LODGE AT SUNSPOT

MARY JANE BASE AREA

PONY EXPRESS

ZEPHYR EXPRESS

ARROW

GEMINI

ESPRESS

THE VILLAGE AT WINTER PARK

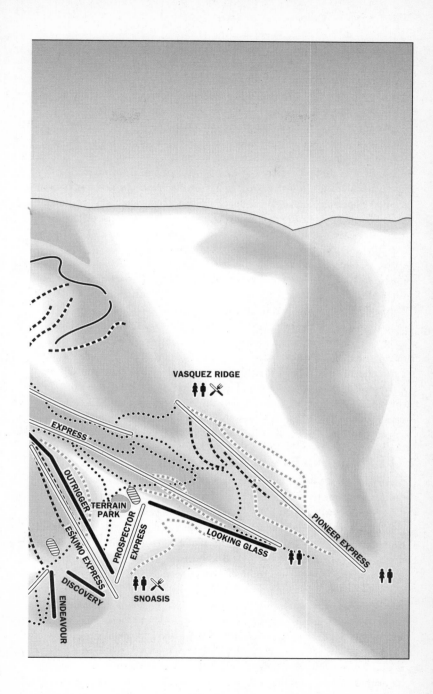

playing a real-estate game in parallel with ski-area operations, as is so often the case. At the end of the 2002–2003, this era came to end, when Winter Park joined the Intrawest family, along with Copper Mountain and such out-of-state powerhouses as Whistler/Blackcomb, Tremblant, Stratton, Snowshoe, and real estate developments elsewhere in snow country.

But Intrawest has a reputation for enhancing resorts that it takes over, and the odds are that Winter Park will still remain a very special place to ski. It is a mecca for expert skiers in search of a challenge, but it also introduces to the sport more beginners to skiing and snowboarding than any other Rocky Mountain area. It has also developed the finest handicapped skier program in the country and may be the last ski area in the U.S. West that you can reach by ski train, week in and week out.

Winter Park lies just on the north side of Berthoud Pass, a 11,315-foot gap in the ranks of high, rounded mountains lining both sides of I-70, Colorado's main auto route across the Rockies. Winter Park-bound visitors branch off this freeway about halfway between Denver and the Continental Divide, turn north, and zigzag up and over the recently widened Berthoud Pass through steep, densely timbered slopes. This is classic Colorado front range country, with dark green mountains, narrow, shadowy valleys, and, for the motorist, slow and twisting roads. The road winds down the far side of the pass into an open rolling valley called Middle Park, and there is Winter Park. It is novel to drive downhill to a ski area, alerted only by a few big signs and a couple of ski runs barely seen through the trees, and turn off a small highway onto an even smaller "way" in search of the area's base facilities and parking lots. Nothing about your arrival at Winter Park will make you think that it's really a big ski area.

The Shape and Feel of the Mountain

There are two bases and two distinct, although interconnected, main mountains. You reach the first base area off the highway via a fairly narrow, winding access road. This is Mary Jane, named after an old mining claim. About a mile farther along is the main base area of the original ski mountain, Winter Park proper. Most of the terrain is out of sight from the bottom—from either bottom. Additionally, Vasquez Ridge on the far side of Winter Park seems to qualify as a separate peak, but as it has no road access, the division into two ski areas—Winter Park and Mary Jane—makes more sense in terms of crafting an image of the place. Winter Park has many outlying day-skier parking lots, an efficient bus system, and thousands of regulars who know the routine and the bus routes.

Mary Jane is Winter Park's more challenging half, where the easiest runs are serious blues, where the big bumps live. This sector, specifically its front-side trails, is almost entirely responsible for Winter Park's reputation among serious, hot, young skiers. The top portion is accessed by three long chairs running parallel up the front face. The middle one, the Summit Express, is a high-speed detachable quad that gets most of the traffic. When weekend skiers fill its maze, some skiers move onto the Challenger and Iron Horse lifts, which are slower, traditional double chairs but provide an alternative to a full maze. All the runs on the front of Mary Jane end up right at the main Mary Jane base.

Mary Jane also has a secondary base at the Utah Junction parking lot and the base of the Challenger double chair. Earlybirds looking for first tracks on Mary Jane's steeps park here and hop on the lift, unworried about its low capacity and conventional speed, because it offers the most direct access to Mary Jane's most spectacular steeps.

Both sides of Mary Jane's front face are equally steep, fierce, or "interesting," depending on your point of view. What the trail map labels as *Mary Jane's Back Side* is more the left flank of the mountain (looking up) than the actual back. It is served by the Sunnyside triple chair. All the runs there dead-end into a long, dull comeback road called *Corona Way.* To avoid Corona Way, take the Sunnyside triple back up, and do laps on the back side, make your way over to the Winter Park, or ski Parsenn Bowl (see below for both). A double chair opens up some lovely, above tree line skiing in Parsenn Bowl, a high, open area behind the former "summit" of Mary Jane. Beyond that lies Vasquez Cirque, which offers some of the steepest bowl skiing in Colorado.

Because the Winter Park side is so spread out, orientation is a challenge on this complex, multisummited, multiridged ski mountain. Every high point seems to offer alternative ski routes down two sides. After a while, you might lose the notion of front and back, realizing that this ski area meanders over numerous ridges and down numerous valleys or drainages. The trail map lists 100 designated trails. Don't take this too seriously; Winter Park is big, but not that big! The task of orientation isn't made easier by the enthusiasm with which the mountain crew seems to have baptized every single slot, opening, gap in the trees, or shortcut from one run to another with a trail name of its own. In a simplified overview, Winter Park (*sans* Mary Jane) would be divided into four zones. The first, directly above the base (making it the front face), has some really serious black and blue-black runs. One of the most visible from the base is *Hughes,* a classic, steep racing trail that always seems to be hosting a competition. A number of easier runs comes back in from the right side, from somewhere around the corner. The Zephyr Express, the quickest route to the summit of the front zone, also accesses the back side of the mountain, an altogether different sort of ski domain with lots of long, inviting, easy blue and green runs. Half the runs drop down into a long valley served by Olympia Express. This valley has runs of its own, and the lift is a key link as the obvious route for Winter Park skiers to access Mary Jane's runs.

The rest of the runs from the Zephyr Express unload tend to curve down around to the right, funneling skiers into a wide, flat area with a large warming hut/restaurant complex called the Snoasis.

Behind Snoasis rises a sort of overgrown hill (or minimountain) served by two short lifts from opposite sides and offering short runs of every difficulty. You can ski here or cross over this minisummit to reach the last skiing zone, Vasquez Ridge. (As an alternative, you can reach Vasquez Ridge also by skiing down below Olympia Express.) Vasquez Ridge is a long, low-angle ridge that offers runs of varying degrees of challenge but all ending with a very long, flat run-out. Served by the Pioneer Express lift, Vasquez Ridge's terrain tends to be friendly, mostly unchallenging, and uncrowded, but it's a major undertaking to get back to the main Winter Park areas via the long Olympia Express.

Crossing back and forth between Mary Jane and Winter Park demands a bit of forethought. The base and the top of Mary Jane are higher than the base and the top of Winter Park. You can easily ski down from Mary Jane's base to Winter Park's base, and do relatively easily from Mary Jane's summit to Winter Park's. Getting from Winter Park to Mary Jane, however, requires two lift rides, even if you just want to move from base to base.

Obviously, less-experienced skiers find the back side of Winter Park more to their liking; dyed-in-the-wool experts head right for Mary Jane, and skiers in between (the majority) can find some runs to their liking almost everywhere on these twin mountains.

Winter Park for Inexperienced Skiers

Winter Park's Groswold Discovery Park, named after the resort's long-term president, is one of the finest learning areas in all the land. From the main Winter Park base, ride the Gemini Express to a broad green-circle paradise served by two slow-moving lifts. All the slopes are very, very gentle, but they are prettier than an average beginner area, because they are away from the congested base and are lined by trees. This gives the feeling of really skiing and being on a mountain—from day one.

The next step is *Parkway,* an easy green trail back to the base area. Better skiers use it as a good warm-up just to get their ski legs back. Try to avoid *Interstate.* Though marked as the "easiest way down," it's altogether too roundabout and too flat to enjoy unless you're a rank beginner. If your first run seems comfortable, take right off for the top via the left-hand base lift, the Zephyr Express. Don't get psyched out by the steeper runs you'll ride over on this chair. All your skiing will take place on mild runs off the top, all directly accessed by the Olympia Express or Eskimo Express.

From the top—a rendezvous point where the Lodge at *Sunspot* is located—head straight back a hundred yards or so. Turn right, down a blue run called *Cramner* or go a little farther, past a line of trees separating these runs, and take the next run, a green trail called *Allan Phipps*. At first, everything on this side of the mountain seems almost the same. As you head down, the runs on the right steepen and those on your left remain flatter. Take your choice. You can also choose whether to contour right around the mountain by following *Allan Phipps* or to continue to go more or less straight down to Olympia Express on *March Hare* or *Mad Tea Party*. Olympia generally offers the best skiing for strong novices or weaker, less-experienced intermediates.

Two other options will help stave off the boredom of always remaining on one part of the mountain. One is to ski down to the Pioneer Express quad, and from its top ski on Vasquez Ridge by sticking to *Gunbarrel* and *Lonesome Whistle*. The blue runs on Vasquez Ridge tend to be more difficult and demanding than the blue runs served by Olympia Express. There's also the Mary Jane adventure suitable for novices and tentative intermediates. From the top of Mary Jane are several very long, very easy, and very scenic green routes back down to the Winter Park side. The best of these is *Switchyard*. There's definitely enough easy skiing to give even timid or inexperienced skiers the sense of exploring a big mountain.

Winter Park for Average Skiers

You're a good solid intermediate. What to expect? Where to go? There are so many runs, aimed in so many different directions, that it's all too easy to waste hours of your skiing day zigzagging around the mountain with no game plan, getting stuck on a lot of the road-like connectors that abound at Winter Park. If you are a fairly strong but not overly bold or ambitious skier, you'll find the most enjoyable upper-intermediate skiing on the two opposite sides of the mountain, the far side of Vasquez Ridge and the back-side slopes of Mary Jane. Many skiers who fit this description either ignore or spend little time on the blue slopes of the middle section of Winter Park above Snoasis, because they are excellent cruisers and great confidence-builders and are easy to reach.

Such Vasquez Ridge blue runs as *Stagecoach, Sundance,* and *Quickdraw* have plenty of character. They twist and turn; their pitch and contour change often; their steeps flatten out before they can psych you out; and when moguls appear, they do so in inviting patches rather than forbidding phalanxes. The only flaw with Vasquez skiing, as on any long ridge, is that runs follow a natural fall line down the flank of the ridge but always feels as if they bottom out too soon. As a result, you'll wind up skiing the flats along *Big Valley* or *Wagon Train* at the end of every good run on Vasquez Ridge.

In fact, it may strike you that the bottom terminal of the Pioneer Express has been placed a few hundred yards too low, at the bottom of the Vasquez Ridge zone; the last stretch seems to be pointless. There was a reason for this design. There is a concept (which might even come to pass some day, if Intrawest still likes the idea) of building a gondola directly from the Town of Winter Park to this section of the mountain, and the Pioneer placement might just have something to do with that possibility. In the meantime, the bottom of the Pioneer Express lift is placed in this unlikely spot where it is accessible to skiers and snowboarders returning from the upper Vasquez drainage, the high, white corniced bowls in the distance that are now known as Vasquez Cirque (see below).

The back side of Mary Jane offers real open-glade skiing through a naturally thinned-out, high-altitude forest in *Wildwood Glade* and *Belmont Bowl.* To reach it from the Mary Jane summit, ski past of the Sunnyside triple unload and angle down *Side Track,* segueing into the trees as the mood strikes you, or drop down to the Timberline chairlift. It leads to the 12,060-foot top of Parsenn Bowl. The upper reaches are tree-free snowfields, which lead into the timber. Several routes, including easy ones like *Juniper* and *Forget-Me-Not* and more challenging ones like *Willet's Way* and *Johnstone Junction,* lead through broad glades. The rule of thumb on Parsenn Bowl is that the farther from the lift you traverse, the steeper the pitch and the tighter the trees.

All of this high-Alpine terrain—Parsenn Bowl, Backside Parsenn off the skier's left of the bowl, and Vasquez Cirque (the latter discussed below but definitely off-limits for intermediates)—comprises a special treat at Winter Park, where most of the front-side forestation is so dense and dark. These open areas behind Mary Jane also offer the best views— sweeping panorama up to the big peaks on the Continental Divide rather than the endless succession of green timbered slopes at which one gazes (and soon comes to ignore) on the front side.

Winter Park is a good place for intermediates to push their skills and comfort levels up, one notch at a time. If you're a pretty fair skier who wants to start challenging steeper and bumpier slopes, take advantage of several trails marked on the trail map with a black diamond within a blue square. These are perfect transition runs on which to test yourself before attacking the real black diamonds. On the Mary Jane side, ski *Sleeper* before trying any of the black runs. On the main front face at Winter Park, try *Hughes* or *Bradley's Bash* (a smidgen harder) before tackling any blacks there. Several runs, including *Mary Jane* and *Cramner,* are partially groomed, so that beginning bump skiers can slide in and out of the moguls as they wish.

A trail map is necessary at Winter Park, a complex and multifaceted mountain, which has a lot to offer but also can be full of surprises, if you don't know where you are. Still, one of the advantages of skiing a complicated mountain is that, if you keep your wits about you, you can find slopes of virtually any difficulty on any exposure.

Winter Park for Very Strong Skiers

There are ski mountains in Colorado where the three-color, national trail-marking system has been skewed so far in one direction or the other that skiers can look at a blue square or black diamond sign and still not have a clue as to what sort of experiences, terrors, or delights await them. By happy contrast, Winter Park's rating system is extremely honest. If a trail is marked black, it is black, which means it's steep and there are plenty of bumps. On Mary Jane in particular, the black runs are not wimpy, but they're not ugly either. By tradition and reputation, Mary Jane's moguls are usually well formed, big and rhythmic, with rounded exit gullies, though with the great increase in mogul-riding snowboarders and short, shaped skis this has changed too. Still, compared to many other areas, Mary Jane's bumps don't get quite so hacked up and chopped off.

Outhouse and *Drunken Frenchman* drop down from the top of Winter Park into Mary Jane. Long and consistently pitched, they are a workout that begin to hint at the big-bump splendor that awaits. Either from the Challenger double or from the Summit Express via *Bellmar Bowl* are such back-side steeps as *Cannonball, Long Haul,* and *Short Haul.* They tend to be even straighter, steeper, and more continuous than Mary Jane's front-side, bump runs side—more fun too, once you're into double black mogul skiing.

Winter Park's black diamonds also signify real high-Alpine skiing. If you are ready, the gullies and short, cliff-like faces of the upper section of Mary Jane, around *Sluice Box* and *Pine Cliffs,* are good warm-ups for tackling the harder bump lines to skier's right. The dividing line between Mary Jane's front and back sides is a long, bumped-out ridge run called *Derailer,* and the area's hardest, best bump runs branch off *Derailer* on both sides.

The most difficult and certainly the most exciting runs in all of Winter Park are the three chutes—*Awe Chute, Baldy's Chute,* and *Jeff's Chute*—that drop off the back side of the *Derailer* ridge. They are reached via a special gate on the side of *Derailer,* furnished with a special and very sobering warning sign. If the conditions aren't adequate, that is to say if there isn't enough snow or the snow is too hard or icy, the patrol closes this gate. Take these runs very seriously. They are very steep, narrow, twisty, and rocky, and a fall could be dangerous. It's a tribute to the spirit of Winter Park management that these runs are marked and often open. As long as skiers and riders can continue to find challenges like this at ski areas, downhill skiing still qualifies as an adventure sport.

Of course, there's more to expert skiing than the pursuit, and mastery, of difficult runs—there's the aesthetic side as well. Experts willing to hike a bit will find a wonderful combination of high-Alpine aesthetics plus steep chutes and mixed open trees in the wilds of upper Vasquez Cirque, a remote drainage behind Parsenn Bowl.

Pass a gate at the top of Parsenn Bowl and make the long shuffling traverse along the ridge top to the Cirque, which is, by far, the Winter Park complex's most extreme terrain, challenging by any measure. If you just want to get the flavor of Vasquez Cirque, drop into *Belle Fourche* or *Boulevard,* single black diamonds relatively close to the access gate. If you are up for true challenge, continue traversing around the rim and dip off the cornice on any of the double-black-diamond steeps: *South Headwall, West Headwall,* or any of the *Alphabet Chutes* in Parsenn Bowl. The breathtaking drops are exciting but relatively short, and they feed into more excellent glades. The ski-out leads to the bottom of the Pioneer Express. To do laps, you need to take that lift, cut down to the High Lonesome Express via a green trail called *Gunbarrel,* and finally drop down to the Timberline chair from Lunch Rock. This makes for quite an excursion. Little wonder that snowboarders tend simply to hike back up the Cirque rather than making the circuitous roundtrip.

Snowboarding

Winter Park has been building and refining terrain features ever since riders demanded such facilities. Rail Yard is a recently reconfigured, highly visible park on Allan Phipps trail. The park begins with a series of jib features as rails, a teeter-totter, and a rainbow rail. The lower portion has two distinct lines, one with traditional features like tabletops and spines. The Rolls, a slope-style park designed for skier and boarder-cross events, features crescents, compression rolls, and spines. Vertigo is the half-pipe located below the terrain park and above Snoasis midmountain restaurant.

Some sections of Winter Park are so flat that they are not at all congenial for riders. Terrain like the Pioneer trails' runouts, *Turnpike, Cranmer Cut-Off,* and of course, *300-Yard Walk* are bad enough with two skis to push off from and poles to help. For riders, they are real slogs. However, the payoff at Winter Park is gorgeous fall-line runs where freeriders and freeskiers simply soar.

Base Facilities and Village

The base facility at the bottom of the main mountain is called the Village at Winter Park. It's a big complex of day lodges with shops and eateries, and, finally, Zephyr Lodge, the first hotel in what will be a legitimate base development directly at the bottom of the lifts. What you see today won't be what you get tomorrow, for Intrawest is known for designing and quickly creating user-friendly, slopeside villages. Expect a condo-dense development built around a pleasant plaza, built-in space for shops and restaurants, and parking out of the way and out of sight.

But for the moment, the Winter Park ski-area base is an interesting hodgepodge of architecture, skier services, and good vibes. Vintage buildings, such as the old Balcony House day lodge with ticket windows and BYO lunchroom, are intact monuments to ski history, with a building style that could be called early Forest Service Tyrolean—but they are scheduled for replacement. Next door, West Portal Station is an impressive cubist structure of corrugated metal and glass—an integrated mini-mall of retail, rental, eating, and drinking spots that really works. Sun decks everywhere face the mountain, and a classic, timeless après-ski scene with collegiate overtones of beer drinking and girl- and guy-watching is under way here long before the lifts close. Beyond is Winter Park's outstanding children's center, including both nursery and kids' ski-school facilities. The kids' program is one of the best in the West. Mary Jane Center is one rambling, functional day lodge, with a big cafeteria, pizzeria, lively bar, and a deck that is too small on nice days.

One of Winter Park's "base" experiences is actually at the summit. The Lodge at Sunspot is a large and attractive lodge with a cafeteria, a sit-down restaurant, and commanding mountain views. Crowded at lunch, it also puts on dinners with access via gondola cars hung on the Zephyr Express cable and an optional mountaintop snowcat tour. Until Intrawest took over, these dinners were offered only on weekends, but there is the possibility of adding more days as Winter Park's resort component increases.

Old Town of Winter Park, just down the road from the Winter Park ski area base and off U.S. 40, offers a few places to stay and play, but most of the services are in the Town of Winter Park. Calling this agglomeration of shops, services, and lodging a town is not sufficient to make it feel like one. The base development is not yet a village, Old Town Winter Park is also tiny, and the Town of Winter Park certainly doesn't feel like a Colorado ski town. This is the big flaw in Winter Park's offering, but it certainly will change.

The Town of Winter Park is an unplanned, underdeveloped strip. This loose collection of random-access parking lots and shopping, eating, and lodging facilities thrown up in the woods on either side of U.S. 40 runs for a couple of miles. It is one of those less-than-urban assemblies where the individual elements may work (for example, there are a couple of wonderful 1940s-style, dark, wooden lodges and a couple of really handsome contemporary condo castles). Still, nothing is tied to anything else, and there's no center, no pedestrian-friendliness, and no harmonious local character. Enough said.

Is it too late? Maybe not. It's easy enough to see why a proper town didn't develop along U.S. 40. For years and years, Winter Park was little more than the classic popular weekend destination for Denver skiers. After a remarkable period of ski-area expansion, Winter Park's mountain facilities are now on a par with Colorado's other destination resorts. Maybe a well-planned development will be created at the base of the mountain or a hot ski town will grow out of the chaos down the road.

Winter Park Data

Winter Park Statistics

Total vertical feet	3,060 feet
Base elevation	9,000 feet (Winter Park)
Summit elevation	12,060 feet (Parsenn Bowl)
Longest run	5.1 miles (combined North Cone to Turnpike)
Average annual snowfall	367 inches
Snowmaking	294 acres
Number of lifts	22: 8 high-speed quads; 4 triples; 7 doubles; 3 moving carpets
Uphill capacity	36,230 skiers per hour
Skiable terrain	2,886 acres
Opening date	Mid-November
Closing date	Mid-April
Snowboarding	Yes

Transportation

By car A 90-minute drive from Denver. Take I-70 west to Empire exit (Exit 232), and drive west on U.S. 40 over Berthoud Pass.

By limo or van Home James operates ski shuttles from Denver International Airport and the resort (85 miles); call (800) 729-5813 or (970) 726-5587.

By train Daily scheduled service to Granby from San Francisco and Chicago on Amtrak's California Zephyr; (800) USA-RAIL. Shuttles meet the train. Also, between mid-December and early April, The Ski Train has service from Denver Friday, Saturday, Sunday, as well as the Christmas- New Year and February holiday periods. It leaves Union Station at 7:15 a.m. directly to the base of Winter Park, and leaves Winter Park to return to Denver at 4:15 p.m. Reservations are required; (800) 729-5813.

Key Phone Numbers

Ski-area information	(970) 726-5514 or (303) 892-0961
Snow report	(970) 726-SNOW or (303) 572-SNOW
Reservations	(800) 729-5813 or (970) 726-5587
	(800) 903-7275 or (970) 726-4118
Websites	www.skiwinterpark.com, www.winterpark-info.com

Lito's TECH TIP

Basic Bumps

Bumps (or "moguls") on a ski slope can delight or frustrate. Personally, I love them, but I know that most skiers don't, which is natural if they have a hard time skiing them. Even if these skiers don't have a hard time turning, they may have a hard time feeling and staying poised and comfortable from turn to turn to turn.

The reason bumps exist at all is because any little high spot or lump on the slope, serving as a natural pivot point, facilitates turning your skis. Skiers figure this out early and use bumps (whether they enjoy bump skiing or not) to trigger or launch their turns. The real problem comes in putting it all together, staying in balance on a moguled slope, controlling your speed in the limited space available, and arriving at the end of one bump turn poised, comfortable, and ready for the next. In a word, finishing a bump turn well is harder than starting that turn.

Start your bump turns the way you always do—only less so. By this I mean that when you cross over the top of a bump, don't pivot your skis as hard as you normally do. Trust in the fact that your skis will follow the scraped-out hollow of the bump's trough. That's right, the round shape of the turn is already there in the rounded shape of the bump's gully; all you need to do is let your skis drift. They will follow the curved gully in an arc that brings you around under the bump.

Most skiers who have trouble with bumps simply over pivot their skis on the very top. They complete the entire turning action in the first foot or two and find themselves out of balance, with their skis jammed sideways or crosswise to the gully at its narrowest point. One reason skiers seem to have a hard time just letting their skis drift on down through the gully is an anxiety about picking up too much speed. It's true, you will go a little faster right in the middle of each turn as you're coming around the side of the bump. But you will finish each turn underneath the bump, where you'll have more room to turn your skis sideways without getting them caught in the gully.

So, this should be your basic pattern for comfortable bump skiing: a slow start, pivoting your skis just enough to get them into the turn; a relaxed middle phase drifting around the bump, letting your skis follow the rounded gully; and finally, an active finish below the bump where you actually turn your skis as far across the slope as you want to slow down. Remember, slow down beneath the bump, not in the middle.

Loveland

Loveland is the closest ski area to Denver along what is known as "the I-70 corridor." Skiers by the thousands drive by this ski area, which is nestled under and spread out above the East Portal of the Eisenhower Tunnel, without pausing. Perceptions notwithstanding, it is definitely worth a stop—either en route to or from Denver International Airport for an extra few hours on a legitimately down-home mountain or even as a worthy destination.

Loveland is a relatively modest ski area, but it is one of the state's oldest. Since it opened in 1937, it has remained a day area, with the nearest lodging in Georgetown, 12 miles away. The main base area is only a stone's throw from the twin tunnels where I-70 plunges under these peaks en route from Denver to Dillon, to Vail, and, ultimately, to Grand Junction and points west. Even from the highway, you can see that just above this base—above the tunnel—everything changes.

Loveland is a real gem that offers some stunning scenery and, even better, a ski experience that's hard to find elsewhere. Loveland has a lot to offer: a high base elevation, grandiose, above-tree line terrain; the world's highest quad chair; Colorado's second-highest average annual snowfall (after Wolf Creek, which does not appear in this guide); and a

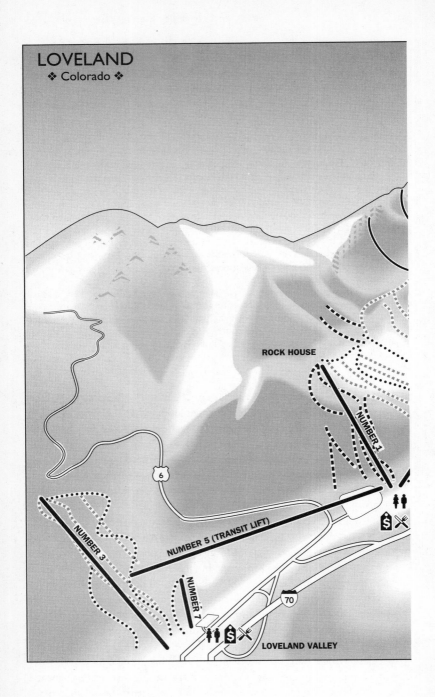

LOVELAND
❖ Colorado ❖

ROCK HOUSE

NUMBER 1

6

NUMBER 3

NUMBER 5 (TRANSIT LIFT)

NUMBER 7

70

LOVELAND VALLEY

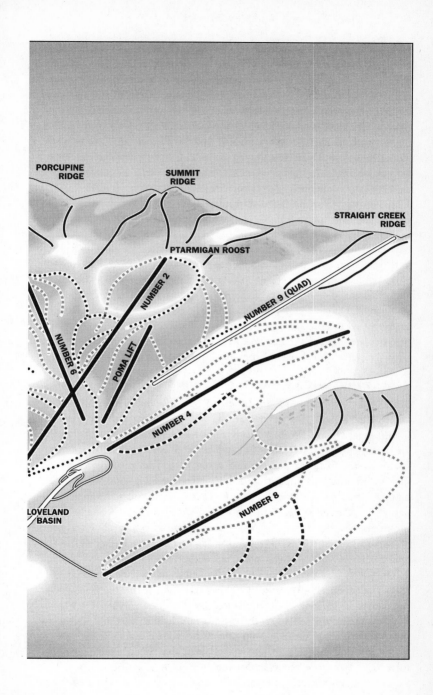

PORCUPINE
RIDGE

SUMMIT
RIDGE

STRAIGHT CREEK
RIDGE

PTARMIGAN ROOST

NUMBER 2

NUMBER 9 (QUAD)

POMA LIFT

NUMBER 6

NUMBER 4

NUMBER 8

LOVELAND
BASIN

steady record of being the state's first or second area to crank up its lifts every ski season. Still, Loveland has not been part of the white revolution of high-speed lifts that has transformed skiing in general and Colorado skiing in particular. Loveland seems virtually deserted on weekdays (except on a powder day when front range schools and even offices are closed). Even on weekends, when the parking lots fill up mostly with Denver cars, it still doesn't seem full or crowded. If you find yourself with some time while traveling to or from a major destination resort, stop at Loveland. To make it easy, the area even sells a reduced-priced ticket good for any four hours during the ski day.

In addition to several fixed-grip quads and triples, the rest of the lifts are old double chairs painted a shade of powder blue that somehow makes them look even older than they are. Even recent upgrades of its base facilities haven't eliminated the area's wonderful old-fashioned feeling. The whole Loveland experience seems to come straight out of another place and time. For one thing, the daily skiing ticket is cheap by Colorado standards. For another, in this age of heightened ski-area liability concerns and general corporate uptightness, there are places at Loveland where the ski-area boundary is left vague, where the distinction between tamed ski area and wild mountainscape is no longer clear. This is exactly what I like most about Loveland skiing.

The Layout and Feel of the Mountain

Strike that word "mountain." Loveland is a bowl or high Alpine basin rather than a peak. It's set among the high summits and ridges of the Continental Divide. Treeline is only a few hundred feet above the parking lot, but the dense forest thins out quickly and disappears altogether in a last scattering of sparse and stunted dwarf trees. The world turns white; snowy basins and distant corniced ridges alternate with windswept, rocky, patchy cliffs. The eye ranges unchecked across wide and wide-open snow basins—an Alpine rather than sub-Alpine world, an unmistakable, high-mountain feeling. Except for the highest headwalls and chutes—some lift-served, some hike-to—Loveland skiing isn't ultra-challenging, but the wild nature of the landscape makes it feel that way.

The ski area has two parts. They are linked by a long horizontal chairlift (Lift 5) that exists only to shuttle skiers back and forth, but hardly ever runs anymore, having been supplanted by shuttle vans. The first section that you see on the left when driving west on I-70 is Loveland Valley. To get to it, turn left at the exit ramp (if coming from Denver). It has a short, gentle beginner slope with its own chairlift that is ideal for those first turns, and a cluster of blue-square runs served by a fixed-grip quad. The valley's biggest plus is that beginners have their own slope, well away from more advanced traffic. Its second-biggest plus is that the blue runs off the quad are flanked by trees, not a trivial thing on blustery, white-out days.

Next is Loveland Basin, which spreads out above the freeway tunnel and is the "real" ski area. Five chairlifts fan out in a semicircle into all sides of the basin above the highway. As you look up from the main base area, the far-left chair (Lift 1) is the steepest and serves respectable, even fierce, black bump runs, as well as a number of interesting blues that sweep around into the center of the basin. While this triple serves Loveland's most technically demanding runs, it is not necessarily where you'll find the most beautiful skiing. Since this section is densely treed, it doesn't share in that high, above-timberline atmosphere found elsewhere at the ski area. Still, the triple is always the first lift to open (in October, usually), but it takes a while for the black runs to open. These runs, Loveland Basin's easternmost, wear double diamonds. *Over the Rainbow* dives down through some steep trees, and *Avalanche Bowl* is wider but equally steep.

To get right into the Loveland feeling, however, hop onto Lift 2, another triple. It serves the middle of an expansive bowl that seems to invite you to ski in any and all directions, which is just what you probably will do. Although named "runs" or "lines" are indicated on the trail map, there are few boundaries between them until you get back down into trails through the trees. The open nature of the terrain quickly tempts you into a more dashing, free-form style of skiing: big-turn cruising, where you look for mountain shapes to turn on rather than just repeating your same old moves down the middle of a well-defined run. The stunted, tree-like vegetation, often resembling evergreen bushes more than mini-trees, gives you widely spaced points of green by which to turn around. Rolls, dips, and gullies lend themselves to flowing, smooth, high-speed skiing. However, if you see a wide patch of untracked snow that tempts you, it might just be one of the snow-filled hollows, so instead of making first tracks, you might find yourself shuffling through the deep till you get back to some pitch.

Just beside the top of Lift 2, you'll see a wooden chalet-like structure. Ah ha, you think, a snack bar or top-of-the-mountain restaurant. Nope, it's a picnic hut called Ptarmigan Roost. Just the idea of a ski area not exploiting this spot and leaving the hut for those who pack their lunch in a rucksack takes you back to an earlier, more romantic era. If you feel like dashing down to the base to buy lunch in the cafeteria and taking it up the lift with you to enjoy, along with the view, at this old-time warming hut, do it.

For years, the top of Lift 2 was the high point of the lift system, but now a fixed-grip quad lift, Lift 9, ascends all the way up to a ridge on the Continental Divide at 12,700 feet. Loveland boasts that this is the highest quad lift in the world. It accesses more wide-open, above-timberline terrain, an area loosely known as *The Ridge*. The uppermost section of this summit cirque is Loveland's steepest lift-served terrain. Strong, ambitious, and well-acclimated skiers can hike even higher and drop into the topmost bowls from high summit ridges at just over 13,000 feet. This is Loveland skiing at its best. You can traverse a long way to the right or left, into and through a number of Loveland's high basins, and you'll explore without keeping score, because, again, the different "runs" all tend to blur together. The real pleasure at Loveland is that sense of not being hemmed in by the boundaries of any particular run. You can head in any direction you please and know it's okay—just over that roll, on the other side of that boulder, beyond that tiny grove of trees, there'll be more open slopes waiting. It doesn't feel like typical Colorado skiing. *Vive la différence!*

Around the Corner, Far Away

Years before Loveland opened The Ridge, there was the skiing in Zip Basin, the farthest right-hand aspect of the overall Alpine basin when looking up from below and on the other side of the interstate from the main base area. Zip Basin is accessed by a fixed-grip quad lift (Lift 8), but is like a private ski area within a ski area, because reaching it requires some effort. You either follow *Zip Trail* from the mid-station of Lift 4 or take a roundabout (but more scenic) route, traversing to the left from the top of Lift 4 and staying high. With this option you actually go around the shoulder of a peak, turn the corner, and come out at the top of a long series of open treeless slopes that constitute Zip Basin. These slopes drop away to the left into a sort of gully way down below you. Surprisingly, you will have skied clear out of sight of the section of the ski area that you just crossed. Still, you can look across the valley and the Interstate to the tiny bumps off Lift 1. Zip Basin, above all, invites you to stay there, around the corner for a number of runs. Its skiing is very much like a miniature version of Vail's Back Bowls, a very Alpine experience.

Even though Loveland itself never seems crowded, Zip Basin seems to get even less traffic. The terrain is continuous, never very steep, and always inviting. It's not always clear where the ski area stops, and it doesn't seem to matter because any line you ski will funnel you down into the natural drainage of a side valley that slants back to the bottom of Lift 8. *The Plunge,* just beneath the Chair 8 unload, is the steepest parcel, while *Zip Basin Street, Awesome,* and *Stardust* are the best wide cruisers. Trees on either side are skiable, especially after a snowstorm. There are two alternatives for getting back to the main ski area on the other side of a four-lane interstate highway. From the top of Lift 8 follow *Zippity Split* back to Lift 4 for an easy but roundabout route. A much faster option is to follow the continuation of *Awesome,* snaking down the creek-bed drainage below the Lift 8 loading area and finishing above the highway on a steep, usually moguled shoulder called *The Face*. From there, a small pedestrian/skier tunnel crosses under the freeway and brings you back to the Loveland base lodge.

Snowboarding

Loveland doesn't really *need* a snowboard park, because its abundant natural terrain features invite riders to let fly. Still, in 2002–03 the area built a new terrain park, with rails, hits, tabletops, and other features.

Loveland Data

Mountain Statistics

Vertical feet	2,410 feet (1,265 lift-served at Loveland Basin)
Base elevation	10,600 feet (Loveland Valley)
Summit elevation	12,700 feet (Loveland Basin; hike to 13,010 feet)
Longest run	2 miles
Average annual snowfall	400 inches
Snowmaking	160 acres
Number of lifts	11: 3 fixed-grip quad chairlifts; 2 triples; 4 doubles; 2 surface lifts
Uphill capacity	12,437 skiers per hour
Skiable terrain	1,365 acres; 100 acres for hiking
Opening date	Late November
Closing date	Mid-May
Snowboarding	Yes

Transportation

By car A 45-minute drive (in good road and weather conditions) from Denver's western suburbs, go west on I-70 to exit 216, just east of the Eisenhower Tunnel.

Key Phone Numbers

Ski-area information	(800) 736-3SKI, (303) 569-3202, or (303) 571-5580 (Denver direct)
Snow report	(800) 736-3SKI, (303) 569-3202, or (303) 571-5580 (Denver direct)
Reservations	(800) 225-5683
Website	www.skiloveland.com

Lito's TECH TIP

Stepping Out: Skiing Off-Piste

Off-piste is a wonderful expression and a wonderful feeling. European skiers call their ski runs "pistes" and use this expression to describe skiing away from prepared runs. This doesn't refer to just powder skiing but skiing in a mixed bag of variable, natural snow conditions. Skiing off-piste demands an adaptable and secure technique to cope with anything from wind-ruffled powder to breakable crust. The high, treeless basins at Loveland, exposed to sun and wind, are perfect places to experience the delights and frustrations of ungroomed, variable snow. Here are a few general tips and strategies to use whenever you ski in tricky, variable snow conditions.

Security first. Maybe the surface will support you, maybe it won't; if you have doubts, ski it slowly—high-speed tumbles are much riskier. Ski it on two feet with both skis equally weighted. This is the opposite of normal packed-slope technique, where you want to be exclusively balanced over your outside ski. But in unknown snow conditions, equal weighting gives you several advantages. If the snow surface has a light, unstable crust, you're less likely to break through with only half the weight on each ski, and if one ski does break through to become trapped inside or under the crust, then you've still got your other ski for support and turning while you try to get it—or them—back together.

For similar reasons, I suggest medium-radius turns in variable and tricky snow conditions.

If the snow seems extremely variable and catchy, you'll probably want to use a smooth, powerful up motion to start your turns. Add that snappy lifting of your outside hand and arm that I mentioned in connection with powder to punctuate this up movement. But don't simply jump in the air and turn your skis and come down hard; a hard landing can trap your skis again in deep, crusty snow. Instead, try to follow your smooth upward extension with an equally smooth progressive sinking to absorb some of the extra pressure of this landing.

In difficult variable snow I make an effort to lean or bank into my turns. This tilts my skis up in the snow and reduces the likelihood of catching an outside edge in the crust. This is not something I'd ever recommend on a packed slope, but it's helpful in heavy, difficult snow.

Summit County

Keystone The closest of the three largest Summit County ski areas to Denver, Keystone has three separate mountains to ski, long fall-line slopes, a superb snowmaking system, and efficient lifts. Keystone is mostly a cruiser's mountain. In addition to the original base village surrounding a frozen lake, a new village center called River Run brings Keystone into twenty-first-century resorthood. A wide choice of additional lodging is near the base or in nearby Dillon.

Arapahoe Basin The highest ski area in Colorado, A-Basin is also the smallest but the most spectacular Summit County ski area. A-Basin is a day area, not a full resort. Usually the last on the continent to close for the season, it's renowned for late-spring skiing in an Alpine, above-timberline setting. A-Basin is skiable on any lift ticket valid at Keystone, Breckenridge, Vail, or Beaver Creek—at least for now.

Breckenridge This former mining town is a popular destination resort, yet it remains the only true authentic historic ski town in Summit County. The ski area is spread out over four mountains and, like the town at its base, can absorb a lot of people. Breckenridge skiing offers a little of everything, plus proximity to Denver and the rest of Summit County.

Copper Mountain In addition to the full spectrum of Colorado-style, groomed-trail skiing, Copper Mountain has a series of intriguing, high, open bowls on a logically laid-out mountain. The village at the base has become a real purpose-built ski village. Located directly off I-70, it is the farthest of the Summit County areas from Denver but the easiest to reach.

Keystone

If there were such a thing as a prize for the most improved ski resort in Colorado, Keystone would win it time and again. During the revision of this guidebook, Keystone has reinvented itself, adding a whole new base

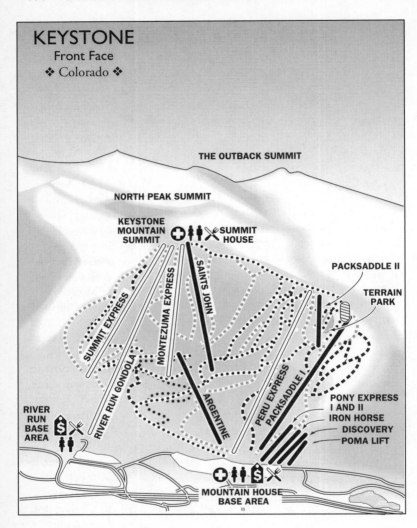

KEYSTONE
Front Face
❖ Colorado ❖

THE OUTBACK SUMMIT

NORTH PEAK SUMMIT

KEYSTONE
MOUNTAIN
SUMMIT

SUMMIT
HOUSE

PACKSADDLE II

TERRAIN
PARK

SUMMIT EXPRESS

MONTEZUMA EXPRESS

SAINTS JOHN

RIVER RUN GONDOLA

ARGENTINE

PERU EXPRESS

PACKSADDLE I

PONY EXPRESS
I AND II
IRON HORSE
DISCOVERY
POMA LIFT

RIVER
RUN
BASE
AREA

MOUNTAIN HOUSE
BASE AREA

village to its already considerable offering and polishing its already polished skier services to a new level.

Keystone is an unlikely success story in Colorado skiing; it's the little ski area that could. Hardly little any more, it has been beautifully organized, developed, and expanded to a degree no one—perhaps not even the visionaries who did it—would have believed possible. Keystone is not a great "natural" ski mountain, being a bit short on both natural snowfall and ideal skiing terrain. This is a densely forested, dark green mountain, so even the Keystone Mountain trail map, which after all is only an artist's idealized conception, looks a good deal greener than that of many other mountains (and I'm talking green forests, not green runs). But Keystone has been cut, carved, groomed, and honed into one of the state's biggest, most successful ski areas. It has consistently broken new ground in skier service, offering Colorado's first giant, modern snowmaking system, the state's largest night-skiing operation, two high-speed gondolas, and the first truly fine-dining mountaintop restaurant. All this has paid off, because Keystone has become both a top-ranked destination resort and a perennial favorite with Denver skiers. The ski terrain spreads over three interconnected mountains, one behind the other. First comes Keystone Mountain, a big, broad flank of forest-lined fairways and groomed sweeps that flow toward the valley for smooth and fast trail skiing. This is the original and main mountain, steadily improved with three high-speed quads and a high-speed, high-capacity gondola. Most runs tend to greens and blues, and it is here that night skiing takes place.

Next comes North Peak, the mountain behind the mountain. This was Keystone's first major expansion with new lifts, new exposures, new views, and generally more challenging skiing. North Peak instantly became a terrific addition to a mountain that was previously too heavily weighted toward novice and low-to-intermediate skiers, but it's been on-line for so long now that it feels as if it was always part of the Keystone experience. With its preponderance of black runs and very inviting bump skiing, it balances the spectrum at the upper end. The Outpost gondola links the Keystone Mountain and North Peak summits. Riders can take it in either direction. The Outpost day lodge perches high on North Peak, near the gondola terminus. The Santiago chair serves most of North Peak's runs, while the Wayback quad climbs up North Peak's back side and is also used by skiers and snowboarders returning from The Outback, Keystone's third linked mountain (see below). Finally, the Ruby lift, an express six-seater, is a faster return from North Peak to Keystone Mountain than the gondola.

The Outback is the most recent addition to the Keystone complex. Think of The Outback as the mountain behind the mountain behind the mountain. In other words, you must cross over North Peak to get there—which makes the Keystone-to-North Peak gondola a true shortcut. The Outback, well served by a single high-speed quad, boasts long runs and true fall lines, a very elegant and satisfying addition to Keystone skiing.

This layout, one mountain after another, tends to put skiers farther and farther from the base, but luckily, the layout doesn't oblige one to take boring roads and catwalks to get from one peak to the next. The "get-there" runs linking the different peaks provide attractive and sustained skiing. So if you're heading over to North Peak or on to The Outback, getting there can indeed be half the fun. Naturally, you'll need a few important strategies to find yourself at the right place at the right

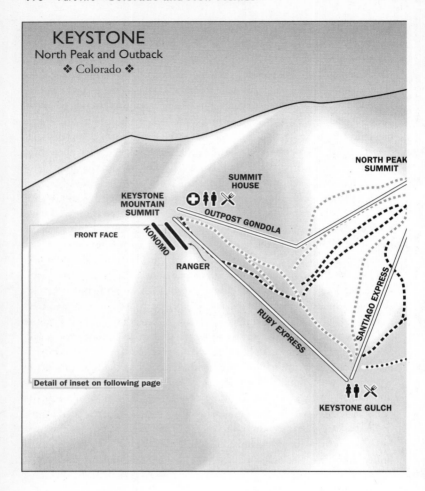

KEYSTONE
North Peak and Outback
❖ Colorado ❖

NORTH PEAK SUMMIT

SUMMIT HOUSE

KEYSTONE MOUNTAIN SUMMIT

OUTPOST GONDOLA

FRONT FACE

KONOMO

RANGER

RUBY EXPRESS

SANTIAGO EXPRESS

Detail of inset on following page

KEYSTONE GULCH

time of day in such a big ski complex, and we'll cover them in more detail a little later.

Keystone, of course, also has two, almost three, villages. The original resort spreads along two sides of Keystone Lake, frozen in winter and maintained as the country's largest ice surface. This attractive development was ultra-modern when it was conceived and it remains, like Keystone's mountains, more a triumph of hard work than of natural advantages. However, it isn't at the base of the ski mountain but linked by free, frequent shuttles.

Some lodging exists at the original Keystone Mountain base, but the most intriguing development is River Run, created by Intrawest, which ironically owns arch-rival Copper Mountain and now also operates Win-

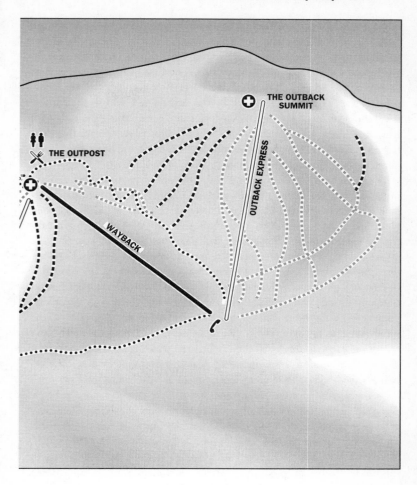

ter Park. The architecture and layout at River Run reflect Intrawest's successful formula: compact mid-rise condos with commercial space on the pedestrian level and parking hidden underneath, welcoming pedestrian plazas, and a harmonious theme (in this case, Colorado mining). Like everything Intrawest touches, the village center at River Run works.

Keystone Mountain: The "Front Door"

Keystone Mountain itself—the resort's first or "front" mountain—is as wide or wider from side to side as it is tall, an impression reinforced by the fact that it has two base locations. You have to start at one of them no matter where you wish to ski. The western portal, the original base and closer to Keystone Village, is focused around an attractive day lodge called the Mountain House, plus limited lodging. Farther east, up the Snake River Valley, is the eastern base—River Run Village—and the gondola rising all the way to the Summit House in one straight shot.

The terrain divides neatly into thirds. The first third, the east side of Keystone Mountain, is served by the River Run gondola and the Summit Express. The center is served by the Argentine lift from the Mountain House base and by two higher chairs, the Montezuma Express quad and the Saints John double. The western side is served by the Peru Express and the two Packsaddle doubles. (Many of the lifts here, as you may already have guessed, are named after historic mine sites.)

The green and blue runs that snake down the front mountain at Keystone are long with relatively few trail intersections, so cross-traffic is seldom a problem. However, there's a remarkable similarity among the long blue runs at the center of the mountain. It's sometimes hard to tell runs like *Flying Dutchman, Frenchman,* and *Paymaster* apart. By contrast, the far-western side, served by the two Packsaddle doubles, has more character than the rest of the front face—not necessarily better skiing, but more distinctive skiing. On a big forested mountain like Keystone, runs can begin to resemble one another. *Packsaddle Bowl* at the top of this sector is unique because it is Keystone Mountain's only real open-slope terrain. Tilted somewhat east, it catches the early sun. Lower down, this far western flank also offers a few serious black slopes, the hardest skiing on the front side—and suddenly you know you're not just cruising another Keystone ski boulevard. While it may seem tempting to ski the center of Keystone's front mountain from top to bottom, you can actually log more miles by doing laps off the Montezuma Express quad on runs like *Flying Dutchman* and *Bachelor.* If you're dead set on skiing long top-to-bottom runs, focus on trails east of the gondola and Summit Express like *Spring Dipper* with its variants, *Santa Fe, Swandyke,* and *Whipsaw. Jackwhacker,* another run of this mode, has been turned into a terrain park. These runs continue down to River Run Plaza. The only problem with this strategy is that the final section of the *River Run* is rarely fun. It is always crowded with terrified traversers, and often is slick or even icy. Fortunately, it's short. Stick to the east side (skier's right) as much as you can.

North Peak: Bumps, Glades, and Great Dining

To reach North Peak, drop down one of three trails from the top of Keystone Mountain into a different world. North Peak is a separate, forested peak behind the main mountain. Here, too, trails have been cut through the trees, but they are a good deal steeper and more stimulating for advanced skiers. A number of runs are also equipped with snowmaking, but—except on highly trafficked *Mozart* (see below), the sole blue-square access from Keystone Mountain—the snow rarely has that scraped feeling of the front mountain, largely because the style of skiing changes back here. Turns shorten, and the terrain demands a more conscious, less straight-ahead style.

The main way down to North Peak is a blue beauty called *Mozart.* It is spacious, inviting, and extremely varied, with random tree islands blocking and then revealing views. The terrain constantly folds and ripples into small micro-gullies, drops, and momentary side hills. An irresistible invitation to playful skiing, *Mozart* is a great name for a great run. Sometimes it seems that the whole world finds it appealing, which is why it often gets skied off. Keystone's newest treat for strong skiers is *The Windows,* a steep gladed sector, skier's left of *Mozart. Diamond Back* and *Mineshaft,* the two black runs that are alternatives to *Mozart,* are usually rivers of black bumps. *Mineshaft* is shorter, but both have a curious sun exposure, and seldom offer good conditions until the bumps soften during the afternoon.

The front side of North Peak (the side facing the back of Keystone Mountain) served by the Santiago Express offers a choice of mostly bumped-out black and blue runs. Surprise: for those skiers who don't yet feel at home with bumps, these are some of the friendliest mogul runs in Colorado. What makes these bumps so easy to ski? It is likely the preserve of steady, sustained pitches rather than drops and flats, and, perhaps, the fact that two categories of skiers are conspicuously absent: inexperienced skiers who wander onto bump runs by accident and chop off the back sides of bumps with panic pivots; and, equally destructive, the real hotshots who ski straighter, faster lines and hammer rounded gullies into narrow slots with the tails of their skis. Snowboarders do affect the shape of the bumps, but they don't seem to gravitate to these runs. These North Peak runs are just the sort of inviting bump terrain that serves as a good introduction for good skiers to the esoteric pleasures of mogul skiing. You'll usually find one or two recently groomed options, but generally the front side of North Peak is all bump skiing of a pleasant, almost relaxing, variety. Don't miss it.

Most North Peak skiers bear left off the lift, but a right turn leads to *Geronimo* and *Cat Dancer,* a couple of steeper trails, and better yet, to two glades. The original glades, visible to the right of the chair as you are riding up, are steepish, double fall-line glades that require a fair amount of snow before they can provide comfortable skiing. Beyond *Cat Dancer* is the recently developed *Cat South Glades.* After a few seasons on the trail map, they still feel virtually undiscovered.

Like Keystone Mountain, North Peak also has a back side, but it's more of a skiers' bridge to The Outback than a skiing zone in its own right. Two parallel blue runs, *Anticipation* and *Spillway,* and a single green trail, *Fox Trot,* lead down to the third and last mountain, The Outback.

North Peak still has a couple of other treats. On its summit, only 20 feet higher than the summit of Keystone Mountain at 11,660 feet, is a beautiful log structure called The Outpost, one of the most handsome mountain restaurants of any Colorado resort. The main eating hall is so attractive that you want to rush right into the cafeteria and fill your tray. But hold on. Next door in the same building is something even better, a sit-down restaurant called the Alpenglow Stube. Nowadays, there are quite a few other sit-down restaurants at Colorado ski resorts but the Alpenglow Stube is a winner. It's not just the charming old-world decor but also the food that is a cut above. Like most fancy on-mountain restaurants, lunch reservations are needed to snare a table, but you can usually be spontaneous, walk in without reservations, sit at the counter in front of the open kitchen, and talk with the cooks while they perform their culinary magic for you. After a long morning blasting down North Peak's bumps or The Outback, a gourmet lunch at the Alpenglow is hardly sinful.

The Outback: Keystone's Third Mountain

The Outback boasts long, beautifully cut lines, which drop straight down the fall line. No distracting or boring flats. No nasty surprises of any sort. The grooming is excellent with a predictable and sustained pitch. In short, for many people, this is probably the best skiing at Keystone.

Elk Run, directly under the Outback Express, is very wide, and the feeling of skiing down a natural crest is delicious. The adjacent runs are all blue with splendid, but never too steep, pitch. Even dyed-in-the-wool experts will probably prefer these long runs to the shorter black ones farther to skier's left from the quad, simply because cruising at this pitch is so rare. The farther out you go, in either direction from the Outback Express, the narrower the runs and the more they begin to resemble glades. This is true both on tough runs like *Timberwolf* and *Bushwacker* on skier's right from the lift, or easier ones like *Wolverine* and *Wildfire* on skier's left. Either way, you can dance through trees along The Outback's outer edges, and the only price you'll pay is a rather longish traverse back to the quad.

In addition, two black-diamond bowls, *North Bowl* and *South Bowl,* are hike-to sections above and behind the top of the Outback Express. They start as relatively short open bowls, funneling into drainages on either side of the mountain with run-outs back to the lift. *North Bowl* is somewhat easier than *South Bowl* and also gets (and keeps) better snow.

Snowboarding

Keystone was Colorado's second-to-the-last anti-snowboarding holdout, but riders have been welcomed for several years. Much of Packsaddle (now called Area 51) has become their province.

Keystone by Night

Night skiing is well known in the East, the Midwest, and the Pacific Northwest, where it's an accepted way for urban ski hordes to get maximum benefit from small nearby areas, but Keystone is Colorado's only major area to offer it. Like everything else the resort does, Keystone has developed outstanding skiing under the lights. The gondola and the Peru Express provide access to 13 well-lit runs. Long eerie runs in the iridescent purple shadows cast by vapor lamps, a tent of high-altitude stars, a carpet of moon-gray snow—all the ingredients needed for a truly surrealistic evening. If you're spending a week in Summit County, this is definitely worth a night just for the change of scenery.

Resort Tips

Skating on the frozen lake is a must. It, too, is lit up at night, and rental skates as well as skating and hockey clinics are available. If you happen to be at the resort on a clear, full-moon night, take a snowshoe tour. It's an experience you won't soon forget, as you move over the snow under the canopy of a starry night sky. Dinner at the **Alpenglow Stube** is also an unsurpassed experience—two gondola rides (blankets supplied), a fine dinner, and cozy ambience. Based on food and service alone, probably the best Keystone dinner is at **Keystone Ranch,** a refurbished log ranch house on what is now a golf course. Fine food and a wine list to match are hallmarks of dinner at the Ranch. Fine four-course dinners are served nightly at **Ski Tip Lodge,** a wood-and-plaster, Austro-Alpine inn that was operated as the region's first ski lodge by Max Dercum, the man who started Keystone, and his wife, Edna. Keystone now operates Ski Tip and has built a modern development too close to it, but once you're inside, the romance and patina live on.

Keystone Village has clean, unpretentious architecture terraced down the hillside from **Keystone Lodge.** When the structure was built, the bold concrete-and-glass main lodge made an architectural statement in ski country, with a series of pedestrian walks and plazas and dramatic views over the skating lake toward the ski mountain. But the village itself just isn't big enough, active enough, or diverse enough to keep visitors stimulated for a whole week. River Run is growing up around the base of the River Run gondola, with handsome condos and attractive shops that are well planned and lively, but they are a well planned development without the patina and eclecticism of a real mountain town. Keystone gives vacationers multi-day visit vouchers for non-skiing activities, making it easier to sample the resort's growing array of off-slope options.

Additionally, from Keystone it is only a short drive or free bus ride from three other serious ski mountains and a couple of other towns.

Copper Mountain is being developed in the River Run mode, and Breckenridge and Frisco are two genuine towns. Even nearer is the Dillon/Silverthorne area with rambling suburban-style developments around Lake Dillon, just off I-70, between the highway and the resort. Even though Keystone has the best accommmodations in the east end of Summit County, a lot of Keystone skiers stay in and around the Dillon/Silverthorne area and save money. A lot of people also like to shop in the brassy Silverthorne factory outlets.

There are also several good restaurants in the Dillon area, but the all-time classic is a barnlike Mexican restaurant and honky-tonk called the **Old Dillon Inn,** located just north of I-70. Generations of ski bums, instructors, and lift operators have found happiness in the dark, dense atmosphere of the O.D.I. Maybe you will too.

Keystone Data

Mountain Statistics

Vertical feet	2,900 feet
Base elevation	9,300 feet
Summit elevation	12,200 feet
Longest run	3 miles
Average annual snowfall	230 inches
Snowmaking	956 acres
Number of lifts	21: 2 gondolas; 1 six-passenger high-speed chair; 5 high-speed quads; 1 fixed-grip quad; 1 triple chair; 4 double chairs; 2 surface lifts; 5 moving carpets
Uphill capacity	35,175 skiers per hour
Skiable terrain	1,861 acres
Opening date	Early November
Closing date	Late April
Snowboarding	Yes

Keystone's lift ticket is also valid at Breckenridge and Arapahoe Basin; limited interchangeability with Vail and Beaver Creek.

Transportation

By car A 90-minute drive (in good road and weather conditions) from Denver. Take I-70 west through the Eisenhower Tunnel to the Dillon exit (Exit 205), then six miles on U.S. 6 east.

By bus or limo Resort Express from Denver International Airport, (800) 334-7433.

Key Phone Numbers

Ski-area information	(970) 496-2316
Snow report	(970) 496-4111
Reservations	(877) 753-9786
Website	www.keystoneresort.com

Lito's TECH TIP

Hard, Icy Snow

It's a matter of regional pride to assert that there are never icy conditions in the Rockies. Of course, it isn't true. But it's certainly fair to say that there is much, much less ice in the Rockies than skiers from both coasts are used to. All mountains experience very "firm" conditions whenever and wherever artificial snow-making systems have been used. Sometimes, as in the case of a World Cup race course, this hard surface is a real advantage; most of the time it's a pain, simply because everyone skis better on perfect, packed powder. Here are a few techniques and tips to help you fight back.

The two main problems that plague skiers on very hard snow are over-turning and over-edging. The first, over-turning, is a natural occurrence because on a slick, hard surface, there is much less friction between skis and snow. That means that once you twist your skis sideways into a turn, they just keep on turning. Nothing slows down or inhibits this turning, pivoting action, and before you know it you are skidding sideways in a straight line rather than carving a clean arc. At this point, most skiers compound the problem by trying to "dig in," or edge their skis harder to stop such skidding. It doesn't work; in fact, the harder, or icier, the slope is, the less good it does to strongly edge your skis. Real masters on hard, icy snow try to edge their skis just enough to hold, knowing that if they overdo it, their skis will immediately start to chatter and slip. So what to do?

Your first step will be to quiet down all your movements, and try to make what I call the minimum start to your turns. That is, simply shift onto the new ski and wait... It takes a second for something to happen but this is exactly what you want: a slow, progressive start to the turn, in which your weighted ski will carve slowly around. If you get impulsive and give one or both skis a powerful twist, then it's all over—you will have initiated a skid, rather than a turn. As long as your skis are primarily slicing forward rather than moving sideways, relatively little edging is required to keep them "on track." Once they've begun to skid out on a very hard, scraped surface, however, no amount of edging will produce a good turn.

Since the edge of your turning ski doesn't bite or grip this "firm" snow very well, the distribution of weight along the edge of that ski becomes critical. If you put too much weight on the front or on the back of your ski, the tail will break loose in a skid. So it is important to distribute your weight evenly along the whole edge of the carving ski, or, to put it another way, to stand evenly on the whole edge of that foot, neither on the ball nor on the heel. One way to maintain this even, unvarying weight distribution is to calm down any upper-body activity, especially arm movement. Spread your arms in a poised, balanced position and keep them there. On icy snow, any sudden arm-hand-pole movement is enough to make your skis skid right out from under you.

And that's your basic strategy for very hard, icy snow. Calm, almost motionless skiing—as though you were skiing over acres of delicate, white eggs, careful not to break a single one with a sudden movement. Try it; it works.

Arapahoe Basin

Arapahoe Basin, or "A-Basin" as it's usually called, has a summit elevation of 13,050 feet and is usually thought of as the highest ski area in Colorado (although Loveland is really in the same league), as well as one

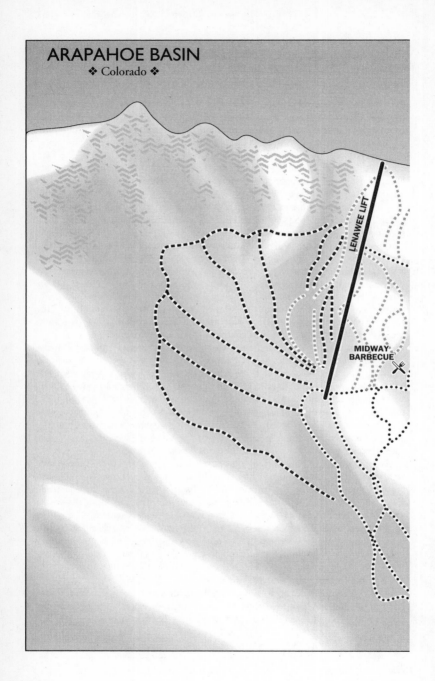

ARAPAHOE BASIN
❖ Colorado ❖

LENAWEE LIFT

MIDWAY
BARBECUE

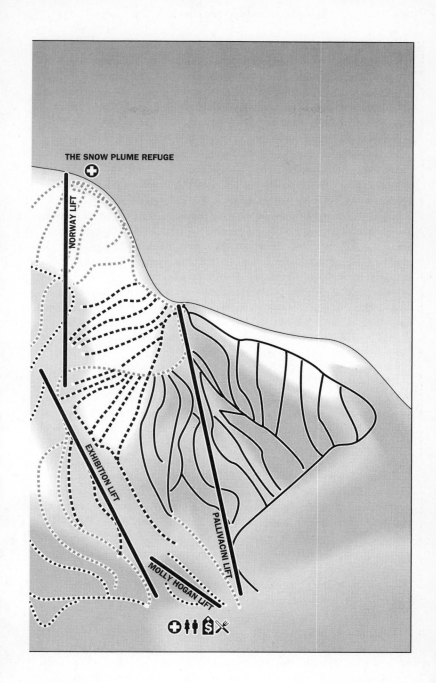

THE SNOW PLUME REFUGE

NORWAY LIFT

EXHIBITION LIFT

MOLLY HOGAN LIFT

PALLIVACINI LIFT

of the oldest. Its season is the longest by several months. Because it's set at a high elevation amid dramatic mountains, it is one of those relatively small ski areas that feels much larger than its statistic indicates.

A-Basin is tucked into a kind of fold just over the western side of the Continental Divide, a few hairpin turns down from the summit of Loveland Pass on what used to be the main road west from Denver. Since the construction of the Eisenhower Tunnel in 1973, I-70 has been speeding motorists under the divide into Summit County, and nowadays many skiers reach Arapahoe Basin by driving up the canyon from Keystone (or taking a shuttle bus from there). The high-Alpine flavor of A-Basin skiing is so different from anything else in Summit County that it certainly merits a discussion of its own. This is genuine, white-on-white, above-timberline skiing in a splendid remote setting—and it is the county's only noncorporate, nonresort ski area. For the time being—through 2003–2004 for sure—any lift ticket or pass good at Keystone is also accepted at A-Basin. Keystone's shuttle buses continue to link the two ski areas, introducing vacationers to the Alpine experience available at A-Basin. How long that arrangement will continue remains an open question. The ski area has obtained permits to install snowmaking, which would provide a reliable early-season start and position it for a summer skiing operation, possibly as early as 2004.

The Alpine Area

Although there are only four full-size chairlifts at A-Basin (plus one wee beginners' chair), the mountain offers a lot of variety without a lot of frills. There are no high-speed lifts, no on-site lodging, no fancy dining establishments, and, until very recently, no machine-made snow. Even without shot-from-guns snow, A-Basin boasts one of the longest ski seasons in the land, usually opening around Thanksgiving and operating into June, often even July. Now, an early start is assured, and summer skiing is a possibility.

The Exhibition triple is the main chair up from the base lodge, and both this lift and the runs it serves are in the forested zone. Above Exhibition lift, the scene changes. The trees thin and rapidly disappear. Skiers can enjoy every square meter of several wide-open, rolling bowls served by two more lifts, the Norway and Lenawee chairs. The Lenawee triple season, a 2001–2002 upgrade from a double, increased the uphill capacity by more than 45% and reduced a major bottleneck. The top terminal of the new lift was realigned to access both the Lenawee and Norway faces.

Pistes packed into this sector are marked a sort of generic blue—with the exception of one easier angled hollow known as *Dercum's Gulch,* named after Max Dercum, who operated Ski Tip Lodge and started both the Keystone and A-Basin ski areas. None of these slopes is really steep, but they are constantly varied and have so much character that no one could be bored. As soon as you go off-piste, you might find powder, corn, crud, or a combination that ratchets up the challenge.

This sort of treeless terrain always provides the option of diving into beautiful short, steep faces right in the middle of an otherwise easy stretch of mountain, pitches that most skiers might avoid but others take advantage of, because everything, literally, is skiable. A-Basin is not really considered a prime novice area, but it does cater to beginners with free use of the Molly Hogan lift. Not only is this a bonus for families or groups with mostly good skiers and a newbie or two, but it is also terrific for anyone just taking up snowboarding or telemarking and wanting to get in some practice turns without shelling out big bucks—or any bucks.

Arapahoe Adventures

A-Basin provides two kinds of adventure skiing: untracked off-piste lines on the East Wall and breathtakingly pure, steep bump skiing in and around Pallavicini.

The East Wall comprises the whole steep mountain flank that arcs around to the right as you look down from the top of the Lenawee lift. It's pretty obvious where the skiing stops, and the steeper rocky mountainside continues toward high craggy ridges that overhang the whole area. This is very impressive, Alpine-feeling terrain. To ski the East Wall, take *Falcon,* the right-most run, from the top of the Lenawee lift, and bear right onto the East Wall traverse through a well-marked access gate.

Since the East Wall, overhung by those steep cliffs, has a high-potential avalanche hazard, the A-Basin ski patrol opens and controls it separately. In terrain like this, it is doubly important to read all the posted signs and obey all closures. From the entrance, the long ski-track traverse leads out across the Wall itself. You choose where you want to peel off. There are no marked runs—just space. Still, areas of the East Wall, for instance, *T.J. Cornice* and the *Tree Chutes* have been named; some of them are marked on the map and some aren't.

The farther out you traverse, the more turns you'll log on this intriguing mixed terrain. You can often climb up above the traverse to access more untracked snow, but check with the patrol first. This is real high-mountain terrain, with rocks to avoid, deep-drifted gullies to scope out, and altogether lots of room to move. The fact that you have to work—that is, walk—for it, makes these lines even more delicious. Where the East Wall blends back into *Wrangler,* an easy green run at its foot, there are often one or more "kangaroo jumps" that are especially popular in springtime— tracked and body-packed by wild-eyed college students in shorts.

If it's chutes you crave, chutes you get by entering North Pole Ridge though a gate above the Lenawee lift unloading area. Ski *North Pole, Willie's Wide, Upper East Wall,* and *Corner Chute,* each one an awesomely steep, rock-rimmed, snow-packed slit in the mountain face, and after you have made it down into the portion of East Wall normally accessed from the traverse, those ungroomed steeps will feel relatively tame!

The bump-skiing mecca lies on the western side of the area, and the Pallavicini lift is bump headquarters. Separated from the rest of A-Basin by a ridge, it tends to feel like a one-lift ski area within the larger precincts of the whole. Possibly, the reputation of Pallavicini is a little exaggerated, but that's natural, because when you look up at it from the parking lot, it seems dead vertical. It is steep, but not as steep as it looks from below. In addition to steepness, Pallavicini traditionally has had great-shaped bumps, because the skiers who are drawn to it are very competent. No one wanders onto this face of the mountain by accident, and those who ski it a lot belong there. With more snowboarders in the moguls these days, they are somewhat less perfect than they once were. First-timers on Pallavicini should find skier's right side to be a little more friendly and forgiving, and a little less steep and forbidding, than the entryways at the top.

If you look at the trail map, you'll quickly spot the Pallavicini lift on the lower right, but where is the storied run with that name? Gone. For years the face to the right of this lift was just called Pallavicini, period, and the steep, gully-like fold in the center was known as Pallavicini Couloir. Nowadays there are a host of names attached to the black (really double black) lines that stripe this face: *Pali Main Street, The Spine, Pali Face,* etc. Still, you don't have to know the correct tag for the part of Pallavicini that you are skiing in order to enjoy it. Around the corner from the Pallavicini lift (skier's right), the runs marked black are mostly the easier blacks.

A-Basin, mindful of its wild and challenging reputation, now promotes its High Adventure Series of clinics and workshops. These include Chris Anthony's Adventure Freeskiing Camps; Arapahoe Basin Slopeside Session with personalized mogul coaching from pro skiers; Snowboard Freeride Session, TeleClinics, Telemark Steep Camps, and the Arapahoe Basin Avalanche School. Programs range from three hours to two days. Call (888) 272-7246, extension 3, for dates and details.

Snowboarding

It sounds like hyperbole to describe any single ski area as a snowboarder's paradise, but with its expansive terrain, tight shots through cliff bands and mid- and lower-mountain terrain, and gullies that are natural half-pipes, A-Basin merits that praiseworthy description. Additionally, the area has a half-pipe, expanded for 2003–2004, but for the freedom of the snows that riders can experience so well, the natural terrain is prime.

Seasonal Tips, Extra Dimensions

The area is indeed open from Thanksgiving or early December on, but in winter, it can be deadly cold and windy. Then, Keystone's tree-sheltered runs are usually a better bet unless a big snowstorm has just passed through. After a storm, Arapahoe has more powder to track up than Keystone, which is not only lower but always more crowded.

The most important piece of advice about A-Basin: Ski there in spring! A-Basin really comes into its own in springtime. The high-altitude sun bouncing off the reflector-oven walls of its high-Alpine bowls quickly transforms the snow into the most consistent corn in Colorado. When other areas are closing in April, the scene at A-Basin is just warming up, literally and figuratively. It's a tradition among good Colorado skiers to treat themselves to an after-the-season ski at Arapahoe. Of course, to participate, change your strategy a bit. No one wants to ski icy moguls in the early morning (see the following Ski Tech pages for more spring-snow strategies). In spring, there is an optimum time slot for almost every exposure.

You'll also want to eat at the **Midway Barbecue,** an outdoor deck at the warming hut on top of Exhibition lift, or bring a picnic and find a flat, dry rock somewhere under the East Wall. On an average-to-good snow year the lifts keep running until June. During a high-snow year, July 4 is the traditional aimed-for closing date. But as May wears on and the snow, even at 12,000 feet, starts to thin out, Arapahoe skiers often drive up to Loveland Pass. With a little hiking along gentle ridge tops, they can usually find beautiful untracked corn-snow lines leading back down to the highway on either side of the pass. Arrange a car shuttle with your bud or hitchhike back up.

One of the most famous (or infamous) out-of-bounds run is a steep, smooth face called *The Professor* that drops down across the road from the A-Basin parking lot. *The Professor* is completely outside and separate from the ski area; it's uncontrolled and can be (and has been) a death trap in winter. Don't take foolish risks for a few powder turns; it's far better to wait until the late spring weather has solidified all the out-of-area slopes around Loveland Pass before hiking out there for an adventure. If the spring corn snow up on the pass is still fairly solid and not mushy in late morning, then it's most likely safe.

Arapahoe Basin Data

Mountain Statistics

Vertical feet	2,270 feet
Base elevation	10,780 feet
Summit elevation	13,050 feet
Longest run	1.5 miles
Average annual snowfall	367 inches
Snowmaking	125 acres
Number of lifts	5: 2 triple chairs; 3 double chairs
Uphill capacity	7,026 skiers per hour

Arapahoe Basin Data (continued)

Mountain Statistics (continued)

Skiable terrain	490 acres
Opening date	Mid-November
Closing date	July 4 is the target, June is virtually assured
Snowboarding	Yes

Transportation

By car   From Denver, Interstate 70 west to Exit 216 (Loveland Pass) via U.S. 6 east, or a 15-minute drive from Keystone via U.S. 6 east.

By bus   Keystone's free shuttle serves the Arapahoe Basin base area.

Key Phone Numbers

Ski-area information	(888) 272-7246 or (970) 468-0718
Snow report	(970) 468-0718
Website	www.arapahoebasin.com

Lito's TECH TIP

Corn Snow and Springtime Strategies

Spring snow conditions can produce both the best and the worst surfaces a skier ever gets to play on or curse all on the same day. Variable, challenging, and sublime, spring snow is the result of repeated daily melting and nightly freezing. During the day this snow goes through three distinct stages.

Early in the morning, spring snow is simply ice; it's not the smooth, polished ice on which racers love to hone their carving skills. Morning ice in spring is lumpy, brutal stuff, with every rut, every track, and every glob of slush thrown up the previous evening turned into a rock-hard obstacle. Icy slopes on a spring morning have no redeeming qualities.

As the snow surface melts toward midday, it mellows into a condition skiers call "corn." Corn snow is to skiers what sweet corn is to the inhabitants of Garrison Keillor's Lake Wobegon, a delight that banishes all the trials of their existence. This is the ultimate snow surface, on which a good skier can do anything. Skis bite cleanly, hold effortlessly, slide smoothly, and come alive.

Alas, perfect corn conditions only last from about 10:30 a.m. to 1 p.m. Then, as the thawing penetrates deeper into the snowpack, corn turns to slush that is challenging, annoying, and occasionally dangerous to ski in. As usual, there are tricks to tame it.

Early in the morning you have two choices: sleep in or head directly for the eastern-facing slopes that have already been thawing in the sun for a couple of hours. Lumpy spring ice can't be tamed and shouldn't be skied. In fact, the idea of watching the sun and choosing your slopes accordingly works all day long. If eastern-facing slopes are the first to "corn up," they are also the first to turn slushy by early afternoon. At that time you should have already moved around to the opposite, western exposures that are just starting to get good.

Unlike lumpy morning ice, afternoon slush can be skied well. The problem is just the opposite of a smooth, icy slope where there often isn't enough friction. Here there is too much resistance to your skis' movement. If you twist your skis violently, they won't skid; they'll simply catch or stick in the glue-like snow, knocking you off balance or worse. The remedy is simple: minimum twisting action and longer turns, allowing your skis to slice forward much more than they move sideways.

On late spring afternoons, moguls can become dangerously soft. The danger, in fact, lies in burying the front of your skis in a soft bump. At that point, only perfectly functioning bindings stand between you and an injury. To avoid this, try to slide diagonally into slushy moguls so that your ski tips never hit the back side of the bump directly. Or better yet, quit early and go swimming. After three hours of sweet corn, why fight it?

Breckenridge

Breckenridge is the princess of Summit County ski resorts. Like nearby Keystone and Cooper Mountain, Breckenridge offers a lot of skiing on an up-to-date mountain, but unlike its neighbors, Breckenridge is also the name of a genuine and historic Colorado town.

So many of Colorado's ski towns were mining towns, yet they're all different. Even today, with T-shirt shops and real estate sales offices fast becoming the tandem common denominator of the American resort landscape, the differing architecture and geography of these ski towns tell very different stories. Aspen was a silver-mining center; Crested Butte, a proletarian coal-mining community; and Telluride, a remote gold camp, while Breckenridge was an early famous placer-mining district. Surreal gravel bars and placer mounds long lined the Blue River, visible on the drive into town from the north. Even though much reclamation work has taken place in recent years and these mounds are disappearing, in winter these ghostly white lumps look like leftover moguls from a vanished race of giant skiers. The Ten Mile Range above town echoes these same domelike shapes in large white rolls that make skiers drool. No need to drool. Peaks 8 and 9 are spider-webbed with lifts; and Peak 10 and the newly developed Peak 7 have one high-speed lift each. Additionally, high-summit bowls of both Peak 7 and Peak 8 are open and avalanche controlled for skiers and snowboarders who are willing to walk uphill for their adventures.

Take your choice: an above-timberline bowl; relaxed and mellow trail cruising; the largest, longest novice slopes; or some of the narrowest and gnarliest bump runs in the state. All in all, Breckenridge is a very well-balanced ski mountain with lots of terrain. The added plus is downtown Breckenridge, a multicolored, Victorian main-street strip running like the border stripe of a handwoven rug beneath mixed layers of condos and forest.

A Breckenridge Overview

Coincidentally, the Ten Mile Range has ten major summits; logically, although prosaically, named Peaks 1 through 10 and numbered from north to south. They rise above the Blue River Valley like a row of giant

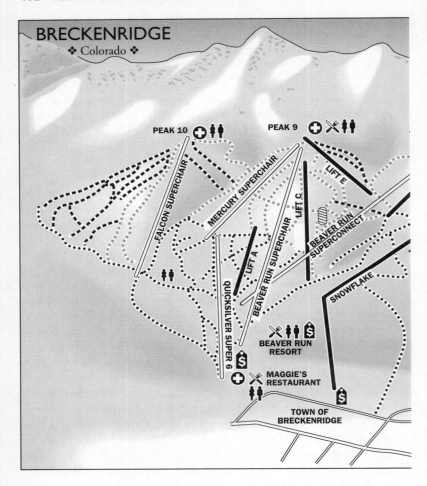

windswept mile markers. The town of Breckenridge lies below the slopes of Peak 9, near the south end of the range. Chairlifts don't reach all the way to the top of this imposing series of peaks. The rounded frontal ridges and the deep-cleft valleys between Peaks 7, 8, 9, and 10 define the playing field at Breckenridge and divide the area into distinct zones to directly shape your skiing day.

Peak 8 was the first of the quartet with lift service. It offers steep skiing on the upper mountain topped by a crown of open bowls, a graceful mixture of sparse timberline trees with open slopes for serious skiers, and some easy slopes near the base. Peak 7, the northward extension of this open-bowl terrain, is now lift served. It is big, exciting, and a magnet for strong intermediate skiers and riders. The deep valley or gully between Peaks 8

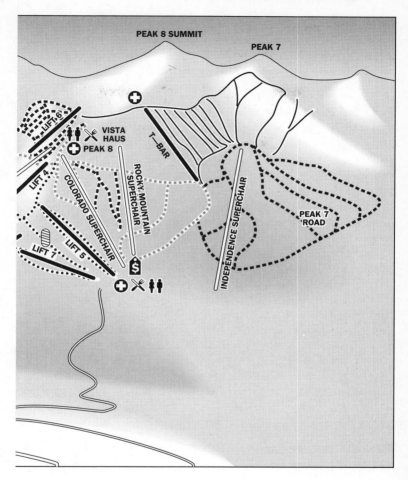

and 9 is an intense area: steep, "rad," and thoroughly bumped out. On both sides of this drainage, but especially on peak 9's North Face, young bump specialists find the tightest, most challenging moguls at Breckenridge—some of the finest in the entire state. The main part of Peak 9, a mountain for the masses, has user-friendly, unchallenging skiing. In fact, the lower half, now served by the country's first line-gobbling double-loading, high-speed six-passenger chairlift, is strictly for beginners. The upper half of Peak 9 is low-key, low-intermediate-level skiing.

Peak 10 completes the Breckenridge spectrum with classic advanced and upper-intermediate terrain: blue and black runs that aren't too demanding but still keep your attention with some bumps, some glades, and some pitches.

Once you understand this zone-by-zone, mountain-by-mountain approach to what can otherwise be a very spread-out and confusing ski area, it's duck soup to tailor your Breckenridge experience to your own level of skill and your own desire for challenge or ease. We'll look at each zone in more detail, starting with the friendliest skiing Breckenridge has to offer.

Peak 9: A Perfect Warm-Up Mountain

Peak 9, the middle mountain at Breckenridge, offers pretty much middle-of-the-road, or middle-of-the-piste, skiing. It's also the closest mountain to town. The lower slopes were equipped with Colorado's very first detach-able chairlift, but by today's standards it wasn't fast enough, and in 2000–2001, it was replaced by a double-loading six-seater called the Quicksilver Super6. The lower mountain, a pleasant maze of extremely gentle green beginners' runs, is Breckenridge's main novice ski zone and is just too flat for experienced skiers. This is also where beginners should take lessons at Breckenridge, because what beginners need most, in addition to a patient instructor, is lots and lots of inviting, suitable terrain.

The Beaver Run high-speed quad that starts just a little uphill from the Quicksilver Super6 rises to the upper part of Peak 9, which is laced with attractive, meandering blue runs. This is the sort of intermediate skiing that doesn't pose any special challenges or offer any special rewards, just basic wandering trails steep enough to slide along at a good clip but never steep enough to make you want to put on the brakes. These runs are exactly what an enormous number of skiers need in order to develop early parallel skills and confidence. Peak 9 is a great learning mountain, and even for better skiers, it's a good place to warm up and get back on your ski legs the first day of a Summit County vacation.

Peak 8: The Peak Experience at Breckenridge

Peak 8 has a good deal more character and variety than Peak 9, or even Peak 10. It is set back from and above town, and its higher elevation partly explains its more Alpine feeling. If you want to drive directly to Peak 8, take a winding ten-minute drive up Ski Hill Road from town— or better yet, take the bus. A skis-on option is crossing from Peak 9. Unless you like bumps, follow an easy blue-square catwalk called *Union*.

Stronger skiers in search of excitement and intriguing terrain will probably spend much of their Breckenridge ski time on Peak 8. Peak 8's lower half is striped with steeper blue and moderate black runs that have big, swooping rolls and dips. Although these are all trails cut through thick trees, they don't seem as closed-in as many forested trails do. At the very bottom of the area are a handful of very easy slopes, but Peak 9 remains a better bet for beginners.

On the far north side of Peak 8 (skier's right), half into and half out of the white world above the timberline, are ten runs collectively known as the back bowls. Accessed from the Snowbird chair (Chair 6), Peak 8's highest chairlift, they are more like designated lines fanning out and down from the lift than real runs. This is an ideal area for creative skiing: threading new paths through partly timbered, partly open, reasonably steep, but never scary, terrain. It's an area to explore as well as just ski.

More magic lives on Peak 8's upper slopes, where the ski area emerges from the trees into wide-open, treeless terrain served by just one modest T-bar. Contest Bowl and Horseshoe Bowl are smooth, steep, white basins that have a peculiar wind exposure that also produces a wonderful wind-packed powder: cold and smooth, hard but grippy, ideal for snappy rebounding turns and a definite rarity in Colorado.

It takes a little gumption to get the most out of Peak 8. From the T-bar that runs up Horseshoe Bowl's north side, you have to traverse out to reach the best lines, but it is worth every step. To the right of the T-bar you'll find a zone of indistinct black and blue lines among patchy high-altitude trees. Runs like *Forget-Me-Not* and *White Crown* feel almost out of bounds, which they almost were until the ski area pushed back its boundaries to include the actual summit ridge and highest bowls of both Peaks 7 and 8. These softly curving white bowls recede back toward higher, farther ridges. Once considered too high, too far, and too dangerous, they are now avalanche controlled. When the patrol gives the green light, you can hike up from the top of the Horseshoe Bowl T-bar to enter *Imperial Bowl* and *Lake Chutes,* backcountry skiing directly above one of the country's largest lift-served ski areas.

Tweener Runs: Bumpety, Bumpety, Bump

The steep sides of the gulch between Peaks 8 and 9 boast the most demanding technical skiing at Breckenridge. Even though most Colorado skiers and most of the readers of this guidebook may not be wild about bump skiing, this zone is worth a special mention because of the importance of freestyle and mogul competition in the Breckenridge story. Breckenridge began to host early international freestyle competitions, fostering the development of this exciting, gymnastic branch of ski competition in a period when it was generally misunderstood and ignored.

The most difficult bump runs are concentrated in two pods. Runs on Peak 7's north face like *Mine Shaft* and *Devil's Crotch* are the wildest, meanest, and the most fun—when you survive them. They are extremely narrow, sometimes only two or three moguls wide, and absolutely unrelenting. No flats, no rest spots. You just get in the groove and go. By comparison, the four double-black diamond runs across the way on the south-facing side of the gulch, from *Southern Cross* to *Mach 1,* seem positively forgiving. They are almost as steep and every bit as moguled, but there's so much more room to maneuver that you are almost overwhelmed with choices. This whole zone provides a serious workout for strong bump skiers.

Peak 10: High Times for High Intermediates

There is no road access to Peak 10. Access is either by skiing across from Peak 9's upper slopes via *Upper Lehman, Briar Rose,* or *Country Boy,* or by riding the Quicksilver Super6 and cutting a sharp left at the unloading area and traversing on *Wellington.* Peak 10, while not nearly as big as 8 or 9, is a perfect complement to the rest of Breckenridge skiing. Peak 10 adds precisely what the central slopes lack: stimulating, upper-intermediate terrain and even some seriously advanced pitches. The most popular Peak 10 skiing—easy blacks and solid blues—are on the south side of the Falcon Superchair.

The surprise treats on Peak 10 are the harder runs to the north of the lift. *Spitfire* and *Corsair* are narrow, steep, and serious, but best of all is *The Burn,* a mountain flank where lightning and a forest fire did the sort of radical tree clearing that ski areas are not permitted to do. In lighter snow years this steep flank of Peak 10 may not be open, but it still gives a lot of character and drama to this end of the mountain. Peak 10 attracts a cadre of loyalists who like to ski long cruisers and steep glades without the crowds.

Peak 7

Though numerically first of the four interlinked mountains, Peak 7 comes last here because it is the resort's newest sector. Inaugurated at the beginning of the 2002–2003 season, it features the resort's second six-passenger chairlift and a lush and lovely web of undulating trails. Most are intermediate cruisers, with a few inviting powder pockets in the trees.

Snowboarding

With a historic break-the-mold freestyle background, Breckenridge was one of the first mountains in Colorado to encourage snowboarding. It remains a major riders' capital, and in fact, Breckenridge terrain park designers have been named the top in North America during *Snowboarder* magazine's Cutters Cup, which has been held there, in addition to major national and international snowboarding competitions. Breckenridge boasts three terrain parks and two half-pipes. The 2,400-foot-long, 300-vertical-foot Freeway Terrain Park on Peak 8 is world-class, with a series of rolled terrain and banked turns, followed by large jumps, tabletops, and spines. The park's Superpipe boasts commanding 15-foot walls and a 27-foot transition. Think of it as Breck's black-diamond park. The Gold King Terrain Park on Peak 9 is designed for mid-level riders, the resort's equivalent of the blue-square park. The newest park, called Swinger Terrain Park and also located on Peak 8, features introductory terrain features and a smaller scale half-pipe designed for nascent freestyle riders and would be marked green if terrain parks were so ranked.

Breckenridge: Townscapes and Town Tips

Breckenridge is an honest, no-nonsense ski town with just enough history on Main Street to let you know it's been here for a long time; enough modern lodging blocks stacked up the hills on either side of Main Street to accommodate an enormous number of skiers; enough garishly painted false fronts to suggest that someone is trying to turn this town into a cutesy little theme park for skiers; and enough locals who still care to make you hope it won't happen. One local calls Breckenridge a "middle-class Aspen," but that doesn't quite capture it, even though Breckenridge prices aren't nearly as alarming as Aspen's or Vail's.

You won't exactly need a map to orient yourself in Breckenridge, since Main Street is where everything is, where everything happens. It's a real walking street: human in scale, full of goodies, and a scene that will certainly take you more than one evening to explore. Many of Breckenridge's most interesting restaurants, nightspots, and shops are either on this main drag or within a block of it. In winter, when the street trees are festooned with lights and the snow sparkles, it's one of the nicest local scenes around.

Breckenridge has accommodations for thousands of visitors. The largest and most convenient is **Beaver Run Resort,** a ski-in, ski-out condo-hotel near the bottom of Peak 9. The nearby **Great Divide Lodge** and the **Village at Breckenridge,** a quartet of stumpy towers (one hotel, three condos) at the base of the Quicksilver Super6, have both been remodeled recently. Across the valley from the lifts is the **Lodge & Spa at Breckenridge,** offering lovely lodging, good spa facilities, and an away-from-the-fray ambience. Elsewhere, you'll find more condos, some very nice B&B's in various price ranges, and even some old-time budget motels.

There's also all sorts of good eating in town. The **Briar Rose** is a place for hearty and well prepared meats, seafood, and pasta, generally considered the best restaurant in town. **Café Alpine** is an upscale restaurant with European cuisine and a terrific tapas bar. **Pierre's Riverwalk** is known for good French fare. Killer breakfasts and abundant Mexican food are served at the **Gold Pan.** When you tire of run-of-the-mill ski-town shopping, check out some of Breckenridge's abundant galleries and even a couple of museums.

Breckenridge Data

Mountain Statistics

Vertical feet	3,398 feet
Base elevation	9,600 feet
Summit elevation	12,998 feet
Longest run	3.5 miles
Average annual snowfall	300 inches

Breckenridge Data (continued)

Mountain Statistics (*continued)*

Snowmaking	539 acres
Number of lifts	27: 2 high-speed six-passenger chairlifts; 6 high-speed quads; 1 triple chair; 6 double chairs; 5 surface lifts; 7 moving carpets
Uphill capacity	36,680 skiers per hour
Skiable terrain	2,208 acres
Opening date	Mid-November
Closing date	Late April
Snowboarding	Yes

Transportation

By car A 106-mile drive (about 90 minutes in good weather and road conditions) from Denver via I-70 west to the Friso-Breckenridge exit (Exit 203), then south on Colorado Highway 9.

By bus or van Resort Express (phone (800) 334-7433) from Denver International Airport. Colorado Springs is 110 miles, either via U.S. 24 and then Colorado Highway 9 over Hoosier Pass, or via I-25, C-470, I-70 and Colorado 9. Timberline Express (phone (800) 288-1375) offers transportation from Colorado Springs Airport.

Key Phone Numbers

Ski-area information	(970) 453-5000
Snow report	(970) 453-6118
Reservations	(970) 593-5260 or (800) 221-1091
Website	www.breckenridge.com

Lito's TECH TIP

A Snowboarding Primer

Few things are as humbling or as stimulating to a good skier as abandoning the security of a sport already mastered to become, once again, an awkward beginner. This is true on cross-country skating skis, on telemark skis, on monoskis, and especially on snowboards. Recently, I strapped on one of these amazing contraptions for the first time and loved it. Here's a little of what I learned.

Which foot forward? Snowboarding, like surfing and skateboarding, is a sideways-standing sport. To discover your natural stance, find an icy stretch of pavement or a frozen puddle, run a few feet, and let yourself slide across it. Which foot do you instinctively stretch forward? That's your front foot on a snowboard.

To get started, pick an easy hill with soft snow. What precisely does one do with a snowboard? There are several competing approaches in snowboarding instruction, but this is what worked for me. Go across the hill first. You will gain more confidence and control more quickly, if you develop a traversing/side-slipping/braking pattern first, before heading straight down the fall line. Unlike skiing, traversing across a slope on a snowboard is quite different depending on which way you're heading. You will have a back-side traverse (back to the mountain) and a front-side traverse (facing the mountain). The back-side traverse is a stronger, easier maneuver, because the high plastic spoilers of most snowboard bindings give you more support in this direction—you can lean back against them to increase edging. On the front-side traverse you feel like you're standing on your toes, and it takes more strength to control the board. Experienced skiers seem to react differently to snowboards than those whose only experience of sliding over snow has been on a board. Instinctively, the skilled skier who tries snowboarding wants to develop strong edge control. The shortest route to this end is to use hard plastic snowboarding boots rather than soft Sorel-type, felt-lined boots and wraparound bindings. Hard boots greatly strengthen your front-side edging.

While you traverse the slope, flatten and sideslip your board from time to time; to stop, push the board away from you, twisting it up the hill, while you let it slip. And—very important—when you get in trouble, sit down! In fact, you can sit down and flip your board around between traverses until you're ready to turn downhill. As in skiing, the downhill turn is the soul of the sport, but don't try it until you feel comfortable just sliding sideways and across the hill. When you're ready, start your downhill turn by committing your body in the direction you want to go—leading with your front hand—and then swivel the board with your feet to catch up to where your body already is. The feeling is almost like falling into a turn, insecure but very effective.

This thumbnail sketch doesn't take the place of lessons, and nowadays most ski schools have become ski and snowboard schools, so it won't be hard to find good snowboarding lessons at most ski areas. Five years ago it would have been a challenge, ten years ago impossible. Good riding!

Copper Mountain

Copper Mountain has long garnered top marks for snow quality and for the natural skier's logic of its layout. But until recently, resort facilities at its base never added up to a successful ski village. In that regard, Copper was an underachiever. But that's history, now that the resort's facilities are rapidly taking shape to match the mountain. This change in Copper Mountain's fortunes is due to its acquisition by Intrawest, the remarkable Canadian ski-resort developer. Intrawest has done an extraordinary job of creating the fabulous and successful base village at Whistler, British Columbia, and revitalizing the base villages at Vermont's Stratton Mountain and Quebec's Tremblant. The new Copper boasts an attractive, integrated, human-scale village. What will ultimately be a $450-million expansion is also integrating three spread-out base areas into a more cohesive whole.

Imagine a mountain, a grand mountain, whose main axis seems to be horizontal rather than vertical, stretching sideways around the fork of an Alpine valley rather than up toward the sky, and you'll get a sense of Copper's paradoxical topography. It sounds weird, but it skis great. Copper must have been designed by the great forest ranger in the sky just to keep different levels of skiers from getting in each other's hair. Looking

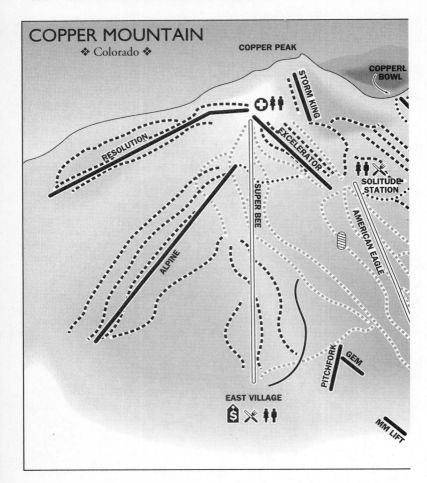

up from the base, you see a beginners' mountain on the far right, a steep bumped-out experts' mountain on the far left, and a smooth gradation of ski terrain in between. High above and out of sight from the base, is a long ridge with two summit points: Copper Peak on the left (east) and Union Peak on the right (west). Copper Peak is slightly higher, but the top Union Peak lift climbs higher than the top Copper Peak lift. Wherever you are on the mountain, you can move one run to the east and the skiing will be a fraction harder, one run farther west and the slope will be a tad easier. No other mountain in Colorado enables skiers to fine-tune the degree of challenge they'll face, or satisfaction they'll receive, on each run quite this easily.

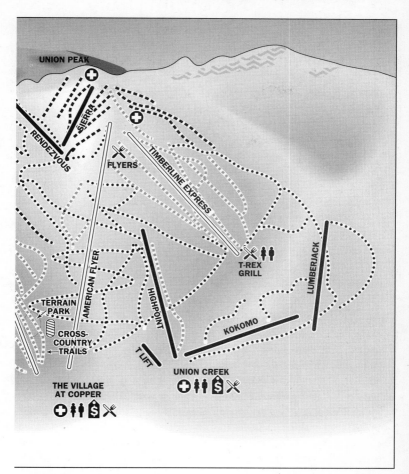

Some Pluses on the Mountain

Copper Mountain has long made serious efforts to open up tantalizing skiing that often seems just out of reach above the tree line; and this has been a grand success. First, came a surface lift to access *Spaulding* and *Hallelujah Bowls,* the handsome, treeless faces below the summit ridge of 12,441-foot Copper Peak. Then Lift S, a chairlift, opened some serious, even magical skiing in *Union Bowl* and on the slopes of Union Peak. Then came Copper Bowl—a large, mostly above-timberline cirque on the back sides of Union and Copper peaks, offering a stunning "back bowls" experience, with over 700 acres and 1,200 feet of vertical in an Alpine setting. Two chairlifts, recycled from the front side, serve these

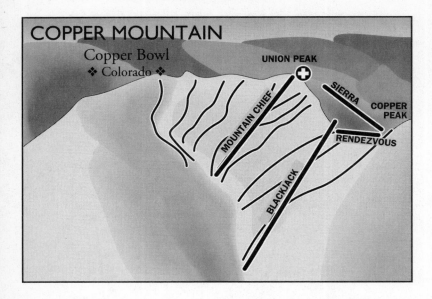

high slopes. Additional high bowls on the flanks of Tucker Mountain, Union Peak, and farther back on Jacque Peak presently are accessible by long traverses or by hiking, but lifts could eventually be built there.

Three base clusters at Copper are now tied together. At the far eastern end (left when looking up) the Super Bee six-seat detachable rises from the East Village, part of the base redevelopment, serving steep, mostly moguled runs. This end of the mountain is really for strong skiers only, but less-skilled skiers can take the six-pack lift and then traverse west to more moderate skiing on the center of the mountain. The traditional center of the older resort development, near the Copper Commons base, is now called the Village at Copper. It comprises the heart of the redevelopment project, right below the center of the wide mountain. This is where most skiers start their day. Two high-speed quads, American Eagle and American Flyer, climb high on the mountain. The American Eagle quad slants up and left, depositing skiers at a halfway point, with a cafeteria called Solitude Station in the heart of a zone with upper-intermediate runs. The other quad, American Flyer, slants up to the right, toward more modest lower-intermediate and novice ski terrain. The final base pod, Union Creek, is still farther right along the base of the mountain. Its lifts serve very easy terrain on the western end of Copper Mountain, headquarters for children's programs and ski school and the sector where true novices skiers should start their day. Along with base redevelopment and lift upgrades, Copper has eliminated the old letter designations from the trail map and given all of the lifts proper names.

Finally, Copper deserves kudos for its early-season slope preparation. It uses its ample snowmaking capacity well, generally opening a limited number of runs with very good cover long before Thanksgiving. The U.S. ski team and other national teams traditionally select Copper Mountain for early-season training, especially when an early World Cup race is scheduled in the Rockies.

Copper for Less-Experienced Skiers

First-time skiers, shaky novices, and families with young children need to report to the recently redeveloped Union Creek base area, on the far right (west) end of the resort. The vastly upgraded Union Creek base lodge is headquarters for skiers and riders plying gentle slopes nearby, while the outstanding new Schoolhouse at Union Creek features a state-of-the-art children's facility, where parents can rent equipment for 3- to 12-year-olds and enroll them for ski or snowboard instruction and lunch.

At Copper, very inexperienced adult skiers can still have a major mountain adventure by riding the American Flyer and then circling around to the extreme far right (or western side) of the area on a gentle green run called *Soliloquy.* This far-west circle tour continues via *Roundabout* or *West Ten Mile* over by the Lumberjack chair, a very quiet, gentle backwater. This makes an enormously long and pleasant run. However, the final return to Union Creek is almost painfully flat, with nature taking care of the slow-skiing injunction. For a better finish, cut right on *Soliloquy* where *Roundabout* branches off and follow *Woodwinds* to the bottom.

For another novice "mountain adventure"—still on all-green slopes but somewhat more demanding—ski down from the top of the American Flyer via *Coppertone* and then either stay on it or branch off onto *Carefree* to the bottom. Your two choices off the top of the Rendezvous triple—*Union Park* or *Wheeler Creek*—are unusually attractive greens and have a totally different, upper-mountain feel than all the other easy skiing on the western side of Copper Mountain.

Copper for Intermediate Skiers

A good bet is the terrain around the Solitude Station at the top of the American Eagle quad. *Copperopolis* and *Ptarmigan* off the Excelerator lift are delightful, and to tell the truth, the black runs between these two are not very black—more like charcoal gray. The two best intermediate cruisers back down the center of the mountain are *Collage* and *Andy's Encore. Bouncer,* once a cruiser, is now a freestyle terrain park.

Calmer intermediates seeking friendly runs rather than speed find lots of choices on the middle mountain. *Main Vein,* under the American Eagle quad, a slow-skiing zone, is a good choice. There is also fine, fairly low-angle intermediate cruising on the center section of Union Peak, which can be quickly reached by taking the American Flyer quad and dropping right down the eponymous *American Flyer* run or *The Moz.* The blue skiing on Timberline will take you several hours to explore, and it's worth it.

Copper for Strong Skiers

Very strong skiers will find happiness clear across the mountain, starting from the day-skiers' lot on the eastern end of the ski terrain, either hopping directly onto the Alpine lift and skiing down to the Excelerator, or on the Super Bee from East Village. The runs off the Alpine and Super Bee lifts are straight and straightforward medium-steep bump slopes. Alpine's trails get less traffic, so the bumps often seem better shaped. For most skiers on this side of the mountain, the goal is the Resolution lift higher up, serving *Resolution Bowl* and a galaxy of black-diamond bump runs on a sloping shoulder off Copper Peak.

But the best skiing of all for strong skiers is in the high bowls above timberline. *Spaulding Bowl* is off the Storm King platterlift, *Union Bowl,* or *Copper Bowl*—take your pick. A nice linkup is to ski *Spaulding Bowl* from the top of the Storm King platterlift and continue down *Highline,* one of four black runs served by the Resolution lift. The exciting runs on Union Peak are obvious exceptions to the sweeping generalization about the skiing getting easier and easier as you move west across this mountain. The only consistent disappointment for strong skiers is *Enchanted Forest,* a mouthwatering area of half-open bowls and thin, sparse trees dropping from the shoulder of *Hallelujah Bowl. Enchanted Forest* is rarely open, because wind scours its ridge-like upper slopes into veritable rock gardens.

Copper Bowl is a splendid, almost treeless playground in its own right. Scooped out of the back side of the ridge linking Union and Copper Peaks, as well as Tucker Mountain, which is not lift served, Copper Bowl offers little headwalls, wide open snowfields, broad cirques and tight chutes, all clad in a black diamond or two. The top portion has no trees; the bottom section tends into glades. All runs funnel into one valley with two double chairlifts, Mountain Chief and Blackjack, providing the return ride to Union and Copper Peaks, respectively.

The gung-ho, go-for-it intermediate skier who loves to ski hard and fast but doesn't really ski well enough to handle blacks with ease tends to stick to the attractive blue runs in the center of the mountain—at least to those that haven't been designated as slow-skiing zones.

Snowboarding

Copper's three terrain parks and world-class superpipe have evolved with the most up-to-date concepts in park design, no small feat given the pace of the rapidly evolving freeride movement. The designs during any given season are a collaborative effort between the Copper Freeride Team, a group of professional and amateur skiers, snowboarders, and Copper's snow-park crew.

The main terrain park, located on Loverly, has three distinct lines: a beginner track on the left with minikickers and small rails. In the center are medium-sized kickers and jumps, and on the right, giant tabletops and a hip feature offer potential for as much air as riders can handle. Halfway through the park is a rail section with various flat, kinked, and rainbow rails, plus a 20-foot quarter-pipe with a fun box on top. Sprinkled throughout the park are additional features of varying sizes and degrees of difficulty, all designed for optimum flow. Copper's 430-foot-long super-pipe at the end of the park has 17-foot-high walls. A smaller, less intimidating terrain park, added in 2001–2002, on the *Roundabout* trail gives newbies a place of their own, where they can hone their skills comfortably before heading to the Loverly Park to hang with the big guns. For skiers and riders who love the limelight, Copper's third terrain park is positioned in full view of The Village at Copper on the *Main Vein* trail. It features a sequence of hits and culminates with the Hollywood Big Air Hit, which is the main source of entertainment for visitors lunching and enjoying the après festivities on the deck of **Jack's Slopeside Bar & Grill.**

Copper Mountain Data

Mountain Statistics

Vertical feet	2,601 feet
Base elevation	9,712 feet
Summit elevation	12,313 feet
Longest run	2.8 miles
Average annual snowfall	280 inches
Snowmaking	400 acres
Number of lifts	22: 1 high-speed 6-place chair; 4 high-speed quads; 5 triple chairs; 5 double chairs; 7 surface lifts
Uphill capacity	30,630 skiers per hour
Skiable terrain	2,450 acres
Opening date	Early November
Closing date	Late April
Snowboarding	Yes

Transportation

By car Right along I-70, 75 miles west of Denver (a 1-hour-and-45-minute drive) to Copper Mountain/Leadville exit (Exit 195). Regular shuttles operate from Denver International Airport.

By bus or limo Resort Express from Denver International Airport, (800) 334-7433.

Copper Mountain Data (continued)

Key Phone Numbers

Ski-area information	(800) 458-8386 or (970) 968-2882
Snow report	(800) 789-7609 or (970) 968-2100
Reservations	(888) 263-5302
Website	www.ski-copper.com

Lito's TECH TIP

Improving Your NASTAR Handicap

Copper Mountain has been associated with the United States Ski Team and with the Alpine National Championships for so many years that I thought it would be appropriate to talk about ski racing in this Tech Tip section. For most skiers, racing is synonymous with NASTAR, the national standard race held at hundreds of ski areas across the country: an open, single-flag, giant-slalom-type race where skiers compete against a base time established by a designated pacesetter. Almost every skier has run a NASTAR race or two, but very few have achieved their full potential between the gates. Here are two simple but vital tips to improve your NASTAR handicap.

Turn early This is the key advice, and it's so simple I'm amazed more skiers haven't figured it out. Don't wait until you reach the flag that you have to turn around before starting that turn. If you start your turn at the flag itself, you will invariably turn too hard (to aim back at the next flag) and, in so doing, you will find yourself skidding down below the optimum line between the two flags. Instead, start your turn well before you reach the flag, curving around in a wider, longer arc, so that when you actually pass the flag, your turn is complete and you are already aimed for the next flag! This way you will be making a rounder, longer turn, but you won't skid down below the optimum line—which is where most skiers lose precious seconds.

Step your turns This one is simple too. Instead of turning both skis, step dynamically to the side on the ski that is going to become the outside ski of your turn. For example, step laterally onto your right ski in order to turn left, and then make your turn completely on that ski. Why? By stepping to the side you can gain a foot or more of extra distance away from the pole, which gives you more room to complete your turn early, without waiting to get by the pole before making your move.

The final result: a smoother run, no sudden jerky turns, no skidding low in your turns, and a better NASTAR handicap. Maybe a gold this year. Five, four, three, two, one ... Go!

Soulful Southwestern Colorado and Northern New Mexico

Crested Butte   A gem! This intimate ski mountain welcomes skiers of all abilities but scores highest with experts looking for all-terrain, ungroomed snow adventures—just about the best steep adventure terrain in Colorado. Crested Butte has two villages, a modern condo complex for close-to-the-lifts convenience at the base of the ski mountain, and a wonderful, well-preserved mining town (that hasn't been turned into a theme park) only a few miles away. Great snow conditions are the norm here. Remote and well worth the trip.

Telluride   Staggeringly beautiful mountainscapes surround this "happening" ski resort. The old mining town of Telluride provides historic funk and charm; the newer Mountain Village on the other side of the ski mountain has deluxe modern accommodations. Skiing is more balanced than the Telluride legend of steep bumps would have you believe. Telluride is relatively hard to reach, but its ace card is the unreal backdrop of the San Juan Mountains.

Durango Mountain Resort   It's a small but easy-to-ski, easy-to-get-around mountain near the attractive Western town of Durango in the heart of Louis L'Amour country. The skiing is mostly middle-of-the-road intermediate blue on relatively narrow runs cut through the forest. This favorite drive-to destination for Arizona skiers offers limited lodging at the base and an abundance of choices in the nearby town of Durango.

Taos   Adventure skiing on a richly complex mountain, justly famous for its steeps. An intimate base village gives a Taos ski vacation an old-time European flavor, but offers something completely different, as dining and lodging in the nearby town of Taos change your vacation atmosphere from Alpine to Hispanic, Pueblo Indian, and historic Southwest.

Santa Fe   A compact but satisfying day-ski area with breathtaking views. There's a good kids' program that makes Santa Fe family friendly. Above all, the ski area is only a short drive from one of the most romantic cities and popular vacation destinations in America—old Santa Fe—an opportunity to mix art, as well as Southwestern culture and cuisine, with skiing.

Crested Butte

In Colorado, Crested Butte is only a medium-size ski resort, but in much of the rest of the country it would be a giant. But it is a "beaut" any way you spell it. The mountain, the resort at its base, and the old town of Crested Butte (a couple of miles away) all nestle together on the southern side of the Elk Range—just a few miles and an overnight ski tour away from Aspen, but seemingly a world away. It's a long day's drive between Aspen and Crested Butte, especially in winter, as one has to circumnavigate three sides of a massive mountain range.

Like all of Colorado's most romantic ski towns, Crested Butte was originally a mining settlement. But men here mined coal, not gold; there's an earthiness and a funky down-home simplicity about the Butte that must have its roots in this particular past. As a coal-mining town, Crested Butte couldn't put on airs, and as a ski town it doesn't choose to; charm yes, glitz no.

What else makes for Crested Butte's very special character? There's the countryside: a broad open, ranching valley that reminds you of long, lonesome Wyoming ranch country. There's the old town of Crested Butte, a few miles away from the base of the ski mountain. It's one of the most vital small towns in the Rockies, one that pulled together to defeat a giant corporation's big-buck plans to turn the southern Elk Mountains into a slagheap strip mine. The town lives its own life behind old-time wooden false fronts, sharing its Main Street with winter tourists instead of turning it over to them. Still, the valley is becoming developed more than some long-time locals might wish, but compared to other resorts, it hasn't gotten totally out of hand—yet. The new town of Mount Crested Butte up at the base of the ski area is fundamentally a tourist-lodging community with modern condos and lodges, which are in no small measure responsible for preserving the charm of old Crested Butte from development pressures that would have altered it irrevocably—and not for the better.

And finally, there's the mountain. It is a curious and handsomely shaped plug of a peak, or "butte," that really is named Crested Butte. There is ski terrain grafted onto it, with a good, if not an ultramodern, high-tech lift system. But for skiers, it boasts a couple of true advantages. First, Crested Butte is blessed with some of Colorado's best weather patterns, which over the long term produce frequent snowstorms alternating with blues skies and sunshine. Second, an experts' mountain, the North Face, right beside the regular ski mountain, pioneered the concept of lift-served adventure skiing and offers the finest such experience in Colorado. Appetite whetted? Let's look closer.

The Way the Mountain Works

Unlike many other ski mountains, Crested Butte doesn't exactly have a front side or a back side as such. Its "front" is the Mount Crested Butte development, but most of the ski terrain is elsewhere. The mountain also has a side valley; an upper "around-the-corner" side (the North Face area that I'm so in love with); a lower "around-the-corner" side (called East River); and—just to confuse matters—a small subsidiary hill of easy skiing that is quite detached from the rest of the mountain across a sort of low saddle—and that's where the skiing largely takes place.

The town of Mount Crested Butte (remember, that's the resort development) sits in a sunny, almost treeless saddle below the Butte itself. The wide, white, open lower slopes just above the building cluster are a lot like Alpine resorts. The distinctive mountain called Crested Butte is a sharp, pointed, art director's concept of a mountain. But the summit that you can admire from the valley floor is as rocky as it is snowy, so the ski area is located just beside and below the sharp peak itself. As you ride one of several lifts out of Mount Crested Butte, the rocky-ribbed peak looms off to your right.

From the base, the Silver Queen Express takes you up as close as you can get by lift to that pointed summit and opens up a steep front face full of classic black runs. Another chair, the Keystone Express, angles up to the left, crossing over and accessing a much gentler part of the front face, with a host of meandering green runs. But where are the blue runs? From the top of either of these front-side lifts, you can drop over a kind of ridge into a parallel valley running sideways and down to the left that is the heart of the intermediate or blue skiing on this mountain.

Paradise is the name of Crested Butte's third high-speed quad lift, which serves Paradise Bowl, a large open arena up at the head of this side bowl—and the first area on your right as you ski down from Paradise lift. But people tend to call the whole shooting match back here Paradise. Runs are all honest blues, longish, with some flatter sections near the bottom, and very pleasant indeed. The Paradise lift not only serves every run in this section but is longer and offers a lot more vertical than the parallel Teocalli lift. The Teocalli lift is useful for getting back to front side and is popular with snowboarders, who ride the half-pipe below.

If you ski below the loading areas of Paradise and Teocalli lifts and trend rightward around the corner, you come to a separate, one-lift section called East River, served by a triple chair and offering somewhat steeper and more continuous runs than those in Paradise. East River's black runs are "light blacks." *Resurrection,* the best of the East River trails,

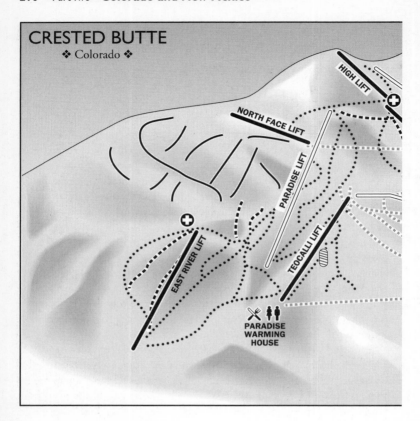

is a tilted boulevard of steep rolling steps. All these runs dead-end near the bottom of a wide river valley and the base of the East River chair.

When you look across to the opposite, south-facing slopes, you'll see long treeless ridges that will make you drool as you stand in the East River lift line. The slopes on this next-door mountain have been stashed away behind a wilderness designation, so all a skier can do is daydream or break out the touring skis.

Crested Butte for Novice and Intermediate Skiers

New or inexperienced skiers and cautious, conservative intermediates can have a great time at the Butte too. Just above the Mount Crested Butte resort development, off to the right as you look toward the mountain, is a small practice lift called Peachtree. It serves wide green slopes completely out of the mountain's traffic pattern. Additionally, all the

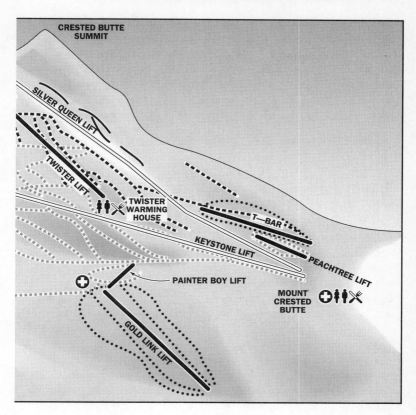

runs underneath Keystone quad lift are friendly, low-angle greens. Their main problem is that better, faster skiers returning to the base from the Paradise and East River areas do use them—and often at a good clip.

Another zone that is tailor-made for lower-level skiers features two lifts that stick out in the direction opposite to everything else on the mountain. The Painter Boy and Gold Link chairlifts are short and serve gentle, open, and sparsely timbered slopes on both sides of a low, round side hill north of the Keystone runs. *Little Lizzie, Splain's Gulch,* and *Topsy* come down the Painter Boy side and are the only runs at Crested Butte right through aspen groves, always a very aesthetic experience. The runs on the Gold Link side of this extra little mountain are all marginally harder and they're rarely crowded. This is a lovely area in which to build mileage and confidence. As homesites have been built up on the Gold Link side, more skiers (and certainly more lift riders) are showing up here.

Skiers ready to graduate to the blue cruising runs in Paradise should first take *Bushwhacker* down to the Teocalli lift. The blue runs off the Teocalli lift, like those off Gold Link, are good for emerging and low-intermediate skiers. When they seem easy, ride the Paradise lift into upper Paradise Bowl, which is considerably steeper. Paradise Bowl offers middle-of-the-road intermediate skiing, while the slightly more challenging blue runs on East River are upper-intermediate terrain for more experienced skiers.

Crested Butte for Strong and Adventurous Skiers

While good skiers at the Butte spend most of their time in the large Paradise area and on the East River runs—which, as the name hints, receive wonderful morning sunlight—very good skiers in search of adventure tend to ski these two zones only for a warm-up and maybe for a little R&R after particularly harrowing runs on the North Face.

Aside from the North Face, described below, another zone of challenging advanced skiing is near the top of the front face. Served by the Twister lift is a group of demanding, well-banked runs. They are perfect racing trails and have been used for the downhill and Super G courses at the U.S. National Championships. Everything is relative, though, because compared to the Extreme Limits, they are simply steep trails with nice fallaways, a sustained pitch, big turns, sweeping views back over moguls and over the valley toward old Crested Butte.

Crested Butte shines in the adventure skiing realm. The ungroomed and wild mountain setting demands judgment and imagination, as well as technique. This sort of skiing is not obvious. Rather, it challenges you to think clearly as well as to move well. If you ski in the North Face section carelessly or foolishly, you could go right over a cliff. The North Face is, in short, very serious. It's a place where you could easily get into trouble, but you also can have the time of your life.

A good way of seeing whether you're up to the North Face is to ski the *Tower 11 Chutes* first. From the top of the Paradise chair, ski the right side of Paradise Bowl until you reach a marked gate in the boundary rope. Then traverse right to the chutes, which are openings in steep forest right under the Paradise lift line. If you feel at home here, then the North Face will be your cup of tea. The logical strategy is to explore the North Face step by step, by skiing farther across it at each run. The first lines lead through *The Glades.* Next you'll traverse across to *High Life,* a long packed-out hiking trail that everybody else follows, and then you'll drop down into the North Face proper. Finally, you'll want to see how far across this vast mountain face you can get and you'll ski *Spellbound Bowl, Third Bowl, Phoenix Bowl,* and the run intriguingly named *Have Skis, Will Trail.*

Don't be misled by the names. The named bowls aren't classic bowls, but rather open faces and wide, steep gullies in a rugged, stair-step face that alternates almost at random between thick timber, cliffs, and couloirs, and sudden, unexpected, and always-welcome minibowls and chutes of snow. A good line on the North Face may take you into and through several of these steep clearings in succession. The steep slot-like faces at the very bottom—like *Cesspool, Last Steep, Staircase,* and *Phoenix Steps*— are the steepest of all and a real challenge to ski well when you are getting tired. There is almost always a best, or most obvious, line down any of these openings, and there are numerous variants. On some of these variants, falling is not a viable option.

Because this is daunting and potentially confusing territory, the area provides guided tours for those who don't feel ready to start exploring the extreme terrain on their own. This is high-energy skiing.

Farther west (to the right as you ride up the Twister or Silver Queen lifts) and the other side of the mountain are some more sections marked with telltale double-black diamonds, a sure sign of excitement at the Butte. These are not cut runs but rather zones to explore. These sections, including *Peel, Upper Peel,* and the lines around them under the big *Banana Funnel,* are unfortunately often closed by the patrol, because wind sweeping around the peak tends to scour off their snow cover. The U.S. Extreme Freeskiing Championships and the U.S. Extreme Boarderfest are regularly held here, but the North Face is generally a safer bet for snow and a much bigger playing field for ski adventure. If skiing powder is your idea of paradise, try to plug Irwin Lodge into your Crested Butte visit. Located in the mountains 12 miles from town, the lodge is accessible by snowcat or other over-snow vehicle. It was renowned for one of the West's premier snowcat skiing operations, with 2,200 skiable acres, 2,100 vertical feet, and an average of 600 inches of snow a year, blanketing fabulous terrain composed of steeps, chutes, bowls, and glades for intermediates and better. The lodge was closed during the 2002–2003 ski season, but new owners came on board in April 2003 and promised to reopen a renovated and improved lodge for 2003–2004. In addition to work on the lodge itself, the new owners needed to buy new snowcats to restart the cat-skiing operation.

Crested Butte for Experts

The most interesting part of Crested Butte is the North Face, a long and rugged mountain face rising in bold, cliff-like steps above Paradise and looming high above East River. This is experts-only country, and Crested Butte was the first Colorado resort to open such hairy terrain. The ski company here deserves a lot of credit for opening this terrain on a regular basis to the skiing public; it did this in a brilliant, cost-effective way. A short, two-minute platterpull ride from *Paradise Bowl* was all that was needed to replace the strenuous half-hour climb that was once the only option to reach the North Face. This ridiculously small and inexpensive lift added some of the most dramatic, serious, ungroomed double-black-diamond skiing imaginable to the ski area and raised Crested Butte into a whole different league! The resort calls this wonderful expert mountain sector its Extreme Limits terrain. The runs named on the trail map are really suggested routes around cliff bands, boulders, trees and just plain steeps. Most skiers refer to the whole sector of the mountain above and beyond Paradise and East River as the North Face, even though there are many separately named areas within it, including a zone called, appropriately enough, North Face.

In addition to being plain challenging, this high, north-facing arena keeps its snow cover relatively well. Added to the exposure and elevation, there's the issue of usage. No one can make laps on the platterpull. The mostly double-black turf feeds into the East River and, peripherally, Paradise sections. It takes a while to ride up the East River chair, slide down to the Paradise Express, and ski to the surface lift, which also has a low capacity.

The ski area received such kudos for opening this sensational terrain that it didn't stop there. In 1991, several seasons after the North Face was established as a legend among Colorado's expert skiers, the High Lift, a T-bar, was installed above the Paradise lift unload. It offers direct access to the *Headwall* and *Teocalli Bowl* behind the Extreme Limits and facilitates access to still another zone of extreme terrain on the front side of the mountain. This section, which added 600 vertical feet to the resort's previously modest vertical, is set in the trough between the ski area and the mountain called Crested Butte. Suspended just below the horn are such steep and narrow double-diamond routes as *Funnel, Banana Peel,* and *Forest.* The single diamond of *Hot Rocks* seems comparatively mild. If you are a strong, adventurous hiker as well as a strong, adventurous skier or snowboarder, ride the top T-bar, shoulder your boards, and climb just under 500 vertical feet to the peak of Crested Butte. The line you'll ski, a steep snowfield on the mountain's back side, isn't visible from the resort—but it will forever be etched in your mind's eye.

Telemarking and Powder at the Butte

Another sort of ski adventure intimately associated with Crested Butte is telemark skiing. The Butte was the birthplace—and today remains a hotbed—of the telemark revolution. This is a hard-to-explain, hard-to-resist mania for skiing even the toughest downhill runs on skis with free-heel, cross-country bindings. You'll probably see more young telemark heroes at Crested Butte than anywhere else in Colorado. Some of the heroes now ski on near-Alpine boards with near-Alpine boots, often not lifting their heels at all, but the tele-mystique still reigns.

Telemark technique is a rediscovered artifact from the dark ages of skiing and Nordic history. Done in a semi-kneeling position with one foot

and ski advanced and the other foot and ski trailing, it is a singularly graceful and very athletic variant of skiing, but it's definitely not for everyone.
In fact, its main attraction, at least at ski areas, is its difficulty; its main
converts are gifted young Alpine skiers who have literally run out of challenges and are looking for something newer and harder. But let me be
more precise: telemarking per se is not so hard. In fact, it is an easy way to
maneuver skinny cross-country skis in soft back-country snow. Doubtless,
the reason that telemark skiing took off in Crested Butte is the amazing
amount of soft powder that falls there. But telemarking down steep runs at
a ski area can be quite an exciting challenge. If you're curious, consider taking an introductory telemark lesson while you're at Crested Butte.

Snowboarding

Crested Butte now has four, count 'em, four terrain parks. One park and
the half-pipe are accessed by the short Teocalli lift. The park along the
Bushwhacker Trail features five rails and three tables; nearby is the 370-
foot-long half-pipe. The Snowdeck Park, opened in 2003, is essentially a
minipark, 70 feet long and 45 feet wide and featuring two rails, a box
jump, and a quarter-pipe. The walk-up park is located near the bottom
of the Keystone lift and is open to snowdecks, skis, snowboards, and
other sliding toys. The Jib Park, built on Warming House Hill, also at
the base area, is as entertaining for spectators as it is for riders and was a
huge success during its inaugural 2002–2003 season. Finally, the Kid's
Terrain Park off the Painter Boy Lift attracts kids of all ages. Adults
wanting to try a rail or a jump are in there as much as the youngsters for
whom it was designed and sized. Crested Butte is always tinkering with
innovations (especially such low-cost innovations as snow features).

Atmosphere, Après Ski, Victuals, and Lodging

Crested Butte is a gem of a ski resort. While the Mount Crested Butte at
the mountain's base plays a vital service role because most of the guest
accommodations are located there, offering hard-to-beat slopeside convenience, it lacks the charm or patina of the historic Crested Butte
downtown. When you feel like a night out, take the shuttle bus or drive
a few miles down the hill into old Crested Butte.

Life pulses up and down Elk Avenue, which is the narrowest main
street in any Colorado mining town, something that gives it an especially intimate character. (The railroad was already operating when the
town was founded, which meant the first town fathers didn't have to
plan extra width on Elk Avenue for long wagon teams and mule trains to
swing around.)

A classic Western ski town has to have a classic locals' bar, and Crested
Butte has two. The **Wooden Nickel** is the hangout of choice for such
ski-area types as patrollers and instructors. Down-valley locals seem to

prefer **Kochevars** (pronounced *Ka-cheevers*) for serious drinking and pool playing; it's still owned by the Kochevar family, who built it in 1900, which makes it the oldest bar in town.

Crested Butte is full of restaurants with great atmosphere, but it's a little shy on restaurants with great cuisine. The best restaurant in town is **Soupçon,** a historic, miniature log cabin in a back alley where you (and only a handful of others) are likely to enjoy some very imaginative and refined French dishes. **Le Bosquet,** located in a small strip shopping center just outside the downtown core, is a runner-up in culinary style but is far more conventional. The **Powerhouse Bar y Grill** is a Mexican restaurant in the town's old powerhouse that serves real *cabrito* on butcher-paper covered tables. **Donita's Cantina** draws its share of Mexican food fans too. If you prefer plain American food, **Slogar** is the place to go. Platters heaped with fried chicken or steak, bowls of potatoes and corn, and mountains of baking-powder biscuits are served family style.

Lodging in old Crested Butte is limited—only a couple of hundred pillows at most—compared to the wide gamut at Mount Crested Butte. A handful of small and charming B&Bs are scattered along the side streets. But the insider's best bet is the **Elk Mountain Lodge,** built in 1919 as an in-town miners' hotel. The lodge has been totally refurbished into a delightful inn. Budget-watchers can't do much better than the **Crested Butte International Youth Hostel,** newly built in 1997 and designed for economy-minded adults who want cleanliness, comfort, and convenience, but don't care much for frills.

At the mountain, Crested Butte's biggest slopeside hotel morphed several years ago into a **Club Med,** designated as a "family ski village," meaning that if you're a nonparent or an empty-nester, you'll probably be happier elsewhere. But if you're traveling with youngsters, Club Med's family friendliness, abundant kids' activities, and all-inclusive pricing are all you need.

If you prefer the charm of a B&B coupled with slopeside convenience, the **Nordic Inn** is a classic ski lodge. The rooms are a bit motel-like, but the public spaces are cozy and charming, the welcome genuine, and the location hard to beat. Elsewhere at the mountain, most of the accommodations are condo-style, either on the mountainside or across the access road and a short walk or shuttle ride to the lifts.

Crested Butte Data

Mountain Statistics

Vertical feet	2,775 feet (lift-served); 3,062 feet (hike to the peak)
Base elevation	9,375 feet
Summit elevation	11,875 feet (highest lift); 12,162 feet (top of peak)
Longest run	2.6 miles

Crested Butte Data *(continued)*

Mountain Statistics *(continued)*

Average annual snowfall	298 inches
Snowmaking	300 acres
Number of lifts	15: 3 high-speed quads; 1 fixed-grip quad; 3 triple chairs; 3 double chairs; 3 surface lifts; 2 moving carpets
Uphill capacity	19,360 skiers per hour
Skiable terrain	1,058 acres
Opening date	Mid-December
Closing date	Early April
Snowboarding	Yes

Transportation

By car The drive from Denver is about 4.5 hours and from Colorado Springs about 3.5 hours. Crested Butte is about half an hour north of Gunnison on Highway 135.

By van or limo Alpine Express from the Gunnison/Crested Butte Airport.

By plane At this writing, Gunnison/Crested Butte Airport is served by Continental, United, and United Express. Some travelers find Montrose, 91 miles from Crested Butte and served by American, Continental, and United, to be an acceptable alternative

Key Phone Numbers

Ski-area information	(800) 810-7669
Snow report	(888) 442-8883
Reservations	(800) 544-8448 or (800) 810-7669
Website	www.crestedbutteresort.com

Lito's TECH TIP

Telemark Skiing

A lot of skiers have seen young telemarkers flashing by in their curious, but elegant, kneeling position. And a lot of downhill skiers have tried cross-country skiing in a track and may even own their own cross-country gear. But even most serious cross-country enthusiasts have never tried telemark turns. Telemarking well in all conditions is a real challenge, but merely learning the turn is easy. If you have a pair of cross-country skis (you don't need special tele-skis to learn the basics) and want to try, do it like this.

First, get used to the telemark stance in a straight run down a very gentle slope. Slide your skis apart, fore and aft, as you drop into a semi-kneeling position: the rear knee almost touching the ski, the front knee bent at 90 degrees. Then rise and slide the rear ski forward as you drop into the opposite kneeling position, front and back legs reversed. Now repeat this kneeling/sliding position a couple of times.

Next, do a couple of fast, smooth wedge turns with your feet pretty close together in a small, narrow wedge. Halfway through one of these wedge turns, drop into the telemark position you practiced earlier, outside ski ahead, inside ski trailing (that is to say, if you're turning right, you'll slide your left ski ahead and let your right ski drop back as you kneel). This wedge-into-telemark works just like a stem christie to sneak you into a beautiful sliding finish, only this time it's a telemark finish to your turn rather than a christie skid. Believe me, it's easy ... if you try it from a narrow wedge.

Next, do a few more of these wedge telemark turns to both sides—fairly long turns, please—letting your skis come around on their own in the telemark position rather than forcing them around quickly. Progressively narrow your wedge more and more while skiing somewhat faster, and in about 15 minutes you'll be guiding a pure telemark turn down your gentle practice hill. A packed-out beginner slope at a downhill ski area is the ideal spot for this eye-opening experiment.

Telluride

Telluride's marketing slogan, "The Most Beautiful Place You'll Ever Ski," is right on the mark—at least as far as Colorado resorts are concerned. The San Miguel River has carved a steep-sided box canyon that is a mind-boggling setting for a ski area. At the end of the canyon nestles a tiny town that has made a transition from a hard-rock mining community to a polished, nationally known resort.

As the United States was celebrating its bicentennial in 1976, the ski area was four years old and the local mine still employed 300 miners. The tunnels are closed now, the mill padlocked, and the miners gone. In the meantime, the town has morphed into a true ski destination. Skiers, tourists, T-shirt merchants, and restaurateurs—plus flocks of real-estate developers and real-estate agents—have discovered this enchanted valley. They, like others before them (including Lito Tejada-Flores who originated this section of this book and shepherded it through its first three editions), were captivated by the place. Lito has written of "the 13,000- and 14,000-foot peaks of the San Juan Mountains ringing the valley and the ski area, or the waterfalls that turn into giant crystal organ pipes in winter, or the sunsets that slant through this east-west canyon like flash floods of liquid gold, or the cockeyed Victorian houses self-consciously spiffy in their new paint and harmonious additions that beef many of them up from their original modest sizes. Telluride is outrageously beautiful every day of the year, even more so in winter."

Today, Telluride is a happening resort, second home of Hollywood stars, and quite possibly the most romantic ski destination in Colorado. From town, the ski mountain looks radically steep (and it is), but actually most of the reasonable skiing is found on the other, much larger side of the ski area. True, Telluride almost certainly boasts a passel of the longest, steepest bump runs in America, but there are plenty of alternatives for every level of skier.

The Shape and Layout of the Mountain

Telluride is a two-sided ski mountain with several bases—two in town and several below and at Mountain Village. The front face, rising dramatically above town, has two bases and two separate lift-access routes. The Coonskin lift is located at the entrance to the town of Telluride and rises up to a midpoint on the long ridge-like crest of the mountain. The old Oak Street lift and the adjacent high-speed, high-tech gondola, together with the Plunge triple (Oak Street lift's continuation) take skiers from the center of town up to the very top, a total of over 3,000 vertical feet. Virtually all the skiing on this front side (known locally as "the face") is serious, dropping straight down the steep fall-line. The sole exception is the zigzag road called *Telluride Trail* that provides a comfortable come-home route for weaker skiers who prefer not to ride the gondola back down into town. The rest of the runs on the front are marked blue or black, but skiers should beware: a blue run on Telluride's face would be black at most ski areas, and a black run here could be double black elsewhere. As for Telluride's double blacks, they are challenging to the max.

However, most people do take the gondola, which is an innovative over-the-top lift linking the town of Telluride with Mountain Village, in the cusp of what used to be thought of as the back side of the mountain. This huge lift has three loading/unloading areas. Station Telluride is in town, beside the bottom of the old Oak Street chair (Lift 8). Station St. Sophia is on the crest of the ridge, not far from the top of the Coonskin chair (Lift 7). Finally, Station Mountain Village is at a large plaza in the eponymous resort center.

For many skiers, the back side is really the main side, because that's where most of the terrain is located. Mountain Village is set in a basin at the bottom of a large, spread-out, and far friendlier parcel of ski terrain for mere mortals. The gondola ride is free for anyone without skis or a snowboard (but requires a lift ticket for use as a ski lift). It operates late into the evening, making this one of the most innovative people-moving systems at any Colorado resort. It ties the towns of Telluride and Mountain Village, eliminating a long round-about drive between the two. Although the gondola didn't open up any new ski terrain, it continues to offer the fastest route from town onto the mountain, and its speed, views, and comfort are bonuses.

Mountain Village is a world apart from quirky, historic old Telluride. Telluride has invested millions into a lift system that links its two lodging cores with complex terrain draped over several mountains and ridges. The large plaza at the Mountain Village gondola base is an entrance point to most of the runs for people staying there. Additionally, a second, lower entrance point serves the few day skiers that Telluride attracts. They reach the Mountain Village plaza via a lower gondola. Finally, the "Chondola," a unique lift whose cables are strung with a combination of quad chairlifts and gondola cars, serves a separate complex of beginner runs, also below the plaza.

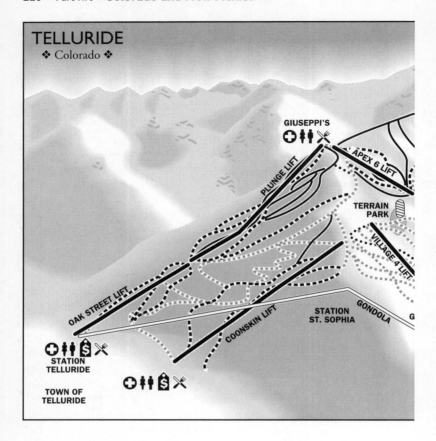

The ski area is draped in separate pods over an amazingly large area, fragmented by a host of natural obstacles: cliff bands, creek beds, and secondary hill-like summits. When you actually total up the acreage of skiing available, it's less than one would expect for such a massive mountain. Curiously, this doesn't matter very much because Telluride's capacity is still bigger than its bed base. Lift lines have never been an issue, which means you can get in as much skiing as your legs can take.

Telluride for Beginners and Novices

The Chondola, that aforementioned quad/gondola hybrid, serves *The Meadows,* a wide practice universe for first-timers, emerging novices, and small children. *The Meadows* are rolling and slightly inclined flats just below Mountain Village. The next step is to explore the trails served by Lift 10, slanting up into thick forest from the Mountain Village. The

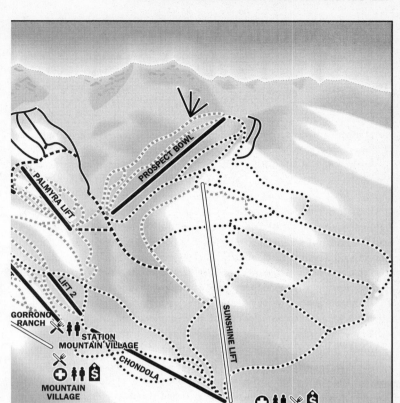

long runs are almost ideal for the sort of mileage that makes progress inevitable. For years, this state-of-the-art, high-speed detachable quad was nicknamed "the lift to nowhere," as it served as a real-estate lift designed to provide ski-in/ski-out access to high-ticket homesites. But with the inauguration of lift service in Prospect Bowl in 2001–2002, it became an access lift to this high basin. One of Prospect's key features is additional novice terrain in a magnificent high-Alpine setting, something new skiers rarely get to experience. Ski down the gentle back-side slope off Chair 10 to the Ute Park chair, serving beguiling beginner and novice terrain laced through the trees in a marvelously scenic location.

Telluride for Intermediate Skiers

From town, most skiers take the gondola and immediately head down the other side. It's good morning strategy to get out at Station St. Sophia and look west toward the large forested bowl that contains Telluride's greatest concentration of intermediate trails. The runs to your left are easier (and *Village Bypass* is absolutely the easiest way down this side of the mountain). *Hermit* and *Smuggler,* straight below, are short and rather steep and occasionally lightly moguled. To the right, are several longer and smoother runs. These wide boulevards offer sustained pitch but no sudden drops. *Butterfly* drops directly down to the big mid-mountain restaurant called Gorrono Ranch, while *Lower See Forever* bears right all the way down to Mountain Village.

At the edge of Mountain Village, Lift 4, a high-speed quad, serves a good chunk of the intermediate skiing. The least-skied run off this lift is *Humboldt Draw,* a lovely half-hidden valley that twists like an outsize toboggan run and is well worth checking out. From the top of Lift 4, you can also traverse to Lift 5, which once again feels like a separate ski area. It's an important one, though, because it features the only consistently easy bump run at Telluride, *Palmyra.* From Lift 5, you can also traverse down and right to Lift 6, which serves another distinct skiing pod or section at what was long the top of the ski mountain.

Prospect Bowl, a long-promised expansion, came on line in 2001–2002 with three lifts, 733 acres of terrain, and an additional 320 vertical feet of lift-served skiing. Much of it comprises big, rolling slopes, some of which are groomed in lovely cruising. Looking up, the right face of the huge, mostly north-facing basin is solid intermediate terrain, cascading off a sub-ridge from Palmyra Peak into a mellow area of open snowfields that feed into newly cut trails and natural glades. Blue-square skiers, enraptured with this peak experience, can gaze across at the steeper Gold Hill slopes and chutes and therefore have something to aim for.

Back to the front, as it were, you might have heard so much about Telluride's famous front-side runs and the classic lifts serving them that you want to sample the old way of skiing there even if you are not the world's best mogul master. From Lifts 8 and 9 (Oak Street and Plunge, respectively), you can follow *See Forever,* a long ridgeline cruiser and the only nonthreatening, nonmoguled, nonblack run off the top. It doesn't have quite as good a view as the name suggests, because it is lined with dense trees for most of its length; "Ski Forever" would be more accurate.

Halfway down *See Forever, Lookout* dives off the ridge and down the front face, and it is certainly the most reasonable run on the front face for average skiers—or what passes for average at Telluride. Wide, usually well groomed, and not truly threatening, *Lookout* really does offer plunging views of the town, which resembles a miniature dollhouse community beneath your skis and provides some of the visual drama of harder front-face runs without the potential trauma. By contrast, *Coonskin* and *Milk Run,* two other front-side runs marked blue, can be very tough when they are moguled.

Bushwacker is almost always groomed, and its north-facing exposure ensures cold, grippy snow, but it's steep and would be a black run anywhere else in Colorado. At the bottom of its long, steep sweep, *Bushwacker* joins the bottom of *Mammoth Slide,* a river of bumps, and the two become a congenial catwalk leading left around the mountain to the lower half of *Spiral Stairs.* This area has been widened, is often groomed, and is not as steep as the top of *Bushwacker.* It takes you down to Station Telluride, and you're home free.

Telluride for Experts

Despite all its intermediate skiing, Telluride has been stereotyped in the folklore of Colorado skiing as an experts' mountain. Fair or unfair? A bit of both. The bell-shaped curve operates here too, and on any given day you'll find more intermediates enjoying themselves on Telluride slopes than experts. But it's also true that the better you are, the better you'll like this mountain. But if this is, in some sense, an experts' mountain, it's also a mountain for a particular breed of expert skier. Telluride is bumper heaven. Its black slopes are very steep and always densely moguled. The awesomely big and deep bumps are really wild—to use the appropriate bump-skiers' vernacular, Telluride's moguls are "gnarly."

There are two main mogul-skiing zones. The first, short and sweet, is off Lift 6, sometimes just called Apex after *Apex Glade,* the large, half-open area to the north of the lift. The skiing is just as interesting as on the front face, but the runs are much, much shorter. *Zulu Queen,* a narrow slot through the woods, is the hardest line; *Silver Glade* and *Apex Glade* are the most fun; and double-black *Giant Steps,* under the lift line, is strictly for showoffs. *Allais Alley* and *Sully's* also bear double diamonds. The terrain off Lift 6 is so bumped up that even the forest area between the mogul runs gets moguled!

The second, legendary bump zone comprises the long black runs coming right off the top and tumbling down the front side toward town in a marathon, nonstop cascade. Although a proliferation of snowboards and shaped skis has changed the way bumps are formed, the best-shaped moguls on the front are traditionally found on *Mammoth Slide,* the worst on *Kant-Mak-M.* Both these runs eventually feed into the middle of *Spiral Stairs,* the granddaddy of all mean mogul runs. *The Stairs,* as the run is known, starts innocently enough, branching off from the top of the *See Forever* ridge. A quarter mile later, the slope simply drops out from under you. The start is breathtaking, and the rest—once you recover from the sudden visual impact of coming over a lip and looking straight down some 3,000 feet—is just as hard. *The Stairs* ranks among the steepest, hardest bump runs anywhere.

Just left of *The Stairs* is *The Plunge.* It's a black diamond too (even though the ski area colored it blue on the trail map, which gets a lot of innocent skiers into trouble), but it's far, far easier than *The Stairs*—and just as famous. In fact, the ski area grooms half of *The Plunge,* leaving half to bump up and giving people who can handle the relentless moguls the opportunity to stay in them the whole way down, but enabling others to bail out for all or part of the run. Still, remember, that it's a special shade of Telluride blue that characterizes *The Plunge.*

Telluride's final treat for expert skiers is Gold Hill. This is an area of steep chutes that, until the opening of Prospect Bowl, required a hike from the top of Lift 6. Now, the new Gold Hill high-speed chairlift ferries skiers to 1,500 vertical feet in just four minutes. It tops off at 12,260 feet, Telluride's highest lift-served spot, well above the tree line, into the bowl area's most challenging terrain and views that won't quit.

The most demanding run in all of Telluride is reached by an access point from the top of the Gold Hill ridge into Bear Creek Canyon. This is more than 3,000 vertical feet of steep and serious terrain, beyond the ski-area boundary and therefore unpatrolled and not avalanche controlled. It is a total commitment, because once you're in, down is the only way out. Consisting largely of chute and tight glade skiing, it requires outstanding off-piste skiing skills, backcountry training, proper equipment (avalanche beacons and shovels for everyone), and the good sense never to ski it alone. It is something most skiers should only read or dream about, but for the elite few who are up to it, Bear Creek is a serious backcountry adventure with the luxury of lift service.

Snowboarding

Telluride's Sprite Air Garden terrain park is exceptional. Relocated in 2003 from the *Butterfly* run above the Gorrono Ranch restaurant to *Lower See Forever*, this huge facility offers more than acres and acres of terrain features. These include an Olympic-sized, 12-foot competition-style half-pipe, plus a variety of tabletops, berms, banks, and pyramids— everything a hot rider, either on one board or a pair of freeskiing shorties, could possibly dream of. With its relocation, the park was tripled in size and modified with the latest jibs, a steeper half-pipe, and other improvements. The layout features three distinct lines, enabling three riders to hit the park simultaneously. Air Gardeners don't even have to hang with the fogies when they are hungry, thirsty, or just want to chill, because the Launch Pad is located right at the top of the park.

Beginner freeskiers and riders can practice in a "pocket park" off the Ute Park chairlift in Prospect Basin. It has rollers, gentle hits, and other features suitable for starters. Additionally, Thrill Hill, a nighttime park provides opportunities to ride on a new type of wheel-less skateboard designed for snow, tubing, snow biking, and snow skating. Gravity Garage is the laid-back lounge and warming hut.

A Tiny Town and Its Treasures

The old mining town of Telluride (including its box canyon) is scarcely more than four blocks wide—though expansion pressure has in recent years pushed development right up to the edge of public land on both sides of the valley. Despite its trendy reputation, Telluride still tries to stay a bit rough around the edges, good-natured, and warm hearted, even if Learjets are now parking at the airport outside town. A car is unnecessary, for there's a free bus in town—and a gondola offers outstanding transportation between town and Mountain Village.

Just what is there to do in Telluride when you're not standing around with a crick in your neck admiring the 13,000-foot peaks that ring the town? **Leimgruber's** is an ever-popular post-Plunge pub with a vast collection of imported German beers. Belly up to the fabulous hand-carved bar in the **Sheridan Bar,** for pure unretouched, unadulterated turn-of-the-century mining-town chic. **Swede-Finn Hall** and the nearby historic railroad depot have each undergone several ownership changes in recent years. Give them a shot, because both are historic and wonderfully atmospheric old buildings.

Actually, Telluride is still too small and too down-home to compete in big-league après-ski, although there are always a couple of bars and clubs with live music and, recently, a lot of live jazz. Among the main-drag favorites are the always-lively **Last Dollar Saloon** (which locals call The Buck) and the **Fly Me to the Moon Saloon** for night owls who hoot to live music. The **Noir Bar,** downstairs from the **Bluepoint,** is a relatively new hotspot for martinis and music. If any sort of show—movie, amateur theatrical, or concert—is playing in the old Sheridan Opera House, one of the most beautiful gold-rush opera houses in Colorado, don't miss it. For the last word in anti-slickness, rent a pair of skates and walk over to the town park to skate on an outdoor oval under the giant cliffs of Bear Creek. It's always satisfying to prowl the art galleries and interesting retail shops lining the main street, though sometimes they seem eclipsed by the storefront sales offices for pricey Mountain Village condos and real-estate agencies selling multimillion-dollar outlying ranch properties.

Telluride has better restaurants than most larger towns. **La Marmotte** is a French restaurant that fits beautifully into a historic brick icehouse located two blocks below Main Street. Another knockout is **221 South Oak** (the address of an old Victorian house), which has refined food in a refined atmosphere at relatively moderate prices. **Honga's Lotus Petal** is in another old house nearby. At the other end of the spectrum, **Baked in**

Telluride, the local bakery, produces the best bagels this side of Katz's Delicatessen. It's the place locals and visitors stop for breakfast or a quick snack. **Sofio's** is Telluride's long-term Mexican classic, while nearby **Eagle's** is all about style and fusion fare.

With the gondola guaranteeing that more people end their day on the south side of town, more spots have opened there. First among equals is **Cosmopolitan,** a sophisticated epicurean temple in the **Hotel Columbia.** If you're into wines, don't miss dinner in its **Tasting Cellar.** The **Wildflour Cooking Company,** in the **Camel's Garden Hotel** right at the Station Telluride gondola base, features excellent fresh-baked treats. High on the mountain, at the apex of the gondola line, is **Allred's,** operating as a private lunch club but serving gourmet dinners.

Mountain Village has its own dining and nightlife options—more subdued, more expensive, more "created" than the eclectic in-town scene. The **Skier's Union Café** on the main plaza dominates the after-ski scene. The **Legends** is the signature restaurant in the **Wyndham Peaks,** the new resort center's major hotel. **Cazwella's** and **9545** get rave reviews—yet interesting shopping is still almost nonexistent. Most skiers staying in Mountain Village still prefer to spend their evenings in downtown Telluride, on the other side of the mountain. Remember that the gondola was designed more as a transportation link than a ski lift and operates late into the night. One has to applaud any resort transportation solution that reduces the use of cars and buses, and this gondola is a bold move that will help keep Telluride an intimate and unspoiled destination a little longer.

In-town lodging options are condos in various price ranges, quaint B&B's in authentic Victorians (plus the **San Sophia Lodge,** a nouveau Victorian of great charm), and several hotels. **The New Sheridan,** a downtown landmark, was already called the New Sheridan"when Williams Jennings Bryan delivered his Cross of Gold speech from its balcony in 1896. Newer—far newer—hotels include the **Hotel Columbia** and the **Camel's Garden Hotel** near the gondola's Station Telluride, the **Ice House** a few blocks away, and the **Hotel Telluride** in a cul-de-sac off the main drag.

Most of the Mountain Village lodgings are condo-style—albeit, luxurious condos. The **Wyndham Peaks Resort & Golden Door Spa** is a full-service hotel, while the newer **Inn at Lost Creek** is far smaller but also quite luxurious.

Telluride Data

Mountain Statistics

Vertical feet	3,530 feet
Base elevation	8,725 feet
Summit elevation	12,260 feet
Longest run	4.6 miles (Galloping Goose)

Telluride Data (continued)

Mountain Statistics (continued)

Average annual snowfall	309 inches
Number of lifts	16: 2 eight-passenger gondolas (1 gondola, 1 Chondola); 7 high-speed quad chairlifts; 2 triple chairs; 2 doubles; 2 surface lifts; 1 moving carpet
Uphill capacity	21,186 skiers per hour
Skiable terrain	1,700 acres
Snowmaking	255 acres
Opening date	Late November
Closing date	Early April
Snowboarding	Yes

Transportation

By car 65 miles south from Montrose; 71 miles north from Cortez, and 125 miles from Durango.

By van From the Telluride, Montrose, or Cortez airports via Alpine Limo, (877) 728-8750, or Telluride Taxi, (888) 212-TAXI. From Montrose, Mountain Limo, (970) 728-9606.

By plane Telluride's own airport has flights from Denver on United Express/ Great Lakes Express and from Phoenix on America West Express. The airport is small and weather-vulnerable, and flights are often diverted to Montrose or Cortez. Montrose currently has daily seasonal service by American, Continental, United/United Express, and America West.

Key Phone Numbers

Ski-area information	(970) 728-6900
Snow report	(970) 728-7425
Reservations	(800) 854-3062
Website	www.telski.com

Lito's TECH TIP

Skiing Super Bumps

Skiing bumps is one thing; skiing extra-big, extra-steep bumps is quite another. As usual, there are a few tricks to it, and, as with an advanced graduate course at a university, there are prerequisites. Unless you can ski medium and small bumps smoothly and efficiently, you'll be floundering on serious bump runs. But given the basics, here's how to adapt to tougher stuff.

On mega-bumps, the slope changes so radically from one moment to the next that you're always playing catch-up with your skis, which tend to drop out from under you in the steep gullies. The solution is faster, more dynamic pole action. By the time your skis have pivoted into the fall line, you should already be reaching straight down the hill with your pole for the next bump. In effect, this pulls your body forward so you can keep up with your skis and, of course, gets you ready for the next turn.

But often in big hard bumps there isn't much room to finish your turn between one bump and the next, so once again speed control becomes an issue. The solution is simply to accept a little more speed and then, periodically, wherever there's room to do so, complete your turn by curving up and over the shoulder of the next bump. This extra uphill hook will cut your speed way back from time to time.

As you ski faster, in bigger bumps, you will often feel yourself compressed, your legs pushed up beneath you, by the force with which you contact the bump. This compression is a natural form of shock absorption, but it only works once. To use your legs as shock absorbers again, on the next bump and the next, you need to make a continual effort to extend your feet and legs back down into the trough as you come over the lip of the bump, stretching out to fill up the available space, and getting tall to absorb the next compression.

Of course, that's not the whole story of super bumps, but it's a good start. You'll find more information, more detail, more help with this and other skiing challenges in my book *Breakthrough on Skis,* a Vintage paperback from Random House.

Durango Mountain Resort

Durango Mountain Resort is the not-so-new name for the former Purgatory, Colorado's most southwestern ski area. It remains relatively small, remote from Denver and the front range, and charming. Located fairly close to Telluride as the crow flies but a helluva long way around by road, it's blessed with typically stunning San Juan Mountain scenery, with panoramic views of granite peaks and deep gorges. Despite some base development, Durango Mountain Resort is still primarily a ski area, with minimal resort life after the lifts close. Durango, the town with which it now shares its name, lies a half-hour drive to the south, where the Animas River flows out of the mountains into the first high, red mesas of Anasazi country. If fate had only put these two together, what a perfect resort it would be.

Durango is a great Western town (more a small city than a town, actually), with an old historic main street, a state college, and enough good shops, restaurants, and lodging to make most ski towns jealous. But you don't get to walk home at night, watching the moonlight painting milky brushstrokes down runs you've just schussed that afternoon. Pity.

The combination still works well, and this duo has been a longtime favorite with skiers from Albuquerque, Phoenix, and elsewhere in the Southwest, as well as with vacationers from Texas, Oklahoma, and farther afield. The Durango ski experience is intimate and low-key rather than challenging and grand, but the skier-service level is high and the natives are friendly. It's hard not to like this destination.

How the Mountain Works

The section of the mountain (which skiers stubbornly continue to refer to as Purgatory) visible from the base faces due east, across the great hollowed-out gorge of the Animas River. A rugged subrange called the Twilight Peaks provides stunning views on the other side of the canyon. This ski area is wider than it is tall, with a tad over 2,000 vertical feet, but stretching so far around to the north side that it gives the impression of skiing on a big and complex mountain.

Chairlifts are numbered in the order in which they were built, but do not indicate their physical relation to one another. The gentle Columbine beginner and snowplay area below the village development features lifts numbered 7, 9, 10, and 11. On the main mountain, just above the base village, Chairs 1 and 6 march right up the front face, which looks, and is, respectably steep. Chair 1 is a high-speed, six-passenger chair, which takes just six minutes from the base to the summit and all but eliminates lift lines at this important spot. Chair 4 slants off to the right, opening up an area of friendly green runs where novices spend most of their time. This lift, currently a double, is being upgraded (possibly to a Telluride-style Chondola), a project that could be completed by the 2004–2005 season. The best time to ski the front face is early to mid-morning in order to take advantage of the direct early light. By late afternoon, the snow is likely to be crusty or scraped—nothing a pass by from a groomer won't cure, but nothing that you really want to ski either.

The front runs are just the portal of this ski area that folds or wraps around the corner to the right into a side valley. The runs on this side of the mountain are served by Chairs 2, 3, 5, and 8 and face almost due north. That makes for a pretty fair trade-off. You either get great views on the front or great snow on the side. Most of the terrain is found on the north side. Since it is quite a bit bigger, during the course of a day, you'll probably wind up traversing from one side to the other a couple of times. The runs called *Parkway* and *Expressway* are the best cross-mountain trails.

The north side of the mountain is naturally zoned into skiing terrain for different abilities. It starts out quite easily with a lot of green runs and easy blues on Chair 2, and the farther back you go, the harder and more stimulating the skiing is. Lifts 3 and 5 serve the middle area of this side mountain, which holds a zone of longer blue runs with a couple of friendly blacks. Finally, by skiing down an expressway of a run called *Legends,* you arrive at Chair 8, which serves a zone called The Legends, the steepest skiing on the north side.

These far-end trails boast Durango Mountain Resort's greatest concentration of black-diamond runs. The two most exciting are *Ray's Ridge* and *Elliot's:* steep, varied terrain with attractive banked sides to play on. The exceptional area near the top, where *Blackburn's Bash* and *Paul's Park* wander through steep, open forest glades presents a nice contrast to the more clearly defined trails on the rest of the mountain.

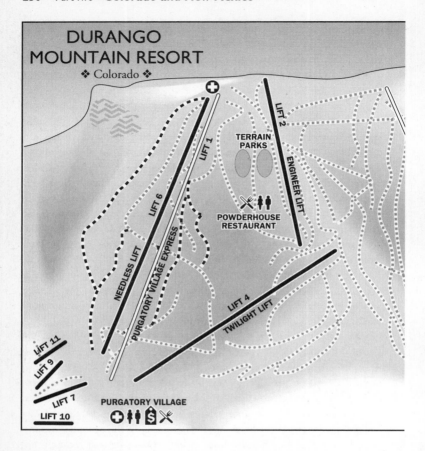

Whether gentle or tough, the resort's runs share a common flavor, a special character that makes skiing intriguing but not effortless. On this stair-step terrain, the pitches of the slopes are seldom continuous. Almost every trail has numerous breakaways and a roller-coaster sequence of steeps and flats with abrupt, sometimes exciting, transitions. They won't get you into trouble, but they do keep you on your toes, then heels, then toes, etc. With this sort of skiing on a real and variable mountain shape rather than slopes of man-made smoothness, you are constantly forced to adapt and adjust to changing terrain. But be careful not to "blind jump" any of these sudden lips where the slope changes angle, or, conversely, not to stop beneath any of these breaks in pitch where a flying skier or snowboarder might nail you.

With the exception of *Dead Spike,* located right in the middle of the northern side of the mountain, the trails tend to be a bit narrower than

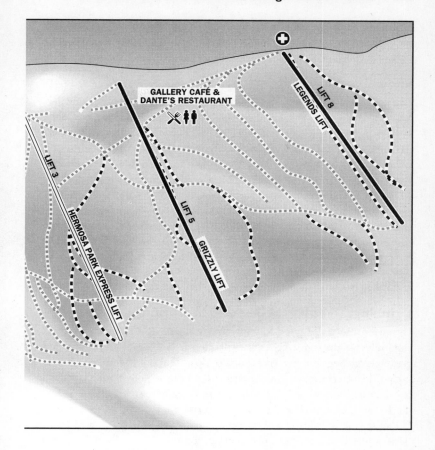

at most Colorado areas. The easiest way to explore some of the remarkable mountains surrounding Durango Mountain Resort is to sign up for a day's powder tour with the San Juan Ski Company, which has permit from the Forest Service for snowcat service to an astonishing 35,000 acres of forested and Alpine terrain. Groups meet at the resort and ride the lift to meet the snowcat, and the return is directly to the resort's base. The skiing includes above-timberline terrain draped off Greyrock Mountain's 12,500-foot summit for sunny days and handsome steep-treed slopes for gray and stormy weather. Seventy-five percent of the terrain is through old-growth forests. This snowcat option has definitely added an element of big-mountain adventure to the resort experience. An enhanced expert adventure is the San Juan Hat Trick. Ski or ride for one day at the resort, then spend two days in the San Juan backcountry, one cat skiing with the San Juan Ski Company and a second at Silverton

Mountain for guided big-mountain adventure on America's newest and most challenging mountain. Book through Durango Mountain Resort as part of a vacation package or directly at (800) 208-2780.

Snowboarding

Durango Mountain Resort has four terrain parks. Just below the Powderhouse Lodge is the Pitchfork Terrain Park, with a 400-foot half-pipe, quarter-pipe, spines, rails, and boxes. The nearby Limbo Slopestyle Park has rails, whalebacks, and various hits. An enhanced and upgraded sound system infuses both parks with the spirit and freedom riders seek. Youngsters have their own little terrain area called the Animas Adventure Trail, which has been improved with replications of historic Animas City building facades and Snow Monster arches, which were created in Durango and now have become a standard for small children's classes around the country. Animas Adventure Trail winds through the trees, and couples fun with a learn-to-slide environment. Finally, the area builds a couple of hits on the Snag Feature Trail, but it becomes more of a place for skiers and riders to create their own mini-park than one pre-configured.

Drinking, Dining, and Dancing in Durango

Despite some really good-looking development at the base of the ski mountain, including a pedestrian plaza that has a great feel to it and great views, there still just isn't much to do at Durango Mountain Resort except ski and sleep. For dinner and entertainment, most guests head to town, either immediately after the last run or after a stop at Purgy's (formerly Farquarht's) at the base of the mountain.

Durango is an easy town to navigate, since it's organized around a traditional street axis. The old section is at the south end of Main, with several blocks qualifying as a historic district. The elegant, historic **Strater Hotel,** one of the most imposing buildings on lower Main Street, is also the fanciest place in town to stay. This grand, four-story, red-brick building is both a treat and a bargain. Comparable rooms in Aspen, with the Strater's all-antique furnishings, would go for three or four times the price. The Strater also houses two other Durango musts: the **Diamond Belle Saloon,** an old-time bar that's still a marvel despite bartenders in corny period costumes, and the **Diamond Circle Theatre,** a classic melodrama and vaudeville stage, where the same corny, old-time costumes are, in fact, just right.

Because Durango is a gateway to Mesa Verde National Park and the Four Corners area, it offers a large number of motor hotels and mom-and-pop motels, which lower their rates in winter, their off-season. Lift/lodging package rates are hard to beat. There are also several charming bed-and-breakfast inns B&Bs in and around town. At the resort, **Joey's** serves Italian food in a casual family atmosphere. Nearby restaurants—**Hamilton**

Chop House, Grizzly Peak Pub, and The Sow's Ear—are mostly of the steak-and-spuds variety. Dining options are far wider-ranging in town. Among them, a wonderfully unpretentious, but very sophisticated, restaurant called **Ken & Sue's** is located at 636 Main Street, and **Chez Grandmere** is tucked in near the railroad depot. Ken & Sue's is a bistro with a knockout combination of creative cooking and modest prices, while Chez Grandmere relocated some years ago from Snowmass and has developed a loyal following. Other good bets are **Red Snapper, Season's Rotisserie Grill,** and **Francisco's Restaurante y Cantina,** the latter for large portions of Southwestern and quasi-continental cuisine. Nearby are a steak-and-seafood place called **Randy's** and a casual bistro called **Meritage,** which serves breakfast, lunch, and light dinners. If you're staying in town, stop for breakfast at **Carver's,** a bakery and microbrew pub. In fact, stop at Carver's after skiing too—or at **Farquahrt's** for pizza, or at **Lady Falconburgh's Barley Exchange** or **Steamworks Brewing Company** for beer and pub food. **The Office,** located in the Strater, is a wine bar-plus that combines sophistication and turn-of-the-last-century ambience.

Durango Mountain Resort's excellent multiday lift called the Total Adventure Ticket allows you to trade in one day of lifts on a four-day (or longer) ticket for a winter ride on the fabled Durango & Silverton Narrow Gauge Railroad, cross-country skiing, snowshoe tours, playing on the SnowCoaster tubing hill, a snowmobile tour, a relaxing day at Trimble Hot Springs, or cat-skiing with San Juan Ski Company. Snowdon, held at the end of January, is Durango's lively winter carnival. As much as anything, it reflects the casual, high-spirited nature of this lively community that has lent its name to a ski resort nearby.

Durango Mountain Resort Data

Mountain Statistics

Vertical feet	2,029 feet
Base elevation	8,793 feet
Summit elevation	10,822 feet
Longest run	2 miles
Average annual snowfall	260 inches
Snowmaking	250 acres
Number of lifts	11: 1 high-speed six-passenger chairlift; 1 high-speed quad; 4 triple chairlifts; 3 double chairlifts; 1 surface lift; 1 moving carpet
Uphill capacity	15,050 skiers per hour
Skiable terrain	1,200 acres
Opening date	Thanksgiving
Closing date	Early April
Snowboarding	Yes

Durango Mountain Resort Data (continued)

Transportation

By car A 30-minute drive north from Durango on U.S. 550. Durango is actually closer to Albuquerque than to Denver.

By plane Durango-Plata Country Airport, 15 miles just south of town and 44 miles from the resort, is served by America West, Continental Express, and United/United Express.

Key Phone Numbers

Ski-area information	(800) 982-6103 or (970) 247-9000
Snow report	(970) 247-9000, ext. 1
Reservations	(800) 979-9742
Website	www.DurangoMountainResort.com

Lito's TECH TIP

Skiing against All Odds

This is not one of my how-to "ski tech" sections but, instead, a note of appreciation, admiration, and genuine awe for the handicapped skiers you'll see on the slopes of Purgatory and other Colorado ski resorts. Calling these skiers blind skiers, one-legged skiers, paraplegic skiers, physically challenged skiers, or adaptive skiers, as we do nowadays, doesn't do justice to the hurdles they have overcome or properly recognize their determination and their very real athletic gifts. The wonderful thing is that so many have become, simply, skiers.

Purgatory, like Winter Park, has a terrific reputation for teaching the disabled to ski. And if you have a friend in a wheelchair or on crutches who you think might love to try skiing, these are the two resorts to consider. Specially trained instructors, using amazing sit-ski contraptions as well as the more usual outriggers for one-legged skiers, can do wonders with people whom common sense tends—wrongly—to classify as permanently excluded from the skiing experience.

There is a very effective program for blind skiers, called the B.O.L.D. Skier program, at many Colorado ski areas. Blind skiers ski with guides who give them verbal information about where to turn and what's coming up on the slope ahead of them. Both the blind skier and the volunteer guide are identified by bright orange bibs.

There are relatively few serious ski-teaching programs oriented especially to the needs of seriously disabled skiers. Purgatory and Winter Park, and nowadays Snowmass, are exceptions. Both Winter Park and Purgatory have been pioneers in this area. Bravo! Hats off to these skiers and to all who have helped them to ski.

For more information on this remarkable program, you can contact the Adaptive Sports Association. ASA runs their Purgatory ski program from a small wooden building just below the base-area plaza, and their phone number is (970) 247-9000, extension 3217. Or you can phone the ASA Durango office at (970) 259-0374.

Taos Ski Valley

Taos is one of those rare ski areas of which you can truly say that they don't make 'em like that any more. The conventional wisdom of today's ski industry says that you just can't build a ski area where 51% of the terrain is expert level. But luckily for us, Ernie Blake, who founded the area in 1955, made a habit of ignoring conventional wisdom. An expatriate Swiss war hero, aviator, and a great skier in his own right, Ernie was a living legend in his own time, and since his death in 1989 he has become simply a legend. To this day, everything about this ski mountain bears his stamp and expresses his vision of skiing—that it is adventure, not just winter recreation. When you ski Taos, you're going to have an adventure—and it will be on skis, for Taos is one of just a handful of resorts remaining in this country to prohibit snowboarding.

The resort is really called Taos Ski Valley—an odd New Mexicanism, calling high-mountains a "valley." Indeed, the highest, snowiest peak in the Sangre de Cristo Mountains that one sees from the town of Taos is called Vallecito Peak, or "little valley" peak. Go figure.

In the late 1990s, the southern Sangre de Cristo suffered a couple of seasons of snow drought, but usually this range enjoys storm after storm of amazingly dry and light powder. Logic would indicate that snow here can't be any drier or lighter than Colorado's, but it seems so. And these are, after all, the southern Rockies, seldom bitterly cold, often sunny. Furthermore, Taos Ski Valley is not only the finest skiing in New Mexico, but one of the handful of really great resorts in the country. It's an unlikely venue. You certainly can't see it from the town of Taos, a Spanish colonial settlement, later a refuge for artists and writers. The Taos Pueblo is still inhabited by Native Americans, and part of the surreal charm of the Taos ski experience. The town's adobe architecture, like its indigenous Spanish and Indian culture, is still largely intact, and to many visitors, Taos feels more foreign, more exotic than France, Austria, or Switzerland. The drive between town and ski resort takes half an hour up a narrow, steep-sided, densely forested canyon, at the head of which is the parking area, a compact Alpine-village base, and a ski area that seems to consist of only a couple of steep runs. Wrong. Taos is full of surprises. Get ready.

The Hidden Shapes of the Mountain

For years skiers arriving at the base of this unconventional resort have been greeted by a large sign that reads: "Don't panic, what you see is just a small portion of our runs; there's a lot of easier skiing farther up, out of sight." It's a good thing, because mostly what you see is *Al's Run,* a steep cascade of big moguls, dropping straight and relentless to the base of two lifts—the only lifts in sight (except for a tiny beginner chair off to one

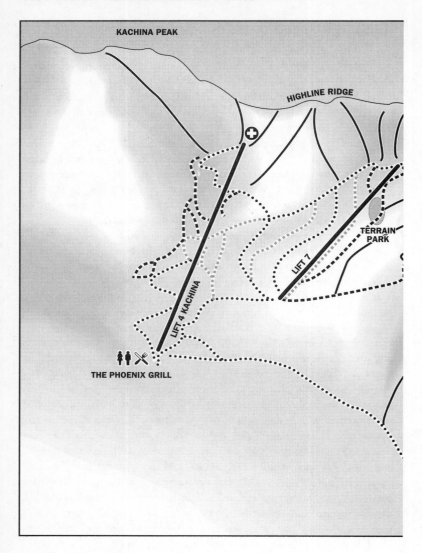

side)—and a faint tracery of other steep-bump runs curving through the forest to the right of *Al's*. It's an impressive introduction to a very complex mountain, full of secrets, full of discoveries.

To understand the shape of the ski mountain that's out of sight above you, imagine *Al's Run* and the lifts that run up it as the ski area's spine or central axis, which continues upward until it runs into a high ridge. This high ridge, virtually at the skyline, divides the mostly north-facing area into two halves: a west side (right, as you are looking up) and an east side (left, again looking up). Both contain large rolling basins, which are

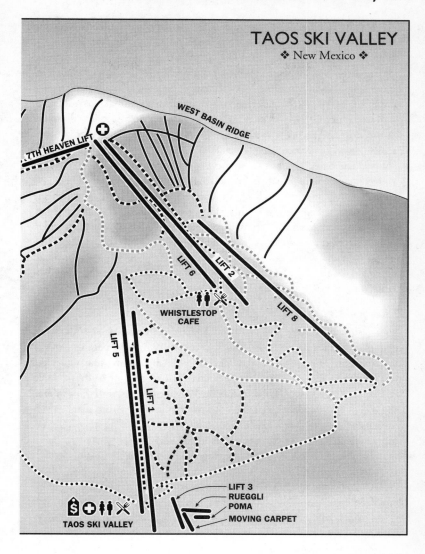

Taos's two intermediate skiing zones, and both basins steepen as they rise in a final sweep to the ridge. Most of the legendary expert and expert-plus runs drop off this ridge. At its far eastern end (again, on the far left on the trail map or as you look up at the mountain), this ridge rises to the real summit of 12,451-foot Kachina Peak, whose immense treeless face provides the most aesthetic, if not the scariest, of Taos's adventures. Your first lift ride on Lift 1, a fixed-grip quad, or Lift 5, an older double paralleling it, takes you right over *Al's Run,* that steep river of bumps, before depositing you on much friendlier terrain high above the valley.

Off to your right is West Basin, a large bowl full of curvy, interesting blue runs and even a few greens, well served by another quad (Lift 8). Above this chairlift, the mountain rises toward the dramatic skyline ridge in a series of steep chutes and gullies that form its upper and western sections, all high-drama, expert skiing. To reach this upper terrain, take Lift 2 or Lift 6, parallel chairlifts that climb toward ski-patrol headquarters, which is fairly high up on the central spine but still well below the topmost ridge. At the top, expert skiers go one way, intermediate and merely "good" skiers another.

When the patrol opens the *West Basin Ridge*, experts start hiking. Ten or fifteen steep, hard-breathing minutes later lead to the crest, where you can start traversing in search of your perfect chute. Traverse right to the exceptionally steep runs off this ridge or left along Highline Ridge, whose runs are generally less wild but still very steep. When the ridge isn't open, experts slide right from the top of Lift 2 across the *High Traverse*, a thin and thrilling line that cuts across most of the expert runs off the West Basin Ridge. It still offers ample vertical and lots of thrills without that lung-busting hike.

Taos for Learning Skiers

A ski resort can hardly exist without a learning area for first-timers and novices, and Taos has one too. Lift 4 serves a very modest beginner hill at the mountain's base. It often lies in the shade, and its main attraction is that beginners are motivated to get better fast to get out of there. A ski school likewise has to offer beginner and novice lessons, and Taos's Ernie Blake Ski School does. But Taos lacks the long inviting flats where novice skiers can log lots of mileage and progress without stress. The terrain just isn't there. So the main reason for very inexperienced skiers to pick Taos is if they are accompanying far better skiers. Don't worry if that's you; you'll still have a good time and still learn a lot about skiing. In fact, under the tutelage of this award-winning ski school and its excellent Yellowbird introduction-to-skiing program, you might just graduate to the blues sooner than you would at resorts with more—and more inviting—green runs.

Another option, if you're not the sort to want a fast-track course to more challenging terrain, is to let your more experienced friends ski at Taos Ski Valley while you drive a half hour over Palo Verde Pass to practice your novice skills at Angel Fire, which has lots of wide-open, low-angle cruising and practice terrain. Another option is Red River, almost due north of Taos Ski Valley but requiring a long-way-around drive. Marketing programs do change, but some seasons, cooperative lift-ticket plans incorporating Taos Ski Valley, Angel Fire, Red River, and even the Enchanted Forest Cross-Country Ski Area have been offered—usually incorporating the words "Enchanted Circle." It's a good way to explore this beguiling region of northern New Mexico—no matter what your skiing level. (And the other two Alpine areas do welcome snowboarders, in case you are one or are traveling with one.)

Taos for Sub-Experts

Let's first look at the skiing that Taos offers to good skiers, so you don't get the impression that unless you eat black moguls for breakfast, this is no mountain for you. Taos really does offer some superb skiing for intermediate and advanced skiers, but not really for lazy, laid-back skiers. This mountain (pardon, a ski valley) challenges every level of skier at every turn.

In many spots, cliff-like black runs seem to loom above or drop below mellower blues and greens, reminding you that however skilled a skier you are, you could always be better. For instance, even if you are skiing beautifully down a blue run like *Upper Powderhorn* (a designated slow-skiing zone), you can look up out of the corner of your eye and see the hotshots demolishing the black bumps of *Castor* and *Pollux* just above. Your ego is not entirely safe at Taos, a ski resort for people who relish the idea of challenge. There's a plethora of stimulating, upper-intermediate skiing but very little low-intermediate or novice cruising.

As soon as you get off Lift 1 from the base, bear right onto *Porcupine* (then a small section of *White Feather*) down to the quad serving West Basin. *Porcupine* is a blue highway sweeping down and left on a small crest with beautiful plunging views and terrific sustained pitch. The most attractive runs, *Lower Stauffenberg* and its several variants, blend a succession of rolls, drops, and short flats just left of the lift line. Stay left in this basin for less traffic and also to avoid the black-run skiers heading for Lift 2 and those continuing to the Whistlestop Café near the bottom of Lift 6.

Most skiers follow *Powderhorn* out of the bottom of the West Basin, but it's worth zigging left into *Bambi Glade,* a green gem, or banking off the sides of *White Feather Gully,* a pleasurable blue. On the other (east) side of the mountain lies *Kachina Basin,* under the high, white backdrop of Kachina Peak. The runs range from green to blue to black, and all you need to remember is that the farther right you ski, the harder the slopes get. Two chairlifts serve this sector.

Honeysuckle is the main access route down to Lift 4 (the Kachina quad). It can be boring and is often crowded. An option is to drop left off *Honeysuckle* to *Totemoff* (blue or green depending on how you ski it) and on to the base of Lift 7. This sector is definitely worth a couple of blue runs before moving on east to Lift 4, which rises into the Alpine. Just below the unload are a few hundred yards of open terrain with stunning views and lots of room to move. Below is a web of blue and black runs ranging from groomers to steep mogul runs. The comeback trail from the bottom of the Kachina lift to the main base area is a green road called *Rubezahl,* longer and flatter than *White Feather* on the other side of the area.

Taos for Gutsy Experts

This is it. Mecca. Only a small handful of American ski resorts—Squaw Valley, Jackson Hole, and Crested Butte—offer the kind of steep, high-Alpine, high-drama adventure skiing that Taos does, but none of the others offers as much of adventure skiing, and no other trail map shows as much black. In fact, there are more dotted black lines (the code for double-diamond runs) than simple black lines on the Taos Ski Valley map.

After a snowstorm, you'll find that it takes the patrol quite a while to complete their avalanche control work on the steep chutes off the *High Traverse* and longer still off the ridge. While you're waiting, go for another kind of treat: powder in the trees. The trail map bears names dropping right off the long spine of Bambi that aren't runs at all, just general routes with names: *Walkyries Chute, Sir Arnold Lunn,* and the *Lorelei Trees.* A few yards past the entrance to any of these areas, you'll be looking for your own line around reasonably spaced trees and always finding it. There's room for hundreds of sets of tracks, all bottoming out at Lift 7. Ride it back up and then take the short 7th Heaven lift back to patrol headquarters, and do the circuit again. New snow or not, when you're ready to test yourself against Taos's steeps off the *High Traverse,* take it step by step. Start with a mere black like *Reforma* or *Blitz,* which are steep slots in a steep forest rather than slots through cliffs. If all goes well, you can ski a little farther across the *High Traverse* (the return via Lift 2 is rapid and scenic).

Somewhere beyond the *West Blitz Trees* and *Spitfire,* the traverse itself starts to get serious: you sidestep gingerly above real cliffs and look down into chutes where missing your first turn would be unthinkable. Many of these ultra-steep gullies are only one turn wide. Still, the snow is usually fantastic—hard, cold, packed powder. Once you're here, you're no longer warming up for Taos's steeps; you're skiing them. If you can handle the likes of *Oster* and *Stauffenberg,* you're ready for the longer but not any harder lines off the *West Basin Ridge* when the patrol says "go." If you want both the views and the cachet of skiing the ridge but runs like those give you butterflies, you are not out of luck. When you reach the ridge, bear left along *Highline Ridge* toward Kachina Peak, where the terrain is merely exciting, but not terrifying.

Sometimes it seems as though Ernie Blake was writing a history quiz when he named his favorite runs. For instance, ask a local who Stauffenberg was, and you'll learn that he was not an Austrian ski instructor, but a tragic figure in World War II. What about a splendid Highline Ridge run, *Niños Heroes?* It was named after martyred Mexican military cadets, the "child heroes." But you will not be doomed as a martyred skier as you dive off the edge onto this steep but welcoming pitch, which is a piece of cake compared with Taos's double blacks.

The finest adventure a strong expert can have at Taos is hiking all the way up Kachina Peak and leaving first tracks on its vast Alpine face.

From below, those hard-earned turns look like a trail of tiny, miniature letters S down the center of the snowfield. Kachina Peak is not often open, so if it is, grab a candy bar for energy and start walking. This is one of the most extraordinary inbounds ski runs in North America.

Perhaps the silliest thing an expert can do here is spend all day pounding the bumps on *Al's Run*. But hey, *de gustibus non disputandum*—no accounting for tastes! In fact, expert skiing at Taos is mostly of the high-Alpine, ski-what-the-mountain-has-to-offer variety: narrow chutes, cliffs and couloirs, rocks and trees, and deep snow, provide the spice instead of the skier-made bumps. But the lower front face and the black runs under Kachina Peak have all the moguls you could want, as many as you want, and as mean as you want. *Al's Run,* in particular, is continuous, unrelenting, and famous. If you're skilled enough to handle it, don't leave Taos without skiing it at least once just to say you did—even if your heart is up on the Ridge.

In addition to this abundance of incredible high-expert turf, Taos Ski Valley boasts arguably the nation's best ski school for learning to handle such terrain. This resort is a bastion of the traditional ski week, where very, very good skiers return year after year to spend five consecutive mornings with the same instructor learning to be even better. The continuity of instruction works wonders. It was inevitable that a ski school on a mountain this challenging would specialize in helping people come to terms with steep and challenging skiing. And why not? Taos skiing is not just for experts, but the fact remains: the better a skier you are, the more you'll love Taos skiing. Check out the resort's lesson-inclusive multiday packages—or better yet, sign up for one. After a week, you'll be skiing better and handling harder terrain than you might have dreamed.

Snowboarding

While Taos prohibits snowboarding, it doesn't ban any size or shape of skis, and the terrain park, called Jay's, on Maxie's Run under Lift 7, packs in tricksters and new schoolers of all stripes. The park features two ramps for air, a hip, a quarter-pipe, and several rails.

Taos Atmosphere

The ski valley's rather minimalist base facilities have matured into a very attractive, somewhat European-flavored mini-village. It'll never grow too much, because there just isn't very much flat land in this high canyon to build on, but there's a lot more than just a base lodge. The resort-center complex serves as a slopeside crossroads, and the medieval murals painted on the sides of some of the buildings reinforce the Swiss connection that Ernie Blake started.

Once you have your bearings on this complex mountain, it doesn't take long to ski down to the bottom for lunch. The choices are good.

The midday meal is a tradition at Taos. In the early years, Ernie Blake stopped the lifts at noon so skiers would return to their lodges for lunch. To reach the resort from West Basin, take any of the runs that funnel into *White Feather*. This long route becomes a road-like catwalk around to the front mountain, below the last bumps above **Edelweiss** and the **Inn at Snakedance.** Taos Ski Valley's three cafeterias (one at the resort center, one on-mountain, and one at the base of Lift 4) aren't much, but **Rhoda's Restaurant,** in the main base, was remodeled in 2003 and offers a pleasant table-service midday dining. Another option, if you are skiing the east side, is to stop for lunch at the **Bavarian Restaurant** near the base of Lift 4.

There are lodges too, wonderful old-style, full-service lodges where you can sleep, eat, and be merry, rather than condos where you just crash after skiing. The classic Taos Ski Valley lodge is the **Hotel St. Bernard,** an oasis of dark wood and French hospitality. The Inn at Snakedance is the largest and most luxurious of the slopeside lodges. Built around the core of the resort's original lodge, it combines traditional Taos Ski Valley Alpine hospitality with Southwestern style. The Edelweiss was rebuilt several years ago, and in a more ambitious style than the original.

Nearby are the **Amizette Inn** and the **Austing Haus B&B.** The valley also offers condominium lodgings in several complexes. But as honestly cool—and convenient—as this tiny community up at the head of the canyon is, the old town of Taos, only a half hour away, is a lot more interesting. It should be; it was founded in 1540. Just drive down out of the canyon is another world, a high desert of sage and scrub, where the ambience is decidedly Native American and Hispanic—adobe buildings, flat roofs, strings of red chilies hanging from protruding timbers, vigas, a central plaza that is sleepy in winter, and nearby, the most photographed and painted adobe church in the West. Taos is a Southwestern fantasy, still more or less intact.

Lodging in town varies from B&Bs in 100-year-old adobes to **The Historic Taos Inn,** a bastion of old New Mexico luxury where every room has its own beehive fireplace. The **Fechin Inn,** just north of the Plaza, is a heralded luxury hotel that debuted several years ago in a historic mansion, and the 25-room **Hotel La Fonda de Taos,** the town's oldest hotel, has completed a six-year remake and now includes a gallery of works by Southwestern artists.

As good as the lodging is, the food is even more unusual. Almost anything you order elicits the query, "Red or green?" Referring to chili, of course. For gourmet meals in Taos, try **Doc Martin's, Lambert's, Villa Fontana,** or **Casa Cordova. Momentitas de la Vida,** along the access road, offers four-star fine dining in a relaxed and lovely setting. Finally, if you're staying in old Taos, grant yourself the luxury of completely forgetting about skiing from time to time and tuning into the pulse of this remarkable place. What other town of only 4,500 souls has so many great bookstores, so many art galleries, and so many concerts and other events? You can find every sort of art in Taos's dozens of galleries and six museums. If your ski vacation brings you to Taos during the Christmas–New Year holidays, stop skiing early on Christmas Day or New Year's Day and watch the ceremonial dances at Taos Pueblo, just outside of town—a trip through time to an earlier America and every bit as special as a perfect run off the ridge.

Taos Data

Mountain Statistics

Vertical feet	2,612 feet (lift served); 3,244 (Kachina Peak, hike-up)
Base elevation	9,207 feet
Summit elevation	11,819 feet (lift-served);
	12,481 to Kachina Peak (hike-up)
Longest run	5.25 miles
Average annual snowfall	312 inches
Snowmaking	648 acres
Number of lifts	12: 4 quad chairs; 1 triple chair; 5 double chairs;
	2 surface lifts
Uphill capacity	15,000 skiers per hour
Skiable terrain	1,294 acres
Opening date	Late November
Closing date	Early April
Snowboarding	No

Transportation

By car Taos is 148 miles (about a 2.5-hour drive) north of Albuquerque via I-25, U.S. 84/285, and State Highway 68, through Santa Fe and Española. Taos Ski Valley is 19 miles (about a 30-minute drive) from Taos via State Highway 150.

By bus or limo From Albuquerque, Faust's Transportation (phone (888) 830-3410), Pride of Taos (phone (800) 273-8340), and Twin Hearts Express (phone (800) 654-9456).

By plane Numerous airlines service Albuquerque Sunport. Rio Grande Air (phone (877) 435-9742) offers commuter air service between Albuquerque and Taos Municipal Airport.

Key Phone Numbers

Ski-area information	(505) 776-2291 and (800) 347-7414
Snow report	(505) 776-2916
Reservations	(800) 776-1111 (Taos Ski Valley) or
	(800) 821-2437 (Taos Central Reservations)
Website	www.skitaos.org

Lito's TECH TIP

Safety on the Steeps

So few American ski resorts offer truly steep skiing that the skills involved are anything but widespread. Here are a few tips that should help already-strong skiers adapt their technique to the sort of steeper-than-usual slopes they'll find at places like Taos Ski Valley.

First, get used to the angle before starting to turn. Do this by sideslipping in a very anticipated position, hips and shoulders turned straight down the mountain, downhill pole extended and ready, just as if you were about to turn. Sideslip straight down a few feet, then set your edges with a quick flick of your knees into the hill. Repeat this a couple of times on the very top of the steep slope you are about to ski. By doing so, your body, and your mind too, will adjust to the angle of the slope before the real action starts. When you do turn, you will have had a foretaste of the all-important control phase at the end of each turn.

Second, make your turns short, quick, and powerful. On very steep slopes, you want to bring your skis rapidly from one almost horizontal position to another one, facing the opposite way, without spending a lot of time in the middle or fall-line phase of the turn. Lingering in the fall -line on steep slopes, you'll pick up too much speed too fast. Start your turns with a snappy, positive up motion (either bouncing up from quick edge set or actually projecting yourself upward with a strong extension of the legs), and then you'll be able to turn your skis into the fall line very rapidly, virtually in the air. When you "land" from this rapid, initial pivoting, try to land softly; don't jam your edges into the steep snow; instead let the skis skid or sideslip. (Over-edged skis tend to accelerate!) Then sink and steer your sideslipping skis (especially your outside ski) quickly around to the horizontal. Spend as little time as possible in the middle, or "belly," of the turn.

And finally, once you start turning, keep turning. Things get out of hand only when you freeze or hesitate between turns. Continuous short turns are the recipe for control on very steep slopes. To eliminate any hesitation, keep reaching your outside/downhill pole straight down the hill—even a little farther down than you usually do, to help balance your body over the downhill ski. Plant that pole without hesitation and you'll find that this triggers the next turn without hesitation. Just as with super bumps, if your hand and pole are late, then you'll be late.

One last piece of advice: Find a practice slope that is very steep but neither long nor dangerous (i.e., no obstacles to fall into), on which to practice these extra-quick, extra-short turns. The top of *Stauffenberg* is no place to start trying to shorten your turns. You don't need much vertical to practice on: three or four turns will do. Take a deep breath, and go.

Ski Santa Fe

New Mexico skiing has a lot going for it: light snow conditions that seem to result more from dry Southwestern air than from bitter cold temperatures, lots of sunshine, and the special flavor of traditional, Hispanic hospitality. The only problem is that there's only one New Mexico ski area that feels like a true Rocky Mountain resort, and that is Taos Ski Valley. The others are either day-ski areas or modest regional resorts rather than destination areas. While the initial intention of this book was to cover only the very best skiing in the West, a few exceptional day areas (as opposed to full resorts) have already slipped in, such as Colorado's Loveland and Arapahoe Basin, and now we're about to visit another: Ski Santa Fe.

What makes this relatively small ski area a real vacation destination is its proximity to the city of Santa Fe with all its attractions. This beautiful city nestles up against the last folds of the Sangre de Cristo Mountains at the very southern end of the Rockies. It is one of the most beautiful and historic cities—and one of the most romantic vacation destinations in America. Add to that the fact that Ski Santa Fe, despite its modest size, is a very friendly ski area that skis and feels like a much bigger mountain, and you have a memorable ski trip in the making, one that will satisfy die-hard skiers and delight any nonskiers in the group or family. We'll look at the two halves of this vacation separately: the mountain and the city of Santa Fe.

A Ski Mountain with a View

The ski area is a 16-mile drive from town on a road that winds through alternate stands of evergreen and aspen. Periodically the forest curtain parts, and you begin to see an immense panorama of high desert country below. At the ski-area base, you're back among the trees, but a few minutes later, after your first or second lift ride, the true dimensions of this valley view become clear. At the top of the ski mountain you are suspended in space some 5,000 feet above Santa Fe. On a clear day, the austere Southwestern landscape spreads out for over a hundred miles. The tall silhouette of Sandia Peak towering over Albuquerque 70 miles away, punctuates the view; still farther away and farther west rises Mount Taylor, one of the Navajos' four sacred mountains; the sawtooth Jemez Mountains decorate the far western horizon. At 12,000 feet, the view is literally and figuratively breathtaking. And what of the mountain beneath your skis?

Ski Santa Fe divides neatly into three parts fanning up and out from the modernistic base lodge (where you'll also find a cool kids' skiing and learning area, Chipmunk Corner, totally separated from all the rest of the mountain traffic). To the right (looking up), the Super Chief quad (Lift 1) takes you up to what feels like the edge of the ski-area basin. Just over the hill, to the right (or south), one sees and senses Big Tesuque Bowl, a large semi-open bowl, dotted with sparse, widespread trees. From the top of the Super Chief, you have your choice of a half dozen long, flowing green and blue runs (with a couple of moguled blacks on your far left). These runs cut through trees flowing well but lacking the expansiveness and drama of the center section of the mountain.

Tesuque Peak is the central high point of the ski area, served by a triple chair (Lift 3) that rises up the ski area's long crest, which is where the fun

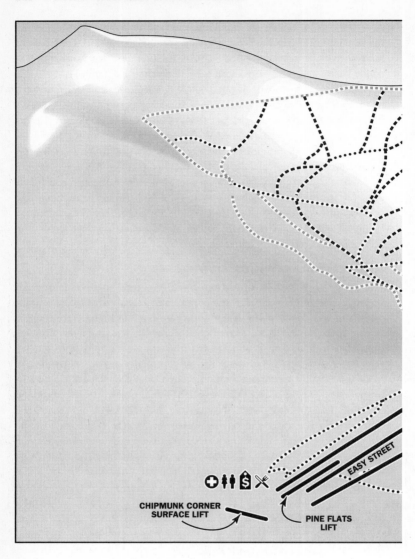

begins. To the right of this lift (again, looking up) the mountain is wide
open. Scattered forests of stunted and twisted trees called *krummholz*
thin out completely toward the top, revealing a wide, white Alpine world
that turns into a fairyland after a storm has frosted the last, isolated,
windswept trees. *Parachute* and *Gay Way*, both wide-cut and groomed
paths, are the two main lines on this side. *Parachute* dives right down the
convex flank of the mountain and steepens progressively to a very

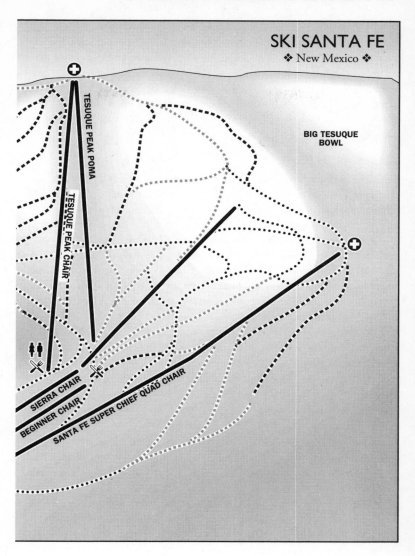

SKI SANTA FE
❖ New Mexico ❖

BIG TESUQUE
BOWL

TESUQUE PEAK POMA

TESUQUE PEAK CHAIR

SIERRA CHAIR

BEGINNER CHAIR

SANTA FE SUPER CHIEF QUAD CHAIR

respectable pitch, while *Gay Way* and its variations meander out to the left and back for a much lower-angle run. The beauty is that you can ski almost anywhere. It's unusual to experience this sort of back bowl, ski-anywhere-you-want terrain at such a small ski area.

On the left side of the Tesuque Peak triple chair (again looking up) are densely timbered slopes that provide a different flavor of skiing altogether. This forested face is accessed from a catwalk called *Sunset,* and although several runs (*Burro Alley, Wizard,* and *Columbine*) have been cut through the steep trees, once again you won't be confined to specific lines. *Tequila Sunrise* is a large, partially gladed and very inviting forest zone rather than an actual run where, if you're a strong skier, you can, and should ski, anywhere. This whole forested face is very legitimately marked black. This steep skiing all funnels down into *Alpine Bowl,* an open-side valley that slants back to the base of the Tesuque Peak triple chair and that is full of friendly blue and green runs.

Getting the Most Out of Santa Fe Skiing

Santa Fe is small enough, so you won't have any trouble figuring it out, but here are a few tips anyway. Inexperienced and learning skiers and novices spend most of their time on the long flats just above the base lodge. This area is served by two lifts: the tiny Pine Flats surface lift (Lift 7) and the longer Easy Street beginner chair (Lift 4). Don't stay on the bottom flats; take the chair right away. Lots of mileage is even more important for beginners and novices than lots of instruction. While there is no easy green way down from the top of Tesuque Peak, there are a number of friendly green routes down from the top of both the Super Chief quad and the Sierra chair (Lift 2), which serves runs cut through the upper part of the trees. The easiest options involve roundabout traverses to the right or left. If you're a novice, don't head straight down, or you'll be skiing blue runs before you're ready.

Good skiers spend much of their time higher on the mountain, often making laps on the Tesuque Peak lift. Take either the Sierra or Super Chief chair for one warm-up run—they both serve almost the same runs—before heading to the top, and then start on *Gay Way.* When you get bored with this wide-open cruising, try the other side of the peak, following *Sunset* in a long zig and a short zag all the way around the steep forested runs mentioned above, in order to access the pleasant blue-green terrain in *Alpine Bowl.*

Strong skiers in search of a challenge should start exploring the forest right next to the Tesuque Peak lift line. A long platterpull lift (Lift 5) in the woods, parallel to the triple chair, runs at peak periods and is a favorite with Santa Fe regulars, because it is actually faster than the chair. It's hard to know where you are in this forested zone unless you're skiing with a local. Run designations like *First Tracks, Avalanche,* and *Desperado* seem to apply equally to a large, steep zone of trees. The snow is protected from wind by the trees and is usually quite good, even though nothing in this area is really ever groomed.

But as exciting as these tree runs are, the world of light and space gives the aesthetic edge to Santa Fe skiing. The boundary between the ski area and Big Tesuque Bowl is not too perfectly defined or rigidly marked, so strong skiers have always allowed themselves fleeting excursions into and back out of this sublime bowl, which funnels down to the highway a few miles below the ski-area base. So if you are tempted to ski it, remember that you don't want to just hike out there and go without a way to return. You can organize your own shuttle by leaving a car at the Forest Service's Big Tesuque picnic area on the access road several miles below the ski area. The ski area has been patiently jumping through all the environmental hoops to put a lift in Big Tesuque and make it an official part of the Ski Santa Fe experience. If and when this happens, it will instantly double the size and quality of Santa Fe skiing.

Santa Fe, the City below the Mountain

Après-ski, Santa Fe–style, is limited by only two factors: your imagination and your pocketbook. Several years ago, the readers of *Condé Nast Traveler* voted Santa Fe "the top travel destination in the world," and while the citizens of Paris or Rio might disagree, that's still a kind of recommendation. In several days, a visitor can barely scratch the surface of this arty, adobe city, with commendable skiing nearby.

Consider staying at one of the great inns, such as the legendary **St. Francis Hotel** or perhaps **La Fonda, Inn at Loretto, Inn of the Governors,** or the **Inn of the Anasazi,** all within easy walking distance of the Plaza. This large central square was the hub of life in colonial Santa Fe more than 400 years ago, and it remains the hub today. Impeccable and imaginative bed-and-breakfast inns are scattered throughout the city and its surroundings. For sightseeing on and near the Plaza, check out the Palace of the Governors, Museum of Fine Arts next door, and the Georgia O'Keeffe Museum around the corner. The Sanbusco Market Center, on the west side of town, is a renascent area of shops and restaurants near the city's old rail yard.

For serious eating adventures, there's no place like Santa Fe. One of the acclaimed temples of Southwestern cuisine is the **Coyote Café,** which lives up to its reputation for innovative fare. Even in winter, reservations can be hard to come by—or there may be a wait. **Aria's** offerings draw from French, Italian, and Spanish inspirations. **Los Mayas** is one of New Mexico's bastions of cuisine from old Mexico. To hobnob with local artists and wannabes, belly up to the bar of **The Pink Adobe** and then have dinner.

Art is found all over town. Small streets around the Plaza are chock-full of galleries and innovative boutiques that would appear to be galleries in any other city. Canyon Road, a narrow street, winds up into the hills and is lined with Santa Fe's oldest galleries in beautiful, crooked, one-story adobes that have inspired generations of painters. Just a short drive north of town, in the neighboring village of Tesuque is Shidoni, a large outdoor-sculpture park and a working bronze-sculpture foundry that keeps the lost wax-casting tradition alive. The city boasts 15 museums—art and other specialties. On the south edge, you'll find a whole district of stunning museums devoted to ethnography, art, and folklore—and even a museum showing toys from around the world. Santa Fe is worth a guidebook of its own, but our subject is skiing. If you're tempted to spend a few days in Santa Fe on your way to and from some Southwestern powder, that's well and good. You won't be disappointed.

Santa Fe Data

Mountain Statistics

Vertical feet	1,703 feet
Base elevation	10,350 feet
Summit elevation	12,053 feet
Longest run	3 miles
Average annual snowfall	225 inches
Snowmaking	275 acres
Number of lifts	6: 1 quad high-speed chair; 1 triple chair; 2 double chairs; 2 surface lifts
Uphill capacity	7,800 skiers per hour
Skiable terrain	660 acres
Opening date	Thanksgiving
Closing date	Mid-April
Snowboarding	Yes

Transportation

By car 16 miles (less than a half -hour drive) from downtown Santa Fe on NM Highway 475. Santa Fe is approximately 1.5 hours by car from the Albuquerque International Sunport via I-25.

By bus or limo From the Albuquerque International Sunport to Santa Fe by Coach USA-Gray Line (phone (800) 256-8991), Santa Fe Shuttle (phone (888) 833-2300), Sandia Shuttle Express (phone (888) 775-5696), or Twin Hearts (phone (800) 654-9456). TMN&O links into the Greyhound system.

By plane Great Lakes Aviation (phone (505) 473-4118) serves Santa Fe Municipal Airport (phone (505) 955-2908) from Denver. Many direct flights from major cities to the Albuquerque International Sunport, including on low-cost, no-frills Southwest Airlines.

Key Phone Numbers

Ski-area information	(505) 982-4429
Snow report	(505) 983-9155
Reservations	(800) 776-SNOW
Website	www.skisantafe.com

Lito's TECH TIP

Protection from the Elements versus Style

Actually there's no conflict here, or there shouldn't be, since skiers who are warm and comfortable move well and look good—and what else is style about?

There are a lot of tricks to staying comfortable on the slopes in all weather that experienced skiers take for granted. Tricks I thought I'd share with you.

Start with your skin. Time was when ski instructors were stereotyped as the bronzed gods of the slopes. Nowadays, a skier's tan is no longer something to be desired. High-altitude sun (remember, even at Santa Fe, you're skiing at 12,000 feet) can do more than sunburn you. There's a very real risk of skin cancer from too much high-altitude sun. So take a tip from today's instructors and use sunscreen with the highest sunblock rating you can find (25 is not too high).

The knit "neck gaiter" is another secret weapon in the fight for comfort on the slopes. It is nothing more than the large turtleneck of a turtleneck sweater—without the sweater. In other words, a tube, knitted wool, or a less scratchy synthetic. These are so small and light you can keep one in an inside parka pocket and put it on only when the wind comes up or the sun goes down. Skiers hide in their neck gaiters on cold days or when they're skiing in clouds of boiling powder, pulling the neck gaiter up to cover mouth and nose as needed.

In the worst stormy conditions, with the wind howling and snow driving horizontally into your face, the combination of neck gaiter, goggles, and a knit hat is all you need to stay snug from the shoulders up. There is a good reason why expert skiers almost never pull up the hood of a parka and secure it around their face. A hood tends to interfere with the free-floating motion of a skier's head, and that's precisely the ability to keep your head level as you ski; ability that gives you a trustworthy, level horizon line for better balance. With the hood of your ski jacket pulled up, you definitely lose some of that balance.

At least half the skiers I know suffer from cold fingers from time to time. If that's you, trade your ski gloves in for a pair of mittens. In mittens, your fingers can warm each other. Don't worry; it is not uncool to wear mittens even if World Cup ski racers don't. Skiers with particularly cold-sensitive hands can also carry small chemical-heat packs in their pockets. Sold under different brand-names in almost all sporting goods stores, these cunning plastic packages come to life when you squeeze them and put out lots of heat for several hours. You can slip them inside your mittens on long lift rides.

Most skiers today know to dress in layers, as many as possible. You'll be more comfortable and warmer when you need to be, if you are wearing lots of layers that trap air between them rather than just putting on your heaviest down jacket for a cold winter day on the slopes. Did you know that on very cold days your feet will stay warmer if you wear an extra-thin pair of socks? Heavier socks make you colder by cutting off circulation. And there's no real reason to buckle the front or toe buckle of conventionally designed boots on very cold days either. Give your toes as much room to move as possible.

Finally, while we're on the subject of boots, no matter what the fashion pages of the ski magazines say, resist the idea of in-the-boot ski pants. Snow always packs in there between pants leg and boot, and of course your feet eventually get wet and cold. In-the-boot stretch pants finger you as a "snow bunny" who never skis deep snow; it is a better look for the base-lodge bar than for the slopes. Look for ski pants with an effective snow cuff that slides easily over the top of your boots and seals them against flying snow. Remember, the ultimate fashion statement on skis is a perfect turn, not a perfect ski suit.

Part Three

Utah and the Northern Rockies

Kurt Repanshek

Imagine Brigham Young in the summer of 1847, sick with fever after a six-month journey across the plains and over the Rocky Mountains of Wyoming and Utah, peering down on the Great Salt Lake from high up in Emigration Canyon (not far from where I-80 today whisks skiers from the Salt Lake Airport to Park City and Deer Valley). He raises himself up on an elbow and utters the immortal words, "This is the place." For nineteenth-century Mormons it was the place—the place nobody else wanted—where they could build their Kingdom of Deseret by turning the abundant snows of the Rockies out of their creek beds and onto lush valley farms.

For mountain men, from Lewis and Clark to Jim Bridger, the ranges of the northern Rockies were the land of beaver, whose pelts made the finest and most fashionable top hats. For prospectors, the Rockies, from Alta to Coeur d'Alene, were the place where 90% of American silver came out of the ground. And for skiers, the Rockies are the big draw, the snow magnet, the really big hills, the really romantic ski towns: the place to ski and snowboard.

After all, this is the place where in 1936, in Sun Valley, Idaho's Pioneer Range, the world's first chairlift was constructed. It was conceived by a designer of conveyor systems for loading banana boats.

This is the place with the highest lift-served vertical in the United States—4,180 feet from base to summit at Big Sky in Montana's Madison Range. And it is home to the recently deposed ex-champ, at 4,139 feet, at Jackson Hole in Wyoming's Teton Range.

This is the place with the most snow in the country, an honor shared by Alta and Powder Mountain in the Wasatch Range, where the average snowfall per season is 500 inches, year in and year out. Let's see: 500 divided by 12, that's over 41.5 feet of snow, and my house is 23 feet high. . .

This is the place with the best snow in the country, maybe the best on the planet. Utah's license plates used to spell it out in no uncertain terms:

Greatest Snow on Earth (before the state switched to more colorful, but less interesting, plates on the theme of rock Arches and the 2002 Salt Lake Games). Utah's snow is regularly on the order of 4–5% water. Melt a quart of it and you get a sip. Scoop it up in your hand and it blows away like dandelion feathers. Pack it down on a ski mountain and your edges slice it like butter: silent, forgiving, effortless.

Utah gets it, as do the resorts farther up the chain. They've all got that continental climate a thousand miles from the Pacific and those winter storms rolling across the western deserts: drying out, cooling down, climbing toward the Continental Divide, where they drop big, stellar flakes, hundreds of which can balance on an aspen twig.

This is the place with some of the most-recognized icons of American skiing—Sun Valley, Alta, Snowbird, Jackson Hole. These places conjure graceful, swooping magic in the minds even of those who have never carved a winter arc. The Rockies also are home to some of the least-known or underappreciated gems in the lexicon, places like Schweitzer Basin and the Big Mountain, Bridger Bowl and Brighton—places where the skiing and riding is so good the locals don't want anyone else to know those places exist.

This is the place, finally, that hosted the Winter Olympics in 2002. Not that Utah needed the publicity or the business. Most of the resorts were doing just fine before the Games arrived. It's just that given the terrain and the snow and the superb transportation links and the fine ski-town amenities and the esprit of the mountain people, there has never been, and may never be again, a more perfect site to stage the games.

All of which is not to say that the northern Rockies are some kind of homogeneous extension of Utah, or of the better-known Rocky Mountains of Colorado, for that matter. The geography is too huge, the weather and the people who live there too variable and independent to classify glibly. Utah's Wasatch Range, for example, is practically an urban mountain range, leaping up as it does 7,000 vertical feet out of a valley with a million residents, and Jackson Hole, hidden by millions of acres of protected wilderness on the southern edge of Yellowstone and Grand Teton national parks, feels like a tiny island of human energy in a sea of rock and sky. Up at the tip of the Idaho panhandle, Schweitzer Basin is slowly emerging out of a slumbering timber and railroading town. The same applies to the Big Mountain high in Montana's Flathead Valley. And Sun Valley, well, Sun Valley is the queen of it all, and she knows it.

Reading the trail maps at any of these mountains is like reading the local history. *Sublette Ridge* and *Rendezvous Bowl* recall the days of the mountain men at Jackson Hole, named for the trapper Davey Jackson. Ski or ride the *Bannock* and *Shoshone* and *Blackfoot* trails at Grand

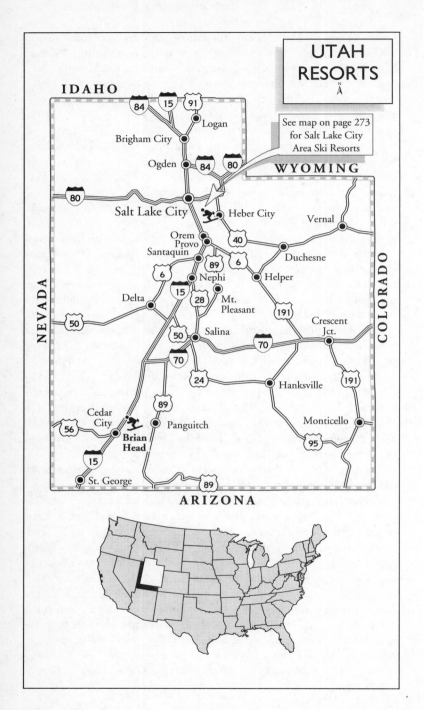

UTAH RESORTS

N

IDAHO

84 15 91
● Logan
Brigham City
Ogden ● 84 80

WYOMING

80

Salt Lake City

See map on page 273 for Salt Lake City Area Ski Resorts

● Heber City
Orem 40
Provo
Santaquin
89 6
● Nephi
6 Helper ●
15
Delta ● 28 Mt. Pleasant ●
50 50 Salina ●
70
70
24
● Hanksville

NEVALDA

COLORADO

Vernal ●
● Duchesne

Crescent Jct. ●
191
191

Cedar City
56 89
Brian Head ● Panguitch
15
St. George ●
89

Monticello ●
95

ARIZONA

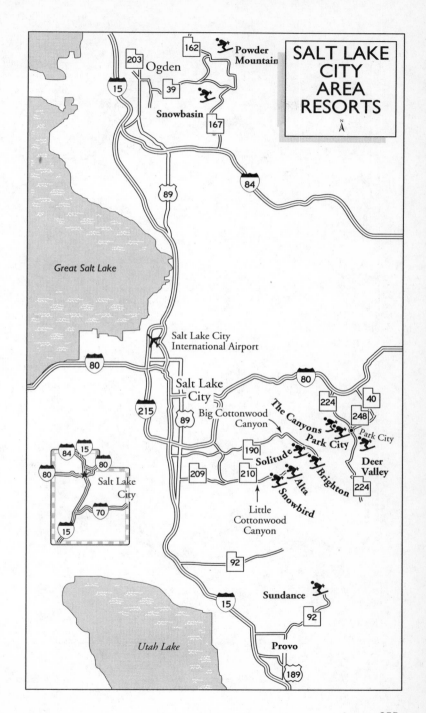

SALT LAKE CITY AREA RESORTS

N

Powder Mountain

Ogden

Snowbasin

Great Salt Lake

Salt Lake City International Airport

Salt Lake City

Big Cottonwood Canyon

The Canyons

Park City

Park City

Solitude

Brighton

Deer Valley

Alta

Snowbird

Little Cottonwood Canyon

Salt Lake City

Sundance

Provo

Utah Lake

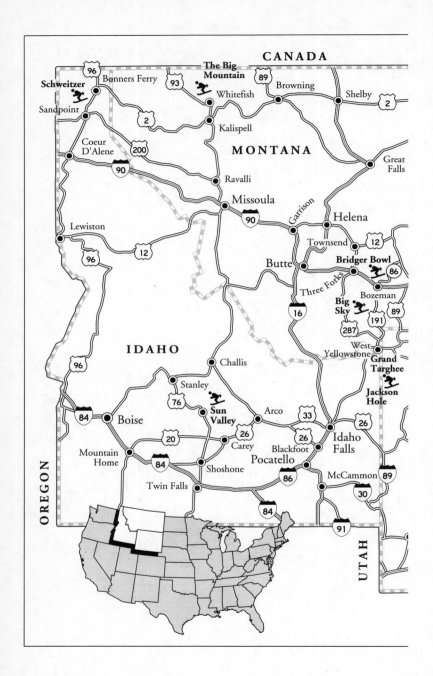

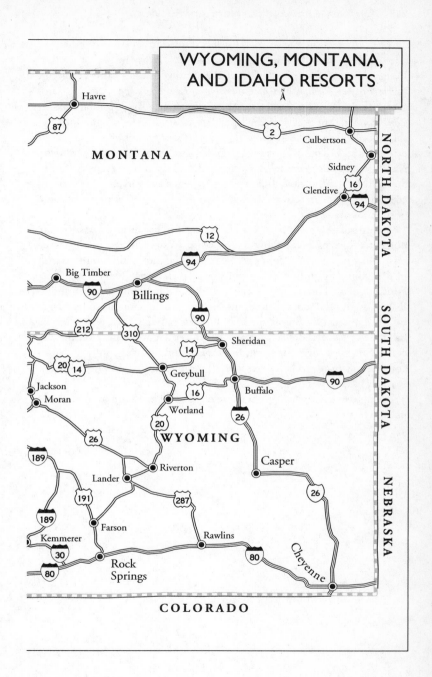

WYOMING, MONTANA, AND IDAHO RESORTS

N

MONTANA

Havre

87

2

Culbertson

Sidney

16

Glendive

94

NORTH DAKOTA

12

94

Big Timber

90

Billings

212

310

90

90

SOUTH DAKOTA

14

Sheridan

20

14

Greybull

Buffalo

90

Jackson

Moran

16

Worland

20

26

WYOMING

26

189

Riverton

Casper

Lander

26

191

287

189

Farson

Rawlins

Kemmerer

30

80

80

Cheyenne

Rock

Springs

COLORADO

NEBRASKA

Targhee and feel the tug of a wilder, less spoiled time. Chief Targhee led a renegade band of Bannocks against the U.S. Army in one of the last Indian wars. Alta's runs echo the names of silver mines from her boom years: *Emma, Rustler, Hellgate, Peruvian, Patsey Marley.* Other ski and snowboard mountains honor the ski pioneers. The Big Mountain has its *Toni Matt* trail in honor of the legendary Austrian who taught with the ski school there. Jackson Hole has *Pepi's Run* for long-time ski-school director and Olympic champion Pepi Steigler. Sun Valley likes to name trails after its famous racing alumni, including, most recently, Picabo Street, the Olympic downhill racer with the flying ponytail and effervescent smile; you can schuss *Picabo's Street* just off the Warm Springs side of the mountain.

From beaver to silver to cattle dotting the big empty expanse, the northern Rockies have followed the classic Western cycle of boom-and-bust. Now it is boom again as the beauty of the mountains and the thrill of the skiing and riding attract stars like Jane Fonda, Ted Turner, Peter Fonda, Glenn Close, Tom Cruise, and the "downhill racer" himself, Robert Redford. Actually, Redford has lived at his Sundance hideaway for 30 years, which almost qualifies him for native status. As a skier, he has known for decades what many in America are just discovering: the combination of high elevation, big mountains, and cold snow born on consistent storm tracks makes the skiing and riding in the northern Rockies second to none.

Choose one, any one. In short order, you will proclaim it, indeed, *the* place.

Little Cottonwood Canyon

Alta A classic in every sense of the word, Alta has huge quantities of soft Utah powder; wide-open, European-style terrain; intimate lodges sandwiched between avalanche run-out zones; tickets priced for the people; and a history that reads like a who's who of American skiing. Some will be put off by the lack of high-speed lifts, the snowboarder ban, and the preponderance of ungroomed slopes, but that's the way Alta likes it: Ski the wild snow, and keep the crowds on the lifts rather than on the trails.

Snowbird Alta's younger, slicker sister is located one mile down the canyon. It has similar snow and superb terrain—especially for very strong skiers and riders—and the notable addition of a swift, Swiss 125-passenger tram to the summit. There is limited beginner terrain, but what they do have is first class. The village is dense and high-rise with a lot of concrete and glass; it is extremely efficient but emotionally cold compared to Alta's historic lodges.

Alta

"A" is for Alta, and Alta *means* Utah skiing to a lot of people.

These people feel about Alta the way a good Muslim feels about Mecca: no skier should die without having made at least one pilgrimage. Those who can, will scrape together as many return trips as possible in a skiing life. Every skier with dreams of deep powder owes himself a trip. At Alta the snow falls deeper and lighter than anywhere else. Anyone with a yen for the truly steep, for chutes and open faces where a pole plant feels like reaching off the edge of the roof, needs to find his way to Alta. Anyone with an appreciation for European-style, above-timberline skiing will recognize a classic in Alta. Anyone with a sense of history who wants to ski the trails where powder pioneers Dick Durrance, Alf Engen, and Junior Bounous skied, will eventually find his way to Alta, a ski resort as timeless and free of fashion as any in the land.

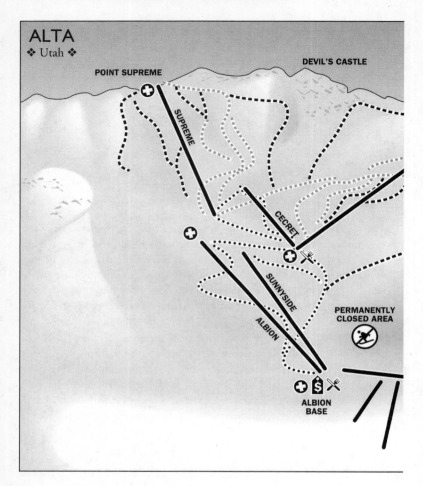

ALTA
❖ Utah ❖

POINT SUPREME

DEVIL'S CASTLE

SUPREME

CECRET

SUNNYSIDE

ALBION

PERMANENTLY
CLOSED AREA

ALBION
BASE

I find I want to use the personal pronoun "she" when I talk about Alta, the way one refers affectionately to a ship or a lover. Alf Engen did this. He said things like, "I love Alta deeply because of her beauty and her variation of terrain." Alta does this to you. She gets under your skin and haunts you with crystalline images and memories of grace. Alta's longtime general manager and past president of Alta Ski Lifts, Chic Morton, put it very succinctly: "Alta has a soul."

Of course, Chic and Alf earned the right to talk about Alta this way. Alf was the director of the ski school for 40 years, and his Alta connection goes back even further than that. It was Alf, out exploring on skis from his CCC post near Brighton in Big Cottonwood Canyon in 1935, who "discovered" Alta and first harbored the thought of turning her delightful, snowy curves into ski runs.

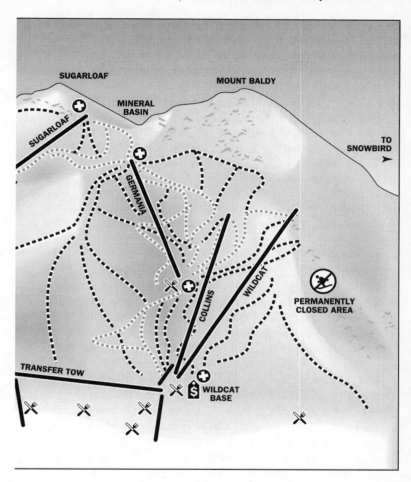

Like many of the first, and best, ski areas in the West—Aspen, Park City, Telluride—Alta was born a nineteenth-century mining camp.

Legend has it that in 1864 a party of soldiers and their wives were picnicking in Little Cottonwood Canyon when one of the women picked up an unusual rock. It was extremely high-grade silver ore. The mines, with names like Emma, Rustler, Hellgate, Peruvian, and Patsey Marley—now the names of some of Alta's most famous ski runs—sprang up overnight, along with a town of 5,000 men and women at the cramped head of the canyon near the base of the present-day Albion lift. (Today there are barely 1,000 beds above the creekside, at 8,500 feet of elevation, and it seems like plenty.)

They were raucous, dangerous days in the silver camp. Alta had seven restaurants, two boardinghouses, three general stores, a school, a blacksmith, two shoemakers, two drugstores, a confectionery, two assayers, four doctors, a minister, a lawyer, three breweries, and twenty-six saloons. Records show there were over 100 shootings in the Bucket of Blood Saloon alone. The miners literally cut down every tree in the canyon for mine timbers and framing lumber. An already fearsome avalanche problem was worsened, and slides rained down unchecked. According to newspaper accounts of the time, at least 74 miners were killed in snowslides between 1872 and 1911. What wasn't destroyed by the avalanches was finished off by a devastating fire in 1878. The town of Alta was leveled. All that remained was "here and there the stump of an old tree . . . only this and nothing more." The old town site was never rebuilt, as the ore had played out in the mid-1880s. A second boom briefly rekindled fevers in 1906–1907, when new technologies allowed the recovery of more silver from old tailings. But that, too, soon died. The Great Depression seemed to snuff all life from the region. Until, that is, Alf Engen skied over the hill and had a vision.

Another character figures prominently in the reawakening of Alta in the 1930s. You'll see his felt hat with a jaunty pheasant feather swept back from the brim, his old wooden skis, and bear-trap bindings in the display case in the Wildcat Ticket Office commemorating Alta's 50th anniversary. His name was George H. Watson, and he was the only man left in Alta when Alf found it. He called himself the Mayor. Why not? He was a majority of one. Watson lived in a shack near the base of the current Wildcat lift. He was the sole proprietor of the defunct Alta United Mines, which owned most of the property Alf coveted as a ski area. The Mayor became Alf's staunch ally in the plan. He was more than happy to deed his 700 acres (as well as nearly 1,000 acres that apparently didn't belong to him) along with his substantial tax bill to the Forest Service, to be developed for winter recreation. Watson stayed on as mayor until he died, in bed, during a snowstorm in the winter of 1952.

From Watson's generosity and the simultaneous formation of the Salt Lake Winter Recreation Association in 1938, Alta was reborn, but by relying on snow from the heavens, not silver from the mines. The nation's second chairlift—actually a converted mine tram near the site of the current Collins lift—opened for business in the winter of 1938–1939. An all-day lift ticket cost a buck and a half.

Things haven't changed all that much in more than 60 years. Alta's ticket prices have always been about 15 years behind the industry standard. Joe Quinney, one of the guiding lights of the SLWRA, is reputed to have told his successors, "What you do for Alta, you do for me. Take what you need to make a living, *but keep the price down.*" This is still Alta's guiding philosophy. The area is run as a family business: pay for improvements when you have the cash, don't go into debt, sell skiing not real estate, and keep the price down.

Utah skiers are spoiled by the low price of Alta skiing. (Brighton and Solitude, the Big Cottonwood Canyon areas to the north, are forced to stay competitive with Alta for the local business, which is to the benefit of skiers everywhere.) Out-of-state visitors are pleasantly shocked. Yet Alta makes a profit every year.

Atop the Wasatch Front, at the head of the canyon, at the top of the heap of American skiing, Alta doesn't feel the need to advertise. So they don't. They did, finally, beginning with the 2002–2003 season, agree to slightly discount tickets for skiers 12 and under. But change comes slowly to Alta, and the locals appreciate that. Amen. Alta's clientele feel themselves to be part of the family. Locals come up from the city on the weekends. Destination skiers, repeat customers most likely, from the far corners of the United States and abroad fill Alta's five lodges during the week. Generations have been returning every winter for decades.

The draw of the place is hard to define, but it surely has to do with the combination of intimacy and grandeur, the homeyness of the lodges, and the unquenchable challenge of the mountain, along with the palpable feel of history, the snow, and, of course, the people. An Alta ski patrolman hit the nail on the head when he told me, "At least when you ski at Alta you know you're dealing with real people and not clones manufactured by the marketing department with pasted-on smiles." Alta is a throwback to simpler times. It is about skiing, real skiing.

Alta's Mountain: An Introduction

Alta occupies two distinct basins, like a big W, with the steep Rustler Ridge in the center. The right-hand spike of the W (looking south) is crowned by 11,068-foot Mount Baldy. The left-hand peak is 10,595-foot Point Supreme. Both basins more or less face north, thus preserving that exquisite dry snow, though there are variations of exposure from east around to west. The only thing Alta doesn't have, inbounds, is a true south-facing slope, but there are plenty to be found across the highway. After every storm local backcountry skiers and snowboarders can be seen hiking the naked white slopes of Flagstaff and Superior for a single run down.

Think of the basins as open books. At the bottom of the right-hand book's spine is the Wildcat/Collins base area. A half mile farther up the canyon, at the foot of the other book's spine, is the Albion base. Both have parking, tickets, rentals, cafeterias, etc. The Wildcat/Collins base is the original ski terrain at Alta. It is generally steeper and bumpier and has more trees than Albion Basin. Albion is far broader, more spread out, and holds the majority of the beginner and intermediate terrain. The two bases are connected by the Transfer Rope Tow, which traverses the almost flat valley floor where the cabins and tent shacks of Alta's boomtown once stood.

Alta *feels* like a huge area even though it has, by Western standards, only a medium-size, 2,020-foot vertical. The reason it skis big has to do with the quality of the choices one faces on the mountain. Every lift ride requires delicious decision-making. For example: I'm at the top of Germania. Do I want to fly down the polished expanse of *Ballroom,* drop down the back side to *Sugarloaf,* hike to the languid snowfields below Devil's Castle, or slide out the *High Traverse* to the still, steep trees of *North Rustler?* Variety is what keeps Alta's employees around for 20 years and more. It's what keeps Alta perennially young—the constant sense of possibility and discovery that are, I believe, at the very core of skiing.

The area's 2,200 acres (no small fiefdom by anybody's standards) are efficiently served by just eight chairlifts: three on the Collins side and five in Albion Basin. It's an effective layout requiring only two lift rides to reach any of the three high points. Alta purposefully doesn't put too many skiers up the hill. "*Roooons* the skiing," Alf once said in his lilting Norwegian accent. Alta refuses to rely on high-speed quad chairs as a means of eliminating the sometimes long lift lines on weekends, although several lifts have been upgraded to triple chairs in recent years and there is a high-speed quad, Sugarloaf, but it's never run at high speed. "We'd just as soon have them in a lift line if it will mean better skiing on the mountain," said Alf. By and large Alta skiers agree. The swooping freedom of an unfettered line on the hill is worth a few extra minutes in line at the bottom. A sign at the base of the Albion lift on busy days says, "Be mellow; we are." And that's the way it is.

Stubborn? Yes. Anachronistic? Perhaps. Mainly Alta is content. And quite sure of its priorities. The downhill experience is number one.

Alta's Justly Famous Steep and Deep

Powder and Alta are practically synonymous. Hardly a week goes by in a normal year that it doesn't snow. The area averages 500 inches a season. Forty-one feet of snow, and most of it is that eiderdown stuff that Utahns rightly call the greatest snow on earth.

The two or three seminal developments in the history of powder skiing were forged here in the 1940s and 1950s. Alf and his brothers, Sverre and Corey, and America's first ski Olympian, Dick Durrance, together invented a deep-snow technique called the Dipsy Doodle. Actually, there was a Dipsy I and a Dipsy II. Both involved stepping from one ski to the other in order to change directions. One used a closed, snowplow-like stance, the other an open-skating stance. They sound awkward today, but they worked. Parallel turns on the long, stiff, wooden skis of the day required fearsome speeds to get the skis to plane and eventually turn. Then in 1948, after coaching the U.S. Olympic team in St. Moritz, Alf came home and thought, why not ski the powder with both feet equally weighted on a stable, balanced platform? Modern powder skiing was born. In the 1950s, Howard Head supplied all the Alta regulars with his revolutionary flexy, metal skis. Engen disciples like Junior Bounous, now the Director of Skiing at Snowbird, refined the movements, quieted the upper body (which no longer needed to rotate strongly to power the skis around), and—voilà!—the efficient and elegant powder style of today. Sometimes when I ski *Alf's High Rustler,* the showpiece powder run from the peak of the ridge right down to the Alta Lodge, I can feel the evolution of this technique.

So where do you go if you are a good skier, and it has just snowed 18 inches last night and you're standing in line with butterflies of excitement in your stomach? First of all, there is no way to ski it all in one day, or two, or ten. But here is one strategy for a new-snow day.

Start on the Collins side. This is the area the patrol opens first. Sugarloaf and Supreme follow in that order. At first glance it looks like the Collins and Wildcat lifts rise to pretty much the same place. But in fact, Wildcat opens up a huge area of expert skiing along the western edge of the resort that can't be reached from the top of Collins. If you like your powder with bumps underneath, stick with Wildcat for a few runs in the morning. *Warmup, Punchbowl,* and *Bear Paw* are humdingers that will keep you bopping and the snow flying.

Most powderhounds head straight for Germania. Even if the *High Traverse* out to *Rustler* is open, I like to make a run or two on Germania before it gets crowded. Some of the best lines are right under and on either side of the lift. The trees to the skier's left (*Fred's Trees*) are quite steep and spaced just so for powder turns. Right of the lift line, the terrain is more open (out toward the spacious glades of *Race Course*), while the region around *Lower Sunspot* harbors dozens of delightful little shots.

When the patrol opens the gates to *High Traverse,* the real Alta experience begins. Double back to the north from the top of Germania and follow the patrol's traverse tracks out along the ridge. My problem is deciding where to peel off: right away into *Sun Spot's* wide acres, or a little farther out to *West Rustler* or *Stone Crusher* or *Lone Pine* or all the way out to *Alf's High Rustler?* Or any of the myriad unnamed lines in between? (Alta has so much skiable terrain, even the patrol doesn't have names for everything. I recently skied a run off Supreme that the patrol called simply "the chute to the skier's right of the little piney ridge"!) Each one looks a little more inviting than the last. The steepest and longest are out near the end. *Stone Crusher* and *Lone Pine* are my personal favorites; they are never bumped up, and the pitch stays at a constant, heart-pounding 35 degrees for over 1,000 vertical feet. *Alf's* is *the* classic, of course. It sweeps to the valley floor like the bell of a horn, starting as a rocky pinpoint and ending at least 200 yards wide at the creek. Because it's such an icon, it is almost impossible, once the season is well under way, to catch it without moguls underneath, a fact that delights mogul lovers to no end.

By this time the Albion side of the Rustler Ridge, known as the Greeley area, is probably open. If you can tear yourself away from another trip down *Rustler,* you will be rewarded with more untracked skiing and some of Alta's longest drops. *Yellow Trail* and *East Greeley* are reached by hiking five minutes from the top of Germania over to the east-facing (morning sun!) side of the ridge. Two of the most exciting runs at Alta, *Gunsight* and *Eddie's High Nowhere,* require a trip out on *High Traverse* about halfway to *Rustler* and then a hike up and over the ridge. The farther out on the ridge you go, the more likely you are to find trackless snow. *Eddie's* soars an uninterrupted 1,800 vertical feet to the bottom of Albion Basin. It takes a little effort to get there—you usually walk the final 100 feet to the notch with skis off—but it's worth every step.

By now you've probably got the idea that hiking, traversing, walking on skis is a big part of the Alta experience. There is plenty of skiing for folks who want never to lift a ski boot out beyond the groomed trails. But for the skier who wants the wild snow and is willing to work just a little for it, Alta is a kind of paradise. In the days following a storm, as the patrol gets around to the other areas, they open up: the huge *Devil's Castle* zone with its undulating convex shapes; the sunny, nearly treeless *Wolverine Peak* area; and so on. When things are really stable, the genuinely extreme *Baldy Chutes* are open to the public, as are the exciting routes off Wildcat Ridge into Snowbird's territory. Speaking of Snowbird, if you bought an Alta-Bird pass, as locals fondly refer to the two-for-one Alta Snowbird Pass, ride to the top of the Sugarloaf chair, head West past the checkpoint that keeps boarders out of Alta and ensures that your pass will let you ski both resorts, and drop into Mineral Basin.

Hardly a winter day goes by that you can't find some powder or one of its slightly less romantic derivatives to sink your skis into. The search is aided and abetted by Alta's front-office philosophy of opening as much terrain as possible as often as possible. It's a kind of throwback to skiing's simpler, less litigious days, and it pervades all of Alta with a warm, adventurous glow.

Oh yes, I almost forgot Supreme. That's what happens to a lot of Alta skiers too. With all the other great steeps, it's easy to overlook this area. (Alta patrolmen who are assigned to Supreme, good-naturedly consider themselves an autonomous sovereignty, independent of the rest of the area.) In fact, Supreme has a wealth of fascinating glades, gullies, chutes, cliffs, and trees, and because it is the last area to open on a new-snow morning (sometimes not until 11 a.m. if control work is heavy on other parts of the mountain) the powder stays and stays.

The lift passes right over some exquisitely steep terrain: the yellow rock cliffs above *White Squaw,* the tubular confines of *Supreme Challenge,* and the gnarled limber pines of *Piney Glade.* The latter two lead into *Sidewinder,* probably the longest and most interestingly serpentine gully run at Alta. All four can be reached without walking a step. Put on your sidesteppin' shoes, however, and you're in for more treats out on the northern ridgeline. *Spiney Ridge* reminds me of steep Squaw Valley or Bear Valley in California's High Sierra: rib-like runs through semidesert rocks and wizened old trees.

Supreme faces mostly west. The light is gorgeous late in the day. The sun may already have set in the Salt Lake Valley, but it is still beaming in low and golden on *Sunset*. All of the Albion side lifts close at 4 p.m. It is possible to catch the last chair on Supreme, ski down, grab the Transfer rope tow, and still catch a late ride on Wildcat, which closes at 4:30 p.m. Time it perfectly and you might even make it up Germania one last time. In the last rays, the *High Traverse* takes on magical qualities.

Lunch on the Hill

There aren't many people still out at 4:30 p.m. A full day at Alta is a full day. One strategy to help you make it through to last run time is to wait on lunch and come back fresh for the final two hours or so. Despite repeated, good-natured chastisement from ski writers, most people still take lunch on the hill at noon. Alta's oldest mid-mountain restaurant, **Watson Shelter,** is long on hearty, moderately priced skier fare but decidedly short on space. **Alf's Restaurant,** in the heart of Albion Basin, offers plenty of indoor and outdoor seating. But from noon to about 1:30 p.m., they can be zooey. I usually pack a granola bar or some dried fruit in a pocket, munch on them at noon and ski through while the lines are short and the slopes practically empty. Then I go in for late lunch. (Watson's chili with cheese, onions, and salsa is particularly satisfying.) Then I go back out rested and ready to close the place down. If you would like to step out of those cold stiff ski boots into some warm sheep-skin slippers and have a nice three-course, sit-down meal around a cozy fire, try **Collins Grill,** located upstairs in the Watson Shelter. Be sure to make reservations, because Collins Grill often fills up with those pesky Snowbird instructors skiing their guests from Snowbird over the Baldy Shoulder for the best lunch break in Little Cottonwood Canyon.

Alta for Beginner Skiers

The Albion Base is the hub for beginner and novice skiers. This is where you can find day-care facilities, the ski school, and the children's ski school. Alta is justifiably proud of the children's center, with its playroom upstairs in the Albion Ticket building and a special dry-land practice room downstairs. Kids who are skiing for the first time have a chance to take skis on and off, practice left and right, learn to walk and sidestep, all on a specially designed carpet with fun instructional graphics built in. They can do this all before ever having to try it outside on the slippery snow.

First-timers—"never evers," in ski school parlance—should always start out with a lesson. There's a handy surface lift reserved for classes just down the hill from the ski school meeting place. Groomed each morning and sheltered from skier traffic, it is an ideal practice slope.

Once rudimentary braking and turning skills are mastered, you have a choice: take either the Albion or the Sunnyside double chairs up into the soft, round shapes of lower Albion Basin. The Albion is almost a mile long, the Sunnyside a little shorter. Both provide access to the three main novice runs. The farthest east, and also the most beautiful, to my mind, is *Patsey Marley.* It takes off at the top of Albion and meanders northwest right down the creek bed at the base of Wolverine Peak, in and out of small stands of evergreens, following the natural roller coasters of the land. *Crooked Mile* zigs back and forth across this gentle, lightly treed terrain. And *Sunnyside,* the farthest west, sweeps over treeless wide humps toward the Alpenglow restaurant and the base of the Sugarloaf lift before turning north again and joining the other two for the final run home. *Sunnyside* is my least favorite; it has a long flat spot in the middle, requiring poling or skating or both, and it's bedeviled by higher-speed traffic from above.

Sunnyside is one of the few traffic problems at Alta. Virtually all of the skiers in the upper basin must exit via the same wide but sometimes congested *Sunnyside* freeway. It's not just the skiers who have ridden up into Albion. A fair number of expert skiers cross over Rustler Ridge, the center of the W, from the Collins side to the powder-rich Greeley area, and they too must descend onto *Sunnyside* for the ride out. This means that the whole soup of skiers, some hell-bent for the Collins base and others just testing the waters with their first wedge turns, are thrown together in, sometimes, frightening combinations. Be alert. Watch for faster traffic from above. When I'm skiing with my children in this situation, I keep to one side or the other, herd them in front of me, and play the role of rear guard.

If conditions get crazy on Albion and Sunnyside—and they can in good weather on the big weekends—try the Cecret chair up in the bosom of the basin. It was put in primarily as access to the intermediate and expert terrain off the Supreme lift. But Cecret is also a well-kept secret for slower skiers seeking a quiet ride through the woods. Two runs, *Sweet 'n' Easy* and *Rabbit,* wander through some of the lushest forests in the area (an area that is making a comeback 65 years after the mountain was denuded in the mining frenzy). *Rabbit* in particular has a fine, deep-forest feel; you might even see the tracks of the snowshoe hare, chocolate brown in summer and pure white (but for the tips of the ears) in winter, with overlarge hind feet for easy movement over snow.

True "learning" skiers should not be tempted to try the Collins Gulch side of Alta. Low intermediates with a sense of adventure, however, should try one blue route off the Germania summit, from the top ease down *Mambo* beneath the glowering face of Baldy into the great cupped palm of the mountain known as *Main Street*. From here bear right through *Meadow* to *Cat Track*, which sweeps back and forth, broomlike, across the face of *Alf's High Rustler*, bringing you gently back to the Collins base. There is nothing very steep on this route, though there are certainly steep, slashing runs all around you. The views—down the canyon to the Salt Lake Valley and across to Sugarloaf and the Devil's Castle—and the huge scope of the terrain make it worth the trip.

Alta for Intermediate Skiers

Intermediates of every kind will find freedom of choice, which is rare this side of the Alps. The reason is the open, sparsely treed terrain. Nearly all the blue trails named and numbered on the map actually include many more miniroutes, so your choices multiply. Take the *Devil's Elbow* trail off Sugarloaf. The line on the map moseys down a delightful succession of bumps, dips, hollows, and soft ridgelines in quintessential Albion Basin style. The number of ways to ski the trail itself, given the inherent playfulness of its path, is practically infinite; this is the polar opposite of bull-dozed, the-best-surprise-is-no-surprise intermediate skiing. The options off either side of *Devil's Elbow*, poking around corners and taking the path less traveled, can add up to a whole day's worth of exploratory fun.

The whole Sugarloaf area is characterized by surprise. In the summer, the land beneath the snow is rock: rock slides, rock chutes, rock bowls, rock gullies. When the prodigious snows fill in the shapes—and Alta, like Bear Valley in California and Arapahoe Basin in Colorado, needs more snow than many areas do to operate—the ski surface becomes a complex, surprising, and fluid sea.

The terrain begs to be explored. Try the whale-like rolls to the right (skier's right) of *Devil's Elbow* just below *Cecret Saddle* (Cecret is pronounced "secret," the misspelling dates to a poorly schooled miner). Or poke around on the *Glory Hole* side of the lift. *Glory Hole* itself is rated black diamond, but that is primarily because of the big bumps that form in its narrow gully. You can escape the bumps if you want to (you can always escape the bumps at Alta with a move to one side or the other) by staying to the left on the gentler, higher ground. The best run for flat-out cruising in this Sugarloaf zone is the aptly named *Roller Coaster*.

On the Collins side of the mountain, the intermediate options appear slightly more limited, but only because they are surrounded by so many black diamonds. In fact, in good snow conditions quite a few black runs can be enjoyed by improving skiers. Among these are *Warmup* off the top of Wildcat lift, *Lower Sunspot*, and the top section of *Bear Paw* before it breaks over the Wildcat face. On one of my first trips to Alta in the late 1960s, I spent a whole morning, run after run, in the spoonlike swales of upper *Bear Paw* and then cut right under the Collins lift to *Meadow*, the always-groomed intermediate thoroughfare in the center of the gulch.

The classic cruiser on this side is the *Mambo/Main Street* combination off Germania. Some people repeat this one all day long. It's a yin/yang kind of run, convex, exposed *Mambo* turning into concave, sheltered *Main Street.* To this I would add *Ballroom,* one of the most awesome settings for a ski run I've seen. From the top of the Germania lift you traverse out onto the face of Mount Baldy. The peak rears up like an impossibly huge wave 600 feet above. The *Baldy Chutes,* almost always in their own blue shade and once described by Alta snow ranger Binx Sandahl as "steep as a cow's face," look practically vertical. (When conditions are just right, the chutes are opened and are skied by local daredevils.) Below the traverse, the *Ballroom* bowl swoops down in an even, unobstructed curve, like the side of a frozen sand dune, all the way to *Main Street.* It's an exhilarating ride.

Should Germania and Sugarloaf get busy—and they are the two most popular lifts with intermediate skiers—make the pilgrimage over to the far eastern edge of the area and the Supreme lift. Supreme is almost never crowded and has some of the least-known and most interesting intermediate and advanced skiing at Alta. There's a whole different feel over here. Ancient limber pines, yellowed and twisted by the elements, haunt the rocky ridgelines. The trees are sparser. There are a few aspens on the sunnier exposures, and parts of the area have the feel of the desert ranges of Nevada or eastern California.

From the top of the Supreme lift you can look east down the back side of the Wasatch Front into the Heber Valley, a region of small farms and cattle ranches surrounding staunchly Mormon Heber City. The skiing off this back side looks pretty tempting, and, indeed, the area is skied periodically by telemarkers and alpine tourers, but the walk out is long and arduous.

Head east from the lift's top terminal and, following a short hike, you'll find yourself in *Catherine's Area,* a mountainside of its own that most skiers never find. Those who make the hike deliver themselves to a powder-choked zone of pocket meadows and pine glades. The pitch isn't extreme, just enough to keep you floating through the deepest of powder storms.

Coming back west, directly off the Supreme top terminal is the *Challenger* blue run. It's one of the few blues that develops and keeps bumps for most of the year. The pitch is unthreatening, so the moguls take on the character of frisky whitecaps at sea rather than the man-eaters you'll sometimes find on *Collins Face,* for example.

Traverse out south of the summit and you'll find two lovely, Colorado-style intermediate cruisers called *Big Dipper* and *Rock 'n' Roll.* This is great teaching/learning terrain, quiet and smooth. Alf loves to take nascent parallelers out here where the big fallaway shapes make turning easy. In between *Challenger* and *Big Dipper* is a marvelous zone of glades and gentle gullies, known as *Sleepy Hollow.* When there is new powder, this is a paradise for intermediates who may not be ready to tackle Alta's

famous steeps but who nevertheless want to play with the feathery sensations of deep snow. Gentler yet is the terrain on both sides of the Albion
lift. This is near perfect, first-timer powder land. I once watched a young
family—Mom, Dad, and two kids—frolicking in the vicinity of *Patsey
Marley* the day after a ten-inch storm. No groomed runs for them. They
bounced from one unskied patch to another, slipping by baby evergreens, bobbing, floating, shrieking with delight, not worrying much
about turning or looking good, but having the time of their lives.

Alta for Expert Skiers

For those experts who just can't get enough within bounds, Alta in
2002–2003 launched snow cat tours into Grizzly Gulch just east of the
resort. This is a gorgeous patch of terrain ranging from steep lines to
rolling swales through evergreens. Until these tours began, the terrain
was touched only by backcountry enthusiasts and skiers who joined one
of Ski Utah's Interconnect Adventures, which comes through the gulch
from Brighton on the way to Alta. Boarders, still banned from Alta
proper, can join in these pricey snow cat forays—$200 for five runs.

Snowboarding

At the time of the printing of this book snowboards were still not
allowed at Alta. Call Alta for current policies.

Alta after Hours

When the day is done and the last powder shredded, long lines of cars
form to go down the canyon (this happens on the weekends only; if it's
mid-week, this is not a problem). If you're staying down in the valley,
this traffic can be a hassle, an unwelcome reminder of the Bay Bridge or
the Lincoln Tunnel. Various plans have been put forth to help relieve the
weekend traffic on the tiny, two-lane canyon road, including monorails
and tunnels through the mountains, but none is likely to be realized
soon, if ever. There is a decent bus system connecting the airport, downtown Salt Lake City, and the resorts in Big and Little Cottonwood
canyons—decent but not great. Check a UTA (Utah Transit Authority)
schedule for routes and times.

If you are driving down, settle in for a slow drive on a busy or very
snowy day; it can take one hour to cover what is normally a 15-minute
drive. The only other option is to settle in at the lounge at the **Goldminer's Daughter** (yes, you can get a drink in Utah; see the "Inside Story"
on Utah's liquor laws, page 339) and wait for the traffic to subside.

Neither is as good an option as staying in Alta in the first place. Space
is limited, so you should reserve as far in advance as possible with Alta
Reservation Service or the individual lodges and condominiums. There
are only five lodges, each with a character and history of its own. The

Peruvian and the Goldminer's Daughter are the least fancy and least pricey. The **Alta Lodge,** hard by the ghost of old Mayor Watson's shack, and the **Rustler Lodge** are more expensive and elegant. The **Snowpine,** Alta's first ski lodge, built by the WPA in 1938–1939, is a rustic, stone jewel. All rooms come with breakfast and dinner included.

My own favorite is the Rustler Lodge. The food is exquisite (a choice of European-style entrees each evening; breakfast buffet with fresh fruits and homemade baked breads and muffins). The view down the canyon in the evening (blue mountain silhouettes against a mauve horizon) is almost enough to supplant hunger. The atmosphere is homey, as if everybody there were part of the same big family that dropped in to visit the Mother Mountain, and we're always welcome. Signs on the outside doors request that you please not let Cec (short for Cecret), the house golden retriever, out during the day.

If you want to go out and sample the dinners at the other lodges, you just have to tell Shawna or Tom in the morning before you go skiing. The only other place to eat in Alta proper in the evening (besides the lodges) is the **Shallow Shaft.** Try their delicious homemade pizzas with pitchers of Wasatch Ale, which is brewed over the hill in Park City.

If you have a car (not at all necessary within Alta), you may want to drive the mile down to Snowbird one evening to sample the fare at one of their fine restaurants. When I'm skiing and staying in Alta, however, I find it exceedingly difficult to rouse myself past the fireplace at the Rustler. After dinner there are always a few knots of friendly conversation around the lounge, buzzing softly about the day's exploits. Then it's off to sleep. Alta is a simple place. Ski hard. Eat well. Sleep well. Ski again. As Chic Morton used to say, "Alta is for skiers." Amen.

Alta Data

Mountain Statistics

Vertical feet	2,020 feet
Base elevation	8,530 feet
Summit elevation	10,550 feet
Longest run	3.5 miles
Average annual snowfall	500 inches
Snowmaking	50 acres
Number of lifts	13: 1 detachable quad chair; 1 detachable triple chair; 2 triple chairs; 4 double chairs; 5 surface tows
Uphill capacity	11,284 skiers per hour
Skiable terrain	2,200 acres
Opening date	Mid-November
Closing date	Mid-April
Snowboarding	No

Alta Data (continued)

Transportation

By car About 45 minutes from Salt Lake International Airport via I-80 and Wasatch Boulevard south to State 210, Little Cottonwood Canyon. Alta is 9 miles up the road at the head of the canyon.

By bus, limo, or taxi From Salt Lake International Airport.

By plane Via major carriers to Salt Lake International Airport.

Key Phone Numbers

Ski-area information	(801) 742-3333 and (801) 359-1078
Snow report	(801) 572-3939
Reservations	(888) 782-9258
Alf Engen Ski School	(801) 359-1078
Website	www.alta.com or info@alta.com

Peter's TECH TIP

Skiing the Deep

I am convinced that the main reason powder skiing is so delightfully addictive is that it slows things down. Powder just naturally creates the kind of situation that tennis players talk about when they're in "the zone" and everything slows down for them. Baseball players speak of being able to watch the seams of a spinning ball. Almost any athlete in the groove sees or feels himself performing in slow motion. In powder skiing, the resistance from all that snow—on skis, boots, legs, and sometimes (especially in Utah) even thighs and bellies—counters the pull of gravity, holds you up, and slows you down.

Have you noticed how powder skiers seem to have a different relationship with the fall line? Without skiing faster, they can ski noticeably closer to the fall line, closer to "the path of water," as Alf would say. The deeper the snow, the more the skier can give in to gravity. Thus all the talk about floating and free-falling, about pillows and cushions and clouds.

The surest obstacle to achieving this state of bliss is our own hurry. Initiate a turn on a packed slope and you can expect near-instant response from your skis. We not only expect it; we are so accustomed to it that our bodies are prepared to balance only so long over that turning ski. Start a turn the same way in deep snow and you will likely fall over before your skis have completed half the arc. The skis have slowed down but you have not. My first suggestion, then, is to cultivate a kind of extreme patience. Practice making long radius turns on gentle, groomed terrain, at slow speeds. This is important because at slow speeds you are forced to stand in balance over your feet. At high speeds you can lean in, bank onto your edges, and get away with it.

Next, find an ungroomed powder slope. Not steep—you're trying to learn to let go, not hold on. Although it may seem heretical, ski in a straight line down the slope and bounce. Bounce your skis up and down in the snow, first with your weight on one ski, then the other, then with your weight equally on both skis. One weighted ski sinks, creating an awkward split. Two skis weighted more or less equally react as one.

Feel the platform that you create down in the snow when you bounce on both skis. In powder, skis don't turn on their edges the way they do on a packed slope; they turn against this platform they create. Push down into the snow; the snow pushes back against the bottom of the ski. Push a ski that's already beginning to turn into deep snow; the snow pushes back, bends it, turns it (and you).

The other basics of turning still apply. You need to unweight (bouncing is one way to do it), so that you can then steer your feet and skis into the turn. This is the part that takes the patience and balance; things take longer to happen in powder. Finally, you need to weight those skis, both of them, through the arc (more patience) to the finish.

Start with one turn at a time: gliding, steering, pressing up to a stop. Start from a shallow traverse, then make subsequent turns closer to the fall line. When this feels comfortable, try linking a few together. Hands and poles—very important—come into play here. Alf used to teach a technique he called the "quickhand" or the "readyhand." At the moment of pole plant, vigorously raise the outside hand and pole in almost an uppercut. The action lightens the skis for easy entry into the turn and positions the hand for the new pole plant to come.

A solid pole plant also helps stabilize the upper body. Shoulders should be square to the fall line. A good powder skier looks very much like a good mogul skier: The upper body is quiet, and the legs and skis move from side to side beneath the trunk. Where a bump skier finishes each turn on the flat spot at the base of each mogul, the powder skier uses the platform of compressed snow at the bottom of his turning motion.

A final word about rhythm. It doesn't make sense on a languid, rolling pitch to impose the jackrabbit rhythm you might have seen employed on *Gunsight*. "Choose the rhythm to fit the hill," says Junior Bounous, an Engen protégé and the first ski-school director Snowbird had. Let the mountain dictate. Balance on both skis. Begin with a strong up motion of the outside hand. Float. Wait. Sink into the soft resistance, and repeat. Soon you, too, will approximate the feeling Bounous has: "Sometimes I find myself yelling or singing a little because powder is the most exciting, exhilarating skiing there is."

Snowbird

Snowbird is to Alta as a Cuisinart is to a good, sharp knife. Alta's sister resort in Little Cottonwood Canyon is a modern, efficient, high-tech, concrete-steel-and-glass counterpoint to Alta's historic, funky, efficient wood, steel, and stone. The differences are largely a matter of style and tone.

Snowbird has the greater vertical, 3,240 feet worth of it, due to both a lower base and a higher top terminal, and perhaps a few more acres of terrain. Snowbird attracts a completely different clientele with its elegant ten-story Cliff Lodge Hotel & Spa, its 125-passenger Swiss tram, and its pricier lift ticket. But Snowbird is not really out to compete with Alta. Snowbird set out to be (and has largely succeeded in becoming) a classy, upscale, European-style resort that is just a mile down the road from what may be the quintessential western American ski experience.

Whereas Alta grew out of the visions of many men—Alf Engen, Mayor Watson, Salt Lake Winter Recreation Association's Joe Quinney,

Monty Atwater, and the men who formed America's first avalanche school (see the "Inside Story," Avalanche Hunters, page 347)—Snowbird is largely the vision of just two men: Alta regular Ted Johnson and Richard D. Bass, the youngest son of Oklahoma oil magnate Harry W. Bass. Johnson advanced the idea, and Bass was the answer to Ted's search for "someone with lots of money and a skier at heart."

Bass made some money in the oil business, had a hand in Vail's early development, then turned his sights on Snowbird, which has been his consuming passion ever since. (Well, perhaps not all-consuming. Between 1983 and 1985, Bass and his friend Frank Wells, who was then president of Warner Brothers, attempted to be the first humans to scale the highest peak on each of the seven continents. It took a tremendous amount of planning, effort, and money. Wells struggled and ultimately failed to reach the highest summit of all, Everest. But Bass prevailed, and in so doing also became the oldest man at the time to have climbed Everest; he was 55. You can read about their adventures in *Seven Summits,* written by Bass and Wells with their friend Rick Ridgeway.

Snowbird sprang into existence, like Venus, more or less full grown during the winter of 1971–1972. The centerpiece was, and still is, the tram, a magnificent piece of steel and cable architecture that connects the Snowbird Center at 8,100 feet with the summit of Hidden Peak at exactly 11,000 feet. There is almost no flat ground here, so the lodges were built into the hillside between Little Cottonwood Creek and the canyon road. They are spacious and sumptuously appointed and remarkably unobtrusive for their mass. The service is impeccable. Bass says, "My underlying dream for Snowbird is the creation of a year-round resort that respects and complements the beauty and inspiration of this natural setting—a place dedicated to increasing human understanding through the enhancement of body, mind, and spirit."

Yes, Dick Bass actually says things like that. And he means every word of it. He's a lover of mountains and what they can do for the "body, mind, and spirit." He's a dreamer. Lucky for us he's practical enough to have turned this particular dream into reality.

Snowbird: How the Mountain Works

Snowbird occupies two side valleys directly down canyon of Alta's ski terrain and a huge back bowl. Like Alta, the horizon line appears as a huge W. Mount Baldy crowns the left-hand point (looking up) at the top of the Alta/Snowbird boundary ridge. Hidden Peak (top of Tram and Mineral Basin Express) is the center spike (Gad/Peruvian Ridge), and the Twin Peaks (at 11,434 and 11,491 feet, two of the highest points in the Wasatch Range) tower over the Gad/White Pine Ridge, the area's western boundary. The western valley is called Gad Valley, the eastern

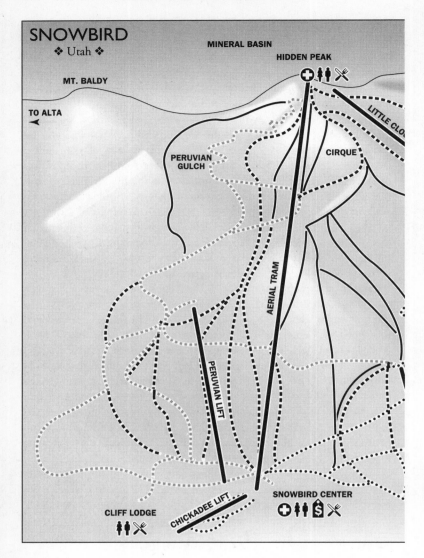

SNOWBIRD
❖ Utah ❖

MINERAL BASIN

HIDDEN PEAK

MT. BALDY

TO ALTA

LITTLE CLO

PERUVIAN
GULCH

CIRQUE

AERIAL TRAM

PERUVIAN LIFT

CHICKADEE LIFT

SNOWBIRD CENTER

CLIFF LODGE

valley is Peruvian Gulch, and the massive 500-acre back bowl is called
Mineral Basin. The gentlest terrain fills the broad, alluvial mouth of Gad
Valley. Up and over on the Peruvian side intermediate, advanced, and
superexpert runs coexist in a melange of forest trails and uncut natural
shapes. Mineral Basin is mainly open bowl skiing/riding with many
interesting gullies and chutes.

The Gad base at 7,900 feet (Entry 1 off the Canyon Road) has a
parking lot but little else. The real base of the resort is the Snowbird
Center, or Tram Plaza as it is sometimes known, accessed from Entry 2.

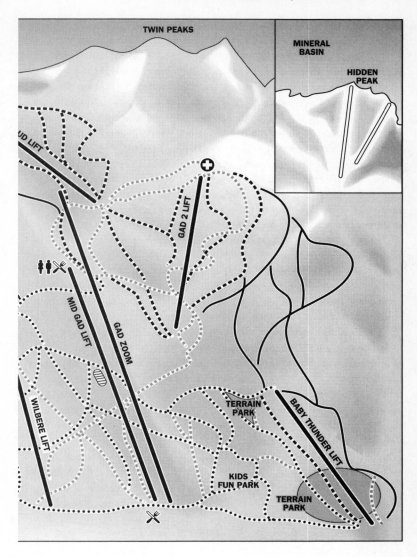

(Entry 3 goes to the Lodge and the Inn at Snowbird, and Entry 4 serves the Cliff Lodge.) At the Tram Plaza you'll find everything on three levels and all under one roof: tickets, mountain school, restaurants, deli, ice cream shop, real estate sales, photography services, medical clinic, post office, sport shops, boutiques, grocery store, state liquor store, pharmacy, and bookstore. This, by the way, is one of the hottest little (three-rack!) paperback bookstores on the planet. They've got Mark Twain, Anne Tyler, Kurt Vonnegut Jr., and Fyodor Dostoevsky. So if you forget your current reading, stop in; it's a browser's treat. My only complaint about the Tram Plaza, and it's a minor one, is that with all the interesting angles and multiple levels, it can sometimes be hard to find your way out to the skiing. Remember, Level 3 is the open-area Plaza Deck where the tram docks, and Level 1 is where you enter from the parking lot.

All of the lodging is clustered near the Tram Plaza; everything is within easy walking distance. Drive in and leave your car parked for the duration. There's even UTA buses for getting to and from the Salt Lake Valley if you want to take in a Jazz basketball game. In general, Snowbird grades its slopes more conservatively than Alta does. Double black diamonds designate runs that are, at times, subject to avalanche activity. These runs are not necessarily steeper than the black diamonds (though some, like *Great Scott* at the upper end of the Cirque, are very steep indeed), but they do tend to be wilder, less visited, more apt to show the extremes of snow, wind, and exposure.

By the same token, I find some of the black diamonds to be eminently skiable—depending on the snow quality—for solid intermediates. Runs like *Primrose Path, Regulator Johnson, Last Choice,* and *Harper's Ferry East* (more on all of these places to come) might not be considered most difficult at Alta, say, or Aspen Mountain. Snowbird has simply chosen to take a conservative overview.

The qualifier "depending on snow quality" looms huge at any area, especially one with large tracts of above-timberline terrain that are exposed to sun and wind. Snowbird enjoys the same superior quality snowfall that blankets most of Utah, but there are days and storms that conspire against certain areas of the mountain while favoring others. *Regulator Johnson,* for example, a classic upper-mountain run, faces the afternoon sun and faces directly into the prevailing winds. On some days it is a bowl of earthly delights, enjoyed by most skiers and riders from intermediate on up; on other days it can be like skiing or riding a giant slab of frozen cod and is definitely recommended for experts only. The same is true for Mineral Basin. Your best bet is to pop your head into the ski patrol hut at the top of the tram and get some advice. There are also ski patrol on almost every tram car. When you load the tram, go to the front of the car (uphill side) and chat with them during the ride up the mountain.

There are seven double chairlifts, three high-speed quads, two surface lifts, and the world-famous Aerial Tram at Snowbird. The tram, which some mockingly call the "cram" for the way it's packed before each uphill jaunt, provides access to almost all of the navigable terrain. The chairs complement the tram by serving each of the six distinct skiing/riding regions. The Chickadee lift rises a brief 142 vertical feet behind the Tram Plaza. It is strictly a beginners' lift and is used mostly for ski lessons. Three lifts serve the vast, easy, lower Gad Valley terrain: Wilbere, Gad-zoom, and Mid Gad. Virtually all of the novice and a good portion of the groomed intermediate terrain is here. Baby Thunder opens more novice/intermediate terrain at the area's far western edge, but has largely been devoted to recycling skiers and 'boarders who time after time attack the terrain park beneath its cables. Growing in the forest here are Rainbow rails, C Rails, fun boxes and a variety of snow features, from spines to tabletops and kickers. While the park lacks a half-pipe, there's a 420-foot-long pipe located on *Big Emma.*

From both the Gadzoom and Mid Gad lifts there are connecting routes to the Gad II lift, which in turn serves a kind of independent fiefdom of blue and black runs through the trees. From the tops of Gadzoom or Gad II (the central belly of Gad Valley) you can reach the Little Cloud lift, which rises 1,300 feet out of this vortex very close to the summit of Hidden Peak. Little Cloud's zone is almost treeless, blinding white bowls of upper-intermediate and advanced terrain. From the tops of Little Cloud or the Ariel Tram you can ski or ride into Mineral Basin and access Mineral Basin Express (MBX). Right next door to MBX is the Baldy Express, which serves a couple novice runs but more importantly connects Snowbird to Alta via Sugar Loaf Pass. The final chair, the Peruvian, climbs a thousand vertical feet into Peruvian Gulch from near the Tram Plaza. It doesn't connect to anything, but it is a superb yo-yo lift, especially for good skiers and riders seeking a bit of mogul madness.

The centerpiece of the area, and the thing that makes Snowbird Snowbird, is, of course, the tram. Built by Garaventa of Switzerland, its blue and red cabins whisk up to 125 skiers and riders at a time up 2,900 vertical feet to the top of the mountain in a mere seven minutes. It is a monumental alpine transport, comparable in this country only with Jackson Hole's tram. It mirrors, as Dick Bass intended, the stunning uphill conveyances of Zermatt and Mürren in the old country.

It is possible, though I don't recommend the practice, to ride to the top via the tram, jump out, race to the bottom in something under seven minutes, and catch the same car on its next return trip to the summit. Certain local fanatics do it all day, every day for most of the winter. No, it's not necessary to yo-yo the tram to get the most out of it, but it is a great way to spend the winter.

Crowds are likely to prevent the practice most days. The tram is justifiably popular. Snowbird regulars measure the wait at the bottom in "trams" or "buckets" or "cars," a two-car wait being typical for a busy weekday or a relatively quiet weekend. A two-car wait means standing in line for anywhere from 8 to 16 minutes, which sounds like a lot for a weekday lift line. But when you consider the vertical gained and the short ride time, it's still a bargain. Chairlift-riding time to the top of Little Cloud Bowl, assuming there are no lift lines, is 15 minutes using Gadzoom and Little Cloud. Consider buying a chair-only ticket if the weather is nice.

The tram is an aesthetic as well as a practical joy. The 125-person limit is cozy but not too terribly tight. The car lifts off imperceptibly and accelerates into space without a sound. The valley of the Little Cottonwood recedes into model dimensions below. You recognize voices and faces from earlier rides. The sea of ski tips becomes vaguely familiar and comforting. The chatter around you rises in anticipation with the elevation.

As the car slows to dock at the summit, the tram operator calls out, "Attention, skiers!" Then he waits, like a teacher waiting for absolute quiet, and continues, "*High Baldy* and *Thunder Bowl* are closed. *Chips* is the easiest way to the bottom of the mountain, and *Lupine Loop* is the easiest way to the bottom of Mineral Basin. Follow the red trail markers on both of these runs. Watch for marked and unmarked obstacles. Check your trail map or see the ski patrol on the peak with any questions you may have. Ski with caution. Have a nice run." The doors open. The noise and energy return, and another wave of skiers and riders clanks across the metal landing platform to the summit snows.

The fact that only 125 people leave the top every seven minutes is another reason that endears the tram to Junior Bounous, Snowbird's director of skiing. "I like that it dumps a limited number of people on the terrain. *Chips* (on the Peruvian Gulch side) is my favorite teaching and free-skiing terrain because it's a very pleasant experience. A wave of people goes by, then it becomes totally silent. I have undisturbed teaching time. *Regulator Johnson* used to be like *Chips* before the Little Cloud chair went in."

Snowbird for Beginning Skiers

Beginning and skiers and riders are the only ones who shouldn't ride Snowbird's tram, although cocky novices won't be entirely over their heads. There is one "green" run (*Lupine Loop*) off of the tram into Mineral Basin. This run is basically a road with a small section of open glades, and you eventually have to take *Chips* back to the bottom of the mountain. (*Chips* is the easiest route off the summit, wandering a leisurely 2.5 miles through Peruvian Gulch; it's so gentle, even timid intermediates should have no qualms.) But this is not to say that novices are given short shrift. The lower Gad Valley has some of the friendliest learning turf anywhere.

Big Emma is the star here. Flowing the full 1,300-foot vertical of Mid Gad lift, *Big Emma* swings beneath the *Gad Chutes* and out onto what I imagine is the jolly, opulent midriff of the mountain. She is as broad as two freeways and as smooth as talc. The lower half, also accessible from the midway unloading station, is gentler still and a lot less crowded. *Upper Emma,* in addition to being prime learning terrain, is also the main highway for better riders and skiers moving around the nose of the mountain to the tram. Pay attention. The slope is so broad and free, it's easy to forget to look over your shoulder.

West Second South is a nice alternative if *Big Emma* gets too zooey. The name refers to the historic red-light district in Salt Lake City, where pleasure came "easy," like the skiing and riding here. (All streets in Salt Lake City are laid out on a grid: east or west of State Street and north or south of Temple. While the system is initially confusing to some new-comers, it is in fact quite orderly.) *West Second South* is really a secluded glade; various fingers dart in and out of little tree clusters, the snow stays soft because of the light traffic, and there is the delicious sense of explo-ration. Follow *West Second South Long* to *Alice Avenue* and on down to Baby Thunder chair. Mid Gad lift serves both *Big Emma* and *West Sec-ond South*. If the lift line there seems to be growing, move over to the Wilbere lift, which rarely has any kind of wait at all. Bounous loves the variety off the Wilbere, including the *Miners Road* novice area.

Snowbird Choices for Intermediates

In fact, if Bounous has only one hour in which to teach a private lesson, he usually heads for Wilbere, a 660-vertical-foot mini-ski area unto itself. Shoot off to the right of Wilbere's top ramp and you can ski either *Big Emma* or sunny, gladed *Wilbere Ridge,* a nice intermediate warm-up. Get off to the left and you're aimed toward the progressively more aggressive bumps of *Harper's Ferry, Harper's Ferry East,* and *Lower Mach Schnell.* The lower third of the area is devoted to easy, smooth pitches—perfect learning slopes.

But Snowbird's wonders are way too enticing to spend much of your time on Wilbere, as nice as it is. Up above, the big shapes and the alpine splendor call. Gad II, Mineral Basin, and the tram beckon.

I am a big fan of the tram, as you have certainly surmised, but I'd like to talk about Gad II for a moment. The lift gains a nifty 1,200 feet in nine minutes, and there's a lot of skiing and shredding waiting when you unload. (Peruvian is the only other chair with this much bang for the buck, but it is primarily expert.) Three of Gad II's runs, draped like white necklaces around this semi-autonomous peak, are prizewinning blues. *Bassackwards* and *Election* both take off toward the center of the big cupped hand that is the upper Gad Valley. *Bassackwards* is the more scenically splendid, coursing out into the open below the yellow rock cliffs of the Twin Peaks. Both runs suffer a bit from their own popularity and are therefore designated as slow skiing/riding areas. The sleeper here is *Bananas*. Sweeping under the boundary ridge along the area's west edge, *Bananas* tumbles down a delightful combination of draws and rolls, then zigs and zags alongside, but effectively out of the way of *Gad-zooks,* the wonderfully named bump run.

Gad II is a cold lift ride. Locals call it "the Fridge." It faces directly north, and its proximity to the Twin Peaks keeps it in the shade during the low sun days of early winter. But that same chilly exposure keeps the snow cold and crisp and guarantees some of the softest snow on the mountain.

To reach the Peruvian side of the mountain from Gad Valley, simply find your way to the Mid Gad Restaurant (all blue runs in the upper Gad Valley except *Bananas* lead there), then take *Big Emma* to *Bass Highway,* a broad, comfy catwalk named for the boss. To get from Peruvian Gulch back to Gad Valley, take the blue highway known as *Rothman Way.* The cutoffs run roughly parallel, one on top of the other like arms crossed over the chest of the mountain. The trail map doesn't make it clear, but it is not possible to ride the Little Cloud lift and then a blue route to the Peruvian side. The Little Cloud stops about 100 vertical feet short and about a quarter of a mile southwest of the Hidden Peak summit. Experts can traverse the top of *Regulator Johnson* to the double-diamond *Cirque.* Skiers and snowboarders have two options to get to *Chips.* One is to ride the tram and the other is to ski into Mineral Basin from the top of Little Cloud and ride MBX up to Hidden Peak. Check on run closures in Mineral Basin before jumping on Little Cloud. On many big-snow days Mineral Basin is for experts only.

Mineral Basin first opened in December of 1999. It added 25% more terrain to Snowbird and improved the skiing/riding 100%. Mineral Basin has 1,500 vertical feet and 500 acres of open bowls, chutes, and some glades and is a great area for strong intermediates and experts. On cold sunny mornings, Mineral is the place to go. With mostly south and east exposure, this area is the first one to be warmed and softened by the sun. Start out by following the *Path to Paradise* road to *Powder Paradise.* The runs are normally machine worked if it is not a powder day. Mineral is normally quite empty between 9 a.m. and 10:30 a.m. Plan your next run during your four-minute ride back up MBX. You can see most of the basin from the lift; you make the choice. If you tire of Mineral, jump on Baldy Express and slip over to Alta. This lift, raised in time for the 2002 Olympics, can drop beginners at the top of a trio of green-belted runs that tie into *Lupine Loop* and a return to MBX or give experts instant access to Alta near the top terminal of the Sugarloaf quad. Be forewarned: Buy an Alta-Bird pass and you better be up for a *full* day of skiing. This pass gives you access to 4,700 acres of terrain, 1 tram, 18 chairlifts, seven surface tows, and, thankfully, 22 restaurants.

If you haven't purchased the "Alta-Bird" pass, when crowds hit Mineral, simply head for the tram.

The tram. Ah, the tram. In my estimation, the tram is the reason to ski Snowbird. Take a minute at the top, walk over to the back-side rim, and peer over. Huge, open bowls plunge into Mineral Basin. The bucolic

Heber Valley and Deer Creek Reservoir (a popular windsurfing spot in summer) lie somnolent to the southeast. Fifteen miles directly south you can make out the Sundance ski area on the shoulder of Mount Timpanogos. Back north, across the sharp V of Little Cottonwood Canyon, Mount Superior dominates a craggy ridgeline. Superior's half-dozen slide paths are among those most likely to close the highway in a big avalanche cycle. From here they look practically vertical, and yet there are tracks made by backcountry skiers and snowboarders who make the walk as a kind of pilgrimage to a steep, untracked Valhalla.

Now that the crowd has gone, you have *Chips* to yourself. No one else will be starting down for at least another five minutes. Ski north down the Gad/Peruvian ridge 100 yards or so, until you can make a right turn. This is *Chips,* a brief road past Gorilla Pass into the pocket below the ridge, then 2.5 miles of open, wheeling, free-flowing terrain to the bottom. It's reminiscent of Alta's Albion Basin; a line on the map indicates the general route, but choices are actually infinite. Poke around, scamper through and around the hundreds of tiny tree islands. One particularly nice whale hump in the upper basin is named *Nacho's Knoll* after a Snowbird rescue dog. A little lower down you'll find yourself in a sunny glade called *Lower Palm Springs,* or so the ski patrol call it; the names are nowhere to be found on the mountain or on the map. Some locals say that 80% of the runs are not even on the map. That is the nature of Snowbird. You can make up your own names; that's the prerogative of the explorer, isn't it?

Snowbird is grooming more and more of Peruvian Gulch these days, which is good news for intermediates. You may find yourself, for instance, following a nicely pitched, groomed path off *Chips* and discover that it is *Silver Fox,* a black diamond on the map. No matter. The same thing may happen on the lower mountain, where some or all of *Chip's Face,* another blackie, may be cut and smooth. Rejoice! Snowbird is one of the rare places where you can find steep, smooth runs, the better to cut loose and feel the weightlessness that experts find here in abundance.

Snowbird for Experts

Snowbird rates 45% of its terrain as most difficult. (The mythical industry ideal, a kind of inverse "perfect" figure, is 25% beginner, 50% intermediate, and 25% expert.) While I think some of that may be slightly overrated, we're still talking about one giant playground for the experts. Let's start with the tram and the skiing and riding it serves and then move on to some separate areas.

The most obvious and inviting steep terrain off the top is found in the Cirque on the Peruvian side of the Gad/Peruvian Ridge. (In fact, the traverse down the ridge—similar in feeling and utility to Alta's High Traverse—is known as the *Cirque Traverse.*) It's a vast bald area, like the inside surface of a teacup, with room for perhaps 200 or 300 clear lines into the gulch. The steepest are near the top, where *Great Scott, Elevator Shaft,* and *Upper Cirque* begin their plunges through a rocky cliff band. *Lower Cirque* is beamier if not quite as steep. For such a large space there are few descriptive names—the patrol refers to specific locations by route numbers. On powder mornings, teams of patrolmen follow pre- scribed routes around the mountain, tossing hand charges into spots (called "shots") known to be prone to sliding. Ergot, one of my favorite runs in Lower Cirque, is known as *Route 2, Shots 11* and *12.* I find it by judging my proximity to *Hotfoot Gully,* a colorful moniker, but one that, again, you won't find on the trail map.

Suffice it to say a strong skier or rider could spend all day blissfully playing in the Cirque. But you wouldn't want to. Not when you can drop off the other side of the ridge into the *Gad Chutes 1* through *13.* This is where a good many of Snowbird's promo pictures are taken; it's a spectacular perch. Twin Peaks hovers like the Breithorn in the back- ground. Down the canyon, the Salt Lake Valley (these days most often under its blanket of smog) stretches away toward the lake of the same name. When a storm has just passed through, the gnarly little survivor trees up here are plastered with rime ice. To ski or ride among them is to weave in and out among so many frozen gnomes.

A little farther down the ridge one comes to *Barry Barry Steep,* and that it is, and to *Wilbere Bowl,* the longest continuous powder line on the mountain. Out at the very nose of the ridge is *Upper Mach Schnell,* a pure north-facing triangle of trees that, because of its distance from the summit, is one of the secret stashes and one of the last places on the mountain to retain powder after a storm. All of the runs from the *Gad Chutes* on down are rated double black diamond, so check with the ski patrol before jumping in.

Little Cloud is another expert area, though, as I have said before, there are a good many days when some runs here could be rated high intermediate: *Regulator Johnson* when the snow is soft, and *Little Cloud* itself, especially early in the season, when the bumps are small or nonex- istent. This is a mammoth zone, probably a mile wide and 1,300 feet high, with very few trees to get in the way; it's a genuine timberline bowl. There are some good bump lines, *Mark Malu Fork* for one, but there are always bump-free lines as well. In the late afternoon, with the sun beaming directly on the slopes, I feel lilliputian here amid the bulging, glacial forms—small, but also possessed of the skier's secret joy at mastering these massive shapes.

Gad II and the Peruvian lift offer the real challenges for mogul mas- ters. To ski moguls well, you have to be able to yo-yo them, up and down and up and down again over the exact same lines until you know their rhythms in your sleep. Peruvian's are the best, if only because the fall lines are truer and longer than the ones on *Gadzooks* and *S.T.H.* (you figure out what it stands for). *Adager* and *Silver Fox,* Peruvian's test pieces, rank with the best bump runs anywhere. The terrain is serpentine, interesting, and fiercely steep. *Primrose Path,* right under the chair, gets more high-intermediate traffic, because the gradient is less severe, and the moguls suffer accordingly. Panicky turns make for sharp, squared-off bumps. (The best "trainer moguls" are on *Harper's Ferry* and *Regulator Johnson.*)

Two of the best expert areas aren't even on the map. When they are open—and they are the last places the patrol opens, after a storm—*Baldy Face* and *Thunder Bowl* are sublime chunks of powderland. Baldy, of course, is the peak on the border with Alta. When the northwest face of this mountain has been favored with new snow and not much wind, it is a jewel. Long, fingerlike chutes cut through spare vegetation and deposit you gently, we hope, in upper Peruvian Gulch near *Chips.*

Thunder Bowl is on the opposite boundary, just off the ridge that separates Gad Valley from White Pine Valley to the west. *Thunder* is a kind of Shangri-la; it's barely visible from the rest of the ski area, and none but the heartiest powderhounds make the trek out from *Boundary Bowl.* Steep meadows and stairstep benches cut through the forest for 1,000 vertical feet before you have to cut back east, across the appropriately named *Pearly Gates,* to the Gad base. To attack it again requires two lift rides, back to the top of Gad II, but if there is powder in the trees, it's worth every minute.

Don't have a lot of time to explore on your own? Want to go directly to the best snow? Sign up for the Mountain Experience, a popular Snowbird program open to expert skiers. You ski with a professional mountain school guide and get a quick line to the powder or other off-trail skiing.

Snowboarding

Boarders who flock to Snowbird tend to have that wild look in their eyes. They don't come for mellow cruising. Instead, they look to the steep, snow-choked chutes and natural terrain features that litter the 'Bird's landscape.

When not in one of Snowbird's recently expanded terrain parks, many riders can be found on the 2.5-mile Chip's Run zig-zagging through Peruvian Gulch. This long and winding run is a boarding bonanza with continuous off-trail cliffs, chutes, and jumps.

When boarders refer to "doing laps," it usually involves some route on or near Chip's Run followed by a trot across the Plaza Deck and back on the Tram.

Pipers looking for air head to *Big Emma,* a 400-foot-long half-pipe located along the trail of the same name.

Expansion Snowbird

One of Dick Bass's dreams is to put a restaurant atop Hidden Peak, with the tram gliding up into the basement, like the one on the Schilthorn in Mürren, Switzerland. With luck, construction could begin in two or three seasons. The Baldy Express that connects Snowbird and Alta was a dream come true. These two rugged resorts share so much in common, and their strengths complement each other so well, that a joint pass was a no-brainer.

As it is, many aficionados consider Snowbird to be nearly perfect— blessed with Utah snow and complex, inviting terrain, as well as the tram, and seated at the top of the world right next to Alta. They'll get no argument from me.

Snowbird Lodging and Dining

Snowbird operates all of the lodging at the resort. You have some basic choices: the condos at the **Lodge at Snowbird,** the **Inn,** and the **Iron Blosam Lodge** or the magnificent **Cliff Lodge.** The condos are similarly appointed and identically priced. The Cliff is Snowbird's centerpiece hotel. Some say its $60+ million remodel job to over 500 rooms a few years ago almost broke Dick Bass. It's a glass palace, modern and severe on the outside, spacious and airy on the inside. A nine-story atrium with full-size trees looks up the slopes of Peruvian Gulch on the building's south side. The hotel is expensive but commensurately luxurious, with a huge staff and service reminiscent of a European grand hotel. The western third of the Cliff has been modified into the "Cliff Club" condominiums with private hot tubs and sumptuous mission-style furnishing.

The absolute best thing at the Cliff is the rooftop pool and hot tub. After a day on the slopes, there's nothing like it. The hot tub holds 20 people, the pool (which is almost as warm) holds 60. You forget you are in the bottom of the sharp canyon; you feel suspended in a power center between the walls, bathed in ethereal light, just floating.

The Cliff is like a small city. It has three restaurants, two lounges, two swimming pools, four hot tubs, an ice-skating rink, and a large, modern game room. Check out the **Aerie** and the **Keyhole** for dinner.

The Aerie is on the Cliff's top floor, California Deco, with fresh seafood specials, live piano in the lounge, and the Aerie Sushi Bar slicing fresh fish nightly during the winter. The Southwestern food at the Keyhole is legit: locally made chips, fresh salsas (ask for hot and you get hot), a good selection of Mexican beers, the largest selection of tequila in Utah, and generous hot plates of Southwestern favorites.

Two of the condo lodges feature fine restaurants as well. The **Bistro at the Lodge** at Snowbird is a popular après-ski bar with the local crowd, and then it turns into a restaurant featuring fine French cuisine. The **Wildflower Restaurant** at the Iron Blosam Lodge specializes in Italian dinners.

My favorite dinner spot is the **Steak Pit** on Level 1 of the Snowbird Center. Great steaks, fish, or chicken served up by very experienced service people who can answer almost any question you have about Snowbird and the history of the canyon. Next door to the Steak Pit is the **Tram Club,** which is a must for après ski.

Lunch, I find, is problematic at Snowbird. The cafeteria fare at the **Mid Gad Restaurant,** the only on-mountain food area, is passable but uninspired. Mid Gad Restaurant does have a large south-facing sundeck, which is a hot spot on those warm spring days. Most people congregate on the big deck of the **Tram Plaza**—you can ski right up to it—where you can munch, indoors or out, then hop back in line for the tram. (Be sure to check out the 200-pound chunk of the Matterhorn displayed on a concrete pedestal near the skiers' bridge. Snowbird and Zermatt are sister resorts, and the Swiss brought a piece of their signal peak for Americans to ponder. Odd, but worth a touch.)

The **Birdfeeder** is your basic Coney Island hot dog/ fries/frozen yogurt stand. I like it. If you want to sit down, the **Forklift** around the corner has good burgers and sandwiches as well as a filling chicken pot pie that really is a floating pancake of flaky crust atop a thick chicken stew. If the weather is gorgeous and the skiing fine, on one of my tram stops I will sometimes grab a deli sandwich from the grocery known as **General Gritts** and carry it with me for lunch at the top of the mountain. One end of the ski-patrol shack—and it's a real shack by Snowbird's architectural standards—is reserved for brown baggers. Just some benches and big windows, but the view is edge-of-the-planet spectacular, eye-to-eye with the Twins across the way.

For a nice sit-down lunch away from the mobs, try the **Atrium** in the Cliff Lodge. You can ski right to the Atrium from *Who Dunnit* to *Cliff Access*. It is located at the base of the 11 stories of windows facing the mountain (hard to miss). You will have a great view of the mountain while eating a hot-buffet lunch and you will almost always be seated immediately. Eat here before everyone finds out about it.

Snowbird Data

Mountain Statistics

Vertical feet	3,240 feet
Base elevation	7,760 feet
Summit elevation	11,000 feet
Longest run	2.5 miles
Longest descent	3.5 miles
Average annual snowfall	500 inches
Number of lifts	13: 7 double chairs, 3 high-speed quads, 1 125-person tram, 2 surface lifts

Snowbird Data (continued)

Mountain Statistics (continued)

Uphill capacity	16,800 skiers/snowboarders per hour
Skiable terrain	2,500+ acres
Opening date	Mid-November
Closing date	Mid-May (conditions permitting)
Spring season	Yes, usually until mid-May
Snowboarding	Yes

Transportation

By car 45 minutes from Salt Lake International Airport (40 minutes from downtown) via I-80, I-215, and Wasatch Boulevard south to State 210, Little Cottonwood Canyon. Snowbird is 6 miles up the road, 1 mile short of Alta.

By bus, limo, or taxi From Salt Lake International Airport.

By plane Via major carriers to Salt Lake International Airport.

Key Phone Numbers

Ski-area information	(801) 742-2222
Snow report	(801) 933-2100
Reservations	(800) 453-3000
Website	www.snowbird.com

Inside Story

Powderbird Heli-Skiing

Is it redundant to have a helicopter skiing service at an area that receives over 500 inches of powder a year? No. Even at Snowbird, those 500 inches get skied out pretty quickly. If you know where to look, you can find soft snow two or three days after a storm by poking around in the trees and rocks. But what about that unimpeded, open-slope experience you see in the pictures? What about skiing untracked powder all day? The only place to live out this dream is in the backcountry, and the easiest way to get there is with the Powderbird Guides.

Wasatch Powderbird Guides offers helicopter skiing to those trackless, inviting realms out beyond the ski-area boundaries. It's expensive, yes, and chancy. Bad weather might mean postponement or cancellation of your reserved heli day. (For this reason, they also have a complex, but workable and flexible, reservations system; call (801) 742-2800.) But if you hit even an average good day, say a five or a six on a scale of ten, you will likely come back bubbling over.

Here's how the day goes. A Powderbird person calls you the night before to confirm. Then that person calls again the next morning; co-owner and chief guide Rusty Daffing will have checked the weather and snow conditions and determined that it's a go for 9 a.m. You find your way to Powderbird's heliport just east of the Cliff Lodge. Inside, it smells of fresh coffee, fruit, and pastries. You are too nervous to eat, but it looks too good not to. Daffing lightens the mood with tales of how some of Snowbird's "easy" runs got their names. *West Second South* was

Salt Lake City's erstwhile red-light district, and *Big Emma* was one of the best-known madams.

The day's skiers are divided into compatible groups. You are issued a rescue beacon and special straps for tying your skis and poles securely together. Outside, pilot and guide go over the safety procedures regarding the Bell Jet Ranger. The $4 million machine revs into action. The roar would seem to blot out the world. You clamber aboard and buckle your seat belt.

Without your noticing, the pilot lifts the bird off. Gently, as if guided by a giant hand, the helicopter climbs to the ridge north of Snowbird and dives over the other side. It banks and stirs the air and sets down on a tiny ridgeline without a bump. Rusty throws his pack to one side, then begins unloading skis. You jump down and crouch around the pack, kneeling in the snow, gloved hands on each other's shoulders like worshipers. Rusty gives the pilot the thumbs up. The bird rises and then bolts toward the canyon floor, prop-washed snow blasting over you like a wave.

Then it's utterly still, jarringly quiet. At your feet, a run called *Meadows Chutes,* a morning run facing the sun, 2,000 vertical feet sparkling, a few aspen trees, shadows down in the creek bottom where the pilot waits, not another skier or ski track in sight. You click into bindings. Breathe twice, deeply. The snow feels like cream . . .

On a typical day you'll ski seven runs like this. Most often they will be in the side canyons of Big Cottonwood, north of Snowbird, west of Solitude, though you may fly as far north as Mill Creek Canyon or as far south as Provo. You may ski runs called *Fat City, Two Guys* (an Italian restaurant downtown in Salt Lake City), *Cardiac Ridge* (120 turns without stopping, if you want), *Holy Toledo,* and my favorite, *The Hall of the Giants,* with its spiraled, spreading, 400-year-old limber pines.

At the end of the day there is cold beer, soup, and sandwiches at the heliport. Voices hum with the day's triumphs and foibles already legend. Nobody seems to want to leave.

Big
Cottonwood Canyon

Brighton   Kids, families, church groups, lessons, night skiing and riding—Brighton likes to call itself "the place where Salt Lake City learns to ski and ride." Recent expansion and redesign have catapulted this small area into the big time, with big snows, big terrain variety—especially strong on winding forest cruisers—plus a couple of big new quad chairs. Brighton is owned by Big Sky's parent company, Boyne USA. There is limited lodging, but the area is only 40 minutes from downtown Salt Lake City.

Solitude   Next door to Brighton and linked via the eponymously named Solbright Trail, Solitude has completed the first phase of what will be the only destination village in the canyon. The mountain itself remains an exquisite, moderate-size day area with long, sunny novice and intermediate trails, gently pitched bowls, and secret steep trees for the wily experts who know to avoid Alta on big weekend days.

Brighton

There'll be 150 first-timers on the broad, gentle base of Mount Majestic every Saturday of the season. At night (Monday to Saturday from 4 to 9 p.m.) more beginners, school kids, novices, and working people in need of an after-hours ski or shredding fix can be seen ghosting in and out of the lights, swishing big christies in the cold, flour-fine snow.

But Brighton is a good deal more than just a learners' hill. It's a kind of mini-Alta (it also reminds me of Colorado's Arapahoe Basin) with largely underutilized intermediate and advanced terrain, Alta-like snow, big views, and nobody but nobody there on weekdays, or on weekends, for that matter, if the weather is snowy, cloudy, cold, windy—anything short of perfection, in other words. Utah locals, you will learn if you are a visitor, tend to be very picky about their ski days. They can't help it; they're spoiled snow snobs who prefer regularly spaced ten-inch overnight dumps followed by cobalt skies.

Out-of-state skiers and riders rarely venture up Big Cottonwood Canyon because there are almost no overnight accommodations up here. (With Alta and Snowbird just over the ridgeline, why bother?) Summer cabins dot the sunny, aspen-studded hillsides on the north side of the canyon, but Brighton itself has only one small lodge and a few rental "chalets." The reasons for this lack of development are threefold: There is a paucity of private land, and there are limited water rights in the canyon to serve development (Big Cottonwood is one of seven canyons that provides the Salt Lake Valley with its potable water); and, frankly, the people of Salt Lake don't want to see a lot of growth in the canyons. They want their wilderness for backcountry skiing and for summer hiking and climbing. As area manager Randy Doyle, a big, comfortable bear of a man, told me, "These mountains are actually pretty small and so close to a huge population base. There are just a lot of uses."

So Brighton is a kind of odd beast, half one thing and half another. On one hand it is a throwback, a low-key, family-oriented, historically significant locals' area. But, on the other hand, the skiing/riding—the terrain, the snow conditions, the potential for personal expression and freedom—is so good that if you could somehow plunk it down in California or Colorado, you'd have a major resort on your hands. In recent years, under the ownership of Boyne USA, which also owns Big Sky in Montana, as well as Boyne Mountain and Boyne Highlands in Michigan, and Crystal Mountain in Washington, Brighton has undergone major upgrades toward that end: high-speed lifts, snowmaking, a spacious new base lodge, and greatly expanded night skiing/riding.

Little Cottonwood has the big reputation. Big Cottonwood is the people's paradise. It's been like this since before the turn of the century. Brigham Young used to gather the faithful up in the canyon for cool, summer meetings. Brighton was skiing before Alta, in part because the canyon was easier and safer to climb. Salt Lake City outing clubs— women in long skirts and men leaning on one wooden pole through their turns—rode the rope tow over by what is now the Majestic run. William Stewart Brighton built a luxury, three-story hotel (with luxury, outdoor, back-to-back six-holers) for miners and then tourists. Tenth Mountain Division troops trained here prior to World War II and before the development of legendary Camp Hale in Colorado. With the highest base in the Wasatch at 8,755 feet and some of the coldest temperatures, Brighton's snow was reliably deep and soft. The people flocked to the end of the road to try this new winter recreation.

And they're still coming, though arguably Brighton's share of the local pie shrunk when Solitude opened in 1956 and, in recent decades, with the completion of the freeway up Parley's Canyon to the Canyons, Deer

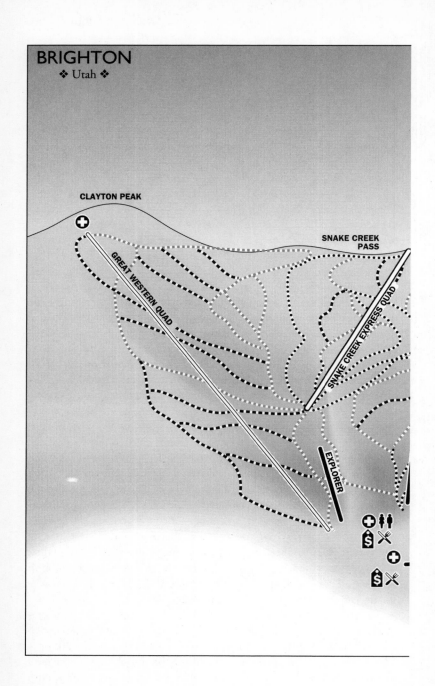

BRIGHTON
❖ Utah ❖

CLAYTON PEAK

SNAKE CREEK PASS

GREAT WESTERN QUAD

SNAKE CREEK EXPRESS QUAD

EXPLORER

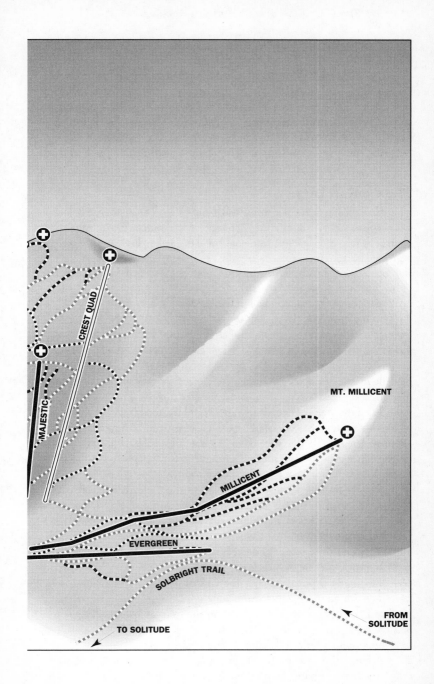

CREST QUAD

MAJESTIC

MT. MILLICENT

MILLICENT

EVERGREEN

SOLBRIGHT TRAIL

TO SOLITUDE

FROM
SOLITUDE

Valley, and Park City Mountain Resort. Perhaps the area's own promotional efforts on behalf of its excellent beginners' terrain and lessons have partially obscured the fact that this is a versatile and intriguing mountain for any level skier/rider. Brighton has become a mecca for snowboard riders due to the exciting terrain of dips, drop-offs, natural half-pipes, and a top-to-bottom maintained playground complete with multiple terrain features, rails, boxes and superpipe. For whatever reasons, Brighton today is an underused ski and snowboard mountain, and that, for as long as it lasts, makes Brighton a find.

The Canyon Drive

The drive through Big Cottonwood Canyon is a treat in itself, and a crash course in the fascinating geology of the range. Quite literally a course—there is a series of information signs at key locations along the highway. It's tough to stop on the way up to a day's skiing, so plan on the way back down to stop and soak in some remarkably graphic examples of big forces at work.

You'll notice that the top half of the canyon has a broad, rolling feel, as if it's been scooped out by a giant hand. In fact, it was, by the Big Cottonwood glacier that was active up until about 30,000 years ago. Then, rather suddenly, the canyon narrows and becomes V-shaped. They call this place the Meeting of the Glaciers. The sign says that several side canyon glaciers met the main river of ice about here, and together they stopped. Big piles of ground-up rock, terminal moraines, lie like dunes on both sides of the road. Then the creek dives into its canyon and the road hugs the rock walls where there is no more valley. (The Little Cottonwood Canyon glacier, by contrast, pressed all the way down to the ancient lake at the canyon mouth. That canyon has a shorter, steeper run overall and shows the characteristic glaciated U-shape from top to bottom.)

Down in the Big Cottonwood narrows there are three more signs. One points out bands of 300-million-year-old Mississippian white marble. The next describes Storm Mountain quartzites and shales, alternating yellow and brown layers that have been grotesquely folded as if they were Silly Putty and then tilted 90 degrees on end. In the curvy throat of the canyon, just above the mouth, a last sign describes a wall of 700-million-year-old blue and purple shales, the bed of an ancient sea elevated by movement along the Wasatch Fault.

From an airplane or even in a car on the freeway between Provo and Salt Lake City, you can see the fault at work. It's almost a ruler line running north and south. The land to the west of the line, except for the alluvial fans of eroded mountain material and the distant Great Basin ranges, is flat as a pancake. (These days, new subdivisions push up the gently tilting planes right to the canyon mouths.) To the east, the mountains are thrown straight up 7,000 feet above the city.

It's as sheer a geological dichotomy as any in North America. The Rocky Mountains west of Denver, although dramatic, climb much more gradually, reaching the 12,000-foot level about 50 miles from the plains.

The Lay of the Land: How the Mountain Works

At the head of the canyon at the end of the road (Brighton's parking lot), the landscape is dominated on the south by 10,452-foot Mount Millicent, a looming pyramid with a very steep north face that is nearly always in shadow, and on the east by 10,750-foot Clayton Peak, the newest skiing at the area. Brighton's eight chairlifts climb up four different aspects of the basin, creating four distinct skiing/riding zones. The farthest west, with its own small base facility and two chairs, is the Millicent and Evergreen area. In the center, on the mountain's north-facing flank, with three chairs, is the Mount Majestic/Crest area. The Snake Creek zone occupies the ridge between 10,315-foot Preston Peak and Clayton Peak to the east. The Great Western Quad, the highest lift, ascends to 10,500 feet, 200 vertical feet short of the summit of Clayton Peak.

The total vertical from the top of Great Western to the base lodge is 1,745 feet. But the more meaningful numbers are those of each of the four areas: Clayton Peak, 1,745 feet; Snake Creek, 1,040 feet; Majestic/Crest, 1,207 feet; and Millicent, 1,125 feet. You can ski or ride from one area to another via access trails, but for all practical downhill purposes, these are four separate mountains.

According to area literature, there are 850 acres of skiable terrain; 1,745 feet vertical and 850 acres doesn't sound like a big area. But Brighton is what I call a Little Big Man. The numbers don't add up to a lot, but the numbers, in the end, lie. Or rather, they don't begin to tell the story. Brighton skis and rides like a big mountain. You want long? The combination of *Lone Star* and *Scout* mambos two miles through the woods. You want naked, oceanic bowls to lose yourself in? Try *Scree Slope* under that monster Millicent face. You want meadows? Secret trees? Exhibitionist bumps right under the chair? You want to jump off powder-coated cliffs? Brighton's got it all. With those choices, does it matter whether you get your skiing or riding in 1,000-foot chunks instead of 2,000 at the "big" areas?

To add to all this, Brighton, by any standard, is a bargain. In order to compete with the other great areas for local business, management has kept lift prices almost ridiculously low. In terms of the cost of skiing, Brighton is (ever so delightfully for us) living at least 15 years in the past.

Brighton for Beginners

Brighton's Intro-Ski programs are anything but retro. The beginner package includes full-day equipment rental, a Majestic/Explorer lift pass, and a beginner lesson, all for less than the price of a lift ticket at most areas. There is also a Works Package for all levels that includes an all-area lift ticket. Half-day and full-day Kinderski packages are available for young riders four to seven years old. Kids ten years and younger ski for free . . . No limits or restrictions and no purchase necessary (only thing is an adult has to get the ticket for them).

Beginner lessons are taught underneath the Explorer Triple, at the far north end of the Majestic base area. The next step up is the Majestic double chair, which, along with the longer and faster Crest quad, serves the lion's share of novice terrain. *Upper Mary* trail to lower *Majestic* is a fine learning slope, moving from the shelter of the woods out into the big, billowing rolls above the lodge. There is a lot of room to experiment here and to play the swales and hollows for the tricks they teach about turning.

The only problem with the Majestic area that I can see is crowding, and then only on weekends—and that, too, has largely abated with the introduction of the Crest people-mover quad and the 2001–2002 addition of the Snake Creek Express quad that replaced a fixed-grip triple.

The Crest also provides a second access to the marvelous, forested Snake Creek terrain. Adventurous novices need brave only one easy blue trail, *Thunder Road,* to reach the green *Snake Creek Access;* or from the Majestic chair they can simply ski or ride off the back side (off the left) to *Hawkeye* or *Snake Creek Access* into a different drainage and a different, quieter world.

There are two wonderful, mile-long novice courses from the top, both great places to rack up the mileage necessary for confidence. They start together on the northeast ridge that divides Big Cottonwood from the Heber Valley drainages to the east. Then they split: *Sunshine* winds deep into the woods, while *Deer Park* opens onto a broad shoulder with views of Mount Millicent's voluptuous timberline terrain. The single route back to Majestic is via the easy green *Hawkeye* road.

The Millicent area sports a couple of green runs as well, but it's a little tougher to get there. The *Milly Access* road is rated blue. It is narrow, and it does twist and dip with some enthusiasm on the way to the Milly base, but unless the snow conditions are unusually hard and fast, I think many novices would enjoy the ride. (Those without good braking skills might want to walk across the parking lot.)

Novices, don't ride the Millicent lift. You'll find only intermediate and advanced runs off the top. The Evergreen lift, Brighton's best-kept secret, is the one for novices. Evergreen is almost never crowded, and the two green runs, *Canyon* and *Main Street,* have a completely different feel from the rest of the mountain. They wander spectacularly through this area's open slopes, solitary Volkswagen-size rocks and scattered trees. *Canyon* is particularly dramatic, waltzing under the mountain's steep face runs. Be aware of experts dropping in from above.

Best Intermediate Skiing

I say that Evergreen (which only runs on weekends) is Brighton's best-kept secret, because it has a little of everything and rarely sees a lift line. The *Evergreen* trail is a delight, slipping through the forest like a hobbit path, unbulldozed, full of character and surprise. Off this lift, you can also get to *Perri's Bowl,* a snaky trough through treeless terrain that invites roller-coaster turns back and forth across its sides. The shapes are quite steep (though they don't stay that way for long), providing intermediates with a challenge that they are often denied at the big ballroom-type areas. Very good skiers love this terrain too. It's sensuous, flowing, and steep enough to make you think of Alberto Tomba carving big, round engraver's cuts in the snow. You can't just stand there; you have to *ski* this one.

If crowds are not a problem, and they rarely are, few intermediates bother with Evergreen, because Millicent is right next door, and it's just the same, only better and bigger. Millicent has almost double Evergreen's vertical and opens up many times as much terrain. Most of it is rated advanced, but there is some fine intermediate cruising on the *Backbone* ridge. This is Brighton's version of the Big Burn: soaring, high-speed stuff, with the mountain falling away on both sides of the broad rib. To the left are the slumbering, white-blanketed Twin Lakes, which are part of Salt Lake City's water supply, and Twin Lakes Pass, a high saddle on the ridge separating Brighton and Alta. The Highway to Heaven, a portion of the Interconnect Trail linking the Big and Little Cottonwood Canyon areas with each other and with Park City (see the "Inside Story," The Utah Interconnect, page 311), is etched across the sheer face of Davenport Hill. To the skier's right, the rollicking, mostly ungroomed pitches of upper Millicent dance away toward *Canyon.* Some, like *Little Milly* and *Chute 2,* become transition grounds for skiers and riders moving up into the advanced ranks. Bumps sometimes form in the gullies, but because the skiing is crafted by landforms rather than trees here, there are always mogul-less alternatives. This is the beauty of alpine terrain. In the summer these pistes are all rock. In the winter, under Brighton's 500 inches of snow, it's all white; you go wherever whim or the fall line leads you.

Snake Creek feels like a different ski area, perhaps Colorado or maybe Maine, except for the unmistakable feel of Utah snow underfoot. These runs are snipped top to bottom from dark forest cloth. Dive in and the white ribbon takes you for a ride. There are few forks in the road or choices to make. Just relax and be taken.

There are half a dozen intermediate rides here, all close to a mile long and all bouncing down a stair-step fall line to the lift base in a bright meadow. Each one suffers the odd flat spot or two, nothing so bad as a walk, but they do interrupt the flow here and there. *Thunder Head* was created when a slide cut loose on Clayton Peak and blasted through

298 Part Three Utah and the Northern Rockies

heavy timber along what was then the area's northeast boundary line. Nature's bulldozer. They are two of the best lines on the mountain. *Thor* and *Pine Martin* have a lovely, private, what-lies-around-the-next-corner feel to them.

Now, thanks to the Great Western quad, there are two ways into *Thor.* Most Great Western terrain is black, but *Thor, Thunder Head,* and *Lone Star*—all fine blues—course the naturally gladed shapes here. Check out the breathtaking view of Timpanogos from the Snake Creek Pass and the awesome view of Snowbird's tram from the top of the Great Western lift.

Snake Creek lacks the transition terrain that Millicent has: the small to medium-size bumps and the smooth steep of a *Perri's* or a *Christy Bowl.* The shapes go directly from long and smooth to short and nasty. To their dismay, far too many intermediates plunge into the bumps of *Doyle's Dive* and find out that it really does deserve its black diamond. But that's okay; the forest wanderers are as good, in their genre, as any in the state. Lower Pioneer and Ziggy have some manageable intermediate bumps, and most of the intermediate bump lessons are taught on Ziggy.

A final alternative for intermediates, or anyone with good basic skills, is to head over to Solitude for part of the day. The two areas sell a combined ticket and are connected by the creatively named *Solbright Trail.*

Expert Skiing

One of the raps against Brighton as a small area is that it lacks the big expert challenges that the major areas have. The irony of this Little Big Man misconception is that not very many expert skiers come to the top of Big Cottonwood Canyon. In fact, the expert skiing is superb, uncrowded, and suffused with a sense of adventure.

If big bumps are your measure of difficulty, however, then you will be disappointed here. The best are on *Doyle's Dive, Exhibition,* and a few gully shots on *Lone Pine* in Millicent Bowl, and *Rockin R* and *Desperado* off of Great Western. But it's because of lack of traffic on the steep, not because there are no steeps. Brighton excels at other aspects of the game: trees, jumps, and both back side and inbounds powder.

Powder, powder everywhere. A Brighton patrolman I know claims that the area "never gets skied out." Quite a statement, especially in light of the fact that Alta and Snowbird are substantially "skied out" the first day after a storm. But if it snows, on average, once a week through the winter, and there aren't enough strong skiers to cut up all the accessible Brighton fluff before the next storm cycle, then he's right. This is Brighton's fate and its great secret.

I experienced a graphic example of this when I was skiing with this same sanguine patrolman on the Snake Creek lift in a snowstorm. He led the way into the trees next to the *Hard Coin* run. Big, red-barked

Englemann spruce stood well spaced for powder turns, the alleys between their trunks extending downhill as far as I could see. The new snow was less than six inches deep, so any old tracks would have shown through. But there were none.

"There are no tracks in here," I exclaimed. "Not even any old tracks."

"Welcome to Brighton." He smiled and pushed off into the virgin quiet.

It's the same in *Saw Buck*. A short traverse to the right off the top and you are in rarely skied, powdery glades and meadows that flow all the way to *Deer Park*. Over on Millicent, the powder is more obvious; there are only a few trees, and the mountain's skin (over rocky bones) is pure white. Out in the bowl beneath the Millicent north face, two runs are identified on the map, *Lone Pine* and *Scree Slope*, but there are literally hundreds of lines. None is as monolithic a shape as, say, High Rustler at Alta, but they make up in quirky playfulness what they lack in sheer size. The ground under your skis is constantly changing. My friend, the patrolman, calls Millicent "a little amusement park."

One of the most popular rides in this "fun zone" pops skiers and snowboarders into the air. Boulders from 5 to 50 feet tall dot Millicent's open landscape. On a powder day, when the landings are pillow-soft, bird men and women are taking flight all around. I am not generally a jumper; I prefer to keep my skis on the ground, but Brighton does something to me. The spirit is contagious, and I find myself winging off small cliffs onto steep powder landings without missing a beat. Or screwing up the courage to jump six feet down into a chute with no other entrance, for the reward of 20 glorious powder turns below.

When the inbounds powder looks like it's mostly chopped up, strong skiers often have the option to go out of bounds, legally. (Clayton Peak used to be one of these zones. Now it is open, and the Great Western Express accesses a baker's dozen of black routes from *Clark's Roost* to *Desperado*.) The Brighton patrol maintains three gates: at the tops of Millicent and Great Western and at the entrance to what is called *Mary's Chutes*, a wild zone between Millicent and the Majestic area. When conditions are deemed safe, the gates are open, and you can use the lifts (and a little walking power) to reach some marvelous skiing.

Most popular is the back side of Millicent, where west-facing powder slopes plunge down uninterrupted to the Twin Lakes. In *Mary's Chutes* one can find perhaps the best jumping grounds in Utah. The area consists of three huge swales, like storm waves at sea, with untold slots and clefts and niches through their cliff faces. I recommend a local guide for the first few trips in; the place is a maze. Very little shows on the map, and there are occasional booby traps. The patrol and the public have an unspoken understanding here: Skiers/riders in out-of-bounds areas will use their heads and the buddy system and, most important, not ski in closed areas. Outside the resort boundaries, gate or no, you are on your own. Backcountry explorers should have knowledge of current avalanche conditions and must have proper rescue equipment.

Snowboarding

Tectonic forces eons ago turned Brighton into a natural fun park, pushing up ridges here, cliffs over there. Then, of course, there are boulders in a wide variety of sizes and shapes that make excellent kickers. But the folks who run Brighton didn't want to settle for Mother Nature's handiwork. The result is a top-to-bottom array of terrain park features that keep boarders and twin-tip skiers doing laps on the Crest Express. At the top, *My-O-My* begins the fun with a series of rails, boxes and jumps. More rails lie in wait on skier's left in the "Great Divide" flats near the *Snake Creek Access* run, and then a sneak through the woods from *Hawkeye*, past *Short Shot* and onto *Face,* delivers those with nerves, and bones, of steel to Big Bertha, a towering hump of a launch pad that gives those aboard the Majestic chair a bird's eye view of crashes and burns. Further down below the chair resides the resort's superpipe, as well as more rails, boxes, spines, tabletops and kickers.

Lunch

In the excitement of skiing, I completely forgot about lunch. (This happens in real life too.) Brighton has three eateries, all at the base: Molly Green's, a private club (in Utah parlance that means they can serve liquor), the Alpine Rose cafeteria, and the Millicent Chalet at the minuscule Milly base. The Chalet is the locals' hangout, with a sunny porch known as "the beach," good pizza, and homemade chili.

Dinner and Overnight in the Canyon

Brighton is so tiny (population about 70 during the winter) that it has just one place for dinner. **Molly's Restaurant and Bar** is a space of joyous eclecticism: two half-scale WWI airplanes (a Sopwith Camel and a Fokker) hang from the cathedral ceiling; carved wooden elephants and cats; flowers on the tables; and cane safari chairs in front of a big fireplace.

The only place to stay right in Brighton is the 20-room Brighton Lodge **Slopeside.** It has a hot tub, a heated outdoor pool, continental breakfast, and a common living room. It's not chic, but it's comfortable and family-affordable. **Brighton Chalet** and **Mount Majestic Properties** rent cabins in Brighton. On Brighton Circle is **Das Alpin Haus Bed and Breakfast.**

Staying in the Valley

And that's about it. There are a couple of chalets for rent near the lifts and a family-style lodge down the canyon at Silver Fork, but generally, people who ski Brighton stay in the valley. Salt Lake City, Murray (at the mouth of Big Cottonwood Canyon), and Sandy (at the mouth of Little Cottonwood) together have over 50 lodging options, 10,000 rooms combined—everything from the Hilton to the Marriott to a burgeoning number of bed-and-breakfasts. The **Doubletree Hotel** downtown and the **Comfort Inn** in Sandy do a good job of catering to skiers' needs.

My pick of the B&Bs is the **Spruces** on 9th East right on the way to Big Cottonwood. The house is a classic carpenter's gothic Victorian built by Norwegian Martin Gunnerson for his family in 1903. In 1915 Gunnerson transplanted 16 spruce trees from Big Cottonwood Canyon around the house. They're still there, all but hiding the place from the street. The house was remodeled to include four guest suites in 1985. The new owners were clever and careful enough to leave a big cottonwood tree growing up through the middle of the new breakfast room roof. Immediately south of the inn is the **Wheeler Historic Farm,** a working museum of nineteenth-century farming techniques that history buffs will love.

Staying in Salt Lake rather than up at the resorts can have its benefits. You're only 10 minutes from the airport and 45 minutes by car from any of seven resorts, an hour if you use the Utah Transit Authority ski buses. In town you're only a matter of blocks away from the Delta Center, where the NBA Jazz play basketball, or Symphony Hall, where Utah's two symphony orchestras perform. Ballet West, which summers in Aspen and winters in Salt Lake, is perhaps the finest company on this side of the Continental Divide. There's a planetarium, a zoo, a theater, galleries, and museums. Here, too, is Utah's number one tourist attraction, Temple Square, where you'll find programs and exhibits on the ongoing saga of Utah's original white settlers, the Mormons and their Church of Jesus Christ of Latter-day Saints.

Salt Lake City is more than just a regional transportation center and the capital of the Mormon state. It's grown manifold in size and sophistication since I first visited over 30 years ago. It's become a near-perfect ski base. A visitor can sample Alta one day, Brighton the next day, and Park City another day, and return to the city in the evenings. Unlike Denver, which is a long way from its good skiing, this city really works as a staging point. If you didn't get your reservation in to the Rustler Lodge early enough this year, you can still ski Alta and then maybe take in the Jazz game that same night.

Brighton Data

Mountain Statistics

Vertical feet	1,745 feet
Base elevation	8,755 feet
Summit elevation	10,500 feet

Brighton Data *(continued)*

Mountain Statistics *(continued)*

Longest run	3 miles
Average annual snowfall	500 inches
Number of lifts	8: 3 high-speed quads; 3 double chairs; 1 triple; 1 rope tow
Uphill capacity	10,100 skiers per hour
Skiable terrain	850 acres
Opening date	Early November
Closing date	Late April
Night skiing	4–9 p.m., Monday–Saturday, mid-December through late April
Snowboarding	Yes

Transportation

By car 45 minutes from Salt Lake International Airport via I-80 and Wasatch Boulevard south to U.S. 152, Big Cottonwood Canyon. Brighton is 14 miles up the road at the head of the canyon.
By bus, limo, or taxi From Salt Lake International Airport and from downtown Salt Lake City.
By plane Via major carriers to Salt Lake International Airport.

Key Phone Numbers

Ski-area information	(800) 873-5512
Snow report	(801) 533-4731, ext. 532
Salt Lake Convention & Visitors Bureau	(801) 521-2868
Website	www.skibrighton.com

Lodging

Brighton Chalets	(801) 942-8824
Das Alpin Haus	(435) 649-0565
Mount Majestic Properties	(435) 647-7063
Reservations, Brighton Lodge	(800) 873-5512

Peter's TECH TIP

Stormy-Day Strategies

Whales in the sky. The first sign of a coming storm is often those long, curving, lenticular clouds, like pods of gray whales arcing up over the mountains. Then the ceiling begins to fall, the wind spits, the sky goes white and lowers until the tips of the peaks—Superior, Patsey Marley, Clayton, and Millicent—disappear into the clouds. The first sharp snowflakes tap against your nylon shell.

For many people the day has ended. It's time for the hot-buttered comfort of the lodge. But for others, the best is yet to come. I am one of the latter, and here's why. Skiing in a storm refreshes me just as the mountain is being replenished. The snow just gets softer and softer as the day progresses. Where before my edges might have made a scraping or a rasping sound on the old snow surface, now all I hear are whispers under the scolding wind. In a storm, both sight and sound are muffled. I rely more on my sense of feel; I am in many ways closer to the mountain and its ever changing gravities.

On stormy days the fair-weather crowds are banished. Those who stay out gain an intimacy with the elements. The civilizing aspects of the sport—the lifts, the snow machines, the fashion—pale before big forces. We are puny and lucky and bold all at once. Skiing in a storm is a little like being on your own planet.

Sometimes the difference between those who enjoy stormy-day skiing and those who don't is simply a matter of equipment. Ideally, your gear should render you immune to the cold and snow, the way a diver in a dry suit can be in the sea but not get wet. Windproof jacket and pants are essential. A one-piece suit is even better; there are no chinks for cold to enter around the waist. You need good warm gloves or mittens, a hat that covers your ears, and goggles (amber or rose for low-light visibility; double lenses still beat a coated single when it comes to fogging). A high collar is nice; even nicer is a high collar plus a neck gaiter—it's more efficient than a scarf for covering up sensitive neck, cheeks, and chin.

A ski buddy of mine calls this the Inside-Inside, Outside-Outside. Inside, you are toasty and dry. Outside, the storm may rage, it may tap against the windows and doors, but it can't get in. You are encapsulated. It's a cozy, wonderful space in which to ski.

On the slopes, if the visibility is bad, ski next to or right in the trees. Their shadows give the snow surface definition. Ski on the lee side of the trees, where the wind is piling the snow up, as opposed to the exposed side, where the new snow is being carried off.

If the temperature is near freezing, bring a plastic garbage bag for sitting on wet chairlifts. The Alta ski patrol motors around on such days with heavy vinyl half skirts hanging to their knees. They flap in the wind and look generally ridiculous, but they keep bottoms dry through a day of lift riding.

If you get cold, take a break, come inside, dry out, and warm up. Have a hot drink, preferably nonalcoholic, as booze will lower your body temperature further. Eat something, fuel up, and then go out again. Ride the tram or the gondola if there is one. But keep skiing. The longer it storms, the more velvety the mountain becomes, and it's all yours.

Want to learn to ski powder? Ski in a storm. Tomorrow when the sun comes out, machines will flatten the lower-angle powder, and the hordes will descend scrambling for the rest. Today, the day before that blue-sky, flashing-colors day, you can take it where you will. Everyone else has gone home, and if you're really lucky and it's one of those beautiful Utah storms where the flakes fall fast and thick, you'll get off the lift at the top and your tracks from the last run will have disappeared.

Solitude

The trail map says a lot about the way a resort perceives itself. For instance, while Deer Valley's map might feature a photograph of the elegant crystal and silver luncheon buffet at Stein's, Solitude's is more likely to feature skiers and 'boarders ripping through powder. Another shot in a recent season's trail map revealed snow-choked Honeycomb Canyon,

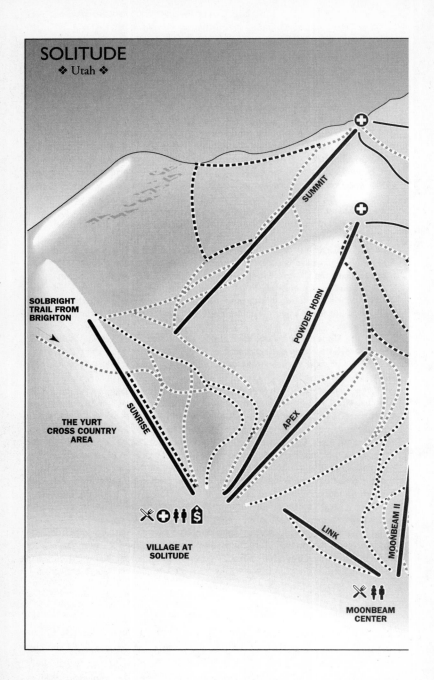

SOLITUDE
❖ Utah ❖

SUMMIT

POWDER HORN

SOLBRIGHT
TRAIL FROM
BRIGHTON

SUNRISE

APEX

THE YURT
CROSS COUNTRY
AREA

MOONBEAM II

LINK

VILLAGE AT
SOLITUDE

MOONBEAM
CENTER

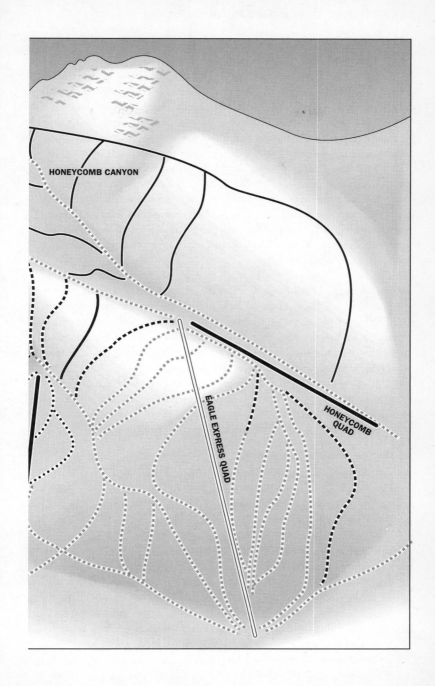

HONEYCOMB CANYON

EAGLE EXPRESS QUAD

HONEYCOMB QUAD

while another depicted one of the new base lodges that mean no long drives after a long day busting down the slopes.

Solitude has transitioned to a four-season mountain resort with a European-style village featuring a variety of dining options, deluxe accommodations and full-service resort amenities. The Village includes the Creekside Condominiums, The Inn at Solitude, Eagle Springs Lodge, the Powderhorn Lodge, the Crossings with its townhomes, and Alpine Creek, another condo property. The slopes are busiest on weekends, when families, school and church groups, and racing teams drive up Big Cottonwood Canyon from the valley. Some days, in fact, the area seems given over to youth. The calendar shows numerous special events designed for children, including family fun days, children's mini-downhills, and chocolate discovery tours as well as ongoing programs like the all-day Ski Academy class. You can ski or ride for half price on your birthday and feel like a kid no matter what your age.

The area is not just for kids, of course. Solitude is an intriguing mountain, not just for beginners but for experts and progressing intermediates as well. Compared to its glittering cousins in Little Cottonwood Canyon, this is an undiscovered powder gem. Some of the expert terrain is so remote and frequently unexplored, it can hide powder caches for weeks. Much of the intermediate skiing/riding is of the free-wheeling, treeless variety. (Big Cottonwood once had over 300 lumberjacks working to supply the wood for a growing Salt Lake City.) For the skier or rider looking to experiment with deep snow for the first time, I can think of few pitches better than *Paradise Bowl,* as wide and unobstructed and inviting a piece of powder real estate as there is.

How the Mountain Works

As it is, Solitude is a taller (2,047-foot vertical), broader (1,200 skiable acres), and more complex ski mountain than Brighton, its older neighbor at the head of the canyon. This complexity of layout, terrain, and traffic patterns actually causes the mountain to ski *smaller* than it is.

The area occupies two side canyons on the left bank of Big Cottonwood Creek plus the broad, sloping shoulder of Eagle Ridge between them. Solitude Canyon is on the east side, a narrow and steeply cut zone of mostly expert terrain. White granite cliffs signaled silver-bearing rock to the nineteenth-century miners. There are 30 to 40 known shafts up here and a few yet to be rediscovered. In the not-so-distant past, a luckless ski instructor found one by skiing into it; he was unhurt.

The majority of the skiing and riding flows off sparsely treed Eagle Ridge like a white blanket flung loosely over the mountain's spine. Two bases, Village at Solitude and Moonbeam Center, rest on the blanket's lower folds.

Honeycomb Canyon runs along the back side of Eagle Ridge, a sharply gouged imprint of glaciers past. Limited access, a purposeful absence of grooming, and a long, long return road make it the least-skied—but most inviting for advanced skiers and riders—part of the mountain. Honeycomb is a good example of how a mountain can ski small. There's 2,000 feet of vertical, but the really interesting skiing—and it is *really* interesting—is also quite short, plunging down either side of the canyon to the gully bottom. Another example is the High Expert area served by the Summit chair. It skis like a mini-Taos—quite steep and densely treed, a 1,200-foot expert's mountain off by itself. Similarly, the mostly intermediate skiing that is served by the Eagle Express quad can function quite independently of the rest of the area. Although the arrival in 2002 of the Honeycomb quad negated a long, slow retreat out of the canyon and greatly improved the mountain's traffic flow and accessibility, Solitude skiers and riders tend to stay put, focusing on one of the mini-mountains to the exclusion of the rest.

Paradise for Beginners

The addition in 1988 of the very low-angle Link lift solved the only thorny beginners' dilemma at Solitude. Before, a skier's first mountain run pretty much had to be up the Moonbeam lift and then down *Main Street,* which is a glorious, wide avenue for learners, except for two short 15-degree pitches. For some people it was too much. The Link is a supergentle four-degree grade.

The realigned Moonbeam II lift opens up more of the kind of high-mileage terrain novices need to improve. It tops out at the base of *Paradise Bowl,* where there is a lot of bald, rolling, alpine-type space. *Main Street* is nice. But it has also been the main drag forever, funneling intermediate and advanced skiers and riders down the mountain as well. The addition of green runs called *Little Dollie, Same Street,* and *Pokey-Pine* give gentle options back to Moonbeam base.

The best option for novices who want to explore another part of the mountain is the Sunrise lift with its two forest meanderers, *North Star* and *Deer Trail.* Care should be taken here, as *Deer Trail* is the only access to and from the Summit lift. Fast skiers, like Mercedeses on the autobahn, sometimes appear out of nowhere.

Blue Solitude

Apex, somewhat of a misnomer, as it climbs but 870 feet to a front-side midpoint, is still one of the best intermediate zones on the mountain. The lift parallels the longer Powderhorn lift and opens up some lovely, gladed slopes that used to be hard to reach. *Alta Bird* and *Stagecoach* drop invitingly from the balding top knoll.

You'll find the mountain's best collection of blue cruisers fanning out from the Eagle Express quad (first high-speed quad in Utah), which reaches its high point on Eagle Ridge. You can attack *Sundancer, Hal's Hollow,* and *Rumble and Grumble,* all fine forest cruisers with character that are meticulously groomed nightly. Also sample the marvelous bowl skiing/riding up above, runs like *Rhapsody, Gravity's Rainbow,* and *Olympia.* Eagle Express is 1,400 vertical feet of groomed bliss. Speed freaks work out their laps here.

Former Solitude ski school director Dean Roberts loves the meander that runs through the bottom of Honeycomb Canyon for intermediates: "If it's groomed! It can be the best thing on the mountain or the worst. If it's groomed, it's great for intermediates, rolling and pitching." But if it's not machine-smoothed—and it isn't always—it can be a tough slog for all but the best skiers. Intermediates should enter the canyon only at the top, off the Summit lift, and not along its steep flanks. There are gates at the tops of the Powderhorn and Express lifts for entry midway into the canyon, but only for very strong skiers and riders capable of knitting their way through tight trees.

The most frequently skied bumps on the mountain are in a string right under the Eagle Express lift. They're hardly pearls for the learning mogul skier; they tend to be, especially on the top half of *Inspiration,* angular and abrupt. Better teaching/learning bumps can usually be found scattered off *Eagle Ridge.*

My favorite blue skiing is in Solitude Canyon off the Summit lift. There's really only one blue run, but it's a dandy. (When *Liberty,* a nominal black diamond, is groomed, it makes a fine top-half alternative.) The primary route is *Dynamite,* and it winds back and forth under the lift through very dramatic and really quite steep terrain: moving under the white cliffs of *Cathedral* (unskiable) and *Cathedral Cirque* (occasionally open for high experts only), skirting the *Headwall,* and dropping down onto the snowy lakebed of Solitude Lake. It reminds me of skiing in Europe; it is scenic, curvy, challenging without being scary, and a real leg-burner if you ski it nonstop.

Solitude for Experts

The heading is entirely apt. Expert skiers here may find themselves surrounded by peace and quiet. There's not a lot of competition on the steeps except for the odd Saturday or Sunday that also happens to be a powder day.

Basically, there are three expert regions: the Powderhorn/Paradise Bowl area, the Summit lift basin, and the Honeycomb Canyon side walls. From the Powderhorn base almost the entire wall of Eagle Ridge is visible on the skyline. It looks expansive and inviting, and it's even bigger when you get up in it. *Concord, Paradise,* and *Vertigo* are just three named fall lines. There are literally hundreds, maybe thousands, more here. You have but to pick your spot, peel off the ridge, and enjoy nearly 1,000 vertical feet of sparsely treed, alpine-style skiing/riding. The pitch modulates between 20 and 30 degrees. It's steep enough to hold your attention but not so steep that you have to hold onto the mountain. This is sublime, cut-loose terrain in the powder.

The Solitude Canyon expert skiing is very different: quiet, steep, exploratory, introspective. Most of it is in the trees and rated high-expert, Solitude's version of the double black diamond or the yellow caution signs in use elsewhere. The old *Courageous* run, now known as *Corner Chute* because it begins at a bend in the ridge where the *Solbright Trail* turns toward Brighton, is a straight, shady corridor through the spruce, which, if it hasn't snowed for a while, develops some tasty bumps. I caught this overlooked corner of the resort two days after a storm and the snow still was deep and fluffy, like pounding through cotton. Almost everything else in the *Headwall* region is wild, uncut, and unnamed. Some of the best tree runs are out the *Evergreen Traverse* (not shown on the map) from the *Corner Chute.* (Evergreen Mountain divides Solitude from Brighton and the Twin Lakes basin. Its western slope constitutes one side of Solitude Canyon.) Skiing north, each shot through the trees looks better than the last, but if you can hold out to the end, there is a special treat: a broad rockslide with room for you and 20 of your friends to match figure eights all the way to Solitude Lake.

On the map there appears to be one and only one route connecting the top of Powderhorn to the Summit area. It's called *Parachute.* The patrol calls it "Terror Chute." You might need a parachute if you are not lucky enough to be the first or second person down after a storm. This radically steep, narrow avalanche gully is rarely open, and even then rarely worth the stress on mind and equipment. There is, however, some exquisite, superexpert exploring to be had in the cliffy woods north of *Parachute.* Ski *Houli's* first, then go back up and ease your way to your right into some of the least trodden snow on the mountain. Forget about a ski route to the Summit lift. Someday they'll have to blast one. For now, ride the Sunrise triple, an almost purely transportational lift, along with everybody else.

Until 2002, Honeycomb Canyon was always a dilemma: Is the skiing/riding good enough on the short, steep upper pitches to warrant the long road back around the mountain? Do you want to end up at the Eagle Express base? In fresh snow and after the patrol has controlled the slides under the Honeycomb Cliffs to the south, the answer was often yes. With the arrival of the Honeycomb quad, the answer now is always yes, as it ferries you back to the top of Eagle Ridge and negates the long, roundabout ski back to the Eagle Express. When *Black Forest,* down the back side from the top of Powderhorn, is good, it is very, very good, and it is also the longest fall line in the canyon. For sheer alpine beauty, you can't beat the long traverse under the cliffs to *Crystal Point.* Dean Roberts will tell you, "It's a lot of work for 20 turns." But what an exquisite 20 turns, through sparkling steep meadows to the creek bottom!

Another time to go into Honeycomb is when there hasn't been new snow for a while. Then the long back side of Eagle Ridge provides near infinite exploring options amid twisted old limber pines. Here, in regions with names like *Here Be Dragons* and *Navarone,* you'll find an occasional jewel of a chute, a rib off the spine, untouched for weeks. Use caution throughout the area; small cliffs and rock bands abound. The new Honeycomb quad makes round trips through Honeycomb Canyon more inviting than ever for experts.

Snowboarding

There is perhaps no greater breathtaking ride in Utah than carving turns down the jagged and striated flanks of Honeycomb Canyon. Riders who search for billowy powder know that Honeycomb packs it in and holds it for days after storms pass.

Although you can hike to the canyon's 10,500-foot summit for added steepness and tight, gnarly chutes, all you need for pure floating through powder is to venture onto *Voltaire, Prince of Wales,* or *Boundary Chutes.* If you want, you can go even farther, into *No Man's Land* and *Crystal Point,* but Honeycomb is so massive and lures so few that you can find a clean line just about anywhere here.

If you're just in search of speed, the long blue cruisers fed by the Eagle Express lift are where to head.

Solitude Lodging

The first phase of the new European-style **Village at Solitude** includes the **Creekside Condominiums** (18 units) and the **Inn at Solitude, which houses 47 hotel rooms plus a spa and conference center. The Powderhorn Lodge** has 82 units featuring one, two and three bedroom condominiums and on its ground level, the rustic pub, **The Thirsty Squirrel.** When the village is complete there will be 560 bedrooms along an 800-foot main walking mall. The skiers that continue to stay in the valley and commute the 30 minutes to ski will have a very unique situation when parking. The ski-in/ski-out parking lot ensures that all skiers only have to walk 100 feet (at most) to get to the slope.

Solitude Data

Mountain Statistics

Vertical feet	2,047 feet
Base elevation	7,988 feet
Summit elevation	10,035 feet
Longest run	3.5 miles
Average annual snowfall	500 inches
Number of lifts	8: 1 quad, 1 high speed quad; 2 triples, 4 doubles
Uphill capacity	12,550 skiers per hour
Skiable terrain	1,200 acres
Opening date	Early November
Closing date	Late April
Snowboarding	Yes

Transportation

By car About 45 minutes from Salt Lake International Airport via I-80 and Wasatch Boulevard south to State 152, Big Cottonwood Canyon. Solitude is 13 miles up the road, 1 mile below Brighton.

By bus, limo, or taxi From Salt Lake International Airport and from downtown Salt Lake City.

By plane Via major carriers to Salt Lake International Airport.

Key Phone Numbers

Ski-area information	(801) 534-1400
Snow report	(801) 536-5777
Lodging	(800) 748-4754
Salt Lake Convention & Visitors Bureau	(801) 521-2868
Website	www.skisolitude.com

Inside Story

The Utah Interconnect

So close are the big five areas on the Wasatch Front—that is, Snowbird, Alta, Solitude, Brighton, and Park City—that skiers have dreamed for years of linking them somehow to create one giant ski circus. It's been done successfully in France—Les Trois Vallées, for example, where one ticket gains you access to three interconnected valleys, numerous villages, and hundreds of lifts. In Switzerland, too, Zermatt is linked over the ridgelines with Cervinia, Italy, to the south. Wouldn't it be great, so the thinking goes, to ski from Alta to Park City, have lunch, and ski back?

One proposal has such a linkup completed with the addition of just three chairlifts. One would climb from the Alta parking lot to Twin Lakes Pass via Grizzly Gulch, thus connecting Little Cottonwood to Big Cottonwood Canyon. The return lift would tie Brighton to the same ridgeline. The third lift would leave

Brighton and connect with Park City in the Scotts Pass/Guardsman Pass area.

Simple, but not so simple. While the ski areas themselves are basically for the idea—assuming the details of avalanche-control work, patrolling, and jurisdictions can be ironed out—the general populace is not so sure. Some see it as a way to further promote the uniqueness of Utah skiing. There is no other place in North America where such a nexus could exist. Others see the plan as harmful and unnecessary. Backcountry skiers would mourn the loss of wilderness in canyons currently accessible only on foot. Local environmentalist groups, most notably Save Our Canyons and the Sierra Club, contend that there are already too many cars in the canyons, and that there are air, water, and large-scale transportation problems to be worked out before such a linkup would be warranted. The flip side of the amazing accessibility of these mountains is that there are numerous and often competing or overlapping uses.

Happily, you can ski from area to area right now, without the lifts, via the Inter-connect Adventure Tour. The five-area tour starts in Park City and passes through Brighton, Solitude, and Alta and ends in Snowbird. It runs Mondays, Wednesdays, Fridays, and Sundays and costs approximately $150. The four-area tour—Snow-bird to Alta to Brighton to Solitude and back to Alta—runs Tuesdays, Thursdays, and Saturdays. Both include guides, all lift passes, lunch at Solitude, and trans-portation back to your starting point.

This is real adventure skiing in the backcountry with some walking and climb-ing, and, if you're lucky, some gorgeous powder turns in pristine settings. I have only skied the four-area loop tour, but I am told that compared to the longer, five-area traverse, it involves more downhill skiing.

We began with orientation and a quick clinic on the avalanche transceiver/rescue beacons we would all wear. Then it was up an early tram at Snowbird, over to Alta and up the Supreme lift. From there we climbed and traversed for perhaps half an hour to the boundary between Big and Little Cottonwood Canyons at Catherine's Pass. From there to Brighton it was all powder, down runs like *Dog Lake Chute* and *Pillow Talk,* names only our guides knew. At Brighton we took the *Solbright Trail* around the nose of Evergreen Mountain to the Solitude base. A lunch of soup, sandwiches, and chocolate chip cookies and we were off again, up Solitude's lift system to the top of Summit. The route from there back over to Lit-tle Cottonwood Canyon follows a long and breathtaking traverse of Davenport Hill, known as the *Highway to Heaven.* For safety reasons we walked it one at a time. There was time, alone on the open slope, to take in the sweep and scale of these mountains, the porcelain bowls dropping away at your feet, the wind-sculpted crests of Patsey Marley and Wolverine peaks across the chasm. How tiny you feel inching along old avalanche paths, where, earlier in the winter, overloaded storm snow released in a monstrous whoosh down to the basin floor.

From Twin Lakes Pass, it is down Grizzly Gulch, a sinuous, shady powder run through meadows and glades to Alta's upper parking lot. Our guides, when pressed, weren't sure they favored the Interconnect lifts, even though their bosses at the Utah Ski Association are strong supporters of the plan. Who can blame them—the way it is is so much fun. I empathize, but I would like to see the Interconnect become a reality someday. The terrain practically demands it. The actual new terrain that would come under the areas' domain is quite small, and the vast new sense of choice and adventure available to the alpine skier, while in no way giving up its Utah charm, would rival the best in the Alps. For more infor-mation, contact Ski Utah Interconnect at (801) 534-1907.

Back Side Wasatch

Park City Mountain Resort   Park City doesn't get the copious snows the front-side canyons receive, but it makes up for that with snowmaking; high-speed six-passenger chairs; fine, rambling, something-for-everyone terrain; and a real reborn mining town with excellent restaurants and clubs, and even a world-renowned midwinter film festival that lures the Hollywood crowd out into the cold and snow. There is every imaginable amenity and range of lodging here, and Park City consistently is rated as one of the top ten mountain resort towns in the United States.

Deer Valley Resort   This ski area made its reputation on service, high-end lodging and dining. Valets help remove the skis from your car racks, there is smoked salmon for lunch at the Stein Eriksen Lodge, and a huge percentage of the trails here are buffed to corduroy perfection every night. The surprise is the hidden expert skiing in sublime aspen and evergreen glades. If you have to ask the price, you're in trouble.

The Canyons   This once-upon-a-time day area is being transformed by the American Skiing Company into a lavish destination resort with a potential 7,200 skiable acres! With a new name and a new future, The Canyons is the closest back-side area to downtown Salt Lake, located between the I-80 and Park City.

Sundance   This is a secluded, idyllic forest village built by Robert Redford on the site of Provo's local ski hill. The ambience is all rough-cut timbers, down comforters, and Remington bronzes beneath the soaring white wall of Mount Timpanogos. The skiing and riding on two connected mountains doesn't quite live up to the tasteful elegance. The terrain is best on Back Mountain, where you just might catch a glimpse of Bob cruising on *Bearclaw*.

Park City Mountain Resort

Park City Mountain Resort (PCMR) is the anomaly among Utah ski areas—a real town, a full-on, mining-era boomtown, like Aspen or Telluride, that has been resurrected by skiing. Certainly Alta was a town, too (and it still is an incorporated municipality), but there was nothing left from its silver glory days when skiing began there in the late 1930s. Park City, on the other hand, counted about 1,000 souls living in its Victorian, gingerbread shacks in 1957 when the last of the unconsolidated mines shut down. People there still drank in the saloons and went to the movies at the Egyptian Theater even though the town was listed in a guidebook to Utah ghost towns; it was quiet but far from dead. Then in 1960 the United Park City Mines decided to develop some of its 10,000 acres of mountainous terrain west of downtown for skiing. It was a visionary move. Park City Mountain Resort opened in 1963.

Today Park City is Utah's ultimate winter destination, putting together an unmatched package of lifts, snowmaking, yearly skier/rider visits, and available tourist beds. All that in addition to the attention the area draws for being the home of the U.S. Ski and Snowboard Team and for hosting big-time ski events like the America's Opening men's and women's World Cup races every November and the annual U.S. Snowboard Grand Prix. The World Cup has never been predisposed to open its season outside Europe, so the World Cup weekend is indeed a public relations coup.

Yet Park City eclipsed the awe of the World Cup's "white circus" in 2002 when it, along with neighboring Deer Valley, played host to the 2002 Salt Lake Winter Olympics. While Park City staged the Olympic slalom, giant slalom and all the snowboard events (to record crowds, too), Deer Valley was the backdrop for the freestyle competitions.

Nordic jumping and bobsled/luge were contested a few miles north of town at the Utah Olympic Park, giving the Park City area a near-monopoly on the Games' skiing, boarding, and sliding competitions. (Snowbasin to the north prevented the sweep by staging the downhill and Super G events.) In the wake of the Games, anyone can soar off the Olympic Park's 18- and 38-meter practice jumps for a minimal cost. The price includes training by Nordic and freestyle jumpers. Check the schedule for times and days.

Park City is certainly the most international of the Utah resorts. It is a multifaceted winter and summer destination like Aspen with prices to match. Park City is one of the few towns in Utah not founded by Mormon settlers in the latter half of the nineteenth century. In many ways, it seems less a part of Utah than almost any other place in the state, and, in fact, its history corroborates the feeling.

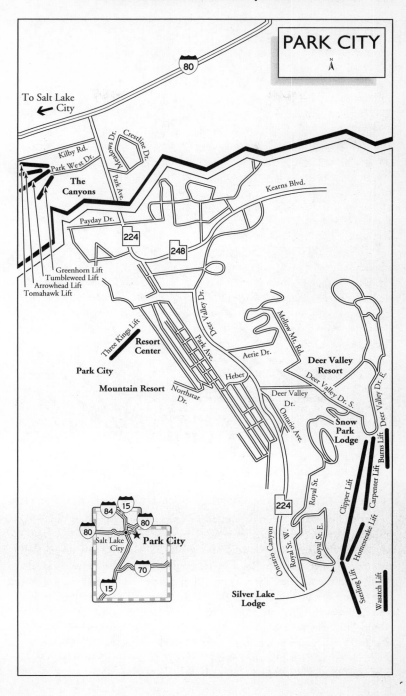

PARK CITY

N

To Salt Lake
City

80

Crestline Dr.

Meadows Dr.

Kilby Rd.
Park West Dr.

Park Ave.

**The
Canyons**

Kearns Blvd.

Payday Dr.

224

248

Greenhorn Lift
Tumbleweed Lift
Arrowhead Lift
Tomahawk Lift

Three Kings Lift

**Resort
Center**

Park City

Mountain Resort

Northstar
Dr.

Park Ave.

Deer Valley Dr.

Aerie Dr.

Heber

Mellow Mt. Rd.

**Deer Valley
Resort**

Deer Valley Dr. S.

Deer Valley
Dr.

Deer Valley Dr. E.

**Snow
Park
Lodge**

Burns Lift

Carpenter Lift

Clipper Lift

Homestake Lift

Ontario Ave.

224

Royal St.

Royal St. W.

Royal St. E.

Ontario Canyon

Sterling Lift

Wasatch Lift

**Silver Lake
Lodge**

84
15

80

80

15

70

Salt Lake
City

★ **Park City**

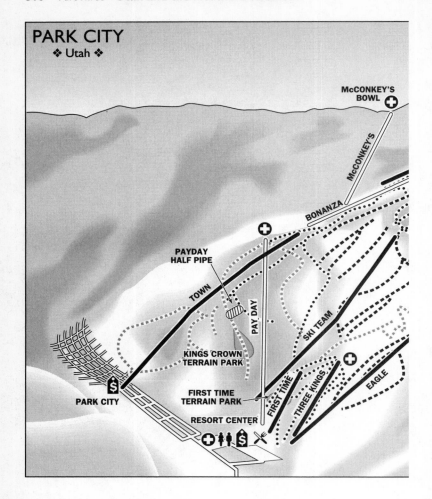

Brigham Young would not allow any of his Mormon flock to prospect for or extract precious metals, so the rich veins of silver under the Wasatch Range went undiscovered until about 1863, when federal troops stationed in the valley forayed up the canyons and literally stumbled upon them. The Park City bonanza, discovered in 1872, was one of the richest ore bodies of all; $400 million in silver was extracted in less than 50 years. Mormon farmers in what was then called Parley's Park could only watch in horror as thousands of immigrant miners swelled the little valley's population to over 10,000 by the 1890s. They were Irish, Swedes, Finns, Cornishmen, Chinese, Scots, and Yugoslavs. Very few were there for spiritual reasons.

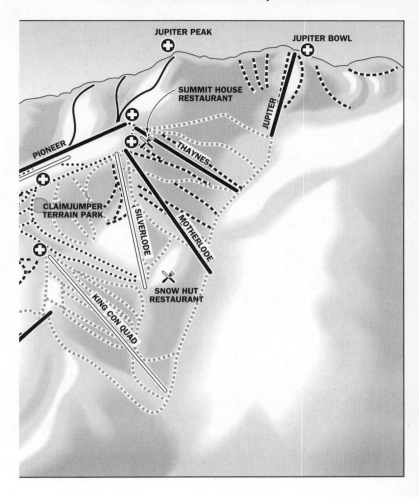

At one time there were 27 saloons on Main Street. During Prohibition the town stayed wet because local mortician George Archer drove his hearse up to Evanston, Wyoming, pulled the shades down, and rattled home loaded to the tassels with whiskey. Park City developed as a kind of cultural and moral nonconformity in Mormon Utah. It was either an oasis or a black hole, depending on your starting point.

The last mine to shut its doors, the Ontario, near the base of the mountain at Deer Valley, is still maintained against the day when metals prices warrant digging again. United Park City Mines no longer runs the ski operation but still owns all the ground. In fact, all three areas on this side of the Wasatch—Park City Mountain Resort, Deer Valley Resort, and the Canyons—are mostly on private land. This means the Forest Service is not involved in anything except plans for possible future expansion into public territory. The difference is certainly not discernible in terms of facilities or the quality of the ski experience. But Park City would not have grown as extensively or as quickly as it did if the ski company had had to wade through the same public procedures as do the areas on the front side of the range. This private-land free hand gives Park City a brashness, a kind of boomtown spirit rekindled that is unique in Utah.

The Back Side of the Wasatch

Although it's on the back side of the Wasatch Mountains from Salt Lake City, Park City is as close, in driving time, as the front-side resorts. The reason is I-80, which charges up Parley's Canyon out of the center of Salt Lake. It's freeway all the way, over the divide and down into the grassy interior valleys, then south at Kimball's Junction on Route 224, an easy lope along the eastern base of the mountains to the resorts.

You're really very close, as the Interconnect flies, to the headwaters of Big and Little Cottonwood Canyons, but the physical differences here are pronounced. The Salt Lake Valley sprawl is missing, and the mountains have a different feel too. It has to do with elevation and orientation.

The Park City base at 6,900 feet is almost 2,000 feet lower than Brighton's. Sage and oak brush dot the dry hills east of town. Two thirds of the ski mountain are carpeted with sun-loving aspens. Ridgelines are softer, more rounded, as if the violent Wasatch upthrust ran out of gas back here. The valleys are gently V-shaped, stream-washed rather than glacier-gouged.

Park City is not in a canyon but at the end of a narrow, flat-bottomed valley wedged up as far as it will go into the hills. The town itself is shoehorned onto the point. It's barely four blocks wide and over a mile long. The valley runs north to south, so the storefronts on one side of Main Street catch the morning sun while the businesses on the other side enjoy direct afternoon light.

The ski mountain has a similar orientation, though the main axis runs more northeast to southwest. It climbs up and away from town on one long ridgeline. Ski runs drape both sides of the ridge like old lace; one side gets the morning light, the other side the late-day glow. Here and there are patches of north-facing terrain, indicated by dense evergreens, sections of dark cloth on an otherwise leafless winter quilt.

Less than a fourth of the 3,300-acre mountain is visible from the valley. Lifts climb out of the monolithic Resort Center base and disappear over the ridge. PayDay, a six-passenger high-speed chair, is the fastest way out of the Resort Center. From the summit, more lifts radiate in all directions, down the ridgeback and over both sides. Generally speaking, the farther back you go, the more difficult the skiing and riding becomes, until finally the ridge peaks in the alpine zone, where four steep Alta-style bowls cap the lift-served skiing and riding right at 10,000 feet. The mountain is much deeper than it is wide, drawing up and away from town until at the top you are probably closer to Brighton than you are to your car at the Resort Center parking lot.

Because of the lower elevation and a possible snow shadow effect, Park City measures about 150 fewer inches of the light stuff than do the front-side areas. Still, 350 inches is more than enough in most years. To guard against cover intrusions on the lower slopes, the area has developed the most extensive snowmaking system in the state. They had to have it when they began hosting World Cup and pro races in mid-November. Now they use it, as many areas around the country have learned to do, to guarantee an early opening.

There is an occasional tendency to confuse the three areas surrounding the old town: Park City, the Canyons (previously called ParkWest and then Wolf Mountain), and Deer Valley at Park City. While they all use the town of Park City as a hub, and visitors often ski all three areas in a single stay, they are actually three separate areas with quite separate and distinct personalities. The Canyons is four miles north of Park City and is quickly evolving into a major destination resort. Deer Valley is just east of Park City, a relatively recent, self-contained resort and real estate development with an unapologetic tilt toward the luxury end of the spectrum. Park City is in the middle of the exuberant boomtown—now a National Historic District—with an equally spirited ski and snowboard operation built on top of the diggings.

Park City for Beginners and Novices

Park City has a nicely self-contained beginner's area to the right of the Resort Center base. Two slow-moving lifts, First Time and Three Kings, glide up the sunny, east-facing slope. Beginning boarders can get their feet under them on table tops and other terrain park features located here on *Pick 'N Shovel*, too, with their own terrain park beneath First Time. There is almost no incoming traffic from above, so skiers just starting out have the whole thing to themselves. This is where the ski and snowboard school teaches first-timer lessons.

Once you've made the transition to novice and you're ready to go up on the mountain proper, the choices multiply wonderfully. Take the Pay-Day six-passenger (six-pack) high-speed chair from the Resort Center, then ski down *Bonanza Access* to the Bonanza Hi-Speed six-pack. Utilizing these two lifts will get you to the Summit House in about 12 minutes. Another option would be to ride the Eagle triple chair, then the King Con Hi-Speed quad, and then the Silverlode Hi-Speed six-pack.

The latter option takes 17 minutes, not including ski and ride time and time in the lift line.

Your goal, whether you ride the six-packs or the other lifts, is an exquisitely long (novices need mileage) green run from the Summit House all the way to the resort base. It's 3.5 miles long, and though it's the designated "easiest way down," don't save it for the last run of the day unless you have plenty of energy left. Start off the top and ski or ride right under the Bonanza six-pack line on *Homerun,* the Champs Elysées of the mountain. You're right on the ridgeback; it's airy and spacious, and in the afternoon your shadow precedes you weaving down the groomed promenade. Halfway down the ridge, turn right onto a switchback detour through the aspens that cut out *Silver Queen* on the steeper nose of the ridge. *Homerun* recrosses the ridge near the base of *Bonanza* and then snakes back and forth a bit through the trees before flowing in a more direct path back to the Resort Center.

It's often a good idea not to ski or ride this route all the way to the bottom. Depending on the time of year and the recent natural-snow history, *Lower Homerun* is likely to be covered with man-made snow—not the stuff people come to Utah to sink their edges into. Consequently, many novices stay on *Claimjumper* to yo-yo the Silverlode area, a north-facing zone with good snow and runs ranging from buffed to bumped. Boarders frequent this circuit as well, to catch some air and grind their edges on the rollers, tabletops, spines, and rails in the park found on *Claimjumper's* inside elbow. Ride the Silverlode six-passenger chair to the Summit House hub, and ride/ski *Claimjumper* for its full crescent mile. The Silverlode is a good area for families or groups with differing abilities who nevertheless want to end up in the same place together. A smorgasbord of novice to advanced runs fans out from the top, then funnels back into one cup at the bottom. The Snow Hut Restaurant serves the crowd at the base of the lift.

And there can be a crowd. It's no accident that this is the place management chose for the West's first six-seater chairlift. If it gets too bad, the novice has two options. One is to ski east, skier's right, off *Homerun* onto the *Mid-Mountain* trail. This takes you by the Mid-Mountain Restaurant (the best on-mountain lunch; more on that later) and down to the base of Pioneer lift. The pokey Pioneer is infrequently crowded; it's slow and serves mainly intermediate and advanced skiing, so novices often overlook it. Adjacent to it is McConkey's Hi-Speed six-pack, which shuttles experts to the top of McConkey's Bowl and the gladed runs that ramble beneath it. But the *Homerun/Mid-Mountain* combination is a nice one, through the trees, strong on morning sun, shadowy in the afternoon with an easy return either to the Summit House or the base via the *Flat Iron* trail.

The other option is to ride or ski the bottom of the mountain while everybody else is up top. This plan works basically from late morning on.

The PayDay six-pack serves all of the *Treasure Hollow* region, including *Homerun*. When the snow is fresh and soft, several blue runs in this domain become easier, notably *Treasure Hollow* and the signature run, *PayDay*.

Park City Intermediate Skiing

Everybody wants to cruise on *PayDay*. It's a good run, almost 1,300 feet of vertical, wide, with a roller-coaster fall line and always plenty of snow, man-made or otherwise. This is where the main snowboard half-pipe is located (the last of the resort's four terrain parks is next door on King's Crown) and where they turn the lights on for night skiing as well (4–9 p.m., seven nights a week from Christmas into March). So it gets a lot of traffic, and traffic means scraped hard snow. For my money the really great cruising—and this is one of Park City's strengths—is on the back side in the *Silverlode* and *King Con* (short for King Consolidated Mine) region and still higher in the Thaynes Canyon realm.

The *Parleys Park* run is a classic intermediate swipe down the fall line. So wide that from one side you are barely aware of the other edge; so smooth, it's like a carpet underfoot. It starts out almost flat, tips just enough down the ridge to get you sailing, then rolls over the crown for a sustained, high-speed ride to the bottom.

More circumspect, but in some ways more interesting, is the *Hidden Splendor* route. It dips and curls along terrain changes from the *Claimjumper* ridge down a gentle sink in the center of the woods. Both drop more than 1,300 vertical feet.

There are a number of steeper groomed runs off Silverlode to the west into Thaynes Canyon. *Single Jack*, *Sunnyside*, and *Prospector* seem to dive over the edge through forests of mixed aspens and evergreens. In between, *Fools Gold* and *Glory Hole* rate black diamonds. They are exactly the same pitch—not too steep for most intermediates—but their moguls are allowed to grow unimpeded. From the trough at the bottom of Thaynes Canyon, you can either ride the Motherlode triple chair and in a reasonable 11 minutes be back to Summit House (so much of Park City's skiing emanates like spokes from this point), or you can keep sliding down the groove another half-mile to the King Con. King Con serves an all-intermediate tract, a large area of smooth-mowed trail skiing. It's quite popular, but I find the runs short compared to Silverlode and Thaynes, and the lower elevation can occasionally bake the snow.

The higher you get, of course, the colder and softer the snow will be. *Single Jack* takes you to the Thaynes chair, the highest, shadiest intermediate quarter on the mountain. *Keystone* carves a serpentine passage through dense spruce and fir near the head of the canyon just below Jupiter Bowl (the snow is always crisp). Or try the *Jupiter Access* trail. It's more than just access to the Jupiter lift; it covers some delightful, lumpy-moraine terrain at the base of the *West Face* and *Fortune Teller* and, for the daring, it's a launching point for some great tree runs that shelter powder stashes days after storms are replaced by blue skies If nothing else, it's worth the peek up into this alpine zone, the cream of Park City's expert offerings.

From the Jupiter base a blue trail leads down the gulch to the Thaynes chair again. There is no groomed descent off the Jupiter ridge, so unless you are experienced in wild snow, powder, or its cut-up cousin crud, don't ride this chair. If you do, either by mistake or through misplaced machismo, *Scotts Bowl* is the lowest-angle return to civilization.

Just above the Thaynes base you'll notice a jumble of tin mine buildings. In Park City's early days skiers had the option of getting to Thaynes via the gondola (and *Single Jack*) or underground through the honeycomb of mine tunnels. They rode three miles in on a miner's train with United Park City miners at the helm. They were then lifted 1,800 feet straight up in a hoist elevator to ground level at the bottom of the Thaynes lift. The route was abandoned 20 years ago, but now with all the talk about Interconnects and the need for traffic solutions in the canyons, the idea of using some of the hundreds of miles of tunnel under the mountains is receiving thoughtful consideration.

What to do when things back up on the Silverlode lift? Move a step uphill to the Motherlode. And when that one gets a little long? Move up another notch to Thaynes. And if Thaynes gets busy? Once again, head over the ridge to Pioneer and McConkey's six-pack. The blues serviced by the Pioneer chair are a little shorter over here, but they're almost invariably quiet. *Comstock, Red Fox,* and *Hawk Eye* are like a different world, flush with the morning sun, bright even when the sun is on the other side because they are cut through aspens and oak brush, with big views to the east at Deer Valley's double cones and south up into Puma and McConkey's bowls. Get some good northern exposure skiing on *Sunrise* and *Buckeye* or test your skills in some off-trail skiing and riding in McConkey's Bowl and the surrounding trees.

When it's time to go home in the afternoon, you can join the commuters on the *Homerun/PayDay* hayride or you can try something different. Turn left off *Homerun* to the top of the Ski Team lift and follow the wide-open ridge to the north. Your shadow should be dancing out in front all the way to the end, where you take *Gotcha Cut-off,* dodge through the aspens, and pop out on *Ladies SL,* for a final set of sweeping esses to the base. Oh, and there's one more option if your lodging is closer to the heart of Old Town than to the new stuff at the Resort Center. You can ski right down into Old Town over the old Creole mine dumps on two runs called *Creole* and *Quit'n Time,* that funnel into a ski bridge over Park Avenue that drops you into the heart of lower Main Street with its lodgings, shops and restaurants. Look for the narrow entrance off *PayDay* to the right.

For townies and visitors staying in Old Town, the Town triple chair at 8th and Park Avenues makes good sense for getting up the mountain in the morning. It's strictly an access chair—you don't yo-yo it—but it'll get you to the Bonanza Access trail and you won't have to drive or ride the Park City Transit shuttle out to the Resort Center.

Park City's massive, village-in-itself base has its advantages—namely being able to find everything around one pedestrian courtyard. The ski and snowboard school is here, lift tickets, Kids Mountain School, Interconnect departures (for skiing and riding to the four areas across the divide in Big and Little Cottonwood Canyons), race clinics, equipment rentals, food—fast and otherwise—and so on.

Park City for Expert Skiers and Riders

Some of the longest and cleanest expert lines on the mountain are also some of the first you see when standing at the base. The so-called *Ski Team* runs—the *Men's* and *Ladies' SL* and *GS* runs, *Willy's Run* and *Erika's Gold*, and the adjacent *Silver King* and *Shaft*—cut strong corridors through the aspen carpet. The Ski Team lift climbs straight to the top of these runs, but there never seems to be anybody skiing or riding them. Why? Because in Park City and the rest of Utah great snow is what you expect and merely good snow is often snubbed. The *Ski Team* runs are low on the hill and face directly east. This snow absorbs a lot of solar radiation. Then, when the sun passes overhead to the King Con side, that same snow freezes hard. If you can catch these runs soon after a snowfall they have a marvelous consistent pitch over true fall lines. Much of the time, however, they are too crunchy to compete with softer snow farther up the mountain.

Bumpers love the Thaynes/Motherlode realm. Runs like *Glory Hole, Double Jack,* and *The Hoist* (all hard-rock mining terms that are particularly expressive, it seems to me, of enthusiastic mogul mashing) provide about 1,000 vertical feet each of continuous bumping action. Closer to town the PayDay lift offers quick access to a couple of nasties called *Widowmaker* and *Nail Driver.* Neither is long, but they are steep, and the bumps, once the season is well under way, become Volkswagen size.

The best-shaped moguls, long and round, the kind made by the best skiers, are generally in the Shadow Ridge area off Jupiter lift. Strong mogul skiers pour down this crescent, 1,100-vertical-foot run all day long, but the bumps never get too sharp or sawed-off and unmakable. Occasionally, there'll be small developing bumps on the *West Face* of Jupiter Peak (if it hasn't filled in with new snow for a week or so) or in the center of Blueslip Bowl, but generally speaking the high bowls don't see enough traffic after the powder is skied out to grow serious lumps. Blueslip is an interesting place. Just up Pioneer Ridge from the top of

Bonanza six-pack, it was out of bounds before the Pioneer lift went in. Forbidden but so inviting. Bounded on one side by aspen glades and on the other by dense spruce, it plunges 500 vertical feet quite suddenly, more precipitously than anything in bounds at that time. After work ski area employees would sometimes sneak down its steep flanks. If they were caught, they were fired, given their blue slips.

Thankfully, it's now open and well-served by the Pioneer chair. The left side, the aspen side, gathers more sun and therefore reaps the subsequent benefits and pitfalls. On the negative side, powder sours more quickly in the direct sun, and in mid-winter the resulting crud can be nearly unskiable. In the spring, however, this is one of the first exposures to "corn up," or go through the cycle of melting and freezing that produces the marvelous, ego-boosting surface known as corn.

The right side, the evergreen side, has a totally different character. The snow stays shady and cold most of the winter. Another wonderful thing happens. Wind-driven snow from over Pioneer Ridge lands here in dense, smooth layers, like a blue-white sheet stretched over the terrain. When this happens, the right side of Blueslip Bowl is a winter equivalent of corn, easy-turning, easy-holding snow on an exhilaratingly steep pitch.

The crown jewels of Park City expert skiing and riding hover regally above everything else. The summit ridge, from Scott's Bowl on the west to McConkey's Bowl on the east, with Jupiter Peak reigning in the middle, encompasses about 600 acres of bowls and chutes and steep trees, the kind of terrain that puts Park City in the same league with Alta and Snowbird. (Before the Jupiter lift went in, in 1976, Park City was an unparalleled novice and intermediate mountain, but it lacked the high-end excitement, the real steep and deep that only happens around timberline where nature sculpts runs by means of rock slide, avalanche, and extreme weather.)

Because this is extreme terrain, not all of it will be open all of the time. The farthest out, Puma and McConkey's, open as avalanche-control work is completed. On a powder morning, locals and deep-seeking visitors will head straight for Jupiter (Payday to Bonanza to Pioneer or Thaynes is the fastest way); there's really no reason to stop anywhere else along the way.

The steepest runs are off to the left of the lift among the spindly trees and cliffs of Jupiter Bowl proper. *Six Bells* is the steepest of the steep. In the mines, six bells signaled "Look out below!" A little farther out on the ridge is the *West Face* of Jupiter Peak, where you'll find beautiful finger-thin lines with scraps of small trees in between to differentiate them. My favorite is *Om Zone.* Ski it with repetitive short turns and you'll be in a happy trance all the way to the bottom of the bowl. It's also a magical place in the afternoon, when golden light floods the face head on.

Thanks to the small knobs and clearings that interrupt the thick forests here, natural kickers and rails abound beneath Jupiter Peak.

Scott's Bowl (off the chair to the right) sometimes has a sizable cornice for the air-minded. Underneath, it is the most spacious of the bowls, and the incline quickly moderates to a relatively mellow pitch. This is the place to go if you're not sure you're ready to test your skills on the hairier runs to the east.

However, if you are quite sure of your skills, then you owe yourself a trip down off the peak. It requires a walk, perhaps ten minutes from the saddle above *West Face,* but this walk earns you the most adventurous terrain on the mountain. Rock ribs with vertical bands of snow in between break up *East Face.* The center chute, *Hourglass,* squeezes down to about one-and-a-half ski lengths at the throat, then opens quickly into the expanse of Puma Bowl. This is heart-pounding skiing and riding, very steep but not particularly dangerous because of the open slopes below.

Chances are good the chutes will already have avalanched by the time the patrol lets you up there—they're that steep. For deeper snow on a more moderate pitch, take McConkey's six-pack and ski the north-facing glades of Puma Bowl or all the way out to the giant scoop that is McConkey's. Here you can weave together 50 powder turns before bumping into the *Woodside* trail and the return to Pioneer or McConkey's six-pack. Everything on the east side of the peak flows into the Pioneer drainage; everything on the west funnels back to Jupiter. Even so, a return trip to Puma land requires only one lift ride.

Many good skiers and riders race to the Jupiter lift and stay there all day. It's a different world up there, separate and challenging. The trip back down, via *Thaynes Canyon* or the *Claimjumper* expressway, with the maze of lifts and other skiers and riders, is a bit of a shock. But it's a pleasant one because it underscores the specialness of the place you've been in.

Snowboarding

PCMR offers something for every rider. There are long, swooping cruisers like *Parley's Park* and *Sunnyside* for speed freaks, and there are wonderfully steep pitches, studded with rock outcrops that make perfect launching pads for those happiest in the air, such as *Fortune Teller, Silver Cliff,* and Jupiter's *Main Bowl.*

But riders who like to fly need not head high up the mountain, as the West's first superpipe lies in wait near the bottom of *CB's Run.* Built for the 2002 Winter Games, this 400-foot-long pipe with 17-foot walls lures the world's best pipe riders to the resort for annual competitions.

Riders who like to jib aren't overlooked, either. Located on King's Crown is a terrain park overflowing with C Rails, S Rails, a dragontail rail, mail boxes, flat bar rails, and snow features.

For natural kickers, try the wooded landscape that lies above and below *Keystone.*

Lunch on the Mountain

The food court at the **Legacy Lodge** serves a selection of hot entrees specials, grilled items, a baked-potato bar, fresh-salad bar, and homemade pizza. The Legacy also has an espresso bar, **The Legends Apres Ski and Ride Bar,** a private club, and a **Brew House.** My favorite on-mountain eating is at the **Mid-Mountain Restaurant.** The building itself is 100 years old and was built originally as a boardinghouse/dining hall for the Silver King miners. In 1987, in an astonishing feat, the ski area cut a new run in order to haul the building 4,000 feet up the mountain to its present location in the aspens near the base of the Pioneer lift. Although it's been completely refurbished, the place retains the essence of its history. It's in the whitewashed interior, the narrow hallways, the old wainscoting and double-hung window sashes. To top it off, the walls are hung with photographic prints, some of them spectacularly sharp, of mining-era scenes. They are the kind of photos that draw you irresistibly in; the miners' faces are more like our own than the distance of history would lead us to imagine. There's a big, sunny deck, and the food is good too. Classic American ski resort fare: pizza, chili, stews, and sandwiches, and, of course, the locally brewed Wasatch Ale, a very respectable red bitter.

The **Summit House,** once an elbow-to-elbow cafeteria, has been redone as a wonderful sit-down restaurant with table service. The views south over Blueslip and McConkey's bowls to Deer Valley can be intoxicating. There's also a small bar here with a handful of tables.

At the bottom of the Silverlode Lift, the **Snow Hut** attracts a more "common man" crowd, with daily specials and crowded tables indoors and barbecue grill productions outdoors on the deck.

In Town: Eating, Sleeping, and Other Forms of Rejuvenation

Tough choices here. There are fine restaurants in some of the slopeside hotels, but I'm going to stick pretty much to the historic Main Street area, which you can cover in under half an hour either on foot or by hopping the clanging little trolley.

Alex's is Park City's only prix fixe French restaurant; it is intimate, decorated in soft pastels with a simple, well-prepared, and reasonably priced menu. For Mexican I like **Nacho Mammas,** located at 1821 Sidewinder Drive, which features Mexican-style dishes combined with unique regional specialties borrowed from throughout the Southwest. For frontier-size steaks and prime rib, try the **Claim Jumper,** owned and operated by the same man (a former Blue Angel fighter pilot) who runs the Mid-Mountain Restaurant.

The most unusual dinner setting in the area comes aboard the **Heber Creeper,** a restored steam train with an elegant dining car that makes a nightly dinner loop through the Heber Valley 20 minutes southeast of Park City.

Getting a drink in Utah is not as complicated as it may seem (see the "Inside Story," Utah Liquor Laws, page 339). Having a drink with a meal is no difficulty. If you want to just sit in a bar and have a cocktail, you can do that too. But there's a twist: Bars that serve wine and mixed drinks over the counter are called clubs, and you'll be asked to become a member. Two-week temporary memberships are available, for about $5, at all the clubs and at most hotel desks. With that one transaction out of the way, you can order a drink. The most authentic, mining-era bar on Main Street is, appropriately enough, the **Club.** Breakfast is a key meal for skiers. For great homemade pastries, croissants, and cappuccinos, the **Morning Ray** on upper Main Street is the place. For an all-American, bacon-and-eggs-and-flapjacks kind of place, try the **Mt. Air Cafe,** a classic diner on Park Avenue near Kearns Boulevard.

The lodging list is long and the choices are multifarious. Park City has about 10,000 guest pillows. For a complete listing call the Park City Chamber Bureau, (800) 453-1360.

A few places of note: **The Alpine Prospector Lodge** is a genuine mining-era boardinghouse remodeled into a ski lodge with budget rates. **The Old Miners' Lodge Bed-and-Breakfast Inn** is chock-full of antiques and serves a full breakfast, and it is next to the Town lift. By far the least expensive lodging option is the **Hidden Haven Campground,** right off I-80 with hook-ups and nightly, weekly, or monthly rates for skiers who bring their lodging with them.

There are untold condominiums and condo hotels in the valley. During the 1970s building boom, some tasteless and shabby units were thrown up, but more protective and historically sensitive controls have since found favor. One of the nicest within walking distance of the main base lifts is the mid-range **Edelweiss Haus.** Unassuming, even homely on the outside, it is very comfortable and has an outdoor pool and hot tub. The huge complex right at the base of the lifts, a kind of hulking mini-city unto itself, is the **Resort Center Lodge & Inn.** It's pricey, but it has everything from ice skating to shops and restaurants, and it's right in the center of the action.

One center of the action, I should say. The Resort Center and old Main Street—about half a mile apart—are twin blazes of light in the winter night air. While the Resort Center tends toward more generic, youth-oriented ski-area music and dancing, Old Town offers more rounded cultural fare.

Film lovers should plan to be in Park City in late January for the Sundance Film Festival. Created by Robert Redford's Sundance Institute as a way to encourage and promote independent filmmaking, the event has grown spectacularly since it moved to Park City in 1985. In the winter of 2003, 20,000 seats were sold for the ten-day festival. Screenings include world premieres, documentary competition, dramatic competition, a rogues' gallery of new American shorts, and special tributes and retrospectives. A scan of audience faces reveals somberly dressed and pasty-faced denizens of the New York and Los Angeles film worlds interspersed with the suntanned and goggle-lined visages of skier/filmophiles. For my money, it's the perfect overlap of culture and sport. At Jackson and Sun Valley they have skiing but no film. In Telluride and Aspen they have film but not during ski season. Park City, true to its nonconformist history, stands apart.

Park City Data

Mountain Statistics

Vertical feet	3,100 feet
Base elevation	6,900 feet
Summit elevation	10,000 feet
Longest run	3.5 miles
Average annual snowfall	350 inches
Number of lifts	14: 4 six-passenger chairs, 1 quad, 5 triples, 4 doubles
Uphill capacity	27,200 skiers per hour
Skiable terrain	3,300 acres
Opening date	Mid-November
Closing date	Mid-April
Snowboarding	Yes

Transportation

By car About 45 minutes (30 miles) from Salt Lake International Airport via I-80 east through Parley's Canyon to State 224 south. Also, Route 189/40 from Heber City and Provo to the south, about 1 hour.

By bus, limo, or taxi From Salt Lake International Airport.

By plane Via major carriers to Salt Lake International Airport.

Key Phone Numbers

Ski-area information	(435) 649-8111
Snow report	(435) 647-5449
Lodging reservations	(800) 222-PARK
In Utah	(435) 649-0493
Website	www.parkcitymountain.com

Deer Valley Resort

Deer Valley is the gourmet ski resort in Utah, and maybe the entire hemisphere. Writers usually talk more about the food here than the skiing. They talk about the cuisine like the smoked trout and caviar at the

Mariposa, the chocolate cheesecake, the valets who whisk your skis off the roof rack when you arrive at the lodge, afternoon tea in front of the fireplace at the Stein Eriksen Lodge, the extremely low 4:1 guest-to-staff ratio, limited ticket sales, machine-buffed snow, padded chairlifts Chateau Laffite Rothschild, and so on.

The resort doesn't mind this kind of talk; in fact, they encourage it. Deer Valley was conceived as a kind of five-star experience, from morning coffee to evening digestive. The skiing is not exactly secondary to the rest of the experience; it is an integral, highly polished part, but no more important a part than the sumptuous food or the elegant service. Deer Valley's well-heeled guests, such as Roger Penske (now part owner), Sidney Poitier, Jane Fonda, Bruce Willis, and Tom Cruise, appreciate it that way.

Interestingly, while Deer Valley is one of the newest Utah ski resorts, the gentler of the area's four mountains, Bald Eagle Mountain, was the site of the first lift-served skiing on the back side of the Wasatch. In 1946 it was called Snow Park, and it was the town rope tow just a short mile east of Park City's Main Street. The development in the early 1960s of the Treasure Mountain Resort (later renamed Park City) west of town made Snow Park obsolete, but the owners of the property sensed that their time would come.

It did in 1981. After years of planning, a triumvirate including entrepreneur Edgar Stern, hotelier James Nassikas, and ski icon Stein Eriksen opened Deer Valley as their vision of an "uncommonly civilized" resort. Stern, who was on the Board of Directors at Sears, was the money man. Nassikas brought to the mountains the exacting standards and fanaticism for service that were his trademark at the Stanford Court Hotel in San Francisco. Stein added his considerable charm and ski experience to the project. Perhaps even more important, he lent it his bankable mystique as the very embodiment of the elegant ski lifestyle.

The opening-day $20 lift ticket (no big deal today, but a skyrocket in 1981) sent ripples through the American ski industry, but so did the ski valets. The place was an instant success, at least in terms of image. Resorts in Colorado and elsewhere around the country scrambled to imitate Deer Valley's gourmet, sit-down lunches and went to school on Deer Valley's skier services. The point was, people of means who ski (and who might be counted on to invest in slopeside real estate) won't blink at the cost of a lift ticket if they are made to feel pampered on and off the hill.

Deer Valley was, and is, the most expensive skiing in Utah. Locals make up but a small percentage of the on-hill traffic. It's the very opposite of Alta's corporate philosophy, which has always been aimed directly at the local skier. But this exclusivity—which includes a snowboard ban—was part of the plan from the beginning. Deer Valley plan to set itself apart has largely succeeded. This is not skiing for Everyman; it's skiing for Privilegedman, or for anyone who wants to feel like aristocracy for a day or a holiday.

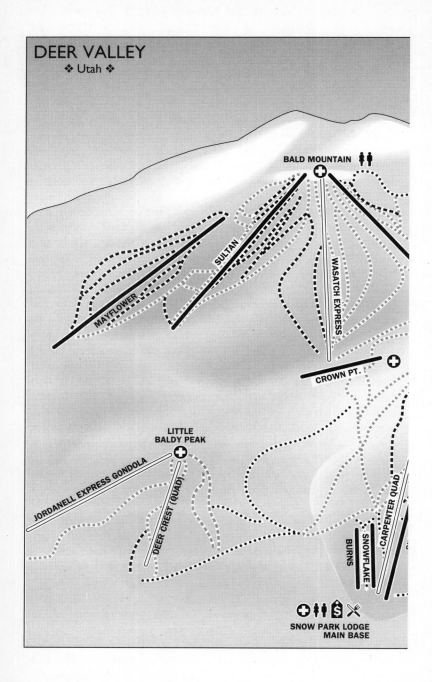

DEER VALLEY
❖ Utah ❖

BALD MOUNTAIN

MAYFLOWER

SULTAN

WASATCH EXPRESS

CROWN PT.

LITTLE
BALDY PEAK

JORDANELL EXPRESS GONDOLA

DEER CREST (QUAD)

CARPENTER QUAD

BURNS

SNOWFLAKE

SNOW PARK LODGE
MAIN BASE

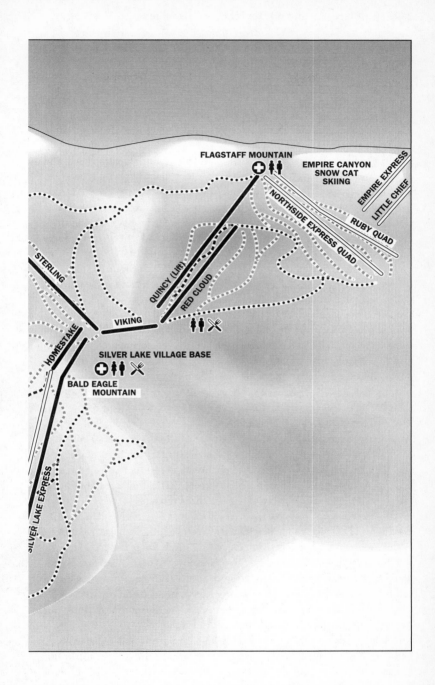

FLAGSTAFF MOUNTAIN

EMPIRE CANYON
SNOW CAT
SKIING

EMPIRE EXPRESS

LITTLE CHIEF

NORTHSIDE EXPRESS QUAD

RUBY QUAD

STERLING

QUINCY (Lift)

RED CLOUD

VIKING

HOMESTAKE

SILVER LAKE VILLAGE BASE

BALD EAGLE
MOUNTAIN

SILVER LAKE EXPRESS

Deer Valley's Four Peaks: Bald Mountain, Bald Eagle, Flagstaff, and Empire Canyon

Deer Valley's skiing, especially the intermediate cruising, is good enough to stand on its own without the luxurious trappings. There is not as much terrain as at Park City, nothing like the expert challenge at Alta and Snowbird, and they don't get the copious snows that Brighton does, but it is still very good skiing.

Of the four principal mountains, Bald Mountain is the southerly and easterly peak, and at 9,400 feet, it is higher than Bald Eagle by 1,000 feet. This is where you'll find the majority of the steeper skiing. To the west is Flagstaff Mountain at 9,100 feet, featuring blue-square cruisers with one notable challenge, the funky, steep *Ontario Bowl*. The newest addition is Empire Canyon at 9,570 feet. This area is the most advanced area at Deer Valley, with eight runs, three bowls, eight chutes, and two lifts. Far below and to the southeast lies Little Baldy Peak, a 7,950-foot-tall stub of a mountain that features a few meandering blue cruisers and three temperate expert runs. Combined, they make up Deer Crest, an extension of Deer Valley conceived largely for the placement of lavish second homes (which have their own private ski runs leading to the public runs). All these areas have a decidedly eastern feel compared to most Utah mountains. They are heavily forested round mounds, with fall-line trails cut down their flanks. Only the very top of Bald Mountain and a distant lip of Empire Canyon show any sign of timberline rock and wind.

The area's total vertical, from the top of Empire Canyon to the bottom of Deer Crest, is 3,000 feet. But you can't ski it in one fell swoop. The more meaningful figures are the verticals of each peak: 1,300 feet for Empire Canyon, 1,960 feet for Bald, 1,200 feet for Bald Eagle, and 900 feet for Flagstaff Mountain. There are 19 chairlifts;ten of the which access the universally well-groomed, uncrowded skiing; and three that are short transportation lifts linking the three peaks.

The access road from the town of Park City splits midway up the hill, leading to two Deer Valley base facilities. Snow Park Lodge at 7,200 feet at the foot of Bald Eagle is the main base. This is where the free parking, the guest service attendants, and the awesome Natural Breakfast Buffet are. The other base at Silver Lake Lodge, at 8,100 feet, snuggles into a saddle between the peaks. The parking here is limited and expensive. Silver Lake is less a base area than a chance for the hoi polloi to hang out next door to the ultra-tasteful Stein Eriksen Lodge.

More roads meander the west-facing, evergreen-and-aspen hillside between the two bases, linking a string of private homes, ski-in/ski-out lodges, and condo projects, including the Stein Eriksen Lodge. One of Deer Valley's design coups is the fact that all accommodations are convenient to every level of ski terrain. A novice staying high on the mountain at

Stein's, for example, rides one short lift and has the entire lower mountain at his ski tips. An advanced skier at the same lodge has but to walk outside, slip into ski bindings, and slide over to the Bald Mountain lifts.

If you begin your ski day at the Snow Park base, check the big signboard outside the lodge for information. It'll tell you which lifts are open. It shows which runs were groomed the night before, which have been left unpacked, and which have moguls on them.

Deer Valley for Beginners and Novices

There is some excellent green terrain here but not much of it, although the meticulous grooming means some blues are also suited to advancing novices.

Wide West underneath the Burns lift (Snow Park base) is a super-gentle beginners' hill. Ski school pretty much takes it over in the middle of the day. The Kinderschule sets up its fun obstacle and terrain garden here as well.

After *Wide West*, ride the Carpenter lift to the top of Bald Eagle and take the *Success* trail for the full ride back to the base. *Success* is aptly named and cleverly cut to weave the easiest route down the hill. Options off the *Success* route include *Little Bell, Last Chance/Silver Dollar,* and *Rosebud.* One of my favorite tours through the Bald Eagle terrain follows *Success* to *Little Bell* to *Dew Drop,* which is marked blue on the map. But it is a nonthreatening blue full of tree islands and the kinds of playful terrain that the more staid greens lack.

Adventurous novices who have done it all on Bald Eagle should make the trip up Bald Mountain to ski *Sunset,* as genial a blue as there is. It lives up to its name, curving toward the sun late in the day. When the temperatures fall, the snow takes on a golden glow.

Little Baldy Peak is a gentle haven for strong novices and fledgling intermediates anxious to avoid crowds. The broad, rolling *Jordanelle* not only offers great views of its namesake reservoir to the east, but skitters from the mountaintop all the way to its base. The result is a long ride that allows improving skiers ample chance to work on technique and balance. From it they can graduate to either *Fairview* or *Silverhill,* similarly broad cruisers that offer greater pitch. True novices benefit from *Deer Hollow,* which encircles the northern half of the mountain on its way back to the Jordanelle Express gondola.

Deer Valley for Intermediates

This is the area's forte, its pièce de résistance. The beginner/novice terrain here is good, but the choices are somewhat limited, and the genuine advanced challenge comes up a little soft. But for sheer, burnished, high-speed, let-'em-run cruising it's tough to beat Deer Valley's combination of uninterrupted fall lines and constant machine grooming.

Look down from the top of any of the four main mountains (you'd think they would have renamed either Bald Mountain or Bald Eagle in the interest of clarity), and the terrain progression is the same. The left side, the western edge, of each peak is the easiest. As you move to your right around the cone to the east, the runs become progressively more difficult.

Bald Eagle has a few blue cruisers that make excellent warm-ups if you are starting your day at the Snow Park base. Cruisers don't necessarily have to be marked blue, or intermediate. Deer Valley grooms some of its black diamonds as well, turning them into buffed autobahns. *Solid Muldoon* has a concave, gully-bottom feel. *Big Stick* starts out across a gladed plateau and then drops over a big roll before merging with other trails on the beginner flats known as *Wide West*. Both descend the full 1,200-foot Bald Eagle vertical, and both are machined regularly to ensure Deer Valley's trademark corduroy texture.

Serious cruisers will head over to Bald Mountain and stay there. The vertical is bigger, and there are at least a dozen swooping dance floors on which to carve your signature. The best is off the Sultan lift, where Bald Mountain's east shoulder falls into *Perseverance Bowl.* This one has a beautiful shape. It sweeps from the steep bowl facedown into a wide concave belly dotted with evergreen archipelagos and splashed with long shadows. The pitch is constant, inviting, and a good deal steeper than blue runs at most areas. But because of the smooth-carpet surface underfoot, the skiing is anything but difficult. In fact, it's deceptively, addictively easy. Some people are enticed into skiing a little too fast for their ability, but almost everyone feels a sense of fluid movement, of grace. It is quite possible on these runs to glimpse in oneself a bit of the elegance that Stein brings to his every movement on skis.

Perseverance isn't the only one. *Tycoon* toboggans this same Sultan terrain on the other side of the lift, where the predominant aspen trees tick by like a picket fence. The Wasatch lift serves some of Bald's most popular cruisers. The busiest is *Nabob,* perhaps because its overall pitch is the gentlest. The three other side-by-side cruisers in this zone—*Keno, Legal Tender,* and *Wizard*—are rarely crowded.

The two main thoroughfares off the Sterling chair, *Sunset* and *Birdseye,* are reserved for slow skiing, but there is one interesting cruiser on the far west (and easiest) side of Bald Mountain. It's called *Emerald,* and it's rated black diamond. The only reason I can see for the designation is that the wind sometimes does the grooming here. It often has a wind-deposited, hard-margarine layer on top that makes excellent skiing once you get used to the ripple effect.

The shorter blues on Flagstaff are no less perfect in their fall-line ease. The runs surrounding the Northside Express quad—*Hawkeye, Lucky Star,* and *Lost Boulder*—are especially attractive for the quick five-minute return ride.

Deer Valley for Experts

Cruising is not just for intermediates, of course. Very good skiers enjoy Deer Valley's polished steeps too. In fact, quite a few of the skiers Deer Valley counts as locals are long-ski connoisseurs from Salt Lake City and Park City who come out of the woodwork when there hasn't been new snow for a while and the slopes are sleek and fast. You will see them on *Perseverance* or *Hawkeye* on their 215-centimeter giant-slalom boards banking huge arcs as if they were stock cars on the oval at Daytona.

But most experts eventually weary of the manicured pitches and go looking for something with a steeper angle than what can be machine groomed, or something with bumps on it, or something with wild snow between the trees. Deer Valley has some of each, and because the area doesn't attract a huge number of advanced and expert skiers, the black zones are often the least crowded places on the mountain.

Deer Valley has worked hard to bend its image as an adrenaline-free zone. There is an "Experts Only" trail map highlighting some of the less obvious tree and chute skiing. There's even an expert enclave west of the existing Flagstaff boundary, known as *Empire Canyon,* that offers challenges equal to those found elsewhere in the state. There is one high-speed quad and one fixed-grip quad, and more lifts are planned. The skiing *Empire Canyon* offers is akin to that found around *Jupier Peak* at Park City or off *99-90* at The Canyons: bowl skiing that tails off into glades as well as narrow, vertigo-inducing chutes.

Riding up the Empire Express quad, you can feast on the treeless mountainside bowl that sprawls so much from west to east that it requires three names: *Solace, Conviction,* and *Domingo.* Utah's trademark powder fluffs deep on this bowl after storms, providing a springy underfooting for turn-after-turn-after-turn from Empire's summit to the aspen and conifer glades near its base. After the storm's fluff has been ransacked, the bowl grows moderate-sized moguls. Head west from the lift along *Orion,* a gentle ribbon of white that skirts the main bowl, and you can lose yourself in the thick forest of *Anchor Trees.* Bypass the forest and you can dive into the somewhat short, but decidedly precipitous, *Daly Bowl* or, even steeper and narrower, *Daly Chutes.* Head east of the lift station and you can plunge into *Lady Morgan Bowl,* a delicious slice of backcountry-esque heaven that's surprisingly overlooked by most skiers. As with Empire Canyon's main bowl, *Lady Morgan*'s bare-naked upper half sprouts conifers and aspens lower down.

Bald Eagle has three black diamonds, not much steeper than the surrounding terrain. They are designated as such because management allows them to grow moguls. *Know You Don't* is longer and better than *Lucky Bill,* although, due to the general caliber of skiers on Bald Eagle, the bumps here tend to be small and tentative. *Champion* is a relatively short steep face that is visible from the base area; this is the mogul run that was used for the 2002 Olympics.

The best bumps are on Bald Mountain, most of them toward the east end. The left side of Perseverance Bowl (looking down) offers a variety of lumpy lines through gladed terrain. The map shows three named trails—*Thunderer, Blue Ledge,* and *Grizzly*—but they tend to blend together. I like them because you can pick your size: big moguls down the concave centers of the drains, smaller bumps out at the edges, or only hints of nascent mogul shapes in the open tree lines that divide the runs.

Only occasionally will you find really big bumps at Deer Valley and then only in a few, highly visible, lift-line locales like *Rattler* or *Narrow Gauge.* Even these don't come close in size and ferocity to the man-eaters on Snowbird's *Silver Fox,* for example. The place just doesn't attract skiers interested in yo-yoing the moguls.

Mayflower, at the far east end of the area, is Deer Valley's truest expert territory when it comes to bumps. It rarely gets steeper than Perseverance Bowl, but it has a wild feel; the grooming machines leave it alone. Near the top of Mayflower Bowl a lone spruce on a rocky outcrop stands as a sentinel above the steepest skiing on the mountain. A good, smooth, windblown base flows around the tree toward the gully-bottom moguls of *Morning Star* below. When there is new snow, *Morning Star* and the parallel *Fortune Teller* and *Paradise* runs are the best powder skiing on Bald Mountain. They do face the morning sun, however, so it's best to get to them before they've had a chance to absorb the rays.

The longest-lasting powder snow at any area is to be found in the trees, and Deer Valley has a wealth of underexplored trees. Once again, it seems that the lion's share of its skiers aren't out to push beyond the (very) comfortable limits of the cruising terrain. A little exploring (with the Experts Only trail map in hand) is therefore often richly rewarded.

There are two kinds of tree experiences here: aspens and evergreens. Aspens love light and hug the east-facing slopes. Occasionally you'll find them on west-facing hillsides and almost never on true northern exposures. The most famous aspen patch in Deer Valley, the one where Stein is frequently photographed for brochures and articles, is the *Triangle Trees* between the Sultan and Wasatch lifts on Bald Mountain. They're easy to find. Turn left off *Tycoon* about halfway down, and you're in a maze of slim, branchless, cream-colored trunks spaced just right for powder turns. In flickering shadow and light, the skiing is hypnotic and mesmerizing, a kind of metronome counterpoint to the giant leaning arcs one makes on the piste.

The evergreens are much more secretive, cooler, and darker. Skiing them is a kind of private investigation. You may spook a grouse, hooting and flapping, from his perch. You will surely see rabbit tracks and probably those of squirrels, chipmunks, and mice. You may not be able to link more than five or six turns in a row before a leafy wall closes in, but there is always the possibility you will find a hidden meadow with 10 or 12 turns that no one has skied this year.

The most accessible evergreens at Deer Valley are the ones between *Grizzly* and *Ruins of Pompeii.* They're spacious with a nice rhythm and good starter trees. (Because Deer Valley is private land, mountain crews have had a free hand in trimming limbs and shaping trees they know will see considerable traffic. Some of the results—bare trunks to eight feet above snow level—look a little like French poodles. But then, they were probably just hoping for a big snow year.)

Over on Flagstaff, *Oompa-Loompa Land* provides some of the easiest tree pitches around, with generous helpings of low-angle powder meadows. *DT's Trees,* on the other hand, are tight firs best left for the fast-twitch set.

You'll find dense, untrimmed forest on the other side of Perseverance Bowl between *Perseverance* and *Hawkeye.* Another good set of trees is on the west side of Bald Mountain between *Emerald* and *North Star.*

On sunny days it's a good idea to work the aspens first, before the sun can change the snow to mashed potatoes, and then slide into the deeper, darker evergreens, which may protect bowers of cold snow for days, even weeks, after a storm.

One final note for Bald Mountain skiers: The upper mountain shuts down like an accordion door, east to west, in the afternoon. Mayflower closes at 3 p.m., Sultan at 3:30 p.m. Wasatch and Sterling stay open until 3:45 p.m. The Bald Eagle lifts run until 4 p.m. It's a shame, but the ski patrol has to do it this way to sweep the flock back to camp before dark.

The Famous Food

Everybody needs fuel to ski, but at Deer Valley satisfying that requirement is closer to art than necessity. Here's the way I would set up my ideal gourmet ski day.

Breakfast at the **Snow Park Lodge,** where they set out what they call their Natural Breakfast Buffet: fresh-squeezed juices, melons, pineapple, fruit salads, croissants, cereals, muffins, hazelnut bear claws, eggs Benedict, and omelets. Serve yourself and sit in a plush oak chair by the window. A waiter comes around to fill your coffee cup whenever it gets low or cools down.

Lunch at **Stein's.** You can't miss it as you fly down the *Birdseye* trail at noon; the tasteful cloth banner reads "Skiers' Buffet," with an arrow pointing into the aspens and Stein's lodge. (Stein does not actually own the lodge, but that is immaterial. He had a hand in its every design detail. His gold and silver medals from the 1952 Olympics and 1954 World Championships are proudly displayed here. His wife, Françoise, has her ultraluxe Bjørn Stova Boutique in the lobby, and Stein prowls the restaurant and lounge every winter day that he is in town. It's quite okay to call it Stein's lodge.) The buffet spread is staggeringly opulent: cream of broccoli soup, Mediterranean lamb stew, Yucatán chili, prime rib, smoked fish and meats, salads, fresh fruits, chocolate cheesecake, apple crisp, two-tone pear pie, all in a setting of white tablecloths, silver service, stone fireplace, and carved wooden doors. You feel funny clanking around the carpet in your ski boots, but that's what everyone does.

Ski some more. Then have dinner at the **Mariposa** in the **Silver Lake Lodge** (huge laminated beams, copper fireplace covers, and flowers in the windows). Reservations are essential. Each night's menu is exquisitely fresh and artfully prepared.

For more casual dining, you could ring up the **Red Banjo Pizza Parlor** on Main Street in Park City. They deliver.

Lodging in Deer Valley

Staying in Deer Valley is designed, logically enough, to be commensurate with the rest of the experience. **Stein's** is the choice abode, for its name, its location on the slopes, the lavishly outfitted rooms and suites, the automatic doors (in case you have skis in hand), the heated sidewalks, and the fact that you can walk the halls in your lush terry-cloth robe (provided) to the wind-screened, heated pool. Plus, it's downright beautiful. The tab will run anywhere from $200 to $1,500 per night.

All of the other lodging in Deer Valley is managed by Deer Valley Central Reservations and includes condominiums, private homes, and the **Stag Lodge.** A huge variety of lodging options and prices exists down the road in Park City.

Deer Valley Data

Mountain Statistics

Vertical feet	3,000 feet
Base elevation	6,570 feet
Summit elevation	9,570 feet
Longest run	2.1 miles
Average annual snowfall	300 inches
Snowmaking	500+ acres
Number of lifts	19: 7 high-speed quads; 2 fixed-grip quads; 1 high-speed gondola; 7 triples; 2 doubles
Uphill capacity	38,320+ skiers per hour
Skiable terrain	1,750 acres
Opening date	Early December
Closing date	Early April
Snowboarding	No

Deer Valley Data (continued)

Transportation

By car About 45 minutes from Salt Lake International Airport via I-80 east through Parley's Canyon to State 224 south. Into Park City and east on Deer Valley Drive for 1 mile. Also, Route 189/40 from Heber City and Provo to the south, about 1 hour.
By bus, limo, taxi, or helicopter From Salt Lake International Airport.
By plane Via major carriers to Salt Lake International Airport.

Key Phone Numbers

Ski-area information	(800) 424-3337 or (435) 649-1000
Snow report	(435) 649-2000
Deer Valley Central	(800) 558-3337 or (435)645-6648
Reservations	
Stein Eriksen Lodge	(800) 453-1302
Website	www.deervalley.com

Inside Story

Utah Liquor Laws

In Brigham Young's time, the Mormon "Word of Wisdom" forbade smoking or chewing tobacco and drinking alcohol (some ascribe caffeine to the list of forbidden fruits). The body had to be kept pure for the work of building the Heavenly City.

Despite popular myth, Utah never was dry and is not now. Aspects of the state's liquor laws may seem complex, even quixotic, to visitors, but it is possible to get a drink here. Once you get used to the system, in fact, it's nearly as practical as anyplace else.

Restaurants with liquor licenses may serve alcoholic beverages of any sort to your table. You used to have to purchase minibottles of hard liquor and a "set-up" (glass and ice), then pour it yourself, but a 1988 revision eliminated that quirk. You may also bring your own "brown bag" liquor or wine to the restaurant. They will provide glasses and charge you a "corkage" fee.

Bars in the traditional sense are called private clubs in Utah. They sell wine, beer, and mixed and blended drinks "over the bar" to members and their guests. Temporary guest memberships are available for a fee (usually $5) to visitors. You can buy them at the club or at the front desk of your lodging. In Park City and Snowbird a single "reciprocal" card is good at most if not all the clubs in town. Some bars, like the ones in the lodges in Alta, will hold your liquor bottle for you, with your name on it, and pour you a drink whenever you like.

Taverns, or beer bars, sell only beer (and 3.2% alcohol beer at that), but brown bagging is permitted.

Sale of packaged liquor is controlled by the state government. There is at least one State Liquor Store in each resort, sometimes in the lodges themselves. They're closed on Sundays and holidays, and they only accept cash. You can buy beer at grocery and convenience stores any day of the week.

The Canyons

The newest of the Utah resorts, the Canyons (formerly Wolf Mountain), has the potential to be one of America's premier ski resorts. The resort was purchased by the American Skiing Company in 1997 with plans to invest $500 million by the year 2005 and expand the skiable area to over 7,000 acres. As of November 2002, the area boasts a fleet of 16 lifts, ranging from an eight-passenger gondola that hauls skiers and 'boarders to mid-mountain to five high-speed quads. There also were two mid-mountain lodges, the more upscale is Lookout Cabin with its fine restaurant, and 3,500 total acres. The first phase of the base village was completed for the 2000–2001 ski season. It delivered the 360-room Grand Summit Hotel and the 125-condominium signature Sundial Lodge. Since then, a privately owned hotel opened next door to the Sundial Lodge with 185 rooms, and it, too, has room to expand.

With the freeway, the Canyons is the closest skiing to downtown Salt Lake City, and the area has capitalized on this fact.

The Shape of the Mountain

The Canyons' ski terrain is strung out along eight mountains that offer a mix of steep-sided ridgelines ringed by blue cruisers. The ridges' parallel crowns run more or less east to west, so there is one shady cool side and one often-as-not burned-out solar side. Two of the best intermediate runs have been carved along the sharp crests of the ridges; they look like flattop haircuts. The longest runs are down the flattop ridges and along the creekbeds in the gullies at their bases. The truest fall lines spill off the sides of the ridge tops toward the gully trails, which pull all the traffic, like metropolitan beltways, around the flanks and toward the base.

This base is unimposing and a little bit deceptive. From the parking lot you see only the bald, nearly treeless tip of the lowest ridge, probably less than 10% of the 3,500 skiable acres. Part of the fun here is discovering the rest, moving back and up, ever farther west until you can go no more, then filling in the blanks on your way home.

There are eight discernible ski zones. The first zone is the terrain you see right outside the Day Lodge. This zone has one quad chair, the Red Hawk quad, which services a boarder/skier cross park and a big air park and some open novice terrain.

Next zone up and back is Lookout Peak, served by the Golden Eagle double. This has some black diamond terrain, but the lift also provides access to one of the most popular intermediate zones at the resort, known as *Snow Canyon,* served by a chair of the same name. The northernmost, and longest zone (actually a separate ridge unto itself) is the Condor region: one blue, three double blues and some very steep blacks, and a whole slew of double black, experts-only trails. The best of these is

Murdock Bowl, a nice piece of timberline, walk-up turf above Condor Peak. Local boarders who prefer their air dished up by natural terrain features head here, as a gully that roams along *Canis Lupis* offers a tight, serpentine half-pipe ride that never fails to please.

Intermediates who are weary from the popular Snow Canyon zone can take a cat track off the back side to the Saddleback area, 1,200 vertical feet of mostly blue glade and tree runs.

The middle zone and the heart of the Canyons is at the top of the gondola at the Red Pine Lodge area. This area is serviced by the Saddleback Express and the High-Meadow lifts. For beautiful intermediate cruising along with many north-facing black runs this is the place. The Red Pine Lodge provides a fantastic place to rest between runs and to have lunch.

Working our way south we come to the fifth zone, which we'll call the Tombstone Express Zone. Serviced by the Tombstone Express Quad, this area has a nice, long blue run, *Another World,* which is good for warming up (beware of the steep drop at the end of the run; it can be avoided by taking *Tranquility*), as well as many short south-facing black runs. Tombstone also has a great double blue called *Cloud Nine* and an easy blue back to Red Pine called *Red Pine Road.* Be aware of your skiing exposure—the southern exposures tend to have much less snow.

The highest zone is the 99-90 area. This area is serviced by 99-90 Express lift and provides advanced black runs in a more Alpine-like setting. Much of this zone is above tree line, and you have the sense of Big or Little Cottonwood Canyon skiing.

Working our way south we have the Peak 5 Zone. This area has steep double blacks, gladed blacks on the northern exposures and long cruising blue runs that will take you to Dreamscape or to the bottom of Tombstone Express.

The southernmost zone is the Dreamscape Zone. This area has beautiful, mellow blue runs that are named to fit the area: *Bliss, Day Dream, Panorama* and *Snow Meadow,* to name a few.

If there's a downside to these zones, it's the time it takes to reach them. Optimists revel in the countless options you encounter between the base area and the top of *99-90* or *Dreamscape,* though pessimists will lament the four lift rides between the base area and your first run on *Dreamscape* or the round-about, occasionally flat path you have to take to go from *Dreamscape* back to *99-90* or *Peak 5.*

Open Bowls for Beginners

I like the Canyon's beginner slopes. Ride the gondola up to mid-mountain and ski *The Meadows, Showtime,* and *Enchanted Forest,* just to name a few. The Perfect Turn Ski & Board School has a meeting area next to the Red Pine Lodge at mid-mountain.

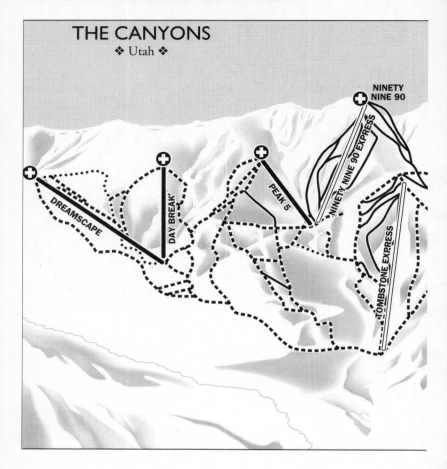

The Canyons' Blues, Intermediate Skiing

There are five intermediate zones where the old ego needn't suffer even a temporary jolt: the Snow Canyon area, the Snow Dancer area, *Another World*, the long and winding *Upper Boa* trail, and the entire Dreamscape area. Snow Canyon can sometimes gum up with people on a busy day. When this happens, head south to the Saddleback or Tombstone region with its dozen or so rolling blues. *Boa,* the longest, most private blue run on the mountain, rolls off the top of Condor into the elbow between the muscular biceps of Condor Ridge and the aspen-dotted forearm of Murdock Peak. Well over a mile long, the top half is delightfully pitched; the bottom half, unfortunately, falls into the cat-track category.

Upper Boa runs alongside a little ravine that, when it fills up with snow, becomes the area's premier natural half-pipe. A completely natural shape,

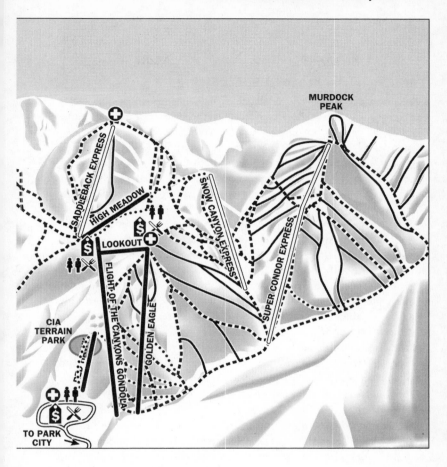

this one is perhaps a quarter-mile long, and fraught with wild surprises: twists and drops and narrows. The locals call it "The James Bond trail."

Dreamscape is rife with ecstasy for cruisers. *Daydream, Panorama,* and the namesake *Dreamscape* blues are built for speed—wide and nicely pitched, each with a handful of tree clusters for contrast. If boredom ever threatens to interfere with those, simply move into *Bliss, McDonald's Meadows,* or *Snow Meadow*, sections of mountain where grooming is forsaken for mogul-building and powder stashes. Boarders beware: the long return to civilization along *Harmony* tests both your momentum and your gliding capability.

The Saddleback Express lift offers a potpourri of terrain. I've had some of my best tree skiing through knee-deep powder cloaked by towering evergreens embraced in "The Pines" that lie just north of the lift. If you prefer aspens over evergreens, head south off the ridge. Mogul-bashers, meanwhile, slice up *Elk Ridge* and *Silver Horse*, while cruisers can make long, looping returns to the lift base on either *Snow Dancer* or *Kokopelli* and *Pine Draw* or *Painted Horse.*

The Call of the Steeps, Expert Skiing

Because most runs flow off the ridgelines, most of the Canyons' steeps are relatively short, fall-line shots from ridge to road (with the exception of the 99-90 area). Similar but ungroomed (hence black) pitches, in fact, surround kestrel, on Condor's north-facing escarpment. *Aplande* is the longest. *Devil's Friend* has the heinous bumps. Snow Canyon also has a popular bump run off its evergreen north side. It's called *Powder Chute,* but all you'll find here are large bumps; it's used as the local mogul-contest site.

The back side, or sunny side, of Condor Ridge features a string of very steep runs through the oakbrush into *E Z Street* gully. You have to lean out from *Apex Ridge* to follow their descent. Like the little girl of the nursery rhyme with the curl in the middle of her forehead, they can be very, very good, but when they are bad, they can be horrid. When there is snow, they are some of the steepest lines anywhere, but the extreme solar exposure and the relatively low elevation pretty much guarantee that there will not be good cover for much of the winter.

The top terminals of the Tombstone and 99-90 lifts also access runs as steep as a cow's face. When snow conditions allow, *Grande* and *DeShutes* just north of the Tombstone lift and *Red Pine Chutes, Charlie Brown,* and *Magic Line* on the northern flanks of 99-90 lead you down steep lines through the trees.

When the powder comes to the Canyons, the best skiing and riding is in the natural bowls: *Dreamscape,* the area's southern boundary, *Murdock Bowl,* up at the area's western boundary, and the 99- 90 area on the far southwestern boundary. *Murdock* and *99- 90* bowls face east-northeast, so it's best to ski or ride them early in a powder cycle.

Dreamscape is an intermediate area that was added in 2000–2001. It takes a while to get there, but the skiing and riding is fun—shot blue and double-blue runs and great glades. It's wonderful powder skiing. The area is accessed by riding Peak 5. Peak 5 also has some fun riding and skiing—blue and double-pitches with trees. It can have some of the best powder on the mountain because the snow stays dry in the trees. Peak 5 also accesses the Colony's ski-in/ski-out five-acre lots and two very long intermediate runs, *Crowning Glory* and *Harmony,* which take you back to Tombstone.

Murdock Bowl is a little different. It too faces the morning sun, but it keeps its powdery texture in stands of aspens and even receives infusions of fresh wind-driven crystals from time to time over the boundary ridge.

To add to its charm, *Murdock Bowl* requires a short but stiff hike of about 500 vertical feet from a saddle below the Condor top terminal. You'll see snowboarders' snaky S-shaped tracks peeling off the hiking trail almost every day of the season. Two-skied trekkers have the option of traversing the full breadth of the bowl to a marvelous, pure line called *Ocelot.* You can't yo-yo *Murdock Bowl,* and it stays pristine for that reason.

The view from the top of *Murdock Bowl* is one of the best on the Wasatch back side. To the east, across Parley's Park, you can see the Uinta Mountains, a rugged and largely wild range culminating in Utah's highest point, 13,528-foot Kings Peak. To the north, the Wasatch rolls toward Snowbasin, and Powder Mountain, the Ogden Canyon areas. To the west, through a notch between peaks, you can catch a snippet of the Salt Lake Valley. To the south (sigh) is the softly curvaceous, timberline terrain of Red and White Pine Canyons (some of the Utah Powderbird Guides' favorite landing sites), and the country the Canyons might have been built on but wasn't quite.

Snowboarding

The friendly jockeying between Park City Mountain Resort and The Canyons for snowboarders might cost the two resorts a substantial amount, but it benefits riders immensely.

At The Canyons, boarders don't even have to step on the gondola to catch some air. Just uphill from the base day lodge is the "CIA" terrain park (aka Canyons International Airport), with more than two dozen rails and roughly 30 snow features, including a 60–65 foot cheesewedge kicker. The fun doesn't go down with the sun, either, as the park is wired for night lights and sound.

If you do board the gondola, though, it'll take you to some of the Wasatch Range's most creative terrain features. Make the trek to *Upper Boa* and you'll discover a twisty ravine that is the area's premier natural half-pipe. Officially known as *Canis Lupis,* but dubbed "the James Bond trail" by locals, the steeply banked pipe rambles for about a mile and tests your reactions with its sudden changes.

Elsewhere at The Canyons are five other natural pipes lying in wait.

Lunch on the Hill

There are four places to eat at the Canyons: one at the base, which tends to be overrun on weekends; one on Lookout Peak, called **Lookout Cabin,** which has the big view; the **Sun Lodge** at the bottom of the Snow Canyon lift; and the most popular lunch spot, the **Red Pine Lodge,** at the top of the Flight of the Canyons gondola. I prefer the Sun Lodge— the food is great, there is an enormous sun-soaked deck complete with barbecue grill, and you avoid the crowds that can jam the Red Pine

Lodge. If you decide to spend the day at Dreamscape, it's not much, but **Chuck's Grill** (outdoor) across from the lift can provide some sustenance to keep you going. For some relaxing at day's end, try **Doc's,** conveniently located in the **Grand Summit Hotel** across from the gondola.

Après-Ski

The Canyons' Euro-style village offers a handful of options, such as Doc's and **Smokie's Smokehouse.** Also, Park City is only four miles away (see the Park City section, In Town: Eating, Sleeping, and Other Forms of Rejuvenation, page 326), and there is an efficient shuttle that runs from 8:20 a.m.–4:45 p.m.

The Canyons Data

Mountain Statistics

Vertical feet	3,190 feet
Base elevation	6,800 feet
Summit elevation	9,990 feet
Longest run	2.5 miles
Average annual snowfall	355 inches
Number of lifts	16: 5 high-speed four-person chairs; 4 fixed-grip quads; 1 eight-person gondola; 1 double; 2 triple; 1 high-speed eight-person cabriolet; 2 surface lifts
Uphill capacity	25,700 skiers per hour
Skiable terrain	3,500 acres
Opening date	Late November
Closing date	April 15
Snowboarding	Yes

Transportation

By car About 40 minutes from Salt Lake International Airport via I-80 east through Parley's Canyon to State 224 south and the Canyons Drive. The Canyons is 4 miles north of Park City.

By bus, limo, or taxi From Salt Lake International Airport, and by regularly scheduled shuttle from the Park City/Deer Valley area.

By plane Via major carriers to Salt Lake International Airport.

Key Phone Numbers

Ski-area information	(435) 649-5400
Snow report	(435) 615-3456
Reservations	(888)-CANYONS
Website	www.thecanyons.com

Inside Story

Avalanche Hunters

When the Forest Service got involved with recreational skiing at Alta in 1938, it was an invitation for disaster. The fine skiing in Collins Gulch and the new chairlift constructed from remnants of a silver ore tram were drawing thousands of skiers into a canyon that had already seen 100 miners die in avalanches.

Turn-of-the-century boomtown Alta was battered repeatedly by slides emanating from Rustler Mountain to the south and Flagstaff and Superior to the north. At the time the situation was exacerbated by the total deforestation of these slopes for mine timbers and building lumber. The trees were making a comeback by the time skiing started, but natural slidepaths, on the ski slopes and hovering above the canyon road, still made being there on certain days a risky proposition. The Forest Service (and Alta Ski Lifts) quite properly felt a responsibility toward these new enthusiasts.

In 1941, they hired Sverre Engen, Alf's brother and fellow competitor on the professional jumping tour, to be Alta's first snow ranger. Sverre's job was to watch the accumulation of snow and determine to the best of his judgment when the avalanche danger warranted closing certain trails on the mountain, and ultimately closing the road from the valley. World War II interrupted Sverre's work, but immediately following the end of the war a not-so-young powder lover, Harvard man, and fiction writer Montgomery Atwater, convinced the Forest Service to hire him as snow ranger.

Monty Atwater wanted to do more than just warn people when things were looking scary; he wanted to understand why snow behaved as it did, and he wanted to see if he couldn't figure out some way to *prevent* dangerous slides. Although not a trained scientist, he nevertheless had a true scientist's curiosity coupled with the physical energy of several people. For a decade, up until the mid-1950s, Atwater wore the multiple caps of father, nurturer, humorist, and one-man gang of American avalanche research.

Atwater noticed that most avalanches occur during or immediately after a storm. He therefore focused his studies on storm measurements and how they affected the snowpack at large. He'd stay up for days and nights during big storm cycles, tromping to his instruments to gauge snow depth, intensity (how fast the snow was coming down per hour), temperatures throughout the storm, crystal types and water content, wind speed and direction. He was the first to accurately describe the formation of the soft slab layers in the snowpack, that made for great powder skiing but that were also responsible for most of Alta's winter (as opposed to springtime wet-snow) avalanches.

He was the first to recognize the potential of explosives in controlling avalanches. Early in his tenure he hiked the mountain in the fall, planting a series of dynamite charges on particularly pesky, cornice-forming ridgelines. Then, in the winter, when the cornices were big enough to threaten slopes below, he blew them up, harmlessly.

But placing bombs for a one-time cleansing was impractical and inadequate. Atwater needed some way to make the slide paths run on a more or less regular basis and therefore compact and stabilize themselves. His first piece of artillery was a nineteenth-century French cannon, monstrous and unwieldy, but he convinced the Forest Service and the Utah National Guard to let him roll it up and down the highway in order to lob shells into start zones high above.

U.S. Army 75- and 105-mm Howitzers were the vogue for a while. Now Alta has a military surplus recoilless rifle permanently mounted on Wildcat Ridge. They use the gun for shooting across the highway at slides that threaten the lodges and the access to Snowbird and Alta. Within the ski area on snowy mornings, patrolmen drop hand charges in known avalanche pockets and fire an air-powered "Avalauncher," a mortarlike device Atwater commissioned in the 1950s. Avalaunchers are much cheaper but somewhat less accurate than the big military hardware. (Ski patrolmen at Snowbasin were practicing with their new Avalauncher a few years back and missed the ridge entirely, sending a projectile through the garage roof of an unlucky Ogdenite five miles away.) Today every ski area and highway department with avalanche problems uses some combination of ordnance and tactics devised by Monty Atwater at Alta.

One morning recently I woke before dawn and joined the Alta ski patrol for the firing of the big gun. It had snowed 17 inches overnight and 26 inches in the last two days. The road was closed. The tiny valley was on "interlodge" alert—that is, all guests and employees were required to stay indoors while the control work was going on.

We shoveled off the gun platform. One man went down in the concrete bunker to hand up ammunition; each shell is about three feet long and weighs 30 pounds. A second man dialed in the exact coordinates of likely start zones on Mount Superior across the way. A third man loaded the shell and locked the breech. I stood as close as possible to the barrel, where the concussive force is smallest, and held my hands over my ears.

The blast was shattering, the predawn sky briefly aflame. It was still too dark to see if our shot had done any good, but a voice over the radio, from an observer down in the valley, said we kicked off a "small" one, 3,000 vertical feet down to, but not over, the highway.

We fired a dozen shots. Gradually, the sky grew pink, then golden. Behind us on the ski trails, teams of patrolmen followed their prescribed routes. The Avalauncher team caused a small but dramatic slab to release on Sugarloaf Mountain, snow pouring over the cliffs like sugar. Another team, cutting across the High Traverse, forced sluffs in *Sunspot* and again on *West Rustler* and *Stonecrusher*. By eight o'clock the road was open, and by nine the first powderhounds were riding up the mountain, eager to ski this new snow with the impunity we have all come to take for granted.

Mysteries still abound regarding snow and snowslides. What causes late releases, for example, days and even weeks after a storm? How and why does the snow change over time deep in the snowpack, creating weaknesses and instability? Research continues here and in Europe and Japan. The Forest Service, sadly, is no longer as committed as it once was to such inquiry. Monty Atwater has moved on, leaving behind most of the avalanche terminology we use today and a wonderful book called *The Avalanche Hunters*. He is replaced by a tiny cadre of dedicated disciples.

Meanwhile, ski slopes have never been safer, and snow remains one of the least understood, most volatile solids on the planet, and one of the most romantic.

Sundance

Over dinner at the Blind Miner in Brighton one evening, I eavesdropped on a telling conversation. The gentleman at the next table had ventured down to Sundance, east of Provo, for a day of skiing. His distaff compan-

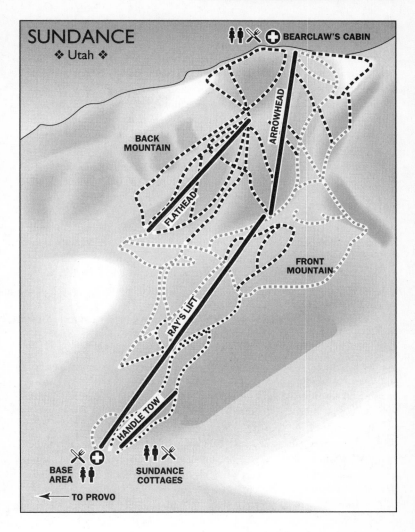

ion lit up instantly. "Did you see *him*?" she asked, eyes as big as saucers.

He, of course, is Sundance's owner and guiding spirit, Robert Redford. Ole Blue Eyes actually lives here. He's been married to a Utah girl for over 35 years and has been a voting resident of Utah County, south of Salt Lake City, for more than 30 years. When he doesn't have to be in New York or Los Angeles, Redford—the outdoorsman, family man, and skier—is home in Sundance. You might just see the star of *Butch Cassidy and the Sundance Kid, Out of Africa, Downhill Racer, Horse Whisperer,* and *All the President's Men* in jeans and running shoes, on his mountain bike, or on the slopes, where he has named three of the runs after his kids. Locals refer to him as Bob.

Sundance feels like a rustic, private club. Menus and guest guides are printed on heavy, textured paper. Area literature makes frequent use of the first person plural, as in "we the Sundance community" and "who we are and what we believe in." And yet the clubbish atmosphere is also welcoming: "We want to help you find those elements of the Sundance experience which will most meet *your* needs, *your* dreams."

Condominiums, called "cottages" (Redford hates the word "condominium"), dot the aspen and spruce forest just west of the ski area base. Small in scale and carefully placed for minimum impact on the landscape and their neighbors, they are constructed of rough-hewn spruce and decorated with down comforters and Indian art. They smell like a forest campsite. All facilities are elegantly spare and discreetly luxurious.

To put Sundance in a Utah perspective: Where Deer Valley's opulence is splendid, self-conscious, and even self-congratulatory, Sundance is purposely understated and thus even more exclusive, a perfect place for one of the most recognizable faces on the planet to disappear into the rough-cut woodwork.

Exclusive though it may be, 80% of the ski business is local. Sundance is just 13 miles from downtown Provo. Provo is Utah's second largest city; it's built on the shore of giant Utah Lake, which is connected via the Jordan River to the Great Salt Lake in the north. Provo has a population of 75,000, is the home of Brigham Young University, and a major hub for mining, agriculture, and manufacturing. Provo folks have been skiing at Sundance (before it was called Sundance) since the 1940s.

At the turn of the century, a Scottish immigrant family, the Stewarts, settled this little side valley off the Provo River to raise sheep on the flanks of Mount Timpanogos. Second-generation Stewarts built a rope tow on one of their mountains in 1947. By the 1950s, it was known as Timphaven and boasted a chairlift, the original rope tow, and a burger joint named Ki-Te-Kai, Samoan for "Come and get it!" (One of the Stewarts had been called to a Mormon mission in the islands.)

Redford bought Timphaven and much of the surrounding land from the Stewarts in 1969 and named it after his most famous movie role. He began the slow process of upgrading the ski facilities and built his own house in a high, south-facing meadow across from the ski hill. In 1980 he created the Sundance Institute "to support and encourage work in independent filmmaking." There is an intimate, 200-seat screening room in the pines by the creek and a cinema workspace where Redford's own *Milagro Beanfield War* was edited. Here film-making labs have been hosted in the past by Paul Newman, Sydney Pollack, and Alan Alda, among others. In 1985, the institute took over sponsorship of the

United States Film Festival in Park City, and the event has since grown into one of the world's premier showcases for new independent films.

In 1981, Redford initiated the project that may be closest to his soul, the Sundance Institute for Resource Management. The IRM has sponsored conferences at Sundance and elsewhere on such topics as water development in the West, the mining of uranium on Indian lands, and offshore oil drilling in Alaska. Redford is a lover of nature and a believer in preserving natural resources (he has been called worse by Utah development interests), and the IRM, he hopes, will help resolve conflicts between use (or overuse) and preservation of America's wild riches.

If Sundance feels more like a mesquite-grill and eco-romantic hideaway than a ski resort, this is why. The cultural, artistic, and environmental concerns of "the community" have always come first. But the skiing can be exquisite as well, and it hasn't been sloughed off as a secondary amenity. Skiing (along with hiking and biking in the summer) is viewed as the physical part of a New Renaissance equation, something that Snowbird's Dick Bass has described as a rejuvenation "of body, mind, and soul." Redford loves to ski, he is good at it, and his hiring of former Demo Teamer Jerry Warren to be director of skiing is a strong sign that he is committed to improving the mountain.

Warren is a local Springville, Utah, boy who used to stow away on the bus up to Timphaven when he was a kid. He became a protégé of Junior Bounous, a Provo native, and spent years teaching at Snowbird under Bounous, where he worked his way to eminence in the rarefied world of international ski instructor associations and demonstration teams. Warren taught Redford's kids to ski and more than once filled the boss's head with enough technical ski talk to make him completely forget the stresses of his public life. Now the two of them are working on ways to integrate some of the Sundance Institute's more idealistic concepts into ski teaching and vice versa.

Sundance's Mountain

Mount Timpanogos dominates the Wasatch skyline above Provo. It is a hulking, monolithic presence with an uninterrupted fall of nearly 8,000 feet from its summit to the valley floor. Horizontal rock bands stripe its upper slopes, giving the mountain a look similar to the Italian Alps. Sundance sits on the southeast shoulder of the big peak, well below the multiple summits (in fact out of sight of the actual high point) but high enough at the top lift terminal to gain a spectacular view of Utah Lake to the south and Deer Creek Reservoir and the Heber Valley to the northeast. Sharp eyes can pick out the back side of Snowbird's Hidden Peak and Alta's Baldy and Sugarloaf; Park City's Jupiter Peak is just out of sight.

Park City is about 35 minutes away, and although the creek that tumbles through Sundance's narrow valley eventually flows west into Utah Lake, the area really belongs to the Wasatch back side. As with Park City's three areas, there is a discernible snow shadow (although 325 inches is more than plenty most years). The morning sun is dominant, and late afternoons are spent in the blue shade of the divide.

Sundance has two ski mountains, one in front of the other. Though the trail map doesn't indicate names for the two peaks, locals call them Front Mountain and Back Mountain. There are three chairs total, one on the front and two on the back, plus a beginners' handle tow. Front Mountain is the easier one, providing all of the beginner/novice terrain with a few blues and blacks thrown in. Back Mountain, which claims the area summit at 8,200 feet, is primarily expert with a smattering of the most popular intermediate runs off the top. Skiing between the two mountains was problematic until 1995, when the new Ray's lift quad solved the lack of linkage between Front and Back.

The Sundance base, at 6,000 feet, is quite low by Utah standards. The exposure is good—mostly north-facing—but the warmer temperatures at this elevation mean the area has a somewhat shorter season than its neighbors. A recently initiated snowmaking program on the lower slopes should help.

Sundance is never crowded. The record busy day was 1,400 people a couple of years ago. The parking lot simply will not hold more, and Bob Redford refuses, even if there were room in the cramped, woodsy valley bottom, to make it bigger. Nice.

The Skiing

Ray's lift has a mid-station where you can get off. This is handy for riders and skiers who want to yo-yo the bottom half of the mountain.

Most ski and snowboard school classes are taught from this station on down. There are a couple of nice greens, *Stampede* and *Center Aisle* that are in sight of slopeside lodging. The *Maverick* run off the Ray's lift summit station is fine, rolling blue terrain. This is also where the race courses are set up.

Above the mid-station on Ray's, the terrain jumps steeply to the Front Mountain high point. All of the skiing and riding here is black diamond and deservedly so. Sometimes *Buntline* is groomed, transforming it into a steep but makeable plunge for intermediates.

Arrowhead, on the Back Mountain, is the best intermediate zone and also the most likely to be busy, as this lift is the only route to the summit.

Most skiers and boarders are intermediates. But as Jerry Warren and Bob Redford readily admit, there isn't quite as much intermediate cruising as they'd like to have. *Bearclaw* is just about it. Two feeder runs, *Jamie's* and *Amy's Ridge,* named for Redford children, add a little variety.

But after a while you find yourself swishing down the same big humps and grooves run after run. Take a break and stop into the Warming Hut on top. The views make the walk out the back door to the outhouses doubly rewarding. There are no trees. It feels higher than it is. The awesome presence to the west is Chablis Peak, one of the false summits of Timpanogos, looming 3,000 feet above the Warming Hut. Provo Canyon drops sharply away to the south, and the rest of the Wasatch stretches to the north.

Inside the hut you'll find stills of the fabled Tenth Mountain Division in training, and leather rucksacks, ice axes, ropes, and crampons—early-day trappings of hardy mountaineers—hang from the rafters. A fieldstone-clad fireplace hugs a wall, and good homemade chili, wraps, soups, and chocolate chip cookies are served at the bar. On the way out the door, there's a separate trash barrel for your recyclable aluminum cans, a typically aware Sundance detail.

Expert Skiing

Experts have more options off the top than do intermediates. *Shauna's Own* (the third Redford progeny) follows the ridgeline east to circumnavigate the marvelously spacious *Bishop's Bowl.* Though the bowl is signed for experts, perhaps a nod to East Coasters, this spacious ballroom can be handled by capable intermediates. Out beyond *Shauna's,* the ridge becomes *Far East* and features a series of very steep, very interesting glade runs through mixed aspens and evergreens to the gully-bottom *Pipeline. Pipeline* is not much more than one snowcat wide. When it is groomed, it is fun; when it is not, it can be a trial.

The return road from *Pipeline* deposits you at the base of Flathead lift. Strong-skiing locals and off-duty ski instructors are enamored of Flathead. You can't get to *Bishop's* or *Shauna's* from here (without also riding the Arrowhead lift), but Flathead has *Grizzly Ridge* and *Grizzly Bowl,* along with several other semifierce black runs. (With a winch cat, a high-tech grooming vehicle that can cut moguls on steeper terrain than regular snowcats, Sundance could groom a fair percentage of *Bishop's* and *Grizzly,* thus opening up new terrain for intermediate skiers.)

The big mogul runs are off the west side of the *Amy's/Grizzly* ridge, down through evergreen corridors to *Bearclaw. Quick Draw, Hawkeye,* and *Junior's* grow some pretty big ones, though they're never in the same league with Alta's or Snowbird's; there just isn't enough skier and rider traffic here.

When you get ready to move around to Front Mountain again, you have two options. Ride out of the hollow on Ray's lift or ski the *Sunnyside Access* road cut around the flank of Front Mountain.

Snowboarding

To skier's left of Arrowhead's top terminal, *Hill's Headwall* is a relatively short, steep pitch, but its natural kickers and aspen glades draw boarders looking for air all day long.

Eating and Sleeping at Sundance

I've already mentioned the cottages hidden away in the trees. There are 37 of them. With the addition of another 15 or so rental cabins, Sundance's bed base can accommodate 225 guests—not enough to create a lift line on even one of the chairlifts. (Sundance will grow, but not very much, according to Jerry Warren. "He [Bob] wants to develop, but he doesn't want to be big, to destroy the close, connected ambience.") Some Sundance skiers stay at Park City and drive over (about 35 minutes) for the day. It's not a bad hour drive from Salt Lake City either. Inevitably, **Provo** is the closest nonresort lodging. The **Excelsior Hotel** on Center Street was recommended to me by the Sundance staff. If you can swing it, though, stay in one of the cottages. They provide the ambience Redford intended for Sundance, and they are among the most charming ski accommodations you'll find anywhere.

If anything, Sundance eating is even better than Sundance sleeping. There are two restaurants in the rustic little General Store building across the creek from the lift base. **The Grill** serves breakfast, lunch, and dinner, while the **Tree Room** serves dinner only. The food is simple and delicious: linguini, tortellini, grilled chicken, fresh trout, pheasant, range-fed lamb. One evening there was a shark-and-clam soup I will not soon forget. Many of the herbs and spices are grown at Sundance Farms over in the Heber Valley. The wine selection is superior to that of most resort restaurants with the possible exception of Deer Valley's.

The Tree Room has a large, dead spruce spearing the ceiling and a nice chunk of Bob's southwest Indian art collection scattered about, including some exquisite Navajo rugs and Hopi kachinas. The Grill is more cowboy, with a big stone fireplace, saddles, and chaps and Remingtonesque bronze buckaroos.

Sundance Data

Mountain Statistics

Vertical feet	2,150 feet
Base elevation	6,100 feet
Summit elevation	8,250 feet
Longest run	2 miles
Average annual snowfall	325 inches
Number of lifts	3: 1 quad; 2 triples

Sundance Data (continued)

Mountain Statistics (continued)

Uphill capacity	5,800 skiers per hour
Skiable terrain	450 acres
Opening date	Late November
Closing date	Late March
Snowboarding	Yes

Transportation

By car From Provo, 13 miles via Highways 189 and 92, the Alpine Loop. From Park City, about 35 minutes south via U.S. 40 and 189. From Salt Lake City, about 1 hour via I-15, off at exit 275, Highway 52 to 189.

By bus, limo, or taxi From Salt Lake International Airport.

By plane Via major carriers to Salt Lake International Airport.

Key Phone Numbers

Ski-area information	(801) 225-4107
Snow report	(801) 225-4100
Reservations	(800) 892-1600
Website	www.sundance-resort.com

Ogden Area

Snowbasin   A maturing gem barely 60 minutes north of Salt Lake City, Snowbasin offers a cornucopia of skiing and snowboarding: expansive bowls, vertigo-inducing chutes, great tree runs, natural half-pipes and terrain parks. So far there are no condos, but you will find a luxurious base lodge and two on-mountain day lodges that might have been plucked from country clubs they're so sumptuous. Little was spared in the lodges' construction; they feature hand-hewn timbers, vaulted ceilings and exposed beams, cavernous fireplaces, marble tabletops, and made-to-order menus. While the lodges are just the places for relaxing between runs or at the end of the day, it's the terrain that defines this mountain, challenging terrain that staged the downhills for the 2002 Winter Olympic Games. The well-oriented lift system, which includes two gondolas, serves terrain that rivals Alta's for variety, surprise, and pure, unbulldozed challenge. Great beginner and intermediate shapes as well. While Ogden can't match Salt Lake City bar-for-bar and restaurant-for-restaurant, you'll still find some appealing accommodations, a nice variety of eateries, and enough watering holes to quench your thirst.

Powder Mountain   With the same snowfall numbers as Alta (500 inches per season) and twice the acreage (5,500 acres, all private land), Powder Mountain delivers on its name. Across Pineview Reservoir from Snowbasin, the area offers snowcat skiing and riding and a return shuttle bus on the back side to keep beyond-the-ropes powderhounds happy. Most of the mountain is gently rounded, great for intermediates—skiers and boarders. Very limited lodging in minuscule, bucolic Eden down the hill.

Snowbasin

Snowbasin is the Alta of the northern Wasatch. That is to say, you'll find steep, open terrain here, with real timberline bowls and jagged peaks that justify the name "Needles." North of Snowbasin, the craggy profile of the range softens; the ridgelines are rounder and less alpine on their way to the Idaho border. So this upthrust, bolting dramatically above Ogden and the Great Salt Lake, is a kind of last hurrah for classic, Alta-like landscape.

Snowbasin, venue for the 2002 Olympic Downhill and Super G, compares favorably with its better-known brethren to the south. This is real Utah skiing—plenty of fine dry snow (400 inches a year), inviting, natural shapes, and not a whole lot of trees to get in the way.

Snowbasin also nearly matches Alta in longevity. In 1936, the city of Ogden turned this watershed basin over to the Forest Service for possible recreation development. In 1940, Forest Service recreation adviser (and Alta pioneer) Alf Engen visited the area and recommended that a ski area be created. They didn't wait around. On December 23 of that same year, Snowbasin held its first race, hosting 75 ski racers.

This part of Utah, north of Salt Lake City and east of the lake, bills itself as the Golden Spike Empire. Representatives of the Union Pacific and Central Pacific railroads drove the final spike, a golden spike, to complete the linkup of the first transcontinental railroad at Promontory, Utah, in 1869. Ogden has been the hub of this transportation/agriculture empire since Peter Skene Ogden, a Hudson Bay Company man and trapping party leader, first camped here in the early 1800s. Now the empire has expanded to include skiing and snowboarding, (which debuted in Utah at Powder Mountain in 1981). The resorts are not nearly as well known or as busy as the central Wasatch heavies (in fact, they are little more than day areas with muscular, destination-area physiques), but that just makes them even better discoveries.

From downtown Ogden, eight miles and 1,000 vertical feet up precipitous Ogden Canyon you pop suddenly into the open and broad snowbound saucer of Ogden Valley. Pineview Reservoir fills the valley lowland. The one town in the valley, Huntsville, sits at the edge of the lake surrounded by rich farmland, soil that not so very long ago (perhaps 25,000 years ago—a mere blink in geologic time) was on the bottom of Lake Bonneville, the huge ancestor to the Great Salt Lake. The valley is ringed by mountains, ancient shorelines cutting strange, straight lines in their foundations. Imagine a teacup of a valley with a rim of peaks. Snowbasin's ski runs pour in from the southwest rim, while Powder Mountain perches squarely on the north slopes.

Snowbasin impressively landed on America's skiing map with the competition of the 2002 Olympics as the resort hosted the downhill and Super G races. And, in return for hosting those races, Snowbasin leveraged a land swap with the Forest Service, a swap that opened the way for a destination village at the base. The area's parent company, the same folks who own Sun Valley Resort and Little America Hotels, know a

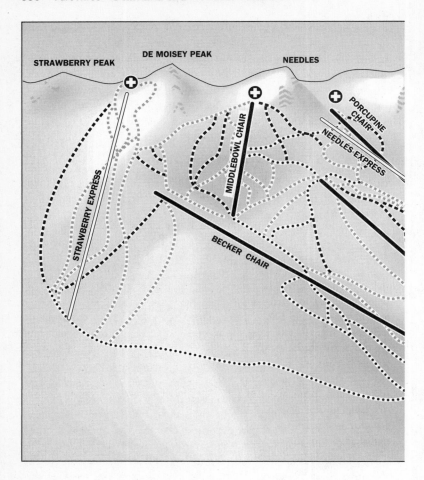

thing or two about luxury destination resorts. Snowbasin foresees a bright future!

Snowbasin's Mountain

Snowbasin proper occupies the center of a freestanding, five-peak ridge. The middle rock, which rises 9,010 feet, is appropriately called the Needles. (The giant molding forces of the Wasatch Fault have turned the rock layers on end, creating vertical striations of snow and stone, ivory and ebony, like a keyboard.) To the west is Allen's Peak, at 9,465 feet, and to the east is Strawberry Peak, at 9,265 feet. The lift-served terrain climbs to 9,350 feet, just below the summit of Allen's Peak and at the top of the Olympic Tram. You will see a small start house on your right as you travel

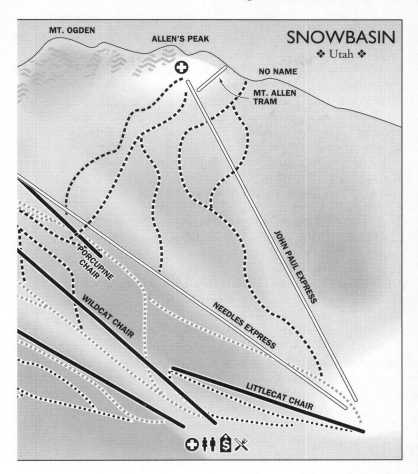

up the 15-passenger tram. This is the start of the Men's Olympic Down-hill. Swiss legend Bernard Russi designed the downhill race courses for the 2002 Winter Olympics and was determined to make this men's course one of the world's toughest. Its precipitous start down *Ephraim's Face*, double fall-line traverses, sweeping turns and air-inducing humps, accomplished that task. If this expert run seems too daunting as you near the top on the tram, don't panic, as you can ride it back down.

Snowbasin has lively intermediate pitches, particularly in *Porcupine* and *Middle* bowls as well as 90% of the Strawberry area. You can ski or ride the bowls in 1,200-foot chunks or follow the two natural drains all the way down for the full 3,400-vertical-foot ride. Strawberry has great cruising from top to bottom giving you almost 2,500 feet of vertical with a nine-minute ride aboard the eight-passenger Strawberry Express gondola back to the top. Beginners have a separate first-time area and a number of fine routes on the mountain as well. Experts will have to look hard for moguls (the old Utah "problem" of too much terrain and too few skiers to bump it up), but there is challenge in the timberline wild snow, in the powder glades, and on the few short steeps sprinkled around the hill. Boarders have endless acres to roam, and the terrain is cut with plenty of gullies, that double as serpentine half-pipes, such as the unlabeled *Gordon's Gulch* that wiggles from *Elk Ridge* over to *Last Chance*.

Nine lifts serve an efficient 3,200-acre layout. Traffic is practically nonexistent. Fall lines flow naturally, like designer clothes on a super model. Alf Engen knew a good ski hill when he saw one.

The Gentle Side of Snowbasin, Skiing for Beginners

The Littlecat lift off to the west of the base lodge is a fine beginners' zone. It has a gentle pitch, lots of room to roam, and is safe from faster traffic. Off to the skier's left from Littlecat is a stand of trees the local children have dubbed *Garfield's* after the cartoon cat. Every year they groove some wonderful hobbit trails in there, mini–roller coasters around the trunks. It's perfect play terrain for kids. Just beware if they say, "Follow me, Dad!" I nearly lost my hat a couple of times to low-lying branches.

After the Littlecat, novices (that is, beginners who have learned to turn and stop) can ride the Wildcat lift up the mountain. From here the *Eas-A-Long* road leads to the wonderfully concave *Bear Hollow* and to *School Hill* and *Snow Shoe,* which add up to 1,300 vertical feet of high-mileage neophyte cruising. Off the other side, the westerly side of Wildcat, *Blue Grouse* is another option. It's marked blue on the map and is steeper in places, but it's well groomed; this is a fine route for lower intermediates and progressing novices.

Blue Grouse also provides access to the Porcupine lift and its easiest blue route, via *Middle Bowl Traverse* and *Board Walk,* off the top. Weather, especially wind and blowing snow, can make this upper-mountain slope more difficult for novices. But it is still possible—a rarity on mountains this big—to ski a gentle blue route top to bottom.

Snowbasin Blues, Skiing for Intermediates

Porcupine, Middle Bowl chair and the Olympic Tram are the upper mountain lifts. Wildcat and Becker serve the lower mountain while Needles Express and John Paul Express travel from bottom to top. Strawberry Express services the Strawberry region, which is east of the base area. Choosing the Needles Express Gondola, it's just a scenic, dry and comfortable nine-minute ride to the top of the mountain. I am partial to the blue skiing and riding up high (as opposed to the lower-mountain blues) because of the fine snow quality and the billowing, ever-varying lines. *Middle Bowl* is loaded with them. *Sweet Revenge, Dan's Run,* and *Bullwinkle* all dart among the isolated trees with a playful esprit; no bulldozer has worked its homogenizing power here.

Over on Porcupine, where there are even fewer trees, *Porcupine Face* and *Race Course* both drop over a precipitous, bald knoll before settling into a cup-shaped gulch. Up here, there isn't a great deal of difference between the blues and the blacks. Some of the expert trails, like *Pork Barrel* right under the Needles, do roll over steeper drops, but by and large, it's the grooming that makes the difference. The blues are kept pretty smooth; the black diamonds are left to nature's whim. The very best intermediate skiing is in the Strawberry Express area. The wide open expanses and beautiful grooming will boost the ego of any intermediate skier or rider. You will be skiing/riding, uninterrupted, for 2,472 vertical feet and have a mere nine-minute gondola ride back up. For experts on their new super carve skis or long alpine boards, this area is paradise. For incredible steeps that open onto treeless flanks that can be choked with powder, venture south to the *Sisters,* or from the top of the lift, make a short hike and traverse to the west behind 9,370-foot De Moisy Peak and drop into *Middle Bowl Cirque* for some steep turns that will deposit you across from the Needles day lodge.

On the lower mountain Becker has the better novice terrain, while Wildcat has the two best intermediate runs in *Blue Grouse* and the glorious *Wildcat Bowl.* Seldom will you see an intermediate groove like this one gouged, as if by a giant spoon, out of the front face of the mountain. (Aspen Mountain's Spar Gulch is the only analogy that comes to mind, and it is shorter and flatter.) *Wildcat Bowl* makes a perfect Super G course for junior racers. Recreational skiers and riders can bank off the ravine's sides at any speed and feel the rush of concave, wavelike gravities.

Advanced Snowbasin

Ski racers in hard turns create artificial gravities in defiance, it seems, of natural forces. Alan Miller, son of longtime Snowbasin ski school director Earl Miller, still remembers a turn the young Phil Mahre made in a race held on *Centennial* trail years before he would become a World Cup and Olympic champion. Mahre apparently cleaved to a line so tenuous that mere mortals would have been off into the oakbrush, but he held it, and the moment stuck in Miller's memory. Racing is a big part of Snowbasin's heritage. In fact, the men's downhill course, *Grizzly,* closely follows the line cut for the 1957 NCAA downhill. The steep trails off the Wildcat ridge, like *Centennial, Bash,* and *Becks,* are perfect for slalom and giant slalom. If there have been no races for a while, these three are likely suspects if you are searching for moguls.

Snowbasin, like Alta, is a powder skier's paradise. There are so many choices, so many lines to be explored on a new-snow morning. You'll

362 *Part Three* **Utah and the Northern Rockies**

find open-slope skiing and riding in upper *Porky's, Main Street, Trappers Trail, Coyote Bowl,* and on either side of the *Middle Bowl* lift line. *Trail 119* is especially nice, plunging over the Roman nose at the base of the Needles. Some of the steepest powder is in the trees off *Philpot Ridge, Allen's Peak,* and *John Paul Trees. Sunshine Bowl* off the east side of the Becker lift is a real sleeper. Like an open book with north-facing evergreens on one page and sun-loving oakbrush on the other, *Sunshine* often harbors untracked snow until late in the day.

Even more tempting is the vast *Strawberry Bowl* domain east of *Philpot Ridge* and the Strawberry Express. Here you will be greeted with 1,400 acres and 2,472 vertical feet of wide-open bowls, gullies, and ridgelines such as the *Sisters* that fall off the resort's southern boundary.

Snowbasin offers classic big-mountain skiing. Thanks to the Salt Lake Games, it's no longer a Little Big Man, just enough out of the way so that its reputation is much smaller than it deserves to be. Rather, it's luring more and more destination skiers who don't mind the drive from Ogden, Salt Lake, or even Park City. And, with the resort's master plan in the works, it won't be long before base lodging is available.

Snowboarding

Snowbasin offers boarders endless acres to roam, and the terrain is cut with plenty of gullies that double as serpentine half-pipes, such as the unlabeled *Gordon's Gulch* that wiggles from *Elk Ridge* over to *Last Chance.*

Boarders were rewarded towards the end of the 2002–2003 season when a terrain park, complete with boxes, kickers, and rails, was installed beneath the upper end of the Porcupine lift, and at press time resort officials were looking for a suitable location for a half-pipe.

Local boarders are partial to *Becker Face* with its natural kickers, tree rails, and natural half-pipe, although the Middle Bowl area also has its share of grinders.

Speed hounds head to the Strawberry area first thing to rip some lines before the sun softens up the snow.

Lodging and Dining Options: Huntsville and Ogden

Huntsville is a sleepy little farming community in the winter, but it does offer a few après-ski options for riders and skiers coming down the hill. By far the most folkloric is the **Shooting Star Saloon** downtown, since 1879 the oldest continuously serving beer bar in Utah, or so Al and Bev will tell you. Al is about six-foot-four, and Bev couldn't possibly be over five feet. Together they serve up 3.2% beer, chips, and wisdom underneath the jackalope nailed above the bar. According to Snowbasin employees, Al and Bev "are like Mom and Dad" to them all. Al and Bev are pretty nice to visitors too.

Finding dinner up in Ogden Valley is a little tougher than finding a beer. The **Jackson Fork Inn,** which also has rooms available, is the place to go for chicken-steak-lobster-style hearty fare. They also do brunch, with eggs Benedict, huevos rancheros, and Belgian waffles. Just down the road is **Chris's,** a cavernous place where you can play pool, drink beer, eat homemade stew, and gander at the world's biggest goose, hanging from the ceiling in front of the fireplace.

Down at the mouth of the canyon in Ogden, I like the **Greenery Restaurant.** They do soups, salads, and things like turkey enchiladas and stuffed spuds for a very reasonable price. Venture deeper into Ogden to Historic 25th Street and you'll discover **Roosters,** a great brewpub with a filling menu, and **Bistro 258** with its inventive cuisine.

Lodging is not as sparse as it was in the valley before the Winter Games. Among your options are the **Jackson Fork Inn;** the **Snowberry Inn,** a charming log-constructed B&B that offers ten suites; **Lakeside Village Condominiums; Moose Hollow** with its condos, and; across Pineview Reservoir toward Powder Mountain, the **Wolf Creek Resort.** Originally a summer-only place, the lodge is now open for skiers too. The units range from adequate to spartan, but there is a hot tub, sauna, and clubhouse, and you get to wake up in the mountains.

Down in Ogden, the **Ogden Plaza Hotel** is a boutique hotel with 137 rooms ensconced in the historic Eccles Building. Purple straight-back chairs and gold-embroidered footstools contrast with the building's original marble flooring, staircases, and walls, lending an art deco fusion to this hotel. If you can, plan your trip for mid-January when the Hof Festival takes over the Golden Spike Events Center. It's a wonderful week of revelry as Ogden celebrates its sister city, Hof, Germany. Live polka music fills the arena, and good German sausages and beer abound. There's folk dancing and yodeling at the events center, and quite a few sweet people in lederhosen strolling about emitting good Bavarian vibes.

Snowbasin Data

Mountain Statistics

Vertical feet	2,959 feet
Base elevation	6,391 feet
Summit elevation	9,350 feet
Longest run	3 miles
Average annual snowfall	400 inches
Snowmaking	580 acres
Number of lifts	9: 2 gondolas, 1 jig-back tram, 1 high-speed quad, 4 triples, 1 double
Uphill capacity	14,650 skiers per hour
Skiable terrain	3,200 acres

Snowbasin Data (continued)

Mountain Statistics (continued)

Opening date	Thanksgiving
Closing date	Mid-April, weather permitting
Snowboarding	Yes

Transportation

By car About 33 miles north of Salt Lake International Airport. Take I-15 north, exit to I-84 east to Mt. Green/Huntsville (#92), and follow the signs to Highway 226. From the north, take the 12th Street exit off of I-15, Ogden to Ogden Canyon; ski area is 17 miles east of Ogden. From Park City, take I-80 north to I-84 at Echo Junction. Continue west on I-84 to Mt. Green/Huntsville (#96) and follow the signs to Highway 226.

By plane Via major carriers to Salt Lake International Airport.

Key Phone Numbers

Ski-area information	(801) 620-1000
Snow report	(801) 620-1100
Ski School	(801) 620-1016
Website	www.snowbasin.com

Inside Story

Aspens

Ronald Reagan may or may not have said, "You've seen one tree, you've seen them all." But it is certainly not true to say, "You've skied one tree, you've skied them all." Skiing an evergreen forest—and in Utah that means mixed Engelmann spruce and alpine fir—is a totally different experience from skiing in an aspen grove. Where evergreen woods are dark and secretive, aspen woods are bright and open. Where evergreens smother sounds with millions of tiny needles, winter aspen glades have no leaves at all and almost no branches; the cries of powder skiers ring across space uninhibited. Skiing around aspens is almost like strolling through an abstract expressionist sculpture, an "installation" of hundreds of cool, slim, gray-green trunks and their hundreds of slim, blue, straight-line shadows.

Adding to the wonder, aspens have "eyes." Actually, they are eye-shaped scars where lower branches have been sloughed off on the tree's climb for light. Some of these eyes have even sent wrinkles into the smooth bark, like smile lines.

Aspens are members of the poplar family, along with willows and cottonwoods and the "Mormon trees" or Lombardy poplars. You'll find them on every ski mountain in Utah, especially in the Park City area and on the lower slopes of Snowbasin. You'll find them in the sun, on east-, west-, and south-facing slopes. Aspens are shade intolerant, although they will occasionally invade a moist north-facing slope—the exception to the rule.

The aspens we see in the Rocky Mountains are known as *Populus tremuloides,* or quaking aspen, because the faintest breeze will set their heart-shaped leaves aflutter. They are deciduous, of course—bare in winter, with pale green leaves in spring and blazing gold leaves in fall. They are an important food source for deer, who nibble new buds, and beaver, who fell aspens for food and lodge-building materials. Look closely and you may find dollar bill–size cuts on some aspen trunks where elk with their great flat front teeth have gnawed their way down from the high country in the deepening fall snows. Early man found that the aspen's inner bark, when chewed or brewed as a tea, was good for reducing fevers. The active compound involved, salicylic acid, became the prime ingredient in aspirin.

Aspens followed the retreating glaciers all over North America. They are aggressive pioneers, filling in newly created habitats such as burned areas or clearcuts. In bright, open spaces their roots send up sucker shoots (all of the trees in a grove are connected underground), and the empty space is quickly filled. In one of nature's great ironies, shade-tolerant evergreens often get a toehold under the aspen canopy. Eventually the conifers, the climax species in the Rocky Mountain ecological cycle, block the aspens' light and take over completely.

So the next time you find yourself gliding through an aspen stand, think of smiling eyes, think sun, think aspirin, and watch the shadows flicker by like the frames of a silent movie.

Powder Mountain

Powder Mountain is a pretty brave name to take in the State of Powder. But in this case, the name is justified. About half an hour from Snowbasin, across Pineview Reservoir on the northern rim of Ogden Valley, Powder Mountain receives an average 500 inches of snow per year, which ties it with Alta and Snowbird for tops in the state.

The storm track is a little different here. Powder Mountain's slopes look down on Cache Valley to the north and an uninterrupted sweep of dairy and ranchland stretching north into Idaho. Northerly storms that might not reach down into the central Wasatch dump an inordinate amount of cold, fine snow on these hills.

Then there is the commitment of Powder Mountain's people to powder skiing and riding. There is a staggering amount of terrain set aside just for wild-snow enthusiasts. You won't find a great deal of lift-served vertical: 1,605 feet by chair and a total of 1,960 feet if you ride the backside shuttle bus. But (and this is a big but) skiable terrain now encompasses about 5,500 acres, making Powder Mountain the single biggest ski mountain in Utah; 2,800 acres are serviced by four chairlifts, one platter lift and two surface tows. 1,200 acres are in the back-side Powder Country realm, and 700 acres are in the snowcat skiing zones beyond the northside boundaries and 800 acres of extreme terrain in the Wolf Creek Drainage. The vast majority of this terrain, all private land, is ungroomed, uncut, unfettered—wild powder country.

Not so long ago, this was all sheep country. Dr. Alvin Cobabe ("*Co* like co-op, *babe* like 'Hi, babe'"—this is a man who is comfortable helping you learn to pronounce his name) and his father ran 3,500 head of sheep and 600 head of cattle on these high ridgelines. One day in 1958 Cobabe,

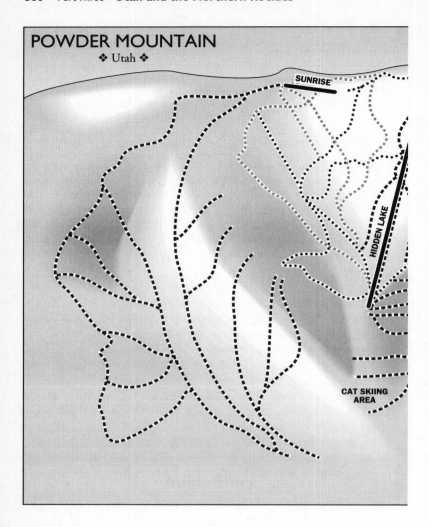

POWDER MOUNTAIN
❖ Utah ❖

SUNRISE

HIDDEN LAKE

CAT SKIING
AREA

who was also an Ogden physician, was riding horseback on Lightning Ridge just west of where the ski area is now, when his companion said, "Boy, that would sure make a good ski run." The first two lifts, Sundown and Timberline, opened in 1972, and it's still a family-run business (although the resort was on the market in 2003). Cobabe's son-in-law is president and general manager, one of his four daughters is involved with the area, and two grandchildren also work there. Now in his 80s, the good doctor has quit his practice downtown and devotes all of his time to the ski business, to the benefit of our physical and mental well-being.

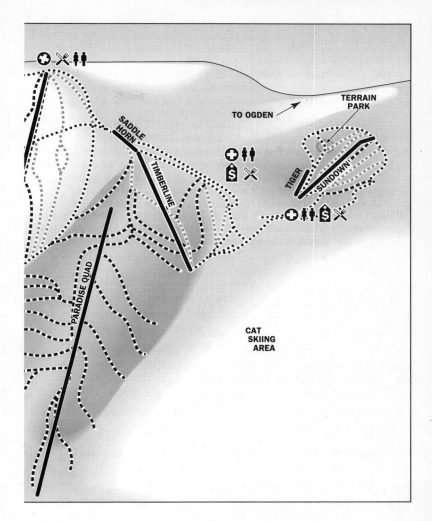

The Shape of Powder Mountain

From Pineview Reservoir and the tiny, one-store town of Eden on its
north shore, the road to Powder Mountain climbs an astonishingly
steep gully into the heart of the mountains. It's a second-gear pull for
most cars and first gear or compound low for many. After a couple of
miles of grinding slowly upward, you round a curve and come rather
suddenly on the Sundown Lodge and the first of three skiing zones. The
Sundown area is the smallest and the gentlest of the three. The
Sundown chair and Tiger surface tow serve a cup-shaped cirque of

northeast-facing beginner and intermediate terrain that is largely separate from the other zones. This is also where the lights blaze after dark for night skiing until 10 p.m.

The road continues beyond the Sundown Lodge, twists back to the east, and ascends the main ridge to the Powder Mountain Lodge and base area. (Imagined from above, the ridges form an elongated question mark: Sundown is in the curl, while the other two zones stretch out along the tail.) The Powder Mountain base is where most skiers, from novice to expert, will begin their day.

Sadly, the road continues up the south side of the ridge to the actual summit of the ski area, where condo projects are scattered in the trees. These provide the only lodging at the area, about 300 beds so far. I say "sadly" because the road snips in half the back-side skiing one can do from the Timberline chair, and the aesthetics of road cuts this high in the mountains leave a lot to be desired. But this is private land, and, as I have said, there is a lot of skiing that isn't affected by roads of any sort.

Adjacent to the Powder Mountain Lodge, the Timberline zone is 900 vertical feet of steep tree shots (with the only moguls to be found on Powder Mountain) and one sublime rolling glen called *Sidewinder*. The Paradise quad, which rises 1,605 vertical feet, climbs along the ridgeline that the neighboring Timberline chair summits more directly. Beneath it, expert runs drop off both sides of the ridge and weave through tree mazes and steep chutes. Farthest east, the Hidden Lake chairlift, the mountain's longest ride at 6,000 feet, opens up a nearly two-mile-wide intermediates,' powder skiers,' and riders' paradise.

The area is so spread out that 2,000 people skiing on a busy day just seem to vanish in the expanse.

Different Slopes for Different Folks, Beginner Skiing

While the Sundown area is not strictly beginner terrain, it is the place for new skiers and boarders just starting out. The Tiger Tow surface lift runs from the day lodge 120 vertical feet up the *Confidence* run. Other trails, like the intermediate *Shot Gun* and the novice *Dead Horse,* merge with *Confidence* up above, so it's not as isolated as it could be. Still, this is the gentlest teaching/learning terrain here.

Skiers and boarders ready to ride a chair will be thrilled by Sundown. Because it is a separate peak, the views from the top are spectacular. Antelope Island rises like a ghost ship out in the middle of the Great Salt Lake. On clear days, you can see mountains in Nevada beyond the lake and the Bonneville salt flats, 140 miles distant. To the east, a knowledgeable eye can pick out peaks in Wyoming, and up to the north the most distant horizons are part of Idaho. The novice skiing on Sundown is limited to three trails—*Confidence, Dead Horse,* and *Slow Poke*—but they are long, mileage-building descents.

Families and groups of mixed ability who nevertheless want to stay together will do well on Sundown because the center of the cirque pitches steeply enough to hold four intermediate blue runs and one black diamond, and everything funnels back to the same lift base. Children under the age of five ski free with their families on Sundown.

Slow Poke stays high on Sundown's west ridge and circles the dish to provide access to the Powder Mountain Lodge a couple of hundred feet above the Sundown Lodge. There is one green run, *Drifter,* in the adjacent Timberline zone. It's a lovely see-forever ridge run, though it seems more blue-green than green. Way out in the Hidden Lake domain are two long, winding greens, *East 40* and the precisely named *Three Mile.* Powder Mountain is so broad that by the time most novices ski or ride over to these trails, they will be able to call themselves intermediates.

Intermediate Skiing

Hidden Lake is intermediate heaven. For about three miles and the full 1,300-foot vertical, you can cruise all day on big swoopers like *Burntwood, White Pine,* and *Hidden Lake Run.* It's cold over here on the north side; the ski patrol calls this lift "Frozen Lake," but that means the snow stays silky. Don't miss the run called *Sunrise* out on the area's east edge. To get there you have to ride the little 100-foot Sunrise surface tow in the saddle. It's well worth it for the views, the late-day sun, and the long, long glade runs that never seem to get skied out. Hardy hikers don't stop on Sunrise Ridge but keep pushing to the eastern edge of the resort where they dive into Cobabe Canyon with its bowls and tree runs. You don't need to be an expert to sample these delights, as *Thimbleberry* and *Buckshot* are geared to intermediates. To return to the lodges from Hidden Lake, your quickest route requires that you ride the Saddle Horn surface lift to the top of Timberline. For a more leisurely return, cruise *Meadow Express,* a wonderfully meandering green, to the Paradise chair and ride it to the top of Timberline.

Expert Skiing

The Timberline zone is primarily black (although the green *Drifter* leads gently down to the lodges). Short, steep fall-line pitches through the trees are called *Dynamite, Exterminator,* and *Runaway.* Together they satisfy the needs of the relatively few mogul mashers here.

The Paradise chair also caters largely to treehounds and bump skiers with blacks that trickle down either side of the ridge and which fill with powder or bumps, depending on the weather. While *Sweet Claim, Medicine Man, Tombstone* and *Saddle Chute* weave through trees, *Quick Shot, Geronimo, Tomahawk, Paradise, Silver Bowl* and *Powder Horn* glide nicely through mostly open meadows.

Expert powder seekers have been discovering Powder Mountain in increasing numbers since the opening in 1983 of what they call *Powder Country* or simply the *Backside*. It was a brilliant stroke. The best steep terrain is on the back side, plunging toward the access road from both the Sundown and Hidden Lake summits. There just weren't any lifts, and the terrain was extreme enough that lifts didn't seem practical. So Cobabe and company decided to open the skiing, when it was safe, and run a shuttle bus up and down the road every 15 minutes to pick up the grinning skiers and snowboarders.

On new-snow mornings the Sundown side, which faces the morning sun (figure that one out), is skied first. Then the hounds move around to the Hidden Lake side, which is even steeper (a good 40 degrees in some spots), more heavily treed, and west-facing. But it never gets completely skied out. There's just too much of it, about 1,200 acres with a maximum vertical of nearly 2,000 feet. I skied untracked snow on both sides of the road one winter, ten days after the last snowstorm.

Snowboarding

Riders long have been welcomed at Powder. In fact, the winter of 1981 saw Powder Mountain become the first Utah resort to welcome snowboarders. While a terrain park can be found off the Sundown Lift between *Confidence* and *Shotgun* and a half-pipe exists alongside the *Hidden Lake Run*, natural half-pipes and terrain features abound. Two natural pipes lie along *Rendevous* and another is in the throat of the long and winding *Cobabe Canyon* run.

Eating and Sleeping

All three day lodges are open for breakfast and lunch. The **Sundown Lodge** stays open through the night-skiing session until 10 p.m. When it comes to après-ski food and spirits, Powder Mountain, like its Ogden Valley neighbor Snowbasin, suffers a bit from its isolation, but there are a few options. Several new restaurants are located in Eden at the bottom of Powder Mountain Road, including **Eats of Eden** (Italian), **General Store** (deli), **Hungry Wolf** (steak, chicken, fish, and pasta dishes) and the **Cellar** (casual pizza/sports bar). Scout out the three eateries in Huntsville (see the Snowbasin section, Lodging and Dining Options: Huntsville and Ogden, page 362), or, as the vast majority of skiers here do, trundle back down the canyon to Ogden. One recommendation that bears repeating is the Shooting Star Saloon in Huntsville, since 1879 the oldest beer bar in Utah. The decor is true western funk, Al and Bev are down-home hosts, and their Shooting Star Burger is a find.

There are approximately 300 rental beds right at Powder Mountain. Demand is strong, though, and short-notice vacancies are rare. For lodging information in the greater Ogden area call the Chamber Bureau at

(800) 255-8824. For reservations, call Golden Spike Empire Travel Region at (800) 554-2741.

Powder Mountain Data

Mountain Statistics

Vertical feet	2,005 lift-served; 1,980 via shuttle bus
Base elevation	6,900 feet
Summit elevation	8,900 feet
Longest run	3 miles
Average annual snowfall	500 inches
Number of lifts	7: 1 quad, 2 doubles, 1 triple, 2 surface lifts, 1 platter tow
Uphill capacity	7,900 skiers per hour
Skiable terrain	5,500 acres 1,600 lift-served
Opening date	Thanksgiving
Closing date	Early April
Snowboarding	Yes
Night skiing	4:30–10 p.m.

Transportation

By car About 55 miles from Salt Lake International Airport via I-15 north; exit at 12th Street, Ogden to Ogden Canyon (State Road 39); Powder Mountain is 22 miles east of Ogden. Or via Trapper's Loop Road from Mountain Green off I-84 east of Salt Lake City.

By airport limo From Salt Lake International Airport.

By plane Via major carriers to Salt Lake International Airport.

Key Phone Numbers

Ski-area information	(801) 745-3772
Snow report	(801) 745-3771
Lodging reservations	(801) 745-3772
Website	www.powdermountain.com

Inside Story

Back Side

Powder Mountain assistant patrol director Dennis Perry met his wife on a rescue off the back side of the Sundown ski terrain. She was planning to ski down to the access road as other skiers had done earlier that day, but she took a wrong turn and ended up in a different drainage. It was a cold, moonlit night. Perry and the search team found her at 2 a.m. fighting through the willows halfway to the valley town of Eden. The two hit it off, and the rest is history.

Would that every backcountry rescue ended so happily. The fact is, backcountry skiing—or off-piste skiing, as the Europeans call it—is a horse of a different color compared to its on-piste, groomed, civilized cousin. The snow can be difficult, crusty, crunchy, sloppy, and heavy; it can embarrass even very good skiers. Or it can be the softest, deepest, most exhilarating snow you've ever encountered. You can get cold skiing out there, very tired, and, even, lost. A trip out of bounds might be the best run of your life, or it might be the worst.

Powder Mountain's back side is not true wilderness. There are signs to aim you the right way, and the ski patrol does sweep the terrain for stragglers at closing time. But—witness the future Mrs. Perry—you can still find trouble out there. Ditto for a sneak peak into White Pine Canyon next to Snowbird or even a day on the Interconnect area-to-area tour. Here are a few hints to make your trip beyond the ropes safer and more enjoyable.

Always go with a partner. Four is an even better number; then if one person gets stuck, someone can stay with him while the other two go for help.

Tell somebody where you're going and when you plan to be back. Set it up so that somebody will miss you if you are late.

Pay attention to the weather. If it's cold or snowing or could get that way soon, bring the gear you'll need to stay warm and dry.

Know where you are and where you plan to end up. Nothing dampens a great powder run quite like overshooting your return traverse and having to slog uphill back to the trail.

Bring along some water and high-energy food, like dried fruit, nuts, or candy. Your friends will think you are a genius. Some back-side skiers go out prepared to survive a night in the open. In a day-pack they carry an extra jacket and a space blanket to conserve body heat. It may seem ultra-cautious, silly even, until you need it.

Talk with the ski patrol about the stability of the snowpack. If there is any question in your mind about the safety of a given slope, don't ski it. *Never* ski in a closed area. Chances are the patrol has a very good reason for closing off a particular slope.

Ski within yourself. Forget looking good; off-piste is not the place for high speeds and hero turns. Ski ugly, if that's what it takes; traverse and kick turn, if that's what it takes. Develop a strong, cautious style, one that will get you down *toute neige, tout terrain,* as the French say, "any snow, any terrain."

Finally, cultivate a backcountry attitude. Respect the winter landscape, respect the steep, the cold, the vagaries of snow, rocks, and trees. The idea, after all, is to go out there, sample the wild, and come back in time for dinner.

Southern Utah

Brian Head Down in "Utah's Color Country," Brian Head attracts skiers from southern California, Nevada, and southern Utah as well as the occasional northerner who's seeking the sun. Two separate mountains, one a fine intermediate cruiser, the other a gentle learning hill, perch at the edge of the red-rock canyon country. Ambience is late-model mall. Lodging consists of two full-service hotels and condos. Families are big, and side trips to Zion and Bryce National Parks (or to St. George for golf) are just down the road.

Brian Head

Fact: San Diego skiers and riders can drive to Brian Head in approximately the same time it takes to reach the quintessential Southern California destination, Mammoth Mountain. On a busy winter weekend it looks as if the beach crowd, minus only the sand, has been transported to the slopes. Snowboarders, those riders of the frozen wave, make up a big portion of Brian Head's business. A full 80% of skier days are logged by veterans of the I-15 route from the greater Los Angeles and Las Vegas metropolises.

Brian Head is the happening place down in Utah's Color Country. It's like another state. Before crossing into Arizona, the Virgin River dips to 2,700 feet in elevation. The climate is semitropical. To the south of Brian Head St. George's palm trees make green splashes against red rocks. You can play golf one day and ski the next.

The Wasatch Range, home to Utah's best-known skiing and riding, remains out of sight to the north. Brian Head sits on the western edge of the high Colorado Plateau, where red-rock highlands meet the dry, beige-colored basin-and-range country that stretches west from here all the way to the Sierras. The land is better known for its national parks than for its skiing or riding. Zion and Bryce Canyons are just minutes away. Capitol Reef, Arches, and Canyonlands National Parks are all within a half-day

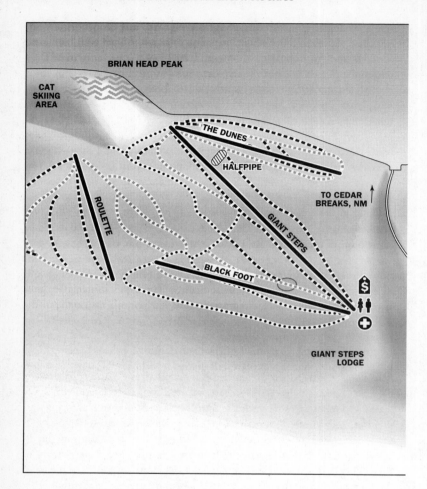

sphere. Portions of Cedar Breaks National Monument are visible from the Dunes (Lift 7) ski terrain. Cross-country ski tours into the pink-and-white columns of Cedar Breaks can be arranged through one of the local ski shops. Locals are fond of skiing to the rim of the monument on moonlit nights, building a bonfire, and watching the night unfold on the edge of the great desert.

Brian Head is isolated, yes, but it is not small. There are 4,000 condo beds; it has a large uphill capacity of 11,000 skiers per hour, and more learn-to-ski and family packages than you could shake a beach towel at. The resort opened in 1965 with a used T-bar and three trailers for a base village.

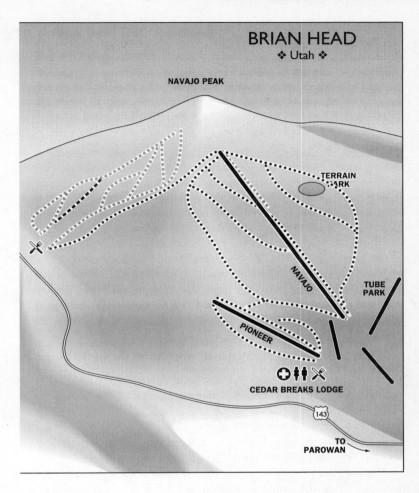

Brian Head is high—the base is 9,600 feet and the top is 11,307 feet—and the same winter jet stream that brings snow to the northern resorts deposits more than 400 inches a year on the forested plateaus. The terrain is not as vast or as spectacular as the glaciated Cottonwood canyons, but the snow quality is unbeatable and the skiing is first rate. Five-hundred thousand San Diegians can't be wrong.

Brian Head Skiing

The skiing takes place on two mountains: a gentle one to the west and a more demanding one to the east. The highway runs north and south through the narrow valley between them, leading to Cedar Breaks,

Panguitch, and Bryce. There are two distinct skiing zones, one on the west mountain, one on the east. Each zone has its own base. They have to, because making the trek across the road and the parking lots from one zone to another is easier said than done. There is a free shuttle system that has recently been improved with larger shuttles and more frequent service, but longtime Brian Head hands admit that the first thing they need is a connector lift or a better way to link the two mountains.

Beginner Skiing

Driving up the quite steep road from the I-15 freeway exit at Parowan, the first skiing and riding you come to is the beginner area, with its two chairlifts and its base, the Navajo Lodge. This is the newer of the two bases, sleek and modern and well set up to accommodate new skiers and boarders, especially children. (There's a terrain garden off to the side that looked like so much fun I had to give it a try.) The Pioneer lift and its trio of debut runs, *First Time, You're Ready,* and *Fun Run,* are as calm a beginner zone as you'll find anywhere. It's completely isolated from faster traffic; you'll never feel a hotshot skier or ripping boarder breathing down your neck. The Brian Head beginner program includes a three-hour lesson with the latest shaped skis for a very reasonable price. Check their website for the current price.

Intermediate Skiing

The Giant Steps Lodge is the main base area. This primarily west-facing zone has four chairs (all triples, including the namesake Giant Steps), the largest vertical at the resort (1,161 feet), and the lion's share of the intermediate and advanced terrain. Shops and services clustered at the Giant Steps base have, wittingly or not, given themselves the perfect California-away-from-home name: the Mall.

A series of mile-long, interconnecting trails weaves through Giant Steps mountain. They are basically quite easy. *Hunter's Run* to *Bear Paw* to *Heavenly Daze* is the easiest, though the intersections sometimes resemble the Hollywood–Golden State freeway interchange at rush hour. *Giant Steps,* right under its namesake chair, is the most popular intermediate route and deservedly so. Skiing and riding it is like floating down an oversize stairway in a Busby–Berkeley musical. The only genuine black diamond is called *Engens* (after the ski pioneer brothers Alf, Sverre, and Corey), and it is never tamed by the snowcats mowing down the moguls. This side of Brian Head is fairly typical of the resort as a whole; it's like a ski parka ski playground. There's nothing particularly grand about the terrain, nothing scary. It's comfortable, uncrowded, a great place to go to learn, to feel unpressured, to feel—in the absence of serious challenge—like a hero, and did I mention uncrowded? Past ski-school director Danny Edwards, talking about powder skiing here, put it in the vernacular: "A foot of new snow is perfect. More than that, it's too flat. Let's face it. Let's get real. We need terrain."

Expert Skiing

Expert terrain, that is. There's plenty of ego-soothing stuff. There are a couple of options now for very good skiers and riders, but they take some work. One is to climb the peak, and, depending on snow conditions, that's a half-hour walk from the top of Giant Steps. (Conditions permitting, a snowcat will take you for a fee.) From the flat mesa top, ski or ride through the gaps in the striated summit cliff bands and down the broad shoulder. Short but exciting. Snow conditions are forever changing, from icy wind crud to premium talcum powder; the peak receives a lot of weather that misses the more sheltered slopes below.

The other option for good skiers and riders is to find a private bower in the trees. There are two fine zones: *Dark Hollow* (big-trunk spruce with plenty of space and a rare, true north exposure) off the north side of the Roulette lift, and *Powder Run* (smaller trees leading to a pair of steeply tilted meadows) off to the left of *Engens* in the Giant Steps region. The ski patrol calls these their "secret jewels." They can be exquisite, but if the snow is old or thin, they can also be nasty. Check with the patrol before you jump in, likewise when walking up to the Peak, and be sure to check out the snowcat skiing in this area.

Snowboarding

Other challenging skiing and riding includes Bear Paw Pitch and five fun terrain parks of varying ability levels where you can get plenty of wall hits, air time, and 360s. A half-pipe is located just off the Giant Steps lift. A freestyle, park a bit gentler than the one on *Bear Paw Pitch*, and an "intermediate" half-pipe is located on Navajo Peak along *Navajo*.

Lodging and Eating at Brian Head

The **Giant Steps Lodge** offers a very basic lunch. The quality of food is not bad, with a simple menu that includes burgers and fish tacos. Next door to the Giant Steps Lodge (downhill) are **Extreme Pizza** and **Bump and Grind.** These small establishments offer reasonably priced good pizza, steaks, pasta, burgers, and great specials. Much better is the cafeteria at **Navajo Lodge;** it's just tough to get there if you've been skiing the east mountain. Don't forget the **Mountain View Deli and Bakery.** You have to have the Brianberry Pie… a locals' bragging-rights special.

Other dining options are the **Lift House,** a reasonably priced steak-and-seafood eatery; the **Cedar Breaks Lodge Double-Black-Diamond Steak House** (Friday and Saturday only); and the **Columbine Café** with steak, seafood, and breakfast buffet.

Parowan, which was settled on Brigham Young's order in 1851 (the oldest Mormon community in southern Utah), provides slightly more distant lodging, 11 miles away. Cedar City, 32 miles south, is a major tourist hub with motels, inns, and cabins galore. The best reason to stay in Cedar City is its proximity to Zion and Bryce, for two unusual, beautiful side trips to a ski adventure.

Brian Head Data

Mountain Statistics

Vertical feet	1,707 feet
Base elevation	9,600 feet
Summit elevation	11,307 feet
Longest run	1 mile
Average annual snowfall	425 inches
Number of lifts	8: 5 triples; 1 double; 2 surface lifts
Uphill capacity	10,500 skiers per hour
Skiable terrain	500 acres
Opening date	Mid-November
Closing date	Mid-April
Snowboarding	Yes
Terrain Parks	5
Snow Tubing	Yes

Transportation

By car 15 miles southeast of Parowan on State Highway 43; 32 miles from Cedar City; 3 hours from Las Vegas; 4 hours from Salt Lake City; and 8 hours from Phoenix and Los Angeles via I-15.

By chartered bus From Las Vegas and Cedar City.

By plane Via major carriers to McCarren International Airport in Las Vegas, with daily connecting flights via SkyWest Airlines to Cedar City.

Key Phone Numbers

Ski-area information	(435) 677-2035, ext. 100
Snow report	(435) 677-2035, ext. 2
Reservations	(888) 677-2810
Website	www.brianhead.com

Inside Story

Side Trips

Brian Head Peak, a flattop snow-and-rock sandwich sitting 400 feet above the ski area's top terminal, looks out over one of the most remarkable landscapes in America. From Cedar Breaks, south to the bottom of the Grand Canyon, a distance of no more than 100 miles, the earth falls away nearly 10,000 vertical feet in a geologic phenomenon called the Grand Staircase. Along the way, billions of years of the earth's history are exposed.

Bristlecone pines, the planet's oldest living trees, inhabit the rim country around Cedar Breaks on the top step, which is easily reached on skis from Brian Head.

The next step down, the Paunsaugunt Plateau, is home to Bryce Canyon National Park. Not really a canyon, Bryce is a series of natural amphitheaters peopled with thousands of goblinesque figures, columns, and pinnacles carved and weathered out of white limestone and orange sandstone.

Southwest of Bryce, the Virgin River gouged Zion Canyon out of rocks that were once wind-deposited sand dunes. The Great White Throne rises straight up 2,394 feet over the grassy valley floor. Farther upriver in the Narrows section, one can touch with outstretched arms both walls of the canyon at the same time. Mountain lions still roam the canyon rims; I have yet to see one, but I have seen roadrunners, eagles, and hawks.

Down go the steps of the Grand Staircase, over the Pink Cliffs, White Cliffs, and Vermilion Cliffs, to the Paria Plateau, overlooking the Grand Canyon. The final step is a big one, 5,000 feet down from the North Rim to the Colorado River. There is no other geologic record like it on earth, so clearly cut are the layers of time. At the very bottom of the canyon, black metamorphic rock, known as Vishnu schist, is estimated to be four billion years old. Grand Canyon National Park is so vast and wild that there are only one or two places to scramble up out of the gorge on the 18-day raft trip from Lee's Ferry to Lake Mead.

All of these places are easy day trips from southern Utah's ski areas, and they are particularly attractive in the off-season (spring and winter) when crowds are sparse and the weather is more bearable.

Another park well worth visiting, though it's not on the Grand Staircase, is Capitol Reef National Park. North and east of Bryce, it was so named because its sandstone domes reminded early geologists of the capitol's architecture, and its colorful, buttressed spires reminded them of coral reefs. You'll find smooth, red-rock cliffs here covered with pre-Columbian petroglyphs as well as Co-Hab Canyon , where polygamists once hid from crusading federal marshals, a place of particular interest to Mormon history buffs.

The Northern Rockies

Jackson Hole "The Big One" has the second-largest lift-served vertical in the United States (behind Big Sky) at 4,139 feet. Not just tall, Jackson Hole has huge breadth of weather, exposure, terrain variety, and challenge, and offers more choices from the top of the famous red tram than at any other lift-served high point in the Rockies. This is adventure skiing and riding with a capital A, complete with a compact base village, the grandeur of the Tetons, and, across the still unspoiled Snake River Valley, good food and good-natured Western hype in the town of Jackson.

Grand Targhee On the other side of the Tetons and facing the sunset (and the spud farms of southern Idaho), Grand Targhee complements Jackson Hole with gentle, undulating, ski- and ride-forever terrain; a cozy, self-contained, hype-free resort; and no crowding ever across 3,000 acres and 2,200 vertical feet. There's no nightlife to speak of and nothing on the hill to scare an expert skier or rider; this is a place to dazzle yourself with your own footwork, eat well, and fall into bed. Plus, there is wonderful snowcat skiing and riding on an adjacent peak.

Big Sky Montana's only master-planned, destination luxury resort sits in the middle of a lot of wilderness within sight of Yellowstone National Park to the south. Big Sky is located on the river where *A River Runs Through It* was filmed and is surrounded by a really, really big sky. Endless low-angle cruising makes a lot of families and intermediates happy. The 1995 opening of a new tram to Lone Mountain's 11,666-foot summit gave Big Sky the vertical crown, by 41 feet, over Jackson Hole and in the process opened an abundance of steep chutes, cliffs, and above-timberline bowls.

Bridger Bowl The midsize, nonprofit, local area for the university town of Bozeman, Bridger became famous as the schooling ground for extreme skiers Scot Schmidt, Doug Coombs, Emily Gladstone, and Tom Jüngst. "Ridge hippies" hike to marvelously intricate steep terrain along the ridge. Mortals find excellent bumps, powder, and groomed snow on the less severe pitches below. It is homey and laid-back—and a real bargain—like the old days. Rooms and eats are 25 minutes away in downtown Bozeman.

The Big Mountain The Big Mountain is a real find up in the northwest corner of Montana by Glacier National Park; it's a long drive from anywhere, but Amtrak runs right through Whitefish, and Kalispell Airport is just 19 miles away. Huge intermediate bowls, rimed "ghost" trees, one super quad, and super reasonable cat skiing off the back side together add up to big skiing. There is some lodging on the mountain; the town is funky and friendly—Aspen 30 years ago. Northern cold and a dearth of sunshine are the only things slowing the rush from Colorado.

Schweitzer Built by skiers from Sandpoint, Idaho, and Spokane, Washington, who were weary of the long drive east to the Big Mountain, Schweitzer is a near twin in scale and possibility: 2,400 feet vertically, 2,500 acres, and myriad lines off the ridges. It has superb intermediate bowl skiing with steeper glades virtually untouched, so few are the experts. Giant, old-growth cedars on the back side, night skiing, a secluded terrain garden for kids, and a beautiful new upscale hotel and base facilities make the journey from anywhere worthwhile.

Sun Valley The queen of Rockies resorts claims the world's first chairlift (1936) and some of the world's longest, most continuous fall-line skiing and has long been a magnet to stars, from Clark Gable to Arnold Schwarzenegger. Most lodging and dining is decidedly and unapologetically upscale, as are the crowds of well-dressed, silver-maned cruisers working their giant slalom skis over manicured steeps. Extensive snowmaking ensures skiing and riding even in low-snow winters, though the mountain is best when new snow blankets the bowls and softens the overused boulevards. The old sheep town of Ketchum has more reasonable housing for Everyskier.

Jackson Hole

When the great Jean-Claude Killy came to race a giant slalom at Jackson Hole in 1967, he pronounced the ski mountain the best in America. Those are strong words, but then Killy had been everywhere. The next year he would win all three alpine gold medals—downhill, slalom, and giant slalom—at the Olympics in Grenoble, France. He won that giant slalom race in Jackson Hole too. So perhaps the glow of victory colored his bonhomie?

I think not. Killy was never shy about pronouncing his own greatness. Neither did he fail to back up his words with results. The same is true of Jackson Hole, a lusty, sprawling, avalanche-prone, weather-enriched and

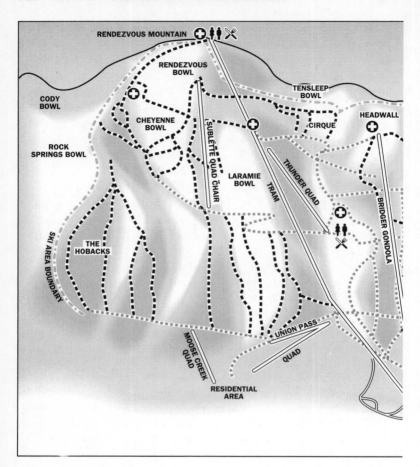

weather-bedeviled, wild-snow mountain that refers to itself in its own literature as "The Big One." Big Sky may now claim the total-vertical title, at 4,180 feet from top terminal to lowest lift base, but Jackson retains the "continuous skiing" vertical crown at 4,139 feet. Uninterrupted! Ski it or ride it without stopping if you can. It is one of those rare places that lives up to the hype and, on many days, gloriously surpasses it.

Bigness is a part of it; history is another. Jackson Hole was the center of the beaver-fur trade in the early nineteenth century and the home to irascible mountain men like John Colter, Jim Bridger, and Davey Jackson. Colter, who left the Lewis and Clark expedition in 1807 on its return from the Pacific, was probably the first white man to see the area around what is now Yellowstone National Park. Back East, his tales of boiling springs, spouting fountains, and sulfurous fumes were ridiculed

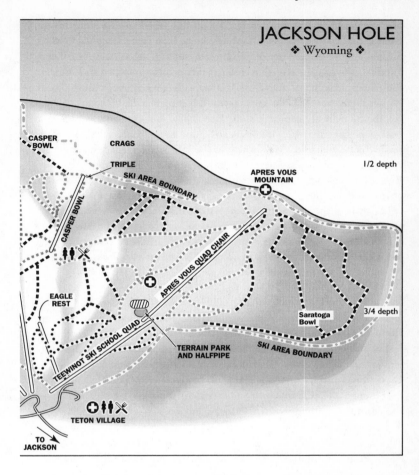

as the work of an unbalanced mind. "Colter's Hell," they called it. But Colter also talked of great numbers of beaver in the high meadows and creeks, and with beaver-fur top hats all the rage in cities around the world, the northern Rockies were soon crawling with trappers.

South of the Yellowstone Plateau, a trapper named Davey Jackson laid claim to a spectacular valley that was almost perfectly flat and surrounded on all sides by mountains. In those days, such a valley was called a "hole." Jackson shared his with a few Flathead Indians in the summer and a lot of elk in the winter. Eventually, the valley of the upper Snake River became known as Jackson's Hole.

With the beaver almost gone by 1840, men's millinery fashion changed to silk, and Jackson Hole slumbered until the formation of Yellowstone and Grand Teton National Parks. A thriving summer tourist business still left Jackson desolate for nine months of the year, until a Californian named Paul McCollister, with help from Colorado's Willy Schaeffler and Alta pioneer Alf Engen, strung the first lifts on Rendezvous Mountain. Killy arrived to race the next year, and Jackson Hole's reputation as a skiers' mecca—as well as a haven for moose, bear, elk, and, yes, beaver—has grown steadily since.

Today, with an airport just minutes away, Jackson Hole is poised to post some big skier/rider numbers and join the top ranks with household names like Aspen and Vail. Growth in the 1990s has startled the old guard and sparked controversy here as it has everywhere in the trendy Rockies. But two things will probably help Jackson Hole retain its funky, Western charm: the proximity of national-park land never to be developed and the wild nature of the ski mountain, with its bitingly cold mid-winter temperatures, its ridiculously steep terrain, its occasional wind and fog, and its waist-deep snows. More than any other ski terrain in the Lower 48, Jackson Hole feels like the Alps. Killy was right—this is a *serious* mountain.

The Lay of the Land

Imagine yourself in a balloon at 10,000 feet over the Jackson Hole valley. The Snake River runs a shallow, braided course from north to south through the eastern flats of Grand Teton National Park. The town of Jackson wedges into the mouth of Cache Creek Canyon near the south end of the valley. Frozen Jackson Lake stretches away to the north. Everything on the ground is coated with snow.

Straight ahead to the west, the Jackson Hole ski area plunges from the summit of Rendezvous Mountain to the valley floor. The famous Swiss-made aerial tram connects Teton Village at the base with the 10,450-foot peak. To the right (north), the somewhat lower summit of Après Vous Mountain (8,481 feet) is also festooned with lifts.

Lifting your gaze farther to the north, you see the sharp granite peaks of the three Tetons: South, Middle, and Grand. French trappers on the Idaho side of the range named them the Three Breasts, and indeed, from that side the resemblance makes some sense. From the Jackson side, they look like nothing so much as serrated shark's teeth. Indian tribes knew them as the Hoary-Headed Fathers and the Three Brothers. At 13,770 feet, the Grand Teton is by far the tallest rock in what is arguably the most dramatic upthrust in the Rockies. Given the number of automobile ads shot here—to give just one example—there must be few in America who have not subliminally absorbed the Tetons' stunning silhouette.

Behind the Tetons and west almost to the Idaho border sits Grand Targhee Resort, with its major snow accumulations and views of potato-rich Teton Valley. In fact, to get there, you have to drive into Idaho and then go back east just barely across the Wyoming border on the sunset slope of the range.

Due north of your balloon, the great hump of the Yellowstone Plateau spreads across 4,000 square miles, taking up the entire northwest corner of Wyoming and parts of Idaho on the west and Montana to the north. The world's first national park, Yellowstone, attracts increasing numbers of winter visitors, as does the nearby Big Sky resort. Some come to view the bison, moose, wolves, and the elk. Others ride snow coaches or snow-mobiles in to see Old Faithful. Still others cross-country ski into what remains, especially in winter, a vast, nearly roadless wilderness.

It's a 12-mile drive from the town of Jackson to the Teton Village base. Skiers and riders stay at both places. The Village tends toward con-dos, upscale inns and full-service hotels, including the world's only Four Seasons Resort & Residence Club located at a ski resort. Jackson, while it has gained tone in recent years, is still long on less-expensive motels and bed-and-breakfasts.

The mountain itself, for all its mega-acreage, retains a simple layout. There is just one base, out of which radiates the tram, the gondola, and two of the eight chairlifts. The easiest skiing and riding flows down from the north through the lower meadows of Après Vous Mountain. The vast majority of intermediate terrain resides on the upper two-thirds of Après Vous and just south, in the Casper Bowl region. Farther south, under the Bridger Gondola, the Gros Ventre Valley cuts a deep gouge through the gut of the mountain. Gros Ventre means "big belly," and it was the name of a local Indian tribe. South of Gros Ventre and beneath the tram's spi-dery cables, Jackson's vaunted expert terrain dominates, although there are a smattering of escape routes for the less bold. And when the bold themselves get to feeling cramped inbounds, Jackson's open-gate back-country policy allows access to uncountable acres of expert terrain. Among these hinterlands are three hourglass-shaped canyons south of the marked terrain: Rock Springs, Green River, and Pinedale. These wild snow preserves are open only when the ski patrol deems them safe.

The mountain looks vaguely like a fan, three miles across at the ridgeline, with the gentlest skiing and riding on the right leading to pro-gressively more daring and higher-elevation terrain to the left. Every-thing faces, more or less, east and into the morning sun. This is good for warming up the spirit and the snow on cold mornings. But it is not nec-essarily good during warm spells or low-snow years. In fact, Jackson's exposure would never work down south in Colorado, where east- and south-facing slopes can remain bare even at 10,000 feet. But here in northwestern Wyoming, with colder temperatures and a more oblique winter sun, the snow quality remains (mostly) exquisite.

Skiing and riding Jackson Hole artfully often involves judging solar angles and moving to appropriate exposures. If the open, largely treeless southern slopes are too soft, just swing around to the north-facing, shadier sides of the bowls. There are nine major bowls, two purely intermediate, inside the everyday boundaries. Each has exposures from north around to south—everything but true west. So searching out or hiding from the sun is a puzzle Jackson Hole riders and skiers love to master.

Finally, I think it is instructive to look at Jackson Hole's mountain not as a series of runs laid out down the hill, as many eastern (and western) American ski areas appear to be. Look at the mountain as the massive fault block that it is, mostly bare of trees and covered with snow like a thick white rug thrown down by the gods over the rocky bones of the land. Runs, per se, don't exist here. Some areas named on the trail map—*Cirque,* for example, or the *Hobacks*—are so big that one could take literally hundreds of ways down and hundreds of possible lines. You follow the shapes underfoot, dodge the occasional aspen or conifer, and let your skis or board seek the ever-changing fall line. You could spend weeks, months, or whole winters here and not know every line. That's the definition of a big mountain.

Starting Out at Jackson Hole, Beginner Skiing

Jackson's reputation as a magnet for cliff jumpers may have unfairly obscured its gentler side. Beginners don't need a lot of terrain to get started on, and Jackson's Eagle's Rest and Teewinot chairs provide plenty of long, well-groomed moving sidewalks. Eagle's Rest, with its namesake run, plus *Pooh Bear* and *Antelope Flats,* is the true first-time beginners' chair. It takes off near the Bridger Center, a family-oriented structure that houses a ski and snowboard shop, ski and snowboard rentals, ski gear, lockers, child-care center, ski school, and lift ticket offices. The ski school meeting place is right out front. Just steps away is the Cody House Kids Ranch, which offers one-stop shopping for childcare, lessons, and gear rentals. You can drop skis, boards, skiers, and riders off at the door, then return a short distance to day parking in the upper lot. (The lower parking lot, the first one you come to off Teton Village Road, makes more sense for skiers or riders who plan to ride the tram up Rendezvous Mountain.)

First-time beginners should always take lessons. There is so much to gain by doing so, and so much wasted time likely if you don't. Jackson's ski and snowboard school was run for 20-plus years by Pepi Stiegler, an outgoing Austrian who won three Olympic medals in 1960 and 1964. Olympic champion Tommy Moe, following his dramatic performance at the Lillehammer Games, succeeded Pepi and now serves as the resort's ambassador. After Eagle's Rest, the Teewinot Ski School Quad (the name is Shoshoni for "pinnacles") climbs a very gradual three-fifths of a mile up Après Vous. *Lower Werner* and *Lower Teewinot* trails shouldn't scare even the most timid novice, but they do have to accommodate occasional faster riders and skiers coming down off *Upper Werner* and *St. Johns.* Both are equipped with snowmaking to guarantee good cover.

Wide-Open Intermediate Spaces

One piece of the (theoretically) perfect terrain progression Jackson Hole lacks is the transition zone between novices and genuine intermediates. By novices I mean second-day skiers and riders or more timid veterans who can turn and stop on green runs but can't yet handle steeper pitches and higher speeds. Generally speaking, Jackson's slopes tend to leap directly from very gentle to exhilarating and wide-open cruising.

There is one marvelous route off the top of Après Vous lift that is perfect for transitional intermediates. Taking Togwotee Pass Traverse to South Pass Traverse means sweeping back and forth across a big chunk of the mountain for six glorious miles. This route is an exquisitely long and varied access road. It's a great way to give yourself the tour. The route intersects much of the intermediate terrain served by the Après Vous lift, so you have an opportunity to check out the snow conditions, the grooming, and the look and feel of runs you may wish to try later.

Novices and low intermediates should under no circumstances attempt the terrain off the tram. That is not to say you shouldn't ride the tram once and then turn around and ride it back down. The trip up is an experience in itself, especially on a clear day. (On a snowy day or a big powder day, the tram packs full like a sardine can; it's tough to secure a spot by a window. Even if you do luck out, the steamy breath of all those powderhounds makes seeing anything merely wishful thinking.) The top is another story, though. With good weather, the panorama, not to mention the altitude, can be breathtaking. The Tetons leap up to the north. Cody Peak and Cody Bowl (named, of course, for Buffalo Bill) look like a many-layered chocolate cake to the south, and to the east the valley floor, so far below, really does look like a hole.

Solid blue intermediates will find Jackson Hole a kind of heaven. The percentage of intermediate terrain may lag behind that allotted to experts (50%), but the length and quality of the runs compare with any of the cruising magnets, from Snowmass to Big Sky.

The easiest descents will once again be found on Après Vous. *Upper Werner, Hanna,* and *Teewinot Gully* have the wide-open, big-mountain feel that so epitomizes Jackson. Over in the Casper Bowl region, *Easy Does It* or *Timbered Island* to *Sundance Gully* provide 2,200 vertical feet of mellow, bump-free sliding, bigger than most whole mountains. To get to Casper, slide across from Après Vous on the *Togwotee Pass Traverse* or follow *Sundance* from the top of the Bridger gondola and take the *South Pass Traverse.* Casper is such a hit with intermediates that Jackson's only full-fledged, on-mountain restaurant sits near the base of Casper lift. For those who want to add a bit more pitch—and Jackson's spaciousness inspires swooping, hawk-like skiing and boarding—the choices are myriad and spread across the mountain. Starting on the right again (looking at the trail map), two beautiful burners roll down the shape of Après Vous. *Moran* to *Lower Werner* would make a super giant-slalom course, pitching like mammoth ocean swells from flat to steep to flat skiing and riding with smooth transition. *St. Johns,* over on the east side of the Après Vous high-speed quad, is rated double blue, not because it's any steeper really, but for its narrower, serpentine course through sparse glades.

The runs are a little shorter over on Casper. Left or right at the top of the chair, everything is tilted just right for linking big turns with no fear of dropping off the edge of the world (which, as we shall see, is *not* the case on some of the black-diamond runs). North of the Casper high point, *Sleeping Indian* and *Wide Open* may grow occasional bumps— good, round intermediate ones. South of the chair most everything is groomed. *Camp Ground* and *Timbered Island* are especially nice as they meander through sheltering stands of evergreens. Beware *Sundance Gully* at rush hour, which is usually just late in the afternoon. Skiers and riders returning to base from the Gros Ventre/Thunder lift areas spill into the gully, adding high-speed traffic to the more cautious right-laners.

Next up for intermediates is the great central gut of the mountain, the *Amphitheater,* between the Bridger gondola and the Thunder chair. This region is not exclusively blue, as the Casper terrain primarily is, but I believe it is the finest pure intermediate terrain on the mountain, par- ticularly for stronger intermediates. You get there by sliding the *Amphitheater Traverse* from the Casper top station or *Lupine Way* from the top of the Bridger gondola. Quite solid skiers and riders can also get there by riding the tram and navigating the fickle *Rendezvous Bowl* to *Gros Ventre Traverse.* I say fickle because, even though *Rendezvous* is a black diamond on the map, depending on snow and visibility it can rate anywhere from a relatively easy blue to a nasty, white-out, wind- whipped, genuine expert trail.

Once at the top of Thunder lift, a fixed-grip quad, the choices are European in scope. South of the ridge defined by the tram line, *Grand* plunges through fields of mostly buried treetops. It's usually groomed and fast. *Laramie Bowl,* which used to be all expert, now sports an intermedi- ate route right down the throat. It's an exciting trip, especially for skiers and riders new to Western, big-bowl skiing. Both *Grand* and *Laramie Bowl* drop onto *South Pass Traverse,* which leads back to Thunder base.

The choices off the north side of the ridge are even better. The snow is colder and shadier, and the main route, *Upper Amphitheater,* descends some of the most interesting, constantly changing terrain anywhere. The first north-facing drop below *Expert Chutes* offers lines from relatively easy on your right to steep and bumpy if you swing around to your left. Then the route dives through a series of big rolls and funnels perfect for banking, letting the terrain ski you. Finally, it spits you onto the giant

Amphitheater plain, where you can turn or not turn. In fact, it's a great place to mess with terminal velocity, a surprisingly accessible and instructive reality even for intermediate skiers. Just pick a quiet moment, stand tall and forward on your feet, like a bowsprit, and let 'em roll. On a pitch like *Amphitheater* you will stop accelerating at about 25 or 30 miles per hour, when your weight and gravity and the air pushing against you have reached equilibrium. It's a very freeing sensation. You can actually lean against the air. A caution: Try this only in uncrowded situations and only where you feel completely comfortable letting the skis run. *Lower Gros Ventre,* the main route back to the Village, is generally not the place to experiment with terminal velocity. It's a great snaking gully in which to go fast, but it can be busy and the pitch is generally too steep to eschew turning altogether.

Amphitheater and the Thunder lift are so popular you may run into lift lines here in the heart of the day; try the Sublette quad chair for shorter lines. One final intermediate option, and it's a good one for skiers and riders who can handle *Laramie Bowl:* At the bottom of the bowl you'll find the Sublette quad chair, another fixed-grip quad. (Detachable quads can move up to twice as fast.) From the top here, you can cut a long, scenic semicircle around *Cheyenne Bowl.* The route slices beneath Rendezvous Bowl on Hanging Rock trail, then out along a high ridge to *Rendezvous Trail,* a double blue with no big surprises, just a long, consistently fine ride back to the Sublette lift and *South Pass Traverse,* the all-important artery connecting most sections of this mountain.

Jackson Hole for Experts

The aerial tram is the key to Jackson's expert skiing and riding, and the tram society is the soul of the enterprise. Forty-five people load into each of the fire engine–red cars. Some of the veterans inevitably moo as the last two or three ski patrolmen back into the crowd like human cattle prods and slide the door closed. Skis clack together, boots shuffle for room, nylon shoulders swish against other nylon shoulders, and finally the lot of you swings gently away from the dock and glides up the cable 2.4 miles and 4,139 vertical feet in ten minutes.

Steamy breath fogs the windows. The pros bring napkins from Nick Wilson's Cowboy Cafe next door and stuff them into their goggles. This way moisture from your forehead doesn't condense on the inside of the goggles. Before I learned this trick, I stepped out at the top on a cold morning and found I had the optical equivalent of shower-stall glass for goggles. It took me ten minutes inside the warming hut to chip them clear.

At the top, the same 45 people trundle out and down the metal stairs to the snow. This is the great beauty of the tram. For ten minutes, until the next car reaches the summit, the world is yours. Just you and 44 buddies with all of Rendezvous Mountain at your ski tips.

You could slide down the *East Ridge* a couple hundred yards and watch the bird men and women leap into *Corbet's Couloir.* Depending on recent storm and wind conditions, it may be anywhere from a 5- to a 25-foot drop from the cornice to the first turn. Four out of five of the skiers I watched launched right out of their bindings on impact, sailing into the shady blue snow and strewing gear in what is known in the parlance as a "yard sale." One in five touched down at the right place at the right angle and survived to arc high-speed turns between the yellow rock walls and out into the sunlight at the bottom.

One of my favorite runs is down the *East Ridge,* past *Corbet's,* to *Tensleep Bowl,* a luscious, low-angle field dotted with rocks the size of houses at various angles of repose, giving the place the look and feel of a tumbling glacier. The powder stays untracked here longer than in most other spots on the mountain.

Beyond *Tensleep,* you have the option (that's the great thing about Jackson—you always have multiple options) to drop into the steep rollovers of *Expert Chutes* or to circumvent them and cut to the easy throat of *Upper Amphitheater,* or to traverse out into the vast, treeless teacup known as the *Cirque.* The *Cirque* faces east and south, so it absorbs a lot of solar radiation, which means slush and/or ice on some days. But if you catch it early on a powder morning, what a ride! Nearly 1,000 vertical feet of uninterrupted, laundry-chute steep, falling-dream turns to the calm at the center of *Amphitheater.* Not for the faint of technique or heart. But, like a lot of Jackson's steeps, give it a couple of days and it will raise the level of your game.

You'll find Jackson's mogul meisters clustered primarily on the Thunder lift, where north-facing shots through the trees generate big, soft, stair-step bumps. *Paint Brush, Thunder,* and *Riverton Bowl* are the main pitches. *Tower Three Chute,* when it's open—and it isn't open when the snow is thin or too hard—is a kind of litmus test of extreme mogul skiing. One slip and you're in for the full ride to the bottom.

There are more good bumps in the three bowls south of the tram: *Rendezvous, Laramie,* and *Cheyenne.* The bumps tend to develop on the north slopes, where the snow stays soft. The south-facing sides of the bowls (to the skier's/rider's left) receive more sun and less traffic. There are always bump-free lines to be found in each of the bowls.

Below *Cheyenne Bowl* is a very special zone called *The Hobacks,* which includes a series of three, almost treeless, 2,000-foot ridges and the gullies between them. They are saved just for powder mornings when conditions are perfect. Moguls don't have a chance to grow, so every time *The Hobacks* are open, it's a thigh-burning, powder-breathing, whipped-cream orgy: the best lift-served pure-powder terrain in the Rockies.

The only thing to rival it might be the out-of-bounds country just beyond Jackson Hole's southern boundary. You can see into *Cody Bowl* from the top of the tram. This is where the U.S. National Powder 8 contest is staged every March. Teams of two skiers from all around the West lay down the most rhythmic, perfectly shaped eights they can. When it's all over, 2,000 exquisitely braided turns cover the face like an Early American rug.

You can walk to and ski *Cody,* as well as *Rock Springs, Green River,* and *Pinedale* bowls, in this progression to the south. Avalanche locators are highly recommended. In 2000, Jackson instituted an "open gate" policy for entering the backcountry. The ski patrol has no jurisdiction and does not take responsibility for the out-of-bounds areas. What a concept! Bravo, Jackson, all resorts should learn from you.

Snowboarding

Boarders are at home everywhere on the mountain, cruising both inbounds and out in search of powder and kickers. Few pack hard boots and long carving boards, preferring instead to free ride in all directions. The resort's terrain pipe, complete with an array of rails, boxes and snow features, is stashed next to the Après Vous lift, as is the superpipe.

One of the West's best natural pipes, though, runs the length of *Dick's Ditch*, a snaking gully nestled between the Bridger Gondola and the tram. Running 1,500 vertical feet, the gully provides ample launching opportunities, as well as more than a few good hits. Come mid-March, the gully is the backdrop for a banked slalom race that draws boarders and two-plankers.

Lunch on the Hill

Thunder habitués often don't want to stop skiing; they're having so much fun, but in the end they can't resist the good smells emanating from a tiny shack next to the chair. There used to be a more substantial eatery here, but a huge avalanche—a rare 100-year phenomenon—swept it away. Now there's this little **Thunder** snack shack and a smattering of picnic tables in the sun. The folks inside serve up killer hot chocolate on those cold powder days. If it's nice out, I like to take my time with a melon-size bread bowl that's filled with homemade stew or soup of the day. Not to worry about the next avalanche. Improved control techniques and better patrol access to start zones on the Headwall have all but eliminated the risk.

If you're skiing Casper, the **Casper Restaurant** at the base of Casper chair offers better-than-average cafeteria fare and a spacious sunny deck. Beginners are pretty much consigned to the village base, but this is no gastronomic loss. **Nick Wilson's** in the Clocktower Building has great chili, fries, and homemade baked goods. You can find the obligatory, postprandial espresso just inside the double doors of the slope-side **Village Center.**

One more place to grab a quick lunch. (This mountain is so good, you'll not often be tempted to linger over a Euro-style feast.) This is in the low building hunkered onto the summit of Rendezvous Peak. It houses the ski patrol room and a small eatery called **Corbet's Cabin.** The name resonates for Jackson aficionados as the name of the legendary mountain man and as the moniker given to Jackson's most infamous cliff jump, the airborne entrance into *Corbet's Couloir.*

The food here is minimalist; it's really just fuel to get you back out into the powder. Most is prepared in advance, and all of it must be shuttled up in the morning via the tram. But this is not in any way a criticism. I've had a cold drink and a monster oatmeal-raisin cookie up there that I believed at the time to be ambrosia from the gods.

For those who may have ridden the tram with no idea whatsoever of where they'd like to go, Jackson has a very nice tour service called the Mountain Hosts. Every hour on the hour mountain-orientation tours leave the top of the mountain. Mountain Hosts are also available at the Clocktower building at the base.

A final note on the tram. The first tram leaves the dock at 9 a.m., and the final car departs at 3:30 p.m. Be in line early if it's a powder day. New snow of eight inches or more brings the local hounds out by the hundreds.

Dining in Teton Village and in the Town of Jackson

The most famous place in the Village to go for an after-ski beer is the **Mangy Moose,** the raucous, barn-like, longtime local hangout. The Moose has whole airplanes hanging from the ceiling and ancient skis nailed to the walls, live music, good munchies, and a surprisingly varied average-priced dinner menu. Another option for drinks and food is **Beaver Dicks** in the **Inn at Jackson.** The **Alpenhof Lodge,** right across from the tram building, serves continental specialties featuring veal and wild game. The newly remodeled **Resort Hotel of Jackson** (formerly known as the Sojourner) serves great barbecue in **The Pub** downstairs and fine fare in **Henessey's** upstairs.

Down in the town of Jackson informal Western cuisine is the norm. **Bubba's Bar-B-Que Restaurant** serves up such succulent ribs that there's usually a line waiting in the cramped but happy entry. Happy in part because you can bring your own six-pack to Bubba's, and what better way to while away the time until your table is ready?

The **Cadillac Grille** has in recent years carved a niche with its Art Deco atmosphere, huge burgers, and salad bar.

A couple of blocks off the main square with its famous elk antler arches is the **Lame Duck.** They serve very credible Chinese food and offer private tearooms and take-out orders.

A visit to Jackson would not be complete without a visit to the **Million Dollar Cowboy Bar** right in the Town Square. It has Western dancing and saddle barstools. Most locals wouldn't be caught dead in the place. They are more likely to be down at the **Americana Snow King**

Resort in the **Shady Lady Saloon** boogying to the best live music in the valley—everything from reggae to the newest alternative rock.

Jackson Hole Data

Mountain Statistics

Vertical feet	4,139 feet
Base elevation	6,311 feet
Summit elevation	10,450 feet
Longest run	4.5 miles
Average annual snowfall	500 inches
Number of lifts	11: 1 aerial tramway, 1 gondola, 2 high-speed quads, 4 fixed-grip quads, 1 triple, 1 double, 1 Magic Carpet
Uphill capacity	12,096 skiers per hour
Skiable terrain	2,500 acres
Opening date	Early December
Closing date	Mid-April
Snowboarding	Yes

Transportation

By car About 90 miles east of Idaho Falls, Idaho, on U.S. Highways 26 and 89, and 270 miles north of Salt Lake City, Utah, on U.S. Highway 89. The START Bus connects the town of Jackson with Teton Village from 7 a.m. to 11 p.m.; $2 each way.

By plane Via American, Delta, SkyWest, Continental Express, United, and United Express from Salt Lake City and Chicago. The Jackson Hole airport is 10 minutes from both the town of Jackson and Teton Village. Airport and many lodging shuttles service all flights.

Key Phone Numbers

Ski-area information	(307) 733-2292
Snow report	(307) 733-2291
Jackson Hole lodging	(800) 443-8613
Jackson Hole reservations	(800) 443-6931
Website	www.jacksonhole.com

Inside Story

Ski the Big One

Longtime Jackson Hole marketing director Harry Baxter had sought for years to find a proper vehicle to convey just how big Jackson's skiing was. He wanted to show that "dollah for dollah" (Harry is a transplanted New Englander with infectious smile lines), "you get more skiin' at Jackson Hole than any other area in the country."

His idea: Give a personal achievement award called Ski the Big One to anyone who racks up 100,000 vertical feet or more in a week of skiing. The prize is a Ski the Big One pin with a certificate written in calligraphy by Harry's wife, Martha.

Ski 300,000 feet or 500,000 feet or a million feet over time and you can receive bronze, silver, and gold belt buckles. Harry has 27,500 names in his computer, names of people who have reached at least the first level. They've given out 340 gold belt buckles since the program started. It is a privileged club, and just one more manifestation of the extended-family atmosphere that, along with the less formal Tram Society, gives Jackson the comfortable feeling of reunion.

The 100,000-foot goal is really not that daunting given Jackson's ultimate uphill weapon, the 4,139-foot vertical of the tram. Harry proved it himself with an awesome 66,000-foot-vertical day on 16 tram rides a few years back. You need only average 17,000 feet per day for six days to chalk up 100,000 feet for the week. That's a leisurely two or three trams, plus a few laps on the Thunder, Après Vous, or Casper lifts. The system works like this: Pick up a Ski the Big One score-card with your lift ticket for the week, simply mark the chair rides as you ride them, and then total the vertical at the end of the day (everybody's on the honor system). Then, at the end of your stay, present your card and vertical total at the Guest Services Desk in the tram building to receive your certificate.

While you're there, take a minute to glance through the record book. Eighty-two-year-old Charlie Nebel from New Jersey made his million in 11 weeks of skiing over two years. His 79-year-old wife wrote, "He's crazy, just skis too fast for me!" Then there is Sadamitsu Tanzawa, who got his gold in 30 days. He said, "I had only two ski seasons. So I hurry to achieve." A nine-year-old Californian named Mary Wholey racked up a million feet in three seasons of skiing with her num-bers-mad parents. There is a Swedish couple who managed 150,000 feet in just three days. "Those were three hard, smooth, clear days," Harry assured me. I received my certificate in February 1985, when I totaled 157,806 feet in five days at Jackson. I am especially proud of my numbers because almost every one of those turns was two feet under the snow. That week the heavens would not stop snowing. I woke up every morning to another helping of fresh powder. Since the visibility was not the best, my favorite route, down *Rendezvous Bowl* to *Ten Sleep Bowl* to *Gros Ventre,* was decidedly slow. I had to work hard to reach my goal, and I couldn't help it that every turn was a slow-motion powder baptism, the shim-mering stuff flowing over my shoulders like white silk scarves.

Grand Targhee

It wasn't too long ago that Grand Targhee's address said a lot about the place: Grand Targhee Resort, Alta, Wyoming, via Driggs, Idaho. While you no longer need to append "Driggs, Idaho" to Targhee's address, you still can't get there from here without really meaning to. State borders, those clean, straight lines favored by early Western mapmakers, don't mean much when it comes to a genuine identity.

Named for both the Grand Teton that looms directly to the east and a renegade chief of the Bannock tribe in the 1870s, Grand Targhee sits, technically speaking, in far-western Wyoming. But its soul resides a cou-ple of miles across the border in Idaho. The quickest way to get there is from Jackson Hole, on the eastern side of the Teton upthrust. Just drive over 8,431-foot Teton Pass, beneath the awesome sweep of Glory Bowl (a very large avalanche path that doubles as a springtime hike-and-ski mecca for local hard cores), and then down through Victor, Idaho (population 292), and north into the Teton Valley. From Driggs, with its square, Western storefronts and woodsmoke haze, drive back east onto the western slope of the Tetons to tiny Alta, Wyoming. It's simple, and it takes about an hour to drive in good weather. Arriving from Idaho Falls to the southwest takes about 90 minutes, while the drive from Bozeman, Montana, up north, takes much, much longer.

The trip is worth every minute. Targhee is one of the last unpolished jewels of American skiing and riding. It is a beautiful, spacious, well-designed, modestly priced, family-oriented mountain that just happens to get more powder than most resorts in the Rockies. The average is just over 500 inches per season. Targhee's long-time motto has been "Snow from heaven, not hoses." In truth the resort can make snow around the lifts at its base and the beginner's area to ensure early season coverage when the upper mountains are already buried but the base area is wanting.

On my first trip I skied around taking care not to nip the branches of the little evergreens that dot the slopes like toy soldiers on white bed sheets. Then somebody told me they were actually the tops of mature, 20-foot trees. So prodigious are the snowfalls that fully one-third of Targhee's mountain (1,000 acres) is reserved for snowcat powder skiing and riding. On the other 2,000 acres—1,200 of which are designated ungroomed powder reserves—you can ski and ride 9:30 a.m. to 4 p.m. off trail, never cross your own tracks, and never even see your skis under the surface.

But Targhee is no Jackson Hole; it is no magnet for the cornice-jumping, extreme-skiing Doug Coombses of the world (although the inbounds Peaked Chutes do provide some "Jackson Hole" type of terrain). Most of the terrain is tilted a few degrees shy of scary. Seventy percent of the map is rated intermediate, and the area has developed a reputation as a near-perfect place to *learn* to ski powder, to touch a tentative toe onto the off-piste.

The base village is designed around skiing families, conservative Idahoans for the most part, but it is developing a growing destination clientele from elsewhere. Everything is clustered in one woody meadow: three lodges with room for 440 guests, four restaurants, one bar, a fitness center and spa, an outdoor ice rink, an outdoor pool, two hot tubs, a Nordic center with 15Ks of groomed trails, a tubing hill, rental and retail shops, a video arcade, a general store, the children's center, and . . . and that's it. Eat, sleep, play games, and ski or ride powder. What else do you need?

The Big Picture

Back when mountain men combed the Tetons for beaver, the Teton Valley was known as Pierre's Hole. Trappers from French Canada were the first in the region, and it was they who named the granite peaks cresting the range *les Trois Tetons,* the three breasts. On this western side the spiky, pink granite fins dominate far more dramatically than they do on the

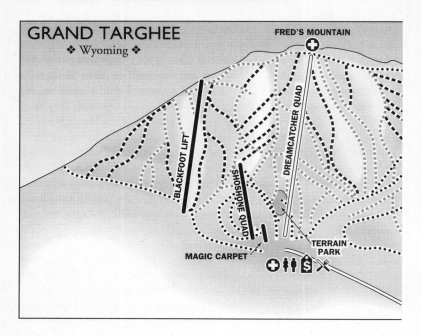

Jackson side of the crest. When late afternoon sun pours across the valley, turning snow the color of cherry blossoms, and the Tetons become a rich apricot color, it's easy to agree with past Targhee ski-school director Gene Palmer, who calls this "the *Grand* side of the Tetons."

Palmer was a typical display of the genuine Western ambience that pervades Targhee. (Everybody here wore cowboy hats before Billy the Kidd dreamed of donning his.) Palmer lived down the road in Rexburg, Idaho, and was a spud farmer in the off season. He was so country he was embarrassed a few years ago to drive down the streets of his hometown with those new, pink K2 skis tied to his station wagon roof.

Palmer's domain was known as Fred's Mountain, which hosts three of Targhee's four chairlifts. Next to it is Peaked Mountain, a mixed realm of lift-served and snowcat terrain. Both mountains are part of the same uniformly tilted fault block. The front side (west side) is perfectly angled for skiing and riding. The back side is closed, a jagged layer cake of cliff bands plunging into South Leigh Creek Canyon. Adding to the front side's skiability is an ancient burn that sheared most of the trees. So what you have now are long, near-naked ridges—more like wrinkles, really—scoring the full 2,200-foot vertical with shallow, inviting bowls and the gullies between. Names on the trail map sometimes refer to whole drainages where a skier or rider might scribe any of a hundred lines. Big chunks of real estate have no names at all. Although there are groomed

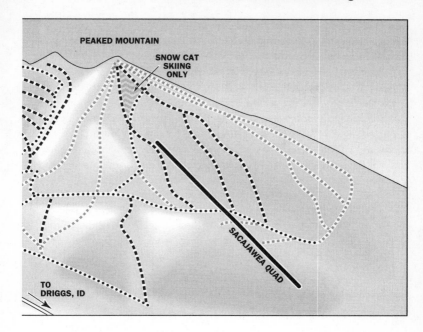

runs here, a nod to skiers and boarders who feel more comfortable with corduroy underfoot, most of the terrain is wide open, fluid, sculptural, the way a Michelangelo marble is devoid of straight lines.

There are four chairlifts; four chairs for 2,000 acres. A supremely simple and efficient layout. Everything flows back to the center of the compact village. Until recently, there were not enough riders and skiers to result in lift lines here. Due to increasing notoriety, the number-one chair, the old base-to-summit Bannock double, sometimes used to back up. Now its successor, the high-speed detachable Dreamcatcher quad, has taken care of any lines.

Beginners: A Separate Place

Few areas of any size can match the quality and safety of Targhee's beginner terrain. A gentle Magic Carpet surface tow serves a short run right outside the Kid's Club cabin at the edge of the village. This is where they teach the first-timers gliding maneuvers, turns, and stops.

A few steps away, the Shoshone quad chair climbs 1,800 feet through sunny aspen glades to the main learning runs. *Big Horn, Little Big Horn,* and *The Meadows* are completely free of faster traffic as they arc back to the base, while *Big Scout* ventures into the zone around the base of the Dreamcatcher quad and thus intersects intermediate routes off the upper mountain. *Big Scout* in particular serves as a return thoroughfare for riders and skiers coming down off the popular *Sitting Bull* ridge. But true beginners and novices who stay north of the Shoshone chair will never feel the swoosh of speeding commuters.

The wide-open glades below *South Street* are marked "Intermediate Powder Area." Powder Reserves with no trails or names per se, these are places that never feel the weight of a grooming machine. Depending on the pitch, they are designated as advanced, intermediate, and even beginner powder areas. Yes, a beginner powder area! It's off the Shoshone lift to the far right as the skier descends. No turns required. Just stand in balance and feel the ski tips bend and float as you run straight through snow that hisses and sparkles and leaves soft, blue trenches where you pass.

A final option for novices seeking a top-of-the-mountain adventure: The *Teton Vista Traverse* runs from the top of the Dreamcatcher lift along the summit ridge of Fred's Mountain, with the huge views of the Grand, Middle, and South Tetons, and then down the V-shaped gully that divides Fred's from Peaked Mountain all the way to the base. At 2.8 miles, it's the longest route on the map and a great, sweeping green tour.

Intermediate Nirvana

The huge majority of Fred's Mountain is rated intermediate. That's 1,500 acres of deliciously, consistently tilted blue terrain. No cliff bands, no surprised faces, hardly a mogul in sight. Just some of the best, big-mountain cruising to be found in the West.

Most of it pours off the summit ridge and is accessed by either the Dreamcatcher or the shorter Blackfoot lift to the north. With few trees to interfere, the runs follow the fall lines in two major concave drains and atop the three ridges that, like chubby fingers, define them. South of the Dreamcatcher lift, the two most dramatic ridge routes, *Crazy Horse* and *Wild Willie,* dive side by side for nearly 2,000 vertical feet. The treeless expanse and the continuous rolling pitch have a European feel. The other big ridge off the Dreamcatcher summit is called *Sitting Bull.* It runs along the top edge of the area's primary mogul chutes, a collection of steeps known as *The Good, The Bad, The Ugly* and the *East Woods.*

As good as the ridges are, the gullies are even more interesting. *Ladies Waist* snakes between *Wild Willie* and *Wandering Moose,* a horizontal twister that is the mountain's best half-pipe, one that offers run after run of playtime for boarders and skiers alike. Riders in search of something a bit nastier jump into *Nasty Gash,* another snaking, high-rimmed gully. Off either side of the Blackfoot lift, *Blackfoot Bowl* and *Chief Joseph Bowl* offer the rarest of intermediate treats: wide-open, groomed skiing and riding in the cupped palm of the mountain, plus the playful terrain idiosyncrasies—banks, rolls, and occasional tree islands—that give shape to a descent.

In between the groomed blue runs are miles of intermediate powder reserves. Here the terrain flows like a rumpled white linen tablecloth gently tilted downhill with humps and swales amid pockets of evergreens and aspens. Try one whipped-cream turn off the packed trails, or, if you can, spend a month sleuthing the soft areas. These are probably the most accessible and the most reliable and least threatening powder zones in the Rockies. The biggest is the vast *Sunnyside Bowl* under the Dreamcatcher lift. But, as the name implies, this exposure receives a lot of solar during clear periods and may not have the best snow quality. Wind, as area personnel will readily admit, is also a factor. Targhee faces straight into the oncoming weather with no buffer ranges; thus, the extraordinary snowfalls. But it also means some storms roar through with winds that ripple the snow surface into a variety of slabs and crusts, some more forgiving than others. The exposed ridgelines are generally hardest hit. The best snow usually settles on the lee shoulders and in the trees. In fact, the returning forests cluster almost exclusively in northside lee pockets.

That's where intermediates should look for the most forgiving powder. The *Lost Warrior* and *North Boundary* areas to the skier's far right off the Blackfoot lift protect bowers of deep snow in the lee of aspens and evergreens. In a windy period, the lower-elevation slopes offer the best protection. The Powder Reserve below *South Street,* for example, stays relatively sheltered.

Strong intermediates who particularly want to master, or at least grow comfortable in, powder should consider a day or two on Peaked Mountain, riding one of the area's three snowcats to uncut stashes (see "Inside Story," Snowcat Skiing, page 402). Recent evolutions of powder skis have made floating in the deep stuff much more accessible to nonheroes. The skis are affectionately known as "fat boys," and their greater surface area, nearly twice that of regular Alpine skis, floats you up high in the snow, helping to reduce resistance and grease the turns. Targhee's ski shop has fat boys to rent.

The preponderance of terrain on Peaked Mountain is intermediate as well, and there are more trees here than on Fred's. Snow quality improves with shade, and the definition provided by the trees helps visibility during storm or fog episodes. Sign up for half or full days with the cats. Expect eight to ten runs for approximately 10,000 to 20,000 vertical feet. Full days include a guide, snack, and lunch. Special half-day powder lessons are also available. Targhee encourages snowboarders and telemarkers to ride with the cats too.

Thanks to the March 2002 arrival of the Sacajawea quad, Peaked Mountain no longer is accessed only by those hauled there aboard a snowcat. The lift doesn't climb to the 9,700-foot summit of Peaked, but it does open up nearly 1,300 feet of vertical, nicely sloped terrain that's dotted with aspen glades and evergreen sentinels. The 500 acres served by the lift are embraced by *Northern Lights* and *Dreamweaver,* two opposing J-shaped cruisers that encourage long, swooping arcs from top to bottom. Between these runs the bulk of the terrain is a collection of meadows, glades, and gullies, an expanse with no mandatory approach. Rather, it's terrain designed and begging for exploration. Spend your first few runs on this side of Targhee and you'll enjoy solitude while exploring, as most skiers and boarders head straight to the Dreamcatcher lift.

Targhee for Expert Skiers

For several years Targhee hosted advanced ski clinics with the Northface Extreme Team, comprising two sets of extreme-skiing, film-starring brothers, the Des Lauriers and the Egans. One of the four kicked off a terrifying cornice avalanche on a permanently closed section of Peaked Mountain for the film cameras a couple of years back. But other than this piece of genuine hazard, I'm hard pressed to think of where the brothers could go on this mountain to teach steep technique. Powder, yes, of course. But really steep? I'm not sure. Just to skier's right of Sacajawea's top terminal there are some chutes and steeps that fall off Peaked's northern flanks, but beyond that, experts are left largely to focus on their powder techniques.

There are two semiprecipitous zones on Fred's Mountain where most of the black diamonds are clustered. One drops from the *Sitting Bull* ridge. The trees are relatively thick here, and the snow is cold and soft. *Headwall, The Good, The Bad,* and *The Ugly* fall straight and steep into *Chief Joseph Bowl.* The last two, *The Bad* and *The Ugly,* grow the biggest moguls on the mountain.

The other expert zone hugs the south border of Fred's, where gentle, south-facing snowfields nose over into the Teton Vista Traverse. Here you'll find a series of short, steep shots through tree fingers known as *Lost Groomers Chute, Patrol Chute, Instructor's Chute,* and so on. The term "chute" may be a teensy bit misleading, especially if you are familiar with *Alta Chutes* at Jackson Hole, for example. These are nowhere near the elevator-shaft category, but they do roll over nicely and can be a real challenge in hard or windblown conditions.

In any event, the goal at Targhee is not the search for base-baring steeps. Good riders and skiers are rewarded the same way intermediates are, with hundreds of acres of wild-snow terrain, an abundance of terrain that practically guarantees a new sense of freedom and expression.

The North Boundary glades hide many days worth of powder lines. On the other side of Blackfoot lift *Steam Vent* and *Fallen Timber* offer myriad lines through random, maverick trees. The biggest expanse is off to the south of Dreamcatcher, where empty, oceanic shapes almost never get completely tracked out. There is no name on the trail map, but the ski school calls this area *Instructor's* after the many powder lessons taught there.

Good skiers and boarders who do not link up with the snowcats for at least one day are missing a rare opportunity. While Peaked's terrain never reaches the steepness of the Monashees, the alchemy of so many linked turns on a virgin canvas will change you and bring on random cries of delight.

There are those for whom even the semi-wilderness of the snowcat preserve is not enough. For these intrepid solitude seekers and backcountry powder skiers and riders, Targhee is a fine base from which to explore the west side of the Tetons. For a little (or a lot) of guidance, contact Rendezvous Ski and Snowboard Tours in Alta, Wyoming, at (307) 353-2900 or (877) 754-4887. They know the landscape better than anyone, and they maintain three cozy yurts in the high country for overnight tours to exquisite free-heel terrain.

Snowboarding

The rumpled lay of the land at Targhee offers some long and winding gullies that offer just about as much as any groomed half-pipe you'll find. *Ladies Waist* and *Wandering Moose,* both found on Fred's Mountain, are nice and deep and serpentine. A more challenging ride can be found in the concave bowels of *Nasty Gash,* a tight cleft running between Fred's Mountain and Peaked Mountain.

For pure cruising through feathery powder stashes, boarders flock to the terrain that falls below the Blackfoot Traverse. Here lie acre-after-acre of powder fields. True, the terrain isn't incredibly steep, but it's wide open and always inviting. For steeper shots, head into Chief Joseph Bowl.

Targhee Dining

All five eating establishments at Grand Targhee are located in the **Rendezvous Base Lodge,** where they've successfully included a little something for everyone. At the top of the heap, **Targhee Steakhouse** (named for the original avalanche transceiver worn by ski patrolmen) is the fine-dining restaurant. A notch down in price and panache, **Wild Bill's** serves pizza and sandwiches. **Snorkels** is the popular stop for latte lovers, cappuccino cravers, espresso addicts, and pizza/calzone connoisseurs. The chef is in at 4 a.m. everyday, baking pastries and starting the soup of the day. Finally, there's **Wild Bill's Grill** for quick breakfasts, express grill, salad bar, and so on.

The **Trap Bar** ("It's so much fun, you get trapped") has moved upstairs, where a new deck lords over the base and offers glorious views of the mountain.

Down the road in Alta, the **Teton Teepee** offers a nice dinner alternative. The Teepee is a family lodge with guest rooms in a circle around a soaring central fireplace and living/dining room. The Melehes family accepts reservations from nonguests for dinner. The camaraderie is a throwback to the days when everyone stayed at full-board lodges. The hearty food is served family style: great steaming bowls of soup, platters of meat, baskets of rolls, all passed hand-to-hand along with introductions and tales of the day.

In Driggs, the locals' favorite is the **Royal Wolf,** a pub and dining room with a delightfully incongruous menu, including a couple of very good Thai dishes.

Grand Targhee Data

Mountain Statistics

Vertical feet	2,800 feet (lift-served), 2,800 feet (cat skiing)
Base elevation	8,000 feet
Summit elevation	10,200 feet
Longest run	2.8 miles
Average annual snowfall	500 inches
Number of lifts	8: 2 high-speed quads; 1 fixed-grip quad; 1 double chair; 1 moving carpet; 3 snowcats
Uphill capacity	3,600 skiers per hour
Skiable terrain	2,000 acres (lift-served), 1,000 acres (cat skiing)
Opening date	mid-November
Closing date	mid-April
Snowboarding	Yes

Transportation

By car About 1 hour northwest of Jackson, Wyoming, over Teton Pass, via Highways 22 and 33. About 1.5 hour northeast of Idaho Falls, via U.S. Highways 26, 31, and 33.
By plane Via major carriers to Jackson, Pocatello, or Idaho Falls.

Key Phone Numbers

Ski-area information	(800) TARGHEE
Snow report	(800) TARGHEE
Lodging information	(800) TARGHEE
Website	www.grandtarghee.com

Inside Story

Snowcat Skiing

If heli-skiers drink Dom Perignon, then snowcat skiers settle for garden-variety champagne. They don't imbibe as many vertical feet each day, and they don't thrill to the power of flight.

But snowcat skiers do enjoy a number of advantages over their airborne brethren. First, they never fall out of the sky, and second, they never get weathered out. Storms that ground the flyboys just make skiing better for the cat skiers, and you can cat ski for a fraction of the cost of heli-skiing: under $300 a day on Targhee's Peaked Mountain, including a snack and lunch. A day at Great Divide Snow Tours in Monarch, Colorado, costs only $80. By contrast, a typical heli-ski day will run $550–$750 or more.

Snowcat skiing is often more accessible than heli-sliding. Many U.S. operations work the back sides of some pretty decent lift-served terrain. Targhee is one. Aspen is another where cats ply the untrammeled Little Annie region behind Aspen Mountain. Big Mountain, Montana, is another. They've got a special deep-snow tree preserve on the north side of the mountain open only to cat skiers.

The cats, of course, are those growling, diesel-powered grooming machines retrofitted with comfy cabins on the back for carrying up to a dozen skiers. The Targhee cats can accommodate ten skiers plus the guide; Big Mountain's cat has a six-person gondola welded onto the back. A cat-skiing day feels very much like a heli-skiing day, only slower. Guides comb the backcountry for the best-quality snow. You clamber out, click in bindings, and drop into that creamy place where your skis never really touch bottom, where gravity lowers you like a gentle hand, and cold crystals fill every wrinkle in your grin.

On the way back up you chat up new friends while having a quick snack and a drink of water. The cat lurches to a stop, everyone trundles out, and you do it all again, never once crossing another skier's track. Depending on the terrain and the skill level of the group, cat skiers can make up to 15 runs a day. Eight to ten is the average; by then most people are ready for the hot tub.

If the weather is good, lunch is served on the snow: hot soup, tea, sandwiches, chocolate, fruit. Targhee's guides lay out a sumptuous spread inside a high-altitude yurt, which is a circular cloth tent that serves as a warming hut, midway down the slopes of Peaked. The food tastes like ambrosia in the sharp, high-elevation air. It is also essential fuel. Powder skiing all day will leave you limp of leg and emotionally spent. It is time so well spent you may be back for more. The powder-skiing high is among the most addictive in the known world, and the snowcat is the surest route—short of your own foot power—for reaching the heights.

Big Sky

Thirty years after sliding its first chairlift under its first fanny, this enclave in an otherwise empty corner of southwest Montana has joined the ranks of such ski-resort names as Alta, Aspen, and Park City. A base village growing in a measured, conservative pace, it boasts a mammoth vertical with some of the steepest ski terrain in the land at the apex, and it ranks as a true value destination for families, offering free skiing and lodging for children to age ten.

At the outset, the resort's developers went out on a bold marketing limb and took the name of the "big sky" state. Skiers of a certain age remember that Big Sky was the brainchild of former NBC anchorman Chet Huntley. Eventually, ownership passed to Boyne USA, a family-owned company that has caused the ski mountain and its attendant facilities to grow slowly, albeit steadily, while visitor numbers remained modest. But more recently, almost like a child who has blossomed suddenly into adulthood, Big Sky became the biggest, classiest, brassiest, and perhaps best-known ski destination in the northern Rockies. The reasons have to do with location, vision, and arguably the most exciting lift in America, the Lone Peak Tram.

Vision first. In the sixties, Huntley, a Montana native, set out in search of a major recreational property. He found it on the West Fork of

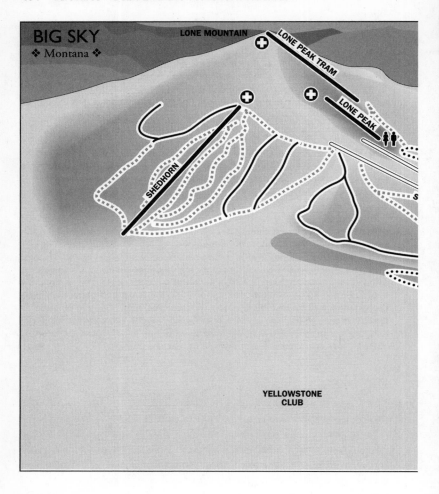

the Gallatin River, northwest of Yellowstone National Park and south of Bozeman, a sleepy agricultural center and home to Montana State University. He was actually a minority owner with less than 1 percent of the stock, but his deep-pocketed, Blue Chip corporate partners funded the purchase of 11,000 spectacular, empty acres on and around Lone Mountain. The first three chairlifts and a gondola opened for business in 1973. Then in 1974, just four months after the lifts cranked up and only a few days before the grand opening of the slopeside Huntley Lodge, Chet Huntley succumbed to lung cancer, and the big investors soon decided to sell. The buyer was Boyne USA, the Michigan-based corporation that now also owns Boyne Mountain and Boyne Highlands in Michigan.

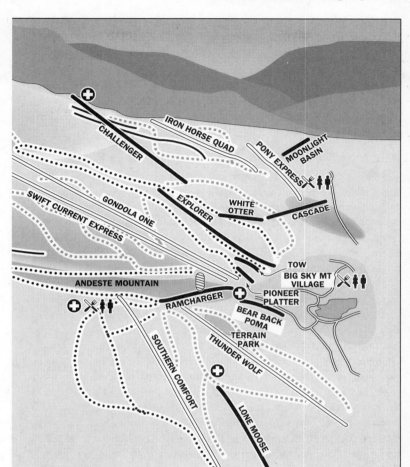

The Boyne folks have serious visions of their own, because today Big Sky boasts over 3,600 acres of varied ski terrain and a wide-ranging lift system to service it. Big Sky and Jackson Hole are the northern Rockies' vertical leaders. At 4,350 feet, Big Sky's "total" vertical involves a math trick. To experience Big Sky's total vertical, you have to ski from the peak to the village—a substantial 3,650 vertical feet—then ride up onto adjacent Andesite Mountain and ski to the terrain's lowest point. Jackson Hole's 4,129-foot vertical is continuous, offering top-to-bottom skiing (get off the Rendezvous Peak tram and don't stop until you reach Teton Village). When comparing these two giants in the greater Yellowstone area, think of them as continuous skiable vertical versus total vertical feet. Big Sky's hot expert terrain complements previously developed chunks of novice and intermediate cruising.

Big Sky's location, between Bozeman and the northwestern reaches of Yellowstone National Park, turns out to be a fortuitous blend of isolation and accessibility, wilderness and notoriety. When you are on the mountain, or in the base village during certain times of light, there is a palpable, almost islandlike sense of seclusion. It's as if the cold, the quiet, and the arc of the sky were indeed bigger than other places you've been.

The Last, Best, Famous, Still Mostly Empty Place

Big Sky is surrounded by impressive sweeps of wilderness, millions of acres' worth, protected forever—and tens thousands of acres of land being developed into exclusive gated resort communities. This corner of Montana resonates a certain romantic chic that is growing more and more recognizable as the outside world discovers it. Ted Turner's place is just to the north, and Peter Fonda's ranch sits just out of sight to the east. Californians by the Lexus-load fall in love with the landscape.

The Yellowstone Club, a posh private ski and golf resort right at Big Sky's doorstep, "welcomes" anyone with, say, a quarter of a million dollar initiation fee and two to several million to buy and build on a parcel of land there. What writer William Kittredge called "the last best place" has become the best-known place in a big, formerly empty but rapidly changing state—and nothing exemplifies these changes more than the exclusive, gated developments like Yellowstone Club. Perhaps surprisingly, however, the states from which Big Sky draws most of its patrons are still North and South Dakota—solid mid-American families and students who pile into vans and pickups for their annual trek across the Plains to the mountains. This combination of Midwestern, Boyne values and big-bucks glitz has turned Big Sky—more than any other resort—into a schitzy place. Farm families from North Dakota, for whom Big Sky is "only" a 12-hour drive from their homes, share chairlifts with well-heeled entrepreneurs who fly in on their private jets.

Three world-famous trout streams flow north off the Yellowstone Plateau toward Bozeman and I-90. From east to west they are the Yellowstone, the Gallatin, and the Madison Rivers. Big Sky is just off the Gallatin, the stream they used to film *A River Runs Through It*. The Madison Range, which divides the Gallatin from the Madison drainages, is Big Sky's backyard. In the center of the chain, Lone Mountain rears its volcanic-looking cone to 11,166 feet, easily the highest summit around. The cosmopolitan glitz of Aspen and the freeway urbanity of Vail may seem both still a long way off, and may, in fact, never reach the high valleys of the Madison and Gallatin ranges. I fervently hope so, but when I look at the seven-figure vacation homes infesting the landscape, I'm not sure.

The Layout and the (Changing) Landscape

Big Sky's lodging and services are clustered in two locations. The hotel, condominium, and dining options are concentrated in Mountain Village at the base of the lifts. Wrapping around the base of the ski mountain are several newer and more opulent housing pods with condos, pivate homes, and a sprinkling of lodges. Of these, the Moonlight Basin area with convenient access lifts is the most densely developed. Meadow Village, a few miles down valley near the bottom of the resort's access road, has additional condo and private-home rentals sprawled in a side valley—and as of 2003–2004 anticipates firing up its own high-speed chairlift. And down at the river confluence in Gallatin Canyon are a number of motels and guest ranches. Lone Mountain Ranch, a separate enterprise and one of the country's premier cross-country skiing destinations and a summer guest ranch, sits high on the valley's shoulder, overlooking Meadow Village.

The Lone Mountain summit offers such a spectacular panorama that it is a sightseeing attraction, even for those who ride the tram back down rather than attempt the super-challenging ski runs. On a clear day, you can see Grand Teton, a commanding peak 100 miles to the south, if you know which serrated bump to look for. Nearer views include the Spanish Peaks, which cut a rugged, white-crested swath across the northern skyline, and the peaks of the Taylor Hilgard Wilderness to the south, between Big Sky and the massive vault of the Yellowstone Plateau. To the west and far below are the winter-golden fields bordering the Madison River, with the Tobacco Root Mountains behind. The only signs of man's presence, besides the ski trappings, are the occasional clear-cut blocks snipped out of the forest carpet—and increasingly, monster homes on private land.

In fact, much of the valley land, including Lone Mountain, is private, courtesy of railroad land grants in the nineteenth century. This is a double-edged sword for Big Sky's developers. On the one hand, private land on the ski mountain makes it easier to build new lifts and trails without having to wade through the red tape of the public lands approval process. Thus the quick implementation of the tram, the likes of which we will probably not see on public-lands ski areas. Similarly, the Iron Horse quad chairlift, attendant trails, and homesites have been carved out of the private, 25,000-acre Moonlight Basin Ranch, and the aforementioned 13,400-acre Yellowstone Club boasts "private powder" served by its own lifts, a golf course and of course, homesites.

On the other hand, the region's private land developers, being free of many constraints, too often have exhibited disregard for riparian and other ecological issues. Building moratoriums have been issued, and fines have been levied to curtail irresponsible development. Hopefully, developers will be more careful in the future. In any case, there will surely be more clear-cutting, more construction inappropriate to the scenic values of the nearby wilderness, more private gated communities, and more of a them-versus-us sense growing between long-time Montanans and moneyed newcomers for whom "privacy" and "luxury" are the greatest values. Still, more of Big Sky's surrounding land is becoming legal wilderness. An activist environmental community has pressured the government into protecting undeveloped land and also negotiating conservation agreements with many of the region's landowners. In any event, Big Sky will always be a strikingly beautiful place.

Big Sky for Beginners

But most vacationers don't get embroiled in land-use issues. They come to ski or snowboard, and the resort offers it in abundance for all levels of skill. Big Sky has made a big push to lure families. Like other Boyne USA resorts, it invites kids ages ten and under to ski and stay free. The resort hosts an independently run Handprints day care program. The ski school has fine children's classes. and much of the learning terrain is excellent and sufficiently segregated from faster traffic.

The moving carpet tows provide the explorer double chair access to a brace of low-angle greens, such as *Lone Wolf, White Wing,* and a third green run that branches off the top of *Explorer* and merges with *Mr. K,* the excellent novice route off the top of the gondola.

Moving up from the Explorer chair, novices have just one option on Lone Mountain, and that is the aforementioned *Morning Star/Mr. K* combination. Beginners can ride the gondola right up to tree line and then slide down over 1,500 vertical feet and nearly two miles over wide, beautifully prepared boulevards that go on and on and on. Elsewhere at Big Sky, novices treasure the runs of Southern Comfort (see descriptions of intermediate terrain, below).

Big-Time Intermediate Skiing

Big Sky has long held a reputation as a super intermediate mountain—three interconnected intermediate mountains, in fact. The RamCharger high-speed quad right out of the base provides the quickest access to intermediate terrain on Andesite Mountain and to the back side, served by the Thunder Wolf high-speed quad. The skiing is long, smooth, and deliciously pitched for giant-slalom cranking. The runs are beautifully prepared, and one soon grows to appreciate the added gravity.

On the front side, *Silver Knife* and the broad *Ambush* run under the lift and are guaranteed coverage thanks to snowmaking. A couple of very interesting blues off to the west side of the lift, the spacious *Hangman's* and the looping roller coaster known as *Africa* with good front-side bumps, need more natural cover to open. There is a very nice escape route for novices skiing the gentler back-side Southern Comfort area (or for beginners who really didn't mean to be riding up on Andesite). That run, eponymously called *Pacifier,* snakes through the woods on a long and winding road back to safety. Two chairs on the back side access two distinct zones. The Southern Comfort triple returns lower-level intermediates to the Andesite summit from a perfectly sequestered, uniformly tilted, sun-worshiping green zone. It boasts a quartet of the gentlest, widest, best-groomed, least-crowded green-circle runs at Big Sky: *El Dorado, Sacajawea, Deep South,* and *Ponderosa* that run the full 1,250-foot vertical and provide a lot of mileage at the stage when learning skiers really need it. The 12-minute ride back up is a long one, but most Southern Comfort denizens appreciate the recovery time.

By contrast, the Thunder Wolf quad races over 1,700 vertical feet in five-and-a-half minutes. You barely have time to glance down at the sublime, mostly wide-open terrain sailing below. It accesses one of Big Sky's best sectors for stronger intermediates. *Elk Park Meadows,* off the ridge of the same name, starts off by skirting the lip of the *Mad Wolf* mogul field, and then dives through the trees over three big rolls and out into a long, sweeping, giddy field dotted with huge, maverick Douglas firs standing sentinel over the whoops and hollers. Skier's left on *Elk Park* is always groomed smooth. Out in the expanse to the right, various gullies and side hills and rollicking natural shapes are left wild. This makes for some superb powder dancing for intermediates and an increasing number of experts who are hip to the warm exposure and the protection from wind. Elk Park feeds directly to the bottom of the Thunder Wolf quad, so skiers can do a huge number of reps on it.

Go right from the Thunder Wolf unload to return to *Elk Park Ridge* or drop into *Mad Wolf,* which is rated black diamond, and except for the topmost pitch, drops gently enough to keep the moguls round. The best intermediate bumps at Big Sky grow on the lower two-thirds, and there are many ways in and out of the bumps from *Elk Park* on the left side. Go left at the unload and you'll reach *Big Horn,* a long, easy ride between forest walls that suddenly turn 90 degrees and drop into a shady, north-facing bowl and gully system, complete with high banks for banking big, lazy, high-speed turns back to the bottom of Thunder Wolf.

Blue-square offerings on Lone Mountain's lower slopes have a very different flavor. Dropping through the trees on either side of the gondola are *Crazy Horse, Lobo,* and *Calamity Jane.* They are relatively narrow, wavy, fall-line cruisers with the occasional bump run cut a little more steeply between them and have a decidedly Eastern feel. One of Big Sky's two original gondolas remains to serve this terrain, but it is essentially rendered obsolete by the parallel (and much faster) Swift Current high-speed quad chair. At mid-mountain, Shedhorn's trees provide good stormy-day cover and yet another cruising zone for intermediates with a bit of wanderlust.

Most intriguing for sturdy intermediates is the terrain off the Lone Peak triple, just below Lone Mountain's summit cliffs and couloirs. This huge, Euro-style, above-the-timber bowl is genuine big-mountain skiing, with all its attendant beauties and vagaries: high winds, deep snow, shapes created by the rocks below and not by any tree-cutter's hand.

Two routes off the top, *Never Sweat* and *Upper Morning Star,* are groomed to guarantee a packed route down, but in the right conditions, the whole 180-degree bowl can provide good skiing. Sometimes high winds smooth and pack the whole thing, creating unlimited lines around twisted, dwarf pines, but when powder falls unmolested by retreating tempests, *The Bowl* surely is one of the sweetest, easiest intermediate fall lines in the Rockies. In the spring, there are few sensations finer than banking the serpentine corn-snow walls of *Never Sweat,* which feels like skateboarding the inside of a mammoth, porcelain bathtub.

Flat Iron Mountain, which also provides access to those people living or staying in the Lone Moose Meadows area, is an isolated ski hill. The base of Lone Moose chair is only at 6,800 feet, so expect less snow depth on this part of the mountain and possible earlier spring melt-off.

Expert Zones from A to Z—and Beyond

Big Sky, once knocked as a white-bread mountain—from an expert's point of view at any rate—was jazzed up with the addition of some of the West's most dramatic chute skiing, the A–Z Chutes off the Challenger chair. In fact, movie-star extreme skiers Scot Schmidt and Tom Jüngst switched allegiance from Bridger Bowl north, a place of legendary steeps, to test their skills here when the chutes were opened.

As you ride the Lone Peak triple through the gut of *The Bowl,* your eye is drawn to the string of chutes, raked like claw marks into the south-facing ridge to the right. These are the *A–Z Chutes.* There are indeed 26 of them, more or less, depending on how snow fills in between the rocks. Years before the tram, hot skiers from Bozeman, including a few extreme stars, regularly made the drive down to Big Sky just to ski them. The chutes are still there, of course. They've just been superseded by the extreme riches offered up by the tram.

It takes work to reach the *A–Z Chutes,* and nobody gets there by accident. From the top of the Challenger chair, it's a straightforward hike of a few hundred feet, followed by a ridgeline balancing act of up to a quarter mile to the chosen snow slot. The most popular routes are the closest before reaching the *A–Z Chutes* themselves, called *The Pinnacles,* for the rust-colored outcroppings that frame the descents. All of the chutes, from *The Pinnacles* up through *Z Chute,* face south around to east, so variable snow conditions, including sun and wind crusts, should be expected.

You don't have to hike to find wonderful advanced and expert skiing. The Challenger chairlift accesses more than vertical 1,700 feet and a plethora of true steeps off the northern prow of Lone Mountain. This is an experts' playground and the prime fallback when wind shuts down the summit tram. There are three zones to explore, each a different aspect. Drop off the ridge to the east into *Little Tree* basin, which begins as a near-featureless porcelain hip and then funnels into a series of slots through the craggy, white-bark pines, many gnarled by the wind. The biggest openings are skier's left, and the farther right you go, the tighter and steeper the lines. Finish by taking the intermediate *Bert Road* back to Challenger base.

The middle zone faces northeast and is named *Rock Tongue.* The snow here is shaped underneath by pure rock that cuts like a glacier from the ridge into the forest below, leaving a swath of open, undulating terrain. *Kurt's Glade,* the most accessible drop from the ridge, is so steep that a fall on hard snow can result in a long slide to the basin below. *Little Rock Tongue* and *Big Rock Tongue* drop through shallow rock fins and are not always filled sufficiently for skiing from the top. The lower half of the lolling "tongue" offers some super, treeless powder and crud skiing.

The third zone, also on skier's left, drops into Moonlight Basin. The slopes face true north, meaning that the snow is some of the softest and best protected on the mountain. The sun hardly shines here in midwinter, and when it does, it comes from directly behind, so that you might ski with your own shadow projected 100 feet or more down the slope ahead. *Moonlight Highway* off the top takes a fair amount of wind, as do all the tree line ridges, but the effect can be exquisite, with smooth, granular snow that carves like soap and rarely develops into moguls. Lower down in the trees, bumps do form in the soft snow, but because they are shaped by good skiers, the net effect is rhythmic and playful. A new lift in Moonlight Basin might change the way this sector is skied. You can exit *Moonlight* back to the Challenger chair via *Fast Lane* or continue on *Bad Dog, Powder River,* or *Snake Bite* to the Iron Horse lift.

Blue Room, War Dance, Mad Wolf, Crazy Raven, Rock Pocket, and *Snake Pit* are among the handful of black-diamond treasures sprinkled among the greens and blues off the RamCharger and Thunder Wolf chairs. Some are steep mogul drops, others are winsome glades of respectable pitch. They don't have the Lone Montain or Challenger rep, but they don't get the traffic either.

The Mystique of the Tram

In 1996 Big Sky installed the Lone Peak Tram, a 15-passenger, single-stage, European-style lift that rises just 16 feet short of the 11,166-foot Lone Mountain summit. The philosophy behind such a low-capacity lift was to retain uncrowded slopes, providing backcountry skier/rider density on lift-served terrain. The tram pushed Big Sky into the pantheon of big-vertical, super-steep mountains, and many true expert skiers now never even give Challenger a second look. Such is the allure of the tram and the awesomely steep, never-groomed terrain that it serves.

At the top, you feel as if you've been thrust up on to the tip of the world. To descend, you have four options: Descend the sprawling, treeless *South Face;* work your way down the east ridge to one of the six *Gullies;* tackle the real test pieces like the serpentine *Big Couloir* twists through the cliffs off the mountain's northwest ridge or; if discretion becomes the better part of valor, ride the tram back down. There is no disgrace in this, and in fact, many less-skilled Big Sky visitors ride up just for a look without ever intending to ski down.

The broad *South Face* of Lone Mountain is the place to start. Once you have committed, there is no turning back, for it features more than 2,000 vertical feet before you even reach the top of another lift. *Liberty Bowl* slides off the summit at the gentlest pitch, but it is ungroomed and far from gentle. The center line usually fills with whitecap bumps. Off to the sides, cutup powder turns to crud in the sun. Move east across the face, and the going gets steeper and steeper. None of this is easy-street skiing. *Thunder, The Wave,* and *Dictator Chutes* (*Marx, Lenin,* and *Castro*) plummet a good 1,000 feet before moderating at tree line. *Marx* has been the site of at least two recent U.S. Powder 8 Championships, and when you look at the near-vertical parcel and imagine a pair of skiers etching perfectly linked turns into new snow, you build a new image of teamwork and great skiing. *Castro's Shoulder* at the far south end of *Dictator Chutes* at 50 degrees is reputedly the steepest named pitch on the mountain.

South Face skiers have the option to take *Duck Walk* road around the peak's burly shoulder to the front side, to the Lone Peak triple and another tram ride, but most one-timers continue downhill into an additional 1,400-foot groomed vertical to the bottom of the Shedhorn double chair, relieved to be in a blue-square zone again. At the end of the day, everyone exits from the back side via the *Duck Walk* road to the village side of the mountain.

Above *The Bowl,* just to the left and right of the tram (and visible from it), are The *Gullies* (One through Six) and the *Big Couloir.* They really mean business, and make up some of the hairiest terrain in the land. Just to get to the top of *Big Couloir,* you have to check in with the ski patrol, have a partner, and carry avalanche-rescue gear. A helmet is a good idea, too, for a slide into the rocks on either side is not a palatable option. Slip and you're in for a long, scary slide, but ski these intoxicating drops well with care and respect, and they will raise the level of your game. Everything else—the black diamonds at other ski areas—will seem like child's play.

Snowboarding

Ambush Meadows boasts Big Sky's big terrain park served by the Ram-Charger lift. For 2003–2004, plans were to excavate the half-pipe into the slope itself, so that it can be constructed and maintained without piling up a great deal of natural and machine-made snow. Additionally, a playful natural half-pipe runs down the right side of *Lower Morning Star,* where a shaded gully provides endless banks, lips, and spines to play on.

A wooden bench outside the Dug Out Restaurant atop Andesite Mountain, where three lifts converge, comes equipped with screwdrivers and pliers for use by anybody who wants to adjust a DIN setting, fix a boot buckle, or alter the stance on a freestyle board. Though such benches have become common to give snowboarders a place to click in, the tools are a once-common courtesy before the days of lawsuit madness.

Dining Big Sky

The **Dug Out Restaurant** atop Andesite Mountain is the *only* food right on the slopes: Polish dogs and picnic-table dining indoors or out. But they really don't need high-altitude restaurants because most of the skiing funnels directly back to the Mountain Village. At the gondola base, the **Mountain Mall** contains eleven eating establishments, plus retail and rental shops. It is a bit odd to clunk along in ski boots with scores of mall rats. But the indoor ambience is a big plus in cold and stormy weather, and the whole thing has a relaxed feel. Besides, it allows for a choice of smaller eateries under one roof.

In nice weather, the big metal deck outside the **Lone Peak Café** is a happening place. Bring food out from any of the eateries inside or order burgers and other casual food from the cafeteria. **Mountain Top Pizza,** which sells by the slice, is a locals' favorite. The Bing Lee family serves Chinese at the **Twin Pandas** restaurant. After skiing, **Dante's Inferno** is the place for live music, beers, and munchies, and **Rooster's** boasts vintage telemark decor and killer margaritas.

Thirty seconds of walking away from the mall, the **Huntley Lodge** and the **Summit at Big Sky** offer more atmospheric dining. The **Peaks Restaurant** at the Summit serves contemporary food in a contemporary Euro-Western/modern American setting, and the **Carabiner Lounge** is a pleasant watering hole. The Huntley Lodge dining room serves breakfast and dinner only in an expansive room with tall windows that overlook the slopes, while adjacent **Chet's Bar** has nightly entertainment and live poker games. (Yes, low-stakes gambling is legal in Montana. You even see it at gas stations and truck stops.) The bar itself is a hand-carved, 100-year-old, solid oak beauty, discovered by Huntley in Anaconda, Montana.

One night you owe it to yourself to travel down to the valley for dinner. **Lone Mountain Ranch's** dining room is situated in a gorgeous log bin, where a gourmet chef prepares fine seafood, beef, buffalo, and wild game entrées. (See "Inside Story" following this chapter.) Further downhill is **Buck's 4T,** probably the finest restaurant in any **Best Western** motel in the land. Game and other hearty dishes are house specialties, and the atmosphere—with trophy heads and rustic artifacts—reflects the Montana spirit.

Big Sky Data

Mountain Statistics

Vertical feet	4,350 feet
Base elevation (Mountain Village)	7,500 feet
Base elevation (Lone Moose)	6,800 feet
Summit elevation (Lone Mountain)	11,150 feet
Longest run	6 miles
Average annual snowfall	400 inches
Number of lifts	18: 1 15-person tram; 1 gondola; 4 quad chairs; 4 triples; 5 doubles; 3 surface tows
Uphill capacity	20,000 skiers per hour
Skiable terrain	3,600 acres
Opening date	Thanksgiving
Closing date	Mid-April
Snowboarding	Yes

Transportation

By car One hour south of Bozeman, Montana, via Highway 191; 3 hours north west of Jackson, Wyoming, via West Yellowstone on Highways 22, 33, 32 and 191; 6 hours north of Salt Lake City via Interstate 15 and Highway 191.

By plane About 43 miles from Bozeman's airport, which is served by Delta, Horizon, Northwest, SkyWest, and United/United Express airlines. Taxi and van service from the airport.

Key Phone Numbers

Ski-area information	(406) 995-5000
Lodging	(800) 548-4486
Snow report	(406) 995-5900
Websites	www.bigskyresort.com

Inside Story

Lone Mountain Ranch

Cross-country skiing consistently ranks first on all those exercise charts of calories burned per hour of exercise. And it's true. The whole body is involved in the diagonal striding/poling, kick-and-glide of classical track skiing—the real-world antecedent of the Nordic Track indoor exercise machine or the highly aerobic and energetic skill of skating on Nordic skis.

At the Lone Mountain Ranch, a few short miles down the hill from Big Sky's Mountain Village (and also accessible by free shuttle), the cross-country art has been honed to perfection. Fifty-five guests stay in 23 log cabins, some dating back to the ranch's founding in 1915. They all eat together in the soaring glass-and-log dining room. And they all come to ski the 65 kilometers of groomed trail that radiate into the surrounding national forest. The trails are the key. The ambience is convivial, the food is superb, and the staff is genuinely friendly and involved, but it is the trails—like magic carpets—that bring 80% of the guests back year after year. The ranch also welcomes nonguests to come ski and eat.

Start from the back door of the ski shop, with its busy waxing bench and its warm, not altogether incongruous, smell of blueberry muffins and melted blue wax. The tracks are set up so you can run (or walk) along in the preset grooves—called diagonal striding or "classical technique" skiing—or skate on the wide, smooth skating lane, like a corduroy sidewalk, on one side.

After a short climb in the woods, the trail bursts out onto a great bald ridge, like a white whaleback with split-rail fences and the meadows of the West Gallatin valley below. No worries. There is no possibility of getting lost; the track winds into the distance and inevitably back to the lodge. Your only choices are whether or not to stop here for a drink of water, or stop among those aspen trees, or stop up ahead where the view of Lone Mountain and the Madisons spreads out like a movie backdrop of a mural in blues and whites. Miles fly by beneath your skis; 5, 10, 20 miles like creek water. On the final downhill plunge to the lodge, the skis turn as the trail turns, ending back at the ski shop. If you're staying at Lone Mountain Ranch, it's hot tub time; and later, dinner beneath the elk-antler chandeliers. Then fall in under the quilts and dream of caressing the hills with your feet.

Bridger Bowl

A small ad in the ski magazines a number of years back featured the requisite, red-clad powder skier in mid-float. The text read: "Don't Let Our $25 Lift Ticket Fool You! We're Bridger Bowl, a nonprofit ski area in Bozeman, Montana. We have no owners to pay. Experience skiing like it used to be . . . a big mountain with over 2,000 feet of vertical for $25/day."

Nonprofit? Big-mountain skiing for $25 a day? Well, not any longer. A single-day lift ticket in 2002–2003 climbed to $35 a day, but on a multiday package and if you're willing to jam four into a motel room, it is still possible to ski and sleep for as little as $39 a day.

Bridger Bowl has been likened to "a classic '57 Chevy"—unchanging, a little long in the tooth but still possessing in abundance the virtues that made skiing great in the first place. Bridger boasts superb terrain, good natural snow, plenty of programs for kids and students, a homegrown management team that is relaxed, friendly, and frankly uninterested in real estate sales, and finally, a mystique surrounding its exceptional extreme terrain. Ski movie-star, extreme-skiing champions who developed their craft on The Ridge include Scot Schmidt, Doug Coombs, Emily Gladstone, and Tom Jüngst—and anyone with the guts and the skill can ski there.

Throughout the West, serious skiers know Bridger to be a last haven for a dying breed of hard-core, committed, first-chair-to-last, 130-days-per-season ski bums. It is the quintessential locals' mountain. Locals started the ski hill during the 1954–1955 season, and locals still run it. Longtime general manager Terry Abelin was a patroller at Bridger, and he answers to a board of directors comprised of his friends and neighbors.

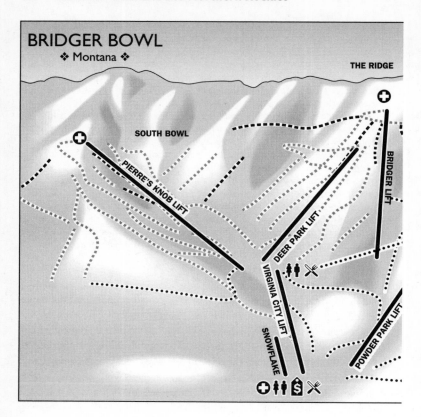

Joining the nonprofit Bridger Bowl Ski Area, Inc., requires only that you be a Montana resident and pay a $25 initiation fee and a $1 annual membership fee. With that, you are a voting member of the association, eligible to election on the nine-member board of directors. The nonprofit status allows the area to keep prices down to nearly 1957 levels—thus the $35 daily ticket and an adult full-season pass of only $505 in 2002–2003 ($370 for midweek skiing only). A remarkable 3,600 locals hold season passes, a big number in a university town of some 30,000 residents (plus just over 11,000 students).

Down in Bozeman, a blue beacon atop the venerable Baxter Hotel lights up whenever there is an accumulation of one or more inches of new snow, and the recorded snow report indicates not just snowfall, but also windspeed at both the base and summit, so that Ridge rats know which exposures are snow-loading and which are losing cover to a scouring wind. When skiers come up the quick 16 miles from town to the

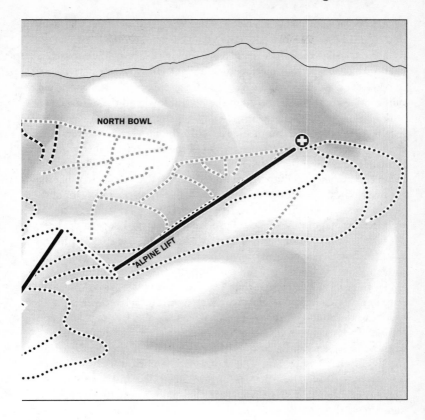

mountain, they are rewarded with some of the best skiing and arguably some of the best skiing value north of Alta, Utah, (another unpretentious, debt-free, community-based ski area with a penchant for keeping frills and prices down).

The Lay of the Land

The Bridger Range pokes a long, narrow finger across the horizon north of Bozeman and I-90. By Colorado standards, these peaks are modest, with summits below 9,000 feet, and the ski area occupies an enormous east-facing basin within that range. The view from the upper runs and especially from The Ridge, at the ski area's apex, is huge in all directions. The wonderfully named Crazy Mountains shine to the east; the Tobacco Roots blaze bright white to the west; the Spanish Peaks hide Big Sky to the south; and the Absaroka and Bear Tooth mountains loom to the southeast on the border of Yellowstone National Park. With inversion clouds covering the valleys (a common phenomenon on cold, high-pressure days), the wild, 360-degree sweep feels like Montana, pre–Lewis and Clark.

On the trail map, the ski area's layout couldn't be simpler: one base, six chairlifts, one new mid-mountain restaurant, and by the start of the 2003–2004 season, a second new day lodge at the base. In reality, the terrain is more complex, divided into the North Bowl and the South Bowl, with a sub-ridge dividing them and cliff bands above. The runs sweep up in a natural progression from the easiest in the meadows and trees near the base lodge, to the mid-range terrain in the midsection, then to more difficult turf up near the tree line, and finally to the steepest terrain in the rocks and avalanche gullies. As you drive toward the mountain, only the lift lines indicate that it is a ski area. The skiable terrain weaves sinuously through natural clearings, along tree-free drainages, and flirts with the tree line. From a bird's-eye view above the Jim Bridger Lodge at the base, the whole thing spreads out like a fan, with the 70 or so named runs on 1,500 skiable acres, pouring down the fall lines to a central point. No hidden zones, no back sides, and nothing you can't see at a glance.

From ground level, a first-time Bridger visitor might need some orientation. Which lifts go to what sort of terrain? The answer isn't obvious, thanks to the abundant forest. The Virginia City (VC), Snow Flake, and Powder Park beginner lifts climb from the base to the lion's share of beginner/novice terrain. The Snow Flake beginner lift, just to the left of the VC lift, has a whopping 40 feet of vertical on a 400-foot run, which leaves a nice 10% grade—perfect for first-time skiers and boarders.

The Powder Park chair, which is the main access to higher lifts, angles toward North Bowl to the right as you are looking uphill. Higher up, and not visible from the base, is the Alpine lift, serving a mix of long novice and intermediate trails. The Virginia City lift, just to the left of the base lodge as you are looking up, directly serves beginner terrain and also leads toward the South Bowl.

The Virginia City chair unloads at a mid-mountain lift confluence—and you can also ski down to it from the top of the Powder Park chair. At this confluence are the bottom of the Deer Park and Pierre's Knob, as well as the Deer Park Chalet restaurant. The Pierre's Knob and South Bowl lifts climb the mountain's mostly intermediate south flank. Right in the trail system's center, pushing up the ridge separating the North and South Bowls, are the Bridger and Deer Park lifts. A network of cat tracks makes it relatively straightforward to move from one zone to another, but because the area is much wider than it is high and because the lifts are quite long and relatively slow, most skiers stake out a region and stay there a while.

Bridger Beginners

Learning skiers should start out on Virginia City with several choices, including *Missouri Breaks, Moose Meadows,* and *Bridger Run.* Unlike the other novice trails that meander through the scenic woods, *Moose Meadows* is so broad you can yo-yo it dozens of times and pick out a different line each time. Bridger's real wealth of easy skiing drapes the Powder Park and Alpine lifts like languid strings of pearls. *Sunnyside* is the wide central boulevard off the top of the Powder Park lift, with *Mogul Mouse, Mully Road,* and *Lower Limestone* feeding in from the side. The Alpine lift accesses long (up to three-mile) descents (via *Crazy Women* and *Timmy's Road*) through the muffled, cold-snow forests along the area's north boundary. *North Meadows Road* to *Limestone* to *Summer Road* carries the gentlest grade. *Porcupine* loops right off the top and joins *Alpine Run* under the chair. Alpine is also a good lift for novices who want to stay high above the occasional inversion clouds blanketing the valley.

Bridger for Better Skiers

There are a number of fine intermediate routes off the Alpine chair as well. The most interesting are in the *Three Bears* area, a generous open-palm bowl below *Three Bears Chutes* with the same wild feel (but not the same steep pitch) as the hike-to terrain above. The Bears are named *Papa Bear, Mama Bear,* and *Baby Bear* according to the depth and volume of the snow. The *Three Bears* and *Alpine Face* funnel together onto *Alpine Run,* so you can repeat them ad infinitum if you want. Another nifty intermediate route on Alpine is the *Powder Park* area off the *Three Bears Traverse* south (right) off the lift's top terminal. This is not a run so much as an adventure through timberline glades and a big, open park dropping onto the *Mogul Mouse* green run. On a powder day, this is the perfect place for deep-snow neophytes to find untracked snow for unhurried practice.

Most intermediates, though, stick to either the Bridger/Deer Park or the Pierre's Knob lifts. Bridger climbs up the spine of the center ridge. Drop to the right of the lift into the spacious *North Bowl,* an expanse of treeless, naked, go-anywhere-you-want-to-point-'em skiing. There is even a route in the bowl called *Freedom. North Bowl* grows some of the best intermediate bumps on the mountain, though you always have a choice; there's so much room, you can always opt for bumps or no bumps.

South (skier's right) of the Bridger lift, the Deer Park chair skirts the side of the center ridge and serves an interesting variety of rolling timberline terrain and snaky shots through the trees. Skier's left, *Deer Park Face, Hanton's Hollow, Powder Horn,* and *Boothill* are rated blue and are usually groomed. The far south end of South Bowl is Pierre's Knob, served by a lift of the same name emanating from the Deer Park confluence. Pierre's accesses to the invitingly pitched south flank of *South Bowl.* The middle is often kept mogul free with a smooth swath groomed down the gut, as is *Emile's Mile* just to the right. These two, along with *Missouri Breaks* to *White Lightning,* provide some of the longest and best cruising at Bridger, with intriguing micro-terrain and little dips and rolls that give a descent playfulness and flavor.

Like *North Bowl, South Bowl* is allowed to develop bumps in the hollows where they form naturally. The pitch is never so steep that the moguls become scary. These are good learning grounds, and you can always bail out to something smooth next door. For bumps with a little more tilt, try *Coulter's Crawl* and *Psychopath,* skier's left of *South Bowl.* These are outruns for steeper chutes off The Ridge, and the bumps are usually well formed by good skiers.

Expert Bridger

The Ridge carries unquestionable cache. Its mystique grew slowly but steadily through the 1970s and 1980s as self-professed "Ridge hippies" rode the aging Bridger lift and hiked the final 400 vertical feet to chutes with names like *Sometimes A Great Notion* and *The O's* (short for the Orgasms). Some of them lived whole winters on one month's salary from fishing in Alaska. Some rode their bikes to the mountain every morning with skis on their backs. They developed a skiing style that, because of the walking and the narrow snow-choked hallways between the rocks, was more efficient than flashy; it was all about grace and nonchalance, no wasted movement, and continuous turns where no panicking or seizing up is allowed. Don't waste your energy in one burst; use it over a whole day. It's a way of skiing that most people are too hurried and impatient to learn.

Intermediates should, under no circumstances, attempt the hike to The Ridge. There are no easy ways down, only very steep, rocky, and tricky drops with nothing remotely like an escape route. Everything qualifies as the "no fall zone." Not to worry, though, you can't get up there by accident. The ski patrol's rather foolproof screening procedure requires skiers and snowboarders to have working avalanche transceivers, verified by an electronic sensor. In addition, everyone must carry a shovel (to dig out a buried companion) and go with someone who has been there before. The Ridge is serious business.

Not all experts feel comfortable on the elevator-shaft steepness of most Ridge lines either. The 400-vertical-foot hike, known as the *Stairway to Heaven,* discourages many who may not have the breath or the quads. However, many regulars do laps. In fact, Bridger mounts an annual King and Queen of The Ridge competition, with the winners accomplishing the most round-trips. In 2003, the top man made 20 runs and the top woman 19. For details about The Ridge, see "Inside Story" on page 423. For the moment, let's look at lift-served expert options below The Ridge.

From the Bridger lift, runs like *Bronco* directly beside the lift and *Sluice Box* and *Ptarmigan* on skier's right, tend to develop sizable bumps and pose as good a fast-twitch challenge as any in the Rockies. Drop off the ridge into North Bowl for great bumps in *The John* and *Easy Money*. Steep but shaded to keep the bumps soft, this duo lures Bridger's mogul maniacs.

Farther south, *Avalanche Gulch* and *The Nose* are like gale-tossed seas. The *Deer Park Road* leads to a traverse into the midpoint on these monsters, but to get even higher, take the *High Traverse* off the top of Bridger lift. There *Avalanche Gulch* plunges like a drainpipe with Volkswagen-size stair steps on which to set an edge, but a piste is often groomed down the center for sublime cruising. Beyond *Avalanche,* the trail shrivels to a darting path through twisted survivor trees. Roots and rocks require dancing feet until you come to any of a dozen double-diamond chutes known collectively as *The Nose*. They're not on the trail map, but they've all got names like *Deviated Septum* and *Nasal Cavity*. Return via *South Bowl Run* to the Deer Park lift.

Many experts like to yo-yo the Bridger lift, repeating runs on *Bronco, Ptarmigan, Out-Of-Site,* or *Easy Money,* which is easier now that the Powder Park chair is in place. Bridger was shortened (from the bottom), allowing for the installation of more chairs and a subsequent upping of capacity to the area's high point.

If Bridger lift is too busy, chances are Deer Park or Pierre's Knob are not. *Lower Avalanche Gulch* and *Devil's Dive* offer some good, steep bumps south of the Deer Park lift. Over on Pierre's, there is some sweet glade skiing on *South Boundary* and a rash of genuinely gnarly tree lines on *Flipper's* and the north-facing pitches below the chair. A great option is to hike above Pierre's to *The Fingers* for additional terrain on those powder days. More glades are found all the way on the other side of the ski area below Sawmill Gulch. Relatively gentle, little-used, and packed with untracked snow for days after a storm, they offer great end-of-day skiing, ending right at the base lodge.

Snowboarding

Bridger Bowl has no man-made terrain park or half-pipe. It's not necessary, because so much of the mountain is nature's own terrain park. The dips, glades, little snow-filled drainages that ride like natural half-pipes, and generous glades are dreamy terrain for free riders. Tricksters have been known to build their own kickers and hits in the trees, totally unauthorized and completely unofficial. Riders, with their softer boots and light boards, have a definite advantage when it comes to hiking to The Ridge. Everywhere on the mountain, they snake through small openings between trees and rocks and turn on a dime.

Good Eats

Bridger's Ridge hippies are famous for eating on chairlift rides—the better to squeeze in one more trip. If you want to stop moving for a while and unbuckle your boots, stop at the mid-mountain **Deer Park Chalet,** the multipurpose **Jim Bridger Lodge** at the base, or the new, as-yet-unnamed base facility slated to open for 2003–2004.

The original 1957 Deer Park Lodge was replaced in 1996 by a handsome new chalet with more than twice the seating and the same popular soups, stews, and homemade breads. Perhaps, say in 2035 or so, Bridger will build a third Deer Park Chalet.

The Jim Bridger Lodge, built in 1988, houses a ski school, rentals and retail ski shops, day care, reservations, and a very serviceable second-floor cafeteria with high ceilings and big windows looking onto *Moose Meadows*. It's comfy yet utilitarian, befitting a nonprofit community. Adjacent **Jimmy B's** bar serves excellent hot sandwiches and beer by the fireplace.

For après-ski activities, most locals and visitors head down valley to the myriad offerings of town. (There are a few beds in Bridger Canyon in private cabins and lodges, but most visitors stay in Bozeman in the moderately priced motels and inns.) The **Cateye Café** and **Hofbrau,** known as the Hof, are locals' hangouts. The **Bacchus Pub,** a classic old place, serves brews, salads, soups, and burgers. **Montana Ale Works** is a happening smoke-free microbrew pub with good food, suds, and billiards. For a white-tablecloth dinner, try **John Bozeman's Bistro** or **Looie's Down Under** on Main Street. The **Spanish Peaks Brewery & Italian Café** serves microbrewed beers and mounds of good Italian food. The **Leaf and Bean** and the **Rocky Mountain Roasting Company** are the places to go for gourmet coffees, and **Mackenzie River Pizza** does gourmet pies.

Bridger Bowl Data

Mountain Statistics

Vertical feet	2,000 feet lift-served, plus 400 to 600 feet to hike on the Ridge
Base elevation	6,100 feet
Summit elevation	8,100 feet
Longest run	3 miles
Average annual snowfall	350 inches
Number of lifts	7: 1 quad; 4 doubles; 2 triples
Uphill capacity	7,300 skiers per hour
Skiable terrain	1,500 acres
Opening date	Early December
Closing date	Early April
Snowboarding	Yes

Transportation

By car 16 miles (20 minutes) up Bridger Canyon (State Highway 86), from Bozeman, Montana. Bozeman is just off I-90 between Billings and Butte, and 1½ hours north of West Yellowstone via Highway 191.

Bridger Bowl Data (continued)

Transportation *(continued)*

By bus Greyhound serves Bozeman, with a terminal on East Main Street. Motels and hotels in Bozeman are served by ski-area shuttle service for a nominal fee.

By plane Via major carriers, including Delta, Northwest, Horizon Air, SkyWest, and United to Bozeman's Gallatin Field, with connections via Salt Lake City, Minneapolis, Denver, and Seattle.

Key Phone Numbers

Ski-area information	(406) 587-2111
Snow report	(406) 586-2389
Reservations	(800) 223-9609
Website	www.bridgerbowl.com

Inside Story

Joining The Ridge Hippies

Bridger Bowl's creaky old lifts got a boost with the recent addition of a new fixed-grip quad. The Powder Park lift serves mostly green runs, but area managers promise that no lift will ever breast The Ridge, this cliff- and chute-strewn curtain that hangs above the lift-served skiing. "The quads that take you there," says Bozeman writer and photographer Gordon Wiltsie, "will have to be your own." Anyone without a decent set of quadriceps, and lungs to match, need not attempt the ascent, which begins near the top of Bridger chair at 8,100 feet. The route parallels an old surface lift that the ski patrol rigged up long ago. The ascent route is called the Stairway to Heaven, the one and only way up. Look closely and you'll see the line of steps cut by countless ski boots that headed to the powder.

Before starting, however, you must pass the ski patrol shack, outside of which is an odd-looking appendage, like a microphone. If your avalanche transceiver is working, a buzzer and light signal the OK to proceed. You must also have a shovel in your pack and a partner who knows the terrain above, or you will be asked to stay on the lift-served terrain below. Once through the electronic gate, you begin to climb. No switchbacks, no fooling around with moderate grades; this sucker only goes straight up. If you are carrying your skis over a shoulder, your tips will brush the snow in front; that's how steep it is. Short skis and snowboards don't have the same problem, but one of the indicators of long-time Ridge hippies is the small shovel packs they use to affix their skis.

As the track narrows through rock walls in a section called the Pearly Gates, each step is a big pull up. These stairs would never meet code. Chances are they were formed early in the season by locals in a hurry. You have no choice but to follow in their footsteps. To venture off to the side would be to wallow in waist-deep fluff.

The speed record for the 400 vertical feet straight up is under ten minutes. If you do it in 20, you are doing well. Even then, and even on the coldest days, you are sweating by the time you reach the top. It's a good idea to wear moisture-wicking (hydrophobic) underwear and to layer your outerwear so you can peel off as you go and then add more at the top.

From the top of the Stairway to Heaven, The Ridge stretches north and south for a mile in either direction. To the north, it snakes its corniced way to a high point of 8,700 feet. *Hidden Gully* is no more than 12 feet wide through its rock-walled top section only to fan out onto the spacious *Apron* above the Alpine lift.

To the south, the Ridge wanders by *Patrolman's,* the shortest walk and the quickest way back to the Bridger lift. From there it's up and over *The Nose* and out toward the area's south boundary, where parallel shafts called *The Fingers* and *The Three Virtues* plummet into *South Bowl.*

Then down one of the so-called *Bridger Chutes,* full of twisted, gnomish, survivor trees, and on to *Three Bears Bowl* and a face full of deep, soft, wind-blown snow called *The O's* that stands, appropriately enough, for orgasms. Back across *North Bowl* to the Bridger lift and up again to the Stair chair.

The Nose, one of the premier runs on The Ridge, starts with a pitch called *Test Face* that is deceptively mellow at the beginning and rolls down gradually, steeper and steeper. The trees on the sides appear to be stepping off the edge of the world. Eventually, *Test Face* plunges over a cliff, but by peeling left into *Exit Chute,* a narrow drain spills out into the moguls and the relative civility of *Avalanche Chute.*

Some Ridge hippies pump a dozen runs a day on the Ridge, eating out of their anorak pouches on chairlifts, stopping only to shed a sweater or share a water bottle. You can do the Ridge that way, or you can treat it as a backcountry tour, an adventure, and a change to the inbounds routine. For me, on that particular day, two was enough. After the Ridge, riding through the fog on the lower trails was like flying; it was so easy and natural that it seemed we were somehow cheating gravity.

The Big Mountain

This destination resort in Montana's far northwest corner is referred to as Big Mountain Ski and Summer Resort or as The Big Mountain. Whichever name you use, it certainly is big. At 3,000 skiable acres with another 1,040 acres in the permit area, it is second only to Big Sky, Montana's biggest ski area. But the name?

The Whitefish community members who sold shares and volunteered their labor to put up the first T-bar in 1947 wanted to call it Hellroaring Ski Area after the creek drainage where the first skiing was done in the late 1930s on the back side of the current development. But propriety and a marketing logic said people might not flock to a place called Hellroaring, and so we have The Big Mountain.

It rises to a rounded, balding 7,000-foot summit between bucolic Whitefish Lake and the railroad/timber/summer-vacation town of Whitefish on the west and the higher, sharper peaks of Glacier National Park to the east. This resort has a great location at the north end of the burgeoning Flathead Valley, with ample snow, sublime natural terrain, and weather that can be so challenging that, until recently, nobody except the denizens of the 49th parallel knew about the place. Cold and fog combine into rime ice, turning the trees near the summit into rimed phantasmagoric creatures in a white-on-white ballroom. More often than not, you just barely see these snow ghosts. Blue sky days are as rare as lift lines.

The mountain's natural gifts were readily apparent to the postwar Whitefish Chamber of Commerce, which wanted to expand business past the fall hunting season and into winter. Those attributes were fine enough to attract a ski hero the caliber of Toni Matt, who came up from Sun Valley to run the ski school and cut some of the first trails. Matt was the Austrian super skier who was the first (and still the only) person to schuss the 1,000-foot Headwall at Tuckerman Ravine on New Hampshire's Mount Washington, making him an instant and enduring legend.

Matt arrived, as do about 5% of today's skiers, on the train. Whitefish, population 6,000, is a major stop on the Amtrak's daily Empire Builder line, following the old Burlington Northern route between Seattle and Minneapolis. Seattle skiers figure they can save two nights' lodging on a trip to Big Mountain by taking the night train that arrives in the morning in Whitefish, only eight miles from the mountain, and returning home snoozing on the night train, to save another night's lodging. Maximize the skiing; minimize the expense. This is not to say that Big Mountain is pricey. Both the mountain and the town have a down-home, mid-America kind of freshness and prices to match.

U.S. gold medalist downhiller Tommy Moe grew up skiing at The Big Mountain before moving to Alaska and the on to U.S. Ski Team. A signed poster of Moe in the Hellroaring Saloon, at the base of the high-speed quad chair, bears the inscription, "To my friends at The Big Mountain, where I learned to ski FAST." That he did. The whole town went fairly crazy when Moe won Olympic gold and silver at Lillehammer in 1994. His mother and stepfather still live here. His stepfather, now retired, once drove a snowcat on the mountain.

While many skiers opt for downtown après-ski, the mountain base offers a traditional brand of camaraderie. The Hellroaring Saloon is housed in the Chalet, the original lodge on the mountain, which in the 1950s, offered a room, all your meals, and a lift ticket for one price. Skiers were a brother- and sisterhood then. Everyone was in this new snow-sliding adventure, and that's pretty much the feeling you can still get at The Big Mountain. The Hellroaring Saloon bristles with great old wooden skis and sepia photographs. If you buy one of their baseball caps, you get one free beer per day for the rest of your life.

The Moguls Pub at slopeside opens a free keg every Monday after skiing hosted by the ski school, and, at this writing, has taken over another Big Mountain. With the Bierstube, the ski patrol's favorite bar, making way for a new conference center, the presentation of the weekly Frabert Award now takes place at Moguls. This award is given every Wednesday for the klutziest move of the week. (Frabert, by the way, is a toy monkey encased in plaster casts and slings that hangs over the bar.)

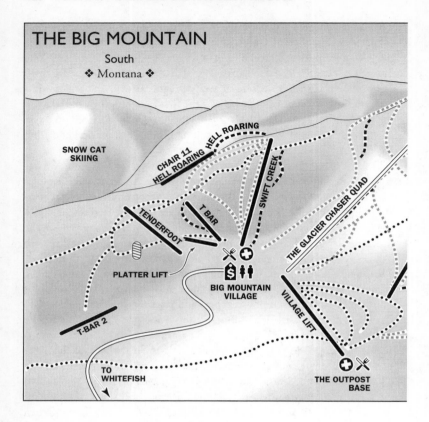

THE BIG MOUNTAIN
South
❖ Montana ❖

SNOW CAT
SKIING

CHAIR 11
HELL ROARING HELL ROARING

SWIFT CREEK

TENDERFOOT

T BAR

THE GLACIER CHASER QUAD

PLATTER LIFT

BIG MOUNTAIN
VILLAGE

T-BAR 2

VILLAGE LIFT

TO
WHITEFISH

THE OUTPOST
BASE

The recipient might be an employee or a visitor who has somehow—wittingly or not—stumbled into the brotherhood.

Glacier Village, a long-promised resort development at the base of the lifts, now has more than 400 lodging units, including two luxury condominium lodges, Kintla Lodge and the brand new Morning Eagle. Bargain hunters and those who like the in-town scene stay down the mountain in Whitefish. An excellent local transit system called SNOW—Shuttle Network of Whitefish—makes town–mountain connections simple. The million acres of nearby Glacier National Park, the exponential growth around Flathead Lake and nearby Kalispell, The Big Mountain's hero terrain and its quick quad to the summit spell bigger visitation for the future. Some longtime locals already complain about the Aspenization of Whitefish. While the area certainly is attracting new home-owners, second and otherwise, calling it Aspenization seems a little extreme.

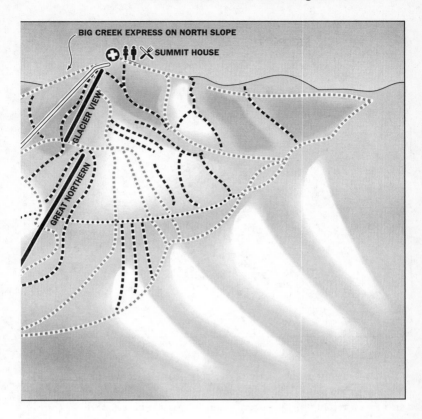

One thing that will probably save The Big Mountain from overcrowding is that northern Rockies weather, which means cold, wet, and snowy winters. In fact, one of the most oft-seen accessories on locals is called Butt Flaps, a foam and nylon item resembling an apron worn in reverse (and invented by local patroller Kerry Critendon) to keep the posterior dry on chairlifts in cold, wet conditions. Perfect for riding chairs all day in the fog, chill, and dumping storms of The Big Mountain. Those are the conditions, after all, that make the stuff under your skis so silky soft and silent.

The Big Layout

What was once a gaggle of eclectic buildings flanking a big day-skier parking lot is finally—after years of planning and promise—morphing into Glacier Village. It is taking shape at the traditional base area at the bottom of the Glacier Chaser high-speed quad lift, which speeds to The Big Mountain summit.

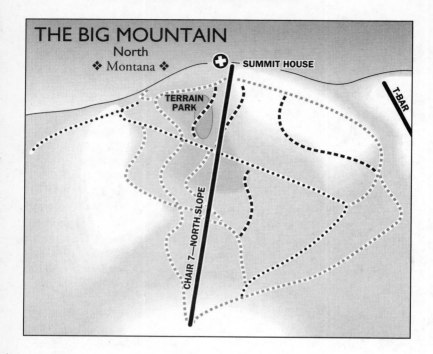

THE BIG MOUNTAIN
North
❖ Montana ❖
✚ SUMMIT HOUSE
T-BAR
TERRAIN PARK
CHAIR 7—NORTH SLOPE

The Outpost is the name of a second base, lower in elevation and slightly to the south, at the bottom of Chair 6 (the Village chairlift). It includes a restaurant, sun deck, ticket windows, ski school desk, patrol room, lockers, and parking. With the development of Glacier Village, it is increasingly important for day skiers. Good skiers will probably never see the Outpost base. They will head straight up the Glacier Chaser high-speed quad and its 2,088 vertical feet to the 7,000-foot summit. From there everything is down; simple. One summit gives you the choice of four directions: north onto the North Slope with its 1,200 feet of vertical; south into the two huge, largely intermediate bowls; west into the Big Ravine and its long cruising; or east onto most of the area's protected and somewhat hidden black diamonds. All trails, except those on the North Slope, eventually feed down to the bottom.

When the light is good here, it is very, very good. Most of the terrain spills south and west from the summit. These exposures would likely not be skiable down south in Colorado, for example. But here, with the lower sun angle and the generally colder temperatures, there is little problem. The winter sun beams unobstructed, and that means the afternoon light paints a golden magic.

The Big Mountain is also the rare Rockies ski area to offer night skiing. On Friday and Saturday evenings, it provides a fantasy of front-side skiing off Chairs 2 and 3 under the lights. A bonus is that any day ticket is valid through the evening (which at this writing means until 9:00 p.m.). On full-moon evenings, you can combine dinner at the summit restaurant and moonlight skiing. It's a fantastic experience, and you don't need to be a fantastically strong skier to have it.

Beginners Ski Free

The Village Lift, which serves all-beginner terrain and also takes pressure off the more congested beginner and intermediate runs above Glacier Village, is free all the time for everybody. The hook, of course, is to get people hooked on skiing or snowboarding, and then entice newbies into lessons and lifts up the mountain. A lower-mountain lift ticket (good on the Swift Creek, Tenderfoot, and Easy Rider chairlifts) serves mostly green and blue runs, plus a couple of easy blacks for the courageous.

The runs above the Outpost base served by the free lift, offer ample room for any number of first-timers. *Beargrass, Huckleberry Patch,* and *Chipmunk* are rated double green, the easiest of all. *Tenderfoot,* with its slightly steeper greens of *Alpinglow Alley* and *Question Mark,* is the next step up in the terrain progression.

Grandest of all for novices is *Easy Street,* a green route from the mountain's summit. It straddles The Big Mountain's east ridge for a mile and then turns back toward the village for another mile and a half on a gentle cat track. At two-and-a-half miles, it's one of the longest descents on the hill.

Another long, gentle run nicknamed *Around the World* curls off the west ridge. Parts of it are rated blue, but it is always groomed, broad, and easy enough to be a good transition route for novices and low-level intermediates. The route starts on the tree line boulevard called *The Big Ravine,* continues down the green-circle *Interstate,* and finishes blue again on *Hibernation,* one of the runs cut for the original 1947 T-bar. Spectacular views, lots of mileage, that top-of-the-world sensation, and the opportunity to ride the quad add up to a near perfect low-angle cruiser.

The Big Mountain's Big Cruising

The opportunity for flat-out, let-it-roll, high-speed cruising is one of The Big Mountain's big strengths. *Toni Matt, Ptarmigan Bowl, Inspiration,* and *Moe Mentum* are all groomed nightly, creating top-to-bottom roller coasters to die for. *Toni Matt* is particularly sweet as it dives off *The Big Ravine* and onto a broad, convex ridge that serpentines right to the base of the Glacier Chaser quad. To the skier's right is *Good Medicine,* a spacious, low-angle gladed run that is rated black diamond, but solid intermediates can handle it in powder or spring conditions. To the left is *Ptarmigan Bowl,* also rated black, but the groomed swath down the center means there are tasty, smooth giant slalom turns for intermediates as well.

The same is true for *Inspiration* and *North Bowl* farther east around the front side of the mountain. Inspiration plunges the full 2,500 feet, for the greatest vertical on the mountain, from the summit all the way to the Outpost base. When the Glacier Chaser quad was installed in 1989, it changed traffic patterns at The Big Mountain—patterns now so ingrained that they seem always to have been there. Though there is rarely a lift line on this main lift, if you are looking for less crowded slopes, you may venture back to the older lifts (Chairs 2, 4, and 5) that serve primarily intermediate terrain. Numbers 4 and 5 (respectively named Great Northern and Glacier View) are little used since the quad covers the same distance to the peak in half the time, but the skiing is underrated. The route off Chair 4 from *Langley* (part of the National Championship downhill cut by Toni Matt in 1948) to *Corkscrew* to the glades of *Powder Trap* is superb, and there's usually nobody there.

A word about the term "glade." Back East, a glade is any wooded area with room enough to squeeze a pair of skis through. In Colorado and elsewhere in the Rocky Mountain region, glades are often created by thinning trees or even cutting down whole forests with a few clusters of trees left here and there for ambience. At The Big Mountain, the entire upper half is peppered with small, rime-encrusted trees with enough room between them to make a mistake, recover, and choose a new path without fear of smacking into anything. It's a liberating kind of tree skiing for both intermediates and experts.

Most of the runs on the North Side are also rated blue. *Black Bear* and *Marmot* are black and bumpy at the top, gentling to blue on the lower portions. Shorter than some of the front-side cruisers, they wind between walls of trees and usually boast some of the best snow on the mountain. The north-facing altitude that keeps the snow also chills the body, so the 1997 upgrade of Chair 8 (Big Creek Express) into the area's second high-speed quad was welcome indeed. A seven-minute ride is tolerable, even when the wind whistles straight down from Canada.

Bumps? Hmmm. This mountain is so big and there are so few skiers that bumps just don't happen consistently. The best intermediate bumps are usually on *Lower Mully's* off Chair 2. *Heap Steep* and *Powder Trap*, two relatively short open glades off Chair 4, also grow shaggy most winters and the groomers leave them be. How refreshing to find an interesting mountain where you don't *have* to ski bumps!

The Big Mountain's Hidden Steeps

At The Big Mountain, big-time cruising is not reserved for intermediates. With the quick return speed of the Glacier Chaser detachable quad, experts certainly like to rip off a few laps on the *Bowls*, *Toni Matt,* and *The Big Ravine*. The rush of speed and the wide-open, undulating shapes are the closest most of us will ever get to free flight. This is hero stuff, Tommy Moe stuff, and stuff for anybody else who likes to feel like a hero.

Mostly concentrated at the east end between *Easy Street* and *Inspiration,* the steeps flow into the *North Bowl* drain from the two ridgelines. This is by no means a small pocket; the dozen named black diamonds harbor countless lines between them, enough for many months of concentrated exploring.

The steepest front-side shots are the double diamonds called *East Rim* and *Haskill Slide. East Rim* features a couple of launchable rock outcroppings on what is otherwise a baby-smooth, cliff-free mountain. *Haskill* is genuinely jump-turn steep, the kind of pitch where air is beneath your ski bases. The rest of the runs are steep, but not scary, openings through the trees. From *Inspiration,* starting with a mellow but shady rollover into *Fault 1* or *Fault 2,* the snow stays cold and deep here. Then, after a brief traverse, it's down again into the funky mixed woods of *Movieland* or *Elkweed.* As noted before, bumps are not a big part of the ski experience here, but if you really want to find some, try the back side of the mountain, where *Marmot, Black Bear,* and *Bighorn* cut narrow swaths through trees and grow substantial moguls. *Bighorn* funnels skiers down a frighteningly steep tree chute. It feels more like one of Stowe's Front Four than a Western powder mountain—except for the snow, that is, which on this shady side of the peak stays cold and dry—and, in fact, is often the best on the mountain. One of the coolest things for advanced and expert skiers to do at The Big Mountain is sign on for snowcat skiing. Combine laps on the Big Creek Express with snowcat shuttles over to Flower Point for a phenomenal bargain compared with comparable cat operations elsewhere. With at least four people on the cat—and there are usually far more than that—the cost in 2002–2003 was just $60 per person per day, plus a lift ticket.

The cat accesses 500 acres of rolling terrain—a symphony of steep drop-offs, funky traverses, open areas, and glades of various degrees of thickness. The terrain feels wild and untamed, and it's always a shock to slide onto the run-out back to the chairlift. The cat skiing operation is handled by The Big Mountain Ski and Snowboard School. When conditions are favorable, it might just be one of the best days on snow of your entire life.

Snowboarding

The Big Mountain's terrain park dominates the Silvertip run and features table tops, major hits, berms, and gap jumps. Freeriders use the complex contours of the mountain like a natural terrain park. The Big Ravine can be thought of as nature's own half-pipe. Riders love to weave through the sparse trees near the summit and the denser glades below, while cliff bands and rock outcroppings serve as launching pads for The Big Mountain's single-plank air force.

Eating at the Big Mountain

Here's a list of recommended restaurants in the resort area:

Moguls Bar & Grille. Slopeside espresso bar, free keg Monday après-ski, courtesy of the ski school.

Summit House. Breakfast, lunch, cocktails, and a special German Bavarian Buffet dinner on select Wednesdays and every Saturday night on top of the mountain.

Cafe Kandahar and Snug Bar. Finest dining in the area in the Kandahar Lodge near the mountain. Reservations recommended.

Hell Roaring Saloon. Burgers, beer, nachos, and ski memorabilia in the historic Chalet building.

The 'Stube. Home of the Wednesday night Frabert "Clod of the Week" Award, sandwiches, videos, great beer and ale selection, live entertainment.

Serrano's. Downtown Whitefish; free appetizers from 5 to 6 p.m., Mexican fare, live music.

The Great Northern. In Whitefish; good, inexpensive Tex-Mex.

The Big Mountain Data

Mountain Statistics

Vertical feet	2,500 feet
Base elevation	4,500 feet
Summit elevation	7,000 feet
Longest run	3.3 miles (Hell Fire)
Average annual snowfall	335 inches
Number of lifts	11: 2 high-speed quad; 1 fixed-grip quad; 5 triples; 1 double; 2 T-bars
Uphill capacity	13,000 skiers per hour
Skiable terrain	3,000 acres, plus 1,000 acres of snowcat terrain
Opening date	Thanksgiving
Closing date	Early April
Snowboarding	Yes

Transportation

By car About 126 miles north of Missoula and I-90 via Highway 93 to Whitefish. The Big Mountain is 8 miles northeast of Whitefish.

By bus From the Whitefish Amtrak station and from Glacier Park International Airport. The SNOW bus, operated by The Big Mountain, offers free shuttle service between Whitefish and the ski resort.

The Big Mountain Data (continued)

Transportation (continued)

By train Amtrak serves Whitefish twice daily (once each direction) on its western Empire Builder route between Chicago/Minneapolis and Seattle/ Portland.

By plane Delta, Horizon Air, Northwest and Big Sky Air fly into Glacier Park International Airport near Kalispell, 19 miles from the resort.

Key Phone Numbers

Ski-area information	(406) 862-2900
Snow report	(406) 862-7669
Reservations	(800) 858-5439
Flathead Convention &	(800) 543-3105
Visitor Association	
Website	www.bigmtn.com

Inside Story

Dealing with Cold

The fanciful "snow ghosts" that populate the upper reaches of the Big Mountain wouldn't last in a warmer clime. In fact, they'd probably never be created in the first place. Rime is water or cloud moisture supercooled to below its freezing point that somehow survives in liquid form until it bumps into something like a tree on a summit ridge. Then it sticks as solid ice and adds to the white-on-white sculpture garden through which we ski on the Big Mountain and on ridgelines at Bridger Bowl, for example, and Schweitzer Mountain in Idaho's northern panhandle. Rime usually forms as a storm is leaving the area, when colder, high-pressure air sweeps in to replace the low-pressure storm front.

So what strategies can you bring to the mountain to deal effectively with cold temperatures? Three things: Generate heat, keep it in, and know when to bail.

First, give your body all the fuel it needs to generate its own heat. Eat a hearty breakfast loaded with complex carbohydrates—cereals, whole grain toast, and muffins—and fats. Yes, fats; have butter, milk, yogurt, cream cheese on your bagel, bacon, sausage. Fats give your body quick energy and generate lots of warmth. High-altitude climbers and Arctic explorers eat butter by the stick. Don't worry, you'll be burning it off and then some.

Second, keep moving on the hill. Ski on runs that make you work rather than just stand and ride. Ski some bumps. Whatever it takes to keep the heart rate up and the blood flowing.

What you wear to keep in the heat is extremely important. (Battery-powered boot warmers are another form of energy consumption. If you have chronically cold toes, give these boot warmers a try; they work.) First, keep your core well insulated. That means layers of polypropylene, silk, wool, or down around your trunk, where your mass is. If your hands and feet feel cold, chances are your core is not warm enough. Frostbite occurs when your body automatically reduces blood flow to the extremities in an effort to keep the central core warm.

After your mid-section, pay attention to your head. We lose up to 40% of our body warmth through the head and neck. All those brain cells firing at once, I guess. A good wool or pile hat and—most underestimated of all ski accessories—a fuzzy, warm neck gaiter or scarf will keep you feeling impervious in the nastiest cold. Oh, yes, goggles are much warmer than glasses.

A wind-resistant outer shell will cut the wind-chill factor out of the equation. Most of the new waterproof/breathable fabrics and coatings, such as Gore-tex and Ultrex, do a super job of boxing out wind. Denim doesn't do it. Wool by itself won't either. You need an outer layer from neck to ankle with a tight enough weave to stop the wind. Perversely, a truly waterproof garment, like a rain suit, will keep the wind at bay, but you will end up colder in the end. Your perspiration—and you will sweat even on the coldest days—cannot exit the impermeable fabric and will leave you clammy and colder on the inside. That's the beauty of breathable outerwear and hydrophobic (water-hating) fabrics next to your skin. Perspiration water vapor is transported outward layer to layer, eventually to the atmosphere, while your skin feels dry and therefore warmer.

Finally, hands and feet. Mittens are warmer than gloves, though a bit more awkward. Those little hand-warmer packets filled with powdered pepper really do work. Placed on a palm inside a glove, they'll keep your hands warm for hours. As for the feet, adding more socks or thicker socks is usually counterproductive. Thin wool socks that allow room for toes to move and blood to flow are usually warmer than thicker socks that may restrict capillary flow.

When you're out skiing on a cold day, have your buddies check any exposed skin—like the cheeks and the tip of nose—for frostbite. They will show as a spot of pure white, like the snow. Take off your mitten and hold a bare palm against the spot. Don't rub; the skin really is frozen. In a few seconds the color should come back. Watch each other carefully, and go inside if the nipped spots reappear.

That's the final thing. Go inside. Have a hot drink, though nothing alcoholic; that'll just lower your core body temperature further. Fuel up with a Power Bar or something sweet. Stand next to the fire. Warm up from the outside in and the inside out. Nobody's paying us to suffer out there. Skiing is supposed to be fun. If you're prepared, even when it's well below zero, you can defy the elements and slip through the cold like a hot knife. But if it gets too bad, in spite of your best polar bear imitation, just bag it. Head for the hot tub. Read a book. The sun will be out tomorrow.

Schweitzer

Idaho's Schweitzer Basin, or Schweitzer Mountain Resort as it is now called, is an almost spooky physical twin to the Big Mountain, its neighbor four hours east in Montana. It is also a big mountain. Big, as in 2,500 inbound acres, the most in Idaho, even more than Sun Valley. Big, as in 2,400 feet of vertical, big snow numbers and a long season (there is a little snowmaking, but nobody's quite sure if it's ever been used). And big, as in wide-open, primarily intermediate pitches with rime-encrusted "snow ghosts" in the summit bowls.

Even Schweitzer's birth is linked to the Big Mountain. Jack Fowler, a local dentist, was returning from a rather wet and foggy ski weekend in Montana in 1960 when he pulled over in Hope, Idaho, to stare in wonder at the then-inaccessible, snowy ridgeline bowls above Schweitzer Creek. Three years later Fowler and partners cranked up the first lifts.

Both mountains rise above newly trendy, reawakened timber towns; Schweitzer's is Sandpoint on the west shore of Lake Pend Oreille. To get to both mountains, you have to ascend long, switchbacking roads that go through rugged country. The road to Schweitzer is even longer and steeper than the Big Mountain's snaking 11 miles from the lakeshore to the base lodge. Both mountains have much more skiing than they have skiers. Until recently, Schweitzer was almost completely unknown outside the Pacific Northwest.

Just get a load of these ski area marketing slogans (I am not making these up): "Fish the big hole, ski the big bowl," or "Ski the big potato," and "Ski Schhhhweitzer."

Well, that last one just might come back in favor someday, because Schweitzer, like the Big Mountain, is no longer a locals' only destination. The secret is out. Here's why: In 1990 the resort launched a ten-year, $100 million expansion plan. First, they pushed a new high-speed quad chair dubbed the Great Escape from the base up to the ridge where Schweitzer's two huge bowls come together. Next, they replaced the rickety, original day lodge with a shiny 40,000-square-foot skiers' and riders' center complete with cafeteria, shops, kinder care, and five-minute massages. (Habitués of the original lodge, designed in 1963 by one of Schweitzer's early boosters, remember that when the band really got going on the top-floor Bierstube, pitchers of beer would bounce right off the tables.) Next door to the day lodge is an 82-room, luxury hotel that gave the mountain instant "destination" panache. That panache grew in 2002, when the White Pine Lodge and its 50 slopeside condo units opened its doors

The resort was able to do all this so quickly because the area is all private land—no public-land agencies to petition or battles to fight. Future terrain expansion, condo construction, and so on will also take place on private ground, so the pace will be set by project economics. The lobby of The Selkirk Lodge looks like a comfy, upper-middle-class living room: cartoons on the TV, checkerboards on the tables, kids lounging on couches waiting for Mom and Dad to hurry up and get ready to ski. Kids under the age of 12 on packages with their families stay and ski for free. *The Enchanted Forest* terrain garden is one of the best children's learning zones anywhere. There are video arcades and movies for the off-hours, and kids seem to be the prime beneficiaries of the Friday and Saturday night skiing. The service is friendly and informal everywhere you go.

Accessibility is still the big factor in keeping the numbers low. Recent yearly totals of about 180,000 skier days would amount to a big week at Vail. The nearest airport is in Spokane, Washington, which is 80 miles away. The nearest population centers are Seattle, Washington, and Calgary, Alberta, both about seven hours away. So for now Schweitzer is

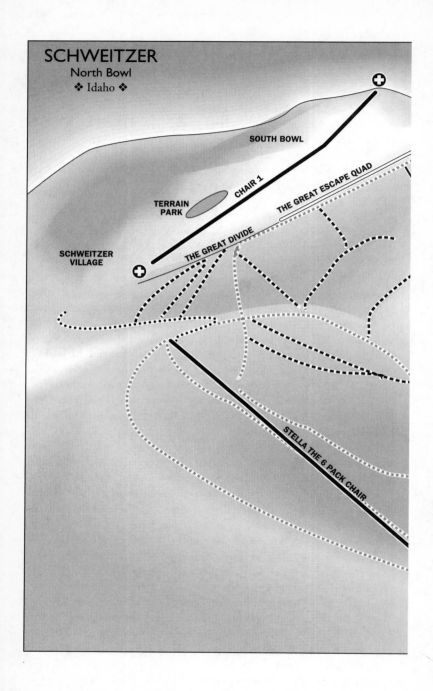

SCHWEITZER
North Bowl
❖ Idaho ❖

SOUTH BOWL

TERRAIN PARK

CHAIR 1

THE GREAT ESCAPE QUAD

THE GREAT DIVIDE

SCHWEITZER VILLAGE

STELLA THE 6 PACK CHAIR

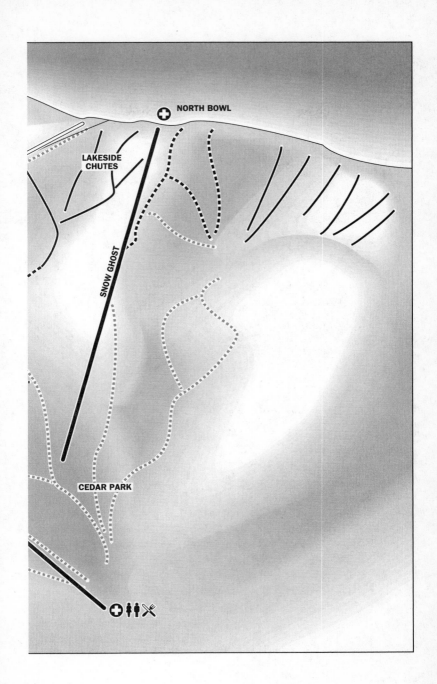

NORTH BOWL

LAKESIDE CHUTES

SNOW GHOST

CEDAR PARK

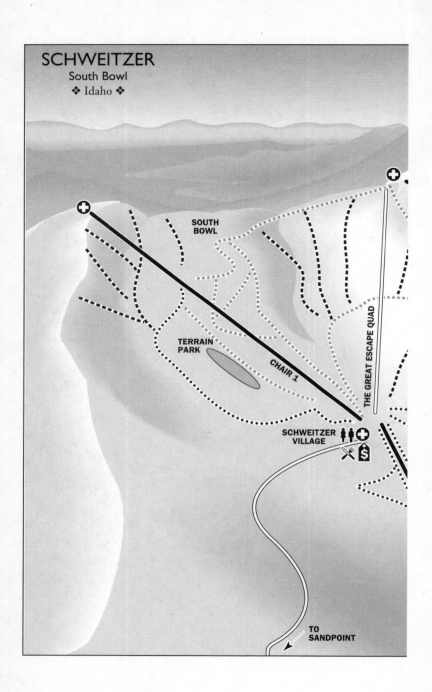

SCHWEITZER
South Bowl
❖ Idaho ❖

SOUTH
BOWL

THE GREAT ESCAPE QUAD

TERRAIN
PARK

CHAIR 1

SCHWEITZER
VILLAGE

TO
SANDPOINT

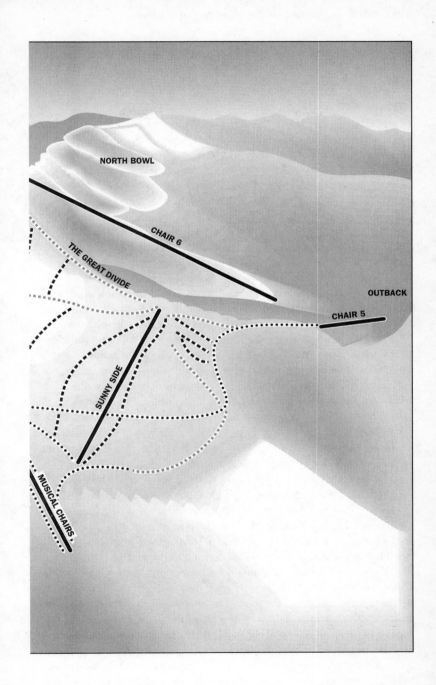

NORTH BOWL

CHAIR 6

THE GREAT DIVIDE

OUTBACK

CHAIR 5

SUNNY SIDE

MUSICAL CHAIRS

pretty much yours to share with the Sandpoint locals. But, like other beautiful areas previously deemed inaccessible—Telluride, Colorado, comes to mind—watch out. Spontaneous discovery may be just around the corner.

Room with a View

From the Selkirk and White Pine lodges, and indeed from just about everywhere on the mountain's front side, which is known as South Bowl, there is an unobstructed view of Lake Pend Oreille, Idaho's biggest lake. It is 43 miles long and 1,000 feet deep in some places, but it is just a remnant of a much bigger ice-age lake that stretched all the way to Missoula, Montana, 10,000 years ago. Because of the lake's depth, the U.S. Navy built a training center here during World War II, for, believe it or not, testing submarines.

This big, east-sweeping view is down Schweitzer Gulch, named for a demented Swiss trapper who lived in a cabin here around the turn of the century. Always formal and polite, he was nevertheless discovered to have trapped a number of Sandpoint's pet cats and turned them into cat stew. He twice appeared out of the fog at night and without a word took the reins from a young woman on horseback and led her home from work. Soon after, he was led away to an asylum, but the name lives on.

From up on the *Sky Edge* trail at 6,400 feet, a more complete panorama unfolds. You are in the southern folds of the Selkirk Range, one of the famous north-south trending heli-skiing ranges of British Columbia. To the east, the Cabinet Mountains define the border with Montana. Far to the south, you can see pieces of the Bitterroot Wilderness. The Pack River flows into Lake Pend Oreille from the north. The Clark Fork River (a gorgeous drive on State Highway 200 to Missoula) feeds the lake from the east. Pend Oreille River drains the lake to the west on its way to meet the Columbia River.

The mountain layout is one of the simplest you'll find. There are two bowls, Schweitzer (South Bowl) and Outback Bowl (North Bowl). The village is in South Bowl, with 1,700 vertical feet above the lodges and 592 vertical feet below in the Musical Chairs beginners' area. The 2,400-foot maximum vertical is measured in North Bowl from the summit ridge to the Outback cafeteria in the bottom of the drain.

Of the four chairlifts in South Bowl, two climb to the Great Divide and access North Bowl. The two North Bowl lifts, Stella and Snow Ghost, will both bring you back over the top and home. There is no way to ski or ride from the Outback base back around to the front; to return to your room you need to ride one of the two lifts back up and then head down.

The uniform cup shape of both bowls makes trail designation simple: The easiest pitches are in the bottom, the intermediate tilts reside in the middle elevations, and almost all the black diamonds drop from the ridges—short, but oh so sweet.

Happy Trails to Beginners

The Musical Chairs beginners' area drifts down the gully below the Headquarters Day Lodge, so you don't have to ride any over-the-snow conveyance until you reach the bottom of the chair. Just strap 'em on and go. Of course, true beginners, or "never-evers," should always take a lesson first thing to get grounded in the basics. Both runs served by the chair, *Happy Trails* and *Enchanted Forest,* are rated green. *Enchanted Forest* features added man-made shapes—mounds, waves, and darting routes through the trees—designed especially for kids. There is a remnant pocket of old-growth cedars, dark and special, where resort personnel teach environmental awareness.

Above the day lodge, in the immensity of South Bowl, the easiest way down is *Crystal.* It's a beauty, slicing in a big semicircle through the timberline glades and back to the center. It starts at the midway unloading station on Chair 1. Beginners, don't make the mistake of riding all the way up; there are no green runs off the ridge. Although, if you do forget to get off, the escape route down *Ridge Run* to upper *Gypsy,* while rated blue, is certainly manageable for most novices.

There are no greens in Outback Bowl, although *Vagabond* and *Cedar Park* are exquisite, wide, scenic runs suitable for all but the newest neophytes. The problem is getting off the Great Divide ridgeline and down to *Vagabond* in the belly of the basin. The easiest route, *Down the Hatch,* is a solid blue. Here's a good transition run for progressing novices: Ride Sunny Side to *Teakettle Trail,* which traverses the upper glades and then dips into the concave fun of *Lower Stiles.*

Intermediates in the Zone

Intermediates should not have any trouble finding a zone that combines comfort and challenge. There are three ways to go right out of the ticket line, depending on your whim and the snow conditions.

Most people bolt straight up the quad, the Great Escape, and decide on the way up. You can turn right off the top and down the Great Divide and into North Bowl. You can go left toward *Upper Stiles* and the big open spaces on the east-facing side of South Bowl, or you can scoot out *Gypsy* to the north-facing blues under Chair 1.

Let's take the front side first. *Upper Stiles* is marked as a black diamond on the trail map, but it almost always has a groomed swath down the center, turning it into that rarest of birds, a steep, smooth run that intermediates and experts alike can soar. The only problem with the east-facing runs on either side of the quad is their tendency to soak up the solar, when it is out, and go crunchy overnight. For that reason, I prefer the blues around to the left (looking up the mountain): the big boulevard of *Ridge Run,* the steady sweep of *Charlies,* and the always interesting, intertwining glade routes of *Sam's Alley.* These guys are in shade most of the day, and the snow is soft and cold and therefore forgiving. You can reach them either from the quad or from the midway unload on Chair 1.

The longest intermediate routes are in the Stella region. These are the cruisers: *Vagabond, Cathedral Aisle, G3,* and *Zip Down.* Fifteen hundred and fifty vertical feet per lap. Soft, north-facing snow. Big trees. Big fun. There are more big trees on *Zip Down,* which is another must for its spacious, groomed, roller-coaster spirit. As long as we're on musts and since we're in Idaho, you really owe it to yourself to have a baked spud with all the trimmings—from sour cream to chili to chutney—at the Outback. The indoor picnic tables might be jammed and the windows steamy, but, especially here, there's nothing quite as tasteful as a tater. And when the weather allows, you can escape the indoors by grabbing a table out on the covered deck, preferably one near the firepit.

The easiest way out of North Bowl is *Cat Track* to *Village* from the top of Stella the 6 Pack chair, a green waltz all the way. With the exception of a few genuinely precipitous chutes cutting north and south, there is not a lot of terrain in these ski- or ride-anywhere bowls that strong intermediates cannot handle in the right snow conditions. That caveat is key, however. *Upper Sam's Alley,* for example, may be intermediate heaven with a light frosting of new snow on a firm base, or it might be a full-on death struggle in deep, crusty, or windblown snow. Use good sense and don't hesitate to venture into inviting-looking glades, which are about as user-friendly here as any trees in the land.

Expert Ridges

Like Bridger Bowl, Schweitzer's steeps are concentrated almost exclusively on the top 400 to 500 vertical feet. Unlike at Bridger, you don't have to walk for any of it. With Chair 1, the Snow Ghost chair and the Great Escape quad rising to strategic high points along the ridges, you can shuffle off and go immediately down the best fall lines on the mountain. The very best are the chutes strung out like the folds of a curtain along the far side, the north-facing side of South Bowl. There are no rocks or cliff bands to speak of, just smooth, straight-ahead drops through gnomish survivor trees that are often unrecognizable under their coats of wind-driven ice. *A Chute* starts just left of Chair 1 at the top. Then comes *B Chute, C Chute,* and the remaining *South Bowl Chutes.* There is so much skiing on this face alone that explorers will find untracked snow for days or weeks after a storm.

One thing you won't find is moguls. Oh, there are a few here and there, on *The Face,* for example, and maybe *White Lightning,* and a few short pitches in the North Bowl. But by and large, they just don't have a chance to form—too much terrain and too few skiers.

One of the finest runs in new powder conditions is the *Lakeside* area of North Bowl. I say Lakeside area because the scale is too huge to call this a single run. Hundreds of skiers and riders could lay down tracks side by side and never cross each other's lines. A hundred turns high above Colburn Lake, *Lakeside* is like the *Big Burn* at Snowmass with occasional dead snags and clusters of tiny trees standing like toy soldiers here and there, except *Lakeside* is bigger and steeper than the *Big Burn.* I don't know if it was logged at one time or burned, but for good skiers and riders looking to heli-ski for the price of a lift ticket, this is the place.

If and when you tire of *Lakeside,* try exploring either side of this massive opening, particularly the north-facing runs that peel off the Great Divide. Between *Whiplash, Shoot the Moon,* and *Debbie Sue,* there's a whole week's worth of poking around in the powder. Nothing scary: no cliffs, little avalanche danger, no inescapable drains or slogging back to civilization. Everything leads back, eventually, to Snow Ghost or Stella the 6 Pack chair. Be sure to check out *Glade-iator* and *Kathy's Yardsale* off the back side of Stella for some exciting high-level glade skiing on north-facing slopes.

Everything depends, of course, on snow conditions, how the wind blows, what the sun influence has been, where the white carpet is forgiving, and where it turns harsh. When conditions are right, some of my favorite expert skiing happens on the mellower, sunny exposures of *Sundance* and *Upper* and *Lower J.R.* They're rated black diamond because the snow you find is always a roll of the dice.

A breakable sun crust can be hell to bash through, but a solid sun crust (or wind crust), one dense enough to support your weight, can provide the smoothest imaginable platform. The trees in the quad region are gnarled and well spaced. To dance a reactive, ever-changing line between them—on any consistent surface, and without having to worry about your brakes—is a gift. The kind of gift that is generously forthcoming at Schweitzer.

Snowboarding

Boarders who feel better in the air than on the snow gravitate to Chair 1 and disembark at the mid-station, for just below lies the Stomping Grounds terrain park. Outfitted with rails, fun boxes, tabletops and a 250-foot-long half-pipe, the Stomping Grounds quickly draws a crowd. A more natural playground with some nice kickers can be found along Kathy's Play Ground, which is accessed by the Stella lift on the back side.

Eating at Schweitzer

Mealtime at Schweitzer is largely an informal process—dash in, grab something to keep you going through the afternoon, and bolt back out to the slopes. If you're working up an appetite in Outback Bowl, your only option for sustenance is the **Outback Restaurant** at the very bottom of the drainage. This is really little more than a cafeteria—crowded with picnic tables on the inside, more enjoyable under a dazzling sun out on the deck, which features a fire pit to temper the temperature. The usual grill items are available, though a baked potato topped by a variety of trimmings is a Schweitzer tradition.

Your other options include the **Chimney Rock Grill,** which was given a makeover heading into the 2002–2003 season. Among the additions to the restaurant, which is located inside the Selkirk Lodge, was a new chef who redesigned the menu to give it a regional cuisine flair that relies heavily on fresh, locally produced ingredients. The restaurant was recently awarded *Wine Spectator's* 2003 Restaurant Wine Award.

If you're in a rush and can get by on a cup of coffee and a fresh-baked pastry, head to the **Mojo Coyote Café,** also in the Selkirk Lodge. This coffee shop also offers hot breakfast items and daily lunch specials. The **Lakeview Café** is the main cafeteria in the day lodge. Prefer pizza? Then head over to **Thor's Pizza** in the village's Lazier Building. It's a great place to enjoy a pepperoni pie and pitcher of beer.

A sandwich and soup, salad, even rotisserie chicken can be had at **Spuds on the Run** in the White Pine Lodge. Sate your sweet tooth at the **Alpenglow Deli and Ice Cream.**

St. Bernard is a long walk down the road. It offers informal, family-style dining.

In Sandpoint

Eichardt's Pub and Grill offers delicious pub fare with nightly fresh seafood specials. Their tagline is "the pub with personality," and it's a popular local's hangout. Eichhardt's offers live music on many nights and is smoke free on Tuesdays and Wednesdays.

Java Adagio, a great coffee fix, is located near the Cedar St. Bridge, a covered bridge market.

Jalapeños is the call if you are looking for Mexican food.

Spud's, located next to Starbucks, has great chicken, salads, and excellent steaks.

Swan's Landing features upscale Northwest dining on the lake.

Schweitzer Data

Mountain Statistics

Vertical feet	2,400 feet
Base elevation	4,700 feet at Village; 4,000 feet at Outback
Summit elevation	6,400 feet

Schweitzer Data (continued)

Mountain Statistics (countinued)

Longest run	2.7 miles, the Great Divide
Average annual snowfall	300 inches
Number of lifts	8: 1 high-speed 6-pack; 1 high-speed quad; 4 double chairs; 2 handle tows
Uphill capacity	8,092 skiers per hour
Skiable terrain	2,500 acres
Opening date	Late November
Closing date	Mid-April
Snowboarding	Yes

Transportation

By car Eleven miles from Sandpoint on Schweitzer Basin Road; 80 miles (90 minutes) from Spokane, Washington, via I-90 to Highway 95 North; 7 hours from Seattle via I-90, and 7 hours from Calgary, Alberta, via Highway 95 South.

By plane To Spokane International Airport, which is served by Horizon, Morris Air, Northwest, Delta, United, and Continental airlines. Coeur d'Alene Airport, 45 miles south of Sandpoint, is served by Empire Airlines.

By train Via Amtrak daily east-west service through Sandpoint. Schweitzer will arrange transfers from airports and Amtrak station with advance notice.

Key Phone Numbers

Ski-area information	(208) 263-9555
Snow report	(208) 263-9562
Reservations	(800) 831-8810
Website	www.schweitzer.com; e-mail: ski@schweitzer.com

Inside Story

Fog

On a sunny day you may not notice the poles with their Day-Glo circles set at regular intervals along the North Sky Edge and along the sides of other easier routes at Schweitzer. On a foggy day, though, they may save your life.

Perhaps it's the ski area's proximity to Lake Pend Oreille, but Schweitzer, along with its spiritual and geographic cousin the Big Mountain on the shores of Whitefish Lake in Montana, suffers an occasional day when the clouds roll in so thick and soupy, you may not see the next snow ghost or your friend two turns ahead of you. And thus the poles, set just far enough apart so that you can see the next one glowing faintly through the gloom. Follow them and you will not fall off any unexpected precipices. Slalom your way faithfully with your fellows—who appear and vanish and reappear like gray ghosts out of the periphery—and you will eventually bump into civilization.

If, on the other hand, you know perfectly well where you are—on the groomed headwall of *Upper Stiles,* for example—and you choose to leave the security of the disks, you may open yourself to a skiing epiphany. With no visual cues, no horizon to play off, you will have a hard time pinpointing the fall line. Sometimes your skis fall away easily into a turn, and sometimes they hang up stubbornly as if pushing against an unseen bank. Are you moving across the hill or glancing more directly toward the center of the earth? Gravity becomes a wider, vaguer tug than you remember. Speed is just the wind peppering your cheeks, and without sight you must depend on your sense of feel instead.

Your skis are, in fact, your best source of information. Trust their messages: Lighter means they are falling off; heavier means they are climbing slightly. If they are riding flat to the snow, the pitch is gentle; if they are up on a thin edge, the slope is dropping away. Even without the advance warning of sight, this information is enough; it is instant and true. You can begin to concentrate on just riding your skis, staying in trim aboard them. That's your job—to stay more or less vertical, fore-and-aft and side-to-side, above your own sliding, hungry feet.

I say hungry because they will soon be ravenous for sensation. The other senses are shut out. You smell nothing but the clean, mid-cloud dankness. The wind and the billions of water droplets muffle even the sound your skis make on the snow. Your collar grows stiff with frozen breath. You snuggle your chin down in your neck gaiter and tune in as best you can to the stimuli from the ground. You let go of the vision thing.

After a while it is like a falling dream. Only you are in control. Falling through the cloud, suspended, making no discernible progress toward the valley. Just falling, and carving the air. Balancing, hanging as if by a string. Turn after turn, untouched by distance or time.

When it's done and you finally bump into the lodge or the base of a lift, or other skiers pierce your reverie with their forms and shouts, you feel relief, but you also feel cheated. You realize you don't need to see to ski. Your feet are smarter than you thought, and that pure visceral touch is as rich as the brightest blue-sky view.

Sun Valley

Sun Valley started it all. It is the beginning point for every Rockies ski story and, indeed, a keystone in the story of modern skiing around the world.

In 1935 there were no ski resorts in the United States. There were a few ski tows, mainly rope tows, driven by old Ford and Dodge motors and looped around rear-drive axles to drag intrepid skiers up New England pastures, Canadian sugarbushes, and even a few timberline passes out West. Even the Alps were not much more sophisticated. Yes, the Brits did play in the snow, skating and sleighing at elegant hotels in St. Moritz and Gstaad, and Ernest Hemingway did ride the cog trains up Swiss passes only to swoop back down on skis to the village and the inevitable wine lunch. But downhill skiing, and ski resorts as we know them, didn't yet exist.

Enter a young Averell Harriman, chairman of the board of Union Pacific Railroad and an avid skier. Harriman very much wanted to increase passenger traffic to the West and decided that a European-style winter destination resort would be just the ticket. So he hired an Austrian count, Felix Schaffgotsch, to scour the mountains for the perfect location, with the caveat that it be accessible by rail.

Count Schaffgotsch spent the winter of 1935–1936 on tour with his knickers and six pairs of hickory skis. He rejected Washington's Mount Rainier because all the surrounding land was publicly owned. He nixed Oregon's Mount Hood as too wet. Aspen flunked because its base elevation at 8,000 feet was considered too high for strenuous Alpine exercise. Jackson Hole was deemed inaccessible.

The good Count was about to return as a failure when a Union Pacific representative in Idaho wired him to take a look at the area around Ketchum, an isolated sheep and cattle ranching town at 6,000 feet elevation with a dwindling population of 270 souls. Schaffgotsch arrived on a new-snow day with the sun dazzling the rounded, nearly treeless slopes of the Pioneer Range. Very little wind found its way through the protective rings of peaks. Due to the nearness of the desert and the long, dry route storms took in getting there, the snow Schaffgotsch found was too dry to make good snowballs; it was mostly air, the better to float down on skis.

The location was perfect, and Harriman wasted no time implementing his plan. By New Year's Eve 1936, the luxurious Sun Valley Lodge had already hosted champagne banquets for the likes of Sam Goldwyn, Errol Flynn, and Claudette Colbert. Guests stepped off the train and twirled around the glorious ice rink or swam in a glass-enclosed, circular pool under the stars. Even more amazing for skiers, Harriman had built the world's first chairlift, engineered by a designer of conveyor systems for loading banana boats in Central America. Replace the banana hook with a single chair, add a safety bar and a blanket for your lap, and up the mountain you go.

Sun Valley changed skiing forever, making it glamorous. Hemingway moved into room 206 in the Lodge to finish *For Whom the Bell Tolls.* A carefully orchestrated marketing program brought the most glamorous Hollywood stars of the day to ski and be seen: Clark Gable, Ingrid Bergman, Gary Cooper, Sonja Henie, Jimmy Stewart, Marilyn Monroe. They even made movies there. Henie and John Payne starred in a 1941 romance *Sun Valley Serenade,* which still screens three times a week in the rooms of the Lodge and the Inn and at the Opera House, a short walk from the Lodge. Virginia Hill, a former mistress of gangster Bugsy Seigel, had shoe boxes full of cash delivered to the Lodge by limousine each month. She later fell in love and ran off with one of Sun Valley's handsomest ski instructors, Austrian Hans Hauser.

In those days most ski teachers in America were Austrian, disciples of the great Hannes Schneider, founder of the Arlberg School in St. Anton, Austria. When I first visited Sun Valley in 1963 (on the overnight train from Los Angeles), I wanted nothing more than to ski like ski school director Sigi Engl, who coursed the mountain with effortless élan. Every turn was the same, beginning with a crisp edge check and then a hop of

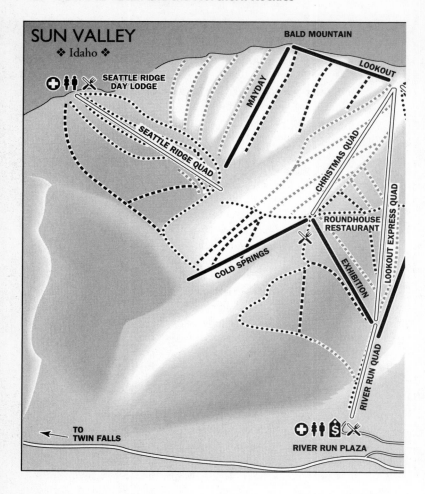

the tails up off the snow and across the fall line, his wool gabardine slacks creased to perfection, feet and knees so tight together it was as if they were sewn in place.

More than the social swirl, the long, long uninterrupted trails of Bald Mountain dictated that the great skiers of several eras put in their time at Sun Valley: Norwegian super skier and founder of Alta, Utah, Alf Engen; America's first ski Olympian, Dick Durrance; master teacher and film-maker Otto Lang; Aspen pioneer Freidl Pfeifer; Toni Matt; Stein Eriksen . . . the list goes on and on. More recent shining stars have included Christin Cooper, GS silver medalist in the 1984 Olympics, and Picabo Street, silver medalist in downhill at the 1994 Lillehammer Games, gold

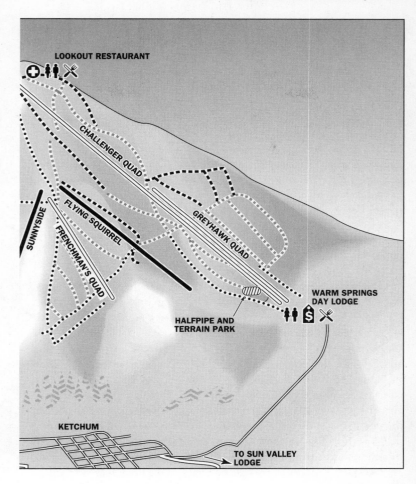

medalist in Super G at the 1998 Nagano Games, and World Cup downhill champion for 1995 and 1996.

The Austrian connection still runs strong. When Arnold Schwarzenegger goes skiing, it is in Sun Valley. Last time I skied on Baldy, I met Adi Erber, Arnold's private instructor when the muscled one is in town. Adi is Austrian, with a movie-star cleft chin, bright smile, and the requisite romantic accent. "Mr. Schmooth," Arnold calls him.

Gone are the boiled wool jackets and jaunty Tyrolean caps, but the spirit of *gemütlichkeit* still pervades the valley. The Ram Bar is still the place to hoist a beer and carve your initials in the thick wooden tables. There is still jazz every night in the elegant Duchin Room at the Lodge.

There is elegant dining on the mountain and off, and a pace and an ambience that owes more to its European predecessors than to its Western, sheep-town roots.

In recent years, the skiing has undergone a greater change than any other aspect of life along the Big Wood River. Bald Mountain has always been recognized as one of the finest natural ski hills in the West, with 3,400 feet of lift-served vertical (3,260 feet of it continuous skiing) and a plethora of unobstructed, rock-free, sinuous fall lines in three directions off the summit. But Sun Valley, some years, has a problem with snow. The name says it all: Sun Valley averages 280 days of sunshine per year. Eighty percent of the days in ski season are sunny. The sagebrush-covered hills immediately south and west of Baldy tell the tale another way: Sagebrush cannot live in a climate much wetter than 16 inches of rain per year. This is the edge of the Great Basin, 210,000 square miles of desert, including most of Nevada, Utah, eastern Oregon, and southern Idaho. Sun Valley—unlike Alta or Grand Targhee—doesn't advertise its average annual snowfall totals. (It receives 220 inches, versus 500 for Alta and Grand Targhee.)

This was a problem neither Harriman nor Schaffgotsch had counted on, and it contributed to a slow decline for the grande dame of American ski resorts. Union Pacific never made any money on the project; Harriman's interest turned to politics, and the area was sold. Neglect tarnished the glamour until current owner Earl Holding decided to do something about nature. Beginning in the late 1980s, Holding invested $18 million in a state-of-the-art snowmaking system—top-to-bottom, 640 acres, covering runs up to three miles long. Then he made access to that guaranteed snow twice as easy by installing high-speed quad chairs all over the mountain, seven of them to date. One chair, the Challenger, roars up 3,144 vertical feet on the Warm Springs side of the mountain in ten minutes. Together, Sun Valley's fleet of lifts can haul a mind-boggling 26,780 skiers and 'boarders—the population of a decent-sized town! — uphill every hour, more lift than any other resort can boast.

You can exhaust yourself in half a day skiing and riding Baldy now. A good many people try, bombing down the Warm Springs and Seattle Ridge groomed pistes on long, quiet skis and Alpine carving boards designed to go fast. When it snows, jump into the famous bowls—*Christmas Bowl, Easter Bowl, Sigi's Bowl, Mayday Bowl*—or try out the bumps on *Exhibition* where Warren Miller shot his first ski footage in the 1950s. When it doesn't snow, join Arnold, Clint Eastwood, and Demi Moore on the baby-bottom-smooth, perfect runs under the sun.

Royalty of the Hollywood kind, the European ski-god kind, and the New York railroad magnate kind, made Sun Valley. Now it almost feels as if the reverse were true: People go to Sun Valley hoping the place will somehow bestow a special grace on them, and more often than not, it does.

Hemingway Country: The View from the Top

Papa loved to fish the Big Wood River that cuts right along the base of Bald Mountain on its way south out of the Pioneer Range. The old town of Ketchum sprawls at Baldy's foot, while a half-mile away up Trail Creek to the northeast the village of Sun Valley just about fills a once-empty sheep meadow. In truth, the two have all but grown together in recent years; the whole resort is referred to as Sun Valley, though the folks in Ketchum like to think of themselves as a crustier Western zip code.

The utterly treeless knob south of the Sun Valley Lodge is Dollar Mountain, the original ski hill and the place where that first chairlift groaned into being. Dollar is still a key component in the overall ski scene; it's the primary teaching hill for the Sun Valley Ski & Snowboard School, with a private beginner's area. Four chairs and a handle tow ply the 638 vertical feet to the summit at 6,638 feet. But next to Baldy across the valley, it is just a bump.

Baldy rises from the river, at an elevation of 5,750 feet to 9,150 feet in a single, steep, mostly forested mound with naked bowls capping the ridges facing south and east. From the sumptuous log and glass Seattle Ridge Lodge near the summit, you can see most of southern Idaho— from the sagebrush plains around Twin Falls to the south to the Pioneer and Boulder Peaks east of Sun Valley, Galena Summit to the north, and endless rows of the jagged Sawtooth Range to the north and west.

The skiing divides into four major zones: the shady northwoods of Warm Springs; the sharp V of the River Run drainage on the east; the bowls; and the mellow avenues of Seattle Ridge farthest south. It's hard to get lost on this mountain; there are only two ways on and two ways off. Fourteen lifts spread the crowds out (an average day is 3,500 people) over the 2,000 acres of skiable terrain.

River Run is the original base, and it sports a huge base lodge and skier services plaza to go along with the parking and high-speed quads. The other base is at Warm Springs, where another day lodge (opened in 1992 with oak-paneled ski lockers and computerized boot-drying service) presides at the foot of the Challenger quad. Warm Springs feels like an exclusive European hunting lodge with gourmet food and prices to match, but don't despair. Irving's Red Hots, Chicago-style wieners, inhabit that little shack across the street. There is very limited parking at the Warm Springs base, but a good local shuttle hustles skiers from the big park-and-ride lot at the corner of Warms Springs Road and Saddle Road. The bus service is excellent throughout the valley. Yellow Sun Valley buses run continuously between the Village, Baldy, and Dollar Mountain. Blue-and-white municipal KART buses connect Ketchum, Sun Valley Village, the Baldy and Dollar bases, and most major hotels.

Beginner Skiing

Although there are a dozen or so green-circle designated runs on the Baldy trail map, this is not a mountain for true beginners. The standard designations have been ratcheted up a notch. The Seattle Ridge greens, for example, while perfectly smooth, would still rate blue on most other mountains. And the blues in the bowls—*Christmas, Mayday, Lefty's*—would no doubt be black diamonds elsewhere. So, beginners beware, start out on Dollar Mountain, and when you can cruise *Graduation* with impunity, you are ready to move up to the big hill.

Dollar for Your Thoughts

Some areas have segregated beginner zones off to the side. Sun Valley has a whole beginner's mountain practically right outside the Lodge door. Dollar is the original ski mountain in the valley, and it's got enough variety and challenge to keep many an intermediate happy as well. The only reason more good skiers and riders don't spend much time, if any, on Dollar is the outstanding big hill across the way. In fact, if Dollar Mountain were transposed to the Midwest somewhere, it would be a major resort.

Part of the fun of Dollar is knowing who has schussed this hallowed terrain before you. There's a marvelous black-and-white photo in the Lodge hallway—a must for any history buff—of Clark Gable and Gary Cooper straight running in the spring powder on Dollar, wearing identical brimmed caps and pressed white jackets. The Lodge corridor also boasts wonderful shots of Lucille Ball, Marilyn Monroe, Ricky Nelson, Jackie O., and a slim Liz Taylor; the hit parade goes on.

All made tracks on the Quarter Dollar, Half Dollar, or Dollar chairlifts and took the sun on the deck out in front of the Dollar Cabin at the base. The terrain is perfect: treeless, north-facing, with infinite microterrain choices from the *Cabin Practice Slope* to meandering *Hidden Valley* to slightly steeper and blue-rated *Face of Dollar*.

The huge majority of skiers you will see here are participating in ski school, but there are other very good reasons to come and ski Dollar. Families with children can ski together here with no worries about high-speed interlopers and no chance to get separated or lost. The pace is more old-fashioned; the chairs are all leisurely old doubles and triples. One more reason to check Dollar out: when there is new powder blanketing the valley, you can bet all the hotshots are ripping it up on the Big Mountain. But on Dollar the snow lies sparkling, intact, and waiting for the few skiers who will claim their Dollar's worth of uncontested fresh tracks in *Sheepherder* and *Sepp's Bowl* and the other historic lines.

Suits Cruising, Intermediate Skiing

With the coming of the quads and the man-made snow, Sun Valley has earned a reputation as a quintessential cruising mountain. In fact, in my opinion it offers the finest in ballroom skiing with its wide-open spaces and reliable fall lines. It was always pretty good for rolling fast over the shapes until your own quads were screaming. But now, thanks to the fast chairs, you can double or triple your vertical in a day. Plus, decades of clearing the slopes of pesky stumps and rocks and the fastidious snow farming means that bothersome interruptions like bare spots, base-tearing obstacles, and moguls never enter the picture.

The runs serviced by Challenger were designed for speed. They hug the fall line with little divergence and are buffed to perfection nightly. While skiers and Alpine boarders soar down these broad avenues, soft-boot aficionados from time to time dart into the trees in search of kickers and jumps. *Warm Springs* run remains the gold standard for Western cruising: three miles long, over 3,000 vertical feet with nary a break—no flats, no roads, no divergence from its pure, fall-line charge to the river. It's so long that they divided it into three sections on the map, *Warm Springs Face, Mid Warm Springs,* and *Lower Warm Springs.* Most of it is rated blue and the bottom is green, but it's all relative. Elsewhere, this kind of persistent pitch would warrant a black diamond. But because it's kept smooth, intermediates thrill to big gravity and experts rip the high-speed shapes. One of the traditions sadly no longer in effect is the awarding of the Sun Valley Two-Star pin for skiing *Warm Springs,* top to bottom, without stopping or falling.

On a busy day, it seems thousands are trying to accomplish that very thing all at once, all of them wearing the latest one-piece suits and riding expensive, vibration-absorbing shaped skis. You might spy silver-maned Bobby Burns, inventor of The Ski, a popular ski brand in the 1970s, and a man who has a heli-ski lodge named after him in the Canadian Rockies. You might spot Sylvester Stallone arcing turns through the gully. You see, the stars never really abandoned the place; they were just hiding out until the skiing became irresistibly good.

If *Warm Springs* gets a little hectic, try *Limelight,* which plunges even more steeply over a series of stair steps before joining *Warm Springs* halfway down. Another option is *Greyhawk,* a broad, steep, finely groomed expressway that departs from *Mid Warm Springs* and lets you roar down to the lift. Or smooth your way out on *Upper College,* the gentler pitched ridge to the east, and then hard down *Flying Squirrel* again to meet the *Warm Springs* funnel to the base. The last section of *Warm Springs* is hash-marked on the map, meaning it's a slow skiing and riding area, and they really mean it. Traffic from a half-dozen major thoroughfares converges here, and you need to go slow and watch your back.

Much less crowded than *Warm Springs* is the *River Run* gully bounded by *College* on the north and the *Round House Ridge* on the south. The cruising is not as long, and it takes two chairs, River Run and the Lookout Express, to reach the top, but the payoff comes in relatively quiet trips down blue-square runs like *Canyon* and *Blue Grouse* and the *River Run* itself, which is a wonderful, deep-throat, bank-sided gulch reminiscent of Aspen's Spar Gulch.

Novices moving up to intermediate skiing and riding on Baldy should start in this zone. The floor of the drain under River Run lift is a good place to start. Then climb higher and follow *Upper* and *Lower College* to the *Lilly Marlane* cat track and back into the gut of the zone for a really long, varied descent. On the other side, take the Exhibition lift up the steep north-facing pitch to *Round House Slope* and *Olympic Lane,* a twisting forest route back to the gully. (Some of Sun Valley's best bump skiers spend time here, and you can watch them—without having to negotiate the same terrain—bopping under the lifts on *Exhibition* and *Holiday.*) Or continue south from the top of Exhibition on *Gun Tower Lane* across the vast lower bowls to the Seattle Ridge lift and its huge novice/intermediate area.

Some nice intermediate terrain on Baldy opened during the winter of 1994–1995 between *Warm Springs* and *River Run.* It's called *Frenchman's Gulch.* It has its own high-speed quad and five blue-square runs through the trees between *Lower College* and *Flying Squirrel.* The northeast exposure is perfect for holding cold, crisp snow; and the location helps siphon off a bit of the *Warm Springs* crowd. Take note: There is no egress from the bottom of *Frenchman's.* You have to ride to the top and exit either into the *Warm Springs* or *River Run* basins.

The reason Seattle Ridge has become such a popular addition to the mountain—besides the gourmet pastas and the heated, glassed-in deck of the Seattle Ridge restaurant—is the miles and miles of easy-swinging, groomed terrain served by the Seattle Ridge quad. *Broadway, Christin's Silver, Southern Comfort,* and *Gretchen's Gold* (named for Sun Valley's 1948 Olympic gold medalist Gretchen Fraser) are all covered by the computer-driven snowmaking system and buffed to talcum by the big machines. Many intermediates just stay here all day. To get home, you take *Lower Broadway* to the old Cold Springs double chair, which lifts you up and out, back into *River Run.*

Looming above the boulevards of Seattle Ridge, the bowls and their myriad possibilities may or may not beckon intermediates. Due to their sunny exposures, you can't count on snow cover, except on *Christmas Ridge,* where the snow guns have poached out into the semiwild. When the natural cover is good, groomed swaths down *Christmas* and *Mayday* and *Broadway Face* make this terrain a real treat for intermediates. At other times and conditions, the bowls' rugged, unshaved nature is best left to very good skiers with wild-snow experience. If at the top you change your mind, you can always ski the summit ridgeline back to Seattle Ridge.

Expert Exhibition

I've already mentioned the kick that experts get screaming down the ultra-smooth groomers in the *Warm Springs* area. There's nothing like it anywhere. But after a while, good skiers want some variety, and Baldy has it in spades.

The bowls are the best, when the snow is there. They flow at a delicious pitch, steep but not too steep, finger after nude finger, gully after treeless gully, across a mile of ridge. *Christmas* is the longest, dropping from the Lookout Restaurant all the way to the base of the Cold Springs lift. *Lookout* and *Easter* bowls are the steepest. Connoisseurs yo-yo the Mayday chair's 1,600-foot vertical and work the lines on either side; powder if the snow is new, bumps if the snowpack is old and deep, north-trending snow ribbons between the sage if the sun has been doing its thing.

The moguls on the north-facing hillside of *River Run* gulch are classics, the biggest and best-formed on the mountain. *Exhibition* is aptly named; generations of bump meisters have shown off underneath the chairlift of the same name. *Holiday* sports some of the steepest bumps on the mountain. (The official, steepest bumps at Sun Valley cascade down *Inhibition* in the *Lower Christmas Bowl* region, but they suffer the fickle snow-cover syndrome over on the sunny side.) The most interesting mogul shapes, to my mind, are those on *Upper River Run,* where the trail drops over the mountain's prow like a frozen river at spring breakup, tumbling through a shady tree alley.

But interestingly enough, Sun Valley is not really a bumper's mountain in the sense that Telluride and Aspen are; in big snow years, sure, years when the bowls are full and creamy, and the moguls have a chance to build and shape from storm to storm. It takes a lot of natural snowfall to carve a good mogul field, and the processes involved in making and grooming artificial snow pretty much preclude turning those runs over to bumps. Besides, the majority of Sun Valley's customers are not looking for mogul madness; they're after the big smooth, and that's what they're getting.

Snowboarding

Boarders who head to Sun Valley's slopes do so mainly for speed. And they find plenty of that on the runs serviced by the Challenger lift—runs like *Greyhawk, Warm Springs Face,* and *Limelight.*

Here on the Warm Springs side of the mountain also is where the resort is investing in a playground for boarders. A 300-foot-long supepipe below *Race Arena* gained Forest Service approval for the 2003–2004 season, and at press time the resort also was seeking permission to put a terrain park in the same area.

Eating at Sun Valley

Trademark Sun Valley architecture exists at the **Warm Springs Lodge,** an opulent structure that offers decidedly upscale cafeteria-style dining. When weather allows, you can dine on barbecue out on the patio. If the lodge's prices are beyond your budget, head across the street to **Irving's Red Hots,** which features sodas and Chicago-style wieners. It's a favorite of local race brats, snowboarders, and anyone in a hurry.

On the mountain, linen-covered tables, silverware, and crystal can be found in the historic **Roundhouse,** the original, tiny, deck-encircled restaurant on the mountain at the top of Exhibition and Cold Springs lifts. Reservations are recommended at this beautiful structure, in which gourmet meals are enjoyed around a cozy fireplace. Inside the **Seattle Ridge Lodge** you'll find huge logs, pink granite bathrooms, silent carpet, heated decks, and a surprisingly reasonable restaurant serving mesquite grill, fresh pastas, and salads, all that along with spectacular views from the summit ridge.

The highest food on the mountain can be found in the **Lookout Restaurant** cafeteria at the top of the Challenger, Christmas, and Lookout quads. Have an early or late lunch here, as the crowds around the holidays can be suffocating. Over on Dollar, the **Dollar Cabin** cafeteria at the base offers lunch with the ghosts of Gary Cooper and Marilyn Monroe.

In the Village

The Lodge Dining Room serves continental cuisine, where you still see couples in evening dress (though it is not required).

The Ram Bar in the old Challenger Inn (now called the Sun Valley Inn), serves good Austrian gemütlichkeit, beer, and accordion music.

Trail Creek Cabin where Hemingway drank; the quality of the food varies, but the ambience is killer. Ride the sleigh from Sun Valley Lodge, but not on a night that's minus 5 degrees.

Bald Mountain Pizza & Pasta is great for family dining, complete with a game room.

In Ketchum

The Pioneer is an old Ketchum watering hole on Main Street with classic Western fare, steaks, trout, etc.

Michel's Cristiania is the new glitzy place in town serving continental cuisine and game specialties.

Sun Valley Data

Mountain Statistics

Vertical feet	3,400 feet
Base elevation	5,750 feet

Sun Valley Data *(continued)*

Mountain Statistics *(continued)*

Summit elevation	9,150 feet
Longest run	3 miles
Average annual snowfall	220 inches
Snowmaking	645 acres
Number of lifts	14 on Baldy: 7 high-speed quads; 2 doubles; 3 triples; 2 surface lifts; 5 on Dollar Mountain: 3 doubles; 1 triple; 1 surface lift
Uphill capacity	26,780 skiers per hour
Skiable terrain	2,054 acres
Opening date	Late November
Closing date	Late April
Snowboarding	Yes

Transportation

By car About 300 miles north of Salt Lake City via I-15 and I-84 to Twin Falls, then north on Highway 75 through Hailey to Ketchum; 150 miles from Boise, via Highways 20 and 75. From the north through Salmon and Stanley on Highways 93 and 20.

By plane Via Horizon Air and SkyWest to Hailey's Friedman Memorial Airport, 17 miles from the resort. Gateway cities for major carriers include Boise, Idaho Falls, and Twin Falls, Idaho, and Salt Lake City, Utah.

By bus Via available charter from gateway cities; complimentary pickup for Sun Valley Company guests at Hailey Airport. Ski company and municipal bus service around the resort village and Ketchum.

Key Phone Numbers

Ski-area information	(208) 622-4111
Snow report	(800) 635-4150
Reservations	(800) 786-8259
Sun Valley Express	(800) 634-6539
Website	www.sunvalley.com; www.sunvalleyexpress.com

Inside Story

Ski Schools

The strong Austrian flavor to the Sun Valley ski school is no accident, and it isn't just because Averell Harriman's scout in the resort's formative years was Austrian Count Felix Schaffgotsch. In the 1930s, almost every ski school in America owed at least some fealty to the great Hannes Schneider, who had developed the first real systematic ski-teaching method at his school in St. Anton. It was called the Arlberg method, and for nearly 30 years it was almost universal.

Schneider sent protégés to start ski schools around the world—Sepp Ruschp to Mount Mansfield at Stowe, Vermont; Sig Buchmayr to Peckett's-on-Sugar Hill, New Hampshire; Hans Hauser and Friedl Pfeifer to Sun Valley. Otto Lang became a kind of filmmaker/roving ambassador for the Arlberg method.

Back then skis were wooden, long, stiff, and heavy, and the boots were leather, soft, and imprecisely clamped to the skis. Turning technique required that you drive the skis through a turn with a powerful rotating of the upper body and arms, like a bus driver twisting a three-foot steering wheel. Then you needed to unweight, often hopping the tails completely off the snow, to begin a direction change. The skis worked as one, feet and knees clamped tightly together. The finished product, which everyone in ski school in those days hoped fervently to imitate, was stylish, elegant, and fiendishly difficult to master.

As ski equipment got better, so, too, was there room for new and divergent teaching theory. In the 1960s, the French National School rose to prominence on the theories of George Joubert and the race results of Jean-Claude Killy. Boots had buckles instead of laces, though they were still made of leather, and skis were built of much more responsive metal laminates. The French showed how to direct the skis with the lower body while keeping the upper body quiet. Several ski schools in the United States still show strong French influence, including Squaw Valley in California, and Loveland in Colorado.

In the 1970s, the Italians became fashionable following the successes of Gustavo Thoeni. Riding on even better fiberglass skis and in stiffer boots, Thoeni and the Italian School demonstrated how a wide, balanced stance and strong edging by the outside knee resulted in superior turns.

Also in the 1970s, the national schools of all the Alpine nations—Switzerland, Austria, France, Italy, Germany—plus the United States and Japan, got together every couple of years to show off their newest teaching theories. Precision ski demonstration teams in matching uniforms competed informally but with great pageantry for bragging rights to the newest and most innovative methodologies.

In 1974 to the surprise and chagrin of the traditional powers, the U.S. team of PSIA (Professional Ski Instructors of America) demonstrators stole the show with their unveiling of the American Teaching Method. This was the first teaching system that was totally student-oriented, completely learning-based; and, most shocking of all to the Europeans who had invested decades in competing national styles, ATM subjugated form to pure function.

Gone was the need to imitate a particular style, or affect a look. ATM focused instead on the key skiing skills—balance, gliding, edging, and pressuring the ski—that *all* effective skiing embodies. ATM rocked the Europeans and became the standard at virtually every ski school in America.

So now when you go take a lesson at Sun Valley, for example, your instructor may be from Austria (he might even be Arnold's instructor), and he may have an elegant, feet-together Austrian style when he free skis, but the lesson he gives you will be pure American Teaching Method, with an emphasis not on what you look like but on the core skills you need to make skiing easier and more fun—to develop basic skills to the point that your own personal style shines through.

Part Four

California and the Pacific Northwest

Seth Masia

Hot Rocks and Cold Water

From the San Bernardino range east of Los Angeles to the Alaska Range, the skiable bits of the North American Pacific Rim stretch out over 2,000 miles. It's a procession of volcanos; some lively, some dormant, most extinct. Fly up the West Coast, and on a clear day you can count the cones: Mount San Gorgonio, Mount Whitney, Mount Humphreys, Mount Ritter, Freel Peak, Mount Rose, Lassen Peak, Mount Shasta, Mount Scott, Three Sisters, Mount Hood, Mount Adams, Mount St. Helens, Mount Rainier, Mount Baker, Mount Garibaldi. They continue north into the vast wilderness of British Columbia and Alaska. Rising 10,000 to 14,000 feet, these mountains force the moist Pacific winds high into the cold upper atmosphere, pulling huge falls of snow out of the air.

When a winter storm boils over from the Gulf of Alaska, a five-day blizzard can drop ten feet of snow on sunny California and 15 feet on the wet forests above Seattle and Vancouver. In a good snow year, two-day storms happen every week. A typical big-mountain ski area gets 40 feet of natural snow each winter.

Because the storms are wet, the snow is often thick. Locals call it Sierra cement. It beds down into a dense, bulletproof base that can last beyond August. While skiers elsewhere in North America hang their gear in the garage at tax time, West Coast skiers can count on a sunscreen season that lasts until May at Squaw Valley, June at Alpine Meadows, July at Mammoth, and until the first snow in October at Mount Hood and Blackcomb.

Wet snow does not mean that the Pacific Rim resorts never get powder days—above 8,000 feet the snow can be light enough to breathe. Even when it has some weight, local skiers know how to glide through the stuff as if it were Utah fluff.

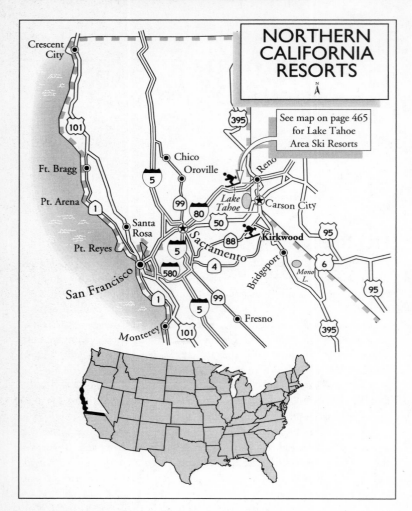

West Coasters treat muck the way Vermonters ski ice: We adjust. Muck is easier to ski, of course, if the slope is steep enough to keep you planing. Finding that steep terrain is no problem on the West Coast. Pushed upward by fire below, the Pacific Rim volcanos are growing and dynamic. They swell, shudder, and occasionally burst (Mount St. Helens is proof that geologic processes move swiftly here). Scientists say that Mount Lassen was once 35,000 feet high; it must have been some bang when the top blew off.

Hyperactive geology can create scenery of vast verticality—think of Yosemite Valley, Shasta, Rainier. It also builds rugged, high-relief ski terrain,

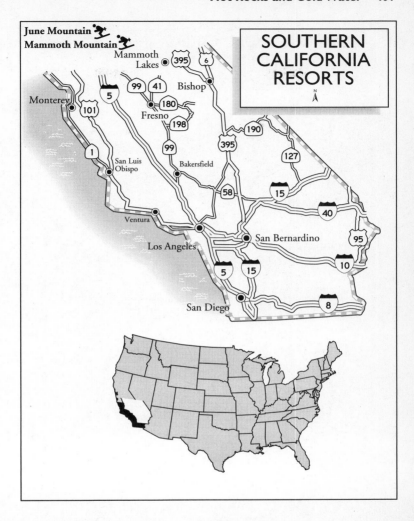

an incredible variety of it. And that's what this section is about. Why ski on the West Coast? The terrain is why.

First of all, you can't have a broad variety without establishing that the expert terrain is truly difficult. At West Coast areas, the standard is high. The black diamond runs are usually natural couloirs or cliff faces. Farther east (with the exception of a couple of hairball places like Jackson Hole and Snowbird), this kind of terrain would be labeled double black, or simply closed. The stem-christie skier can get down most Rocky Mountain black diamonds; on the left coast, the same skier is likely to arrive at the bottom of Headwall or Cornice Bowl sliding on nylon instead of on skis.

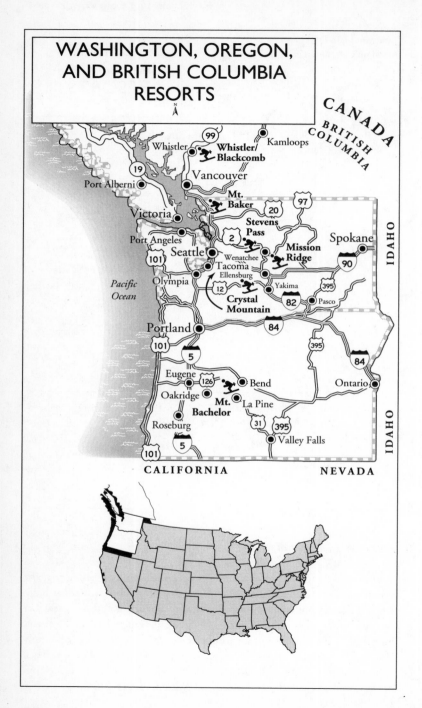

WASHINGTON, OREGON, AND BRITISH COLUMBIA RESORTS

N

CANADA

BRITISH COLUMBIA

Whistler

Whistler/ Blackcomb

Kamloops

99

19

Vancouver

Port Alberni

Mt. Baker

20

97

IDAHO

Victoria

Stevens Pass

Port Angeles

2

Spokane

Seattle

Wenatchee

Mission Ridge

101

Tacoma

90

Olympia

Ellensburg

Pacific Ocean

12

Yakima

395

Crystal Mountain

82

Pasco

Portland

84

101

5

395

Eugene

126

Bend

84

Oakridge

Mt. Bachelor

La Pine

Ontario

IDAHO

Roseburg

31

395

5

Valley Falls

101

CALIFORNIA

NEVADA

The steepest terrain here is simply steeper, and the reason is our geology. The Rocky Mountain ranges are older, more weathered; ski areas there tend to top out on nicely rounded summit snowfields (think of Vail, Aspen, Snowmass, Sun Valley). West Coast areas invariably build their lifts to narrow ridgelines, so a powder run out here often starts with a big first step into thin air (think of Blackcomb's Couloir Extreme, Squaw's Siberia Bowl, Mammoth's Cornice Bowl). Elsewhere in the United States, ski areas try to sculpt most of their runs into ego-boosting intermediate boulevards. West Coast ski areas normally let the runs drop over natural contours, and where those contours dive through rocky chutes, so do the skiers. Of course, there's plenty of easier cruising, but out West the ego stuff begins at the bottom of the summit bowl. You can't always hop on a lift and be certain you'll find an easy (or at least an intermediate) way down; it doesn't work that way. The only way off the top may very well be over the cornice. So this section is for two kinds of skiers.

First is the hardbody looking for gravity-powered thrills, the skier who will revel in the freedom the coastal ski areas provide to ski truly dangerous terrain. For each lift and peak, I'll show you how to squeeze the contour lines closer together.

Second is the skier who wants to have fun without scaring himself stupid. For each lift and peak, I'll show you how to find the sane cruising terrain.

Finally, you can't learn these mountains well with a casual visit; there's simply too much to absorb—too many fall lines, too many exposures, too many avalanche paths masquerading as "lines." At the biggest mountains it takes the professional patrollers years to learn even the names of all the shots.

To a large extent, this section depends on the accumulated knowledge of real locals. A local is someone who has spent a lifetime memorizing the shape of a single mountain. The real local can get off the summit in a white-out as easily as you can find your own bathroom in the dark. These skiers have guided me into their own secret lines and explained the subtleties of the storm patterns. This section owes much to their mental space-maps.

The Sierras and Tahoe

Mammoth Mountain   This is the soul center of southern California skiing. The highest lift-served ski mountain on the West Coast, Mammoth gets the deepest snow—and the biggest crowds. It is vast and varied, with precipitous summit bowls and easy cruising down low. Mammoth's boisterous nightlife is a kind of snowy Mardi Gras.

June Mountain   Mammoth's sister area, a half an hour north, is the reverse of the coin: It is serene and secluded, with miles of easy terrain on the upper slopes and good expert steeps below. It's a romantic and private destination for honeymoon skiers.

Bear Valley   Insulated from the rush of resort towns, Bear Valley offers a laid back retreat, and a vast, steep powder bowl.

Kirkwood   Lift-served adventure skiing an hour south of Tahoe, Kirkwood is a remote high valley with good snow and dozens of steep chutes off the two-mile ridgeline.

Sierra-at-Tahoe   Sierra-at-Tahoe is two ski areas in one: classic, steep Sierra tree skiing at one end and broad open Colorado-type cruising at the other, all served by modern high-speed quads. No lodging and no village here, but it's a great day-skier destination for Sacramentans and Tahoe-area visitors.

Heavenly   Head in the clouds, feet in the Tahoe casinos, Heavenly boasts California's biggest vertical, with intermediate cruising and big bump runs on the California side and steep bowls and tree skiing on the Nevada side. An awkward lift layout guarantees long lines on weekends, but that's changing. Cheap lodging and great nightlife in Stateline casinos.

Alpine Meadows   A friendly, family-oriented area backed up to the Sierra Crest. There is an excellent variety of terrain on two peaks, with a low-pressure atmosphere. There's no nightlife and little lodging at the base area—Alpine skiers stay in Tahoe City, six miles south.

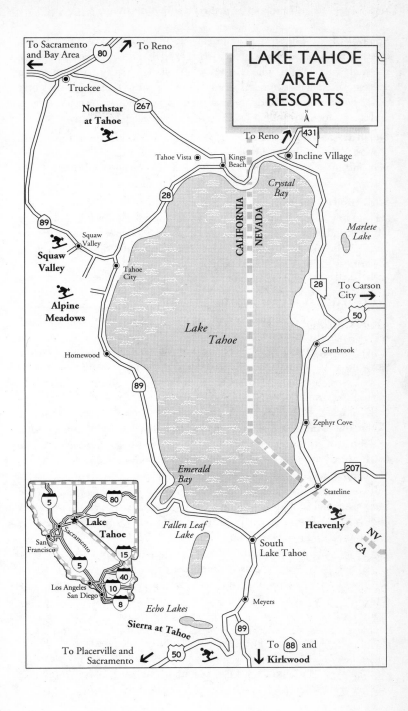

Squaw Valley   The steepest, most macho mountain on the West Coast, this area has a fast, efficient lift system to keep lift lines minimal even when the trails are crowded. The relatively short but very steep terrain provides spectacular challenge in good weather, but it is nearly unskiable on storm days, thanks to high winds and avalanche danger. Squaw attracts athletes, and the go-for-it attitude is reflected in an overheated bar scene.

Northstar-at-Tahoe   This is a comfortable condo community built around a lovely family ski area. Northstar's front side is ideal for beginners and intermediates, while the back-side cruisers give advanced skiers a workout. There's good dining on site and in nearby Truckee.

Sugar Bowl   Perched on Donner Pass, Sugar Bowl is the oldest major ski area in California. It's a favorite powder stash for knowledgeable locals who take advantage of the area's proximity to Sacramento and make the dash up the hill when conditions are prime. Limited on-site lodging in the atmospheric Sugar Bowl Lodge.

Mammoth Mountain

The psychological center of California skiing, Mammoth Mountain is a sort of high-altitude extension of the SoCal beach scene. Six hours from the city along Highway 395, the town of Mammoth Lakes fills up every weekend with tanned, athletic Los Angelenos. They overflow the base lodges, clog the lifts, and party through the night at dozens of bars and restaurants around town.

It's actually an easy six hours. Highway 395 arrows across the Mojave Desert and climbs gradually up the Owens Valley. That's 300 miles of dry, straight road with no stoplights. Beyond Bishop—a good place for a late snack on a Friday night—the road climbs steeply to 7,000 feet; drivers brave snowpacked roads for only the last 30 miles into Mammoth Lakes.

If coming by air, plan to catch a charter flight from Long Beach to the Mammoth Lakes Airport, or fly to Reno for a three-hour drive down Highway 395 from the north (in mid-winter much of this drive can be on snow-packed roads).

At 11,053 feet, Mammoth is the highest lift-served peak on the West Coast, and most years it gets the best, the driest, and the deepest snow. With about 3,500 acres of skiable terrain, 150 named trails, and 27 lifts sprawling over 3,100 vertical feet, it's also among the largest single ski mountains in the United States. The top of the ridgeline, stretching for a couple of miles west of town, consists of precipitous bowls and steep, narrow chutes; it's paradise for an expert but no place for the timid. Down low, sheltered in forests of huge ponderosa pines, are long, rolling intermediate and beginner trails. In between you'll find every kind of open glade, buffed-out cruiser, or mogul field a skier could ask for.

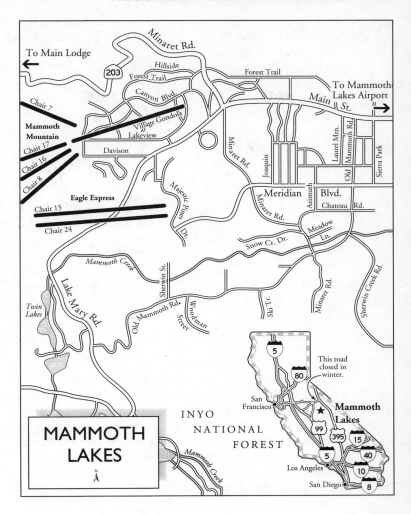

There are four ways to get onto the mountain: at the rambling old Main Lodge (drive up Minaret Road, or take the Red Shuttle); at the Stump Alley Express (on Minaret, a mile closer to town); at the more modern Canyon Lodge (take Canyon Boulevard or the Blue Shuttle); or take the Eagle Express gondola from the Eagle Lodge Area (at the head of Meridian Boulevard, served by the Yellow and Green Shuttle routes).

There's plenty of free parking near both base lodges, and Mammoth does a creditable job of keeping the roads clear. I like to get up early, park close in, and have breakfast at the base lodge while waiting for the lifts to open at 8:30 a.m. Driving up Minaret Road at 7:30 a.m., I've often seen coyotes trotting home after a night-long feast in the base-lodge dumpster.

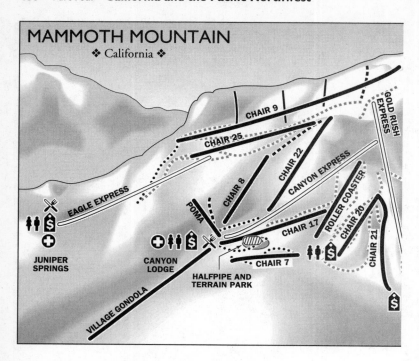

The Little Eagle Lodge lifts serve the east end of the Mammoth complex, consisting of long, gentle beginner-intermediate cruisers like *Bridges, Christmas Tree, Manzanita,* and *Holiday.* (Bridges is also the name of a condo complex alongside the trail.) From the top of Eagle Express, ski down to Chair 9 for the long ride up into the high bowls below Dragon's Back Ridge, where experts find uncrowded skiing for days after a storm. You can jump on Chair 25 to the top of Lincoln Mountain; there's one easy way down from Lincoln, appropriately labeled *Relief.* The rest of the peak is steepish, consisting of chutes, mogul faces, and expert-level tree skiing.

Canyon Lodge is a massive three-story building with locker rooms, cafeterias, retail and rental shops, and ski patrol and ski school offices. Four lifts fan out from the hut. Chair 7 serves a secluded network of beginner trails that are removed from the main flow of high-speed traffic. Chair 8 can put you into some short intermediate terrain or return you to the Little Eagle Lodge complex. Chair 17 goes to some easy intermediate cruisers. Ride Canyon Express, a high-speed quad, for transport out of the Canyon complex toward the summit or Stump Alley Express area.

From Chair 8, Canyon Express, or Chair 17 you can reach Chair 22, the most popular route to the top of Lincoln Mountain. Chair 22 goes straight up Lincoln's steepest face, and on a powder day, you'll find the best tree skiers in town yo-yoing this chair.

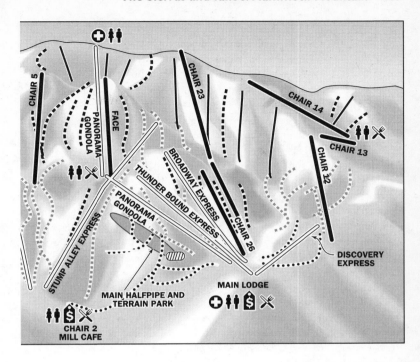

Four lifts branch out from the Stump Alley Express area. Gold Express and Chair 21 serve some nice long intermediate cruisers sheltered in the woods on the lower flanks of the mountain—this is a great place to ski on a storm day. Stump Alley Express goes to the open slopes above the McCoy Station; ride these lifts to access the summit or the Main Lodge.

The Main Lodge—four stories of shops, offices, and restaurants, all spreading out from the Panorama gondola base station—is the jumping-off point for most people who want to ski the summit. From here the gondola rises 2,140 feet to the top; get off at mid-station if you don't want to ski the expert-level summit chutes.

Four more lifts move traffic away from the Main Lodge. Thunderbowl Express and the high-speed Discovery quad are for beginners. Broadway Express serves *Broadway* (the main route back to the lodge for most intermediate skiers) and a variety of steeper, expert-rated cruising trails.

Another route to the summit is via Chair 26 (serving the lower half of the mountain) to Chair 23, which is engineered to climb through the cornice to the summit.

Farther out, in the woods beyond Discovery Chair, is Chair 12, serving the intermediate terrain of White Bark Ridge. Ride Chair 12 to reach the distant Chair 14 outpost at the far western end of the complex.

About the Weather

Like any California ski area, in a big snow year Mammoth is occasionally prey to the monster three-day blizzard. The powerful winds accompanying these storms can close the upper lifts, but there's plenty of uncrowded skiing lower down (most Mammoth skiers are fair-weather folks). Another tactic on storm days is to head up the road to June Mountain, where trees shelter the lifts right to the summit.

Best Beginner Skiing

The best beginner skiing is off Chair 7 near Canyon Lodge; the runs are out of the main flow of traffic; its main trails, *Hansel* and *Gretel,* are prime terrain for learning. At the Main Lodge, the Discovery high-speed quad chair serves the same purpose. Use *Jill's Trail.* There's one beginner trail, *St. Moritz,* that winds down from McCoy Station so adventurous newcomers can ride the gondola up there for lunch. Be aware that expert skiers, moving fast, may cross your path as *St. Moritz* zigs across trails like *Mambo* and *Patrolman.*

Best Intermediate Skiing

The best intermediate skiing is on *St. Anton,* of course, as well as on *Lost-in-the-Woods* and *Wall Street,* a couple of tree-sheltered cruisers off Gold Rush Express. *Bridges, Holiday, Manzanita,* and *Juniper,* the long trails paralleling Eagle Express, stretch out over two miles of relaxed skiing.

On a storm day, if you want to stay out of the wind and near the hot chocolate, the best bets are Chairs 8 and 17, serving the short but rolling trails near Canyon Lodge.

Best Expert Skiing

The best expert skiing is on Mammoth's summit. The summit rises 1,000 feet above the tree line and provides some of the hairiest chutes in North America. There's one way down for intermediates: *Road Runner* follows the ridgeline to the west, eventually descending toward Chair 14. From *Road Runner,* experts can peel off down the reasonably wide (and normally bumped-up) *Cornice Bowl,* or through the narrow shots called *Climax, Hangman's Hollow, Dropout, Wipeout,* and *Philippe's Couloir.* From the top of the gondola, traverse east to reach the popular *Dave's Run* (named for Mammoth founder Dave McCoy) or the scary *Huevos Grande.*

On storm days, when the summit is closed due to high winds, you'll find prime powder in the relatively sheltered tree runs off Chair 22 on Lincoln Mountain, on Canyon and Roller Coaster lifts, or, closer to the Main Lodge, off Broadway, Goldrush, and Stump Alley Express lifts. After the storm, savvy locals find untracked snow off Dragon's Back Ridge above Chair 9.

While it's marked as an intermediate trail, *St. Anton* is one of the great high-speed cruisers—a long easy groomer perfect for arcing big GS turns from the top of Face Lift Express all the way back to the Main Lodge, 1,700 feet below.

Snowboarding

Mammoth now has three terrain parks, including half-pipes. The beginner park is at Canyon Lodge, the intermediate, at South Park, is on Roller Coaster West, and the pro-quality Main Park drops from Thunder Bound lift at the Main Lodge.

Most Convenient Lodging

You have two choices for ski-in/ski-out lodging: the new **Juniper Springs Lodge** at the foot of the Eagle Express lift, and **The Bridges** condo complex, 100 yards up the hill. Just a minute's walk across the parking lot from the Main Lodge sits the **Mammoth Mountain Inn,** with 200 hotel rooms. A dozen different condo developments spread out within walking distance of the Canyon Lodge parking lot; check with central reservations (phone (800) 367-6572) for availability. Motels are abundant where Canyon Boulevard, Lake Mary Road, and Minaret Road meet at The Village, just a short drive from either the Main Lodge or Canyon Lodge.

Best Eats

Most on-mountain food service is strictly cafeteria-style, but you can get a real sit-down lunch at **Parallax Grill** in McCoy Station or at the **Mountainside Grill** in the Mammoth Mountain Inn. Mammoth Lakes offers dozens of restaurants, ranging from pedestrian pizza joints and Mexican restaurants to rather deluxe dining. The most romantic spot in town is **Skadi** (phone (760) 934-3902, $15 and up), occupying the old site of the Cask and Cleaver in Sherwin Plaza II. Skadi serves continental and American cuisine and offers great views of the mountain. A locals' favorite is **Whiskey Creek** (phone (760) 934-2555, $18 and up), serving prime rib, pasta, and so on. Whiskey Creek has a dance floor and the best wine list in town. **Ocean Harvest** (phone (760) 934-8539, $16 and up) is famous for very fresh fish. My favorite place for family dining is **Angel's** (phone (760) 934-7427, $6 and up), a warm and friendly spot serving everything from barbecue to chicken pot pie. For the best breakfast in town, it's the **Matterhorn** (phone (760) 934-3369).

Mammoth Mountain Data

Mountain Statistics

Vertical feet	3,100 feet
Base elevation	7,953 feet

Mammoth Mountain Data (continued)

Mountain Statistics (continued)

Summit elevation	11,053 feet
Longest run	3 miles
Average annual snowfall	385 inches
Snowmaking	477 acres
Number of lifts	29: 1 express six-pack; 8 express quads; 1 quad; 7 triples; 5 doubles; 3 gondolas; 4 surface lifts
Uphill capacity	50,000 skiers per hour
Skiable terrain	3,500 acres
Opening date	Early-November
Closing date	June
Snowboarding	Yes

Mammoth shares its lift ticket with June Mountain (but June Mountain ticket is not valid at Mammoth).

Transportation

By car From Los Angeles, 5 hours via U.S. Highway 395. From Reno, 3 hours via U.S. Highway 395.
By air Commuter airlines to Mammoth Lakes Airport, 7 miles away.

Key Phone Numbers

Ski-area information	(800) MAMMOTH or (760) 934-0745
Snow report	(760) 934-6166 or (888) SNOWRPT
Reservations	(800) MAMMOTH or (760) 934-0745
Website	www.mammothmountain.com

June Mountain

It happens every Friday night from October to June, and it's terrifying; the Mojave Desert is transformed into an extension of the Los Angeles freeway system. The usually desolate Route 395 is packed solid with cars rushing north in bumper-locked precision, all carrying skiers bound for the little town of Mammoth Lakes. There, skiers jam onto Mammoth's lifts and pour like lemmings down its slopes. They turn Mammoth, the second largest ski mountain in the United States, into an anthill. At day's end, Los Angelenos convert the whole area into a disco—neon spandex, sunglasses in the dark, hairdos that defy gravity.

If this is not your scene, you need to drive 20 miles farther north to the High Sierra valley of June Lake. Here, June Mountain's slopes cascade down a classic glacial profile. The mountain is a reasonably flat plateau on top, steepening sharply into a precipice down low.

The hamlet of June Lake is popular with fishermen and hikers in the summer, so it offers a surprising variety of lodging in the form of condos, motels, and cabins, all within a mile of the lifts via shuttle bus (there's no ski-in/ski-out lodging). Best dining is at the **Carson Peak Inn** (steak and seafood) and the **Fern Creek Grill** (traditional American). Traffic is rarely a problem—on the roads or trails—in this beautiful little valley. Quiet and romantic, it's a perfect couples' getaway, with or without kids.

June offers 2,600 feet of vertical, but the lowest 1,100 feet, known as the Face, is so steep as to be unskiable by nonexperts. Ride Chair J1 up to the mid-station June Meadows Chalet and examine what the Face has to offer—it is heady deep powder or intimidating bumps.

The upper runs are much friendlier. There are two peaks, Rainbow Summit and June Mountain. Most of the beginner and intermediate terrain rolls down the face of Rainbow, served by Chairs J6 and J4.

On June Mountain (Chair J7) the runs are decidedly tougher. Drop into any of half a dozen steep chutes (the best is called, aptly, *Powder Chute*), blast down the wide-open slopes of *Matterhorn,* or take on *Sunset,* which starts out steep and then rolls out into a blanket of skiable bumps.

June's summit rises to 10,135 feet, and the trees go all the way to the top. This means that when winter storms close the upper half of Mammoth, pushing 20,000 crazed Los Angelenos together on the lower slopes, most of June remains sheltered, skiable, and uncrowded.

Best Beginner Skiing

Silverado, winding a couple of miles from Rainbow Summit, may be the longest true beginner trail in the West. Most of the terrain off Chair J2, rising from the June Meadows Chalet, is easily handled by new skiers.

Best Intermediate Skiing

There are half a dozen runs that qualify as sweet, don't-stop-now cruisers: *Bodie, Comstock, Gunsmoke,* and *Rosa Mae* on Rainbow and *Sunrise* and *Matterhorn* on June Mountain.

Best Expert Skiing

My favorite high-speed cruiser is *Schatzi,* a classic giant slalom course that begs for linked high-speed turns. Go fast. Go faster. After a storm, of course, grab your widest skis and hit *The Face, Carson,* and *Gull Ridge.*

Snowboarding

The superpipe and main Jib Park are on Chalet—look for them while riding Chair J2. Find another jib park at the summit, along *Schatzi.*

June Mountain Data

Mountain Statistics

Vertical feet	2,590 feet
Base elevation	7,510 feet
Summit elevation	10,135 feet

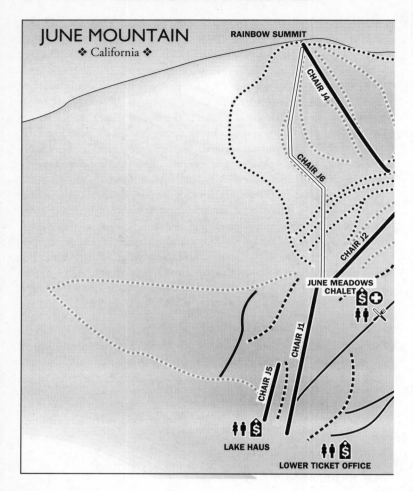

June Mountain Data (continued)

Mountain Statistics *(continued)*

Longest run	2.5 miles
Average annual snowfall	250 inches
Number of lifts	8: 2 quads; 5 doubles; 1 rope tow
Uphill capacity	10,000 skiers per hour
Skiable terrain	500+ acres
Opening date	December
Closing date	April
Snowboarding	Yes

June Mountain shares its lift ticket with Mammoth Mountain; the June Mountain ticket is valid at Mammoth with an upgrade charge.

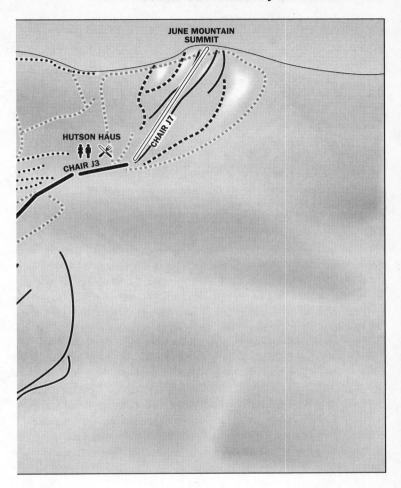

Transportation

By car From Los Angeles, 6.5 hours via U.S. Highway 395; from Reno, 3 hours via U.S. Highway 395.

By air Reno's Cannon International Airport or commuter airlines to Mammoth Lakes (25 miles).

Key Phone Numbers

Ski-area information	(888) JUNEMTN or (760) 648-7733
Snow report	(760) 934-2224
Reservations	(760) 648-7584
Website	www.junemountain.com

Bear Valley

Bear Valley sits 30 miles due south of Lake Tahoe, and 12 miles south of Kirkwood. But because there are no north-south roads along the crest of the Sierra, Bear lives in a serene world of its own, decades removed from the hustle of Tahoe. In the winter, State Route 4 dead-ends at Bear. With no through-traffic, no casinos, and nothing to do but enjoy the deep snow across 1280 acres of classic Alpine bowls, Bear is a sweet retreat. It's laid back and relaxed, with easy cruisers for the family and heinous challenging plunges for experts.

Today's low-key atmosphere belies a rowdy past. A toll road opened over Ebetts Pass in the 1860s and local miners named Mount Reba for Reba Blood, whose parents ran the toll station at Bear Valley Meadows. In 1952 the area was purchased by the Orvis family, ranchers from the San Joaquin Valley. They pastured cattle here in the summers. The bucolic era ended abruptly in 1967, when the Orvis brothers partnered with logger Maury Rasmussen to open the Mount Reba ski area.

In 1967, of course, the San Francisco hippie culture was at its peak. The sexual revolution had hit full stride, and a series of young marketing geniuses turned Bear Valley into party central. Resort manager Dave McTaggart gave free passes to airline stewardesses, on the theory that single men would follow—and they did. Club Med built a lodge. McTaggart flew in travel writers and fixed them up with dates. He ran a national ad campaign ("Ski Bear") featuring nude skiers, including one of his several wives. McTaggart left in 1969, after his Tamarack Lodge burned to the ground in a natural gas explosion. The ski hill then hired Olympic medallist Jimmie Heuga to run promotions. Jimmie invented the celebrity race, flying dozens of Hollywood stars to Bear's private airstrip. (After pulling off a massive real estate scam in Aspen, McTaggart surfaced years later as executive director of Greenpeace.)

The jet-setters are gone, and now no one bothers to plow the Bear Valley airstrip during the winter. Except on holidays, the area has a sleepy, comfortable feel. The day lodge is roomy but simple and functionally comfortable. The lifts are fixed-grip doubles and triples—nothing fancy. But the slopes are uncrowded. At the time this was written, the ski area was for sale, and the potential buyers have talked about putting in some high-speed lifts and modernizing the lodge.

Essential navigation: The "base lodge" at the parking lot is really a mid-mountain day lodge (at 7,750 feet elevation—1,150 feet above the lowest lift station and 745 feet below the summit). Walk out of the lodge and the beginner terrain stretches before you, off Cub and Super Cub chairs. Or ride the twinned Bear or Kuma chairs to the summit for all the intermediate cruisers, lacing the Upper Mountain and Backside.

Experts have two main choices: Descend from the day lodge directly into the precipitous Snow Valley runs (the east end of the lower mountain), then ride the Kodiak chair back out; or pop over to the Grizzly chair (serving the west side of the lower mountain) to ski Grizzly Bowl. Alternatively, go to the Bear Top summit and cruise down *Mokelumne* and *West Ridge*. From this knife-edge ridgeline, you can jump into a dozen named chutes and several dozen un-named tree shots between them.

Visitors to California, take note: Mokelumne is pronounced moo-KAH-la-mi.

Weather Notes

Bear Valley sits at roughly the same elevation as the North Tahoe ski areas, and, on average, gets the same kind of snow. A broad-front major storm will bring the same quantity of snow. However, Bear is separated from Tahoe by three high ridges, so minor storms may come to Bear and not to Tahoe and vice versa. Don't depend on a Tahoe forecast for Bear Valley; call Bear for the local snow report (209) 753-2301, extension 2.

Best Beginner Skiing

Fanning out above the day lodge are *Rodeo, Ego Alley,* and *Cub Meadow,* all served by Cub and Super Cub chairs.

Best Intermediate Skiing

Head for Bear Top summit (8,495 feet) and ski over to the back side. Here you'll find half a dozen long intermediate cruisers sweeping 950 vertical feet down to Hibernation chair. The lift line runs, like exhibition runs everywhere, grow show-off bumps. The main drags—*Bear Boogie, Goldilocks, Satisfaction, Shady Grove,* and *Westworld*—are groomed often. A few steeper shots are labeled as expert-level runs: *Tigger's, Big John,* and the *Blue Jay Way* glade.

On the front of the upper mountain, the longest blue cruiser is the ridge run, *Mokelumne West.* It arcs around to bring you back to the base lodge area via *Lodge Run.* In the other direction off the summit, Tuck's Traverse take you out to the eastern edge of the trail complex, with *Sugar, Lonely Pine,* and *Hog Back* descending alongside Koala Chair.

Upper intermediates who want a challenge should test their skills on the short, steep Feather Duster, reachable via Tuck's Traverse or off the Koala chair.

Bear's longest run is the three-mile *Lunch Run,* descending from Bear Top summit to the Bear Valley Village. There's no lift back—you have to ride the bus, which leaves the Village parking lot about every half hour. It's a great way to end the day, though, if you're staying in the Village. And if you're parked in the upper lot, above the day lodge, finish your day with a ride up Koala chair, then ski *Hog Back* and *Water Tank* back to your car.

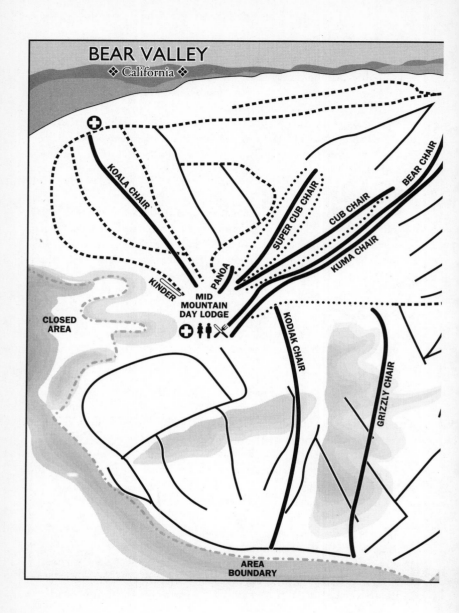

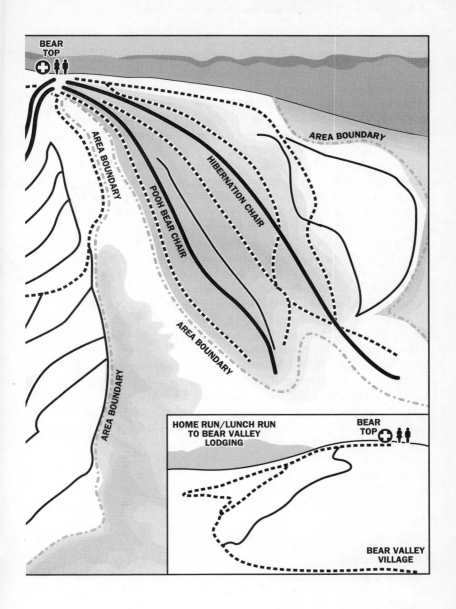

BEAR TOP

AREA BOUNDARY

AREA BOUNDARY

AREA BOUNDARY

HIBERNATION CHAIR

POOH BEAR CHAIR

AREA BOUNDARY

AREA BOUNDARY

HOME RUN/LUNCH RUN TO BEAR VALLEY LODGING

BEAR TOP

BEAR VALLEY VILLAGE

Best Expert Skiing

Most of the expert skiing is on the lower mountain, where there are no easy routes unless you're willing to traverse endlessly across one of the two broad, steep bowls. The two bowls—Snow Valley to the east and Grizzly Bowl to the west—are separated by a massive rocky spine the locals call Lunch Rock. You'll recognize it by the concrete gun mount anchored to its peak: this is where the avalancheros used to fire off their 105mm recoilless rifle to pick the cornices off the surrounding ridgelines.

The steepest shots here are the short *Hari Kari* and *Cec's* above Snow Valley, and the farthest (southernmost) chutes off West Ridge. My favorite shots off West Ridge are *Six Dead Trees* (the glade just past *Other Half*) and the 45-degree *Uptight*. Because the Ridge itself is a fairly steep descent, you'd think that these far chutes might be shorter—but they're not, because the floor of the bowl falls away even more steeply than the ridge. In fact, they're quite long, each dropping about 800 feet only to dump out onto a couple of rolling bowls called Parasite Pitch and Strawberry Fields, which are pretty steep themselves.

The skier indimidated by narrow chutes can find plenty of wide-open steep shots down the middle of the lower mountain bowls. On a powder day the whole area is a paradise, but if you're up early enough to get first tracks, you can't go wrong simply following the fall-line under one of the lifts. The slot to skier's right of Kodiak chair (not shown on the trail map) is called *MTKKK,* and the lift line drops through the sweet *Freefall.* Follow Grizzly chair from Red Baron into Hangar and across Maury's Meadow.

On the upper mountain, a network of short chutes plunge down The Face, right under the two summit lifts, Bear and Kuma chairs. Hotshots will find lines down Kuma Rock or thread the trees on Andy's in the forest to skier's right of Bear Chair—it descends into Sherwood Forest. Watch the exit here: the woods end abruptly in a rope designed to keep you from knocking down the beginners getting off Cub chair.

Most of the forest dropping from Tuck's Traverse offers good short tree shots. Peel off to right of *Cornice* run and you can skirt the *Cave Rock.* Yes, it has a cave, and yes, local teenagers hide out there for illegal purposes.

Out of Bounds

The Bear Valley ski patrol takes a very practical stance on out-of-bounds skiing: they like it. Most of the area boundaries are "soft"—that is, penetrable—so long as the OB terrain sits above a lift loading station. If you can ski back into the main part of the ski area, you're on avalanche-controlled territory, and you can be rescued without too much effort. There's plenty of good soft-boundary OB skiing, to wit:

Northeast of Tigger's (above Hibernation chair) lies a whole complex of tree lines—*King's Realm, Boys' Stuff,* and *Girls' Stuff.* Return to the main area above the bottom of Hibernation Chair.

North and east of the parking lot, beyond the east edge of *Hari Kari,* lie the lower slopes of Mount Reba and the Horse Canyon terrain. When the snow is good, follow the Grizzly Road cat track around the back side of the cliffs. A favorite line, just outside the soft boundary, is *Snowshoe Thompson.*

Finally, slide off the south side of Bear Top summit, as if heading for *Home Run,* and turn left into *Apple Knockers.* Or slip off the back side of *Nastar* run and zig through the cliff bands. Both shots come out at the Bear Valley Village lake, and you'll ride the bus back.

Absolutely forbidden is The Zones, the wedge of cliff bands and glades lying between *West Ridge* and the intermediate *Westworld* run. This is avalanche territory, but more importantly, there's no way to haul a toboggan out of the gulley and up to Pooh Bear chair. Go into The Zones, and it's all downhill for another 2000 feet to the Mokelumne River in the Wilderness Area—where no motorized rescue is allowed.

Snowboarding

The Vans half-pipe takes advantage of a natural pipe called Groovy Gully, just below the steepish *Cornice* and Porridge Bowl terrain off Bear Top summit.

Most Convenient Lodging

Bear Valley offers no ski-in, ski-out lodging. The **Bear Valley Lodge** sits two miles down the road at Bear Valley Village; it offers a regular shuttle bus up to the day lodge, and you can ski down at the end of the day via *Lunch Run* or *Home Run.* Weekend rates for hotel rooms start at $135 per night (call (209) 753-2327).

The neighboring **Base Camp Lodge,** home of the Mountain Adventure Seminars guide service, offers bunk and dorm room starting at about $65 on weekends. The Base Camp has its own pub and dining room (call (209) 753-6556).

Another couple of miles down the road brings you to **Tamarack Pines Inn and Lodge,** a family-oriented bed-and-breakfast with rooms of various sizes starting at about $70 per night on weekends (call (209) 753-2080).

The hamlets of Dorrington and Arnold, 23 and 28 miles from the lifts, offer half a dozen motels, B&Bs, and lodges, plus about eight condo complexes. You'll find a good current directory to these properties at http://bearvalley.com/lodging_index.htm.

Best Eats

The dining room at Base Camp Lodge is a favorite locals' hangout, and **The Creekside Grill** in the Bear Valley Lodge provides standard restaurant fare in a pleasant atmosphere. Also in the Village, the **Bear Valley Pizza Co.** offers live music on big weekends.

Strung out along Route 4 through Dorrington and Arnold you'll find a dozen cafes and pizza joints. Well-recommended by mountain locals is the **Snowshoe Brewing Co.** in Arnold (call (209) 795-2272).

Bear Valley Data

Mountain Statistics

Vertical feet	1,900 feet
Base elevation	6,600 feet
Summit elevation	8,500 feet
Longest run	3 miles
Average annual snowfall	450 inches
Number of lifts	11
Uphill capacity	12,000 skiers per hour
Skiable terrain	1,280 acres
Opening date	Late November
Closing date	Mid-April
Snowboarding	Yes

Transportation

By car from Oakland/Berkeley: 3 hours via I-580 east to I-25, then north to Stockton. Exit to Route 4 and drive 2 hours east through Angels Camp to Bear Valley.

Key Phone Numbers

Ski-area information	(209) 753-2301
Snow report, option 2	
Website	www.bearvalley.com

Kirkwood

Journalists who write about California love to point out that if the state were an independent nation, it would have the seventh largest economy in the world. The Golden State ranks right up there in industrial strength with Germany and France. Reading this, you'd think the state were paved with high-tech factories and industrial-strength farms. In fact, as you travel eastward in from the coast, the state quickly grows emptier and wider and becomes more nineteenth century in its atmosphere. In the Sierra foothills, the economy is based not on silicon chips and stealth bombers but on winemaking, gold panning, and river rafting. In the high mountains, the economy vanishes altogether, except for a few ski resorts tucked up in isolated valleys.

None is more isolated than Kirkwood, 100 miles east and 7,800 feet up from Stockton and Sacramento, 30 miles south of Lake Tahoe, and 100 years back in time. Kirkwood is named for Zachary Kirkwood, a cattle rancher who opened, in 1864, a way station on the lonely road over the mountains between Carson City and Stockton. The legend is that the inn was situated where El Dorado, Amador, and Alpine counties meet, and the bar itself wasn't nailed to the floor. That way, whenever a county tax collector showed up, the liquor business could be skidded across the room into another jurisdiction.

In 1972, when the first ski lifts were built at Kirkwood, Pacific Gas and Electric declined to pay for power lines into the valley. So while Kirkwood lies in the most populous state in the Union, it is an anomaly—the high valley too remote for rural electrification. The ski area built, and still runs, its own diesel-fired generating station. This puts a natural limit on the area's growth, though there's plenty of electricity to run the new condo hotels.

Because of the elevation, Kirkwood snow does seem lighter and drier than what you get at most Tahoe areas. With a higher base—about 1,700 feet above the surface of the lake—Kirkwood is one of the first places to count on for good powder when the storms come through.

Kirkwood's base village is growing fast. It now boasts three luxurious ski-in/ski-out lodges and several hundred condo units. Nonetheless, the nightlife is not what you'd call rip-roaring—only two of the four restaurants have bars. In 2002, when Kirkwood began selling a $300 season pass, business boomed and the summit lifts grew crowded. Fortunately, Kirkwood built a new high-speed lift, Cornice Express, the same year.

Meanwhile, people come to Kirkwood to ski; pure and simple. The weekend crowd comes mainly from California's Central Valley, and it tends to be families and kids from small local colleges. While most vacationers stay at South Lake Tahoe, a Sierra storm is a good reason to sleep in one of the condo units; it's a lot more fun to be first on the lift on a snowy morning than it is to get stuck behind a snowplow for 30 miles.

The college kids are drawn by Kirkwood's reputation for wild skiing. With just 2,000 feet of vertical, Kirkwood offers a surprising network of steep, exciting trails, all dropping from a mile-long ridge. Ride Cornice Express (6) or Wagon Wheel (10) to the ridge top, and choose your route back down: some of the runs are wide, easy cruising, but you don't have to look far at Kirkwood to find heart-stopping narrow chutes between ridgeline cliffs. On a powder day, you can drop weightlessly for 1,500 vertical feet down some of these couloirs.

Around the corner, on the east side of Thimble Peak, you'll find Sunrise lift (Lift 4), serving the broad, rolling cruiser run called, misleadingly, *Elevator Shaft,* plus a huge, wide-open bowl apparently labeled expert because there's too much of it to groom.

Best Beginner Skiing

Stick to Bunny lift (Lift 9), serving four out-of-the-way learner runs west of Timber Creek, home of Kirkwood's learn-to-ski program.

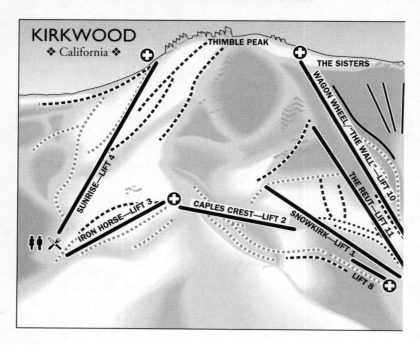

Best Intermediate Skiing

The Sunrise runs—*Elevator Shaft* and *Happiness*—offer great, wide-open cruising. Solitude lift (Lift 5) serves the lower, easier sections of half a dozen long trails cascading off the ridgeline.

Hole-in-Wall lift (Lift 7), rising from the Timber Creek Lodge at the west parking lot, serves mostly easy, sheltered intermediate terrain.

Best Expert Skiing

One of my favorite descents in all of California is *The Drain,* an immense natural half-pipe. You get there by dropping through (or traversing under) the Sisters, a cliff band a couple of hundred yards west of Lift 10. Then you ski one of the six marked chutes—*All the Way, Notch, Sisters, Schaeffer's, Saddle,* or *Cliff.* All six point more or less into *The Drain.*

Most experts head immediately to Cornice Express lift and follow the ridge west out toward Sentinel Bowl. On the way, peer down into *Jim's* and *Chamoix* chutes. To the skier's left of Sentinel are a series of steep glades, the *Rabbit Runs,* which dump you out onto the intermediate Trubee Creek trails.

The final group of steep shots can be reached from Lift 4. Turn right at the top, traverse over to *Larry's Lip,* and, snow conditions permitting, peel off into *Thunder, Two-Man, One-Man,* or *Bogie's.*

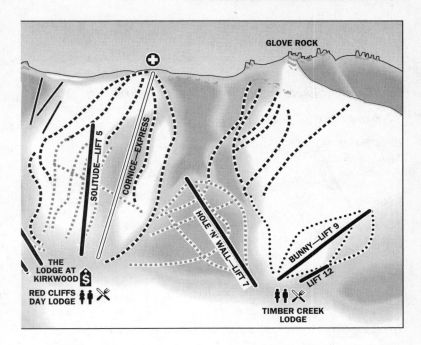

On storm days, the ridge lifts may close due to high winds. Ride the Reut (pronounced "root," named for trailbuilder Dick Reuter) and ski the short, steep runs below Norm's Nose.

Snowboarding

The half-pipe and terrain park are on the old Race Course trail, to skier's right of Lift 5. You can also get there by riding the Cornice Express, then on descent cut right from *Zach's Run.*

Convenient Lodging

Over the past couple of years, Kirkwood has finished work on three handsome ski-in/ski-out lodges: the **Snowcrest,** the **Lodge at Kirkwood,** and the **Mountain Club,** featuring a health club, spa, and underground parking. More condos are under construction. For reservations, call (209) 258-7389.

Best Eats

For Old West atmosphere and a wildly eclectic menu—featuring hamburgers, ribs, pasta, lamb, and seafood—go to the old **Kirkwood Inn;** for charm and a nicely varied menu, try **Caples Lake Resort.** Within the ski area complex there's the **Timber Creek Lodge** for pizza and pasta, family style, and **Monte Wolf's** deli in the mountain village. The place for real sit-down dining within the base area is **Off the Wall,** in the Lodge at Kirk-wood. It's open for lunch daily and dinner on weekends. **Bob's Grill,** in the Sun Meadows complex across the road from Chairs 5 and 6, serves lunch and dinner. It's a sports bar with burgers, salads, sandwiches, and beer.

Kirkwood Data

Mountain Statistics

Vertical feet	2,000 feet
Base elevation	7,800 feet
Summit elevation	9,800 feet
Longest run	2.5 miles
Average annual snowfall	500 inches
Number of lifts	12: 2 quads; 7 triple chairs; 1 double chair; 2 surface lifts
Uphill capacity	17,905 skiers per hour
Skiable terrain	2,300 acres
Opening date	Mid-November
Closing date	Late April
Snowboarding	Yes

Transportation

By car From Reno, 90 minutes via U.S. Highway 395 to Route 88; from South Lake Tahoe, 35 minutes via U.S. Highway 50 to Meyers, then Routes 89 and 88; from Stockton, 2 hours via Route 88.

Key Phone Numbers

Ski-area information	(209) 258-6000
Snow report	(877) KIRKWOOD
Reservations	(800) 967-7500
Website	www.skikirkwood.com

Sierra-at-Tahoe

Tahoe area locals—and this includes savvy Sacramento skiers—have a couple of deep secrets, places they like to sneak off to for uncrowded powder skiing. At the north end of the lake, off I-70, it's Sugar Bowl; at the south end, on Echo Summit off U.S. Highway 50, it's Sierra-at-Tahoe.

A generation of skiers found its way up the twisting two-lane highway from Placerville to ski at the family-owned Sierra Ski Ranch. The place was a low-key joy—no lodging, no bars, no hoopla, just 2,000 acres of wide-open cruising on West Bowl and hair-raising steeps and tree skiing on the face of Huckleberry Mountain. In 1993 the area was purchased by Fibreboard, the parent company of Northstar-at-Tahoe. Fibreboard changed the area's name and installed a bar (the Sierra Pub) but didn't touch the nearly perfect skiing. Today the area is owned by Booth Creek, which also runs Northstar, at the north end of Lake Tahoe. Booth Creek offered cheap season passes, and Sierra boomed—the place can now burst at the seams on weekends.

Vern Sprock, who founded Sierra, designed the trail system with taste and intelligence. Beginners have their own area with three lifts and half a dozen trails just above the base lodge. There's even a short beginner trail down the back side. Intermediates and advanced skiers get eight immense rolling cruiser trails served by a couple of mile-long lifts in West Bowl. If skiers want to check out the view from Huckleberry, they can ride to the top and descend safely via a neat network of easy trails on the back side, served by two short lifts. Experts get a vast area of steep tree skiing, laced with three precipitous trails and served by two more mile-long lifts. There's something exciting for everyone.

There's nothing wishy-washy about Sierra's trail markings: the beginner terrain is very easy; the intermediate terrain is truly broad and inspiring; the expert terrain, like that at Squaw Valley, should be attempted only by skiers with good technical skills and mucho self-confidence.

Cruising skiers should head directly down *Marmot,* west of the base lodge, to pick up the Slingshot high-speed quad lift. From the top, Powderhorn trails cascade away, dividing as they fall into a network of wide-open trails—*Dogwood, Bashful, Pyramid,* and *Beaver*—that invite easy, relaxed skiing or lose-your-hat speed, about 1,500 vertical feet of it.

Steep skiers should slide east of the base lodge to ride the Grand View Express quad. Here you'll find 1,600 feet of vertical on three very steep trails—*Castle, Preacher's Passion,* and *Dynamite*—plus a lot of very hairy skiing among the pines.

Beginners can ride to the top of Huckleberry, too. There's a rambling, easy way down along the ridgeline that is appropriately labeled *Sugar'n Spice.* But beginners will also find a nice variety of trails off the Nob Hill and Rock Garden lifts, and off the gentle Easy Rider Express quad.

The best place for lunch on the mountain is at the Grand View Bar and Grille at the summit of Huckleberry. It feels remote because it is. In nice weather the entire Tahoe Basin is visible from the Grand View Bar and Grille. Below the restaurant a warren of intermediate trails descends through the scrub pine and manzanita to Eldorado lift (it takes you back to the summit) or to Short Stuff lift (it goes to the top of Nob Hill, located in the saddle between Huckleberry and West Bowl).

Beginners can descend the back side, too, via the gentle *Wagon Trail.* It's a scenic treat for folks usually confined to a couple of acres of ski school terrain.

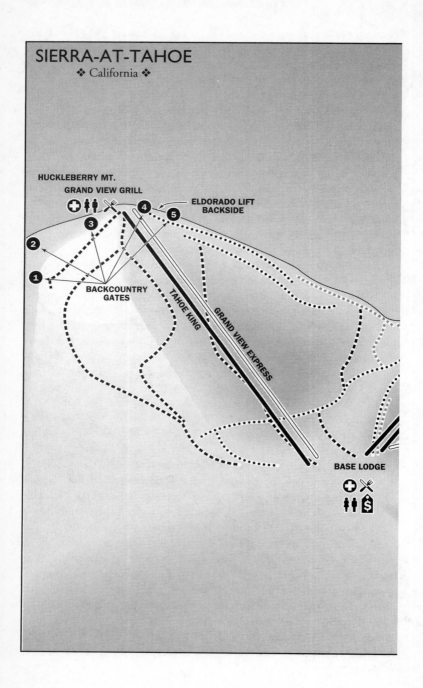

SIERRA-AT-TAHOE
❖ California ❖

HUCKLEBERRY MT.
GRAND VIEW GRILL

ELDORADO LIFT
BACKSIDE

BACKCOUNTRY
GATES

TAHOE KING

GRAND VIEW EXPRESS

BASE LODGE

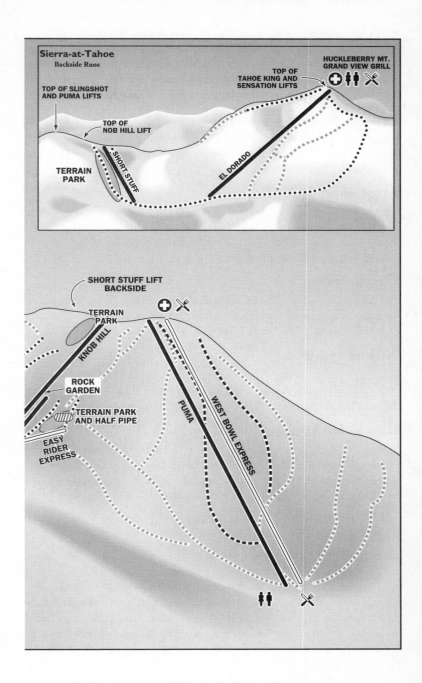

Sierra-at-Tahoe
Backside Runs

HUCKLEBERRY MT.
GRAND VIEW GRILL

TOP OF
TAHOE KING AND
SENSATION LIFTS

TOP OF SLINGSHOT
AND PUMA LIFTS

TOP OF
NOB HILL LIFT

SHORT STUFF

TERRAIN
PARK

EL DORADO

SHORT STUFF LIFT
BACKSIDE

TERRAIN
PARK

KNOB HILL

ROCK
GARDEN

TERRAIN PARK
AND HALF PIPE

EASY
RIDER
EXPRESS

PUMA

WEST BOWL EXPRESS

Best Beginner Skiing

First-timers stick to Easy Rider Express and the *Broadway* trail. Ambitious, athletic newcomers have come to the right place: Sierra offers more skiable variety, off the Nob Hill and Eldorado lifts and along *Sugar'n Spice*, than almost any other mountain.

Best Intermediate Skiing

For speed, try *Dogwood* and *Beaver,* or *Powderhorn* and *Bashful* in West Bowl. For relaxed skiing, try *Powderhorn* and *Pyramid.* For scenery, try *Smokey* and *Coyote* on the back side.

Best Expert Skiing

For raw speed, there's *Clipper* and *Horsetail* in West Bowl. For adrenaline, it's *Preacher's Passion* and *Dynamite.* For out-of-your-skull deep powder, ski the trees on either side of *Preacher's Passion* or venture through the new backcountry gates along *Eastabout* and *Upper Wagon Trail.*

Snowboarding

The new superpipe and a new snowskate park inhabit the terrain under Rock Garden lift, and there are two more terrain parks off the summit of Nob Hill, one of them stretches the length of Short Stuff lift.

Getting There

U.S. Highway 50, from Placerville heading west, or heading east from South Lake Tahoe, is the only way in. Expect traffic to move slowly when the road is snowpacked, and remember to carry snow chains.

Convenient Lodging

There is no lodging—no base village, no condos, no hotels. For now, Sierra-at-Tahoe is for day skiing. **Strawberry Lodge** sits in splendid isolation on Highway 50, five miles west of the ski area. Most overnight visitors lodge in South Lake Tahoe, which is about 12 miles east over Echo Summit. There's free shuttle service.

Best Eats

The **Grandview Grill,** at the summit, offers Mexican, Asian and American dishes, and you get a spectacular view across Lake Tahoe.

In the Base Lodge there are several options for a variety of meals. The **Bake Shoppe** offers full, cooked-to-order breakfast, and the **Front Porch** on the open air deck can handle all of your caffeine requirements. Lunch is covered by any of the following places: **The Sierra Pub** features specialty foods, wines, microbrews and a full-service bar; the **Aspen Café** provides grilled entrees at modest prices; and **Cheeseburger in Paradise** serves grilled island favorites on the main deck. At Grandview, the aptly-named **Grand View Bar and Grill** offers upscale California-Asian cuisine in the awe-inspiring presence of Lake Tahoe. To meet a craving for barbecue, head for the West Bowl where you'll find satisfaction at the **West Bowl Smoke House BBQ.**

Sierra-at-Tahoe Data

Mountain Statistics

Vertical feet	2,212 feet
Base elevation	6,640 feet
Summit elevation	8,852 feet
Longest run	2.5 miles
Average annual snowfall	480 inches
Number of lifts	10: 3 express quads; 1 triple chair; 5 double chairs; 1 moving carpet (children's)
Uphill capacity	15,000 skiers per hour
Skiable terrain	2,000 acres
Opening date	Mid-November, depending on natural snow
Closing date	Mid-April
Snowboarding	Yes

Sierra-at-Tahoe shares a lift ticket with Northstar-at-Tahoe.

Transportation

By car From San Francisco, 4 hours via I-80, then U.S. Highway 50; from Sacramento, 90 minutes via U.S. Highway 50; from Reno, 90 minutes via U.S. Highway 50.

Key Phone Numbers

Ski-area information	(530) 659-7453
Snow report	(530) 659-7475
Reservations	(800) 288-2463
Website	www.sierratahoe.com

Lito's TECH TIP

A Revolution in Skis

It's no secret that skis look different these days. The wide tips and tails and proportionately narrower waist of a new generation of skis have become ubiquitous at ski resorts across the country, and actually around the world. Curiously, this new geometry in ski design has given rise to the term "shaped skis," although our classic skis were anything but shapeless. They too had a waist that was narrower than either tip or tail; but modern skis have exaggerated this shape to a greater degree, and with impressive results.

Are you already skiing on shaped skis? If not, I can predict that you soon will be. These new skis are a dream come true. They literally make everything you try to do on skis easier. Carved turns and skidded turns are both cleaner and simpler. Although they are somewhat shorter than traditional skis, they are also more stable, so you will feel steadier at high speeds. Shaped skis can actually make you a better skier. They'll expand your horizons, your technique, and the limits of your performance on snow. How? Why?

It's simple. The sidecut or side curve of skis has always been what made them arc graceful turns across the snow. The wide tip bites deeper into the snow than the rest of the ski and pulls you into the start of your turn. At the same time, the narrow waist is pressed out into the snow by the skier's weight so that the ski itself becomes bent into an arc—that's why skilled skiers always make such an effort to transfer their weight to the outside ski of each turn: to bend the ski. Then, instead of tracking forward in a straight line, your ski wants to track in an arc, following its own curved shape. Voilà, a carved turn.

Carved turns have always been an expression of polished, expert skiing. Carved turns look great, and they feel even better. By carving the end of each turn you can control your speed without skidding and without fatiguing your legs. Yet until recently, skiers had to ski very fast to create enough energy to bend their skis and carve.

Today, on shaped or super-sidecut skis, skiers discover that their skis will bend into smooth arcs at much slower speeds, at any speed really, because most of that arc is already present in the deep curve of the ski's edge. Shaped skis have put carving within reach of virtually every skier. And if you are already an expert, if you already know how to carve turns, you will soon discover that your carving skills are amplified and refined by these new skis. Mine certainly have been.

What's the downside of this extreme shaped-ski geometry? I've been skiing on super-sidecut skis for three seasons now and I have yet to find any disadvantages. Their wide tips offer greater flotation on powder. Their deep sidecuts make your turns through moguls quicker and more secure. Above all, you can carve perfect arcs on the snow that you never thought possible. These skis are not a fad; they are here to stay. World Cup racers are winning international races on shaped skis. Instructors are having more fun than ever before on shaped skis. And I'm betting that you will too. Remember, these new skis don't work differently than classic skis, they just work better!

Naturally, there are a host of small, easy to master tricks for getting the most from your new shaped skis (subtle techniques like "phantom edging"). I've condensed my experience teaching hundreds of skiers on these stunning new tools into a one-hour videotape, *Breakthrough on Skis III, The New Skis* (available from Western Eye, (800) 333-5178). But even without specialized instruction, I know you will feel the difference. Shaped skis will change your life as a skier—for the better. That's a promise.

Heavenly

Heavenly, boasting a skiable vertical of 3,500 feet, offers the highest lifts in the Tahoe region. Heavenly keeps its feet in the roaring casino towns at the south end of the lake and its head in the thin air at over 10,000 feet. The mountain claims 4,800 acres of terrain (nonsense—that would make the place bigger than Vail, Mammoth, Whistler, or Blackcomb, and it ain't). Heavenly is sizable enough, though, to sprawl across the Stateline—there are base lodges on the Nevada and the California sides, and you traverse sovereignties by riding to the summit.

The ski lifts were built from the launching pad of what already looked like, in the mid-1960s, runaway development based on casino and summer resort business. The twin cities of Stateline, Nevada, and South Lake Tahoe, California, are pretty garish by ski area standards—at night you can read a newspaper anywhere along the main drag by the light of the neon signs. The Nevada side, supported by casinos, has gone in for massive high-rise hotels. The California side runs to sprawling two-story resort motels. The whole effect is of busy suburbia.

In December 2000, Heavenly opened a new gondola. It can zip you from the heart of the stateline casino district at 6,223 feet, to the base of Tamarack Express at 9,156 feet, in under 12 minutes. From there, ride another four minutes to the top of the Nevada-side trail network, or scoot over to the California trails.

The gondola launches from what amounts to Heavenly's first true resort village: 34 acres of shopping malls, hotels, skating rinks, and even a movie house—when it's finished. For now, the Park Avenue project, like Squaw Valley's Intrawest village, is a construction zone.

Also, note that the gondola isn't actually skiable. No trails descend to the Park Avenue village. If you're staying there, plan to ride the gondola down at the end of the day. Beginners should avoid the gondola altogether; it serves no easy trails.

In 2002 the mountain was purchased by Vail Resorts, and the huge ski resort company set out to fix Heavenly's awkward lift system. The network of lifts and trails has been as confusing to the initiate as the Los Angeles freeway system. It has centered on a few critical interchanges, where skiers have to ride lifts up out of gulleys. On a busy weekend, skiers often gridlocked at these junctions, standing bumper to bumper to use the high-speed quads. Using the mountain's full vertical without stopping for a lift line or shuffling across a long flat was impossible. The worst bottleneck is the marshalling yard in the gulley behind Monument Peak (the top of the California Lodge Tram). This mid-mountain cul-de-sac—the bottom of Waterfall, Powderbowl, Patsy's and Groove lifts—is a kind of Grand Central Station where anyone headed either up or down the mountain, from or to California Lodge, has to wait in line for a short but slow lift ride. There is a skiable intermediate trail out of this hole, but it involves a quarter mile of skating, poling, or shuffling along the top of Roundabout trail to use it. Heavenly's brochures boast of the longest continuous descent on the West Coast—5.5 miles—but this includes the flat walking tours in and out of the Monument Peak gulley.

So beginning in the summer of 2003, Heavenly began replacing, realigning and adding new lifts and expanding on-mountain lodges. Eventually, Vail expects to spend $80 million on new projects over a six-year period. The mountain has applied for permits to build:

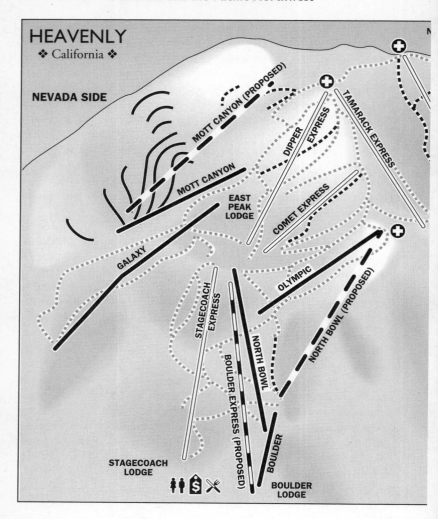

- A surface tow to move folks from Sky Deck along the cat track to the marshalling yard at the base of Patsy's, Groove, Waterfall and Powderbowl lifts. This speeds the return from the Nevada side to the California Lodge, because you'll no longer have to choose between poling across the flats or standing in line for the Sky Express or Canyon lift—and skiing the long Ridge Run and crowded Maggie's—to ride out of the hole.

- Another transport lift from Sky Deck to the top of the Gondola, providing direct access to Tamarack Chair. This provides a fast alternative route to the Nevada side and relieves the crowds on Sky Express and Canyon lift.

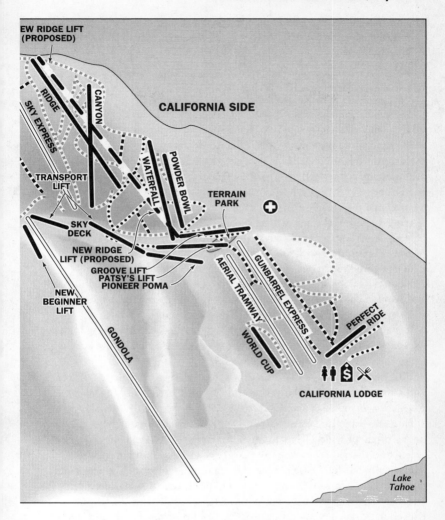

- A new high-speed quad lift from the Boulder Lodge. This Nevada-side entry point is currently served by two fixed-grip lifts—and the upper one, North Bowl, is long and slow, especially on a powder day when you itch to get off and get going.

- A new high-speed quad lift from the bottom of North Bowl to the top of Olympic Chair. It will greatly improve access to some of the best tree skiing in North America, not to mention the classic Olympic Downhill cruiser.

- A new high-speed quad to replace the existing slow Waterfall and Ridge lifts (it will go from the top of the tram to the summit). This is the key development—it should fully relieve the traffic jams at Grand Central Station.

- A replacement for the Mott Canyon lift, running to the top of Milky Way Bowl, roughly doubling the value of the precipitous expert-only chutes in Mott and Killebrew Canyons.

- A couple of beginner lifts on the easy slope at the top of the Gondola, giving the ski school a lot of valuable new real estate.

There'll be some new trails, too.

What this all means, simply, is faster transport uphill and downhill; so we'll spend more time skiing, less time riding and standing. You'll zip to the summit from the California side in two fast lift rides, instead of two fast ones and a slow haul. In theory, a fast powder skier could leave California Lodge at 8:30 am and arrive, fairly winded, at the bottom of the Mott Canyon lift by 9:00 am.

How quickly Vail can get these projects approved and built remains to be seen. For now, we've sketched the proposed lifts in on our own trail map as dotted lines—when you get to the ski area, pick up a new trail map. It's going to change every year for the foreseeable future.

Heavenly's huge snowmaking system now extends from the California and Nevada base lodges all the way to the summit, providing the full skiable vertical on both sides, even in California's drought years.

In a good snow year, Heavenly offers some of the best tree skiing in the world, and on the Nevada side, Mott and Killebrew Canyons are as steep as anything at Squaw Valley or Kirkwood.

This said, Heavenly's real strength is its endless intermediate cruisers. You can roll for miles along rhythmic classics like *Olympic Downhill, Ridge Run, Big Dipper,* and *Canyon.*

Heavenly can also be an inexpensive place to vacation. The big casino hotels often provide cheap rooms and meals (subsidized by the gamblers), and there's always free shuttle service to the mountain.

Heavenly has four base lodges: the main lodge on the California side (at the head of Ski Run Boulevard); the gondola base in Stateline; and the Boulder and Stagecoach Lodges on the Nevada side near the summit of Kingsbury Grade (Nevada Route 207). Coming from Reno on a weekday (80 minutes), the quickest way to Heavenly is via U.S. Highway 50. But when weekend traffic snarls the roads in Stateline (and the weather is good), it's quicker to follow U.S. Highway 395 south to Routes 206 and 207, and use the Boulder or Stagecoach parking lot.

There are three mid-mountain lodges: Top of the Tram above the California base lodge and Sky Deck and East Peak Lodge in the sheltered hollows halfway up the California and Nevada sides.

For now, there's no fast way to the summit. From the California side, you'll ride three lifts to get to the top of Sky Express, and from the Nevada side three or four, depending on where you start. Beginners should enter from the California side or go to Nevada's Boulder Lodge; there's no marked beginner terrain at Stagecoach. You'll find a teaching area at Boulder, and another off to the south side of the California parking lot.

The three lifts rising from the California base lodge serve some pretty severe expert terrain. The Tram and Gunbarrel lifts both go to Monument Peak; World Cup lift goes halfway up and serves the World Cup race trail. The trails descending from Monument are long, steep, and often heavy with moguls. Intermediates may want to bypass *The Face, Gunbarrel, East Bowl,* and *Pistol* in favor of cruising the easy *Roundabout* cat track.

Use Waterfall or Powderbowl lifts to ride out of the gulley below Monument. Beginners will find easy cruising here on *Mombo Meadows, Maggie's Run,* and *Swing Trail.* Intermediates and experts should turn left and follow the signs toward Sky Deck.

On the way, you'll pass the loading stations for Ridge and Canyon lifts, both of which go to *Ridge Run,* with its unsurpassed views of the Tahoe Basin. Also accessible from here is a network of rolling and interesting intermediate trails cut through the scrub pine and manzanita—*Liz's, Yahoo, Betty's, Canyon,* and *Steamboat.*

If you pass up Ridge and Canyon lifts, you'll come to Sky Express, the high-speed route to the summit. From here, cruise *Ridge* or *Liz's,* or take *Ellie's,* a delightful high-speed roller coaster. When the snow is deep, there's great tree skiing on either side of *Ellie's;* at this elevation, nearly 10,000 feet, the woods are naturally thin. To get to the Nevada side, ride Sky Express and turn left onto *Skyline Trail.*

Skyline Trail exits near the top of Nevada's Dipper Express. You can turn left down *Dipper Knob* and partake of the wide cruising terrain above the East Peak Lodge or turn right into the expert terrain in Milky Way Bowl, leading down to the truly severe chutes in Killebrew and Mott Canyons.

From these upper slopes of the Nevada side, Heavenly provides one of the grandest views in all of skiing. You look 6,000 feet down into the Carson Valley and can see halfway across Nevada.

Enter Heavenly from the Nevada lodges, and your first lift rides will take you to the ridge above East Peak Lodge. Here you can scoot down *Pepi's* to ride the high-speed upper lifts (Dipper and Comet Express) or hit the truly wonderful lower cruisers, *Stagecoach* to the east of Stagecoach Express, and *North Bowl* to the west of North Bowl lift. *North Bowl* takes you to Olympic lift, the only way to get to *Olympic Downhill,* one of my favorite high-speed intermediate cruisers. On a storm day, the nicely spaced ponderosa glades on either side of *Olympic* make some of the prettiest tree skiing you'll find anywhere.

Below East Peak Lodge, there's more of this sheltered cruising terrain off Galaxy lift, but to get there, or anywhere, you'll have to ride Dipper or Comet out of the gulley. From the top of Comet, cruise *Jack's, Comet,* or *Little Dipper* back to East Peak Lodge, or follow *49er* back to Sky Deck and California.

From Dipper Express, there are more options: *Orion* back to East Peak, *Big Dipper* to the Galaxy lift network, or *Milky Way* down to Mott and Killebrew Canyons.

The two canyons are very steep and often unstable and should be attempted only by confident experts, and only through the nine designated access gates. Avalanche safety is a serious consideration here; crossing a control fence may get you more than a dressing down by the patrol—it may get you buried. To exit from the Canyons, traverse left to Mott Canyon lift.

For lunching, **Sky Deck** is a great picnic site in nice weather, but it's outdoors. In wind, clouds, or snow, plan to do lunch indoors at the **East Peak Lodge** or at **Top of the Tram.** Or head to one of the base lodges: **California, Boulder** or **Stagecoach.**

Exiting the Mountain

Tired legs often turn rubbery on *The Face* and *Gunbarrel,* and the *Roundabout* cat track can be very crowded after about 2:30 p.m., so consider riding the tram down. If you park at one of the Nevada lodges, skiing down is easier, but remember where you parked: When you cross under Stagecoach or North Bowl lifts, make every left turn to find Boulder Lodge and every right turn to reach Stagecoach Lodge.

Many skiers leaving the mountain get stuck in one of the gulleys and have to wait in a lift line to climb out. It is possible to ski the entire vertical from the top without riding a lift. On the Nevada side, follow the ridgeline (*Sand Dunes* trail) to *Crossover,* then turn left to find *Olympic Downhill.* On the California side, turn right at Sky Deck and skate along the flat *Maggie's* cat track, then cross far to the left at the Monument Peak gulley to *Roundabout,* and follow it around to *Pistol* and *Gunbarrel.* You can also ski *Ridge Run* from the summit and stay left to cruise down *Powderbowl* and *Mombo* to *Roundabout.*

The gondola offers a sane exit path for folks lodging near the Park Avenue development at Stateline.

Best Beginner Skiing

The beginner slopes at Boulder Lodge are less crowded and more relaxing than the California scene, but there's more variety and challenge on the Mombo Meadows complex off Powderbowl lift. Ride the tram down at the end of the day; to get there, you'll have to ride the short Patsy's or Groove lifts.

Best Intermediate Skiing

My favorite cruising is *Olympic Downhill,* which is accessed by a new high-speed quad, Stagecoach Express. To maximize skiing time, use the *Dipper/Orion* trail network off Dipper Express (Nevada side) or *Liz's* and *Canyon* off Sky Express (California side).

Best Expert Skiing

For raw challenge, try *Mott Canynon* and *Killebrew Canyon.* For powder in the trees, try *North Bend,* or the woods alongside *Olympic Downhill* (on a storm day), or *Ellie's* (after the storm). For high-speed cruising, take *Olympic Downhill* or *Ellie's.* For bumps, take *The Face* into *Gunbarrel* and *East Bowl.*

Snowboarding

The terrain park lies beneath Patsy's lift.

Convenient Lodging

Heavenly offers some of the cheapest good lodging in North American ski resort areas, because rooms in the big casino hotels (**Harrah's, Caesar's, Harveys,** the **Horizon**) are to some extent subsidized by gambling. The hundreds of smaller motels in the area, many with their own casinos, have to compete on room rates. None of the hotels provides much in the way of traditional ski-lodge ambience, but they're comfortable and efficient, with free shuttle service to the mountain so you can avoid traffic and parking hassles. The big hotels also offer good restaurants and Vegas-style shows with Hollywood headliners, so there are plenty of ways to spend the money you save on the room.

But if you come to Heavenly simply to ski hard and enjoy the mountain scenery, a couple of lodges are situated within walking distance of the lifts: **Ridge Tahoe** and **Eagle's Nest Inn** near the **Stagecoach Lodge** and **Tahoe Seasons Resort** near the California tram building. And, of course, there's the plush new village at the base of the gondola.

Best Eats

There are literally dozens of good restaurants in town. My own picks are the **Christiana,** across the street from the California parking lot, which serves continental cuisine (this is the closest place for a good meal if you stay at the Tahoe Seasons); the **Chart House** on Kingsbury Grade (steak/seafood); **Chevy's** and the **Cantina Bar & Grill** for Tex-Mex and Southwestern cuisine; the **Edgewood** (at the golf course); **Fresh Ketch** at Tahoe Keys, a marina-style restaurant (guess what they serve); and, at the tops of the big casino hotels, with great views of the mountains and lake, **Harrah's Summit** and **Harvey's Llewellyns.** I also like **Nepheles** on Ski

Run below the **California Lodge:** here you can rent a private hot tub
and work out the kinks before tucking into a fine continental meal.

Heavenly Data

Mountain Statistics

Vertical feet	3,500 feet
Base elevation	6,540 feet California; 7,200 feet Nevada
Summit elevation	10,067 feet
Longest run	5.5 miles
Average annual snowfall	360 inches
Number of lifts	29: 1 gondola, 5 high-speed quads, 1 high-speed six-pack; 1 aerial tramway; 8 triple chairs; 5 double chairs; 6 surface lifts; 2 moving carpets; more under construction.
Uphill capacity	33,000 skiers per hour
Skiable terrain	4,800 acres (patrolled)
Opening date	Mid-November
Closing date	Late April, early May
Snowboarding	Yes

Transportation

By car One hour from Reno via U.S. Highway 50; 2.5 hours from Sacramento via U.S. Highway 50; 4.5 hours from San Francisco via I-80 to Sacramento, then U.S. Highway 50.

By bus Free shuttle bus from most Lake Tahoe hotels. Tahoe Casino Express from Reno-Tahoe airport—$19 one way.

By air Major carriers to Reno-Tahoe International Airport (70 miles, frequent bus service).

Key Phone Numbers

Ski-area information	(775) 586-7000
Snow report	(775) 586-7000 (press 1)
Reservations	(800) 243-2836
Website	www.skiheavenly.com

Alpine Meadows

Alpine Meadows, a friendly and unpretentious medium-size area, sits in the canyon just south of Squaw Valley, backed up to the Sierra Crest. Alpine offers the same snow, the same precipitous summit bowls, and the same gentle plateau runs as its neighboring Tahoe resorts. But it's not as overbuilt as most, and it has managed to retain an intimate atmosphere. While the upper bowls and steep tree runs provide some of the most exciting skiing in the region, Alpine tends to play down its expert terrain in favor of its lovely, rolling intermediate cruisers. Management loves to cater to families; it maintains one of the friendliest ski schools in California and even grooms special training runs for young bump skiers.

Alpine's permit area covers about 2,000 acres spread across two peaks—Ward Peak (8,637 feet) and Scott Peak (8,289 feet). The resort also offers two separate base areas. The main lodge (6,840 feet), complete with cafeteria, bar, ski shop, and locker rooms, sits at the head of Alpine Meadows Road off Highway 89, 12 miles south of Truckee and 6 miles north of Tahoe City. The Sherwood base area offers limited parking and a snack bar, but it functions as a convenient back-door entrance for folks lodging on the west shore of the lake. You can reach it from Highway 89 south of Tahoe City.

Because Route 89 is a winding two-lane highway subject to blockage by both avalanche and traffic accident, it clogs with traffic each morning and evening, especially on weekends. The absolute worst time to travel is Sunday evening, when the entire sporting population of northern California tries to funnel through Truckee and onto I-80 for the slow trip over Donner Pass. If it's snowing, have a leisurely dinner before joining the exodus.

The best way to avoid traffic hassles is to stay over in the Alpine Meadows condos or in Tahoe City and travel on Monday morning. Staying in Tahoe City means making a right turn out of the Alpine Meadows road for a short, easy trip back to the hotel and a nice dinner at Jake's on the Lake (steak and seafood) or Wolfdale's (French and Japanese fusion) or River Ranch (game and steak) right at the base of the Alpine Meadows Road.

While Alpine's total vertical from the main lodge to the summit is modest—less than 1,800 feet—the lofty base elevation, combined with a sizable snowmaking capacity, means that Alpine can count on good coverage from mid-November right through to early June. In fact, the area has been open on snowmaking trails on Halloween, and a July 4 ski race is not unheard of. A big snow season means summer skiing, but it also means the risk of a Monster Sierra Storm, which can close the area for two or three days at a time. When a storm hunkers down over the lake, the roads close, too. Bring a good book and your powder skis because when the weather lifts, you'll have the ski area all to yourself until Highway 50 and I-80 reopen.

Eight of the twelve lifts load near the base lodge. Beginners have an area all to themselves, served by Subway and Meadow chairs and Tiegel Poma. (There's also a Magic Carpet lift for kids—Alpine counts it as a 13th lift.) Intermediates can cruise any marked run off Roundhouse, Kangaroo, or Hot Wheels chairs. Most advanced skiers can hop right onto the high-speed Summit Six for the six-minute trip to the top of Alpine Bowl.

The Chalet Restaurant is another jumping-off point on the front of the mountain. Located alongside *Weasel Run* in the sheltered gulley between Ward and Scott Peaks, the Chalet sits near the loading stations for Yellow chair (serving intermediate terrain) and Scott chair (now a

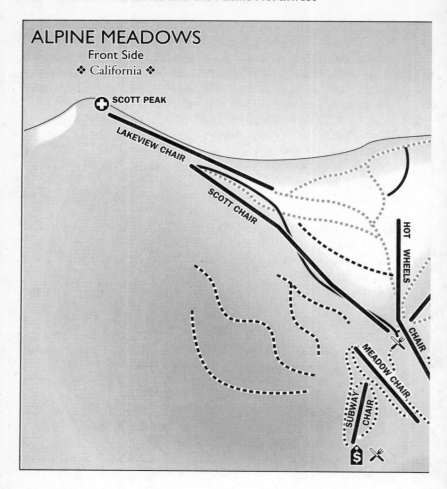

triple chair, offering access to the intermediate Lakeview and Back Bowl areas and to the steep *Scott Chute* and *Promised Land*).

Two chairlifts serve the Back Bowls—Sherwood chair, rising from the West Shore parking lot to a shoulder of Ward Peak, and Lakeview chair, which rises to the summit of Scott Peak.

Best Beginner Skiing

Alpine runs a friendly, competent ski school, and its beginner runs—served by Subway and Meadow chairs—are close to the main lodge and largely sheltered from the wind. Beyond this zone, though, there are no beginner trails. Unlike most ski areas, Alpine never bothered to build an easy way down from the summit. New skiers should stay near the base area.

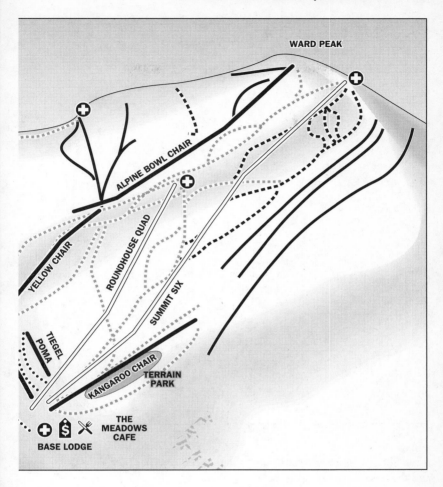

Best Intermediate Skiing

Like to cruise on big, wide-open rolling terrain? Alpine has some of the best nonstops. You can pile up mileage at a stunning rate simply by riding the fast Summit Six, descending in big GS turns via *Alpine Bowl* and *Red Trail*. On the back side, ride Lakeview chair and cruise on *Twilight Zone* and *Outer Limits,* both offering breathtaking views of the Tahoe basin.

Best Expert Skiing

On a powder day, go straight up Scott chair and head for the glades of *Promised Land* and *Gentian Gulley.* After the snow stabilizes, *Beaver Bowl* and *Estelle Bowl,* reachable by traversing from the Summit Six, are magnificent. Never ski this terrain when avalanche danger is high—

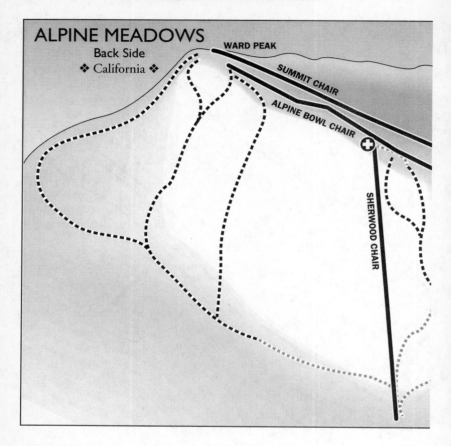

Alpine has had more than its share of avalanche fatalities over the years, and these bowls can slide all the way to the parking lot.

An easily accessible expert challenge is *D-8 Chute* into the steep Wolverine Bowl, then down *Waterfall,* which usually comprises the best bump skiing on the mountain.

Alpine also offers plenty of steep and narrow chutes. The most public of these is *Scott Chute,* directly under Scott chair, where local hotshots show off. Shorter yet steeper terrain can be found by traversing along the ridgeline from the top of Alpine Bowl chair, into *Keyhole, High Yellow,* and, best of all, *Our Father.*

From Alpine Bowl chair you can also pop over the top of the ridge to ski *Sun Bowl* and *CB Chute;* the adjoining *South Face* is skiable from Sherwood chair on the back side. Because these areas face south, they crust up early after the sun comes out and turn to wonderful corn in the spring.

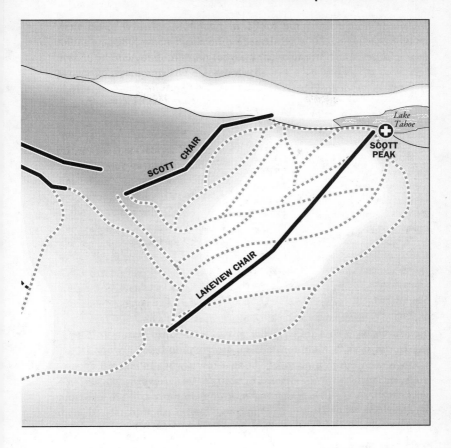

Snowboarding

The Kangaroo Chair serves a long stretch of terrain park and half-pipe challenges. You can buy a $19 ticket valid for the Kangaroo Chair only.

Convenient Lodging

Neither of these base areas is a resort village per se; within a quarter-mile of the main lodge you'll find a dozen condo units, but there's no commercial development until you roll a couple of miles down the access road to Highway 89. Here, nestled around the bridge that crosses the Truckee River, are a ski shop, a deli, some more condos, and the atmospheric old **River Ranch,** with its bar, restaurant, and hotel rooms. For weekend skiing, the River Ranch should be the first choice for comfortable, convenient lodging and meals. Most Alpine Meadows skiers stay in Truckee or Tahoe City motels (a good bet is **Granlibakken Resort** in Tahoe City or **Sunnyside Resort** in Sunnyside), or they travel around the lake from one of the big resort hotels on the Nevada side, either at **Incline Village** (half an hour by road) or **Southshore** (an hour). All these lodges are served by the Tahoe Area Rapid Transit (TART), which connects with the Alpine Meadows shuttle bus. Hours of bus operation can vary with weather and road conditions, so call ahead for details.

Alpine Meadows Data

Mountain Statistics

Vertical feet	1,800 feet
Base elevation	6,8350 feet
Summit elevation	8,637 feet
Longest run	2.5 miles
Average annual snowfall	495 inches
Number of lifts	14: 1 high speed chair; 1 express quad; 4 triple chairs; 5 double chairs; 3 surface lifts
Uphill capacity	16,000 skiers per hour
Skiable terrain	2,000 acres
Opening date	Mid-November
Closing date	After Memorial Day
Snowboarding	Yes

Transportation

By car Four hours from San Francisco; 2 hours from Sacramento; 1 hour from Reno via I-80 to Truckee, then south on Route 89. Turn right at Alpine Meadows access road. From Lake Tahoe locations, to Tahoe City via Routes 89 or 28, then continue north on Route 89. Turn left at Alpine Meadows access road.

By bus TART and shuttle bus.

By plane Via most major airlines to Reno-Tahoe International Airport.

Key Phone Numbers

Ski-area information	(530) 583-4232 or (800) 441-4423
Snow report	(530) 581-8374
Reservations	(800) 949-3296 or (800) 441-4423
Website	www.skialpine.com

Lito's TECH TIP

To Wax or Not to Wax?

That is the question. To wax or not to wax? And there is only one answer: a resounding yes. I know that a lot of skiers aren't thrilled by speed, have no desire to ski faster than they already do, and believe that waxing skis is only for racers or experts in search of ever more speed. Even if you are the calmest skier on the hill, I'd like to encourage you to wax your skis (or have your local ski shop do it), and then keep them well waxed. Why?

Waxing doesn't automatically make you ski faster. Paradoxically, one can ski much slower on a well-waxed pair of skis than on skis that aren't waxed. That's because waxing merely makes skis slippery; it reduces the friction between skis and snow. And that in turn means that it takes less force, less muscle power, and also less speed to make a waxed ski turn. It's true. A well-waxed pair of skis responds to the slightest twisting action of your feet like a well-trained horse to a slight touch of the rein. Even if you've never been lured by the thrill of speed, every mountain has a few boring flat spots you have to get across—gliding or walking—and waxed skis will let you slide across these flats while your friends are pushing with their poles, and skating or shuZing to keep moving.

How often should you wax your skis? Spring snow is more granular and wears wax off the bases of your skis more quickly than cold winter snow; but if you possibly can, I'd recommend getting your skis waxed every few skiing days. For most skiers that means every weekend. Whatever level skier you are, you will be amazed at the difference in your skiing performance.

I mentioned having your ski shop do it. Why not just buy some wax and put it on yourself? Ideally, wax should be melted and ironed onto the bases of your skis—"hot waxing," in ski jargon. This can be done with an old second-hand iron, or with any number of high-tech gizmos that ski shops keep around to melt and apply wax. The hot wax penetrates the pores of your plastic ski bases and lasts a lot longer than wax that is just rubbed on. Once the hot wax is melted into the bases of your skis, it should then be scraped down to a very, very thin layer. And finally, depending on the type of snow, it can be "structured." That's a strange expression for scratching tiny micro-grooves into the ski's base with a very fine wire or plastic bristle brush. The purpose of this "structure" (this almost invisible texture of tiny grooves) is to break up the suction due to water in the snow, suction that can slow your skis considerably. Water in the snow? Indeed. We used to think that water in the snow was only a factor in late spring, when the snowpack begins to melt. Not so. Research has shown that the pressure a skier puts on the snow can momentarily melt a minuscule layer of water, just under the ski's bases. And "structuring" or texturing the running surface of your skis will eliminate the drag of this tiny film of water.

So you can see that a good wax job is more complex than one might think. And we haven't discussed the problem of selecting the perfect wax for today's conditions. You're probably better off to take your skis to a shop at first (ask a ski instructor for the name of the best shop in your area). Later, if you decide to get serious about waxing your own skis, my advice is to pick one of the main brands of wax and stick to it for at least a season, discovering through trial and error just what colors and blends of that wax produce the smoothest-running skis.

Of course, waxed skis will run much faster than unwaxed boards, if you're looking for speed. But waxed skis just plain ski better too. Getting your skis waxed and keeping them waxed may do more for your technique than a private lesson.

Squaw Valley

Squaw Valley has a reputation—the ultimate macho, bad-boy mountain. The steep walls of KT-22, Cornice II, Palisades, Siberia, Granite Chief, and Tram Bowl have trained several generations of racers and extreme skiers. Olympic medalists Jimmie Heuga and Tamara McKinney grew up at Squaw, as did dozens of other U.S. Ski Team members.

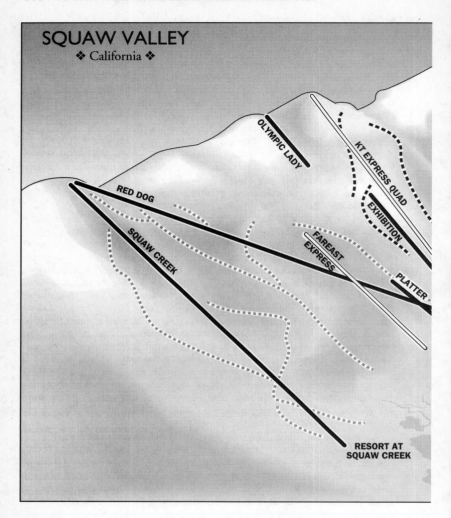

Television and the movies have contributed to Squaw's image. Site of the 1960 Winter Olympics (the first televised winter games), Squaw was also the training ground for Warren Miller, who shot his early films here. Cliff-leaping stuntman Rick Sylvester, who occasionally skis in James Bond films, lives and trains at Squaw. No modern ski film is finished until it includes footage of Scot Schmidt, Glen Plake, Kevin Anderson, Robby Huntoon, Mike Slattery, or Tom or Lizzy Day dropping through the rocks of Palisades.

This rowdy history rankles Squaw's management. Alex Cushing, who, with Wayne Poulsen, founded the place in 1949, would much rather

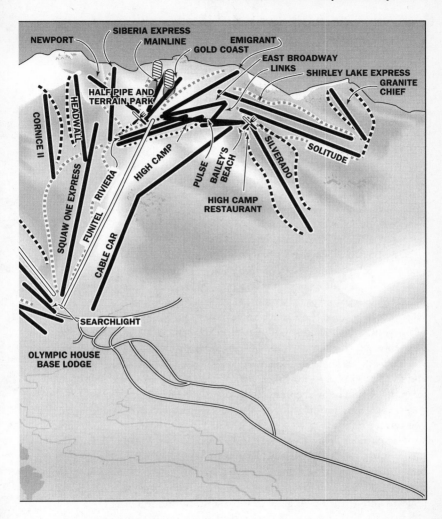

attract a crowd of civilized, reasonably disciplined citizens. In recent years he's rebuilt all the lifts and restaurants, knocking off the rough edges in favor of friendly efficiency. Much is made of the fancy skating rink and swimming pool at High Camp, hovering 2,000 feet above the base lodges. A helpful fact is that Squaw's 30 lifts now constitute the fastest single-mountain lift system in North America (only the combination of Whistler and Blackcomb can move more people upward in an hour).

Squaw is growing. Intrawest, the large Canadian company that owns Whistler/Blackcomb, Panorama, Mammoth, and Copper Mountain (plus a number of ski resorts in the East), has begun construction on a new village with underground parking, 640 residential units, and about 80 shops and restaurants. The construction zone occupies 13 acres of the vast paved parking lot. To help smooth traffic around the construction, Squaw has installed a six-passenger transport chair, dubbed Far East Express. It will take you from the east end of the parking lot to Snow King.

Skiers have been delighted to find that the restricted parking has cut down on lift crowding. Traffic shouldn't be a problem up on the mountain: the lift system has been augmented again. The new Funitel, which replaced the gondola in 1998, makes the two-mile trip from the base area to the Gold Coast in eight minutes—and the 28-passenger cars hang from two cables, so the wind won't swing them much. In theory, the Funitel can operate in winds up to 75 mph, so transport to and from the upper mountain is possible in all but the worst of Sierra blizzards. Beginners and nonskiers can transfer between the Gold Coast and High Camp restaurants on the Pulse lift.

None of this is the reason Squaw regulars return year after year after year. The real reason is Squaw's huge extent of genuinely steep terrain. The mountain now claims about 4,000 acres of skiing, which may or may not be true; a few years ago they claimed 6,000 acres, then backed off. I have no way of measuring the actual acreage, but it's probably a bit smaller than Mammoth, which claims 3,500, and on the same scale (or larger) than Heavenly, which claims 4,800. The important thing is that Squaw is so vast that it takes an expert skier at least a couple of hours to ski from one end of the complex to the other; ski patrolmen take two solid seasons to learn the mountain well enough to be considered useful employees.

Squaw can be intimidating to the new arrival. From the parking lot, you can see only about 10% of the skiable terrain, including some of the steepest parts of Snow King, KT-22, Cornice II, and Headwall. Plus the theoretically unskiable cliffs under the Cable Car (Rick Sylvester skied one of the narrow chutes there in 1968, dropping like a waxed rock for the first 500 feet). All the intermediate skiing is out of sight on the broad plateaus and gentle bowls above the two mid-station restaurants.

Squaw does a lousy job of trail marking; trail names aren't even listed on the official trail map, and if you ask a local for directions you may get several different names for any given trail because the ski school and ski patrol tend to have their own naming systems. Instead of naming trails, Squaw tends to name various areas of the mountain after the peak or the lift that serves it. Lifts, rather than trails, are given green-blue-black designations, so it's especially important to keep your wits about you. It's easy to cruise onto a lift and then find yourself on terrain you didn't expect. That's why this chapter is longer than the others in this section; I've tried to make up for the general vagueness of Squaw's own nomenclature.

Driving to Squaw is easy in good weather, via I-80 from the Bay Area (3.5 hours) or Reno (1 hour), then south from Truckee for 12 miles along the winding two-lane Route 89, following the banks of the Truck-ee River, with a right turn onto the Olympic Valley access road. In stormy weather, when Donner Pass may close, the trip from Sacramento and San Francisco can take all night.

I like to get there before 8 a.m., park close in, and have breakfast at Dave's Deli or Mother Barclay's (both in the Olympic House base complex); there's also a coffee shop in the Cable Car building, where you can get a croissant and latte while waiting to load on the lift. Locals avoid morning lift lines by parking near Children's World (the day care facility at the southeast corner of the parking lot behind the Far East Center) and riding Far East Express to get into the trail network. This route is wonderfully convenient for parents—drop the kids at Children's World and scoot straight up Far East.

Squaw has two base areas and two mid-mountain lodges. At the base (elevation 6,200 feet) is the Resort at Squaw Creek, with its Squaw Creek chair (you will not be allowed to park here unless you are registered at the hotel), and the Olympic House complex, served by the Cable Car (also called the tram by locals), the new Funitel, Red Dog, Exhibition, KT-22, and Squaw One Express. Far East Express and the beginner lifts—the pony tows and Searchlight—also originate here.

At mid-mountain (elevation 8,200 feet) you'll find Gold Coast Lodge at the top of the Funitel, and High Camp Bath & Tennis Club (the good-weather home of the ski school) at the top of the Cable Car.

Here are Squaw's major "neighborhoods," working from east to west:

The Resort Runs are served by Squaw Creek chair. The area is named for the Resort at Squaw Creek, the plush 500-room hotel at the bottom of the Squaw Creek lift. There's mostly intermediate cruising terrain here, but if you drop off the ridgeline to the north, you'll find very steep tree skiing and bump runs. There are no beginner runs here.

Snow King Mountain, also called Red Dog, is served by the Red Dog and Papoose chairs. Mostly steep, race-course terrain (this was the site of the women's Olympic GS courses), Snow King has intermediate trails winding across the bottom of Olympic Lady to emerge above the Olympic House base lodge. It's the normal transfer route from the Resort at Squaw Creek to the main lift network. The last 300 yards of this trail are steep, so it's not recommended to beginners, who, instead, should ride the shuttle bus.

Olympic Lady is the very steep mountain hidden between Snow King and KT-22. Because the lift loads in the secluded gulley above the base area and because the Olympic Lady terrain is never groomed, this area remains a secret hideaway for Squaw's local experts. There's fantastic bump skiing, tree skiing, and powder here. Intermediate skiers shouldn't bother—there's no safe way down. Olympic Lady was the site of the Olympic women's downhill in 1960.

Exhibition serves a steepish and very public bump run overlooking the main lodge and provides access to the steeper Schimmelpfennig Bowl. The bowl was the men's slalom stadium during the Olympics but now serves as a bump run and exit route for skiers descending the Nose of KT-22. Advanced intermediates will be comfortable here when the face of Exhibition has been groomed. Exhibition offers no beginner terrain.

KT-22 (named for the 22 kick turns executed by Sandy Poulsen when her husband, Squaw Valley pioneer Wayne Poulsen, first hauled her up there) is world famous for its magnificent steep terrain. The runs are rarely groomed. Get off the lift and turn left into *GS Bowl;* it's very steep but also very broad, so there's plenty of room to recover when you get in trouble. Follow the ridgeline back under the lift line (a hazardous route at best) to reach the Nose and the Fingers cliffs. Turn right off the lift and drop off the edge into *Chute 75,* a long exhilarating couloir of perfectly consistent pitch. One relatively easy trail follows the ridgeline to the west toward *Saddle* (this is the exit route for intermediate skiers). Drop off the ridge to the north to find precipitous descents in the appropriately named *Rock Garden* and *Dead Tree.*

Squaw normally grooms an intermediate escape route down *Saddle,* reachable via the ridgelines from KT-22 and Cornice II lifts. Just to the west of *Saddle's* low point is an irregular bowl called *Enchanted Forest,* usually my first destination on a good powder morning.

The western descents from KT-22 and the *Saddle* trails descend to *Mountain Run,* the main route off the upper mountain. Situated just below the *Mountain Run* road cut are Cornice II chair and Headwall lift. Cornice II serves some of the steepest face skiing at Squaw. The intermediate exit route from the top of the lift is to turn left and follow the ridgeline east toward *Saddle;* experts can drop off the ridge into the *Horse Trails* area, descend the *Classic* and *Hourglass* chutes, or simply ski the steepish Cornice II face (one of the great lines on a powder day is directly under the Cornice II lift line). From the top of Cornice II local nutcases can climb a few yards and jump into *Light Tower* (also called *Bell Tower*), reputed to be the steepest lift-served chute on the hill. Experts and advanced skiers only on Cornice II.

Headwall chair goes over the northern shoulder of Cornice to the saddle at the east end of Squaw Peak. Turn left here onto the broad, smooth *Sunbowl,* a wonderful intermediate cruiser that's best on powder days and in spring corn. *Sunbowl* exits onto *Horse Trails* or *Saddle.* The other intermediate exit from Headwall chair is straight ahead, onto *Chicken Bowl,* the wide landing field for bodies falling off the Squaw Peak Palisades. Most skiers getting off Headwall chair make a 180-degree turn and follow the cat track 100 yards east to *North Bowl, The Nose,* or *Headwall*

Face. North Bowl starts as a very steep face, usually bumped out, and flattens out to merely steep; it all overlooks the Gold Coast Restaurant, so make your best turns. *Headwall Face* is quite steep and, since it lies under the lift, also very public. Both faces are left ungroomed. My favorite run off Headwall is *The Nose,* the convex spine that separates Headwall from *North Bowl.* The bumps are longer and more rhythmic, and it leads straight down to the high-speed Siberia quad.

Because it overlooks the great Gold Coast/Mainline plateau (cruising ground for Squaw's intermediate skiers), *Siberia Bowl* attracts a lot of ambitious advanced skiers. The bowl is groomed frequently, but because it's steep and fast, it bumps out quickly. The escape route is to the north, along the ridgeline to the *Mainline* and *Gold Coast* runs. The ungroomed portions of *Siberia Bowl* are strictly expert. Newport chair serves Siberia's lower, gentler slopes.

Mainline and *Gold Coast* serve the rolling intermediate runs above Gold Coast Restaurant. Most of these trails are wide and gentle, with easily visible dropoffs, but beware the heavy cross-traffic near the restaurant.

Emigrant chair goes, of course, to the summit of Emigrant Peak. Intermediates have two choices here: Turn left and ski back toward *Gold Coast* or go straight ahead and follow the cat track around to the right to *Attic,* a steep but wide and smooth trail leading toward the high-speed Shirley Lake quad. Experts can duck back under the Emigrant lift line and pound down the very steep *Funnel* (beware the rock band hidden under the snow in the middle) or follow the road toward *Attic* and peel off to the left to descend the tree runs on the back side of Emigrant. There's no beginner terrain off Emigrant Peak.

The easiest terrain at Gold Coast consists of a couple of wide, gentle, and consistent runs served by the East Broadway chair. These are pleasant low-intermediate runs, used for ski school classes and practice. Somewhat more varied and challenging intermediate terrain can be found at High Camp lift, which starts alongside *Mountain Run* a few hundred feet downhill from the Gold Coast Restaurant.

The best beginner terrain at Squaw is on the three ski-school lifts clustered on the High Camp plateau: *Bailey's Beach, Links,* and *Belmont.* Because of the high elevation (8,200 feet), High Camp gets dependable snow. You reach this area via the Cable Car; beginners should plan to ride the Cable Car back down at the end of the day.

North of the High Camp plateau are two lifts suitable for intermediates—Shirley Lake and Solitude—and two for experts, Granite Chief and Silverado.

When the wind is from the west, as is usually the case, Shirley Lake and Solitude are sheltered. Shirley, a high-speed quad, serves the lower slopes of Emigrant's north side and five tree runs that are really wide boulevards separated by thin stands of ponderosa and silver fir. Solitude's trails loop far to the east to give lower intermediates an easy way down and feature one advanced-to-expert bump bowl directly under the lift. *Solitude Bowl* itself, near the top of the lift, makes a good introduction to steep skiing because it rounds out nicely to a flat runout.

Beyond the bottom of Shirley Lake lies Granite Chief chair. All the terrain off the top is quite steep. Turn left and follow the ridgeline until one of the many lines down the bowl looks appealing, or turn right and peel off down *Secret Bowl*. After a storm, this is the last terrain secured by the avalanche patrol, and powder skiers find untracked lines in the trees by traversing farther and farther across the flanks of Granite Chief Peak.

Just east of High Camp Bath & Tennis Club, the terrain plunges away in the precipitous *Tram Bowl*. Experts drop through the cliff band, and advanced skiers can cruise the bowl by skirting below the Bailey's Beach tennis courts to the Broken Arrow saddle and then turning left. This is all delicious powder skiing after a storm, and it opens whenever Silverado chair is running.

The final lift is Broken Arrow, which loads near the bottom of Siberia Express alongside *Mountain Run* and takes you to the top of *Broken Arrow Bowl*. Never groomed, *Broken Arrow* is a magnificently long, rolling expanse of expert chutes, glades, and ridges, facing mostly east and south. It's hidden from the general run of traffic on *Mountain Run,* so it's rarely crowded, but the southern exposure means the powder turns crusty and heavy within a few days after a storm; only strong powder skiers should go there.

Tricks of the Trade

On a crowded day, the fastest way up the mountain will be to bypass the lines at the Funitel and Cable Car and ride Squaw One Express to Siberia Express. Avoid traffic jams by parking behind the Far East Center, and ride Far East Express into the trail network.

At the end of the day, skiers elbow their way down *Mountain Run*—it's an ugly mob scene. Intermediates can skirt the worst of it by skiing down *Sunnyside* on the north side of the valley. Experts have more fun: From High Camp, traverse around Broken Arrow Peak to ski *Sundance* (locals still call it *Tower 16*) under the Funitel, or go straight to *Broken Arrow* and follow the ridges and gullies all the way back to the base lodge bars.

Best Beginner Skiing

In good weather, the High Camp plateau can't be beat. In bad weather, go to Alpine Meadows, because the limited beginner terrain on Exhibition/Searchlight chair is intolerably crowded.

Best Intermediate Skiing

When it's uncrowded, *Mountain Run* is a wonderful cruiser (it was the men's downhill course in 1960). Otherwise, the Shirley Lake tree runs give you the most challenge and the most skiing per hour, thanks to the high-speed lift.

Best Expert Skiing

My favorite runs in powder and corn are the glades on either side of the Granite Chief lift line, the hidden shot off the north side of Emigrant Peak called *McGoo's Madness, Broken Arrow,* and the two *Noses* on *Headwall* and KT-22. On a storm day, the best skiing is *Poulsen's Gulley* (under Red Dog chair) and the forests on either side, and *Enchanted Forest* off KT-22.

Snowboarding

The huge half-pipe and terrain park occupy most of the terrain to skiers right of Mainline lift.

Convenient Lodging

Until the new village complex opens, Squaw still has only five hotels, of which the most comfortable are the **Squaw Valley Lodge,** the **Resort at Squaw Creek,** and the **Olympic Village Inn.** The Lodge is a big modern condo/hotel complex complete with covered parking, pools, and exercise and weight rooms. It sits just behind the Olympic House base area and offers ski-in/ski-out convenience. The Resort at Squaw Creek is a plush 500-room hotel with its own shopping mall, three good restaurants, a ski shop, a skating rink, and a health spa. The Resort, too, is a ski-in/ski-out lodge, with its own base area and lift, though beginner skiers will have to ride the shuttle bus over to the main base area because all the linking ski runs are intermediate or higher. The Olympic Village Inn is a short walk from the main base area (or you can ride their shuttle); built as athlete housing for the 1960 Olympics, the place was thoroughly renovated in the early 1980s and is now a picturesque, rambling condotel with a very good dining room.

Most Squaw Valley skiers stay in Truckee or Tahoe City, but weekend traffic jams on the access road and Route 89 are so appallingly bad that if you can afford to stay in the valley, you should.

Best Eats

On the mountain there are good cafeterias at **High Camp** (with a spectacular panoramic view to the north, east, and south), **Gold Coast,** and **Olympic House.** You can have good sit-down lunches at **Alexander's** (High Camp), **Salsa** (Olympic House), and **Bullwhacker's** (Resort at Squaw Creek).

Several good restaurants have set up recently within the valley. I like **Glissande** (continental) and **Montagne** (Italian) at the Resort at Squaw Creek, the dining room at the Olympic Village Inn, and **Graham Rock's** (eclectic haute cuisine) in the old Poulsen House at the northeast corner of the parking lot. For cheap eats, nothing beats pizza at the **Les Chamois,** the traditional après-ski hangout for ski instructors and patrol persons. The new Intrawest Village offers **Fireside Pizza, Starbucks,** and the plush **Plumpjack Balboa,** a nouvelle cuisine bistro imported from San Francisco. For a casual lunch try Balboa's deli adjunct.

On a snowy evening, the better part of valor lies in dining in the valley, rather than fighting the standstill traffic clotted all the way into Truckee. Traffic thins out after 8 p.m., so choose a designated driver and relax.

Squaw Valley Data

Mountain Statistics

Vertical feet	2,850 feet
Base elevation	6,200 feet
Summit elevation	9,050 feet
Longest run	3.2 miles
Average annual snowfall	450 inches
Snowmaking	400 acres
Number of lifts	34: 1 cable car; 1 funitel; 1 pulse gondola; 3 high-speed six-packs; 4 high-speed quads; 1 fixed-grip quad; 8 triples; 9 doubles; 4 surface lifts; 2 moving carpets
Uphill capacity	49,000 skiers per hour
Skiable terrain	4,000 acres (claimed)
Opening date	Mid-November
Closing date	Memorial Day or later
Snowboarding	Yes

Transportation

By car From Reno, 1 hour via I-80 to Truckee, then Route 89; from San Francisco, 4 hours via I-80 to Truckee, then Route 89; from Sacramento, 2 hours via I-80 to Truckee, then Route 89; from Lake Tahoe area, Route 28 or 89 to Tahoe City, then Route 89 north.

By bus Shuttle bus from most Lake Tahoe and Reno hotels.

By air Major carriers to Reno-Tahoe International Airport (40 miles).

Key Phone Numbers

Ski-area information	(530) 583-6985 or (888) SNOW-321
Snow report	(530) 583-6955
Reservations	(800) 545-4350 or (888) SNOW-321 or (866) 818-6963
Website	www.squaw.com

Inside Story

Sierra Cement

Sierra Cement. It doesn't sound very inviting, that term for the heavy, wet, maritime snow that sometimes falls not only in California's High Sierra, but also up and down the West Coast ranges. I suppose it isn't very inviting, especially compared to fluffy Utah powder.

But skilled Far-West skiers develop a kind of affection for the stuff—nothing improves your skiing more than responding to challenging conditions, and Sierra Cement is a major challenge.

After learning to ski in western Switzerland, I began my ski-teaching life in this country at Squaw Valley, and I was soon wrestling with Sierra Cement. The result was an unexpected plus: Having made my peace with this awkward, heavy snow, I then discovered that I could ski untracked snow anywhere else in the world, easily. It was a tough apprenticeship, but one that worked. I should say too, to dispel a baseless rumor, that Sierra Cement is far from the only kind of snow that falls on these West Coast ranges. It's merely one end of the full spectrum of snow (the heavy, wet end) that West Coast skiers can encounter in the course of a season. And it's only really a challenge in its unpacked state; once it has been packed and groomed, it's just, well, snow.

But you'd like to ski this stuff, or to ski it better. You wake up in the morning and look at a mountain covered with three feet of snow overnight, and you feel thrilled until you go out on the porch and discover you can squeeze water out of a snowball—ugh! Sierra Cement. Let's give it a go. Are you ready?

Naturally you want to approach this wet Western snow like powder, with your weight evenly distributed over both skis. The next thing you need is a steeper-than-normal slope. This heavy wet snow will slow you down—so much so that if you aren't on a steep slope, you may wind up having to walk downhill through it. So steepness becomes an additional part of the challenge. In the Rocky Mountains you can ski powder on very gentle pitches (true powder is so light that it doesn't slow you down much), but not out here, not on Sierra Cement. So let me suggest a couple of confidence-building exercises before you attack a steep slope of Sierra Cement directly. Begin with a few uphill turns, to get used to the extra resistance of the snow. Traverse down and across that steep slope; flex your legs deeply; and make a turn to a stop by extending your legs down and away from you. That's right, an uphill christie by extending your legs and pushing out the tails of your skis. This is a powerful move. It would be out of place, excessive, on a packed slope; but in two feet of untracked Sierra Cement it works great. Now practice a few more of these special uphill christies from steeper and steeper traverses, until finally you can turn out to a stop from a run straight down the fall line, straight down the hill.

Now we're ready to tackle the start or launch phase of our turns in this heavy snow. My suggestions: Use a little more speed than normal; make a very powerful up movement or lift at the start of the turn (to break your skis loose from the grip of this heavy snow); and finally, bank your whole body in the direction you want to turn. Banking is curious. It's often a mistake, a problem, in modern skiing since it tends to put too much weight on the inside ski. But here, in heavy deep snow, it works wonders. As you bank your body in the direction of your turn (the way a bicyclist or motorcyclist leans into a turn), you also bank your skis against the snow. And the resistance of this heavy snow against the tilted or banked bases of your skis will actually push you around, into the turn.

In short, the recipe for success in skiing untracked Sierra Cement is threefold; exaggerated (powerful but smooth) movements, a little more speed than normal, and a steeper slope. It will take time before you can relax in this heavy wet snow, but the first step is simply to turn in it, no matter how crudely. Then with increasing success, increasing confidence, you will be able to smooth out and refine your movements. You'll find out just how much power you need, just how far to bank into the turn. And you'll also discover that skiing hard conditions is one of the great thrills of our sport. Sierra Cement provides that thrill.

Northstar-at-Tahoe

For years Northstar, created in 1972 on logging company land, built its reputation on family skiing. The huge, gladed bowl above the Lodge at Big Springs was perfect for turning the kids loose: all traffic coming off its gentle cruising runs had to pass the lodge, so a watchful parent had no trouble rounding up the herd at the end of the day.

Well, those kids grew up and wanted more challenging skiing. Northstar obliged by opening a high-speed quad lift to serve eight back-side trails of leg-burning length and pitch. Between these trails lies some of the sweetest tree skiing at the lake. Mom and Dad can no longer depend on the kids to cycle past the lunch deck every half hour; it's too tempting to get lost in the woods. Future plans call for additional lifts that will open new terrain rolling down toward the existing Schaeffer's Camp cross-country trail—and a new pedestrian village.

For now, the lift layout is still pretty simple: From Northstar Village, ride the gondola up to the Lodge at Big Springs or take the Echo lift to the same destination. The base village (it has a mini-mall with shops and services alongside the short walk from parking lot to gondola entrance) is simple and woodsy; it's a pleasantly low-key entrée, thanks in large measure to the fact that pedestrian traffic all moves in one direction: toward the gondola in the morning and toward the parking in the afternoon.

From the Lodge at Big Springs, at the top of the gondola, the real skiing begins. Beginners have a choice of three short lifts (Bear Paw, plus Bear Cub and Chipmunk, which are reserved for the ski school), all isolated behind the Lodge at Big Springs. Intermediates and experts can hop on the Vista high-speed quad (it goes up the east side of the bowl), Lookout lift (up the west side), or Arrow Express (right up the middle). All three lifts serve a mix of intermediate and advanced slopes; none is too scary for gutsy kids.

Northstar has two summits: Mount Pluto and Lookout Mountain. During the summer of 2000, Northstar installed the Lookout Mountain Express chair, serving 200 acres of true expert terrain on the north side of Lookout—so named for its spectacular view across Martis Valley. Lookout claims 1,200 vertical feet of bumps, steeps, and glade skiing, with five marked trails. To get there, ride the Poma lift from the top of the lookout double chair.

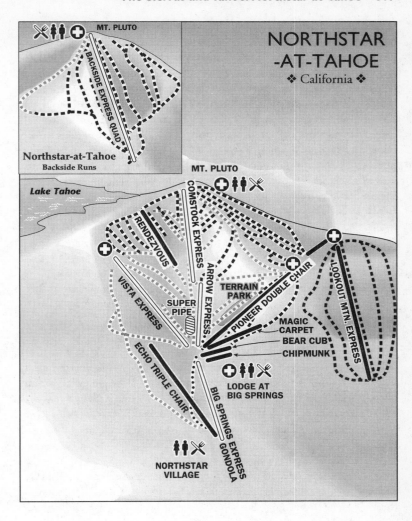

To get to the Mount Pluto summit (and the back side), ride Arrow Express and Comstock Express (serving the upper half of the front bowl).

The runs off the East Ridge, served by Comstock and the shorter Rendezvous triple chair, are marked as expert terrain, but they're just steep enough to keep your skis sliding easily in powder. These trails—*Grouse, Flume, Crosscut, Tonini's, Chute, Dutchman,* and *Delight*—are about perfect for learning to ski powder, and experts will enjoy popping off the trails into the glades.

The West Ridge runs—*Corridor, Plunge, Ax Handle, Stump Alley, Luggi's, Jibboom,* and *Flying Squirrel*—are a bit steeper for a short upper section, then flatten out into easy intermediate cruising.

Back-side runs are served by the back-side Express lift (some locals may still refer to this area as Schaeffer's Camp, but that name is more properly applied to the cross-country complex farther down). When groomed, these runs allow you to set up a consistent GS rhythm and crank 30-mile-per-hour turns for a solid mile and 1,860 vertical feet. When the Back-side trails are bumped out, youngsters will pound on down. Boomers stick with the GS turns but move them into the woods, where the trees are spaced perfectly to accommodate that natural medium-radius turn, in powder or corn snow. No worries here about bursting between close-set trees to fall off a cliff. Except for a couple of road cuts near the bottom, the terrain is of remarkably consistent pitch. Think of the back side as user-friendly expert skiing.

The Back-side runs are generally similar in pitch and width; of course, those that closely parallel the lift (*Iron Horse, Polaris, Rapids,* and *Burnout*) are a bit steeper than the trails that loop to the south (*Rail Splitter, Sierra Grande, Challenger*) and north (*Promised Land* and the easy *Lookout Road* cat track). Don't relax as you near the bottom: while the terrain flattens out on the return trails, the traffic is heavy here so they bump up a bit. It's easy to come honking off *Iron Horse* going mach schnell and find yourself bouncing through a minefield.

Exiting the Mountain

Village Run gets very crowded at the end of the day. While the terrain is very easy, beginners should consider riding down on the gondola—it's an uncomfortable sensation to fall in the middle of the trail with expert skiers whizzing past both ears. Intermediate and advanced skiers can follow *The Woods* to the base village. It's truly hidden away and sees light traffic.

Best Beginner Skiing

Village Run is that rare animal: the long beginner cruiser; and it's pleasant skiing until the crowds get rowdy in late afternoon. Otherwise, stick to the Bear Paw terrain.

Best Intermediate Skiing

You can find this almost anywhere on the front. If you like long cruisers, take *West Ridge* to *Luggi's* to *Lumberjack* to *Main Street*—that drops you 1,800 vertical feet back to the bottom of Arrow Express. The longest trail on the mountain—roughly two miles and 2,200 vertical feet—is *East Ridge* to *Logger's Loop* to the *Woods*. Just turn left at the top of *Comstock* and then make every right turn all the way down.

Best Expert Skiing

This can be found in Backside's trees and in the much steeper glades off Lookout Mountain, in powder or corn. The trees, generously spaced, can soak up dozens of powder freaks after a storm. On Lookout, the steepest, gnarliest trails are *Gooseneck* and *Boca. Prosser* and *Martis* usually provide good high-speed groomed steeps.

Snowboarding

The superpipe is located on *Drop Out,* just above the mid-mountain lodge alongside Arrow Express lift. Another terrain park follows *The Gucley,* along Pioneer Chair.

Convenient Lodging

Northstar provides the best assortment of ski-in/ski-out lodging in California, with 262 condo units at slopeside or within walking distance of the gondola. A friendly shuttle service cycles past all the Northstar condos, making it easy for families to cut the teens loose to find their way out and back, morning and evening. The advantage to staying right in Northstar, rather than at a Truckee or Tahoe City lodge, is that you avoid Tahoe's spectacular weather-caused traffic snarls. Getting to and from Northstar from Reno or Sacramento involves creeping through Truckee via Highway 267, a tense experience when the roads are slick, and impossible when Donner Pass closes. Getting there from the lake means driving Highway 267 over Brockway Summit (7,200 feet), which can be impossible without four-wheel-drive or chains. When weather threatens, allow extra travel time.

Best Eats

Timbercreek seems to be the favorite at Northstar, featuring honey-barbecued salmon and rack of Sonoma lamb. In Truckee, I like **Cottonwood** (phone (530) 587-5711) for nouvelle cuisine in a rambling old roadhouse setting, the **Left Bank** for French specialties, and **Jordan's Pacific Crest.**

Northstar-at-Tahoe Data

Mountain Statistics

Vertical feet	2,280 feet
Base elevation	6,330 feet
Summit elevation	8,610 feet
Longest run	2.9 miles
Average annual snowfall	350 inches
Number of lifts	17: 1 express gondola; 5 quad chairlifts; 2 triple chairlifts; 2 double chairlifts; 4 moving carpets; 3 surface lifts
Uphill capacity	21,800 skiers per hour
Skiable terrain	2,420 acres
Opening date	Mid-November
Closing date	Mid-April
Snowboarding	Yes

| **Northstar-at-Tahoe Data** (continued) |

Transportation

By car From Reno, 45 min. via I-80 to Truckee, then Route 267; from Lake Tahoe area, via Route 28 to Tahoe Vista, then Route 267 over Brockway Summit (7,200 feet); from Sacramento, 2 hours via I-80 to Truckee, then Route 267; from San Francisco, 4 hours via I-80 and Route 267.

By air Major carriers to Reno-Tahoe International Airport (40 miles).

Key Phone Numbers

Ski-area information	(530) 562-1010
Snow report	(530) 562-1330
Reservations	(800) 466-6784
Website	www.northstarattahoe.com

Sugar Bowl

Sugar Bowl is a trip back in time. Built in 1939 by an alliance of San Francisco socialites and Walt Disney, the Sugar Bowl Lodge remains a picturesque warren of dark, narrow corridors and stairwells, with warm, luxuriously appointed rooms and lounges, and, of course, a formal dining room. If I still entertained any hope of impressing my spouse with old-time courtly sophistication, I'd burrow in here for a few second honeymoon nights.

Part of the charm of the place is how you reach it. Sugar Bowl is the closest major ski area to Sacramento and the Bay Area (it's about three hours from the Bay Bridge), but you can't, strictly speaking, "drive in." Instead, you turn off I-80 at Soda Springs, cruise three miles up Old Highway 40, and pull into the parking structure on the right. Unload the car and climb on the old Magic Carpet gondola for a ride across the Union Pacific railroad tracks to the ski area.

Until 1994 this was the only way to enter Sugar Bowl. Since then, with the opening of the Mount Judah expansion, a new access road lets you park right at the bottom of the Jerome Hill Express and Mount Judah Express Quad.

Sugar Bowl is medium-sized (1,500 acres, 1,500 vertical feet) but contains a nice variety of terrain for beginners and experts. The great attraction for most Sugar Bowl skiers is the quality of the snow. The whole Tahoe region is famous for monumental dumps and 40-foot snowpack, but Sugar Bowl gets more. Royal Gorge, a chasm 4,000 feet deep carved by the American River, points straight at the back side of the ski area and funnels Pacific storms so that the clouds spill right over the top of Mount Lincoln, Sugar Bowl's summit. The result is average snowfall of about 500 inches, or 41 feet. As you drive up Old Highway 40, look at the old houses along the roadside; they're all built with a second entrance on the upper floor or with a long wooden tunnel out to the road. The U.S. Forest Service maintains its national snow research laboratory in town.

So Sugar Bowl is a good bet for powder skiing and a relatively easy drive during a moderate Sierra storm; coming from the Bay Area, you don't have to cross Donner Pass. If the road is open to Soda Springs, it's open to Sugar Bowl.

Sugar Bowl has two separate base areas: Mount Judah and the Lodge. The Mount Judah side is simple: the Jerome Hill high-speed quad, named for the railroad heir who built the Magic Carpet gondola, and the Mount Judah Express quad serve 900 vertical feet of mostly intermediate cruising terrain (when groomed, these trails can tempt experts to maintain high-speed GS turns all the way down). To reach the main lift complex, turn right when getting off the lift and follow the easy *Pioneer Trail* to *Christmas Tree Lane;* this will put you at the Mid-Mountain Day Lodge, with access to Christmas Tree and the new Silver Belt Express lifts.

From the Lodge, most skiers ride the short Nob Hill fixed-quad lift. From there, turn right and descend to the Disney Express or Crow's Nest lifts, both serving the 7,900-foot ridge of Mount Disney, or turn left and follow the cat track to the Mid-Mountain Day Mount and Mount Linclon Express to the summit of Mount Lincoln (8,383 feet). Also accessible here is Christmas Tree lift, serving mostly beginner and intermediate terrain.

To return to the Mount Judah base area, ride Christmas Tree lift and follow *Harriet's Hollow* or *Jerome Bound* back to *Pioneer Trail.* From the top of Mount Lincoln, take *Bill Klein's Schuss* into *Harriet's Hollow.*

When the weather is good, I head straight up Mount Linclon Express. A traditional ski race used to descend through the *Silver Belt Chute* just under the summit and then dive down *Steilhung* (I raced in the very last Silver Belt race, held in 1989 during a classic Sierra blizzard, with no distinguished result). The summit chutes *Fuller's Folly* and *The '58s* (named for the big avalanche of 1958) are short but genuinely hair-raising. The groomed runs off Mount Lincoln (*Hellman's Chute* and *Rahlves' Run* and *Crowley's*) are rolling, rhythmic intermediate challenges. Beginners should *not* go to the summit because there is no easy way down.

Christmas Tree lift serves mostly intermediate cruising runs, with a couple of long easy beginner trails (*Sleigh Ride* and *Cat Walk*). Especially on *Cat Walk,* be careful of expert skiers exiting at high speed from the Mount Lincoln runs. You'll find the race arena off Christmas Tree, too.

On a stormy day, I head up Mount Disney Express. From here you can turn left and ski the long steep East Face runs (*Sugar Bowl, East Face, Bacon's Gully,* and *Market Street*), all of which exit above the Mid-Mountain Day Lodge. Turn right and cruise the bowls and tree runs toward Crow's Nest lift (*Disney's Nose, Avalanche, Eagle, Donald Duck, Pony*

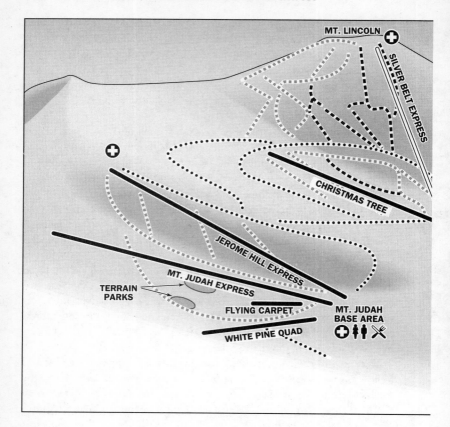

Express). Riding Crow's Nest on a powder day, you can find first tracks until closing time on *Montgomery* and *MacTavish* and in the woods alongside *Mad Dog* and *Overland*.

Best Beginner Skiing

If you're on the Village side, Nob Hill has the ski school and best practice terrain. On the Mount Judah side, find five new beginner runs off White Pine. The nice thing about the lift network is that there are easy ways to get around the mountain between the two base areas and Mid-Mountain Day Lodge by using the Nob Hill, Christmas Tree, and Jerome Hill lifts.

Best Intermediate Skiing

For challenge, try the eastern trails on Mount Lincoln (*Hellman's Chute* and beyond). For cruising, ski the Mount Judah runs.

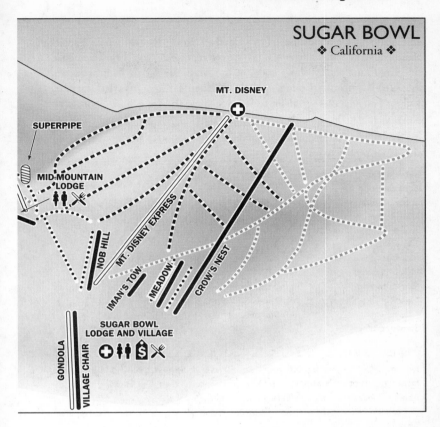

Best Expert Skiing

For challenge, ski *Silver Belt* and *Fuller's Folly* on Mount Lincoln. For bumps, it's *Bacon's Gully*. For trees, go over to the glades alongside *Donald Duck* and *Crow's Face*. Look for the short steeps off the Pacific Coast: *East Face, Roller Pass, Judah Bowl,* and the *Pacific Coast Glades*.

Snowboardings

The superpipe is located just above the midmountain lodge, and two elaborate terrain parks decorate the runs beneath *Mount Judah Express*.

Convenient Lodging

Stay at the **Sugar Bowl Lodge** if you can possibly get in. Otherwise, stay in Soda Springs or Truckee (15 minutes east over Donner Pass; note that Old Highway 40 occasionally closes during the winter, so you might have to backtrack through Soda Springs and pick up I-80).

Best Eats

The only choice for dinner is the **Lodge Dining Room,** where gentlemen still wear jackets (ties are no longer required). You'll find standard ski-resort lunches, cafeteria style, at the **Main Lodge** at Mount Judah, the **Mid-Mountain Lodge,** and the **Village Lodge. Java Juice** at the Village Lodge serves espresso, fruit smoothies, and fresh baked goods.

Sugar Bowl Data

Mountain Statistics

Vertical feet	1,500 feet
Base elevation	6,883 feet
Summit elevation	8,383 feet
Longest run	3 miles
Average annual snowfall	500 inches
Snowmaking	375 acres
Number of lifts	12: 7 quads; 3 doubles; I surface lift; I gondola
Uphill capacity	23,540 skiers per hour
Skiable terrain	1,500 acres
Opening date	Mid-November
Closing date	End of April
Snowboarding	Yes

Transportation

By car From San Francisco, 3 hours via I-80 to Soda Springs, then Old Highway 40; from Sacramento, 1.5 hours via I-80 to Soda Springs, then Old Highway 40; from Reno, I hour via I-80 to Soda Springs, then Old Highway 40.

By air Major carriers to Reno-Tahoe International or Sacramento Metropolitan Airport.

Key Phone Numbers

Ski-area information	(530) 426-9000
Ski school	(530) 426-6770
Snow report	(530) 426-1111
Website	www.sugarbowl.com

The Pacific Northwest

Mount Bachelor A big volcano with interesting, rhythmic skiing in nearly all directions from the summit, Bachelor has a swift, efficient lift system and snow that lasts until July. There's no base village; skiers stay in the lovely, relaxing town of Bend.

Crystal Mountain The great secret of Washington skiing, Crystal Mountain is a big, wild mountain in the shadow of Mount Rainier, 90 minutes from Seattle. Crystal's steeps and tree skiing are world-class, the snow reliably deep but Northwest-sloppy. There is intimate rustic lodging but a limited nightlife.

Stevens Pass There is dependably exciting day skiing at Stevens Pass with easy fun cruising on the front side and a vast natural bowl out back to soak up the adventurous. There is no base village and no lodging accommodations.

Mission Ridge On the east side of the Cascades, Mission Ridge gets the lightest, driest snow in the Northwest. The area is rarely crowded, but the lift system is crude. Happily, it serves some classic terrain, with plenty of long cruisers and good, steepish chutes and tree skiing.

Mount Baker A pocket wonderland hidden south of the Canadian border, Mount Baker has world-record snow depths and intensely steep terrain.

Mount Bachelor

Mount Bachelor ranks among the top ten resorts in the United States for skier visits, even without a lot of "destination" skiing by Easterners. This fact may startle folks from back East, but it's a tribute to the fanaticism of Oregon's hardbody locals, who can "Just Do It" until the mountain finally closes after Memorial Day weekend.

Not that destination skiing would be a bad idea. While Bachelor has no proper base area village, the tidy little city of Bend, 20 miles down the road,

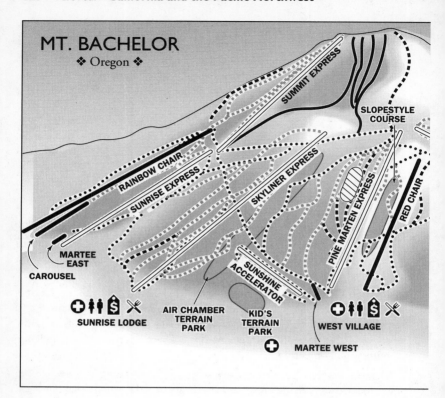

makes a hospitable vacation getaway. You can get to Bend via Highway 26 and 97 from Portland, via Highway 20 from the west or east, or Highway 97 from the south. From Bend, follow Century Drive Highway west and south out of town to the ski area. None of these roads develops any special traffic problem. Free parking is close to the lodges. There's a shuttle bus from the park-and-ride lot in town. Fares run $3 each way from Bend.

Bachelor is a dormant volcano whose forested, gully-etched lower slopes collect snow in six-foot drifts. It is one of a group of dramatic peaks (Mount Jefferson, Three Sisters, Mount Bailey) that makes central Oregon such a startlingly beautiful landscape. The upper slopes provide a geology lesson, bristling with cinder cones, plugs, and half-pipes that once roared with lava flows. Over half of the 3,365 vertical feet lies above timberline, and those broad slopes are a testing ground for high-speed skiing—every turn begs you to bank your skis against some lunar-landscape protuberance.

Bachelor is big—3,686 honest acres, with ten lifts, including seven high-speed quads. The lifts fan out from the summit, making a full skirt

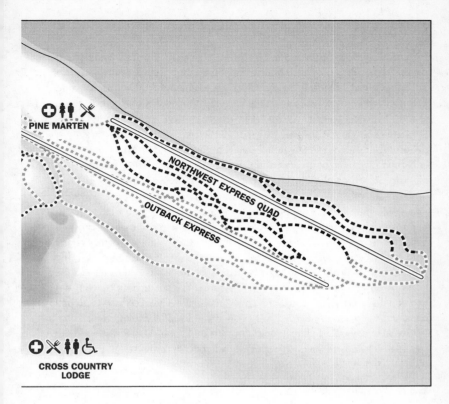

around the entire northern perimeter of the cone. Access is via two base lodges, Sunrise at the east end of the complex and West Village Day Lodge a mile out at the end of the auto road. Each lodge is a full-service facility, with its own cafeteria, rental shop, ski school office, beginner lift, and high-speed quad access to the upper mountain.

From Sunrise Lodge, the fastest route into the trail system is via the Sunrise Express high-speed quad. The lift takes you 800 feet up to timberline, and here you can catch Summit Express to the top or hit the easy cruisers back to Sunrise Lodge. Another option would be to turn right off the lift and follow the *West Village Getback* road that crosses over to the West Village Day Lodge; en route it crosses most of the lower mountain runs. Peel off down *Cliffhanger, Pat's Way, Chipper, Dentist,* or *DSQ* to reach Skyliner Express, which goes 1,316 feet up the hill to serve most of the trails between the two base lodges.

From the West Village Day Lodge, ride Pine Marten Express to Pine Marten Lodge, the large mid-mountain cafeteria. From this point you can reach just about any trail on the lower mountain, either directly or by turning off the *Summit Crossover* catwalk (*Summit Crossover* goes straight to Summit Express lift).

Pine Marten also provides access to the Outback complex, which comprises half a dozen very long, rolling, cruising runs dropping almost 1,800 feet and is served by the Outback high-speed quad lift. Beyond Outback, the Northwest Express quad—the longest lift on the mountain at 2,400 vertical feet (it's 1.7 miles in length)—serves eight gladed intermediate trails carved through the dense, sheltering forest.

Summit Express takes you to the top to enjoy the 360-degree view encompassing most of Oregon and northern California. Three intermediate fall-line cruisers parallel the lift. Experts can pick their way through the lava outcrops at the summit, then drop through the chutes into the *Cirque,* a vast steep amphitheater full of entertaining cones, ridges, and rills.

Storm days present fewer problems at Bachelor than at most exposed West Coast mountains. Because the six lower mountain express chairs end at timberline, they're sheltered from the wind. Roughly half the mountain's vertical and about two-thirds of its skiable acreage can be skied through all but the most severe storms. I've spent days messing up the powder drifted alongside the trees on the Pine Marten and Outback runs, and warming up every hour or so at the Pine Marten Lodge.

On busy days, Red chair (paralleling Pine Marten) and Rainbow chair (paralleling Sunrise Express) provide relief from crowds on the high-speed quads.

Best Beginner Skiing

Sunshine Accelerator is a high-speed quad exclusively serving easy learner terrain. Carrousel lift, at Sunrise Lodge, is the other beginner lift. *Skyliner* and *Marshmallow* are long easy cruisers designed for beginners.

Best Intermediate Skiing

For the longest cruise, pick up *Healy Heights* or *Beverly Hills* from the summit and continue into *Carnival* or *Flying Dutchman* below timberline—the combination gives you well over two miles of nonstop skiing. Similar terrain can be found on *Cliffhanger, Chipper, DSQ, Kangaroo,* and *Ed's Garden.*

Best Expert Skiing

For challenge, try the steep and narrow *Summit Chutes* and (on the back side of the summit) *Cow's Face.* The *Cirque* is endlessly entertaining, steep, and narrow. For moguls, check out *Downunder West.* On a powder day *Boomerang* provides good pitch and deep drifts sheltered between the Outback forests. Those woods offer spectacular, deep powder on storm days.

Snowboarding

The superpipe runs beween *Tippy Toe* and *Canyon* runs, off Pine Marten Express. The *Slopestyle* course runs down *Grotto Trail,* near Red Chair. Another major terrain park, Air Chamber, runs to skier's left of Skyliner Express lift, and there's a smaller park, for kids, under the Sunshine Accelerator beginner lift.

Convenient Lodging

Your best bets are the **Inn at the Seventh Mountain** and **Sunriver Lodge,** both about 15 miles down the road. Sunriver has its own airstrip, a handy item if you happen to fly your own plane. **Entrada** sits halfway between the Inn and the town of Bend.

Best Eats

On the mountain, all three lodges have good cafeterias. The Pine Marten Lodge, at mid-mountain, has four eateries: **Scapolo's** for pizza; **Pinnacles** for pastry, coffee, and smoothies; **Skiers Palate** for Northwest cuisine; and the **Pine Marten Grill** for broiler, deli, and Japanese specialties. In town, my favorites include the **Deschutes Brewery** (burgers and microbrew) and the picturesque **Pine Tavern** (traditional American).

Mount Bachelor Data

Mountain Statistics

Vertical feet	3,365 feet
Base elevation	6,300 feet
Summit elevation	9,065 feet
Longest run	1.5 miles
Average annual snowfall	350 inches
Number of lifts	13: 7 high-speed detachable quads; 3 triple chairs; 2 surface lifts; 1 moving carpet
Uphill capacity	23,000 skiers per hour
Skiable terrain	3,683 acres
Opening date	Mid-November
Closing date	May
Snowboarding	Yes

Transportation

By car From Eugene, 2.5 hours via Route 126, then east on U.S. Highway 20; 3.5 hours from Portland via U.S. Highway 26, then south on U.S. Highway 97; 6 hours from Seattle/Tacoma via I-5, then U.S. Highways 26 and 97; from northern California via I-5 to Weed, then north on U.S. Highway 97.
By plane Major airlines to Portland or United Express to Redmond, Oregon.
By bus Free shuttle bus from Bend.

Mount Bachelor Data (continued)

Key Phone Numbers

Ski-area information	(800) 829-2442 or (541) 382-2442
Snow report	(541) 382-7888
Reservations	(800) 987-9968
Website	www.mtbachelor.com

Crystal Mountain

Crystal Mountain is a 7,000-foot peak just east and a little north of Mount Rainier, literally in the volcano's evening shadow. Crystal shares Rainier's weather, pulling copious snow out of storms tracking in from the Gulf of Alaska. While Crystal's powder often falls al dente, the mountain provides plenty of pitch to keep expert skiers moving through it.

Crystal is also the best-kept secret in American skiing. Who would believe that you could take an area with 2,300 acres of skiable terrain, 3,100 feet of steep vertical, ten lifts, and 30 feet of snowfall in an average year and hide it in such a way that folks in the Midwest and California have never heard of it? Crystal owes some of its obscurity to the fact that there are smaller Crystal Mountains in Michigan (375 vertical feet) and in British Columbia (600 vertical feet). Outside the lucky state of Washington, skiers may simply be confused.

Getting to the big Crystal means a 90-minute drive from either Seattle or Tacoma. To navigate from Enumclaw, pick up Route 410 to the east and climb this two-lane forest track along the Greenwater and White rivers until the road ends. Turn left and drive six miles up the ski area access road. During the winter months, Crystal is the only destination on this route, and the only traffic will be skier traffic. Carry chains for use on the steep access road. You can also ride the weekend bus from Seattle, Bellevue, Tacoma, Renton, and Enumclaw (call (800) 665-2122 for reservations).

The ski area sits below a ridgeline that crests at four different places, making for lots of subsidiary ridges and intervening bowls to catch and shelter the powder. While the mountain is wild, with a potentially confusing diversity of bowls and chutes, the lifts are laid out intelligently. Most lower lifts—especially Discovery and Quicksilver at the head of the valley (to your left as you look up from the base lodge) are of a gentle to moderate pitch and are appropriate for beginners and low intermediates. The third lift here, Gold Hills, serves a broad intermediate slope designed for setting slalom and GS courses. The upper lifts, those going to the ridgeline, serve mostly advanced and expert terrain, with a few long, rolling cruisers, but nothing appropriate for new skiers or even for hesitant intermediates. Two huge backcountry areas provide plenty of natural snow challenge for experts.

If Crystal has a drawback, it's the weather. When the weather is nice, the grooming crews turn the cruising runs into smooth carpets, and the views of Rainier and the surrounding Cascade ridges are superb. But when a three-day Gulf of Alaska storm rolls in, visibility in the bowls drops to nil in snow and fog. Experts revel in steep powder chutes and glades, but intermediates bog down in heavy Cascade concrete. You don't get 350 inches of snow in an average year without enduring storm cycles. I've talked with Seattle-area skiers who complain that in their years of skiing Crystal they've never seen the sun, and then there are others who swear the weather's always fine. The trick is to live in the Seattle-Tacoma area and to go skiing on the day after the storm breaks.

Parking is plentiful and free, but only the early arrivals get to park close in at the upper lot. The lower lots stretch half a mile away down the road, which means a ride on a shuttle or a long uphill trudge to the lifts. The base lodge climbs the hill, too—buy your lift ticket at the bottom of the steps before heading up toward the lodge and lifts, or you'll just have to cycle back later and start the climb over again.

Crystal is waiting for Forest Service approval to build new lifts and a summit tram, which should solve the village traffic flow problems. For now, the fastest way up the mountain is via the Chinook Express six-person chair, to the Rainier Express high-speed quad. This route puts you at Summit House, the mountaintop restaurant. Ski straight ahead into Green Valley, a big rolling bowl stitched with two groomed intermediate cruisers. Turn right and follow the fast *Iceberg Ridge* into steep *Iceberg Gulch* (this shady, sheltered gulley is often icy) or the long, steep plunges back to the base area called *Bull Run* and *Exterminator.* The southeast face of the peak, on either side of Rainier Express, is a broad collection of glades and bowls called *Last Scream* (south of the lift) and *Sunnyside* (north of the lift, leading toward *Iceberg Gulch*). There is a relatively easy intermediate run looping back to the base of Rainier Express—the popular *Lucky Shot.* You can get there by turning right when you get off the lift, following the ridgeline about 100 yards, and cutting right to follow the cat track back under the lift. *Lucky Shot* meanders out into a broad bowl, then steepens briefly before the trees close in to funnel everyone back toward Rex. Watch for cross traffic just above the lift station.

The Green Valley runs collect at the bottom of Green Valley Express, serving both *Green Valley* and the more secluded (and steeper) Snorting Elk Bowl. *Northway Ridge,* a cruiser, follows the area's northern boundary back to Green Valley lift; as you ski it, check out the views into the North Back Country bowls and ridges. Intermediates should return to the lift base; experts can continue down the ridge as it turns into the very steep *Right Angle.* Intermediates can exit Green Valley from the bottom of the lift via the long, looping *Kelly's Gap* road.

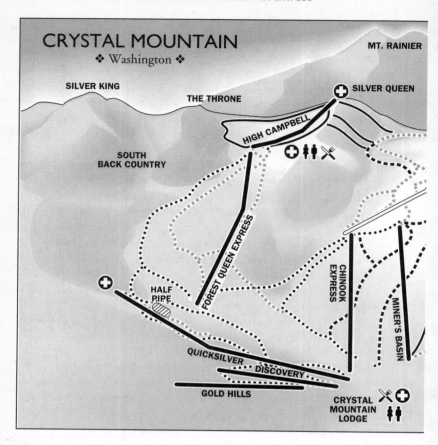

From the top of Chinook Express, take a left and follow the signs back to the Forest Queen. From here, three long intermediate cruisers (*CMAC, Magoo,* and *Downhill*), and the easy 3.5-mile *Queens* descend to the base arc. Above the Forest Queen, the High Campbell double lift goes to Silver Queen, Crystal's highest summit (7,002 feet), with truly steep expert shots into Campbell Basin (to the south of Grizzly Ridge) and onto the north face (north of Grizzly Ridge). When the snow is stable, experts can hike over the Throne into Avalanche Basin and South Back Country.

The Back Country areas are avalanche-controlled but not groomed. Don't bother going into either area unless you're confidently expert in natural snow, tight chutes, and trees; never go in unless avalanche danger is low, and never ski alone.

South Back Country terrain generally requires hiking to reach Avalanche Basin, Silver Basin, or the flanks of Silver King and Three Way Peak. Exiting

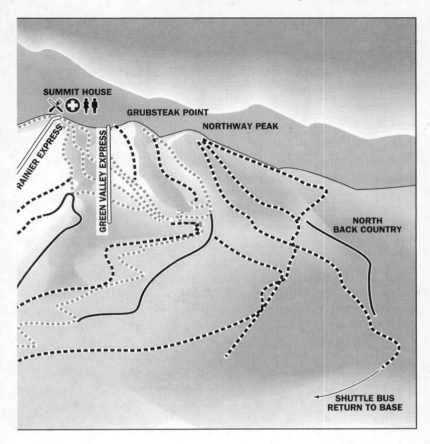

the area means skiing the steep woods overlooking the head of the valley.

North Back Country is more accessible—just drop off Northway Ridge into Paradise Bowl, or make the short walk over Northway Peak to ski the farther bowl lines or the tree lines below *Brand X*. You get back to the base area along the I-5 cat track or ski *Lower Northway* to the shuttle bus pickup that is about a mile down the access road. Buses run about every half-hour.

Best Beginner Skiing

New skiers train on *Discovery*. Novices can cruise *Quicksilver* and *Tinkerbell* on the Quicksilver lift and *Queens* on Forest Queen. *Broadway* and *Skid Road* are easy ways down from Chinook Express and Miner's Basin lifts, but mind the fast traffic exiting the upper mountain, especially at lunch and closing hours.

Best Intermediate Skiing

The best of Crystal's intermediate skiing comprises *Green Valley, Lucky Shot,* and *Downhill.*

Best Expert Skiing

For high adventure, it's the Back Country areas. Hook up with a group of locals for expert guidance. For high-speed cruising, try *Green Valley, Downhill,* and (when groomed) *Iceberg Ridge* and *Gulch,* and *Bull Run.* For bumps, ski *Exterminator* and *Sunnyside.* For tree skiing, try the K2 Face.

Snowboarding

The new half-pipe is near the top of *Quicksilver* lift.

Convenient Lodging

Crystal Village has only three hotels plus two small condo complexes. All are situated within walking distance of the lifts. For hotel reservations call (888) 754-6400; for condominium reservations, call (888) 668-4368. At the base of Crystal Mountain is **Alta Crystal,** offering chalet-style accommodations. For reservations, call (800) 277-6475.

Best Eats

At the base, visit the **Cascade Grill** in the Day Lodge for breakfast or lunch, or for table service lunches, there's **The Bullwheel** on the top floor of the lodge. On the mountain, the **Summit House** (at the top of Rainier Express) serves pizza and pasta. For deli and sit-down dining, try the **Snorting Elk** at the Alpine Inn (soup, sandwiches, chicken, and steak).

Crystal Mountain Data

Mountain Statistics

Vertical feet	3,100 feet
Base elevation	4,400 feet
Summit elevation	7,012 feet
Longest run	2.5 miles
Average annual snowfall	340 inches
Number of lifts	10: 2 high-speed quads; 2 high-speed detachable six-person lifts; 2 triples; 3 doubles; 1 children's surface lift
Uphill capacity	19,110 skiers per hour
Skiable terrain	2,300 acres
Opening date	Mid-November
Closing date	Mid-April
Snowboarding	Yes

Crystal Mountain Data (continued)

Transportation (continued)

By car From Seattle or Tacoma, 90 minutes via Route 167 to the Puyallup area, then Route 410 east.

By bus Daily service from Kent, Auburn, and Enumclaw. Call the ski area for schedule.

By air Major carriers to Sea-Tac Airport.

Key Phone Numbers

Ski-area information	(360) 663-2265
Snow report	(888) 754-6199
Website	www.skicrystal.com

Stevens Pass

When the Great Northern Railroad built its tortuous switchbacks up the Wenatchee River, over the pass, and down the Skyhomish, the deep snow made it nearly impossible to keep the tracks open in winter. In 1910, a nine-day blizzard triggered avalanches that swept two stalled trains into the river, killing 100 travelers. It still snows like that on Stevens Pass. January 1990, for instance, yielded 242 inches (20 feet)! In the course of that winter, the highway department cleared 191 avalanches off the road. In an average year, the place gets 415 inches of snow.

The ski area has been popular with Seattle day skiers since its first rope tows were strung after World War II. In the late 1980s, Stevens opened the vast Mill Valley area on its back side and transformed from a little intermediate hill into a major site for adventure skiing.

Stevens Pass now boasts 1,125 skiable acres and ten lifts—major-league stuff for a day area with no lodging. Driving up U.S. Highway 2 from the Seattle-Everett area (about 90 minutes from Seattle), you get a queasy Twilight Zone sense that you've made a 3,000-mile wrong turn and wound up in New England. The town of Startup (where you start up the pass, of course) even has a white church and steeple. The misty weather, clapboard houses, and twisting two-lane roads are vintage Vermont. But look closer and the trees are unmistakably bigger, the rivers wilder, the verticals more profound than anything in the East.

At the ski area, a short hike from the parking lot takes you past a new day lodge, completed in the summer of 1999. It features a food pavilion, a bar and lounge, guest services, and ticketing. The modern steel-and-glass, three-story base lodge is also up-to-the-minute, with spotless lounge areas and a first-class cafeteria featuring an unlimited variety of deli sandwiches.

The terrain is equally varied and it's nice that each lift serves a specific type of terrain. Three of the older lifts have been completely converted

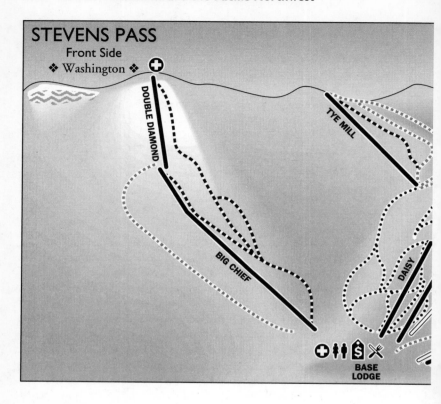

and redesigned; two have been converted into high-speed quads, and the Tye-Mill lift has been changed to a triple chair with a redesigned loading area. Beginners will be happy on Daisy lift, intermediates on the long Skyline and Brooks lifts, and experts on Big Chief and Hogsback lifts.

The front side of Stevens, with its seven lifts, is pretty good for mainstream skiing, with a nice mix of cut trails and some small glades. But the Mill Valley back side is a huge, wonderful bowl, cleared years ago of most of its hemlock and silver fir by a lightning-strike fire. Like Vail's back side, the bowl is roughly subdivided into drainages—Corona Bowl, Pegasus, and Polaris—with long hogback ridges between them.

My own favorite shots are along the perimeters. On the right side going down, the power-line cut called *Borealis* has exactly the same pitch as the wonderful clear-cuts you stumble across in Canada's Cariboos. On the left, the ski-area boundary follows Polaris Creek, a narrow gully into which the snow drifts deeply with each storm. The creek forms a perfect half-pipe. Bank off the sides or jump the right-hand edge onto Andromeda Face.

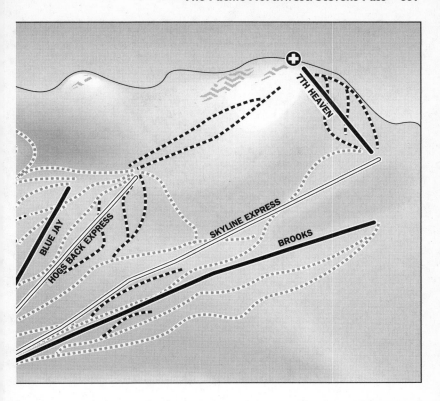

The back side is served by two long lifts, Jupiter and Southern Cross. Southern Cross is actually an extension of the front-side Double Diamond lift. The cable runs from one terminal up over the summit and down to the other terminal. Everyone gets off at the top, regardless of which direction you're riding. Stevens Pass simply got two lifts for the price of one motor.

Best Beginner Skiing

You can find this on anything off Daisy lift.

Best Intermediate Skiing

For long groomed cruising, try *Aquarius* in Mill Valley and the easy rolling trails along Skyline and Brooks lifts.

Best Expert Skiing

For challenge, ski the short, steep chutes off Seventh Heaven lift, and several more off Double Diamond. For high-speed cruising, it's *I-5* and *Aquarius,* on the back side. For powder, it's all of Mill Valley after a storm.

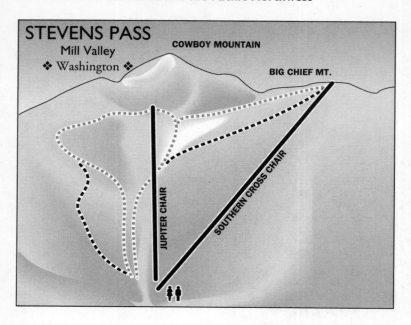

Snowboarding

The Bent Monkey terrain park includes a superpipe. Find it to skier's left of Brodes Chair—where it's also accessible from the high speed Skyline lift.

Convenient Lodging

There is none, but Leavenworth, a resort town with plenty of motels and some good restaurants, lies 34 miles to the east—the wrong direction for Seattle skiers. For folks from the city, it's usually easier to head home on Saturday night.

If you do opt for Leavenworth, try the Icicle Inn, Der Ritterhof, or the **Enzian.** The German names are not accidental—Leavenworth does its level best to look like a Bavarian village.

Best Eats

At the mountain, the new day lodge cafeteria does a great deli act. In Leavenworth, try **Kristall's** for family-style dining and **Katzenjammer's** for steak and seafood.

Stevens Pass Data

Mountain Statistics

Vertical feet	1,800 feet
Base elevation	4,061 feet
Summit elevation	5,845 feet

Stevens Pass Data (continued)

Mountain Statistics (continued)

Longest run	1.5 miles
Average annual snowfall	450 inches
Number of lifts	10: 2 high speed quads; 1 quad; 4 triples; 3 doubles
Uphill capacity	15,210 skiers per hour
Skiable terrain	1,125 acres
Opening date	Late November
Closing date	Mid-April
Snowboarding	Yes

Transportation

By car From Seattle, 90 minutes via Route 522, then west on U.S. Highway 2.

Key Phone Numbers

Ski-area information	(206) 812-4510
Snow report	(206) 634-1645
Website	www.stevenspass.com

Mission Ridge

Smack in the middle of Washington, 6,000 feet above the town of Wenatchee on the Columbia River, lies a horseshoe canyon called Squilchuck (not much of a name). The ski area at the head of the canyon is Mission Ridge (nearby Mission Peak was named for the French priests who worked among the local Indians in the 1860s).

Bowls and glades cascade down both sides of the canyon from the 6,770-foot summit. Skiable vertical is a modest 2,200 feet, but the full vertical is skiable in a single, long, giddy run from most points along the three-mile circumference of the horseshoe. This means that the number of lines is nearly unlimited.

You can cruise the groomed trails that loop and bank up the lower walls of the canyon or traverse along the ridge and drop into broad, steep powder fields like Bowl Four or through the chutes of Bomber Cliffs.

Mission Ridge has only four chairlifts, but they fan out around the canyon to serve the entire 2,000 acres of terrain. Almost anything with snow on it is skiable here, a circumstance that tends to breed hard-core skiers. Scot Kauf, a former mogul pro champ, mastered his craft at Mission Ridge; and Bill Johnson, the first American to win a World Cup downhill, trained here en route to the U.S. Ski Team. The current generation is represented by U.S. Ski teams Slalom, Star, Tour, and Rothrock.

It's a 12-mile climb from Wenatchee and a three-hour drive from Seattle. The remote location puts Mission Ridge out of reach of all but those smart skiers who are determined to find good snow and uncrowded lifts.

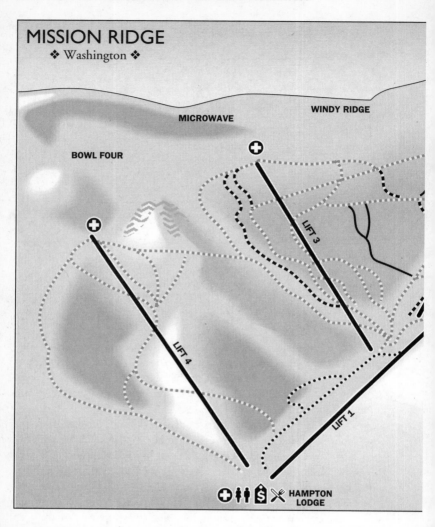

A typical Saturday draws about 2,500 skiers, and since the lifts haul 4,300 skiers per hour, the crowd can count on half a dozen runs before lunch.

Bomber Bowl is named for the Army Air Force B-24 Liberator that crashed here in rain and fog back in 1944. A hunk of the plane's wing is mounted on posts in Bomber Bowl.

A rollicking roller coaster, *Bomber Bowl* run skirts the base of Bomber Cliffs. If you know the terrain well enough to anticipate the landings off the numerous blind jumps, you can let your skis run. You can also turn right off *Bomber Bowl* and plunge down *Bomber Chutes* or *Ka-Wham*, all labeled as double diamonds. Locals consider *Nertz*—to the right of

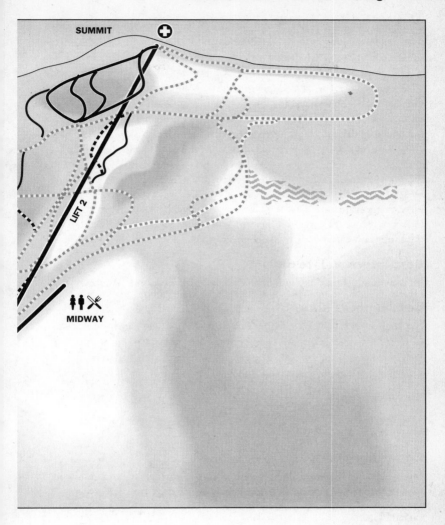

Bomber Bowl—one of the prime bump runs. The pitch—about 30 degrees—is just right, and it sits in full view of Lift 2 so that a knee-proud young *Nertz*-pounder will always have an audience.

On the east side of the canyon, the big cruising runs are *Skookum, Toketie, Kiwa,* and *Tillikum.* They flow more or less parallel to Lift 3. These are the first runs to be groomed after a storm, so the ungroomed shots between them are the first target for powder moles. Most of the lower runs are flatter and easier cruisers or beginner terrain.

The Castle Face cliffs off Lift 4—and the area above Lift 4—offer some of the mountain's best skiing. Follow the ridgeline eastward from the summit to *Bowl 4* and peel off the rim rock for the long, consistent blast to join up with the *Chak Chak* and *Sitkum* cruisers. But be aware that *Bowl 4* is technically out-of-bounds and is not patrolled. Check with the ski patrol before heading there.

The canyon gets an average of about 12 feet of natural snow each winter. That's only half of what they get at Crystal Mountain, which is some 70 miles by air to the west at the same elevation. But because Mission Ridge is on the eastern, desert-facing slope of the Cascades, the natural snow here is considerably drier and lighter than on the ocean-facing slope. It averages 10% density—closer in quality to Rocky Mountain fluff (6–8%) than to Cascade concrete (up to 15%). It's powder heaven in Pacific terms.

Best Beginner Skiing

New skiers train on *Mimi,* which is served by Lift 1. If Mission Ridge lacks anything, it's expansive beginner terrain—unlike most local areas, the mountain caters mostly to advanced skiers.

Best Intermediate Skiing

Intermediates should try out *Bomber Bowl, Skookum,* and *Toketie.*

Best Expert Skiing

For challenge, try *Bomber Cliffs, Chutes,* and *Ka-Wham* and the trees in *Central Park* and *Castle Peak Face.* For powder, ski *Bowl 4.* For bumps, it's *Nertz, Lemolo,* and *Lip Lip.* For fast cruising on groomed terrain, try *Tillikum* and *Bomber Bowl* plus *Elip* into *Sitkum.*

Snowboarding

The terrain park—new for the 2003–2004 season—is located on Katsuk run, near the top of lift 2.

Convenient Lodging

Mission Ridge has no lodging on site. Out-of-towners stay at hotels in Wenatchee (try **West Coast Hotel, Red Lion, Cedars Inn, Rivers Inn**).

Good Eats

At the mountain, the **Hampton** base lodge serves the usual cafeteria fare; also located here is **McGlinn's** for sit-down dining, including local microbrews and regional wines. The **Midway Café** at the bottom of Lifts 2 and 3 serves gourmet pizza and soup, plus salads and barbecue.

Mission Ridge Data

Mountain Statistics

Vertical feet	2,200 feet
Base elevation	4,570 feet
Summit elevation	6,770 feet

Mission Ridge Data (continued)

Mountain Statistics (continued)

Longest run	5 miles
Average annual snowfall	Estimated at 136 inches
Number of lifts	6: 4 double chairs; 2 tows
Uphill capacity	4,300 skiers per hour
Skiable terrain	2,000 acres
Opening date	Early December
Closing date	Early April
Snowboarding	Yes

Transportation

By car From the Seattle/Everett area, 2.5 hours via U.S. Highway 2 or I-90 to U.S. Highway 97, then Route 2; from Spokane, 3 hours via U.S. Highway 2.

By bus Free weekend bus service from downtown Wenatchee.

By air Horizon to Wenatchee (18 miles).

Key Phone Numbers

Ski-area information	(509) 663-6543
Snow report	(800) 374-1693 or (509) 663-3200
Website	www.missionridge.com

Mount Baker

By comparison with the other resorts in this book, Mount Baker is tiny. But by virtue of its wild terrain and wilder weather, it looms large in reputation.

During the winter of 1998–99, 95 feet of snow fell on Mount Baker. It's a world record for shiploads of snow at a lift-served ski area. Locals surfed through the winter sucking air through snorkels. Crews had to dig out the lifts almost daily.

That massive snowfall settled down to about 40 feet of base. If you want to see what that looks like, just ride Mount Baker's Chair 6. About two-thirds of the way up, the record-setting snowpack is marked on a lift tower. More to the point, look at the ladders on the uphill sides of the towers: They're twisted by the weight of the snow.

You probably won't find a 40-foot base when you visit Mount Baker. In a "normal" year the area closes with only about 30 feet of snow on the ground. What you will find, when the snowclouds lift, is some of the most amazingly vertical scenery in North America, along with a unique concentration of steep terrain and rowdy natural half-pipes.

Mount Baker is a sort of private club for expert skiers and snowboarders. The nearest lodging and nightlife lies 17 miles away in sleepy Glacier, Washington, and the resort has to generate its own electricity, which obviates the installation of high speed lifts. So this isn't exactly a

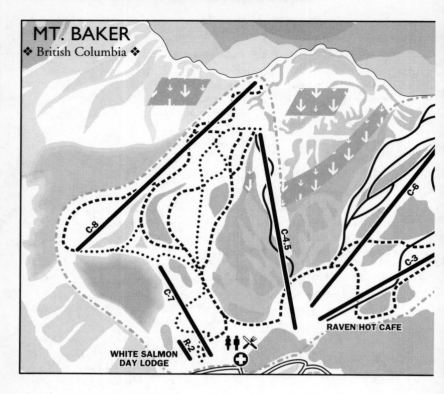

destination resort. Instead, the mountain draws a crowd of bawdy youngsters dedicated to one thing: finding the awesome powder line through that next chute. The core population here is pure of soul and single-minded in pursuit of the next plunge. To get there, they ride a collection of Model T lifts and hike into some truly scary out-of-bounds wilderness.

Local mountaineers began ski touring here beginning around 1927, setting out from the luxurious Mount Baker Lodge in Heather Meadows. The lodge burned down in 1931, but skiers kept coming, and the first rope tow opened in 1931. It wasn't exactly friendly terrain for beginners. It takes guts and strength to slog through the huge accumulations of heavy Coast Range snow. On a powder day, you need serious pitch to keep up planing speed, at least on traditional-width skis. Fortunately, that pitch exists everywhere you look. Over the decades, lots of local kids learned to ski here, but any beginner above the age of 12 would have the sense to be terrified.

The scene changed dramatically after 1982, when some of the first snowboarders discovered the natural half-pipes. Snowboards float on the Cascade Crud where skis tend to sink out of sight. In 1985, Tom Sims

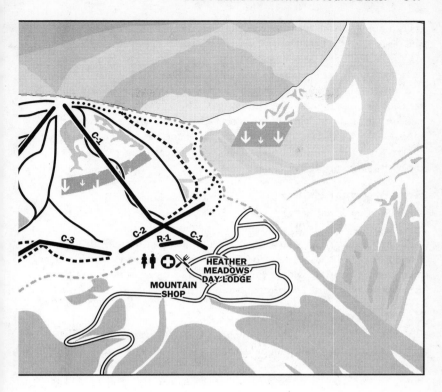

and some buddies set the first of the Legendary Banked Slalom races down *The Chute,* a steep couloir under Chair 1. Today snowboarders outnumber skiers here on most weekends.

The Layout

Mount Baker offers two base areas and two summits. Beginners should head straight to the upper area, where the Heather Meadows Day Lodge (open only on weekends and holidays) serves the terrain beneath Panorama Dome. Just above the lodge, Chairs 2 and 3 provide access to a halfdozen gentle trails. Intermediates can ride Chair 1 to the Panorama Dome summit, but the only user-friendly routes from the top will be the groomed cruisers labeled *Austin* and *Blueberry.* Everything else involves at least a short steep pitch or a squeeze-play between overhanging cliffs.

Most intermediates will launch from the modern White Salmon Lodge, beneath the Hemispheres summit. White Salmon serves as the day lodge all week long. From here, you must ride Chair 7, which can be a bottleneck on busy days. Turn left at the top of the chair and follow *Otto Bahn* trail to the Chair 8 terrain—a network of groomed cruising trails looping off the Hemispheres summit. Or turn right from Chair 7 and descend to the broad gulley between the two peaks. Here three chairs fan upward: Chair 4 back toward Hemispheres, Chair 3 toward Heather Meadows, and the long Chair 6 to Panorama Dome.

It sounds simple enough, but the intervening terrain is broken by a series of cliff bands and avalanche closures. The rolling intermediate terrain off Chair 8 ends abruptly to skier's left of *Nose Dive* trail, where it plunges over a cliff into the steep tree shots some locals refer to as The Library. Turn right at the top of Chair 6 and it's easy to get stuck above the cliffs on the north face of Panorama.

Best Beginner Skiing

From Heather Meadows Day Lodge, descend to the gentle valley serves by Chairs 2 and 3. You'll spend most of the day on the Chair 2 quad. If it's a weekday, you'll have to get here via a roundabout route: Ride Chair 7 and follow *Expresso;* near the bottom, stay to your left and scoot over to the Chair 3 extension, which will take you up to the shoulder leading to *Heather Meadows.* Follow *Mitz's* down to Chair 2.

Best Intermediate Skiing

Best bet for cruising is to cycle on Chairs 4 and 8, the two fixed quads. *Daytona* is a rolling cruiser looping under Chair 8 along the area boundary. *Easy Money, White Salmon* and *Nose Dive* also follow Hemisphere's northeast ridge, falling off to the left toward the base area. Stay to the left as you near the bottom to return to Chair 4 and the summit; turn right to hit the White Salmon Lodge for lunch and the short Chair 7.

Between these trails lie a dozen or more short steep powder pitches, some of them lightly gladed. It's great terrain for learning advanced and expert terrain skills, because you can dive off the gentle groomed terrain into a short challenge, and dive right out again.

A sweet diversion off Chairs 4 and 8 is the long, straight natural half-pipe leading into *Nose Dive* run (some of the locals call it *Crack Pipe*). It's fun to dive in here for rhythmic medium-radius turns.

Best Expert Skiing

Off Chair 4, bragging rights belong to those who've negotiated the long couloir called *Gabl's;* or bail out to skier's right into *The Library Chutes.*

Chair 6 accesses a number of easier tree runs and open faces. *Entrance, Sticky Wicket,* and *Canuck's Delux* are shelving runs, with steep bits and glades, ideal for learning powder skiing skills. The upper shots exit into *Razorback Canyon,* a groomed shot between cliffs, intimidating for its narrow width rather than for its pitch. You don't want to pour through here in company with a pack of out-of-control intermediates.

Turn right off Chair 6 for the broad steep *North Face* or *Gold Mine* runs; to skier's right of *Gold Mine* (skier's left of Chair 6) is a nicely unmarked glade with some of the best sheltered tree skiing on the mountain. It dumps you onto *Honkers* trail for the run back to Chair 6.

Also reachable from the top of Chair 6 is the truly scary and exhilarating *Chute*—but before diving in there, inspect it carefully while riding Chair 1. The *Chute* can fill up with huge blocks of ice falling off the cornice on its west rim, and unless the chunks are covered with about six feet of new snow you'll want to plan your route with care.

Out of bounds

The top of Hemispheres offers a wilderness gate through which hikers can ascend The Shuksan Arm, a sharp spine climbing southeast toward the Mount Shuksan summit. Within a quarter mile, you can dive off the cornice into a dozen different steep chutes and traverse back into the ski area onto *Daytona* run, above the Lift 8 loading station. All the OB terrain at Mount Baker has the potential for massive avalanche, and helicopter rescue is *verboten* in the wilderness areas. So the patrol won't let you depart unless you can prove you know what you're doing and are properly equipped.

Snowboarding

Mount Baker maintains a massive and entertaining terrain park, Blood Alley, to skier's right of *Easy Money* trail. It's hard to miss.

Convenient Lodging

It's all down the road. Closest lodges are the **Snowline Inn,** the **Mount Baker Inn,** and the **Glacier Creek Lodge** in Glacier (17 miles), but you'll find another two dozen hotels, condo complexes and motels strung out along the Mount Baker Highway. Cheapest way to stay is to check into one of the big roadside motels (**Motel Six, Val-U-Lodge**) along I-5 in Bellingham.

Best Eats

On the mountain, you have only three choices: the two base lodge cafeterias and the snug little **Raven Hot Café** at the bottom of Chair 4.

For dinner, out along the highway, the choices are more entertaining. In Glacier, **Graham's Restaurant** (call (360) 599-1964) does steak, burgers, fresh fish and salads; across the street is the charming **Milano's Pasta & Pizza** with deli sandwiches as well as nice Italian specialties. Further downstream, at Maple Falls, find the **Frosty Inn** steak house and the rowdy **Fuego** bar.

Mount Baker Statistics

Mountain Statistics

Vertical feet	2,200 feet
Vertical feet	1,589 feet
Base elevation	3,500 feet
Summit elevation	5,089 feet
Longest run	1.75 miles
Average annual snowfall	645 inches
Number of lifts	7 chairs; 2 rope tows
Uphill capacity	11,000 per hour
Skiable terrain	1,000 acres
Opening date	Mid-November
Closing date	End April (weekends only in April)
Snowboarding	Yes

Transportation

By car Take I-5 to Bellingham and use exit 255. Follow Highway 542 east about 80 minutes (56 miles). From Seattle, driving time is 2.5 hours. From Vancouver, 2 hours: follow Highway 1 east to Abbotsford; cross the U.S. border to Sumas and take Highway 547 south to Highway 542 east.

By bus Baker Shuttle on weekends and holidays. Call (360) 380-8800 for reservations.

Key Phone Numbers

Snow report	Bellingham (360) 671-0211
	Seattle (206) 634-0200
	Vancouver (604) 857-1515
Reservations	800-709-7669
	http://www.mtbaker.us/info/accom.html
Website	mtbaker.us

British Columbia

Whistler/Blackcomb This is North America's biggest ski complex, in every way: extent and variety of terrain, vertical feet, and lift capacity. A modern, cosmopolitan village bustles all day and all night. Whistler Village, two hours north of Vancouver, rivals the great European resorts for sophistication and scenic grandeur. The mountain surpasses everything else on this continent for sheer leg-burning scale and challenge.

Sun Peaks The old Tod Mountain resort above Kamloops has grown up into an ultra-modern full-service village, with skiing—most of it intermediate cruising—on three peaks.

Kicking Horse Whitetooth, at Golden, bursts its bounds: A 4000-vertical-foot gondola launches skiers into a vast Valhalla of spectacular bowls and couloirs.

Fernie This Edwardian coal-mining town is like Aspen in 1960, with a joyous nightlife. The sprawling mountain offers plenty of terrain at all levels, and powder skiers will love its gladed bowls.

Panorama This hidden giant offers 4000 feet of vertical, plentiful powder bowls, a comfortable modern base village, and no crowds, ever.

Whistler/Blackcomb

Stand between the base stations of the Whistler Village gondola and Blackcomb's Excalibur gondola; they're only a few yards apart, and between them they can take you to more contiguous lift-served terrain than you'll find anywhere else in the Western Hemisphere.

Between them, Whistler and Blackcomb Mountains, located two hours north of Vancouver, provide over 7,000 acres of skiing; an even mile (5,280 feet) of vertical, a third of it above timberline; 33 lifts, half of them high-speed chairs and gondolas; four glaciers, with runs up to seven miles long. Most of the lower mountain trails are laid out as endless

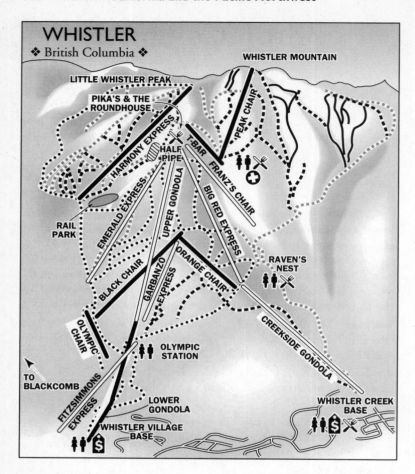

intermediate cruisers; up top experts can find everything from hairball chutes and cliff bands to broad, gentle powder bowls. The complex is simply bigger than anything outside of Europe, and like the European resorts, it attracts a cosmopolitan crowd; on the lunch deck you'll hear French, Japanese, German, Italian, Chinese, and Korean, and, of course, English. The ski terrain is so vast that even a very good skier isn't going to see all of it in a week. The descriptions for these two ski areas are broken out into separate sections that follow this combined introduction.

Whistler Resort (the term includes Blackcomb Mountain) is also clearly one of the cleanest, most efficient, most pleasant places to ski on the planet. Part of the appeal is that Whistler Resort is new. The first lifts went in at Whistler Mountain in 1966, but construction really got rolling in 1980, when Blackcomb opened. By 2003, the village boasted over 115 hotel/condominium lodges, small pensions, and B&Bs, as well as over 93 restaurants and a dozen discos.

Most skiers get to Whistler by driving up Canada's Highway 99, the Sea-to-Sky Highway from Vancouver. It's a 75-mile, two-hour trip (about five hours from Seattle counting traffic delays at the border), on good broad pavement with no mountain passes to cross. In good weather, the wonderful views across Georgia Strait toward Vancouver Island are distracting. Try to keep your eyes on the winding road. In bad weather, the road will be wet and possibly snowpacked, and, as everywhere in the Northwest, invisibly treacherous black ice is a possibility in spite of road salting. Mind your speed or the Mounties will. Canada posts speed limits in kilometers, and for some reason this baffles a lot of Murricans. Eighty kph is 50 mph.

If driving sounds like a hassle, there's hourly bus service from the Vancouver Airport.

Whistler Village sits at 2,000 feet above sea level, which is great for folks who haven't been doing their aerobic exercises. It means you sleep drenched in oxygen: none of those sleepless nights that distress sea-level lungs at 8,000 and 9,000 feet in the Rockies. By the same token, winter storms often bring rain to the village. Don't panic; this usually means snow a few hundred feet up the mountain. The summits get over 350 inches of snow a year—good, dense Gulf of Alaska snow that lasts through May. At this latitude (52 degrees north) winter days are short, so the lifts close at 3:30 p.m. Your legs will have given up by then. In March, hours extend to 4 p.m.

As in a narrow Alpine valley, most of the Village lodges are within walking and skiing distance of the lifts. There's also lots of free parking within a couple of hundred yards of the base areas, but on busy days the lots can clot with traffic. My preference is to park the car at the lodge and rely on the shuttle buses, if only because there are too many bars between the trail's end and the parking lot at the end of the day.

Convenient Lodging

Among others, you'll find ski-in/ski-out lodging at **Woodrun, Greystone, Chateau Whistler** (Blackcomb), **Delta Whistler, Powder's Edge,** and **Westbrook** (Whistler Village).

Best Eats

Among the dozens of good restaurants, I've had great meals at La Rua (continental), **Thai One On** (Thai), and **Monk's Grill** (steak and seafood).

Whistler Mountain

Whistler Mountain has two base areas, each a village in its own right. The mountain shares Whistler Village with Blackcomb Mountain, and it has Whistler Creekside all to itself about four kilometers south down Canadian Highway 99 toward Vancouver. Day skiers from the city can avoid village traffic hassles by parking at Creekside.

From Whistler Village, ride the Fitzsimmons Express chair, or take the Whistler Village gondola, rising 3,800 feet to Roundhouse Lodge, a 50,000-square-foot lodge with gourmet food and more than 1,700 seats. The gondola is the second tallest lift in North America (only the Jackson Hole tram in Wyoming serves more vertical), and it goes only to the timberline, which is about two-thirds of the way up the hill.

You can reach Roundhouse Lodge from Whistler Creekside by riding the Creekside gondola to Mid-Station (at about 4,300 feet) and then the Big Red Express.

The best bet for a newcomer to Whistler is to join one of the guided 40-minute tours offered every day at 11:30 a.m. They meet at the Guest Satisfaction Centre near the Alpine lightboard.

Most of the terrain below Roundhouse Lodge consists of broad, rolling intermediate cruising trails. You might expect to find wonderful tree skiing here, but in fact it's a temperate rain forest—below timberline the trees grow so close together as to make the woods impenetrable.

A favorite high-speed cruiser for strong locals is *Franz's*, usually groomed like an undulating superslab for over three miles back to Whistler Creekside. Less ambitious skiers head for *Jolly Green Giant,* half as long, and cycle back to the top via the Emerald Express. There are even a couple of impossibly long beginner trails from Roundhouse Lodge— the easiest way down is via *Upper Whiskey Jack* past the Green Express to *Olympic Run*—all the way to Whistler Village.

Above lies the High Alpine, a huge expanse of terrain served by the Harmony Express quad and the Peak quad. The high alpine consists of seven immense bowls. In general, only experts should ride the Peak into Whistler and West bowls. In good weather, Symphony bowl offers plenty of gentle terrain for new skiers and is easily accessible off Harmony Express. Harmony and Glacier bowls supply a good mix of intermediate piste skiing and spectacularly varied natural-snow steeps. This part of the world contains many cliff bands, so ski with a level-headed friend.

Best Beginner Skiing

Most new skiers will train on Olympic chair near the village gondola's Olympic station. But easy trails wind all the way from the top of Little Whistler Peak (6,900 feet), off Harmony Express. In good weather an athletic novice should be able to make the seven-mile run from the top via *Burnt Stew* and *Sidewinder*—it's an adventure. Beginners can also descend from Roundhouse Lodge via *Ego Bowl, Whiskey Jack,* or *Pony Trail.*

Best Intermediate Skiing

Intermediates can ski up top on *Harmony Ridge* and the *Glades,* both off Harmony Express; below Roundhouse Lodge, try *Bear Paw* and *Franz's.* For an incredibly long run, ride the Peak to the summit (7,160 feet) and pick up *Highway 86.* It's about three miles back to *Franz's,* and then another couple to Creekside or the village.

Best Expert Skiing

For challenge, explore the couloirs at the top of Glacier and West bowls, the short steep chutes on *Harmony Horseshoes* and (especially in powder) *Waterfall.*

For powder and bumps, ski the sheltered *Boomer Bowl,* a huge funnel necking down into the trees; you get there from Harmony Ridge. *Seppo's,* a consistent fall-line shot under Garbanzo Express, is nicely sheltered, so the powder drifts in deep for good storm skiing.

For high-speed cruising, blast down the aforementioned *Franz's.* Beginning at the top of Orange chair and Garbanzo Express, cruise *Dave Murray Downhill* and *Bear Paw.*

Snowboarding

Whistler's half-pipe and rail park lie below Roundhouse Lodge on GS Trail.

Best Eats

If you're driving up from Vancouver in the morning, grab breakfast on the mountain at Creekside. You can have lunch at Roundhouse Lodge, at the **Raven's Nest Restaurant** located at the top of the Creekside gondola, or at the **Garibaldi Lift Company Bar & Grill** at the village gondola base. The **Chic Pea** serves lunch at the top of Garbanzo Chair. For early birds, **Fresh Tracks** breakfast is served at dawn each day at the Roundhouse Lodge—you ride up the Whistler Village gondola in the dark, pound down the all-you-can-eat breakfast, and hit the groomed trails ahead of the crowd.

When the lifts close, check out **Dusty's Bar & BBQ,** serving up cold beer and hot music since 1965.

Blackcomb Mountain

Newer and a bit taller than Whistler, Blackcomb Mountain offers a trail layout that lies more consistently in the fall line. The fastest way up the mountain is from Blackcomb Base—take the Wizard Express to Solar Coaster Express. Between them, the two chairs lift you 3,900 feet to Rendezvous at the timberline.

The other gateway to the mountains is at Whistler Village. Here, the Excalibur gondola rises only 1,600 vertical feet to the bottom of Excelerator chair. From the top of Excelerator, ski rolling cruisers down to *Solar Coaster,* but mind the high-speed traffic merging from *Black Magic* and *Sorcerer.*

Blackcomb has its own daily mountain tour, leaving the top of *Solar Coaster* at 11:30 a.m. From the top of *Solar Coaster,* you'll find some of the best rolling cruiser trails in the world. Appropriately, one of the finest is named *Cruiser;* it drops off the Rendezvous ridge and pours the full 3,900 vertical feet (about three miles) back to the base lodge. Another niftily rhythmic groomer is *Choker;* exit to *Slingshot* or *Gear Jammer* for the rush back to base, or rest while riding back to Rendezvous aboard Catskinner triple chair.

On sunny days, follow the *Expressway* or *7th Avenue* cat track around to the base of Blackcomb peak, where 7th Heaven Express chair serves a broad powderfield leading into half a dozen broad swaths through the thin woods at timberline. The skiing here is deluxe in springtime corn.

At the top of 7th Heaven, Horstman Hut perches on the spine of the mountain overlooking Horstman Glacier. Descend to the glacier via *Blueline.* The upper half of Horstman, served by two T-bars, is of consistently intermediate pitch, and it presents no special challenge except in flat light, when it's easy to become disoriented. Below Horstman T-bar, though, the routes down grow narrow and steep; you'll ski to one side or the other of the impressive cliff band called the Great Pyramid, then dive between the trees at timberline and pound bumps down to Glacier Creek. From here, pick up Glacier Express lift and ride 2,000 vertical feet back to the glacier or ride Jersey Cream Express back to Rendezvous. You can also ride Crystal chair into a secluded network of half a dozen intermediate and advanced runs below the Crystal Hut restaurant.

The longest run on the mountain—some seven miles long—is *Blackcomb Glacier.* To get there, ride the Showcase T-bar at the head of Horstman Glacier and pop over the back. *Blackcomb Glacier* beckons, half a mile wide. You'll descend a couple of thousand feet of easy intermediate skiing, then a short bit of steeper stuff at the foot of the glacier. At timberline, all the lines converge into an endless easy run-out through the woods, looping for miles back to Excelerator Express and the base.

Best Beginner Skiing

New skiers train on Magic chair at the Blackcomb Base and can graduate to *Green Line* off Catskinner chair (*Green Line* is actually an easy cat track winding all the way from Horstman Hut to the bottom of the mountain).

Best Intermediate Skiing

You can find the best intermediate skiing on the dozen long, rolling groomers alongside Solar Coaster, Excelerator, and Wizard chairs; *Southern Comfort, Panorama,* and *Cloud Nine* on *7th Heaven;* or *Blackcomb Glacier.*

Best Expert Skiing

For challenge, Blackcomb has its share of hairball experts-only terrain. Most famous is the *Couloir Extreme,* better known to locals by its original designation, the *Saudan Couloir.* The couloir starts at an honest 50-degree pitch and "flattens" after 50 meters to a more rational 40 to 45 degrees. You'll drop about 1,000 feet before the terrain rounds out at the bottom of *Jersey Cream Bowl.* Between storms, the couloir bumps out nicely with round long-ski moguls. To get to the couloir, follow the ridge top down from Horstman Hut; the couloir will open on your left. Can't miss it.

If you skip the couloir and follow the right side of the ridge farther, it will bring you to Secret bowl, ending in the chutes called *Pakalolo;* this is terrain for experts who leave their brains at home.

Here's some more terrain your mother warned you about: at the top of Horstman Glacier, you can traverse below the cliffs overhanging Glacier Express lift and cross the ridgeline via *Spanky's Ladder* into *Garnet, Diamond,* and *Ruby Bowls*—steep routes funneling among the cliff bands, about 1,500 feet of exhilarating descent to *Blackcomb Glacier.*

For high-speed cruising, try anything groomed along *7th Heaven, Catskinner,* or *Solar Coaster,* right down to the village.

For bumps and powder, ski the broad stretch below Horstman Glacier and the Heavenly Basin.

Snowboarding

A long terrain park sprawls beneath Catskinner Chair, with a half-pipe near the bottom.

Special Traffic Precaution

At the end of the day, everyone exits via *Lower Merlin's* (to Blackcomb Base) or *Village Run* (to Whistler Village). If you're nervous about being rear-ended, consider downloading on Wizard Express or Excalibur.

Best Eats

For on-the-mountain eats, there's the **Wizard Grill** in the Blackcomb Day Lodge. There are cafeterias at Glacier Creek and Rendezvous (Rendezvous also has a nice sit-down restaurant called **Christine's**), and good, hot soups are served at **Horstman. Crystal Hut** serves a 1950s-style menu including wood-oven-roasted vegetables, meat loaf, salmon or trout fillets, and fresh-baked fruit pies, plus daily specials like roasted salmon and shepherd's pie.

Whistler/Blackcomb Data

Blackcomb Statistics

Vertical feet	5,280 feet
Base elevation	2,214 feet
Summit elevation	7,494 feet
Longest run	7 miles
Average annual snowfall	360 inches
Snowmaking	359 acres
Number of lifts	17: 1 high speed gondola; 6 high speed quads; 3 triple chairs; 7 surface lifts
Uphill capacity	29,112
Skiable terrain	3,414 acres
Opening date	Late November
Closing date	Late April
Snowboarding	Yes

Whistler Statistics

Vertical feet	5,020 feet
Base elevation	2,140 feet
Summit elevation	7,160 feet
Longest run	7 miles
Average annual snowfall	360 inches
Snowmaking	215 acres
Number of lifts	16: 2 high speed gondolas; 6 high speed quads; 2 triple chairs; 1 double chair; 5 surface lifts
Uphill capacity	29,895
Skiable terrain	3,657 acres
Opening date	Late November
Closing date	Mid-June
Snowboarding	Yes

Whistler and Blackcomb lift tickets are a combined ticket, giving skiers dual-mountain access.

Transportation

By car From Vancouver, 2 hours north via Highway 99; from Seattle, 4 hours via I-5 to Highway 99.

By bus Maverick Coach Lines several times daily. Perimeter Bus service to Whistler Village hourly.

By air Major carriers to Vancouver International Airport.

Key Phone Numbers

Guest relations	(604) 932-3434 or (800) 766-0449
Administration	(604) 932-3141
Snow report	(604) 932-4211
Reservations	(800) 777-0185
Website	www.whistler-blackcomb.com

Lito's TECH TIP

Ski Tuning without Tears

Ski tuning is a little like going on a diet or getting more exercise. A lot of skiers know they should do it but somehow don't get around to it. I'm hoping that this simple explanation will do the trick, push you over the brink, and encourage you to get your skis tuned, then keep them in perfect, or near perfect, shape. Why bother? For the simplest of reasons. You'll ski better, much better, on well-tuned skis. Often, when I noticed that one of my ski-school students wore about the same size boot as I did, I would suggest that we trade skis for a run or two, just out of curiosity. Half the time I could barely make a turn on these skis which, at Vail, were often very expensive models, the latest Rossignols, K2s, and other top-of-the-line skis that I knew should ski wonderfully. The problem was always tuning, or rather lack of it.

Here's what happens to skis that makes tuning vital. Early in the season, alas, there are always rocks showing somewhere, poking through the snow cover like mines ready to grab your skis and gouge them. A few scratches and gouges aren't that bad, but often you'll get a scratch right alongside the edge of your ski. This makes that edge dig deeper into the snow. So the ski, at least when turning in one direction, tends to "rail in" and virtually refuses to turn. A lot of skiers simply adjust to this frustrating situation, hopping their skis a little, or generally "horsing" their skis around with a lot of extra body English. Those same early-season rocks can also bash the metal edges of your skis, creating big jagged burrs that catch in the snow and interfere with the smooth sliding and gliding of your skis. A burr on the inside edge of either ski can be enough to block or break the smooth sliding action of the ski in a turn.

And then there's the damage done by just plain skiing, continuous skiing, week-end after weekend, all season long. What happens is that the base of your skis wears down more in the center than it does near the edges. This happens all sea-son long, but especially in granular spring snow conditions. The base then becomes concave or hollow. A ski in this condition is sometimes called a "railed" ski. This too causes the edges to grip excessively, hanging up the turn. What can you do?

The early-season state of your skis' bases is easy to monitor. Just run your fingers along the edges of your skis every time you take them off. They should be silky smooth to the touch. If you feel any jagged burrs, the remedy is dead simple. Just whip a small sharpening stone out of the pocket of your ski suit and rub it over the damaged edge (first parallel to the base, then parallel to the side of the ski). I'm not kidding. I always carry one of those little $2.50 Carborundum stones in my pocket until the snow gets deep and the rocks disappear in January or February. (By the way, an ordinary file won't take these burrs off your ski edge. The burr is "case hardened" from the heat of its contact with the rock, followed by the quenching effect of the cold snow. Only a sharpening stone can smooth out the torn edge.)

Long-term wearing down of the skis' bases (or the presence of a scratch or groove right next to an edge) demands more draconian measures. Take your skis in to the best tuning shop you can find (ask an instructor for a recommendation) and have them redo the bases completely. That means grinding the bases off smooth and flat with a high-tech base grinder (most likely made in Switzerland), and then touching up the job with a hand file to make sure the machine hasn't introduced any small burrs of its own. Unlike waxing, you only need to have your skis tuned a couple of times a season, not every week.

Is it worth it? You bet! A good ski tune-up by a real pro is probably the best bargain in skiing. I love to tune my skis by hand, and after years of practice I'm pretty good at it. But I can't do as good a job as one of the Montana base grinding machines that are now standard at most well-equipped shops. These machines can also put a so-called bevel on your ski edges. What's that? Beveling means that instead of the base being perfectly flat, it is filed to be a tiny bit convex—the opposite of the hollow or railed bases that you need to correct. The theory is that a slight bevel (1 degree or 1.5 degrees) is enough to make the skis initiate or start turns more easily. And it works on most, if not all, skis. If beveling your skis is an option, ask the shop for a 1-degree bevel. Don't overdo it. Of course, the shop will also wax your skis after tuning them. And you will feel like a new skier.

Fernie Alpine Resort

William Fernie, a Scots-born gold prospector, had followed gold rushes around the world: to Australia, California, and British Columbia's Fraser River Valley. But when his brother Peter got a government contract to build a road across Crowsnest Pass, Fernie realized that his fortune lay in the coal deposits on the pass. By 1887, the Fernie brothers had staked their claims, and in 1897 a railroad had been built through the pass to carry coal from the new mines. The town of Fernie, on the Elk River, sprang into being to serve the railroad and the mines, and thousands of loggers worked the forested slopes to supply timber for mine shorings and railroad ties.

The mines have a tragic history of explosions, fires and cave-ins. The town itself burned to the ground in 1904 and again in 1908, but was promptly rebuilt—the last time largely in brick. Hence the Edwardian architecture of the historic downtown district. Veteran skiers roll into Fernie's snowbound streets for the first time and experience a time warp: the place looks like Aspen circa 1958. Come back at midsummer, after the snow has melted away, and you'll find that many of the streets remain unpaved.

The mines were the basis of a healthy local economy, exporting coal worth about $1.3 million daily (in U.S. dollars). Local workers could afford to ski, and a ski club put up a rope tow in 1961, followed by a chairlift in 1963. Ski school director Heiko Socher took over as manager and eventually bought the place, cutting most of the upper mountain runs himself. In 1998 he sold the lifts to Resorts of the Canadian Rockies, which runs a dozen ski areas across the Great White, and the following year the company installed two brand new lifts in Timber Bowl, roughly doubling the lift-served terrain.

The result was a big mountain: 2800 vertical feet and 2500 acres—with a dependable average snowfall of 350 inches (29 feet). The powder literally draws skiers from around the world: Most of the ski-bum jobs in town are held by kids with Australian and Kiwi accents. They form the core of a rocking downtown social life.

Basic Navigation

The upper mountain consists of no fewer than five vast bowls, all backed up against a precipitous and largely unskiable 7000-foot ridge-line (the highest lift tops out at 6,500 feet). From east to west, the bowls are named Siberia, Timber, Currie, Lizard, and Cedar; and happily enough at least one route down the center of each bowl is marked for either beginner or intermediate cruising. Except for Cedar Bowl, everything funnels back via half a dozen easy beginner superhighways, to the base area at 3,500 feet.

The steep stuff consists of the trails and slopes cascading off the ridge-lines between the bowls, so an expert needs to know the names of the ridges. From east to west, these are Siberia, Diamond Back, the Polar Peak ending in *Stag Leap* and *Skydive* trails, North Ridge, and Snake Ridge.

The Weather

It's British Columbia. A typical winter day means the town lies under a dismal gray cloud. You could look out the window and pull the quilt over your head; bad move. Jump on the lift and, as you rise above 4000 feet, you climb out of the cloud into brilliant sunshine.

Then there are days when snowclouds get trapped against that ridge-line: you can have good visibility down below and white-out on top (this is why the top of Timber Bowl is called White Pass).

Fernie has more than its share of local ghosts and tall tales, and most of them are said to explain weather phenomena. Ask a bartender to explain The Griz, a half-human character who brings snow by firing his rifle into the clouds. Ask, too, about the weird horsehead "ghostrider" clouds which often pour off the Lizard Range

Fernie's ridgelines and bowls face due north, while the sides of the bowls—where the steep stuff lies—face east and west. This means that regardless of where the wind blows and where the sun shines, someplace on the mountain you'll find great snow.

Locals dress for powder and they're seldom wrong.

The Tour

To access the east end of the complex (Siberia Bowl, Siberia Ridge and most of Timber Bowl), use the fast Timber Bowl quad lift. Pop over onto the Siberia side for the delightfully long *Falling Star,* skiable by most low intermediates and rolling almost three miles all the way back to the base area. Traverse high under the radio tower and you get the marvelous *Morning Glory,* an exhilarating gladed powderfield. Move further to skier's left and you get a double-diamond cliff band called *Hell's Gate.* Or just follow Siberia Ridge, which finishes with a long spine-jarring mogul run.

Or go higher, turn right off the top of Siberia and ski the intermediate trails down to White Pass Quad. While riding to the top of the lift network

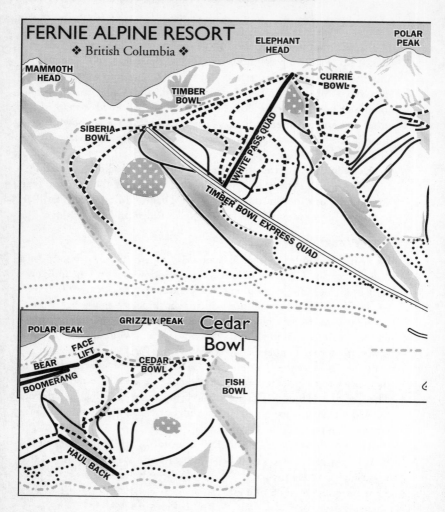

(at 6,500 feet), gaze up at the astonishing Elephant Head—the ridgeline has the shape of an elephant's head and tusks (on your left, rising to withers and rump along a half-mile of inaccessible ridgeline).

At White Pass Summit you've got a myriad of choices. About a dozen different tree runs can take you back into Timber Bowl in intermediate style (try the glades between Highline and Silver Lining) or in expert funk (Black Cloud). Take the leg-burning *Diamond Back* down the ridgeline all the way to the base area. Or turn into Currie Bowl and pick one of the broad intermediate cruisers down into the easy *Gilmar Trail*.

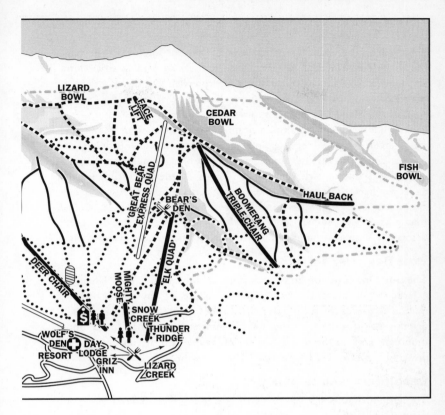

Or traverse far onto the west side of Currie to hit *Cornice Chute* and the steep woods between Currie Creek and Stag Leap.

Beginning at Stag Leap, you're skiing the "old" lift-served terrain—the traditional trails reachable, without hiking, from the top of North Ridge. To get there from the base, ride the fixed-grip Elk Quad, then scoot over to the Great Bear Express. From here you have access to all of the immense, wide-open Lizard and Snake Bowls. On the Lizard side, almost everything is marked for intermediate skiers—except for the traversing cat roads which give beginners an easy way down. Experts will want to follow the Great Bear lift line and peel off into the steep glades of Sunny Side (the west side of Lizard Bowl).

Cedar Bowl is quite different. Four broad cruisers (*Cruiser, Cedar Centre, Trillium,* and *Blueberry*) funnel into the bottom of the bowl. Don't get sucked into the double-diamond *KC Chute,* to skier's left of *Cedar Centre.*

Several days after a storm, you may still find good powder by taking the high traverse across the top of Cedar Bowl onto Snake Ridge. The double-diamond, east-facing *Steep and Deep* drops forever off the ridge, but the seldom-travelled *Red Tree,* skirting the westernmost area boundary, may harbor the last of the untracked powder. On the other side of the rope lies serious avalanche country—the tenure (Canadian for permit area) of the Island Lake Lodge snowcat operation.

Which leaves the vast complex of mostly expert terrain on the big diamond-shaped wooded face cascading eastward from North Ridge. Heiko Socher cut a big arcing trail here, and from town it looks like a boomerang, so that's what it's called, along with the fixed triple lift that hauls you back to its top. Naturally, neighboring trails got Aussie names: *Boomerang Ridge, Kangaroo,* and *Wallaby.* Interspersed are *Linda's Trail* (named for Mrs. Socher) and *Kodiak.* All these trails start out pretty damn steep, then level out toward the bottom into blue-green cruisers.

Best Beginner Terrain

The entire lower mountain is marked green. You can ride Deer Chair and explore to your heart's content without encountering anything scary other than expert skiers blasting past you en route to another lift ride. In self-defense, you owe it to yourself to ride Timber Bowl Quad to the upper mountain and ski the scenic wonder of *Falling Star.* It's also easy to get down Lizard Bowl via *Lizard Traverse* to *Dancer* to *Dipsy.*

Best Intermediate Skiing

The groomed runs off White Pass Quad—*Highline, Silver Lining,* and *Down Right*—can be counted on for delicious snow, as can the lines down Lizard Bowl from the Great Bear lift: *Bow* and *Cascade.* If it's groomed, the roller-coaster power line to skier's right of Elk Quad lift is great fun.

Best Expert Skiing

Some of the steepest runs angle northwest off the ridgelines, and their exposure means they often harbor dry, windpacked powder. In Timber Bowl, try *Big Bang* and *Mitchy Chutes,* in Currie Bowl find *Gotta Go* and *Anaconda,* in Lizard Bowl it's *Easter,* and in Cedar Bowl look for the glades of *Cedar Ridge.* On a powder day, any of the tree runs—and they are endless at Fernie—can be upgraded to expert heaven.

Snowboarding

The half-pipe and terrain park run on either side of Deer Chair, near the base area.

Most Convenient Lodging

The most luxurious of the ski-in/ski-out hotels is the **Lizard Creek Lodge** (call (877) 228-1948), which also features the nicest dining room on the mountain. Next door, the **Griz Inn Sport Hotel** (call (800) 661-0118) offers some real bargains, with smallish hotel rooms starting at $100 Canadian per night at high season. Within a short walk to the lifts are dozens of condo units and—even more fun—a cluster of privately-run chalets which operate like bed-and-breakfast places. I like the **Black Bear Chalet** (call (250) 423-5023). Buddy up to the owner-manager and you might get a guided tour of the powder shots. Book through the central reservations number: (800) 622-5007.

In town—about five miles down the road—are the motels. For a back-in-time experience, check into the **Royal Hotel** in old downtown. This elegant pile, built in 1910, has been luxuriously renovated. And it will put you near the live music in the downtown bars.

Best Eats

In town, locals pick **The Wood Bistro** for top French cuisine (phone (250) 423-7749), **Ferrelli's** for classic Italian (call (250) 423-4824), and **The Old Elevator** for nouvelle cuisine (call (250) 423-7115). The **Royal Hotel** harbors a good steakhouse (phone (250) 423-7743). Asian food? That's the **Curry Bowl** for Indian, Thai, and Japanese dishes (call (250) 423-2695). A favorite ski-bum hangout is **Rip 'n' Richard's Eatery** (burgers, pizza, and pasta) out on Highway 3 at 4th Street (phone (250) 423-3002).

Fernie Alpine Resort Data

Mountain Statistics

Vertical feet	2,811 feet
Base elevation	3,500 feet
Summit elevation	6,316 feet
Longest run	3 miles
Average annual snowfall	348 inches
Number of lifts	10
Uphill capacity	13,700 skiers per hour
Skiable terrain	2,500 acres
Opening date	Early December
Closing date	Mid-April
Snowboarding	Yes

Transportation

By car From Kalispell, Montana: 2 hours via Highway 93 across border. Turn east on Highway 3 (Crowsnest Highway) to Fernie.

From Calgary, in good weather: 3 hours via Route 2 south, then west on 22X and south on 22. Turn west on Route 3 through Crowsnest Pass and through Sparwood to Fernie. In bad weather, 3.5 hours via Route 2 south to Fort Macleod, then west on Route 3 to Sparwood and Fernie.

By air Commuter airlines to Cranbrook, 50 miles away.

Fernie Alpine Resort Data (continued)

Key Phone Numbers

Ski area information	(250) 423-4655
Snow report	(250) 423-3555
Reservations	(800) 258-7669
Websites	Ski resort: www.skifernie.com
	Town: www.fernie.com

Kicking Horse

Kicking Horse is only as old as the millennium, but it's already a legend among rowdy young powderhounds. You won't find better cheap vertical anywhere.

The railroad junction at Golden, B.C., lies at the head of one of the world's longest wetlands—200 miles of river and marsh—stretching along the Columbia River beyond the U.S. border. The walls of the valley are formed by the Purcell and Kootenay ranges. The mountainsides grow timber. The wetlands throw off fog. Climb above the fog and what you see is sunlit snow, thousands of square miles of the stuff, out to the horizon and climbing to knife-edge 9,000-foot ridges. It looks like infinity. The logging town used to have a little ski area here called Whitetooth. Now, following construction in 2001 of a 3,800-vertical-foot gondola, the town has a nearly digestible bit of that infinity. In 2002 a summit lift went in, boosting the vertical to 4,133 feet—all skiable in a single steepish shot.

Kicking Horse is a lonely miracle. There's nothing else here—no pedestrian mall, no discos, restaurants, boutiques. The tortuous access road crosses a one-lane bridge, and you'd better yield to downhill traffic there, because the truck may have no brakes left. What greets the eye at the 3,900-foot base area is a muddy parking lot, a couple of construction trailers, and a small but handsome new day lodge, two old lower mountain chairlifts and a brilliant high-speed gondola straight out of Star Wars. The gondola cable climbs into the gloom above—it might easily be rolling upward to orbit.

How this all came about is a lucky bit of bartering. At the other end of Canada, the huge Dutch construction firm Balast Nedam landed a contract to build a nine-mile bridge from New Brunswick to Prince Edward Island. Part of the deal is that Balast Nedam is to reinvest some of their profits in Canada—and why not in a huge new ski area? The town of Golden, afflicted by the collapse of the local logging industry, approved the project overwhelmingly and Balast Nedam set about putting new lifts up above the old Whitetooth ski area. The new name comes from Kicking Horse Pass and the Kicking Horse River on the other side of the valley, so named for the tethered horse which nearly killed Sir James Hector when he and John Palliser camped here in 1858 while looking for a railway

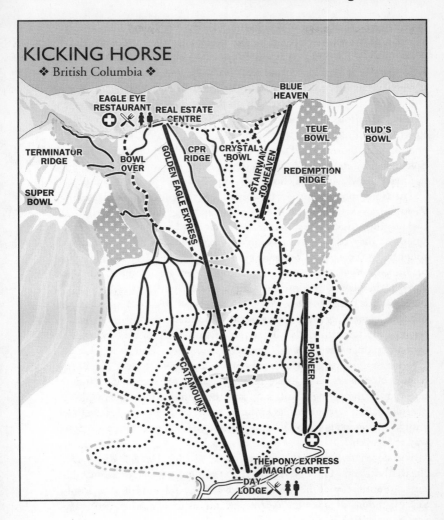

route across the mountains. (And why were they exploring so far north? The British government thought more clement routes to the south were too close to the border with the very expansionist United States.)

The Layout

The upper mountain—all the new terrain opened by the gondola and the Stairway to Heaven summit quad—consists of three long, steep ridgelines backed up against the Continental Divide, which at this point runs more or less southeast to northwest. This means that the three ridgelines run downward to the northeast, providing faces exposed to the southeast (morning sun!) and northwest (dry powder three days after the storm!).

Naturally, the three ridgelines form four vast bowls—from south to north, the major features are Super Bowl (no lift access yet), Terminator Ridge, Bowl Over, CPR Ridge, Crystal Bowl, Blue Heaven Ridge, and Feuz Bowl. North of Feuz Bowl, and west of the Divide, lies heli-ski country: it's the domain of Purcell Heli-Skiing operator Rudi Gertsch.

New arrivals should head straight up the gondola. Yes, much of the terrain is precipitous, but there's a beginner run that winds down Crystal Bowl for 6.2 miles all the way to the base. *It's a 10* is ten kilometers long and marked 10 on the trail map. Each of the bowls off the top of the gondola has an intermediate cruiser to the base: Sluiceway in Bowl Over and, in Crystal Bowl, you get a choice of Cloud Nine or Northern Lights.

The view from the top of the gondola, at the comfortable Eagle's Eye Restaurant, is staggering. The view going up the gondola is sobering. On the way up, look at the steep south-facing tree shots off CPR ridge. About 15 marked lines are accessible from the crest of the ridge, all with roughly the same pitch. You can ski one of the upper lines (*Golden Spike* or *Tunnel Vision*), then traverse left into the next group, and so on, until you exit the bowl in the intermediate *Knee Deep* trail.

As you ride the gondola, look south across Bowl Over to the sicko chutes off Terminator Ridge. Until they get a lift up there, the north-facing Terminator couloirs are strictly hike-to terrain, and ought to be: It takes dedication to plunge down *Truth, Dare,* and *Consequence* chutes.

From Eagle's Eye, descend northbound into Crystal Bowl. The north-facing couloirs off CPR Ridge mimic the lines off Terminator, and are reserved for the young, the strong, and the stupid. Most skiers will simply follow *It's a 10* into the easy rolling terrain at the bottom of the bowl, with its scattered glades. Stay left of *It's a 10* to find the summit lift, Stairway to Heaven.

The dozen tree runs on the south side of Blue Heaven Ridge carry "heavenly" names like *Epiphany* and *Amen*. Once again, the strong skier can start at the top of the ridge and move left at the bottom of each shot. Slip off the north side of *Blue Heaven* and, as on the other two ridges, you're in gnarly steep couloir country. The runout at the bottom of the wall is the boundary line.

The serious woods begin at the bottoms of the bowls, and this is where experts head on storm days. Below Crystal Bowl in the forests between *Briggs, Bubbly,* and *Euphoria* runs, find dozens of great powder lines, sheltered from the wind. To reach this terrain, you first need to ski Crystal Bowl. In a serious storm, when the upper mountain is on wind hold, ride the old Pioneer lift (from the north end of the base complex) to get steep sheltered powder off *Porcupine* and *Kicking Horse* runs.

Below Bowl Over, nature has provided something grand. In July 2000, while the gondola was under construction, a freak windstorm cleared a couple of hundred acres of forest on the lower flank of Terminator Ridge.

What looks like forest on the trail map is now a series of shallow gulleys and modest ridges, entirely bare of trees. Find the blow-down between *Hail Mary* trail and the gondola lift line. It's just the right pitch for big terrain-following GS turns.

Best Beginner Skiing

It's a 10 has to be the most exciting green trail in North America, but if you need variety, find a dozen easy cruisers off Catamount Lift from the base lodge.

Best Intermediate Skiing

Sky Crystal Bowl, if only because you can yo-yo on the summit quad. In need of an interminable cruiser? Follow *Cloud Nine* out of the bowl along *Tailspin* and into *Wiley Coyote* for a four-mile leg-burner to the bottom of the gondola.

Best Expert Skiing

Expert skiing is everywhere you look! *Kicking Horse* seems designed as an adrenaline junkie's private playground. My personal favorites are the south-facing tree runs off CPR and Blue Heaven Ridge, and the powder stashes off Bubbly.

Snowboarding

Oh, yes, there's snowboarding. But don't look for a terrain park here. All the pipes at Kicking Horse are natural.

Convenient Lodging

My first choice is the two deluxe suites upstairs from the **Eagle's Eye Restaurant.** Book one of these (for about $1,500 Canadian a night) and you get a first-class dinner. More to the point, you wake to that view across the top of the world, first tracks in the morning, and a ski guide for the day. Barring that, the ski-in/ski-out property is the **Whispering Pines** condos, starting at about $106 Canadian, per person, including lift ticket. Yes, for the price of a day pass at Aspen or Vail, you can ski Kicking Horse *and* stay in a nice three-bedroom condo.

Cheaper deals are available in town, at about a dozen different motels and bed-and-breakfast places. I rolled into Golden with no reservations and scored a motel room, with Jacuzzi, for $30 in U.S. currency.

Best Eats

The base lodge cafeteria is comfortable and the food is good. And there's a cute little yurt with a snack bar near the base of the Stairway to Heaven lift. But it baffles me why anyone would pass up a chance to lunch in comfort at **Eagle's Eye,** looking out at the kind of view you'd have atop Mount Blanc.

In town, the choice is between about a dozen uninspiring diners and two or three real restaurants. Try the **Cedar House** (call (250) 344-4679) for seafood, steak and pasta, or cruise Downtown, on the north side of the river, check out **Apostoles** and **Packers Place** on Ninth Avenue North; on the south side of the river, restaurant row is on 9th Street, where you'll find (among a scattering of family restaurants) the **Kicking Horse Grill** and **Mad Trapper Pub.**

Kicking Horse Data

Mountain Statistics

Vertical feet	4,133 feet
Base elevation	3,900 feet
Summit elevation	8,033 feet
Longest run	3 miles
Average annual snowfall	275 inches
Uphill capacity	5,000 skiers per hour
Skiable terrain	2,600 acres
Opening date	Mid-December
Closing date	Mid-April
Snowboarding	Yes
Terrain parks	Look at the mountain, bro'

Transportation

By car From Calgary 2.5 hours: Highway 1 west to Golden; at interchange, take Highway 95 south and turn right at Kicking Horse sign.

By bus From Calgary and Banff: Bus departs daily from Calgary airport at 6:30 p.m., departs Banff 8:30 p.m., arrives Golden 10:30 p.m.; return trip leaves Golden 5:20 a.m. Call Kicking Horse reservations for information.

Key phone numbers

Ski-area information	(250) 439-5400
Snow phone	(250) 439-5400
Reservations	(866) 754-5425
Website	kickinghorsesresort.com

Sun Peaks

In 1961, Kamloops businessman Harry Burfield pulled together a group of local investors and installed a lift up Mount Tod. Despite the availability of gentle slopes on friendly nearby peaks, they sited their lift on a steep meadow. It arrowed up through the forest and across a precipitous bowl. Precious little intermediate terrain could be seen—if you couldn't ski the ungroomed plungers with names like *Freddy's Nightmare* and *Challenger,* you were in trouble. There was no easy way down. Burfield and his buddies already knew how to ski. They wanted a place where local kids could learn to race, and they didn't anticipate catering to tourists.

Burfield, who died in a plane crash, wouldn't recognize the place today. Since 1991, the lift operation has been owned by Nippon Cable, the lift manufacturer; and the owner has strung sufficient lifts to turn Tod into a three-peak, 3,400-acre complex with many miles of consistent, ballroom cruising runs. The plush new village consists of 26 hotels and lodges with an international clientele. After a European tour operator pointed out that Todt is the German word for death, the new owners changed the name to Sun Peaks.

Today Sun Peaks is best known as the home of its leading citizens, Canada's World Cup heroine Nancy Greene and her husband, Al Raine. Raine was one of the key figures in developing Blackcomb Mountain and Whistler Village; the couple now operates their Cahilty Lodge in the heart of the village. These retired racers keep Sun Peaks' endless intermediate trails from turning woosified: No one seems to object to using any cruiser as a challenging GS course.

The Layout

The three mountains are Tod (still characterized by gladed gulleys and steep summit bowls above timberline) and the lower, rounded, forest-sheltered Sundance and Morrisey. Nearly all the expert runs are on Mount Tod. Sundance features half a dozen blue cruisers. The new Mount Morrisey complex, which opened in the fall of 2002, specializes in entertaining gladed intermediate runs.

Local skiers driving up from Kamloops often park at the original base area and ride the Burfield Quad—the resort's longest lift—into the network of expert and upper-intermediate trails at Tod Mountain's Top of the World summit. But most visiting skiers stay in one of the new resort village hotels, and access Tod's forested east shoulder via the Sunburst Express, which serves half a dozen long blue cruisers—and a fan of six expert runs, each with its own pitch and rhythm. Up top, between the Burfield and Sunburst lifts, is the shorter Crystal triple chair, offering access to eight or nine short steep expert runs cascading into a hidden gulley. The western shoulder of Mount Tod's summit is served by a T-bar for access to some intermediate powder lines.

Each of the three peaks offers an easy way down: A long beginner trail loops off each summit to follow an area boundary gradually back to the base. Navigating between the three lift systems involves long cat track tours through the woods. Happily, these connector routes have a good pitch, so commuters don't have to walk much; and they're well marked, so if you can read you shouldn't get lost. Burfield Outrun, for instance, goes to the bottom of Burfield Quad, and Mount Morrisey Connector goes to Morrisey Express.

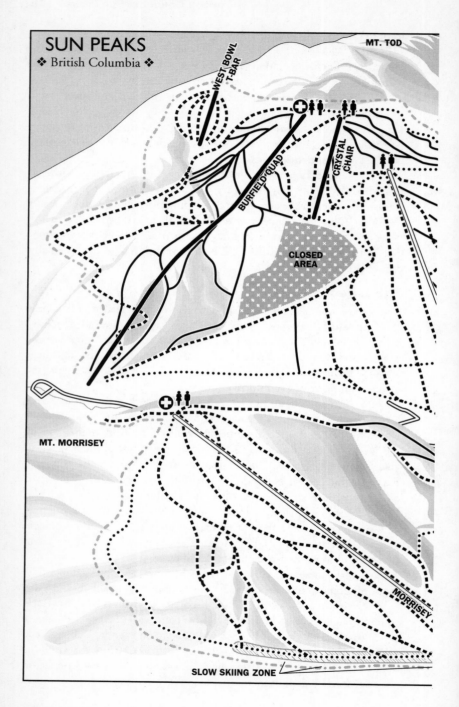

SUN PEAKS
❖ British Columbia ❖

MT. TOD

WEST BOWL T-BAR

BURFIELD QUAD

CRYSTAL CHAIR

CLOSED AREA

MT. MORRISEY

MORRISEY

SLOW SKIING ZONE

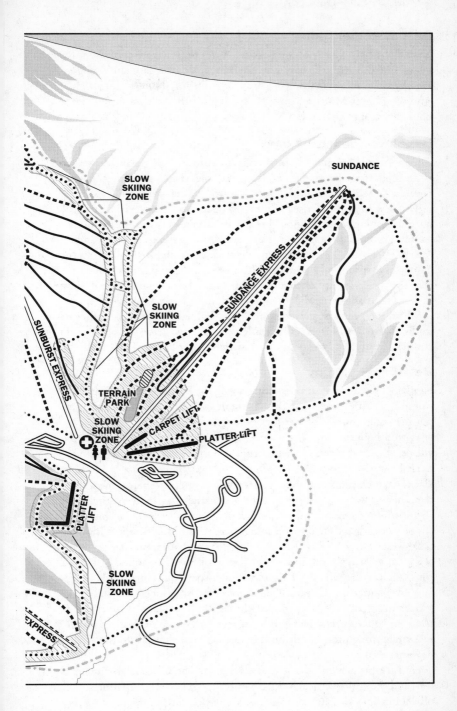

Best Beginner Skiing

New skiers have plenty of long excursion routes off the top of the three peaks. On Burfield, the easy way down is *5 Mile;* on Sundance, choose *Homesteader* (turn left from the top of the lift) or *Rambler* (turn right). And off Mount Morrisey, turn left getting off the lift and hug the area boundary along *The Sticks.*

Best Intermediate Skiing

The most convenient traditional cruisers—broad, well-groomed avenues —descend from Sundance Express, and the glades on either side of Grannie Greene's are a prime place to learn powder-skiing skills.

The new Mount Morrisey Express lift opens up a huge expanse of easy, nonthreatening forest skiing. The woods have been thinned out enough so that grooming machines can operate between the trees. The result is "groomed glades," giving intermediate skiers a chance to loop turns among the spruce and hemlock. If you're just learning to ski powder, Morrisey offers plenty of chance to dip in and out of the sheltered snow in the woods adjoining the groomed glades.

Way out on the east shoulder of Mount Tod, far from the main flow of traffic, West Bowl offers a big gentle powder bowl served by its own T-bar. It's a good place to go hide and work on your natural-snow skills.

Best Expert Skiing

Sun Peaks has a snow cat operation serving the bowls below Mount Tod's summit, at 7,060 feet, and this is where you'll find the lightest, driest powder (call (250) 578-5542 for booking information).

Within bounds, three main zones are of interest to experts. From the village, the most accessible expert runs drop to skier's left from the Sunburst Express lift line. *Cariboo, Bluff, Sting, Intimidator, 5th Avenue,* and *Broadway* look similar on the trail map, but as you move across the mountain they grow progressively steeper—each trail has its own pitch and rhythm. When groomed, these six encourage race speeds—and you'll usually see a practice course set up somewhere within this group. With their northwest aspect, the woods between these trails harbor powder for several days after each storm. And it's possible to pile up huge mileage on these runs, because they all cycle back to the high-speed Sunburst quad.

Above Sunburst, Crystal Chair serves the wide-open Crystal Bowl (skier's right) and the steep gladed chutes *Hat Trick, Sacred Line, Headwalls,* and *Bushwacker.* The longer, steeper *Green Door, Chute,* and *Spillway* angle trough the woods on the west face and dump into the *5 Mile* beginner trail back to the village.

Find leg-burners by skiing Burfield Quad. The lift rises about 2,800 feet, and the entire vertical is skiable nonstop via several steep routes. Peel off the lift line via Highway 22 into *Challenger,* or follow *Juniper Ridge* down the *Nose* into *Roller Coaster* or *Expo.* On the east side of *Juniper Ridge, Kukamungas, Sunnyside,* and *Toilet Bowl* offer morning sun, or in the spring, first corn snow. To avoid exiting into the long, intermediate *7 Mile* runout to the base, bear left onto *Round A Bout* and pop back into expert terrain below the Burfield midstation.

Experts shouldn't avoid Sundance Express and Mount Morrisey. Sundance offers a steep gulley called *Peak-A-Boo,* and the "groomed glades" on Mount Morrisey are great fun for fast cruising.

Snowboarding

Find the expert's terrain park and half-pipe right under the Sundance Express lift line. Below and to skier's right between *Sunshine* and *Sun Catcher* runs is an easier terrain park for beginners and kids.

Convenient Lodging

Nearly every property in the village can be considered ski-in/ski-out. This includes seven or eight large modern hotels and about twice that number of townhomes and chalets. Most of these places have gone up since 1991, and the village has the functional, faux-Alpine feel of a miniature Whistler or Vail. I like the **Cahilty Lodge,** but the **Sun Peaks, Sundance, Delta, Fireside, Hearthstone,** and **Heffley Inn** are equally comfortable. The plush **Pinnacle Lodge** verges on grand luxe.

Best Eats

There's a summit cafeteria at the top of Sunburst Express, but because most of the terrain is reachable with a single lift ride from the village, most skiers go to the base for lunch. Most of the hotels have on-site restaurants. I recommend **Val Senales** (fresh seafood) at Sun Peaks Lodge, **Macker's** (steak, pasta, and pizza) at the Cahilty, **Servus at Creekside** (Austrian, Canada-style) at the Hearthstone, and **Bottom's Bar** at the Sundance.

Sun Peaks Data

Mountain Statistics

Vertical feet	2,891 feet
Base elevation	3,933 feet
Summit elevation	6,824 feet
Longest run	5 miles
Average annual snowfall	208 inches
Uphill capacity	9,000 skiers per hour
Skiable terrain	3,400 acres
Opening date	Late November
Closing date	Late April
Snowboarding	Yes
Terrain parks	Yes

Sun Peaks Data (continued)

Transportation

By car   From Vancouver (4.5 hours), take Highways 1 and 5 through Kamloops. 19 km north of Kamloops, turn right at Hettley Creek and follow the signs to Sun Peaks.
By shuttle   From Whistler, call (250) 578-7842 for schedule and reservations.
By bus   From Kamloops, call (250) 377-8481.
By air   To Kamloops, Air Canada flies daily from Vancouver, Calgary, and Edmonton.

Key phone numbers

Ski-area information	(250) 578-7222
Snow phone	(250) 578-7232
Reservations	(800) 807-3257
Website	sunpeaksresort.com

Panorama

If you absolutely had to get away and hide from the world—sweep your sweetie off to some hidden glen where no one could find you, and ski your brains out for a few days—where would you go? I'd go to Panorama.

Panorama is well hidden. Imagine a 2,000-acre mountain with 4,000 feet of vertical, completely invisible from the nearest towns and highways. Imagine that it's three-and-a-half hours from the nearest big airport. To get there from Calgary, you have to drive at least an hour beyond either Fernie or the Banff area resorts. Because those areas are closer to the city, they tend to filter out the day-skier and weekend skier crowds.

Panorama has no lift lines. It's probably the least-known 4000-foot lift system on the continent. The long groomers—Panorama has them in spades—keep their corduroy longer. You can still find untracked powder lines several days after a storm.

The thin crowds and simple lift system mean it's also a sane environment for family skiing. It's hard for kids to get lost here, but the steep stuff offers more than enough challenge to keep teenagers happy.

Like most of BC's interior resorts, Panorama started off modestly. In 1962 a trio of Swiss-born loggers from the tiny town of Windermere decided they needed some Alpine skiing. Guy Messerli, Karl Strobl, and Fritz Zehnder cut some trails up the gentle slopes above Toby Creek and strung up a rope tow. Local skiers bought into their fledgling company and the first chairlift was built in 1967. The founders are commemorated in some of the trail names: *Messerli's Mile, Fritz's, Strobl Strasse,* and *Zehnder Way.*

In 1993 the resort was sold to Intrawest, the huge development company that now operates Whistler-Blackcomb, Canadian Mountain Holidays, Mount Tremblant, Mammoth Mountain, Copper Mountain, Winter Park, Stratton Mountain, and a dozen more mountain villages and golf resorts. Intrawest began building an elaborate base village descending in terraces to the creek—and began opening new terrain on the mountain.

The first step was to offer some rowdy steep powder skiing in the steep bowl just east of the summit ridge—the terrain now called Extreme Dream. In 2002 Intrawest doubled the terrain to 2,850 acres by opening Taynton Bowl, a complex of gulleys previously reserved for heli-skiing. Lift access remained a problem: After exiting the Taynton Trail, it took the better part of an hour to work your way back up the lift system to the summit.

In the summer of 2003, Panorama finally fixed that. The old Horizon fixed-double and Champagne T-bar disappeared, replaced by a high-speed quad. The Summit T-bar is gone, replaced by a longer fixed-grip quad launching from the bottom of Schober's Glade. It's now possible to ride from the village to the summit in about 20 minutes, or from the bottom of Horizon lift to the summit in about 15 minutes. This doesn't mean you can yo-yo the whole 4,000 vertical feet, but it does mean that on a powder day you can put up 30,000 vertical feet before lunch.

The Layout

Navigation is very simple at Panorama. There's only one peak, one village, and one main route to the top. In general, beginners should stick to the lower mountain, skiing off Mile 1 Express, or trying the low-intermediate cruisers off Sunbird triple. The new Horizon Express serves several blue highways, which snake along parallel to the ridgeline and roll off toward Sunbird base. From here, anything to right of *World Cup Way* trail (the downhill course) dumps you into the chutes of Extreme Dream, so if you want more easy cruising, head west (skier's left) using *Schober's Dream* or *Canadian Trail* toward Sun Bowl, at the far west end of the trail network.

Schober's is also the route to the Summit Quad. The summit face offers half a dozen thinly gladed tree runs, and there's one intermediate route down, labeled, cleverly, *Getmedown*. The real action is in the two steep bowls, Extreme Dream and Taynton. It is possible for an intermediate skier to stage an inspection tour of the Extreme Dream terrain: pick your way along the sharp ridge called View of 1000 Peaks, then follow *Messerli's Mile* to *Madson's Mile* or *Ostrander*.

Best Beginner Skiing

Horseshoe and *Showoff* are the big easy avenues, but they also carry rush hour traffic before lunch and in late afternoon. If the speeders coming off the upper mountain bother you, scoot over to *Stinger* and *Ski Tip Way*.

Best Intermediate Skiing

The classic groomed cruisers include *Schober's, Skyline, Rollercoaster,* and *Millenium. Schober's Glade* has traditionally been a great place to learn tree skiing skills, but the new Summit Quad runs through the neighborhood and it remains to be seen if the terrain will grow big bumps when it sees more traffic.

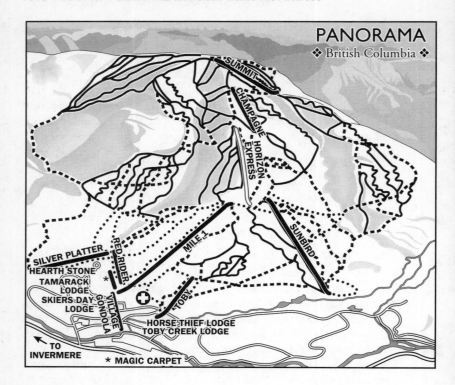

Best Expert Skiing

For steeps, go to the summit chutes (*Trigger, Gunbarrel, Zone 2*) in Extreme Dream. Powder hounds will revel in the bowls and gulleys off Taynton's Outback Ridge. *Lifeline, Black Bear,* and *Tacky* are classic bump runs, though the traffic pattern may change now that *Lifeline* no longer runs under a lift. You'll also find good bumps in steep shots between the glades under Summit lift. For great tree skiing, go to *Duthie's, Moore Glade, Tree Time, Gunner's,* and *Marshall's.* Timberline goes all the way to the summit, so you can find plenty of tree skiing almost anywhere. Try *Hideaway* to skier's right of *Schober's Glade* and *Cliff Glade* to the left of *Old Timer.*

Heli-skiing

RK Heli-Ski operates from the heliplex upstream from Toby Creek Village. The company flies six-seat A-Star and 14-seat Bell 212 helicopters into the vast wilderness of the Bugaboo and Purcell ranges. Half-day excursions start at $600 Canadian (call (800) 661-6060, (250) 342-3889; **rkheliski.com**).

Snowboarding

To yo-yo the half-pipe, ride the short Toby chair from just above Horsethief Lodge, and turn left from the off-ramp.

Convenient Lodging

Ski-in/ski-out lodging is available at the four hotels clustered about the base of Mile 1 quad: the plush **Taynton Lodge, Ski Tip Lodge, Panorama Springs** (favorite with kids because of its elaborate heated water park), and the cheaper **Pine Inn.** Modest-priced digs at **Horsethief Lodge** and **Toby Creek** require a short walk downhill and a ride on the Village Gondola.

Best Eats

On the mountain, plan to lunch at the **Summit Hut** or **Elkhorn** snack bars. You've got just half a dozen choices for dinner: **The Great Hall** in the Ski Tip Lodge functions as the base lodge during the day, serving burgers, salads, and pizza. It's probably the most sensible place to take a pack of rowdy kids. A more civilized family destination is the **Starbird,** where the menu runs to steak, fish, and veggie dishes.

Find an adult atmosphere at the **Toby Creek,** specializing in steak and seafood, or trek down to the **Heli Plex Restaurant** for continental dining, including game dishes. Or get a burger-and-beer at the **Jackpine** or **T-Bar.**

Panorama Data

Mountain Statistics

Vertical feet	4,000 feet
Base elevation	3,800 feet
Summit elevation	7,800 feet
Longest run	2.9 miles
Average annual snowfall	187 inches
Snowmaking	40%
Number of lifts	10: 1 carpet; 4 surface lifts; 2 double chairs; 1 triple chair; 1 hi-speed quad; 1 gondola
Uphill capacity	9,000 skiers per hour
Skiable terrain	2,847 acres
Opening date	Mid-December
Closing date	Mid-April
Snowboarding	Yes
Terrain parks	Yes

Transportation

By car   From Calgary (3.5 hours): Highway 1 west, then south on 93 to Radium Hot Springs. Turn south on 95 to Invermere and follow signs to Panorama.
By bus   From Banff: $70 Canadian; call (403) 609-8226 for booking.

Key phone numbers

Ski-area information	(250) 342-6941
Snow phone	(250) 342-6941
Reservations	(800) 663-2929
Website	skipanorama.com

Index